THE SOLUTION

ONLINE RESOURCES INCLUDED!

CourseMate — Engaging. Trackable. Affordable.

CourseMate brings course concepts to life with interactive learning, study, and exam preparation tools that support MGMT4.

FOR INSTRUCTORS:
- First Day of Class Instructions
- Custom Options through 4LTR+ Program
- Instructor's Manual
- Test Bank
- PowerPoint® Slides
- Instructor Prep Cards
- Engagement Tracker

FOR STUDENTS:
- Interactive eBook
- Auto-Graded Quizzes
- Flashcards
- Games: Crossword Puzzles, Beat the Clock
- Videos
- Student Review Cards
- PowerPoint® Slides
- Cases & Exercises

Students sign in at
www.cengagebrain.com

SOUTH-WESTERN
CENGAGE Learning™

MGMT4
Chuck Williams
Butler University

Vice President of Editorial, Business:
Jack W. Calhoun

Editor-in-Chief: Melissa Acuña

Executive Editor: Scott Person

Developmental Editor: John Choi,
B-books, Ltd.

Product Developmental Manager,
4LTR Press: Steven E. Joos

Brand Executive Marketing Manager,
4LTR Press: Robin Lucas

Editorial Assistant: Ruth Belanger

Marketing Director: Keri Witman

Sr. Marketing Communications Manager:
Jim Overly

Marketing Manager: Jonathan Monahan

Production Director: Amy McGuire,
B-books, Ltd.

Sr. Content Project Manager:
Tamborah Moore

Media Editor: Danny Bolan

Frontlist Buyer, Manufacturing:
Arethea Thomas

Production Service: B-books, Ltd.

Sr. Art Director: Tippy McIntosh

Internal Designer: Ke Design, Mason, OH

Cover Designer: Tippy McIntosh

Cover Image: © Vincenzo Lombardo,
Getty Images

Text Rights Acquisitions Specialist:
Audrey Pettengill

Text Permissions Researcher: Elaine Kosta

Photo Rights Acquisitions Specialist:
Deanna Ettinger

Photo Researchers: Charlotte Goldman;
Dana Freeman, B-books, Ltd.

For product information and technology assistance, contact us at
Cengage Learning Customer & Sales Support, 1-800-354-9706

For permission to use material from this text or product,
submit all requests online at **www.cengage.com/permissions**
Further permissions questions can be emailed to
permissionrequest@cengage.com

Library of Congress Control Number: 2010942407

Student Edition ISBN-13: 978-1-111-22131-7
Student Edition ISBN-10: 1-111-22131-6

South-Western
5191 Natorp Boulevard
Mason, OH 45040
USA

Cengage Learning products are represented in Canada by
Nelson Education, Ltd.

For your course and learning solutions, visit **www.cengage.com**
Purchase any of our products at your local college store or at our
preferred online store **www.CengageBrain.com**

Printed in the United States of America
1 2 3 4 5 6 7 15 14 13 12 11

Brief Contents

© iStockphoto.com/Josh Hodge Photography

Contents

© Southern Stock/Photodisc/Jupiterimages

Part 2
Planning 80

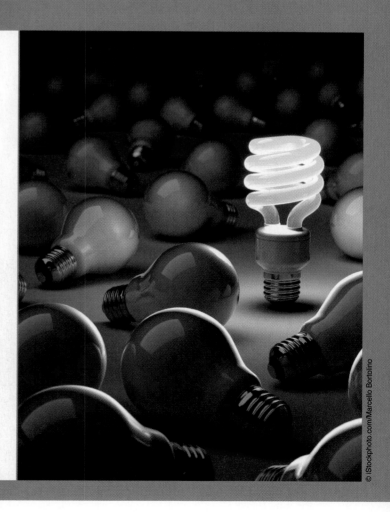

© iStockphoto.com/Marcello Bortolino

Part 3
Organizing 158

© iStockphoto.com/DNY59

Part 4
Leading 240

© Hans Neleman/The Image Bank/Getty Images

Part 5
Controlling 302

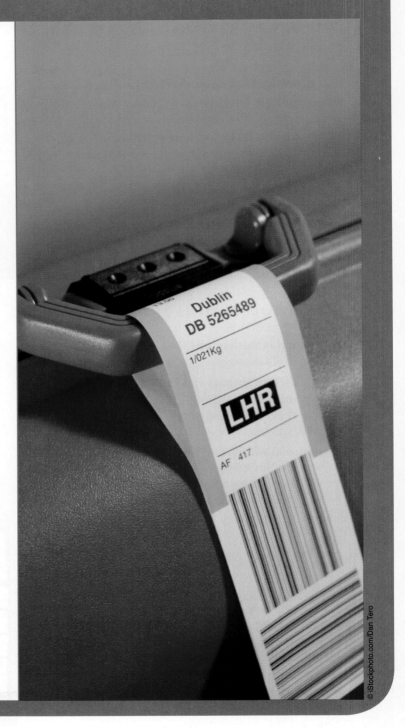

© iStockphoto.com/Dan Tero

"It's easy to read, it outlines important topics, and it's relevant. Thanks for the good stuff on the website, I think it will **really help with tests**.

– Thomas Scholtes, Student at University of Maryland, College Park

REVIEW

HE DID

MGMT4 puts a multitude of study aids at your fingertips. After reading the chapters, check out these resources for further help:

• **Review Cards**, found in the back of your book, include all learning outcomes, definitions, and visual summaries for each chapter.

• **Online printable flash cards** give you three additional ways to check your comprehension of key marketing concepts.

Other great ways to help you study include **interactive management games, podcasts, audio downloads,** and **online tutorial quizzes with feedback**.

You can find it all in CourseMate for **MGMT4**. Login at **www.cengagebrain.com**.

1 | Management

© 81a/Photolibrary/Jupiterimages

LEARNING OUTCOMES:

1 describe what management is.

2 explain the four functions of management.

3 describe different kinds of managers.

4 explain the major roles and subroles that managers perform in their jobs.

5 explain what companies look for in managers.

6 discuss the top mistakes that managers make in their jobs.

7 describe the transition that employees go through when they are promoted to management.

8 explain how and why companies can create competitive advantage through people.

Chapter 1

What Is Management?

management issues are fundamental to any organization: How do we plan to get things done, organize the company to be efficient and effective, lead and motivate employees, and put controls in place to make sure our plans are followed and our goals are met? Good management is basic to starting a business, growing a business, and maintaining a business once it has achieved some measure of success.

To understand how important *good* management is, think about mistakes like these: Mistake #1. A new Chinese plant manager at a factory in South Carolina publicly berates his workers when they make mistakes, creating resentment and alienation among his American workers.[1] Mistake #2. Guidant Corporation, which makes cardiovascular medical products, let forty-five device failures and two patient deaths occur over a period of 3 years before recalling 50,000 defective heart defibrillators, 77 percent of which were already implanted in patients.[2]

Ah, bad managers and bad management. Is it any wonder that companies pay management consultants nearly $240 billion a year for advice on basic management issues such as how to lead people effectively, organize the company efficiently, and manage large-scale projects and processes?[3] This textbook will help you understand some of the basic issues that management consultants help companies resolve. (And it won't cost you billions of dollars.)

After reading the next two sections, you should be able to

1 **describe what management is.**

2 **explain the four functions of management.**

© iStockphoto.com/Mark Coffey

1 ▌ Management Is . . .

Many of today's managers got their start welding on the factory floor, clearing dishes off tables, helping customers fit a suit, or wiping up a spill in aisle 3. Similarly, lots of you will start at the bottom and work your way up. There's no better way to get to know your competition, your customers, and your business. But whether you begin your career at the entry level or as a supervisor, your job as a manager is not to do the work but to help others do theirs. **Management** is getting work done through others. Vineet Nayar, CEO of IT services company HCL Technologies, doesn't see himself as the guy who has to do everything or even as the guy who has to have all the answers. Nayar looks at himself essentially as "the guy who is obsessed with enabling employees to create value." For Nayar, this process doesn't happen by him coming up with every solution and holding everyone's hand at every step. Instead, Nayar creates and encourages opportunities for collaboration, for peer review, and for employees to give feedback on ideas and work processes. Says Nayar, "My job is to make sure everybody is enabled to do what they do well."[4]

Pat Carrigan's description of managerial responsibilities suggests that managers also have to be concerned with efficiency and effectiveness in the work process. **Efficiency** is getting work done with a minimum of effort, expense, or waste. For example, how do millions of Girl Scouts from over 200 councils across the United States sell and deliver millions of boxes of cookies each year? In other words, what makes Girl Scouts so efficient? The national organization, Girl Scouts

> **Management** getting work done through others
>
> **Efficiency** getting work done with a minimum of effort, expense, or waste

of America (GSA), licenses only two bakers, so when GSA changes or improves its cookie offerings, for example, by adding new flavors or making healthier, sugar-free options, it can do so quickly and consistently nationwide. GSA has also designed Girl Scout cookie packages to maximize the number of boxes that can fit in a delivery truck. The national organization optimizes its overall cookie inventory by tracking sales by type of cookie and troop. Because GSA operates efficiently, 2.9 million scouts can sell and deliver more than 50 million cookies in an 8-week period.[5]

Efficiency alone, however, is not enough to ensure success. Managers must also strive for **effectiveness,** which means accomplishing tasks that help fulfill organizational objectives such as delivering customer service and satisfaction to end users. John F. Kennedy International Airport in New York City was notorious for crowded runways, leaving passengers trapped on idling airplanes with no food, no water, and no bathrooms. Recently, however, the airport instituted a runway reservation system, in which each flight is designated an assigned takeoff time, and no plane is allowed to leave the gate until its assigned time. How effective is the new system? Instead of having 40 planes queuing on the runway, now there are only 6 to 8 planes in line for takeoff at a time. And even though flights are still often delayed, passengers can now wait them out at the terminal, where they have access to food, bathrooms, and lounges, rather than inside the plane.[6]

2 | Management Functions

Henri Fayol, who was a managing director (CEO) of a large steel company in the early 20th century, was one of the founders of the field of management. You'll learn more about Fayol and management's other key contributors when you read about the history of management in Chapter 2. Based on his 20 years of experience as a CEO, Fayol argued that "the success of an enterprise generally depends much more on the administrative ability of its leaders than on their technical ability."[7] Although Google CEO Eric Schmidt has extensive expertise and experience in computer technology, Google succeeds because of his capabilities as a manager—not because of his ability to write computer code.

Managers need to perform five managerial functions in order to be successful, according to Fayol: planning, organizing, coordinating, commanding, and

controlling.[8] Most management textbooks today have updated this list by dropping the coordinating function and referring to Fayol's commanding function as "leading." Fayol's management functions are thus known today in this updated form as planning, organizing, leading, and controlling. Studies indicate that managers who perform these management functions well are more successful, gaining promotions for themselves and profits for their companies. One study shows that the more time CEOs spend planning, the more profitable their companies are.[9] A 25-year study at AT&T found that employees with better planning and decision-making skills were more likely to be promoted into management jobs, to be successful as managers, and to be promoted into upper levels of management.[10] The evidence is clear. Managers serve their companies well when they plan, organize, lead, and control. We have therefore organized this textbook based on these functions of management, as shown in Exhibit 1.1.

Now let's take a closer look at each of the management functions: 2.1 planning, 2.2 organizing, 2.3 leading, and 2.4 controlling.

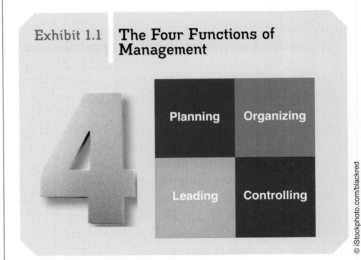

Exhibit 1.1 **The Four Functions of Management**

Planning · Organizing · Leading · Controlling

© iStockphoto.com/blackred

2.1 | PLANNING

Planning involves determining organizational goals and a means for achieving them. As you'll learn in Chapter 5, planning is one of the best ways to improve performance. It encourages people to work harder, to work hard for extended periods, to engage in behaviors directly related to accomplishing goals, and to think of better ways to do their jobs. But most importantly, companies that plan have larger profits and faster growth than companies that don't plan.

For example, the question, "What business are we in?" is at the heart of strategic planning. You'll learn about this in Chapter 6. If you can answer the question, "What business are we in?" in two sentences or less, chances are you have a very clear plan for your business. But getting a clear plan is not so easy. Sometimes even very successful companies stray from their core business. This happened when eBay paid $2.6 million to acquire Skype, which makes software for free video phone calls over the Internet. In 2009, eBay sold Skype. Why? Because eBay's CEO realized it was a poor fit with the company's core e-commerce business, meaning its Internet auction site and its PayPal online payment service business.[11] As a company providing a broad range of technology products, services, and solutions, Cisco began an in-house initiative to create videoconferencing products in 2006. Since then, Cisco's telepresence systems have become a growing staple of its business offerings. Its 2010 purchase of Norwegian videoconferencing firm Tandberg helped add to its core telepresence business, which is now on pace to generate $175 million in annual sales. Therefore, unlike eBay's purchase of Skype, Cisco's purchase of Tandberg made sense as part of its long-term plan to support and grow its telepresence business.[12]

You'll learn more about planning in Chapter 5 on planning and decision making, Chapter 6 on organizational strategy, Chapter 7 on innovation and change, and Chapter 8 on global management.

2.2 | ORGANIZING

Organizing is deciding where decisions will be made, who will do what jobs and tasks, and who will work for whom in the company. On average, it costs more than $10 billion to bring a new pharmaceutical drug to market. So when Pfizer, the 2nd largest pharmaceutical firm in the world, acquired Wyeth, the 11th largest, then CEO Jeffrey Kindler decided to restructure Pfizer's research and development unit into two parts, one for small molecules or traditional pills and one for large molecules or drugs made from living cells. Kindler said, "Creating two distinct, but complementary, research organizations, led by the top scientist from each company, will provide sharper focus, less bureaucracy and clearer accountability in drug discovery."[13] In all, the new company will consist of nine businesses, including primary care, vaccines, oncology, consumer and nutritional products, and pharmaceuticals.

You'll learn more about organizing in Chapter 9 on designing organizations, Chapter 10 on managing teams, Chapter 11 on managing human resources, and Chapter 12 on managing individuals and a diverse work force.

2.3 | LEADING

The third management function, **leading**, involves inspiring and motivating workers to work hard to achieve organizational goals. For Alan Mulally, CEO of Ford Motor Company, a critical part of keeping his employees motivated is to "Communicate, communicate, communicate."[14] Mulally distributed a set of cards with Ford's mission statement printed on it to every Ford employee. He also hosts a Business Plan Review with his top executives once a week to check up on progress. Along with his commitment to communicating the mission, Mulally brings an enthusiastic, hard-working, detail-oriented leadership style to the table, and employees at Ford are buying in. Joe Hinrichs, a manufacturing boss, says, "Alan brings infectious energy. This is a person people want to follow."[15]

Mulally's leadership has brought Ford back from what many thought might be the brink of extinction. In a series of timely maneuvers and shrewd business deals, Mulally secured a $23.6 billion loan and then sold off several noncore brands prior to the recession, which kept Ford sufficiently capitalized as the world economy slowed. And while General Motors and Chrysler were forced to seek government loans and eventually file for bankruptcy, Ford managed to stay afloat on its own, posting healthy profits in 2009 and 2010, well ahead of Mulally's promise to make Ford profitable by 2011.[16]

You'll learn more about leading in Chapter 13 on motivation, Chapter 14 on leadership, and Chapter 15 on managing communication.

2.4 | CONTROLLING

The last function of management, **controlling**, is monitoring progress toward goal achievement and taking corrective action when progress isn't being made. The basic control process involves setting standards to achieve goals, comparing actual performance to those standards, and then making changes to return performance to those standards. Needing to cut costs (the standard) to restore profitability (the goal), major airlines began paying Pratt & Whitney to power-wash the insides of their jets' engines two to three times a year at a cost of $3,000 per wash. Why? Cleaner engines reduce fuel consumption by 1.2 percent and can go 18 months longer before having to be rebuilt for

Organizing deciding where decisions will be made, who will do what jobs and tasks, and who will work for whom

Leading inspiring and motivating workers to work hard to achieve organizational goals

Controlling monitoring progress toward goal achievement and taking corrective action when needed

regular maintenance—at a high cost. Johnny Holley, who manages engine maintenance and engineering for Southwest Airlines, says, "It's more than just a subtle improvement when they wash these engines. A phenomenal amount of fuel can be saved doing this."[17] Indeed, these engine washes will not only pay for themselves, they will save Southwest Airlines an additional $5.1 million in fuel costs on an annual basis.

You'll learn more about the control function in Chapter 16 on control, Chapter 17 on managing information, and Chapter 18 on managing service and manufacturing operations.

What Do Managers Do?

not all managerial jobs are the same. The demands and requirements placed on the CEO of Sony are significantly different from those placed on the manager of your local Wendy's restaurant.

After reading the next two sections, you should be able to

3 **describe different kinds of managers.**

4 **explain the major roles and subroles that managers perform in their jobs.**

3 Kinds of Managers

As shown in Exhibit 1.2, there are four kinds of managers, each with different jobs and responsibilities: 3.1 top managers, 3.2 middle managers, 3.3 first-line managers, and 3.4 team leaders.

3.1 | TOP MANAGERS

Top managers hold positions like chief executive officer (CEO), chief operating officer (COO), chief financial officer (CFO), and chief information officer (CIO) and are responsible for the overall direction of the organization. Top managers have the following responsibilities.[18] First, they are responsible for creating

a context for change. In fact, the CEOs of Citigroup, Merrill Lynch, Home Depot, Starbucks, Motorola, and JetBlue Airways were all fired within a year's time precisely because they had not moved fast enough to bring about significant changes in their companies. Indeed, in both Europe and the United States, 35 percent of all CEOs are eventually fired because of their failure to successfully change their companies.[19] Creating a context for change includes forming a long-range vision or mission for the company.

Once that vision or mission is set, the second responsibility of top managers is to develop employees' commitment to and ownership of the company's performance. That is, top managers are responsible for creating employee buy-in. Third, top managers must create a positive organizational culture through language and action. Top managers impart company values, strategies, and lessons through what they do and say to others both inside and outside the company. Above all, no matter what they communicate, it's critical for CEOs to send and reinforce clear, consistent messages.[20] According to General David Petraeus, communicating clear strategies and objectives was critical to leading a successful turnaround in Iraq. Once the big ideas have been identified, Petraeus says, "You just echo and re-echo it in every forum, in every communications opportunity you have."[21] Similarly, top managers, like Ford's Alan Mulally, who employ these communication strategies in business will be more successful in getting the message across.

Finally, top managers are responsible for monitoring their business environments. A. G. Lafley, now retired CEO of Procter & Gamble, believes that most people do not understand the CEO's responsibilities. Says Lafley, "Conventional wisdom suggests that the CEO was primarily a coach and a utility infielder, dropping in to solve [internal] problems where they crop up. In fact, however, the CEO has a very specific job that only he or she can do: Link the external world with the internal organization."[22] This means that top managers must closely monitor customers' needs, competitors' moves, and long-term business, economic, and social trends. You'll read more about business environments in Chapter 3.

3.2 | MIDDLE MANAGERS

Middle managers hold positions like plant manager, regional manager, and divisional manager. They are responsible for setting objectives consistent with top management's goals and for planning and implementing subunit strategies for achieving those objectives.[23]

Exhibit 1.2 **What the Four Kinds of Managers Do**

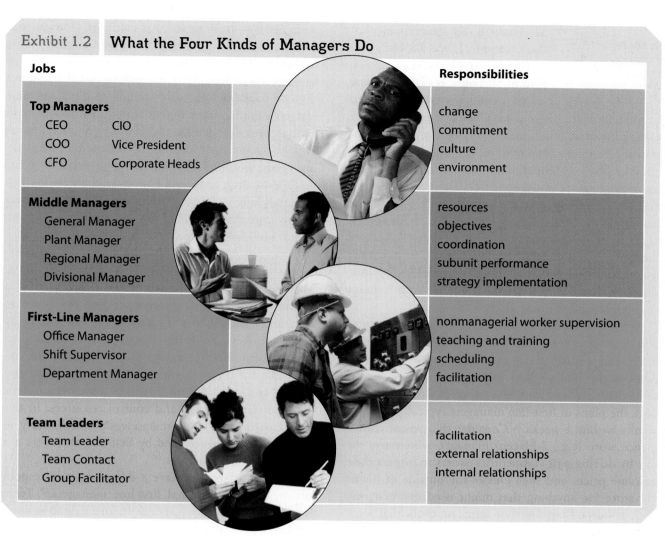

Jobs	Responsibilities
Top Managers CEO — CIO COO — Vice President CFO — Corporate Heads	change commitment culture environment
Middle Managers General Manager Plant Manager Regional Manager Divisional Manager	resources objectives coordination subunit performance strategy implementation
First-Line Managers Office Manager Shift Supervisor Department Manager	nonmanagerial worker supervision teaching and training scheduling facilitation
Team Leaders Team Leader Team Contact Group Facilitator	facilitation external relationships internal relationships

One specific middle management responsibility is to plan and allocate resources to meet objectives.

A second major responsibility is to coordinate and link groups, departments, and divisions within a company. In February 2008, a tornado destroyed a Caterpillar plant in Oxford, Mississippi, the only plant in the company that produced a coupling required for many of Caterpillar's machines. The disaster threatened a worldwide production shutdown. Greg Folley, a middle manager in charge of the parts division that included the plant, gave workers 2 weeks to restore production to pre-tornado levels. He said, "I was betting on people to get it done." He contacted new vendors, sent engineers from other Caterpillar locations to Mississippi to check for quality, and set up distribution operations in another facility. Meanwhile, Kevin Kempa, the plant manager in Oxford, moved some employees to another plant, delivered new training to employees during the production hiatus, and oversaw reconstruction of the plant. The day before the 2-week deadline, the Oxford plant was up and running and produced 8,000 parts.[24]

A third responsibility of middle managers is to monitor and manage the performance of the subunits and individual managers who report to them. Finally, middle managers are also responsible for implementing the changes or strategies generated by top managers.

3.3 | FIRST-LINE MANAGERS

First-line managers hold positions like office manager, shift supervisor, and department manager. The primary responsibility of first-line managers is to train and supervise the performance of nonmanagerial employees, who are directly responsible for producing a company's goods and services. First-line managers are the only managers who don't supervise other managers. The responsibilities of first-line managers include monitoring, teaching, and short-term planning.

First-line managers teach entry-level employees how to do their jobs, and also encourage, monitor,

First-line managers managers who train and supervise the performance of nonmanagerial employees who are directly responsible for producing the company's products or services and reward the performance of their workers. David Brown, CEO of Datotel, an IT and data storage firm in St. Louis, realized that few of his employees were motivated by the employee-of-the-month reward, usually a $25 gift card, a short email, and a notice on the company intranet. To encourage employees, and to show that their efforts mattered, Brown asked his managers to take a less rigid, more personal approach. Datotel's managers, and Brown himself, take the time to thank outstanding employees in person, and even send them handwritten notes in the mail. Stephanie Lewish, who received one of these letters commending her work, says, "It made me feel important to get something so personal and unique, since I'm sure David has several hundred other things swirling around in his head."[25]

First-line managers also make detailed schedules and operating plans based on middle management's intermediate-range plans. In contrast to the long-term plans of top managers (3 to 5 years out) and the intermediate plans of middle managers (6 to 18 months out), the plans of first-line managers typically produce results within 2 weeks.[26] Consider the typical convenience store (e.g., 7-Eleven) manager, who starts the day by driving past competitors' stores to inspect their gasoline prices and then checks the outside of his or her store for anything that might need maintenance, such as burned-out lights or signs, or restocking, such as windshield washer fluid and paper towels. Then comes an inside check, where the manager determines

what needs to be done for that day. (Are there enough coffee and donuts for breakfast or enough sandwiches for lunch?) Once the day is planned, the manager turns to weekend orders. After accounting for the weather (hot or cold) and the sales trends at the same time last year, the manager makes sure the store will have enough beer, soft drinks, and Sunday papers on hand. Finally, the manager looks 7 to 10 days ahead for hiring needs. Because of strict hiring procedures (basic math tests, drug tests, and background checks), it can take that long to hire new employees. Said one convenience store manager, "I have to continually interview, even if I am fully staffed."[27]

3.4 | TEAM LEADERS

The fourth kind of manager is a team leader. This relatively new kind of management job developed as companies shifted to self-managing teams which, by definition, have no formal supervisor. In traditional management hierarchies, first-line managers are responsible for the performance of nonmanagerial employees and have the authority to hire and fire workers, make job assignments, and control resources. In this new structure, the teams themselves perform nearly all of the functions performed by first-line managers under traditional hierarchies.[28]

Team leaders thus have a different set of responsibilities than traditional first-line managers.[29] **Team leaders** are primarily responsible for facilitating team activities toward accomplishing a goal. This doesn't mean team leaders are responsible for team perfor-

© Photolink/Photodisc/Getty Images

Which kind of manager is responsible for teaching the new employees in this grocery store how to do their jobs? Which kind of manager acts as a liaison between the produce department's employees and the employees of another department in the same store?

mance. They aren't. The team is. Team leaders help their team members plan and schedule work, learn to solve problems, and work effectively with each other. Management consultant Franklin Jonath says, "The idea is for the team leader to be at the service of the group. It should be clear that the team members own the outcome. The leader is there to bring intellectual, emotional, and spiritual resources to the team. Through his or her actions, the leader should be able to show the others how to think about the work that they're doing in the context of their lives. It's a tall order, but the best teams have such leaders."[30]

Relationships among team members and between different teams are crucial to good team performance and must be well-managed by team leaders, who are responsible for fostering good relationships and addressing problematic ones within their teams. Getting along with others is much more important in team structures because team members can't get work done without the help of other teammates. For example, studies have shown that it's not the surgeon but the interactions between the surgeon and all operating room team members that determine surgical outcomes. However, at twenty hospitals, 60 percent of the operating room team members—nurses, technicians, and other doctors—agreed with the statement "In the ORs here, it is difficult to speak up if I perceive a problem with patient care."[31] And when operating room team members don't speak up, serious mistakes can occur no matter how talented the surgeon. Consequently, surgeons are using "safety pauses" to better involve members of their surgical teams. The surgeon will pause, ask if anyone has concerns or comments, and address them if need be. Studies show that safety pauses reduce mistakes, such as operating on the wrong leg or beginning surgery with key surgical instruments missing.[32]

Team leaders are also responsible for managing external relationships. Team leaders act as the bridge or liaison between their teams and other teams, departments, and divisions in a company. For example, if a member of Team A complains about the quality of Team B's work, Team A's leader needs to initiate a meeting with Team B's leader. Together, these team leaders are responsible for getting members of both teams to work together to solve the problem. If it's done right, the problem is solved without involving company management or blaming members of the other team.[33]

So the team leader's job requires a different set of skills than those of traditional management jobs. Team leaders who fail to understand how their roles are different from those of traditional managers often struggle in their jobs. A team leader at Texas Instruments reacted with skepticism to his initial experience with teams: "I didn't buy into teams, partly because there was no clear plan on what I was supposed to do. . . . I never let the operators [team members] do any scheduling or any ordering of parts because that was mine. I figured as long as I had that, I had a job."[34]

You will learn more about teams in Chapter 10.

4 Managerial Roles

Although all four types of managers engage in planning, organizing, leading, and controlling, if you were to follow them around during a typical day on the job, you would probably not use these terms to describe what they actually do. Rather, what you'd see are the various roles managers play. Professor Henry Mintzberg followed five American CEOs, shadowing each for a week and analyzing their mail, their conversations, and their actions. He concluded that managers fulfill three major roles while performing their jobs:[35]

- interpersonal roles
- informational roles
- decisional roles

In other words, managers talk to people, gather and give information, and make decisions. Furthermore, as shown in Exhibit 1.3, these three major roles can be subdivided into 10 subroles. *Let's examine each*

Exhibit 1.3 Mintzberg's Managerial Roles

Interpersonal Roles
- Figurehead
- Leader
- Liaison

Informational Roles
- Monitor
- Disseminator
- Spokesperson

Decisional Roles
- Entrepreneur
- Disturbance Handler
- Resource Allocator
- Negotiator

Source: Reprinted by permission of *Harvard Business Review* (an exhibit) from "The Manager's Job: Folklore and Fact," by Mintzberg, H. *Harvard Business Review*, July–August 1975. © by the President and Fellows of Harvard College. All rights reserved.

Managers must constantly scan their environments looking for **information**.

*major role—**4.1 interpersonal, 4.2 informational**, and **4.3 decisional**—and their 10 subroles.*

4.1 | INTERPERSONAL ROLES

More than anything else, management jobs are people-intensive. Estimates vary with the level of management, but most managers spend between two-thirds and four-fifths of their time in face-to-face communication with others.[36] If you're a loner, or if you consider dealing with people a pain, then you may not be cut out for management work. In fulfilling the interpersonal role of management, managers perform three subroles: figurehead, leader, and liaison.

In the **figurehead role**, managers perform ceremonial duties such as greeting company visitors, speaking at the opening of a new facility, or representing the company at a community luncheon to support local charities. Wichita, Kansas–based Cessna Aircraft Company is the largest manufacturer of general aviation planes in the world. When Cessna opened a new 101,000-square-foot jet service facility employing seventy-seven workers in Mesa, Arizona, CEO Jack Pelton flew in to join Mesa's mayor, Cessna managers, and local workers and their families to celebrate the grand opening.[37]

In the **leader role**, managers motivate and encourage workers to accomplish organizational objectives. At RedPeg Marketing, cofounder Brad Nierenberg motivates his employees with company perks such as a three-bedroom beach house that is available to all forty-eight employees for vacations, cold beer in the refrigerator, free breakfast at staff meetings, and trophies and awards for great performance. Once, after the company had met a critical goal, Nierenberg walked into the office with $38,000 in cash, or $1,000 each for his then thirty-eight employees. Said Nierenberg, "I thought, 'I've got to make a big deal out

of this; I can't just put it in their checking accounts because that's not as fun.' I thought it would be cool for them to see [over] $30,000 in cash."[38]

In the **liaison role**, managers deal with people outside their units. Studies consistently indicate that managers spend as much time with outsiders as they do with their own subordinates and their own bosses.[39] When Mike Tannenbaum, general manager of the New York Jets, headed across town to the headquarters of JPMorgan Chase, he wasn't paying JPMorgan CEO Jamie Dimon a social call. Tannenbaum had scheduled the meeting to discuss JPMorgan's risk assessment and acquisition processes. The appointment with Dimon was part of a much broader initiative in which members from all levels of the Jets organization would interact with professionals outside of their fields, such as firefighters, storm chasers, and bankers like Dimon, for the purpose of learning better management and decision-making processes. The Jets are also planning opportunities in the future for JPMorgan employees to visit their facilities. In this case, the liaison role operates in both directions, as managers are initiating interactions with outsiders and outsiders are coming to them.[40]

4.2 | INFORMATIONAL ROLES

Not only do managers spend most of their time in face-to-face contact with others, but they spend much of it obtaining and sharing information. Indeed, Mintzberg found that the managers in his study spent 40 percent of their time giving and getting information from others. In this regard, management can be viewed as processing information, gathering information by scanning the business environment and listening to others in face-to-face conversations, processing that information, and then sharing it with people both inside and outside the company. Mintzberg described three informational subroles: monitor, disseminator, and spokesperson.

In the **monitor role**, managers scan their environment for information, actively contact others for information, and, because of their personal contacts, receive a great deal of unsolicited information. Be-

Figurehead role the interpersonal role managers play when they perform ceremonial duties

Leader role the interpersonal role managers play when they motivate and encourage workers to accomplish organizational objectives

Liaison role the interpersonal role managers play when they deal with people outside their units

Monitor role the informational role managers play when they scan their environment for information

sides receiving firsthand information, managers monitor their environment by reading local newspapers and the *Wall Street Journal* to keep track of customers, competitors, and technological changes that may affect their businesses. Today, managers can also take advantage of electronic monitoring and distribution services that track the news wires (Associated Press, Reuters, and so on) for stories related to their businesses.

Because of their numerous personal contacts and their access to subordinates, managers are often hubs for the distribution of critical information. In the **disseminator role,** managers share the information they have collected with their subordinates and others in the company. There will never be a complete substitute for face-to-face dissemination of information. Yet technology is changing how information is shared and collected. Although the primary methods of communication in large companies are email and voice mail, some managers are also beginning to use social networking technologies like Facebook and Twitter to disseminate information.[41] Serena Software, based in Redwood City, California, uses Facebook to communicate worldwide with its 850 employees. On "Facebook Fridays," employees are given an hour, should they choose, to spend time using Facebook to communicate about themselves or learn about others in the company. Serena Software relies on Facebook so much for recruiting new employees and marketing its prod-

ucts that the social network has become the company's de facto intranet.[42]

In contrast to the disseminator role, in which managers distribute information to employees inside the company, in the **spokesperson role,** managers share information with people outside their departments and companies. One of the most common ways CEOs serve as spokespeople for their companies is at annual meetings with company shareholders or the board of directors. CEOs also serve as spokespeople to the media when their companies are involved in major news stories. When Steve Jobs, founder and CEO of Apple, gives a keynote address or makes a product presentation, he is acting as a spokesperson for the company. Jobs' speeches, all rigorously rehearsed, are famous for capturing the attention of industry experts, Apple fans, potential customers, and analysts alike. When the iPhone was launched in 2007, Jobs described the device as a "revolutionary and magical product that is literally five years ahead of any other mobile phone." At the unveiling of the iPhone 4 in 2010, Jobs described it as "the biggest leap since the original iPhone."[43] As Apple's spokesperson, Steve Jobs uses his platform to communicate his vision to the rest of the world.

Disseminator role
the informational role managers play when they share information with others in their departments or companies

Spokesperson role
the informational role managers play when they share information with people outside their departments or companies

Entrepreneur role
the decisional role managers play when they adapt themselves, their subordinates, and their units to change

4.3 | DECISIONAL ROLES

Mintzberg found that obtaining and sharing information is not an end in itself. Obtaining and sharing information with people inside and outside the company is useful to managers because it helps them make good decisions. According to Mintzberg, managers engage in four decisional subroles: entrepreneur, disturbance handler, resource allocator, and negotiator.

In the **entrepreneur role,** managers adapt themselves, their subordinates, and their units to change. In the past, new drivers at United Parcel Services (UPS)

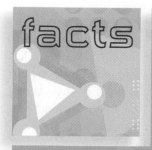

facts

Connect to Your Business

These services deliver customized electronic newspapers that include only stories on topics the managers specify:

Business Wire (http://www.businesswire.com) offers services that monitor and distribute daily news headlines from major industries (e.g., automotive, banking and financial, health, high tech).

CyberAlert (http://www.cyberalert.com) keeps round-the-clock track of news stories in categories chosen by each subscriber.

FNS NewsClips Online (http://www.news-clips.com) provides subscribers with daily electronic news clips from more than 5,000 online news sites.

learned all of the intricacies of their jobs from classroom lectures and reading books, whether it was how to deal with traffic, how to unload their trucks, where to store their keys, or how to fill out paperwork. When the company discovered that nearly 30 percent of trainees were flunking the program, UPS abandoned traditional classroom training for high-tech, interactive training methods. UPS training now includes video game simulators and "kinetic learning" modules designed to allow recruits to practice specific scenarios, such as walking on ice. It even has an 11,500-square-foot facility with a real driving course that teaches and tests UPS driving techniques. Thanks to its new interactive training methods, only 10 percent of driver trainees fail, leading Allen Hill, UPS's senior vice president of human resources, to conclude that the new training methods have "enhanced the probability of success of these new drivers."[44]

In the **disturbance handler role**, managers respond to problems so severe that they demand immediate action. Top managers often play the role of disturbance handler, but shortly before Hurricane Katrina made landfall, Wal-Mart's CEO Lee Scott realized that all of the company's top managers and store managers would have to be effective disturbance handlers in order to serve the company and the communities in which they worked. So Scott sent this message out: "A lot of you are going to have to make decisions above your level. Make the best decision that you can with the information that's available to you at the time, and *above all*, do the right thing."[45] Empowered by their CEO, employees used a fork lift to crash through a warehouse door to get water, broke into a locked pharmacy to retrieve medicine for a hospital, and crashed a bulldozer through the front of a store to obtain supplies that were used to sustain the local community.

In the **resource allocator role**, managers decide who will get what resources and in what amounts. For instance, as the recession that began in the fall of 2008 deepened, companies slashed production by closing facilities, laying off workers, and cutting pay for remaining workers and managers. But when it came to research and development (R&D) spending, the largest firms spent as much on R&D as they did before, despite a fall in revenues of nearly 8 percent. Why did they allocate an even larger part of their budgets to R&D spending in the middle of a recession? Because in prior economic downturns, continued investments in R&D led to the development of successful products such as the iPod and fuel-efficient jet engines. Says Jim Andrew, of the Boston Consulting Group, "Companies by and large realized that large reductions in R&D are suicidal."[46]

In the **negotiator role**, managers negotiate schedules, projects, goals, outcomes, resources, and employee raises. At times, negotiators may have to work with outsiders as well, as in the cases of negotiating settlements in lawsuits and negotiating contract terms in business deals.

What Does It Take to Be a Manager?

i *didn't have the slightest idea what my job was. I walked in giggling and laughing because I had been promoted and had no idea what principles or style to be guided by. After the first day, I felt like I had run into a brick wall. (Sales Representative #1)*

Suddenly, I found myself saying, boy, I can't be responsible for getting all that revenue. I don't have the time. Suddenly you've got to go from [taking care of] yourself and say now I'm the manager, and what does a manager do? It takes a while thinking about it for it to really hit you . . . a manager gets things done through other people. That's a very, very hard transition to make. (Sales Representative #2)[47]

The preceding statements were made by two star sales representatives who, on the basis of their superior performance, were promoted to the position of sales manager. As their comments indicate, at first they did not feel confident about their ability to do their jobs as managers. Like most new managers, these sales managers suddenly realized that the knowledge, skills, and abilities that led to success early in their careers (and were probably responsible for their promotion into the ranks of management) would not necessarily help them succeed as managers. As sales representatives, they were responsible for managing only their own performance. But as sales managers, they were now directly responsible for supervising all of the sales representatives in their sales territories. Furthermore, they were now directly accountable for whether those sales representatives achieved their sales goals.

If performance in nonmanagerial jobs doesn't necessarily prepare you for a managerial job, then what does it take to be a manager?

After reading the next three sections, you should be able to

5 explain what companies look for in managers.

6 discuss the top mistakes that managers make in their jobs.

7 describe the transition that employees go through when they are promoted to management.

5 What Companies Look for in Managers

When companies look for employees who would be good managers, they look for individuals who have technical skills, human skills, conceptual skills, and the motivation to manage.[48] Exhibit 1.4 shows the relative importance of these four skills to the jobs of team leaders, first-line managers, middle managers, and top managers.

Technical skills are the specialized procedures, techniques, and knowledge required to get the job done. For the sales managers described above, technical skills involve the ability to find new sales prospects, develop accurate sales pitches based on customer needs, and close the sale. For a nurse supervisor, technical skills include being able to insert an IV or operate a crash cart if a patient goes into cardiac arrest.

Technical skills are most important for team leaders and lower-level managers because they supervise the workers who produce products or serve customers. Team leaders and first-line managers need technical knowledge and skills to train new employees and help employees solve problems. Technical knowledge and skills are also needed to troubleshoot problems that employees can't handle. Technical skills become less important as managers rise through the managerial ranks, but they are still important.

Human skills can be summarized as the ability to work well with others. Managers with human skills work effectively within groups, encourage others to express their thoughts and feelings, are sensitive to others' needs and viewpoints, and are good listeners and communicators. Human skills are equally important at all levels of management, from team leaders to CEOs.

Because lower-level managers spend much of their time solving technical problems, however, upper-level managers may actually spend more time dealing directly with people. On average, first-line managers spend 57 percent of their time with people, but that percentage increases to 63 percent for middle managers and 78 percent for top managers.[49] When asked how his management style has changed over time, Stephen Sadove, chairman and CEO of Saks Inc., the holding company

Technical skills the specialized procedures, techniques, and knowledge required to get the job done

Human skills the ability to work well with others

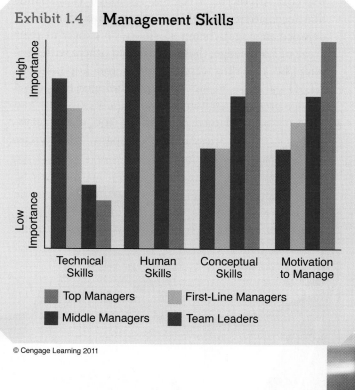

Exhibit 1.4 **Management Skills**

High Importance / Low Importance

Technical Skills | Human Skills | Conceptual Skills | Motivation to Manage

■ Top Managers ■ First-Line Managers
■ Middle Managers ■ Team Leaders

© Cengage Learning 2011

for Saks Fifth Avenue, says, "I spend more time with people and people issues."[50] Compared to earlier in his career, he focuses much more on mentoring, coaching, and developing young talent.

Conceptual skills include the ability to see the organization as a whole, to understand how the different parts of the company affect each other, and to recognize how the company fits into or is affected by elements of its external environment such as the local community, social and economic forces, customers, and the competition. Good managers have to be able to recognize, understand, and reconcile multiple complex problems and perspectives. In other words, managers have to be smart! In fact, intelligence makes so much difference for managerial performance that managers with above-average intelligence typically outperform managers of average intelligence by approximately 48 percent.[51] Clearly, companies need to be careful to promote smart workers into management. Conceptual skills increase in importance as managers rise through the management hierarchy.

Good management involves much more than intelligence, however. For example, making the department genius a manager can be disastrous if that genius lacks technical skills, human skills, or one other factor known as the motivation to manage. **Motivation to manage** is an assessment of how motivated employees are to interact with superiors, participate in competitive situations, behave assertively toward others, tell others what to do, reward good behavior and punish poor behavior, perform actions that are highly visible to others, and handle and organize administrative tasks. Managers typically have a stronger motivation to manage than their subordinates, and managers at higher levels usually have a stronger motivation to manage than managers at lower levels. Furthermore, managers with a stronger motivation to manage are promoted faster, are rated as better managers by their employees, and earn more money than managers with a weak motivation to manage.[52]

ᒫ Mistakes Managers Make

Another way to understand what it takes to be a manager is to look at the mistakes managers make. In other words, we can learn just as much from what managers shouldn't do as from what they should do.

Several studies of U.S. and British managers have compared "arrivers," or managers who made it all the way to the top of their companies, with "derailers," or managers who were successful early in their careers but were knocked off the fast track by the time they reached the middle to upper levels of management.[53] The researchers found that there were only a few differences between arrivers and derailers. For the most part, both groups were talented and both groups had weaknesses. But what distinguished derailers from arrivers was that derailers possessed two or more fatal flaws with respect to the way they managed people. Although arrivers were by no means perfect, they usually had no more than one fatal flaw or had found ways to minimize the effects of their flaws on the people with whom they worked.

The number-one mistake made by derailers was that they were insensitive to others as demonstrated by their abrasive, intimidating, and bullying management style. The authors of one study described a manager who walked into his subordinate's office and interrupted a meeting by saying, "I need to see you." When the subordinate tried to explain that he was not available because he was in the middle of a meeting, the manager barked, "I don't give a damn. I said I wanted to see you now."[54] Not surprisingly, only 25 percent of derailers were rated by others as being good with people, compared to 75 percent of arrivers.

The second mistake was that derailers were often cold, aloof, or arrogant. Although this sounds like insensitivity to others, it has more to do with derailed managers being so smart, so expert in their areas of knowledge, that they treated others with contempt because they weren't experts, too. For example, AT&T called in an industrial psychologist to counsel its vice president of human resources because she had been blamed for ruffling too many feathers at the company.[55] Interviews

© iStockphoto.com/Josh Rinehults

with the vice president's coworkers and subordinates revealed that they thought she was brilliant. Unfortunately, these smarts were accompanied by a cold, aloof, and arrogant management style. The people she worked with complained that she does "too much too fast," treats coworkers with "disdain," "impairs teamwork," "doesn't always show her warm side," and has "burned too many bridges."

The third mistake made by derailers involved betraying a trust. Betraying a trust doesn't mean being dishonest. Instead, it means making others look bad by not doing what you said you would do when you said you would do it. That mistake, in itself, is not fatal because managers and their workers aren't machines. Tasks go undone in every company every single business day. There's always too much to do and not enough time, people, money, or resources to do it. The fatal betrayal of trust is failing to inform others when things will not be done on time. This failure to admit mistakes, quickly inform others of the mistakes, take responsibility for the mistakes, and then fix them without blaming others distinguished the behavior of derailers from arrivers.

The fourth mistake of derailers was being overly political and ambitious. Managers who always have their eye on their next job rarely establish more than superficial relationships with peers and coworkers. In their haste to gain credit for successes that will be no-

ticed by upper management, they make the fatal mistake of treating people as though they don't matter.

The fatal mistakes of being unable to delegate, build a team, and staff effectively indicate that many derailed managers were unable to make the most basic transition to managerial work: to quit being hands-on doers and start getting work done through others. Two things go wrong when managers make these mistakes. First, when managers meddle in decisions that their subordinates should be making—when they can't stop being doers—they alienate the people who work for them. According to Michael Mathieu, CEO of online video advertising firm YuMe, "The worst managers come in and believe, 'O.K., I'm going to control this.' They're very structured. And...that actually stifles high performers."[56] Second, because they are trying to do their subordinates' jobs in addition to their own, managers who fail to delegate will not have enough time to do anything well.

7 The Transition to Management: The First Year

In her book *Becoming a Manager: Mastery of a New Identity*, Harvard Business School professor Linda Hill followed the development of nineteen people in their first year as managers. Her study found that becoming a manager produced a profound psychological transition that changed the way these managers viewed themselves and others. As shown in Exhibit 1.5 on the next page, the evolution of the managers' thoughts, expectations, and realities over the course of their first year in management reveals the magnitude of the changes they experienced.

Initially, the managers in Hill's study believed that their job was to exercise formal authority and to manage tasks—basically being the boss, telling others what to do, making decisions, and getting things done. In fact, most of the new managers were attracted to management positions because they wanted to be in charge. Surprisingly, the new managers did not

Top Ten Mistakes Managers Make

1. Insensitive to others: abrasive, intimidating, bullying style

2. Cold, aloof, arrogant

3. Betray trust

4. Overly ambitious: thinking of next job, playing politics

5. Specific performance problems with the business

6. Overmanaging: unable to delegate or build a team

7. Unable to staff effectively

8. Unable to think strategically

9. Unable to adapt to boss with different style

10. Overdependent on advocate or mentor

Source: M. W. McCall, Jr., and M. M. Lombardo, "What Makes a Top Executive?" *Psychology Today*, February 1983, 26–31.

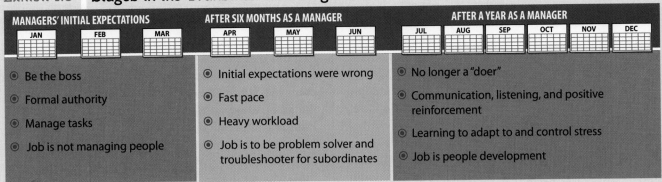

Exhibit 1.5 Stages in the Transition to Management

MANAGERS' INITIAL EXPECTATIONS			AFTER SIX MONTHS AS A MANAGER			AFTER A YEAR AS A MANAGER					
JAN	FEB	MAR	APR	MAY	JUN	JUL	AUG	SEP	OCT	NOV	DEC

MANAGERS' INITIAL EXPECTATIONS	AFTER SIX MONTHS AS A MANAGER	AFTER A YEAR AS A MANAGER
◉ Be the boss	◉ Initial expectations were wrong	◉ No longer a "doer"
◉ Formal authority	◉ Fast pace	◉ Communication, listening, and positive reinforcement
◉ Manage tasks	◉ Heavy workload	◉ Learning to adapt to and control stress
◉ Job is not managing people	◉ Job is to be problem solver and troubleshooter for subordinates	◉ Job is people development

© Cengage Learning 2011

believe that their job was to manage people. The only aspects of people management mentioned by the new managers were hiring and firing.

After 6 months, most of the new managers had concluded that their initial expectations about managerial work were wrong. Management wasn't just about being the boss, making decisions, and telling others what to do. The first surprise was the fast pace and heavy workload involved. Said one of Hill's managers, "This job is much harder than you think. It is 40 to 50 percent more work than being a producer! Who would have ever guessed?" The pace of managerial work was startling, too. Another manager said, "You have eight or nine people looking for your time . . . coming into and out of your office all day long." A somewhat frustrated manager declared that management was "a job that never ended . . . a job you couldn't get your hands around."[57]

Informal descriptions like this are consistent with studies indicating that the average first-line manager spends no more than 2 minutes on a task before being interrupted by a request from a subordinate, a phone call, or an email. The pace is somewhat less hurried for top managers, who spend an average of approximately 9 minutes on a task before having to switch to another. In practice, this means that supervisors may perform thirty different tasks per hour, while top managers perform seven different tasks

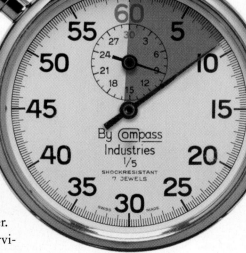

Top managers spend an average of 9 minutes on a given task before having to switch to another.

per hour, with each task typically different from the one that preceded it. A manager described this frenetic level of activity by saying, "The only time you are in control is when you shut your door, and then I feel I am not doing the job I'm supposed to be doing, which is being with the people."[58]

The other major surprise after 6 months on the job was that the managers' expectations about what they should do as managers were very different from their subordinates' expectations. Initially, the managers defined their jobs as helping their subordinates perform their jobs well. For the managers who still defined themselves as doers rather than managers, assisting their subordinates meant going out on sales calls or handling customer complaints. But when the managers "assisted" in this way, their subordinates were resentful and viewed their help as interference. The subordinates wanted their managers to help them by solving problems that they couldn't solve. Once the managers realized this distinction, they embraced their role as problem solver and troubleshooter. They could then help without interfering with their subordinates' jobs.

After a year on the job, most of the managers thought of themselves as managers and no longer as doers. In making the transition, they finally realized that people management was the most important part of their job. One of Hill's interviewees summarized the lesson that had taken him a year to learn by saying, "As many

© Stockbyte/Getty Images

demands as managers have on their time, I think their primary responsibility is people development. Not production, but people development."[59] Another indication of how much their views had changed was that most of the managers now regretted the rather heavy-handed approach they had used in their early attempts to manage their subordinates. "I wasn't good at managing . . . , so I was bossy like a first-grade teacher." "Now I see that I started out as a drill sergeant. I was inflexible, just a lot of how-tos."[60] By the end of the year, most of the managers had abandoned their authoritarian approach for one based on communication, listening, and positive reinforcement.

Finally, after beginning their year as managers in frustration, the managers came to feel comfortable with their subordinates, with the demands of their jobs, and with their emerging managerial styles. While being managers had made them acutely aware of their limitations and their need to develop as people, it also provided them with an unexpected reward of coaching and developing the people who worked for them. One manager said, "I realize now that when I accepted the position of branch manager that it is truly an exciting vocation. It is truly awesome, even at this level; it can be terribly challenging and terribly exciting."[61]

© iStockphoto.com/Todd Headington

MGMT ≠ BOSSY

Why Management Matters

If you walk down the aisle of the business section in your local bookstore, you'll find hundreds of books that explain precisely what companies need to do to be successful. Unfortunately, the best-selling business books tend to be faddish, changing dramatically every few years. One thing that hasn't changed, though, is the importance of good people and good management: Companies can't succeed for long without them.

After reading this section, you should be able to

🔒 **explain how and why companies can create competitive advantage through people.**

🔒 Competitive Advantage through People

In his books *Competitive Advantage through People* and *The Human Equation: Building Profits by Putting People First,* Stanford University business professor Jeffrey Pfeffer contends that what separates top-performing companies from their competitors is the way they treat their workforces—in other words, their management style.[62]

Pfeffer found that managers in top-performing companies used ideas like employment security, selective hiring, self-managed teams and decentralization, high pay contingent on company performance, extensive training, reduced status distinctions (between managers and employees), and extensive sharing of financial information to achieve financial performance that, on average, was 40 percent higher than that of other companies. These ideas, which are explained in detail in Exhibit 1.6 on the next page, help organizations develop workforces that are smarter, better trained, more motivated, and more committed than their competitors' workforces. And—as indicated by the phenomenal growth and return on investment earned by these companies—smarter, better trained, and more committed workforces provide superior products and service to customers. Such customers keep buying and, by telling others about their positive experiences, bring in new customers.

According to Pfeffer, companies that invest in their people will also create long-lasting competitive advantages that are difficult for other companies to duplicate. Indeed, other studies clearly demonstrate that sound management practices can produce substantial advantages in four critical areas of organizational performance: sales revenues, profits, stock market returns, and customer satisfaction.

In terms of sales revenues and profits, a study of nearly 1,000 U.S. firms found that companies using *just some* of the ideas shown in Exhibit 1.6 had $27,044 more sales per employee and $3,814 more profit per employee than companies that didn't.[63] For a 100-person company, these differences amount to $2.7 million more in sales and nearly $400,000 more in annual profit! For a 1,000-person company, the difference grows to $27 million more in sales and $4 million more in annual profit![64]

Another study that considered how investing in people affects company sales found that poorly performing companies were able to improve their average return on investment from 5.1 percent to 19.7 percent and increase sales by $94,000 per employee. They did this by adopting management techniques as simple as setting performance expectations and coaching, reviewing, and rewarding employee performance.[65] So, in addition to significantly improving the profitability of healthy companies, sound management practices can turn around failing companies.

To determine how investing in people affects stock market performance, researchers matched companies on *Fortune* magazine's list of "100 Best Companies to Work for in America" with companies that were similar in industry, size, and—this is key—operating performance. Both sets of companies were equally good performers; the key difference was how well they treated their employees. For both sets of companies, the researchers found that employee attitudes such as job satisfaction changed little from year to year. The people who worked for the "100 Best" companies

Exhibit 1.6 | Competitive Advantage through People: Management Practices

1. Employment Security—Employment security is the ultimate form of commitment companies can make to their workers. Employees can innovate and increase company productivity without fearing the loss of their jobs.

2. Selective Hiring—If employees are the basis for a company's competitive advantage and those employees have employment security, then the company needs to aggressively recruit and selectively screen applicants in order to hire the most talented employees available.

3. Self-Managed Teams and Decentralization—Self-managed teams are responsible for their own hiring, purchasing, job assignments, and production. Self-managed teams can often produce enormous increases in productivity through increased employee commitment and creativity. Decentralization allows employees who are closest to (and most knowledgeable about) problems, production, and customers to make timely decisions. Decentralization increases employee satisfaction and commitment.

4. High Wages Contingent on Organizational Performance—High wages are needed to attract and retain talented workers and to indicate that the organization values its workers. Employees, like company founders, shareholders, and managers, need to share in the financial rewards when the company is successful. Why? Because employees who have a financial stake in their companies are more likely to take a long-run view of the business and think like business owners.

5. Training and Skill Development—Like a high-tech company that spends millions of dollars to upgrade computers or research and development labs, a company whose competitive advantage is based on its people must invest in the training and skill development of its people.

6. Reduction of Status Differences—A company should treat everyone, no matter what the job, as equal. There are no reserved parking spaces. Everyone eats in the same cafeteria and has similar benefits. The result: improved communication as employees focus on problems and solutions rather than on how they are less valued than managers.

7. Sharing Information—If employees are to make decisions that are good for the long-term health and success of the company, they need to be given information about costs, finances, productivity, development times, and strategies that was previously known only by company managers.

Source: J. Pfeffer, *The Human Equation: Building Profits by Putting People First* (Boston: Harvard Business School Press, 1996).

were consistently much more satisfied with their jobs and employers year after year than were employees in the matched companies. More importantly, those stable differences in employee attitudes were strongly related to differences in stock market performance. Over a 3-year period, an investment in the "100 Best" companies would have resulted in an 82 percent cumulative stock return compared to just 37 percent for the matched companies.[66] This difference is remarkable given that both sets of companies were equally good performers at the beginning of the period.

Finally, research also indicates that managers have an important effect on customer satisfaction. Many people find this surprising. They don't understand how managers, who are largely responsible for what goes on inside the company, can affect what goes on outside the company. They wonder how managers, who often interact with customers under negative conditions (when customers are angry or dissatisfied), can actually improve customer satisfaction. It turns out that managers influence customer satisfaction through employee satisfaction. When employees are satisfied with their jobs, their bosses, and the companies they work for, they provide much better service to customers.[67] In turn, customers are more satisfied, too. Indeed, customers of companies on *Fortune*'s list of "100 Best Companies to Work For," whose employees are much more satisfied with their jobs, show much higher customer satisfaction scores than do customers of comparable companies who are not on *Fortune*'s list. That difference in customer satisfaction also resulted in a 1.6 percent higher return on company assets.[68]

You will learn more about the service-profit chain in Chapter 18 on managing service and manufacturing operations.

Higher employee **satisfaction** can often lead to higher customer satisfaction.

STUDENT
Study
Tools

Located at the back of your book:

☐ Rip out and study the Chapter Review Card at the end of the book

Log in to the CourseMate for MGMT at cengagebrain.com to:

☐ Review Key Term Flashcards delivered 3 ways (print or online)

☐ Complete both Practice Quizzes to prepare for tests

☐ Play Beat the Clock and Quizbowl to master concepts

☐ Complete the Crossword Puzzle to review key terms

☐ Watch the video on Numi Organic Tea for a real company example and take the accompanying quiz

☐ Watch the Biz Flix clip from *In Good Company* and take the quiz

☐ Complete the Case Assignment on Starbucks

☐ Work through the Management Decision on checked baggage fees

☐ Work through the Management Team Decision on RFID tags

☐ Develop your skills with the Develop Your Career Potential exercise

2 | History of Management

© Southern Stock/Photodisc/Jupiterimages

LEARNING OUTCOMES:

1 explain the origins of management.

2 explain the history of scientific management.

3 discuss the history of bureaucratic and administrative management.

4 explain the history of human relations management.

5 discuss the history of operations, information, systems, and contingency management.

Chapter 2

In the Beginning

each day, managers are asked to solve challenging problems and are given only a limited amount of time, people, or resources. Yet it's still their responsibility to get things done on time and within budget. Tell today's managers to "reward workers for improved production or performance," "set specific goals to increase motivation," or "innovate to create and sustain a competitive advantage," and they'll respond, "Duh! Who doesn't know that?" A mere 125 years ago, however, business ideas and practices were so different that today's widely accepted management ideas would have been as self-evident as space travel, cell phones, and the Internet. In fact, management jobs and careers did not exist 125 years ago, so management was not yet a field of study. If there were no managers 125 years ago but you can't walk down the hall today without bumping into one, where did management come from?

After reading the next section, you should be able to

1 **explain the origins of management.**

1 The Origins of Management

Although we can find the seeds of many of today's management ideas throughout history, not until the last two centuries did systematic changes in the nature of work and organizations create a compelling need for managers.

*Let's begin our discussion of the origins of management by learning about **1.1 management ideas and practice throughout history** and **1.2 why we need managers today.***

1.1 | MANAGEMENT IDEAS AND PRACTICE THROUGHOUT HISTORY

Examples of management thought and practice can be found throughout history.[1] For example, the Egyptians recognized the need for planning, organizing, and controlling; for submitting written requests; and for consulting staff for advice before making decisions. The practical problems they encountered while building the great pyramids no doubt led to the development of these management ideas. The enormity of the task they faced is evident in the pyramid of King Khufu, which contains 2.3 million blocks of stone. Each block had to be quarried, cut to precise size and shape, cured (hardened in the sun), transported by boat for 2 to 3 days, moved onto the construction site, numbered to identify where it would be placed, and then shaped and smoothed so that it would fit perfectly into place. It took 20,000 workers 23 years to complete this pyramid; more than 8,000 were needed just to quarry the stones and transport them. A typical quarry expedition might include 100 army officers, 50 government and religious officials, and 200 members of the king's court to lead the expedition; 130 stone masons to cut the stones; and 5,000 soldiers, 800 foreigners, and 2,000 bond servants to transport the stones on and off the ships.[2]

Exhibit 2.1 on the next page shows how other management ideas and practices throughout history relate to the management functions discussed in this textbook.

Exhibit 2.1 Management Ideas and Practice throughout History

Time	Individual or Group	Planning	Organizing	Leading	Controlling	Contributions to Management Thought and Practice
5000 BCE	Sumerians				√	Written record keeping.
4000 BCE to 2000 BCE	Egyptians	√	√		√	Planning, organizing, and controlling to build the pyramids; submitting requests in writing; making decisions after consulting staff for advice.
1800 BCE	Hammurabi				√	Controls; using witnesses in legal cases.
600 BCE	Nebuchadnezzar		√	√		Wage incentives and production control.
500 BCE	Sun Tzu	√		√		Strategy; identifying and attacking opponent's weaknesses.
400 BCE	Xenophon	√	√	√	√	Management as separate art.
400 BCE	Cyrus		√	√	√	Human relations and motion study.
175	Cato		√			Job descriptions.
284	Diocletian		√			Delegation of authority.
900	al-Farabi			√		Leadership traits.
1100	Ghazali			√		Managerial traits.
1418	Barbarigo		√			Different organizational forms/structures.
1436	Venetians				√	Numbering, standardization, and interchangeability of parts.
1500	Sir Thomas More			√		Critique of poor management and leadership.
1525	Machiavelli		√	√		Cohesiveness, power, and leadership in organizations.

Source: C. S. George, Jr., *The History of Management Thought* (Englewood Cliffs, NJ: Prentice Hall, 1972).

1.2 | WHY WE NEED MANAGERS TODAY

Working from 8 a.m. to 5 p.m., taking coffee breaks and lunch hours, enduring rush hour traffic, and punching a time clock are things we associate with today's working world. But for most of humankind's history, for example, people didn't commute to work. Work usually occurred in homes or on farms. And as recently as 1870, two-thirds of Americans earned their living from agriculture. Even most of those who didn't earn their living from agriculture didn't commute to work. Blacksmiths, furniture makers, leather-goods makers, and other skilled tradespeople or craftspeople, who formed trade guilds (the historical predecessors of labor unions) in England as early as 1093, typically worked out of shops in or next to their homes.[3] Likewise, cottage workers worked with each other out of small homes that were often built in a semicircle. A family in each cottage would complete a different production step, and work passed from one cottage to the next until production was complete. With small, self-organized work groups, no commute, no bosses, and no common building, there wasn't a strong need for management.

During the Industrial Revolution (1750–1900), however, jobs and organizations changed dramatically.[4] First, the availability of power (steam engines and later electricity) enabled low-paid, unskilled laborers running machines to replace high-paid, skilled artisans who made entire goods by themselves by hand. This new mass-production system was based on a division of labor: Each worker, interacting with machines, performed separate, highly specialized tasks that were but a small part of all the steps required to make manufactured goods. While workers focused on their singular tasks, managers were needed to coordinate the different parts of the production system and optimize its overall performance. Productivity skyrocketed at companies that understood this. At Ford Motor Company, where the assembly line was developed, the time required to assemble a car dropped from 12.5 man hours to just 93 minutes.[5]

Second, instead of being performed in fields, homes, or small shops, jobs were carried out in large, formal organizations where hundreds, if not thousands, of people worked under one roof.[6] In 1849, for example, Chicago Harvester (the predecessor of International Harvester) ran the largest factory in the United States with just 123 workers. Yet, by 1913, Henry Ford employed 12,000 employees in his Highland Park, Michigan, factory alone. With individual factories employing so many workers under one roof, companies now had a strong need for disciplinary rules to impose order and structure. For the first time, they needed managers who knew how to organize large groups, work with employees, and make good decisions.

The Evolution of Management

before 1880, business educators taught only basic bookkeeping and secretarial skills, and no one published books or articles about management.[7] Today, you can turn to dozens of academic journals, hundreds of business school and practitioner journals (such as *Harvard Business Review, Sloan Management Review,* and *Academy of Management Executive*), and thousands of books and articles if you have a question about management. In the next four sections, you will learn about other important contributors to the field of management and how their ideas shaped our current understanding of management theory and practice.

Accounting and the Invention of Writing

Information management and accounting may have a common origin. Sumerian businessmen circa 8000–3000 BCE used small clay tokens to calculate quantities of grain and livestock—and later value-added goods like perfume and pottery—that they owned and traded in temples and city gates. Different shapes and sizes represented different types and quantities of goods. The tokens were also used to store data. They were kept in small clay envelopes, and the token shapes were impressed on the outside of the envelopes to indicate what was inside. Eventually, someone figured out that it was easier to just write these symbols with a stylus on a tablet instead of using the tokens. In the end, the new technology of writing led to more efficient management.

Source: D. Schmandt-Besserat, *How Writing Came About* (Austin: University of Texas Press, 1997).

© iStockphoto.com/Tom Hahn

After reading the next four sections, you should be able to

2 explain the history of scientific management.

3 discuss the history of bureaucratic and administrative management.

4 explain the history of human relations management.

5 discuss the history of operations, information, systems, and contingency management.

2 Scientific Management

Bosses, who were hired by company owners or founders, used to make decisions by the seat of their pants—haphazardly, without any systematic study, thought, or collection of information. If the bosses decided that workers should work twice as fast, little or no thought was given to worker motivation. If workers resisted, the bosses often resorted to physical beatings to get workers to work faster, harder, or longer. With no incentives for bosses and workers to cooperate with one another, both groups played the system by trying to take advantage of each other. Moreover, each worker did the same job in his or her own way with different methods and different tools. In short, there were no procedures to standardize operations, no standards by which to judge whether performance was good or bad, and no follow-up to determine if productivity or quality actually improved when changes were made.[8]

This all changed with the advent of **scientific management,** which involved thorough study and testing of different work methods to identify the best, most efficient ways to complete a job.

*Let's find out more about scientific management by learning about **2.1 Frederick W. Taylor, the father of scientific management; 2.2 Frank and Lillian Gilbreth and motion studies;** and **2.3 Henry Gantt and his Gantt charts.***

2.1 | FATHER OF SCIENTIFIC MANAGEMENT: FREDERICK W. TAYLOR

Frederick W. Taylor (1856–1915), the father of scientific management, began his career as a worker at Midvale Steel Company. He was later promoted to patternmaker, supervisor, and then chief engineer.

At Midvale, Taylor was deeply affected by his 3-year struggle to get the men who worked for him to do, as he called it, "a fair day's work." Taylor explained that as soon as he became the boss, "the men who were working under me . . . knew that I was onto the whole game of **soldiering,** or deliberately restricting output [to one-third of what they were capable of producing]."[9] When Taylor told his workers, "I am going to try to get a bigger output," the workers responded, "We warn you, Fred, if you try to bust any of these rates, we will have you over the fence in 6 weeks."[10] (A **rate buster** was a group member whose work pace was significantly faster than the normal pace in his or her group.)

Over the next 3 years, Taylor tried everything he could think of to improve output. By doing the job himself, he showed workers that it was possible to produce more output. He hired new workers and trained them himself, hoping they would produce more. But "very heavy social pressure" from the other workers kept them from doing so. Pushed by Taylor, the workers began breaking their machines so that they couldn't produce. Taylor responded by fining them every time they broke a machine and for any violation of the rules, no matter how small, such as being late to work. Tensions became so severe that some of the workers threatened to shoot him.

The remedy that Taylor eventually developed was scientific management. The goal of scientific management was to use systematic study to find the "one best way" of doing each task. To do that, managers had to follow the four principles shown in Exhibit 2.2. The first principle was to "develop a science" for each element of work. That meant they had to study each element. Analyze it. Determine the optimal means of doing it. For example, one of Taylor's controversial proposals at the time was to give rest breaks to factory workers doing physical labor. We take breaks for granted today, but factory workers in Taylor's day were expected to work without stopping.[11] Through systematic experiments, he showed that frequent rest breaks greatly increased daily output.

Frederick W. Taylor

Father of Scientific Management

© Bettmann/Corbis / © iStockphoto.com/flyfloor

Exhibit 2.2 Taylor's Four Principles of Scientific Management

First:	Develop a science for each element of a man's work, which replaces the old rule-of-thumb method.
Second:	Scientifically select and then train, teach, and develop the workman, whereas in the past he chose his own work and trained himself as best he could.
Third:	Heartily cooperate with the men so as to ensure all of the work being done is in accordance with the principles of the science that has been developed.
Fourth:	There is an almost equal division of the work and the responsibility between the management and the workmen. The management take over all the work for which they are better fitted than the workmen, while in the past almost all of the work and the greater part of the responsibility were thrown upon the men.

Source: F. W. Taylor, *The Principles of Scientific Management* (New York: Harper, 1911).

Second, managers had to scientifically select, train, teach, and develop workers to help them reach their full potential. Before Taylor, supervisors often hired on the basis of favoritism and nepotism. Who you knew was often more important than what you could do. By contrast, Taylor instructed supervisors to hire "first-class" workers on the basis of their aptitude to do a job well. For similar reasons, he also recommended that companies train and develop their workers—a rare practice at the time.

The third principle instructed managers to cooperate with employees to ensure that the scientific principles were actually implemented. As Taylor knew from personal experience, workers and management usually viewed each other as enemies. Taylor said, "The majority of these men believe that the fundamental interests of employees and employers are necessarily antagonistic. Scientific management, on the contrary, is founded on the firm conviction that the true interests of the two are one and the same. Prosperity for the employer cannot exist through a long term of years unless it is accompanied by prosperity for the employee. Moreover, it is possible to give the workman what he most wants—high wages—and the employer what he wants—a low labor cost—for his manufactures."[12]

The fourth principle of scientific management was to divide the work and the responsibility equally between management and workers. Prior to Taylor, workers alone were held responsible for productivity and performance. But, said Taylor, "Almost every act of the workman should be preceded by one or more preparatory acts of the management which enable him to do his work better and quicker than he otherwise could."[13]

Above all, Taylor felt these principles could be used to determine a "fair day's work," that is, what an average worker could produce at a reasonable pace, day in and day out. Once that was determined, it was management's responsibility to pay workers fairly for that fair day's work. In essence, Taylor was trying to align management and employees so that what was good for employees was also good for management. In this way, he felt, workers and managers could avoid the conflicts he had experienced at Midvale Steel. And one of the best ways, according to Taylor, to align management and employees was to use incentives to motivate workers. In particular, Taylor believed in piece-rate incentives that tied workers' pay directly to how much workers produced.

Although Taylor remains a controversial figure among some academics, his key ideas have stood the test of time.[14] In fact, his ideas are so well accepted and widely used that we take most of them for granted. As eminent management scholar Edwin Locke says, "The point is not, as is often claimed, that he was 'right in the context of his time' but is now outdated, but that *most of his insights are still valid today.*"[15]

2.2 | MOTION STUDIES: FRANK AND LILLIAN GILBRETH

The husband-and-wife team of Frank and Lillian Gilbreth is best known for the use of motion studies to simplify work. Like Frederick Taylor, the Gilbreths had early experiences that significantly shaped their interests and contributions to management.

Though admitted to MIT, Frank Gilbreth (1868–1924) began his career as an apprentice bricklayer. While learning the trade, he noticed the bricklayers using three different sets of motions—one to teach others how to lay bricks, a second to work at a slow pace, and a third to work at a fast pace.[16] Wondering which was best, he studied the various approaches and began eliminating unnecessary motions. For example, by

Companies Still Strive for the "One Best Way"

Don't think scientific management has much to do with today's work life? Think again. Remember the last time you were at the store and the clerk said, "Have a nice day." Chances are the clerk was using a script. Service providers often use scripts to ensure that employees are following the "one best way" of interacting with the customers. At Build-a-Bear Workshops, sales associates are trained to exhibit "must-see behaviors," such as telling customers "Let me show you the Dress Me station!" as opposed to "Would you like to see the Dress Me station?" Scripted behaviors are particularly common at restaurants, such as Olive Garden, where workers must greet the table within 30 seconds of arrival, take the drink order within 3 minutes, suggest five items while taking the order, and check back with the table 3 minutes after the food arrives.

Sources: P. Keegan, "CEO Swap: 2 Best Companies Chiefs Trade Places," *Fortune*, January 22, 2010, accessed July 22, 2010, http://money.cnn.com/2010/01/21/news/companies/build_a_bear_container_store.fortune/index.htm; C. McCann, "Have a Nice Day and an Icy Stare," *Marketing Week*, September 2, 2004, 27.

designing a stand that could be raised to waist height, he eliminated the need to bend over to pick up each brick. By having lower-paid workers place all the bricks with their most attractive side up, bricklayers didn't waste time turning a brick over to find that side. By mixing a more consistent mortar, bricklayers no longer had to tap each brick numerous times to put it in the right position. Together, Gilbreth's improvements raised productivity from 120 to 350 bricks per hour and from 1,000 bricks to 2,700 bricks per day.

As a result of his experience with bricklaying, Gilbreth and his wife Lillian developed a long-term interest in using motion study to simplify work, improve productivity, and reduce the level of effort required to safely perform a job. Indeed, Frank Gilbreth said, "The greatest waste in the world comes from needless, ill-directed, and ineffective motions."[17] **Motion study** broke each task or job into separate motions and then eliminated those that were unnecessary or repetitive. Because many motions were completed very quickly, the Gilbreths used motion-picture films, a relatively new technology at the time, to analyze jobs. Most film cameras, however, were hand-cranked and thus variable in their film speed, so Frank Gilbreth invented the microchronometer, a large clock that could record time to 1/2000th of a second. By placing the microchronometer next to the worker in the camera's field of vision and attaching a flashing strobe light to the worker's hands to better identify the direction and sequence of key movements, the Gilbreths could use film to detect and precisely time even the slightest and fastest movements. Motion study typically yielded production increases of 25 to 300 percent.

Frederick W. Taylor also strove to simplify work, but he did so by managing time rather than motion.[18] Taylor developed time study to put an end to soldiering and to determine what could be considered a fair day's work. **Time study** worked by timing how long it took a "first-class man" to complete each part of his job. A standard time was established after

Motion study breaking each task or job into its separate motions and then eliminating those that are unnecessary or repetitive

Time study timing how long it takes good workers to complete each part of their jobs allowing for rest periods, and a worker's pay would increase or decrease depending on whether the worker exceeded or fell below that standard.

Lillian Gilbreth (1878–1972) was an important contributor to management in her own right. She was the first woman to receive a PhD in industrial psychology as well as the first woman to become a member of the Society of Industrial Engineers and the American Society of Mechanical Engineers. When Frank died in 1924, she continued the work of their management consulting company (which they had shared for over a dozen years) on her own. Lillian was particularly concerned with the human side of work and was one of the first contributors to industrial psychology. She established ways to improve office communication, incentive programs, job satisfaction, and management training. Her work also convinced the government to enact laws regarding workplace safety, ergonomics, and child labor.

2.3 | CHARTS: HENRY GANTT

Henry Gantt (1861–1919) was first a protégé and then an associate of Frederick Taylor. Gantt is best known for the Gantt chart, but he also made significant contributions to management with respect to the training and development of workers. As shown in Exhibit 2.3, a **Gantt chart** visually indicates what tasks must be completed at which times in order to complete a project. It accomplishes this by showing time in various units on the x-axis and tasks on the y-axis. For example, Exhibit 2.3 shows that the following tasks must be completed by the following dates: In order to start construction on a new company headquarters by the week of November 18, the architectural firm must be selected by October 7, the architectural planning done by November 4, permits obtained from the city by November 11, site preparation finished by November 18, and loans and financing finalized by November 18. Though simple and straightforward, Gantt charts were revolutionary in the era of seat-of-the-pants management because of the detailed planning information they provided to managers. Gantt said, "Such sheets show at a glance where the delays occur, and indicate what must have our attention in order to keep up the proper output."[19] The use of Gantt charts is so widespread today that nearly all project management software and computer spreadsheets have the capability to create charts that track and visually display the progress being made on a project.

Finally, Gantt, along with Taylor, was one of the first to strongly recommend that companies train and

Gantt chart a graphic chart that shows which tasks must be completed at which times in order to complete a project or task

---

Exhibit 2.3 Gantt Chart for Starting Construction on a New Headquarters

Tasks	Weeks	23 Sep to 29 Sep	30 Sep to 6 Oct	7 Oct to 13 Oct	14 Oct to 20 Oct	21 Oct to 27 Oct	28 Oct to 3 Nov	4 Nov to 10 Nov	11 Nov to 17 Nov	18 Nov to 25 Nov
Interview and select architectural firm		Architect by October 7								
Hold weekly planning meetings with architects				Weekly planning with architects by November 4						
Obtain permits and approval from city						Permits & approval by November 11				
Begin preparing site for construction							Site preparation done by November 18			
Finalize loans and financing									Financing finalized by November 18	
Begin construction										Start building
Tasks		23 Sep to 29 Sep	30 Sep to 6 Oct	7 Oct to 13 Oct	14 Oct to 20 Oct	21 Oct to 27 Oct	28 Oct to 3 Nov	4 Nov to 10 Nov	11 Nov to 17 Nov	18 Nov to 25 Nov
	Weeks									

Bureaucracy the exercise of control on the basis of knowledge, expertise, or experience

develop their workers.[20] In his work with companies, he found that workers achieved their best performance levels if they were trained first. At the time, however, supervisors were reluctant to teach workers what they knew for fear they could lose their jobs to more knowledgeable workers. Gantt overcame the supervisors' resistance by rewarding them with bonuses for properly training all of their workers. Gantt's approach to training was straightforward: "(1) A scientific investigation in detail of each piece of work, and the determination of the best method and the shortest time in which the work can be done. (2) A teacher capable of teaching the best method and the shortest time. (3) Reward for both teacher and pupil when the latter is successful."[21]

3 Bureaucratic and Administrative Management

The field of scientific management focused on improving the efficiency of manufacturing facilities and their workers. At about the same time, equally important ideas about bureaucratic and administrative management were developing in Europe. German sociologist Max Weber presented a new way to run entire organizations in *The Theory of Economic and Social Organization*, published in 1922. Henri Fayol, an experienced French CEO, published his ideas about how and what managers should do in their jobs (administrative management) in *General and Industrial Management* in 1916.

*Let's find out more about the contributions Weber and Fayol made to management by learning about **3.1 bureaucratic management** and **3.2 administrative management**.*

3.1 | BUREAUCRATIC MANAGEMENT: MAX WEBER

Today, when we hear the term *bureaucracy*, we think of inefficiency and red tape, incompetence and ineffectiveness, and rigid administrators blindly enforcing nonsensical rules. When German sociologist Max Weber (1864–1920) first proposed the idea of bureaucratic organizations, however, these problems were associated with monarchies and patriarchies rather than bureaucracies. In monarchies, where kings, queens, sultans, and emperors ruled, and patriarchies, where a council of elders, wise men, or male heads of extended families ruled, the top leaders typically achieved their positions by virtue of birthright. Likewise, promotion to prominent positions of authority was based on who you knew (politics), who you were (heredity), or traditions.

It was against this historical background that Weber proposed the then new idea of bureaucracy. According to Weber, **bureaucracy** is "the exercise of control on the basis of knowledge."[22] Rather than ruling by virtue of favoritism or personal or family connections, people in a bureaucracy would lead by virtue of their rational-legal authority—in other words, their knowledge, expertise, or experience. Furthermore, the aim of bureaucracy is not to protect authority, but to achieve an organization's goals in the most efficient way possible.

Exhibit 2.4 shows the seven elements that, according to Weber, characterize bureaucracies. First, instead of hiring people because of their family or political connections or personal loyalty, an organization should hire those whose technical training or education qualifies them to do the job well. Second, along the same lines, promotion within the organization should no longer be based on who you know (politics) or who you are (heredity), but on your experience or achievements. And to further limit the influence of

Bureaucracy

Exhibit 2.4 Elements of Bureaucratic Organizations

Qualification-based hiring:	Employees are hired on the basis of their technical training or educational background.
Merit-based promotion:	Promotion is based on experience or achievement. Managers, not organizational owners, decide who is promoted.
Chain of command:	Each job occurs within a hierarchy, the chain of command, in which each position reports and is accountable to a higher position. A grievance procedure and a right to appeal protect people in lower positions.
Division of labor:	Tasks, responsibilities, and authority are clearly divided and defined.
Impartial application of rules and procedures:	Rules and procedures apply to all members of the organization and will be applied in an impartial manner, regardless of one's position or status.
Recorded in writing:	All administrative decisions, acts, rules, or procedures will be recorded in writing.
Managers separate from owners:	The owners of an organization should not manage or supervise the organization.

Source: M. Weber, *The Theory of Economic and Social Organization*, trans. A. Henderson and T. Parsons (New York: The Free Press, 1947), 329–334.

personal connections in the promotion process, *managers* rather than organizational owners should decide who gets promoted. Third, each position or job should be viewed as part of a chain of command that clarifies who reports to whom throughout the organization. Those higher in the chain of command have the right, if they so choose, to give commands, take action, and make decisions concerning activities occurring anywhere below them in the chain. Fourth, to increase efficiency and effectiveness, tasks and responsibilities should be separated and assigned to those best qualified to complete them. Authority is vested in these task-defined positions rather than in people, and the authority of each position is clearly defined in order to reduce confusion and conflict. Fifth, an organization's rules and procedures should apply to all members regardless of their position or status. Sixth, to ensure consistency and fairness over time and across different leaders, all rules, procedures, and decisions should be recorded in writing. Finally,

to reduce favoritism, "professional" managers rather than company owners should manage or supervise the organization.

When viewed in historical context, Weber's ideas about bureaucracy represent a tremendous improvement. Fairness supplanted favoritism, the goal of efficiency replaced the goal of personal gain, and logical rules and procedures took the place of traditions or arbitrary decision making.

Today, however, after more than a century of experience, we recognize that bureaucracy has limitations as well. Weber called bureaucracy the "iron cage" and said, "Once fully established, bureaucracy is among those social structures which are the hardest to destroy."[23] In bureaucracies, managers are supposed to influence employee behavior by fairly rewarding or punishing employees for compliance or noncompliance with organizational policies, rules, and procedures. In reality, however, most employees would argue that bureaucratic managers emphasize punishment for non-compliance much more than reward for compliance. Ironically, bureaucratic management was created to prevent just this type of managerial behavior.

3.2 | ADMINISTRATIVE MANAGEMENT: HENRI FAYOL

Though his work was not translated and widely recognized in the United States until 1949, Frenchman Henri Fayol (1841–1925) was as important a contributor to the field of management as Frederick Taylor. Whereas Taylor's ideas changed companies from the shop floor up, Fayol's ideas were shaped by his experience as a managing director (CEO) and generally changed companies from the board of directors down.[24] Fayol is best known for developing five functions of managers and fourteen principles of management.

The most formative events in Fayol's business career came during his more than 20 years as the managing director (CEO) of Compagnie de Commentry-Fourchambault-Decazeville, commonly known as Comambault, a vertically integrated steel company that owned several coal and iron ore mines and employed 10,000 to 13,000 workers. Fayol was initially hired by the board of directors to shut down the "hopeless" steel company. But, after "4 months of reflection and study," he presented the board with a plan, backed by detailed facts and figures, to save the company.[25] With little to lose, the board agreed. Fayol then began the process of turning the company around by obtaining supplies of key resources such as coal and iron ore; using research to develop new steel alloy products; carefully selecting key subordinates in research, purchasing, manufacturing, and sales and then delegating responsibility to them; and cutting costs by moving the company to a better location closer to key markets.[26] Looking back 10 years later, Fayol attributed his and the company's success to changes in management practices. He wrote, "When I assumed the responsibility for the restoration of Decazeville, I did not rely on my technical superiority. . . . I relied on my ability as an organizer [and my] skill in handling men."[27]

Based on his experience as a CEO, Fayol argued that "the success of an enterprise generally depends much more on the administrative ability of its leaders than on their technical ability."[28] And, as you learned in Chapter 1, Fayol argued that managers need to perform five managerial functions if they are to be successful: planning, organizing, coordinating, commanding, and controlling.[29] Because most man-agement textbooks have dropped the coordinating function and now refer to Fayol's commanding function as "leading," these functions are widely known as planning (determining organizational goals and a means for achieving them), organizing (deciding where decisions will be made, who will do what jobs and tasks, and who will work for whom), leading (inspiring and motivating workers to work hard to achieve organizational goals), and controlling (monitoring progress toward goal achievement and taking corrective action when needed). In addition, according to Fayol, effective management is based on the fourteen principles in Exhibit 2.5.

4 Human Relations Management

As we have seen, scientific management focuses on improving efficiency; bureaucratic management focuses on using knowledge, fairness, and logical rules and procedures; and administrative management focuses on how and what managers should do in their jobs. The human relations approach to management focuses on *people*. This approach to management sees people not as just extensions of machines but as valuable organizational resources in their own right. Human relations management holds that people's needs are important and understands that their efforts, motivation, and performance are affected by the work they do and their relationships with their bosses, coworkers, and work groups. In other words, efficiency alone is not enough. Organizational success also depends on treating workers well.

*Let's find out more about human relations management by learning about **4.1 Mary Parker Follett's theories of constructive conflict, 4.2 Elton Mayo's Hawthorne Studies,** and **4.3 Chester Barnard's theories of cooperation and acceptance of authority.***

4.1 | CONSTRUCTIVE CONFLICT: MARY PARKER FOLLETT

Mary Parker Follett (1868–1933) was a social worker who, after 25 years of working with schools and non-profit organizations, began lecturing and writing about management and working extensively as a consultant for business and government. Many of today's "new" management ideas can be traced clearly to her work.

Follett is known for developing ideas regarding constructive conflict, also called cognitive conflict,

Exhibit 2.5   Fayol's Fourteen Principles of Management

1   Division of work

Increase production by dividing work so that each worker completes smaller tasks or job elements.

2   Authority and responsibility

A manager's authority, which is the "right to give orders," should be commensurate with the manager's responsibility. However, organizations should enact controls to prevent managers from abusing their authority.

3   Discipline

Clearly defined rules and procedures are needed at all organizational levels to ensure order and proper behavior.

4   Unity of command

To avoid confusion and conflict, each employee should report to and receive orders from just one boss.

5   Unity of direction

One person and one plan should be used in deciding the activities to be carried out to accomplish each organizational objective.

6   Subordination of individual interests to the general interest

Employees must put the organization's interests and goals before their own.

7   Remuneration

Compensation should be fair and satisfactory to both the employees and the organization; that is, don't overpay or underpay employees.

8   Centralization

Avoid too much centralization or decentralization. Strike a balance depending on the circumstances and employees involved.

9   Scalar chain

From the top to the bottom of an organization, each position is part of a vertical chain of authority in which each worker reports to just one boss. For the sake of simplicity, communication outside normal work groups or departments should follow the vertical chain of authority.

10   Order

To avoid conflicts and confusion, order can be obtained by having a place for everyone and having everyone in his or her place; in other words, there should be no overlapping responsibilities.

11   Equity

Kind, fair, and just treatment for all will develop devotion and loyalty. This does not exclude discipline, if warranted, and consideration of the broader general interest of the organization.

12   Stability of tenure of personnel

Low turnover, meaning a stable work force with high tenure, benefits an organization by improving performance, lowering costs, and giving employees, especially managers, time to learn their jobs.

13   Initiative

Because it is a "great source of strength for business," managers should encourage the development of initiative, or the ability to develop and implement a plan, in others.

14   *Esprit de corps*

Develop a strong sense of morale and unity among workers that encourages coordination of efforts.

Sources: H. Fayol, *General and Industrial Management* (London: Pittman & Sons, 1949); M. Fells, "Fayol Stands the Test of Time," *Journal of Management History* 6 (2000): 345–360; C. Rodrigues, "Fayol's 14 Principles of Management Then and Now: A Framework for Managing Today's Organizations Effectively," *Management Decision* 39 (2001): 880–889.

which is discussed in Chapter 5 on decision making and Chapter 10 on teams. Unlike most people, then and now, who view conflict as bad, Follett believed that conflict could be beneficial. She said that conflict is "the appearance of difference, difference of opinions, of interests. For that is what conflict means—difference." She went on to say, "As conflict—difference—is here in this world, as we cannot avoid it, we should, I think, use it to work for us. Instead of condemning it, we should set it to work for us. Thus we shall not be afraid of conflict, but shall recognize that there is a destructive way of dealing with such moments and a constructive way."[30]

Follett believed that the best way to deal with conflict was not domination, where one side wins and the other loses, or compromise, where each side gives up some of what it wants, but integration. Said Follett, "There is a way beginning now to be recognized at least, and even occasionally followed: when two desires are *integrated*, that means that a solution has been found in which both desires have found a place that neither side has had to sacrifice anything."[31] So, rather than one side dominating the other or both sides compromising, the point of **integrative conflict resolution** is to have both parties indicate their preferences and then work together to find an alternative that meets the needs of both. According to Follett, "Integration involves invention, and the clever thing is to recognize this, and not to let one's thinking stay within the boundaries of two alternatives which are mutually exclusive."[32] Indeed, Follett's ideas about the positive use of conflict and an integrative approach to conflict resolution predate accepted thinking in the negotiation and conflict resolution literature by six decades (see the best-selling book *Getting to Yes: Negotiating Agreement without Giving In* by Roger Fisher, William Ury, and Bruce Patton).

Exhibit 2.6 summarizes Follett's contributions to management in her own words. She casts power as "with" rather than "over" others. Giving orders involves discussing instructions and dealing with resentment. Authority flows from job knowledge and experience rather than position. Leadership involves setting the tone for the team rather than being aggressive and dominating, which may be harmful. Coordination and control should be based on facts and information. In the end, Follett's contributions added significantly to our understanding of the human, social, and psychological sides of management. Peter Parker, the former chairman of the London School of Economics, said about Follett: "People often puzzle about who is the father of management. I don't know who the father was, but I have no doubt about who was the mother."[33]

4.2 | HAWTHORNE STUDIES: ELTON MAYO

Australian-born Elton Mayo (1880–1948) is best known for his role in the famous Hawthorne Studies at the Western Electric Company. The Hawthorne Studies were conducted in several stages between 1924 and 1932 at a Western Electric plant in Chicago. Although Mayo didn't join the studies until 1928, he played a significant role thereafter, writing about the results in his book, *The Human Problems of an Industrial Civilization*.[34] The first stage of the Hawthorne Studies investigated the effects of lighting levels and incentives on employee productivity in the Relay Test Assembly Room, where workers took approximately a minute to put "together a coil, armature, contact springs, and insulators in a fixture and secure the parts by means of four machine screws."[35] Two groups of six experienced female workers, five to do the work and one to supply needed parts, were separated from the main part of the factory by a 10-foot partition and placed at a standard work bench with the necessary parts and tools. Over the next 5 years, the experimenters introduced various levels and combinations of lighting, financial incentives, and rest pauses (work breaks) to study the effect on productivity. Curiously, however, production levels increased whether the experimenters increased or decreased the lighting, paid workers based on individual production or group production, or increased or decreased the number and length of rest pauses. The question was: Why?

Mayo and his colleagues eventually concluded that two things accounted for the results. First, substantially more attention was paid to these workers than to workers in the rest of the plant. Mayo wrote, "Before every change of program [in the study], the group is consulted. Their comments are listened to and discussed; sometimes their objections are allowed to negate a suggestion. The group unquestionably develops a sense of participation in the critical determinations and becomes something of a social unit."[36]

For years, the "Hawthorne Effect" has been *incorrectly* defined as increasing productivity by paying more attention to workers.[37] But it is not simply about attention from management. The Hawthorne Effect cannot be understood without giving equal importance to the "social units," which became intensively cohesive groups. Mayo said, "What actually happened was

Exhibit 2.6

Mary Parker Follett says . . .

On constructive conflict . . .

"As conflict—difference—is here in this world, as we cannot avoid it, we should, I think, use it to work for us. Instead of condemning it, we should set it to work for us."

On power . . .

"It seems to me that whereas power usually means power-over, the power of some person or group over some other person or group, it is possible to develop the conception of power-with, a jointly developed power, a co-active, not a coercive power."

On the giving of orders . . .

"An advantage of not exacting blind obedience, of discussing your instructions with your subordinates, is that if there is any resentment, any come-back, you get it out into the open, and when it is in the open you can deal with it."

On authority . . .

"Authority should go with knowledge and experience, that is where obedience is due, no matter whether it is up the line or down."

On leadership . . .

"Of the greatest importance is the ability to grasp a total situation. . . . Out of a welter of facts, experience, desires, aims, the leader must find the unifying thread. He must see a whole, not a mere kaleidoscope of pieces. . . . The higher up you go, the more ability you have to have of this kind."

On coordination . . .

"The most important thing to remember about unity is—that there is no such thing. There is only unifying. You cannot get unity and expect it to last a day—or five minutes. Every man in a business should be taking part in a certain process and that process is unifying."

On control . . .

"Central control is coming more and more to mean the co-relation of many controls rather than a superimposed control."

Source: Mary Parker Follett, *Mary Parker Follett—Prophet of Management: A Celebration of Writings from the 1920s*, ed. P. Graham (Boston: Harvard Business School Press, 1995).

More Than Just a Pair of Hands

Like Elton Mayo, 1930s labor leader Joe Scanlon was also an advocate of the worker as more than just a cog in the machine or an extra pair of hands to get the work done. Scanlon argued that the worker could in fact contribute to manufacturing productivity and quality. According to his theory, when problems occurred in the production process, the worker who was directly involved would probably be best qualified to diagnose the problem and find a solution to it. And workers will be more motivated when they are allowed to be a part of implementing solutions to the problems they are dealing with. Scanlon used employee involvement teams to generate ideas for process improvements and implemented gainsharing programs to reward increased productivity and performance. You'll learn more about employee involvement teams and gainsharing in Chapter 10 Managing Teams.

Source: R. Masternak, "Gain Sharing and Lean Six Sigma," *Quality Digest*, December 18, 2009, accessed July 21, 2010, http://www.qualitydigest.com/inside/quality-insider-column/gainsharing -and-lean-six-sigma.html.

that six individuals became a team and the team gave itself wholeheartedly and spontaneously to cooperation in the experiment. The consequence was that they felt themselves to be participating freely and without afterthought, and were happy in the knowledge that they were working without coercion from above or limits from below."[38]

For the first time, human factors related to work were found to be more important than the physical conditions or design of the work. Together, the increased attention from management and the development of a cohesive work group led to significantly higher levels of job satisfaction and productivity. In short, the Hawthorne Studies found that workers' feelings and attitudes affected their work.

The next stage of the Hawthorne Studies was conducted in the Bank Wiring Room, where "the group consisted of nine wiremen, three solderers, and two inspectors. Each of these groups performed a specific task and collaborated with the other two in completion of each unit of equipment. The task consisted of setting up the banks of terminals side-by-side on frames, wiring the corresponding terminals from bank to bank, soldering the connections, and inspecting with a test set for short circuits or breaks in the wire. One solderman serviced the work of the three wireman."[39] While productivity increased in the Relay Test Assembly Room no matter what the researchers did, productivity dropped in the Bank Wiring Room. Again, the question was: Why?

Mayo and his colleagues found that different group dynamics were responsible. The workers in the Bank Wiring Room had been an existing work group for some time and had already developed strong negative norms that governed their behavior. For instance, despite a group financial incentive for production, the group members decided that they would wire only 6,000 to 6,600 connections a day (depending on the kind of equipment they were wiring), well below the production goal of 7,300 connections that management had set for them. Individual workers who worked at a faster pace were socially ostracized from the group or "binged" (hit on the arm) until they slowed their work pace. The group's behavior was reminiscent of the soldiering that Frederick Taylor had observed.

In the end, the Hawthorne Studies demonstrated that the workplace was more complex than previously thought, that workers were not just extensions of machines, and that financial incentives weren't necessarily the most important motivator for workers. Thanks to Mayo and the Hawthorne Studies, managers better understood the effect that group social interactions, employee satisfaction, and attitudes had on individual and group performance.

4.3 | COOPERATION AND ACCEPTANCE OF AUTHORITY: CHESTER BARNARD

Like Henri Fayol, Chester Barnard (1886–1961) had experience as a top executive that shaped his views of management. Barnard began his career in 1909 as an engineer and translator for AT&T, becoming a general manager at Pennsylvania Bell Telephone in 1922 and then president of New Jersey Bell Telephone in 1927.[40] Barnard's ideas, published in his classic book, *The Functions of the Executive,* influenced companies from the board of directors down. He is best known for his ideas about cooperation and the acceptance of authority.

Barnard proposed a comprehensive theory of cooperation in formal organizations. In fact, he defined an **organization** as a "system of consciously coordinated activities or forces of two or more persons."[41] In other words, organization occurs whenever two people work together for some purpose, whether it be classmates working together to complete a class project, Habitat for Humanity volunteers donating their time to build a house, or managers working with subordinates to reduce costs, improve quality, or increase sales. Why did Barnard place so much emphasis on cooperation? Because cooperation is *not* the normal state of affairs: "Failure to cooperate, failure of cooperation, failure of organization, disorganization, disintegration, destruction of organization—and reorganization—are characteristic facts of human history."[42]

According to Barnard, the extent to which people willingly cooperate in an organization depends on how workers perceive executive authority and whether they're willing to accept it. Many managerial requests or directives fall within a *zone of indifference* in which acceptance of managerial authority is automatic. For example, if your boss asks you for a copy of the monthly inventory report, and compiling and writing that report is part of your job, you think nothing of the request and automatically send it. In general, people will be indifferent to managerial directives or orders if they (1) are understood, (2) are consistent with the purpose of the organization, (3) are compatible with the people's personal interests, and (4) can actually be carried out by those people. Acceptance of managerial authority (i.e., cooperation) is not automatic, however. Ask people to do things contrary to the organization's purpose or to their own benefit and they'll put up a fight. While many people assume that managers have the authority to do whatever they want, Barnard, referring to the "fiction of superior authority," believed that workers ultimately grant managers their authority.

Organization a system of consciously coordinated activities or forces created by two or more people

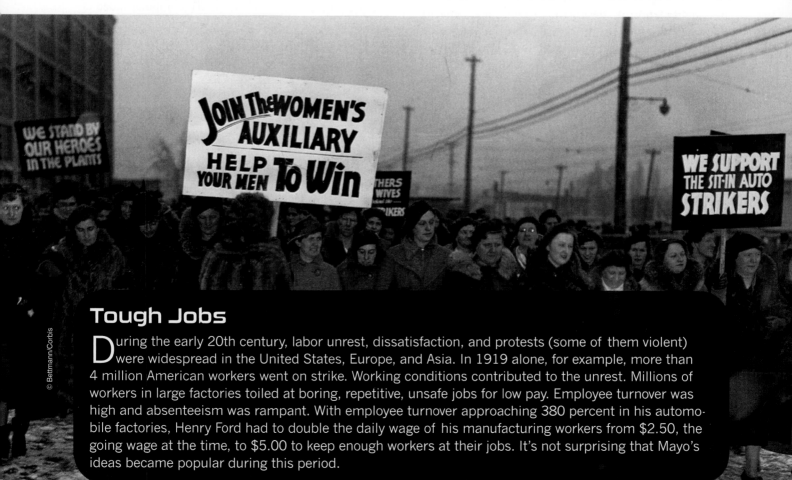

© Bettmann/Corbis

Tough Jobs

During the early 20th century, labor unrest, dissatisfaction, and protests (some of them violent) were widespread in the United States, Europe, and Asia. In 1919 alone, for example, more than 4 million American workers went on strike. Working conditions contributed to the unrest. Millions of workers in large factories toiled at boring, repetitive, unsafe jobs for low pay. Employee turnover was high and absenteeism was rampant. With employee turnover approaching 380 percent in his automobile factories, Henry Ford had to double the daily wage of his manufacturing workers from $2.50, the going wage at the time, to $5.00 to keep enough workers at their jobs. It's not surprising that Mayo's ideas became popular during this period.

5 Operations, Information, Systems, and Contingency Management

In this last section, we review four other significant historical approaches to management that have influenced how today's managers produce goods and services on a daily basis, gather and manage the information they need to understand their businesses and make good decisions, understand how the different parts of the company work together as a whole, and recognize when and where particular management practices are likely to work.

To better understand these ideas, let's learn about **5.1 operations management, 5.2 information management, 5.3 systems management,** *and* **5.4 contingency management.**

5.1 | OPERATIONS MANAGEMENT

In Chapter 18, you will learn about *operations management*, which involves managing the daily production of goods and services. In general, operations management uses a quantitative or mathematical approach to find ways to increase productivity, improve quality, and manage or reduce costly inventories. The most commonly used operations management tools and methods are quality control, forecasting techniques, capacity planning, productivity measurement and improvement, linear programming, scheduling systems, inventory systems, work measurement techniques (similar to the Gilbreths' motion studies), project management (similar to Gantt's charts), and cost-benefit analysis.[43]

Today, with these tools and techniques, we take it for granted that manufactured goods will be made with standardized, interchangeable parts; that the design of those parts will be based on specific, detailed plans; and that manufacturing companies will aggressively manage inventories to keep costs low and increase productivity. These key elements of operations management have some rather strange origins: guns, geometry, and fire.

Since the 16th century, skilled craftspersons made the lock, stock, and barrel of a gun by hand. After each part was made, a skilled gun finisher assembled the parts into a complete gun. But the gun finisher did not simply screw the different parts of a gun together, as is done today. Instead, each handmade part required extensive finishing and adjusting so that it would fit together with the other handmade gun parts. Hand-fitting was necessary because, even when made by the same skilled craftsperson, no two parts were alike. Today, we would say that these parts were low quality because they varied so much from one part to another.

All this changed in 1791 when the U.S. government, worried about a possible war with France, ordered 40,000 muskets from private gun contractors. Because each handmade musket was unique, a replacement part had to be handcrafted if a part broke. One contractor, Eli Whitney (who is better known for his invention of the cotton gin), determined that if gun parts were made accurately enough, guns could be made with standardized, interchangeable parts.[44] So he designed machine tools that allowed unskilled workers to make each gun part the same as the next. Then he demonstrated the superiority of interchangeable parts to President-elect Thomas Jefferson in 1801 by quickly and easily assembling complete muskets from randomly picked piles of musket parts. Today, most products are manufactured using standardized, interchangeable parts.

But even with this advance, manufacturers still could not produce a part unless they had seen or examined it firsthand. Thanks to Gaspard Monge, a Frenchman of modest beginnings, this soon changed. Monge's greatest achievement was his book *Descriptive Geometry*.[45] In it, he explained techniques for drawing three-dimensional objects on paper. For the first time, precise drawings permitted manufacturers to make standardized, interchangeable parts without first examining a prototype. Today, manufacturers rely on CAD (computer-aided design) and CAM (computer-aided manufacturing) to take three-dimensional designs straight from the computer to the factory floor.

Eli Whitney

Inventor of Standardized Machine Parts

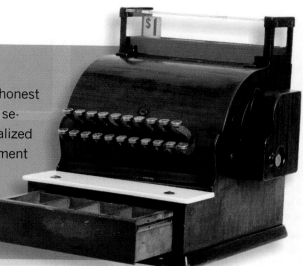

Cash Management

The cash register, invented in 1879, kept sales clerks honest by recording all sales transactions on a roll of paper securely locked inside the machine. But managers soon realized that its most important contribution was better management and control of their business. For example, department stores could track performance and sales by installing separate cash registers in the food, clothing, and hardware departments.

Once standardized, interchangeable parts became the norm, and once parts could be made from design drawings alone, manufacturers ran into a costly problem that they had never faced before: too much inventory. *Inventory* is the amount of raw materials and the numbers of parts and finished products that a company has in its possession. A solution to this problem was found in 1905 when the Oldsmobile Motor Works in Detroit burned down.[46] Management rented a new production facility to get production up and running as quickly as possible after the fire. But because the new facility was much smaller, there was no room to store large stockpiles of inventory. Therefore, the company made do with what it called "hand-to-mouth inventories," in which each production station had only enough parts on hand to do a short production run. Since all of its parts suppliers were close by, Oldsmobile could place orders in the morning and receive them in the afternoon (even without telephones), just as with today's computerized, just-in-time inventory systems. So, contrary to common belief, just-in-time inventory systems were not invented by Japanese manufacturers. Instead, they were invented a century ago out of necessity because of a fire.

5.2 | INFORMATION MANAGEMENT

For most of recorded history, information has been costly, difficult to obtain, and slow to spread compared to modern standards. Documents were written by hand. Books and manuscripts were extremely labor-intensive and therefore expensive. Although letters and other such documents were relatively easy to produce, transporting the information in them relied on horses, foot travelers, and ships. Word of Joan of Arc's death in 1431 took 18 months to travel from France across Europe to Constantinople (now Istanbul, Turkey).

Consequently, throughout history, organizations have pushed for and quickly adopted new information technologies that reduce the cost or increase the speed with which they can acquire, retrieve, or communicate information. The first technologies to truly revolutionize the business use of information were paper and the printing press. In the 14th century, water-powered machines were created to pulverize rags into pulp to make paper. Paper prices quickly dropped by 400 percent. Less than a half-century later, Johannes Gutenberg invented the printing press, which reduced the cost and time needed to copy written information by 99.8 percent. In 15th-century Florence, Italy, a scribe would charge 1 florin (an Italian unit of money) to hand-copy one document page. By contrast, a printer would set up and print 1,025 copies of the same document for just 3 florins.

What Gutenberg's printing press did for publishing, the manual typewriter did for daily communication. Before 1850, most business correspondence was written by hand and copied using the letter press. With the ink still wet, the letter would be placed into a tissue paper book. A hand press would then be used to squeeze the book and copy the still-wet ink onto the tissue paper. By the 1870s, manual typewriters made it cheaper, easier, and faster to produce and copy business correspondence. Of course, in the 1980s, slightly more than a century later, typewriters were replaced by personal computers and word-processing software with the same results.

Finally, businesses have always looked for information technologies that would speed access to timely information. The Medici family, which opened banks throughout Europe in the early 15th century, used posting messengers to keep in contact with more than forty branch managers. The post messengers, who predated the U.S. Postal Service Pony Express by 400 years, could travel 90 miles per day, twice what average riders could cover, because the Medicis were willing to pay for the expense of providing them with fresh horses. The need for timely information also led companies to quickly

System a set of interrelated elements or parts that function as a whole

Subsystems smaller systems that operate within the context of a larger system

Synergy when two or more subsystems working together can produce more than they can working apart

Closed systems systems that can sustain themselves without interacting with their environments

Open systems systems that can sustain themselves only by interacting with their environments, on which they depend for their survival

Contingency approach holds that there are no universal management theories and that the most effective management theory or idea depends on the kinds of problems or situations that managers are facing at a particular time and place

adopt the telegraph in the 1860s, the telephone in the 1880s, and, of course, Internet technologies in the last two decades.

5.3 | SYSTEMS MANAGEMENT

Today's companies are much larger and more complex than their predecessors. They most likely manufacture, service, *and* finance what they sell. They also operate in complex, fast-changing, competitive, global environments that can quickly turn competitive advantages into competitive disadvantages.

How can managers make sense of this complexity both within and outside their organizations? One way to deal with organizational and environmental complexity is to take a systems view of organizations.[47] A **system** is a set of interrelated elements or parts that function as a whole. According to the systems approach, rather than viewing one part of an organization as separate from the other parts, managers should look for connections between the different parts of the organization. Indeed, one of the more important ideas in the systems approach to management is that organizational systems are composed of parts or **subsystems,** which are simply smaller systems within a larger system. Subsystems and their connections matter in systems theory because of the possibility for managers to create synergy. **Synergy** occurs when two or more subsystems working together can produce more than they can working apart. In other words, synergy occurs when 1 + 1 = 3.

Systems can be open or closed. Whereas **closed systems** can function without interacting with their environments, nearly all organizations should be viewed as **open systems** that interact with their environments and depend on them for survival. Therefore, rather than viewing what goes on within the organization as separate from what goes on outside it, managers who subscribe to the systems approach look for connections between the different parts of the organization and the different parts of its environment. Exhibit 2.7 illustrates how the elements of systems management work together.

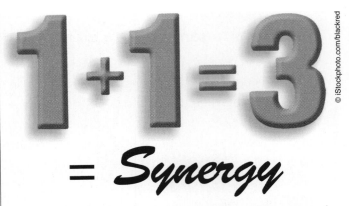

A systems view of organizations offers several advantages. First, it forces managers to view their organizations as part of and subject to the competitive, economic, social, technological, and legal/regulatory forces in their environments.[48] Second, it also forces managers to be aware of how the environment affects specific parts of the organization. Third, because of the complexity and difficulty of trying to achieve synergies between different parts of the organization, the systems view encourages managers to focus on better communication and cooperation within the organization. Finally, survival also depends on making sure that the organization continues to satisfy critical environmental stakeholders such as shareholders, employees, customers, suppliers, governments, and local communities.

5.4 | CONTINGENCY MANAGEMENT

Earlier, you learned that the goal of scientific management was to use systematic study to find the one best way of doing each task and then use that one best way everywhere. The problem, as you may have gathered from reading about the various approaches to management, is that no one in management seems to agree on what that one best way is. In fact, there isn't *one* best way. More than 100 years of management research has shown that there are clear boundaries or limitations to most management theories and practices. None is universal. Though any theory or practice may work much of the time, none works all the time. How, then, is a manager to decide what theory to use? Well, it depends on the situation. The **contingency approach** to management clearly states that there are no universal management theories and that the most effective management theory or idea depends on the kinds of problems or situations that managers or organizations are facing at a particular time.[49]

One of the practical implications of the contingency approach is that management is much harder than it looks. In fact, because of the clarity and obviousness of management theories (okay, most of them), students

Exhibit 2.7 | **Systems View of Organizations**

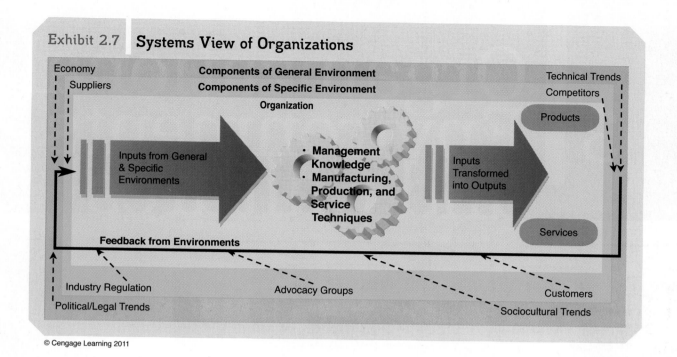

© Cengage Learning 2011

and workers often wrongly assume that a company's problems would be quickly and easily solved if management would take just a few simple steps. If this were true, few companies would have problems.

A second implication of the contingency approach is that managers need to look for key contingencies that differentiate today's situation or problems from yesterday's situation or problems. Moreover, it means that managers need to spend more time analyzing problems, situations, and employees before taking action to fix them. Finally, it means that as you read this text and learn about management ideas and practices, you need to pay particular attention to qualifying phrases such as "usually," "in these situations," "for this to work," and "under these circumstances." Doing so will help you identify the key contingencies that will help you become a better manager.

STUDENT Study Tools

Located at the back of your book:

☐ Rip out and study the Chapter Review Card at the end of the book

Log in to the CourseMate for MGMT at cengagebrain.com to:

☐ Review Key Term Flashcards delivered 3 ways (print or online)

☐ Complete both Practice Quizzes to prepare for tests

☐ Play Beat the Clock and Quizbowl to master concepts

☐ Complete the Crossword Puzzle to review key terms

☐ Watch the video on Mitchell Gold + Bob Williams for a real company example and take the accompanying quiz

☐ Watch the Biz Flix clip from *Casino* and take the quiz

☐ Complete the Case Assignment on ISG Steelton

☐ Work through the Management Decision on scripted service

☐ Work through the Management Team Decision on conflict resolution

☐ Develop your skills with the Develop Your Career Potential exercise

3 Organizational Environments and Cultures

© Biggie Productions/Stone/Getty Images

LEARNING OUTCOMES:

1 discuss how changing environments affect organizations.

2 describe the four components of the general environment.

3 explain the five components of the specific environment.

4 describe the process that companies use to make sense of their changing environments.

5 explain how organizational cultures are created and how they can help companies be successful.

Chapter 3

External Environments

this chapter examines the internal and external forces that affect business. First, we'll examine the two types of external organizational environments: the general environment that affects all organizations and the specific environment unique to each company. Then, we'll learn how managers make sense of their changing general and specific environments. The chapter finishes with a discussion of internal organizational environments by focusing on organizational culture. But first, let's see how the changes in external organizational environments affect the decisions and performance of a company.

Sony is one of the world's top electronics companies because of its ability to innovate, from the first commercially successful transistor radio to the Walkman, the first portable music player. The company has recently experienced a downturn, however, due to elements in its external environment, including heavy price competition in consumer electronics and the development of innovative products such as the iPod and TiVo in the United States. Executives at Sony have responded by generating a shift in the company's internal culture. Engineers from what were once separate divisions of the company are now sharing ideas and working together to develop new products that respond to consumer demand. In particular, customers want their various electronic devices to connect easily to each other and the Internet. Sony has also released the Bravia LCD (liquid crystal display) television, a no-frills response to the demand for lower-priced products.[1]

External environments are the forces and events outside a company that have the potential to influence or affect it.

> After reading the next four sections, you should be able to

1. discuss how changing environments affect organizations.

2. describe the four components of the general environment.

3. explain the five components of the specific environment.

4. describe the process that companies use to make sense of their changing environments.

1 Changing Environments

*Let's examine the three basic characteristics of changing external environments: **1.1 environmental change, 1.2 environmental complexity, 1.3 resource scarcity,** and **1.4 the uncertainty that environmental change, complexity, and resource scarcity can create for organizational managers.***

1.1 | ENVIRONMENTAL CHANGE

Environmental change is the rate at which a company's general and specific environments change. In **stable environments,** the rate of environmental change is slow. For instance, apart from the fact that ovens are more efficient, bread is baked, wrapped, and delivered fresh to stores each day much as it

External environments all events outside a company that have the potential to influence or affect it

Environmental change the rate at which a company's general and specific environments change

Stable environment an environment in which the rate of change is slow

was decades ago. Although some new breads have become popular, the white and wheat breads that customers bought 20 years ago are still today's best sellers.

While baking companies have stable environments, Microsoft, with its Xbox 360 game console, competes in one of the most dynamic external environments: video games. In **dynamic environments,** the rate of environmental change is fast. The external environment of Microsoft's Xbox is dynamic primarily because of changes in gaming technology and competition. At the 2010 E3 Expo video game tradeshow, Microsoft offered new details on its Kinect motion technology. With the success of industry leader Nintendo's Wii console, which picks up motion from its wireless controller, Microsoft and competitor Sony have had to come up with new ideas to stay competitive, such as Microsoft's Kinect, which uses motion capture without any controller input. Sony also has a motion-capture project in the works, and both Nintendo and Sony are working on incorporating 3-D technology in their hand-held devices. The competition has been especially heated of late, as video game sales have lagged the last two years, falling 11 percent in 2010 and 8 percent in 2009. The economic downturn has meant fewer people buying consoles and games. At the same time, there are more social and casual game producers putting games on the market, and more new devices, like Apple's iPhone and iPad, for which independent game makers can release their products. That means more competition for fewer customers. With multiple gaming platforms, new products encroaching on traditional markets, and production costs on top-tier products increasing, the cost of disappointing releases becomes increasingly risky for producers like Microsoft.[2]

Although you might think that a company's external environment would be *either* stable *or* dynamic, research suggests that companies often experience both. According to **punctuated equilibrium theory,** companies go through long, simple periods of stability (equilibrium) during which incremental changes occur, followed by short, complex periods of dynamic, fundamental change (revolutionary periods), which end with a return to stability (new equilibrium).[3]

One example of punctuated equilibrium has affected the U.S. airline industry. Three times in the last 30 years, the U.S. airline industry has experienced revolutionary periods. The first, from mid-1979 to mid-1982, occurred immediately after airline deregulation in 1978. Prior to deregulation, the federal government controlled where airlines could fly, how much could be charged, when they could fly, and the number of flights they could have on a particular route. After deregulation, these choices were left to the airlines. The large financial losses during this period clearly indicate that the airlines had trouble adjusting to the intense competition that occurred after deregulation. By mid-1982, however, profits returned to the industry and grew steadily year after year until mid-1989.

Then, after experiencing record growth and profits, U.S. airlines lost billions of dollars between 1989 and 1993 as the industry went through dramatic changes. Key expenses that had held steady for years, including jet fuel prices and employee salaries, suddenly increased. Furthermore, revenues suddenly dropped because of dramatic changes in the airlines' customer base. Business travelers, who typically paid full-priced fares, comprised more than half of all passengers during the 1980s. By the late 1980s, however, the largest customer base had changed to leisure travelers who wanted the cheapest flights they could get.[4] With expenses suddenly up and revenues suddenly down, the airlines responded to these changes in their business environment by laying off 5 to 10 percent of their workers, canceling orders for new planes, and eliminating unprofitable routes. Starting in 1993 and lasting until 1998, these changes helped the airline industry to achieve profits far in excess of their historical levels. The industry began to stabilize, if not flourish, just as punctuated equilibrium theory predicts.[5]

The third revolutionary period for the U.S. airline industry began with the terrorist attacks of September 11, 2001, in which planes were used as missiles to bring down the World Trade Center towers and damage the Pentagon. The immediate effect was a 20 percent drop in scheduled flights, a 40 percent drop in passengers, and losses so large that the U.S. government approved a $15 billion bailout to keep the airlines in business. Heightened airport security also affected airports, the airlines themselves, and airline customers. Reacting to their financially weaker position and striving to return to profitability, the airlines restructured operations to take advantage of the combined effect of increased passenger travel, a sharply reduced cost structure, and a 23 percent reduction in the fleet.[6] But, just as the airlines were heading toward a more stable period of equilibrium, the price of oil jumped dramatically, doubling—if not tripling—the price of jet fuel, which prompted the airlines to charge for luggage (to increase revenues and discourage heavy baggage) and cut flights that used older, fuel-inefficient jets.

1.2 | ENVIRONMENTAL COMPLEXITY

Environmental complexity refers to the number and intensity of factors in the external environment that affect organizations. **Simple environments** have few environmental factors that affect organizations, whereas **complex environments** have many environmental factors that affect organizations. The dairy industry is an excellent example of a relatively simple external environment. Even accounting for decades-old advances in processing and automatic milking machines, milk is produced the same way today as it was 100 years ago. And although food manufacturers introduce dozens of new dairy-based products each year, U.S. milk production has grown a meager 1.25 percent per year over the last decade. In short, producing milk is a highly competitive but simple business that has experienced few changes.[7]

At the other end of the spectrum, few industries find themselves in more complex environments today than the newspaper business. For a century, the business model for newspapers was relatively simple: sell subscriptions, classified ads, and ads targeted at consumers, print and distribute the newspaper, and then make extremely high earnings. In today's digital age, however, that business model no longer works. For example, digital ads bring in only about 10 percent of the revenue per 1,000 views as single, one-time, print newspaper ads. Likewise, revenue from classified ads, which were extremely profitable for local newspapers, dropped 29% last year because of incredibly popular sites such as craigslist.org, which allow people to post their classified ads for free.[8] Furthermore, because digital content requires almost no cost to distribute or reproduce, there is the widespread expectation that the content itself should be free. But, because the revenue from digital ads is so small, they don't provide enough revenue to cover the cost of "free" online versions of newspapers, such as the *Wall Street Journal,* and the *Times of London,* which now charge subscriptions for on-line access. And while the online version of the *Journal* is profitable, it's unclear whether charging for online content will work for other newspapers. *Mediaweek* senior editor Mike Shields said, "The *Journal* is not free. They never wavered or changed that. That is as key to the success as the content they deliver. That precedent is enviable and hard for someone [else] to copy, particularly if you've been giving away your content for 10 years."[9]

1.3 | RESOURCE SCARCITY

The third characteristic of external environments is resource scarcity. **Resource scarcity** is the abundance or shortage of critical resources in an organization's external environment. For example, the primary reason flat-screen LCD TVs with lifelike pictures were initially six times more expensive per inch than regular TVs, two times more expensive than rear-projection TVs, and 25 percent more expensive than plasma TVs was that there weren't enough LCD screen factories to meet demand. As long as this condition persisted, LCD TV prices had to remain high. With building costs at $2 billion to $4 billion each year, LCD factories were at first a scarce resource in this industry.[10] But as sales of LCD TVs soared, more LCD factories were built to meet demand, and so prices came down as the critical resource, availability of flat screens, became less scarce. Likewise, in many locations throughout the world, water is a scarce resource. This is why a Dow Chemical plant in Texas, faced with water shortages each summer, hired Nalco, a firm that helps companies reduce energy, water, and other natural resource consumption.

© Tetra Images/Jupiterimages / © Donald Nausbaum/Photographer's Choice RF/Getty Images

Simple

Complex

HomeGuides • AUTO MART • TOUCH MART • THE BIG YELLOW BOX • 24 • GOLD • metro FREE DAILY • NOW • FREE

Nalco's water management systems reduced water consumption at Dow's Texas plant by one billion gallons per year.[11] Likewise, working with the Marriott in Mumbai, India, Nalco was able to install a water recycling system that saves 300 million glasses of drinkable water per year from that single hotel.

1.4 | UNCERTAINTY

As Exhibit 3.1 shows, environmental change, environmental complexity, and resource scarcity affect environmental **uncertainty**, which is the extent to which managers can understand or predict the external changes and trends affecting their businesses. Starting at the left side of the figure, environmental uncertainty is lowest when environmental change and environmental complexity are at low levels and resource scarcity is small (i.e., resources are plentiful). In these environments, managers feel confident that they can understand, predict, and react to the external forces that affect their businesses. By contrast, the right side of the figure shows that environmental uncertainty is highest when environmental change and complexity are extensive and resource scarcity is a problem.

In these environments, managers may not be confident that they can understand, predict, and handle the external forces affecting their businesses.

2 General Environment

As Exhibit 3.2 shows, two kinds of external environments influence organizations: the general environment and the specific environment. The **general environment** consists of the economy and the technological, sociocultural, and political/legal trends that indirectly affect *all* organizations. Changes in any sector of the general environment eventually affect most organizations. For example, when the Federal Reserve lowers its prime lending rate, most businesses benefit because banks and credit card companies often lower the interest rates they charge for loans. Consumers can then borrow money more cheaply to buy homes, cars, refrigerators, and HDTVs. In addition, each organization has a **specific environment** that is unique to that firm's industry and directly affects the way it conducts day-to-day business. After more than 20 million unsafe toys, many of them produced in Chinese factories, were recalled, the toy industry spent $200 million to increase the safety of its products.[12] But because that change came from the specific environment (which only influences the particular industry) and not the general environment (which influences all businesses),

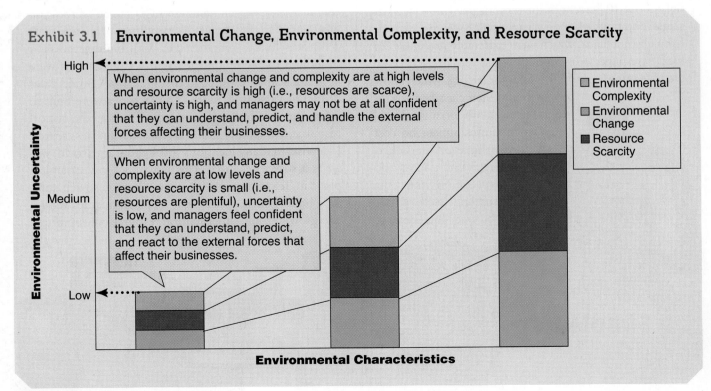

Exhibit 3.1 Environmental Change, Environmental Complexity, and Resource Scarcity

When environmental change and complexity are at high levels and resource scarcity is high (i.e., resources are scarce), uncertainty is high, and managers may not be at all confident that they can understand, predict, and handle the external forces affecting their businesses.

When environmental change and complexity are at low levels and resource scarcity is small (i.e., resources are plentiful), uncertainty is low, and managers feel confident that they can understand, predict, and react to the external forces that affect their businesses.

Environmental Uncertainty — High / Medium / Low

Environmental Complexity
Environmental Change
Resource Scarcity

Environmental Characteristics

© Cengage Learning 2011

only toy manufacturers and retailers, such as Toys "R" Us, were affected. The specific environment, which will be discussed in detail in Section 3 of this chapter, includes customers, competitors, suppliers, industry regulations, and advocacy groups.

But first, let's take a closer look at the four components of the general environment: **2.1 the economy, and 2.2 the technological, 2.3 sociocultural, and 2.4 political/legal trends that indirectly affect all organizations.**

2.1 | ECONOMY

The current state of a country's economy affects virtually every organization doing business there. In general, more people work and wages increase in a growing economy, so consumers have relatively more money to spend. More products are bought and sold in a growing economy than in a static or shrinking economy. Though an individual firm's sales will not necessarily increase, a growing economy does provide an environment favorable to business growth. In a shrinking economy, on the other hand, consumers have less money to spend and relatively fewer products are bought and sold. A shrinking economy thus makes growth for individual businesses more difficult. Because the economy influences basic business

decisions such as whether to hire more employees, expand production, or take out loans to purchase equipment, managers scan their economic environments for signs of significant change.

Some managers try to predict future economic activity by keeping track of business confidence. **Business confidence indices** show how confident actual managers are about future business growth. For example, the Conference Board's CEO Confidence Index is a quarterly survey of 100 CEOs in large companies across a variety of industries that examines attitudes regarding future growth in the economy or in particular industries.[13] Another widely cited measure is the Small Business Research Board's Business Confidence Index, which asks 500 small business owners and managers to express their optimism (or pessimism) about future business sales and prospects.[14] Managers often prefer business confidence indices to economic statistics because they know that other managers make business decisions that are in line with their expectations concerning the economy's future. So if the CEO Confidence Index and the Business Confidence Index are dropping, a manager might decide against hiring new employees, increasing production, or taking out additional loans to expand the business.

Business confidence indices indices that show managers' level of confidence about future business growth

Technology the knowledge, tools, and techniques used to transform input into output

2.2 | TECHNOLOGICAL COMPONENT

Technology is an umbrella term for the knowledge, tools, and techniques used to transform inputs (raw materials, information, and so on) into outputs (products and services). For example, the inputs of authors, editors, and artists (knowledge and skills) and paper, ink, and glue (raw materials) are transformed using equipment such as computers and printing presses (techniques) into this book (the finished product). In the case of a service company such as an airline, the technology consists of equipment, including airplanes, repair tools, and computers, as well as the knowledge of mechanics, ticketers, and flight crews. The output is the service of transporting people from one place to another.

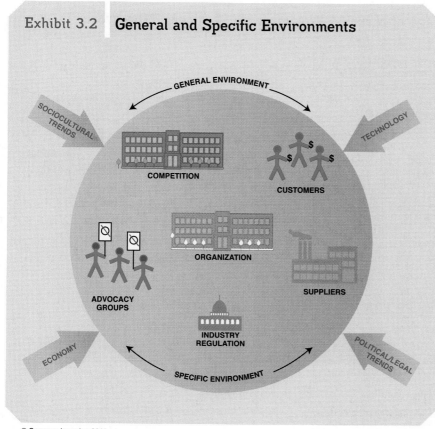

Exhibit 3.2   General and Specific Environments

GENERAL ENVIRONMENT

SOCIOCULTURAL TRENDS

TECHNOLOGY

COMPETITION

CUSTOMERS

ADVOCACY GROUPS

ORGANIZATION

SUPPLIERS

INDUSTRY REGULATION

ECONOMY

POLITICAL/LEGAL TRENDS

SPECIFIC ENVIRONMENT

© Cengage Learning 2011

Technology is an umbrella term for the knowledge, tools, and techniques used to transform inputs into outputs.

Changes in technology can help companies provide better products or produce their products more efficiently. For example, advances in surgical techniques and imaging equipment have made open-heart surgery much faster and safer in recent years. Although technological changes can benefit a business, they can also threaten it. Companies must embrace new technology and find effective ways to use it to improve their products and services or decrease costs. If they don't, they will lose out to those companies that do.

2.3 | SOCIOCULTURAL COMPONENT

The sociocultural component of the general environment refers to the demographic characteristics, general behavior, attitudes, and beliefs of people in a particular society. Sociocultural changes and trends influence organizations in two important ways.

First, changes in demographic characteristics, such as the numbers of people with particular skills and the growth/decline in particular population segments, and changes in cultural norms, such as gender roles, affect how companies staff their businesses. Married women with children are much more likely to work today than they were four decades ago, as illustrated in Exhibit 3.3. In 1960, only 18.6 percent of women with children under the age of 6 and 39 percent of women with children between the ages of 6 and 17 worked. By 2008, those percentages had risen to 63.6 percent and 77.5 percent, respectively.

Second, sociocultural changes in behavior, attitudes, and beliefs also affect the demand for businesses' products and services. With more married women with children in the workforce, traffic congestion creating longer commutes, and both parents working longer hours, employees today are much more likely to value products and services that allow them to recapture free

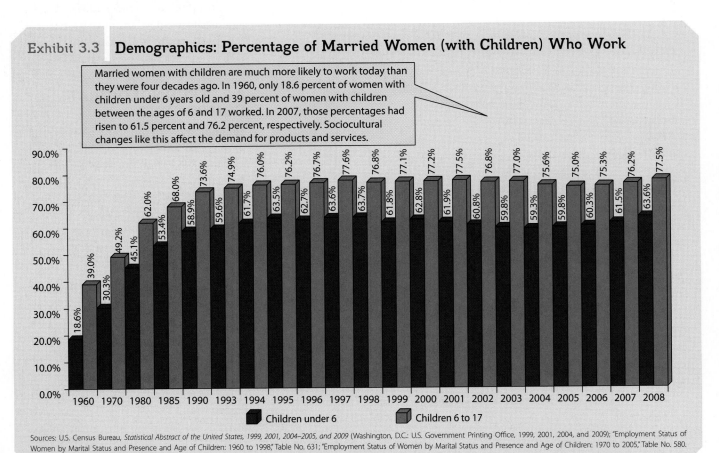

Exhibit 3.3 | Demographics: Percentage of Married Women (with Children) Who Work

Married women with children are much more likely to work today than they were four decades ago. In 1960, only 18.6 percent of women with children under 6 years old and 39 percent of women with children between the ages of 6 and 17 worked. In 2007, those percentages had risen to 61.5 percent and 76.2 percent, respectively. Sociocultural changes like this affect the demand for products and services.

Children under 6   Children 6 to 17

Sources: U.S. Census Bureau, *Statistical Abstract of the United States, 1999, 2001, 2004–2005, and 2009* (Washington, D.C.: U.S. Government Printing Office, 1999, 2001, 2004, and 2009); "Employment Status of Women by Marital Status and Presence and Age of Children: 1960 to 1998," Table No. 631; "Employment Status of Women by Marital Status and Presence and Age of Children: 1970 to 2005," Table No. 580.

time with their families, and families are deliberately selective about how they spend their free time. Thus people—especially working mothers—use numerous services to help reduce the amount of time they spend doing chores and household management tasks. For example, at McGraw Wentworth, a provider of group health care benefits, employees can get on-site laundry pickup and return. IT staffing firm Akraya provides employees with professional home cleaning services.[15]

2.4 | POLITICAL/LEGAL COMPONENT

The political/legal component of the general environment includes the legislation, regulations, and court decisions that govern and regulate business behavior. New laws and regulations continue to impose additional responsibilities on companies. Unfortunately, many managers are unaware of these new responsibilities. For example, under the 1991 Civil Rights Act, if an employee is sexually harassed by anyone at work (a supervisor, a coworker, or even a customer), the company—not just the harasser—is potentially liable for damages, attorneys' fees, and back pay.[16] Under the Family and Medical Leave Act, employees who have been on the job 1 year are guaranteed 12 weeks of unpaid leave per year to tend to their own illnesses or to their elderly parents, a newborn baby, or a newly adopted child. Employees are guaranteed the same job, pay, and benefits when they return to work.[17] Many managers are also unaware of the potential legal risks associated with traditional managerial decisions such as recruiting, hiring, and firing employees. Businesses and managers are increasingly being sued for negligent hiring and supervision, defamation, invasion of privacy, emotional distress, fraud, and misrepresentation during employee recruitment.[18] In fact, wrongful termination lawsuits increased by 77 percent during the 1990s.[19] One in four employers will at some point be sued for wrongful termination. It can cost $300,000 to settle such a case once it goes to court, but employers lose 70 percent of court cases, and the former employee is awarded on average $1 million or more.[20]

Corporations Calculate the Cost of Health Care Reform

The recent health care reform bill, which the President signed in March 2010, has had far-reaching effects within the U.S. business landscape. And while many changes are set to take place, one major area that has been affected is the level of health coverage that major corporations provide their employees. Corporations like AT&T and Caterpillar often help support the health care expenses of employees who get coverage through company-sponsored plans. Under the new legislation, however, the burden of expense for many corporations would increase significantly—in fact, several major corporations including AT&T, Verizon, Caterpillar, and Deere took significant write downs shortly after the law passed. These corporations have also been considering the costs of continuing to offer coverage. If they were to discontinue coverage, the corporations would have to pay a penalty of $2,000 per year per employee, and employees would turn to state-run health insurance exchanges to get coverage. AT&T discovered that it could save nearly $1.8 billion per year if it discontinued coverage and took the charge, and Caterpillar could reduce expenses by as much as 70 percent.

Source: S. Tully, "Documents Reveal AT&T, Verizon, Others, Thought about Dropping Employer-Sponsored Benefits," *Fortune*, May 6, 2010, accessed July 16, 2010, http://money.cnn.com/2010/05/05/news/companies/dropping_benefits.fortune/.

Not everyone agrees that companies' legal risks are too severe. Indeed, many believe that the government should do more to regulate and restrict business behavior and that it should be easier for average citizens to sue dishonest or negligent corporations. From a managerial perspective, the best defense against legal risk is prevention. As a manager, it is your responsibility to educate yourself about the laws, regulations, and potential lawsuits that could affect your business. Failure to do so may put you and your company at risk of sizable penalties, fines, or legal charges.

3 Specific Environment

As you just learned, changes in any sector of the general environment (economic, technological, sociocultural, and political/legal) eventually affect most organizations. Each organization also has a specific environment that is unique to that firm's industry and directly affects the way it conducts day-to-day business. For instance, if many of your customers decide to use another product, your main competitor cuts prices 10 percent, your best supplier can't deliver raw materials, federal regulators mandate reductions in pollutants in your industry, or environmental groups accuse your company of selling unsafe products, the impact from the specific environment on your business is immediate.

Let's examine how the **3.1 customer, 3.2 competitor, 3.3 supplier, 3.4 industry regulation,** *and* **3.5 advocacy group components of the specific environment affect businesses.**

3.1 | CUSTOMER COMPONENT

Customers purchase products and services. Companies cannot exist without customer support. Monitoring customers' changing wants and needs is therefore critical to business success. There are two basic strategies for monitoring customers: reactive and proactive.

Reactive customer monitoring involves identifying and addressing customer trends and problems after they occur. One reactive strategy is to listen closely to customer complaints and respond to customer concerns. Companies that respond quickly to customers' letters of complaint are viewed much more favorably than companies that are slow to respond or never respond.[21] In particular, studies have shown that when a company's follow-up letter thanks the customer for writing, offers a sincere, specific response to the complaint (not a form letter, but an explanation of how the problem will be handled), and contains a small gift, coupons, or a refund to make up for the problem, customers are much more likely to purchase products or services again from that company.[22]

Proactive customer monitoring, on the other hand, means identifying and addressing customer needs, trends, and issues before they occur. Every month, Travelocity, one of the leading travel websites, reviews 30,000 customer surveys, 50,000 emails, and notes from 500,000 phone calls! By using special software from Attensity Corporation that quickly analyzes and identifies trends in mountains of text-based data, Travelocity found that customers who purchased airline tickets on its website were blaming it when airlines cancelled their flights (for example, when not enough tickets had been sold). As a result, Travelocity's website now actively prevents this problem by steering customers away from flights for which only a small portion of available tickets have been sold.[23]

3.2 | COMPETITOR COMPONENT

Competitors are companies in the same industry that sell similar products or services to customers. Ford,

Listen to the Customers When Fighting Trolls

In early July 2010, Activision Blizzard announced that users of the forums for its online video game *World of Warcraft* (WoW) would have to post using their real names. WoW forums had become infamous for "trolls," people who post insulting and critical messages for no obvious reason, hiding behind the anonymity of their user names. This announcement was met with much protest. Some users complained that having to use real names would strip away the anonymity of the Internet and make them accountable for the things they posted. Others worried that whatever they posted on the WoW forum could be searched with Google. They feared that they could be fired from their jobs if their employers were able to monitor their online activity. And other users worried that hackers could track down their personal information to steal their identity or to harm them physically. Some even complained that using their real names would take away the fantasy elements of WoW. Activision Blizzard reacted to these consumer complaints by announcing just three days later that users would be allowed to use anonymous names after all.

Source: C. Morris, "Activision Battles 'Trolls', Backs Down on Privacy Fears," *CNBC.com*, July 9, 2010, accessed July 10, 2010, http://www.cnbc.com/id/38171990/.

© Hemera Technologies/PhotoObjects.net/Jupiterimages

Toyota, Honda, Nissan, Hyundai, and Kia all compete for automobile customers. NBC, ABC, CBS, and Fox (along with hundreds of cable channels) compete for TV viewers' attention. Often the difference between business success and failure comes down to whether your company is doing a better job of satisfying customer wants and needs than the competition. Consequently, companies need to keep close track of what their competitors are doing. To do this, managers perform a **competitive analysis,** which involves identifying competitors, anticipating competitors' moves, and determining competitors' strengths and weaknesses.

Surprisingly, managers often do a poor job of identifying potential competitors because they tend to focus on only two or three well-known competitors with similar goals and resources.[24]

Another mistake managers may make when analyzing the competition is to underestimate potential competitors' capabilities. When this happens, managers don't take the steps they should to continue to improve their products or services. The result can be significant decreases in both market share and profits. For nearly a decade, traditional phone companies ignored the threat to their business from VoIP (Voice over Internet Protocol), that is, the ability to make telephone calls over the Internet. Today, because phone companies were slow to respond, new VoIP competitors have slashed prices and are taking market share using high-speed Internet service.

3.3 | SUPPLIER COMPONENT

Suppliers are companies that provide material, human, financial, and informational resources to other companies. A key factor influencing the impact and quality of the relationship between companies and their suppliers is how dependent they are on each other.[25] **Supplier dependence** is the degree to which a company relies on a supplier because of the importance of the supplier's product to the company and the difficulty of finding other sources of that product.

Buyer dependence is the degree to which a supplier relies on a buyer because of the importance of that buyer to the supplier's sales and the difficulty of finding other buyers for its products. For example, when InBev purchased Anheuser-Busch and renamed itself AB InBev, it became the world's largest brewer, controlling over 25 percent of global beer sales. This gave AB InBev tremendous bargaining power over its suppliers. One of the ways in which it leveraged that bargaining power was to tell its suppliers, who provide everything from malt to hops to yeast, that it would pay them for their product shipments 120 days after being invoiced. With existing contracts providing payment 30 days after being invoiced, that change meant that AB InBev's suppliers would have to wait an extra 3 months to be paid. Delaying payments gives AB InBev an additional $1.2 billion in cash flow per year but at the expense of its suppliers. According to Elisavet Kinsey, who is the commercial and procurement director at MaltEurop, which is one of the world's largest malt producers, the change was simply "unacceptable."[26] There was little, however, that most AB InBev suppliers could do about this change.

As the AB InBev example shows, a high degree of buyer or seller dependence can lead to **opportunistic behavior,** in which one party benefits at the expense of the other. In contrast to opportunistic behavior, **relationship behavior** focuses on establishing a mutually beneficial, long-term relationship between buyers and suppliers.[27] Toyota is well known for developing positive long-term relationships with its key suppliers. Donald Esmond, who runs Toyota's U.S. division, says of suppliers, "I think what they appreciate . . . is we don't go in and say, 'Reduce the costs by 6 percent; if you don't, somebody else is going to get the business.'

Competitive analysis a process for monitoring the competition that involves identifying competition, anticipating their moves, and determining their strengths and weaknesses

Suppliers companies that provide material, human, financial, and informational resources to other companies

Supplier dependence the degree to which a company relies on a supplier because of the importance of the supplier's product to the company and the difficulty of finding other sources for that product

Buyer dependence the degree to which a supplier relies on a buyer because of the importance of that buyer to the supplier and the difficulty of finding other buyers for its products

Opportunistic behavior a transaction in which one party in the relationship benefits at the expense of the other

Relationship behavior mutually beneficial, long-term exchanges between buyers and suppliers

© iStockphoto.com/Eric Robinson

We go in and say we want to come in and help you [figure out] where you can save costs so we can reduce our overall price. So it's a different approach."[28]

How important is relationship behavior? Researchers examined the relationships between auto suppliers and eight major automakers in Japan, Korea, and the United States and found that, in cases where a lack of trust existed between suppliers and buyers, procurement costs could be as much as five times higher than when parties trusted one another. Furthermore, the least-trusted companies were often the least profitable.[29]

3.4 | INDUSTRY REGULATION COMPONENT

Whereas the political/legal component of the general environment affects all businesses, the **industry regulation** component of the specific environment consists of regulations and rules that govern the practices and procedures of specific industries, businesses, and professions. Regulatory agencies affect businesses by creating and enforcing rules and regulations to protect consumers, workers, or society as a whole. The nearly 100 federal agencies and regulatory commissions can affect almost any kind of business. For example, as noted earlier in the chapter, the toy industry spent

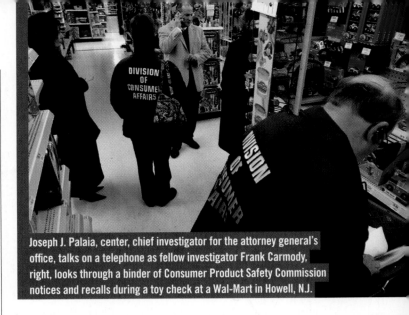

Joseph J. Palaia, center, chief investigator for the attorney general's office, talks on a telephone as fellow investigator Frank Carmody, right, looks through a binder of Consumer Product Safety Commission notices and recalls during a toy check at a Wal-Mart in Howell, N.J.

$200 million to increase the safety of its products after 20 million unsafe toys, mainly produced in China, were recalled because of the presence of harmful chemicals. Following the voluntary recall by toy retailers and manufacturers, new federal regulations embodied in the Consumer Product Safety Improvement Act of 2008 ban phthalates from children's products and require products to be tested for the presence of phthalates before they are sold.[30]

3.5 | ADVOCACY GROUPS

Advocacy groups are groups of concerned citizens who band together to try to influence the business practices of specific industries, businesses,

Fighting the Soda Tax

Changes in the political environment can create a great deal of uncertainty for companies, and even competitors within the same industry will often band together and spend millions of dollars to influence the decisions that are made. For example, in 2010 at least 20 cities and states brought measures proposing new taxes or repeals of tax exemptions on non-alcoholic beverages. The American Beverage Association (ABA), which represents beverage makers such as PepsiCo, Inc. and Coca-Cola Co., spent $688,000 in 2008 lobbying against these measures. As the threat of new taxes increased, however, the ABA ramped up its lobbying efforts, spending $18.9 million in 2009 and $5.4 million in just the first quarter of 2010. Some firms in the industry, however, have explored alternative options. To help cover a budget shortfall in the city of Philadelphia, Canada Dry Delaware Valley Bottling Company offered a $10 million donation to various city health and wellness programs.

Source: V. Bauerlein and B. McKay, "Zeal Fizzles for Soda Tax," *Wall Street Journal*, May 24, 2010, A3.

facts

Federal Regulatory Agencies and Commissions

Consumer Product Safety Commission
Reduces risk of injuries and deaths associated with consumer products, sets product safety standards, enforces product recalls, and provides consumer education **http://www.cpsc.gov**

Department of Labor
Collects employment statistics and administers labor laws concerning safe working conditions, minimum hourly wages and overtime pay, employment discrimination, and unemployment insurance **http://www.dol.gov**

Environmental Protection Agency
Reduces and controls pollution through research, monitoring, standard setting, and enforcement activities **http://www.epa.gov**

Equal Employment Opportunity Commission
Promotes fair hiring and promotion practices **http://www.eeoc.gov**

Federal Communications Commission
Regulates interstate and international communications by radio, television, wire, satellite, and cable **http://www.fcc.gov**

Federal Reserve System
As nation's central bank, controls interest rates and money supply and monitors the U.S. banking system to produce a growing economy with stable prices **http://www.federalreserve.gov**

Federal Trade Commission
Restricts unfair methods of business competition and misleading advertising; enforces consumer protection laws **http://www.ftc.gov**

Food and Drug Administration
Protects nation's health by making sure food, drugs, and cosmetics are safe **http://www.fda.gov**

National Labor Relations Board
Monitors union elections and stops companies from engaging in unfair labor practices **http://www.nlrb.gov**

Occupational Safety and Health Administration
Saves lives, prevents injuries, and protects the health of workers **http://www.osha.gov**

Securities and Exchange Commission
Protects investors in the bond and stock markets, guarantees access to information on publicly traded securities, and regulates firms that sell securities or give investment advice **http://www.sec.gov**

and professions. The members of a group generally share the same point of view on a particular issue. For example, environmental advocacy groups might try to get manufacturers to reduce smokestack emissions of pollutants. Unlike the industry regulation component of the specific environment, advocacy groups cannot force organizations to change their practices. Nevertheless, they can use a number of techniques to try to influence companies, including public communications, media advocacy, and product boycotts.

The **public communications** approach relies on voluntary participation by the news media and the advertising industry to send out an advocacy group's message. Media advocacy is much more aggressive than the public communications approach. A **media advocacy** approach typically involves framing the group's concerns as public issues (affecting everyone); exposing questionable, exploitative, or unethical practices; and forcing media coverage by buying media time or creating controversy that is likely to receive extensive news coverage. In one

of its latest protests, called "McCruelty: I'm Hatin' It," PETA is protesting that McDonald's, which uses 290 million chickens a year, tolerates suppliers' use of inhumane killing methods—hanging the birds upside down, stunning them in water that carries an electrical current, and then cutting their throats. PETA wants McDonald's suppliers to use gas to kill the birds, which it believes is more humane. Paul Shapiro, who heads the Humane Society's factory farming initiative, said, "It causes less suffering than the conventional method, which is archaic and inhumane." However, Marie Wheatley, president of the American Humane Association, disagrees, saying, "There is not definite proof either is more humane. Both technologies are acceptable in

Public communications an advocacy group tactic that relies on voluntary participation by the news media and the advertising industry to get the advocacy group's message out

Media advocacy an advocacy group tactic that involves framing issues as public issues; exposing questionable, exploitative, or unethical practices; and forcing media coverage by buying media time or creating controversy that is likely to receive extensive news coverage

Product boycott an advocacy group tactic that involves protesting a company's actions by convincing consumers not to purchase its product or service

Environmental scanning searching the environment for important events or issues that might affect an organization

minimizing pain and suffering."[31] A McDonald's spokesperson said the company is committed to "humane treatment of animals by our suppliers in every part of the world where we do business."[32]

A **product boycott** is a tactic in which an advocacy group actively tries to persuade consumers not to purchase a company's product or service. When an explosion on one of BP's oil rigs in April 2010 caused massive amounts of oil to leak into the Gulf of Mexico, many American consumers expressed their outrage by boycotting BP gas. Protesters created a Boycott BP website and a Facebook group, and many staged protests outside BP service stations. [33]

4 Making Sense of Changing Environments

In Chapter 1, you learned that managers are responsible for making sense of their business environments. As our discussions of the general and specific environments have indicated, however, making sense of business environments is not an easy task. *Because external environments can be dynamic, confusing, and complex, managers use a three-step process to make sense of the changes in their external environments: **4.1 environmental scanning, 4.2 interpreting environmental factors**, and **4.3 acting on threats and opportunities**.*

4.1 | ENVIRONMENTAL SCANNING

Environmental scanning involves searching the environment for important events or issues that might affect an organization. Managers scan the environment to stay up to date on important factors in their industry. The American Hospital Association, for instance, publishes an environmental scan called "Futurescan" annually to help hospital and health system managers understand the trends and market forces that have a "high probability of affecting the healthcare field."[34] In its 2009 environmental scan, it indicated that consumers are receptive to receiving medical treatment at walk-in clinics at pharmacies or shopping centers; that 80 percent of consumers would like to have online access to information about their medical test results, doctor visits, and hospital stays; that a growing number of physicians will choose to be employed by hospitals rather than go into private practice; and that

regenerative medicine, where medical techniques allow organs and body parts to heal themselves, may be the next major medical treatment.[35]

Managers also scan their environments to reduce uncertainty. Recently, Gatorade created a "Mission Control Center," a room filled with computer monitors and marketing experts, resembling a NASA control center, that constantly monitors social media networks. The monitors display constantly updated visuals that provide real-time information on what people are saying about Gatorade, its competitors, and even sport nutrition in general, within social media networks. This allows Gatorade's marketing team to track how consumers are reacting to its ads and to make quick adjustments based on those reactions. After releasing a campaign called "Gatorade Has Evolved," Mission Control discovered that the ad's song, by David Banner, was so popular that within 24 hours, the company produced and released a full-length version of the song. With such a speedy response that responded to consumers' desires, Gatorade has been able to increase engagement with its product education by 250 percent.[36]

Organizational strategies also affect environmental scanning. In other words, managers pay close attention to trends and events that are directly related to their companies' ability to compete in the marketplace.[37] Knights Apparel, a manufacturer of collegiate-licensed clothing based in South Carolina, recognized a growing concern among consumers—most of the clothes they bought were produced in so-called "sweatshops" located in developing countries where workers were paid as little as $100 per month. Led by CEO Joseph Bozich, Knights decided to respond to the issue by paying a living wage at its factory in Alta Gracia, Dominican Republic. Instead of the legally required minimum wage, Knights' wages are based on the actual cost of living in the Dominican Republic. Although this practice may lead to higher costs, Knights' stance could enhance its position against competitors like Nike and

> Managers pay close attention to trends and events that are **directly related** to their companies' ability to compete in the marketplace.

Adidas. Knights has already received lucrative deals with Duke University, Barnes & Noble, and Follett's, a college textbook store chain. And the apparel manufacturer is likely to attract the growing number of young consumers who care about social responsibility. Says Kellie A. McElhaney, a professor of corporate social responsibility at UC Berkeley, "A lot of college students would much rather pay for a brand that shows workers are treated well."[38]

Finally, environmental scanning is important because it contributes to organizational performance. Environmental scanning helps managers detect environmental changes and problems before they cause organizational crises.[39] Furthermore, companies whose CEOs do more environmental scanning have higher profits.[40] CEOs in better-performing firms scan their firms' environments more frequently and scan more key factors in their environments in more depth and detail than do CEOs in poorer-performing firms.[41]

4.2 | INTERPRETING ENVIRONMENTAL FACTORS

After scanning, managers determine what the perceived environmental events and issues mean to the organization. Typically, managers view environmental events and issues as either threats or opportunities. When managers interpret environmental events as threats, they take steps to protect the company from further harm. For example, now that Internet phone service (VoIP) has emerged as a threat, traditional phone companies have responded by spending billions to expand their fiber-optic networks so that they can offer phone (using VoIP), Internet service, and TV packages just like those the cable and satellite companies offer.[42] For example, last year, Comcast was losing 233,000 cable TV subscribers per quarter, while U-Verse, AT&T's digital TV service, and FiOS, Verizon's digital TV service, were adding 264,000 and 303,000 subscribers, respectively, during the same period.[43]

By contrast, when managers interpret environmental events as opportunities, they consider strategic alternatives for taking advantage of those events to improve company performance. The market for high-end "smart" phones, full-featured mobile phones that also function as handheld personal computers, is growing 30 percent per year. Because of the opportunities in this market, Apple developed the iPhone, a high-end "smart" phone featuring a wider screen and camera and the ability to email, surf the Web, communicate with Bluetooth devices, use faster Wi-Fi networks, and, of course, download and play iTunes music. Apple sold 21 million iPhones in the first 18 months it was on the market, far exceeding its goal of 10 million. Another sign of Apple's success with the iPhone is that it sold nearly 18 million iPhone 4s in its first five months on the market.[44]

4.3 | ACTING ON THREATS AND OPPORTUNITIES

After scanning for information on environmental events and issues and interpreting them as threats or opportunities, managers have to decide how to respond to these environmental factors. Deciding what to do under conditions of uncertainty is always difficult. Managers can never be completely confident that they have all the information they need or that they correctly understand the information they have.

Because it is impossible to comprehend all the factors and changes, managers often rely on simplified models of external environments called cognitive maps. **Cognitive maps** summarize the perceived relationships between environmental factors and possible organizational actions. For example, the cognitive map shown in Exhibit 3.4 on the next page represents a small clothing store owner's interpretation of her business environment. The map shows three kinds of variables. The first set of variables, shown in blue rectangles, are environmental factors, such as a Wal-Mart or a large mall 20 minutes away. The second set of variables, shown in green ovals, are actions that the store owner might take: follow a low-cost strategy; a good value, good service strategy; or a large selection of the latest fashions strategy. The third set of variables, shown in gold trapezoids, are company strengths (low employee turnover) and weaknesses (small size).

The plus and minus signs on the map indicate whether the manager believes there is a positive or negative relationship between variables. For example, the manager believes that a low-cost strategy won't work because Wal-Mart and Target are nearby. Offering a large selection of the latest fashions won't work either—not with the small size of the store and that large mall nearby. However, the manager believes that a good value and a good service strategy can lead to success and profits because of the store's low employee turnover, good knowledge of customers, and reasonable selection of clothes at reasonable prices.

Cognitive maps
graphic depictions of how managers believe environmental factors relate to possible organizational actions

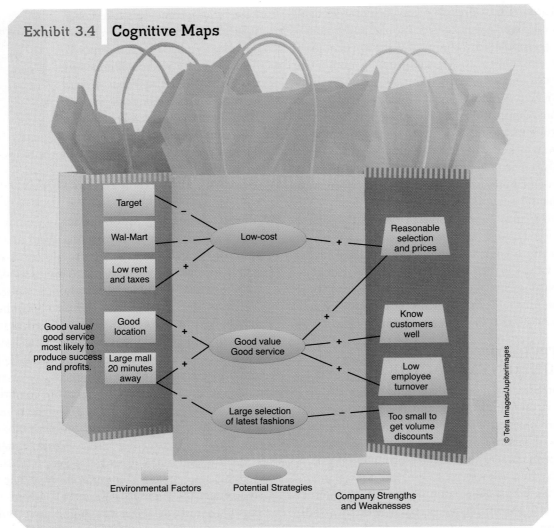

Exhibit 3.4 **Cognitive Maps**

Target

Wal-Mart

Low rent and taxes

Good value/ good service most likely to produce success and profits.

Good location

Large mall 20 minutes away

Low-cost

Good value Good service

Large selection of latest fashions

Reasonable selection and prices

Know customers well

Low employee turnover

Too small to get volume discounts

Environmental Factors   Potential Strategies   Company Strengths and Weaknesses

© Tetra Images/Jupiterimages

© Cengage Learning 2011

Internal Environments

We have been looking at trends and events outside of companies that have the potential to affect them. By contrast, the **internal environment** consists of the trends and events *within* an organization that affect the management, employees, and organizational culture. Internal environments are important because they affect what people think, feel, and do at work. Although innovative new products from Sony's competitors and aggressive cost-cutting in the booming market for high-definition TVs had hurt the company's market share and profitability, its problems were directly linked to its hypercompetitive culture, which discouraged interdepartmental communication and rated designing innovative products, no matter the cost, as the most important contribution to the company. Now, thanks to programs such as "Sony United," which encourage Sony employees in different divisions and locations to work with each other, Sony's culture has begun to change. For instance, Sony's Mexican engineers worked with its U.S. marketing team to design the inexpensive Bravia high-definition TV for the cost-competitive U.S. market. The Bravia sold so well at Wal-Mart that Best Buy asked to carry the TV in its stores.[45]

The key component in internal environments is **organizational culture**, or the set of key values, beliefs, and attitudes shared by members of the organization.

Internal environment the events and trends inside an organization that affect management, employees, and organizational culture

Organizational culture the values, beliefs, and attitudes shared by members of the organization

5 explain how organizational cultures are created and how they can help companies be successful.

5 Organizational Cultures: Creation, Success, and Change

Let's take a closer look at **5.1 how organizational cultures are created and maintained, 5.2 the characteristics of organizational cultures that foster success,** and **5.3 how companies can accomplish the difficult task of changing organizational cultures.**

5.1 | CREATION AND MAINTENANCE OF ORGANIZATIONAL CULTURES

A primary source of organizational culture is the company founder. Founders such as Bill Gates (Microsoft) create organizations in their own images and imprint them with their beliefs, attitudes, and values. Microsoft employees share Gates's determination to stay ahead of software competitors. Says a Microsoft vice president, "No matter how good your product, you are only 18 months away from failure."[46] Although company founders are instrumental in the creation of organizational cultures, eventually founders retire, die, or choose to leave their companies. When the founders are gone, how are their values, attitudes, and beliefs sustained in the organizational cultures? Answer: stories and heroes.

Members tell **organizational stories** to make sense of events and changes in an organization and to emphasize culturally consistent assumptions, decisions, and actions.[47] At Wal-Mart, stories abound about founder Sam Walton's thriftiness as he strove to make Wal-Mart the low-cost retailer that it is today. Gary Reinboth, one of Wal-Mart's first store managers, tells the following story:

> In those days, we would go on buying trips with Sam, and we'd all stay, as much as we could, in one room or two. I remember one time in Chicago when we stayed eight of us to a room. And the room wasn't very big to begin with. You might say we were on a pretty restricted budget.[48]

Sam Walton's thriftiness still permeates Wal-Mart today. Everyone, including top executives and the CEO, flies coach rather than business or first class. When employees travel on business, it's still the norm to share rooms (though two to a room, not eight!) at relatively inexpensive motels like Motel 6 and Super 8 instead of Holiday Inns. Likewise, Wal-Mart will reimburse only up to $15 per meal on business travel, which is half to one-third the reimbursement rate at similar-sized companies. (Remember, Wal-Mart is one of the largest companies in the world.)

A second way in which organizational culture is sustained is by recognizing and celebrating heroes. By definition, **organizational heroes** are people admired for their qualities and achievements within the organization. BOWA Builders is a full-service construction company in Virginia. When it was renovating a large auto dealership, its carpet subcontractor mistakenly scheduled the new carpet to be delivered 2 weeks *after* it was to be installed. Rather than allow construction to be delayed, a BOWA employee kept the project on schedule by immediately reordering the carpet, flying to the carpet manufacturer's factory, renting a truck, and then driving the carpet back to the auto dealership, all within 48 hours of learning about the problem. This story is told and retold within BOWA Builders as an example of heroic customer service. Moreover, the car dealership was so delighted with this extraordinary service that it referred over $10 million in new business to BOWA Builders.[49]

5.2 | SUCCESS AND ORGANIZATIONAL CULTURES

Preliminary research shows that organizational culture is related to business success. As shown in Exhibit 3.5 on the next page, cultures based on adaptability, employee involvement, a clear vision, and consistency can help companies achieve higher sales growth, return on assets, profits, quality, and employee satisfaction.[50]

Adaptability is the ability to notice and respond to changes in the organization's environment. Cultures need to reinforce important values and behaviors, but a culture becomes dysfunctional if it prevents change. Zappos.com is an online shoe retailer that is founded on one principle—make customers happy. To help new employees adapt to a culture based on superior customer service, all new employees, whether website designers or box loaders or corporate lawyers, are required to attend the same four-week training program as the customer service representatives. New hires even spend two weeks taking phone calls from customers, so that they

Organizational stories stories told by members to make sense of events and changes in an organization and to emphasize culturally consistent assumptions, decisions, and actions

Organizational heroes people celebrated for their qualities and achievements within an organization

Exhibit 3.5

Exhibit 3.5 Keys to an Organizational Culture That Fosters Success

Consistency

Adaptability

Clear Vision

Employee Involvement

© iStockphoto.com/Les Cunliffe

can have firsthand experience in providing customers with the best possible service.[51] In cultures that promote higher levels of *employee involvement* in decision making, employees feel a greater sense of ownership and responsibility.

A **company mission** is the business's purpose or reason for existing. In an organizational culture that includes a clear company mission, the organization's strategic purpose and direction are apparent to everyone in the company. Novo Nordisk, a pharmaceutical company based in Denmark, has one clear goal: to cure diabetes. Everything it does as an organization—from research and innovation to marketing to its social responsibility—is geared towards revolutionizing the way diabetes is treated and prevented. Novo Nordisk's mission is about improving the lives of its customers.[52]

Finally, in a **consistent organizational culture,** the company actively defines and teaches organizational values, beliefs, and attitudes. Consistent organizational cultures are also called *strong cultures* because the core beliefs are widely shared and strongly held.

Company mission a business's purpose or reason for existing

Consistent organizational culture when a company actively defines and teaches organizational values, beliefs, and attitudes

Studies show that companies with consistent or strong corporate cultures will generally outperform those with inconsistent or weak cultures.[53] Why? The reason is that when core beliefs are widely shared and strongly held, it is easy for everyone to figure out what to do and what not to do in their efforts to achieve organizational goals. One of the reasons Tony Hsieh, now CEO of Zappos.com, sold his startup company, LinkExchange, was because, "the company culture just went completely downhill."[54] As LinkExchange had grown out of the startup phase, managers had been hiring people based on their skills alone and had ignored the culture that resulted—one in which people weren't excited or passionate about the work they were doing. When Hsieh joined Zappos, culture became the top priority. Gathering input from everyone in the company, Hsieh developed a list of ten core values (for instance, "Embrace and Drive Change" and "Be Passionate and Determined"). Ultimately, the new values gave everyone at Zappos a common corporate language that even carried through to hiring practices. Now, Zappos has prospective hires go through two rounds of interviews: The first to determine experience and technical skills; and the second to determine the applicant's cultural fit based on the ten core values.

Having a consistent or strong organizational culture doesn't guarantee good company performance. When core beliefs are widely shared and strongly held, it is very difficult to bring about needed change. Consequently, companies with strong cultures tend to perform poorly when they need to adapt to dramatic changes in their external environments. Their consistency sometimes prevents them from adapting to those changes.[55]

5.3 | CHANGING ORGANIZATIONAL CULTURES

As shown in Exhibit 3.6, organizational cultures exist on three levels.[56] On the first, or surface, level are the elements of an organization's culture that can be seen and observed, such as symbolic artifacts (e.g., dress codes and office layouts) and workers' and managers' behaviors. Next, just below the surface, are the values and beliefs expressed by people in the company. You can't see these values and beliefs, but they become clear if you carefully listen to what people say and observe how decisions are made or explained. Finally, unconsciously held assumptions and beliefs about the company are buried deep below the surface. These are the unwritten views and rules that are so strongly held and so widely shared that they are rarely discussed or even

Exhibit 3.6 | Three Levels of Organizational Culture

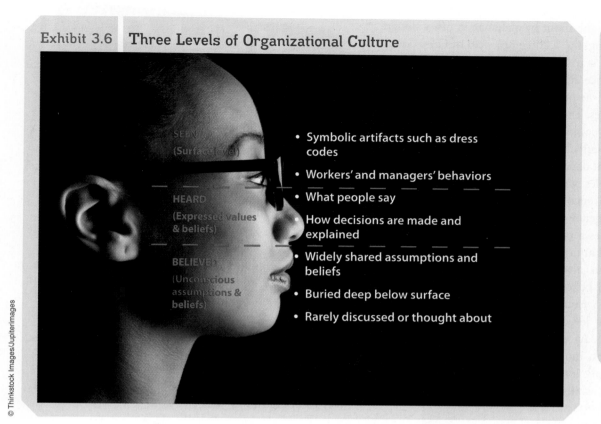

SEEN
(Surface level)

- Symbolic artifacts such as dress codes
- Workers' and managers' behaviors

HEARD
(Expressed values & beliefs)

- What people say
- How decisions are made and explained

BELIEVED
(Unconscious assumptions & beliefs)

- Widely shared assumptions and beliefs
- Buried deep below surface
- Rarely discussed or thought about

© Thinkstock Images/Jupiterimages

Behavioral addition the process of having managers and employees perform new behaviors that are central to and symbolic of the new organizational culture a company wants to create

Behavioral substitution the process of having managers and employees perform new behavior central to the new organizational culture in place of behaviors that were central to the old organizational culture

Visible artifacts visible signs of an organization's culture, such as the office design and layout, company dress code, and company benefits and perks

thought about unless someone attempts to change them or unknowingly violates them. Changing such assumptions and beliefs can be very difficult. Instead, managers should focus on the parts of the organizational culture they can control. These include observable surface-level items, such as workers' behaviors and symbolic artifacts, and expressed values and beliefs, which can be influenced through employee selection. Let's see how these can be used to change organizational cultures.

One way of changing a corporate culture is to use behavioral addition or behavioral substitution to establish new patterns of behavior among managers and employees. **Behavioral addition** is the process of having managers and employees perform a new behavior, while **behavioral substitution** is having managers and employees perform a new behavior in place of another behavior. The key in both instances is to choose behaviors that are central to and symbolic of the old culture you're changing and the new culture you want to create. When Mike Ullman became the CEO of JCPenney, he thought the company's culture was stuck in the 19th century (when the company was started). Employees called each other "Mr." and "Mrs.," casual attire was unacceptable even on Fridays, and any elaborate decoration of office cubicles was reported to a team of office police charged with enforcing corporate décor guidelines. Ullman quickly determined that the company's stringent code

of conduct was, among other things, keeping it from recruiting the talent it needed. Mike Theilmann, the human resources officer, drafted a list of what he called "quick hits," small changes that would have a big impact on the culture. The first of Theilmann's initiatives was a campaign titled "Just Call Me Mike," which he hoped would cure employees of the entrenched practice of calling executives and managers "Mr." and "Mrs." Three JCPenney officers are named Mike, along with nearly 400 other employees at headquarters. Theilmann created posters containing photos of the three executive Mikes along with a list of all the advantages of being on a first-name basis. Top of the list: "First names create a friendly place to shop and work."[57]

Another way in which managers can begin to change corporate culture is to change the **visible artifacts** of their old culture, such as the office design and layout, the company dress code, and the recipients (or nonrecipients) of company benefits and perks like stock options, personal parking spaces, and the private company dining room. When Grey Group, a New York advertising agency, moved to a new office building, CEO Tor Myhren viewed it as the perfect opportunity to change the company's culture. The agency used to be slow, and there was little collaboration. Myhren wanted to create a faster, more nimble, more collaborative culture that would reflect the modern digital age. The change in culture was brought about by a change in office design. In the old building, the 1,200 employees of Grey Group were spread out across 26 stories, and nearly everyone had a private office. In the new building, all the employees were housed in just six stories, and only 3 people had private offices. The new building was designed with lots of open and common space—even many of the partitions between cubicles were removed—in which people from different departments were placed next to each other. Long tables were spread throughout the open office design to encourage spontaneous collaborative meetings. The agency even set up a furnished bedroom to give employees a place to relax and be creative in a different kind of atmosphere.[58]

Cultures can also be changed by hiring people with values and beliefs consistent with the company's desired culture. *Selection* is the process of gathering information about job applicants to decide who should be offered a job. As we will discuss in Chapter 11 on human resources, most selection instruments measure whether job applicants have the knowledge, skills, and abilities needed to succeed in their jobs. But companies are increasingly testing job applicants to determine how they fit with the company's desired culture (i.e., values and beliefs). A key step in hiring people who have values consistent with the desired culture is to define and describe that culture. At advertising agency Partners + Napier, two key corporate values are courage and ingenuity. So how do these values carry over into the hiring process? Applicants must be willing to try new things and learn about the products they're working on. CEO Sharon Napier says about potential hires, "If you don't really want to know how something works, if you don't read a lot, then you're not a very curious person. And in our business you really have to be. If I'm going to put you on an account like Kodak, I want you to learn how to make a photo book…if you're not interested in digging in, then that'll say a lot about you."[59]

Corporate cultures are very difficult to change. Consequently, there is no guarantee that any one approach—changing visible cultural artifacts, using behavioral substitution, or hiring people with values consistent with a company's desired culture—will change a company's organizational culture. The best results are obtained by combining these methods. Together, these are some of the best tools managers have for changing culture because they send the clear message to managers and employees that "the accepted way of doing things" has changed.

STUDENT Study Tools

Located at the back of your book:

☐ Rip out and study the Chapter Review Card at the end of the book

Log in to the CourseMate for MGMT at cengagebrain.com to:

☐ Review Key Term Flashcards delivered 3 ways (print or online)

☐ Complete both Practice Quizzes to prepare for tests

☐ Play Beat the Clock and Quizbowl to master concepts

☐ Complete the Crossword Puzzle to review key terms

☐ Watch the video on Preserve for a real company example and take the accompanying quiz

☐ Watch the Biz Flix clip from *Charlie Wilson's War* and take the quiz

☐ Complete the Case Assignment on Wal-Mart

☐ Work through the Management Decision on responding to tragedies

☐ Work through the Management Team Decision on dog day blues

☐ Develop your skills with the Develop Your Career Potential exercise

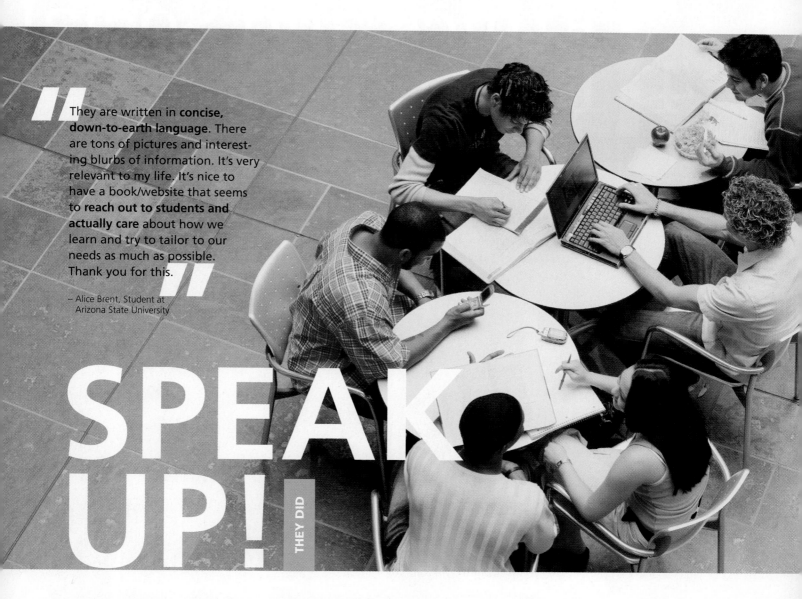

> They are written in **concise, down-to-earth language**. There are tons of pictures and interesting blurbs of information. It's very relevant to my life. It's nice to have a book/website that seems to **reach out to students and actually care** about how we learn and try to tailor to our needs as much as possible. Thank you for this."
>
> – Alice Brent, Student at Arizona State University

SPEAK UP!

THEY DID

MGMT4 was built on a simple principle: to create a new teaching and learning solution that reflects the way today's faculty teach and the way you learn.

Through conversations, focus groups, surveys, and interviews, we collected data that drove the creation of the current version that you are using today. But it doesn't stop there—in order to make **MGMT4** an even better learning experience, we'd like you to SPEAK UP and tell us how **MGMT4** worked for you.

What did you like about it? What would you change? Are there additional ideas you have that would help us build a better product for next semester's principles of management students?

Through CourseMate, you'll find all of the resources you need to succeed in principles of management—**video podcasts, audio downloads, flash cards, interactive quizzes** and more!

Speak Up! Go to CourseMate for **MGMT4**. Access at **www.cengagebrain.com**.

4 | Ethics and Social Responsibility

© Burke/Triolo Productions/Brand X Pictures/Jupiterimages

LEARNING OUTCOMES:

1 identify common kinds of workplace deviance.

2 describe the U.S. Sentencing Commission Guidelines for Organizations and explain how they both encourage ethical behavior and punish unethical behavior by businesses.

3 describe what influences ethical decision making.

4 explain what practical steps managers can take to improve ethical decision making.

5 explain to whom organizations are socially responsible.

6 explain for what organizations are socially responsible.

7 explain how organizations can choose to respond to societal demands for social responsibility.

8 explain whether social responsibility hurts or helps an organization's economic performance.

Chapter 4

What Is Ethical and Unethical Workplace Behavior?

today, it's not enough for companies to make a profit. We also expect managers to make a profit by doing the right things. Unfortunately, no matter what managers decide to do, someone or some group will be unhappy with the outcome. Managers don't have the luxury of choosing theoretically optimal, win-win solutions that are obviously desirable to everyone involved. In practice, solutions to ethical and social responsibility problems aren't optimal. Often, managers must be satisfied with a solution that just makes do or does the least harm. Rights and wrongs are rarely crystal clear to managers charged with doing the right thing. The business world is much messier than that.

across multiple industries, 48 percent of the respondents admitted to actually committing an unethical or illegal act in the past year, including cheating on an expense account, discriminating against coworkers, forging signatures, paying or accepting kickbacks, and looking the other way when environmental laws were broken.[2]

Other studies contain good news. When people believe their work environment is ethical, they are six times more likely to stay with that company than if they believe they work in an unethical environment.[3] According to Eduardo Castro-Wright, vice chairman of Wal-Mart Stores, "Leadership is about trust. It's about being able to get people to go to places they never thought they could go."[4] In short, much needs to be done to make workplaces more ethical, but—and this is very important—most managers and employees want this to happen.

After reading the next two sections, you should be able to

1 **identify common kinds of workplace deviance.**

2 **describe the U.S. Sentencing Commission Guidelines for Organizations and explain how they both encourage ethical behavior and punish unethical behavior by businesses.**

Ethics is the set of moral principles or values that defines right and wrong for a person or group. Unfortunately, numerous studies have consistently produced distressing results about the state of ethics in today's business world. A Society for Human Resources Management survey found that only 27 percent of employees felt that their organization's leadership was ethical. This may be a misperception due to opaque company policies, since 45 percent of HR professionals showed confidence in their leadership's ethics.[1] Nonetheless, the frequency of ethical violations speaks for itself. In a study of 1,324 randomly selected workers, managers, and executives

1 Workplace Deviance

Ethical behavior conforms to a society's accepted principles of right and wrong. Depending on which study you look at, however, one-third to three-quarters of all employees admit that they have stolen from their employers, committed computer fraud, embezzled funds, vandalized company property, sabotaged company projects, faked injuries

> **Ethics** the set of moral principles or values that defines right and wrong for a person or group
>
> **Ethical behavior** behavior that conforms to a society's accepted principles of right and wrong

Workplace deviance unethical behavior that violates organizational norms about right and wrong

Production deviance unethical behavior that hurts the quality and quantity of work produced

Property deviance unethical behavior aimed at the organization's property or products

Employee shrinkage employee theft of company merchandise

Political deviance using one's influence to harm others in the company

Personal aggression hostile or aggressive behavior toward others

to receive workers' compensation benefits or insurance, or "called in sick" to work when they weren't really sick. Experts estimate that unethical behaviors like these, which researchers call *workplace deviance*, may cost companies nearly $1 trillion a year, or roughly 7 percent of their revenues.[5]

Workplace deviance is unethical behavior that violates organizational norms about right and wrong. As Exhibit 4.1 shows, workplace deviance can be categorized by how deviant the behavior is, from minor to serious, and by the target of the deviant behavior, either the organization as a whole or particular people in the workplace.[6]

Company-related deviance can affect both tangible and intangible assets. One kind of workplace deviance, called **production deviance**, hurts the quality and quantity of work produced. Examples include leaving early, taking excessively long work breaks, intentionally working more slowly, or wasting resources. **Property deviance** is unethical behavior aimed at company property or products. Examples include sabotaging, stealing, or damaging equipment or products and overcharging for services and then pocketing the difference. For example, Karin Wilson, who owns the Page and Palette bookstore in Fairhope, Alaska, found that her bookkeeper was using the bookstore's company credit card to pay off her personal credit card and also wrote checks to herself instead of paying publishers for books. In all, Wilson estimates that her bookkeeper made off with $150,000.[7] Employee stealing is more widespread than you'd think. A survey of 24 large retailers employing 2.3 million workers found that 1 out of 28 employees were caught stealing each year.[8]

Theft of company merchandise by employees, called **employee shrinkage**, is another common form of property deviance. Employee shrinkage costs U.S. retailers more than $19.5 billion a year, and employees steal more merchandise than shoplifters (47 percent of theft is done by employees, whereas 32 percent is committed by shoplifters).[9] Shrinkage takes many forms. "Sweethearting" occurs when employees discount or don't ring up merchandise their family or friends bring to the cash register. In "dumpster diving," employees unload trucks, stash merchandise in a dumpster, and then retrieve it after work.[10]

Whereas production and property deviance harm companies, political deviance and personal aggression are unethical behaviors that hurt particular people within companies. **Political deviance** is using one's influence to harm others in the company. Examples include making decisions based on favoritism rather than performance, spreading rumors about coworkers, and blaming others for mistakes they didn't make. **Personal aggression** is hostile or aggressive behavior toward others. Examples include sexual harassment, verbal abuse, stealing from coworkers, and personally threatening coworkers. One of the fastest-growing kinds of personal aggression is workplace violence. More than 2 million Americans are victims of some form of workplace violence each year. According to a U.S. Bureau of Labor Statistics (BLS) survey of 7.4 million U.S. companies, 5.4 percent of all employees experience an incident of workplace violence each year.[11] Between 650 and 1,000 people are killed in such incidents each year.[12]

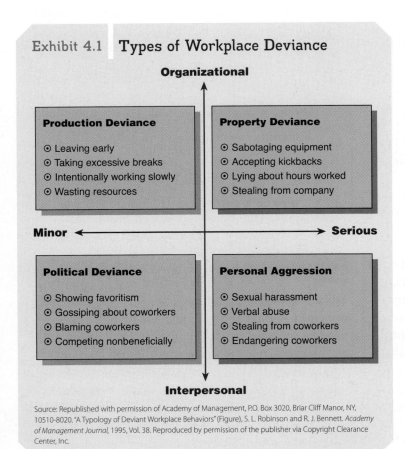

Exhibit 4.1 | **Types of Workplace Deviance**

Source: Republished with permission of Academy of Management, P.O. Box 3020, Briar Cliff Manor, NY, 10510-8020. "A Typology of Deviant Workplace Behaviors" (Figure), S. L. Robinson and R. J. Bennett. *Academy of Management Journal*, 1995, Vol. 38. Reproduced by permission of the publisher via Copyright Clearance Center, Inc.

2 | U.S. Sentencing Commission Guidelines for Organizations

Historically, if management was unaware of an employee's unethical activities, the company could not be held responsible. Since 1991, however, when the U.S. Sentencing Commission Guidelines for Organizations were established, companies can be prosecuted and punished *even if management doesn't know about the unethical behavior*. Penalties for unethical behavior can be substantial, with maximum fines approaching $300 million![13] An amendment made in 2004 outlines much stricter requirements for ethics training and emphasizes creating a legal and ethical company culture.[14]

Let's examine **2.1 to whom the guidelines apply and what they cover** *and* **2.2 how, according to the guidelines, an organization can be punished for the unethical behavior of its managers and employees.**

2.1 | WHO, WHAT, AND WHY

Nearly all businesses are covered by the U.S. Sentencing Commission's guidelines. This includes nonprofits, partnerships, labor unions, unincorporated organizations and associations, incorporated organizations, and even pension funds, trusts, and joint stock companies. If your organization can be characterized as a business (remember, nonprofits count, too), then it is subject to the guidelines.[15]

The guidelines cover offenses defined by federal laws such as invasion of privacy, price fixing, fraud, customs violations, antitrust violations, civil rights violations, theft, money laundering, conflicts of interest, embezzlement, dealing in stolen goods, copyright infringements, extortion, and more. But it's not enough merely to stay within the law. The purpose of the guidelines is not just to punish companies *after* they or their employees break the law, but also to encourage companies to take proactive steps such as ethics training that will discourage or prevent white-collar crime *before* it happens. The guidelines also give companies an incentive to cooperate with and disclose illegal activities to federal authorities.[16]

2.2 | DETERMINING THE PUNISHMENT

The guidelines impose smaller fines on companies that take proactive steps to encourage ethical behavior or voluntarily disclose illegal activities to federal authorities. Essentially, the law uses a carrot-and-stick approach. The stick is the threat of heavy fines that can total millions of dollars. The carrot is a substantial reduction in the fine, but only if the company has started an effective compliance program (discussed below) to encourage ethical behavior *before* the illegal activity occurs.[17] The method used to determine a company's punishment illustrates the importance of establishing a compliance program, as illustrated in Exhibit 4.2 on the next page.

The first step is to compute the *base fine* by determining what *level of offense* has occurred. The level of the offense (i.e., its seriousness) varies depending on the kind of crime, the loss incurred by the victims, and how much planning went into the crime. For example, simple fraud is a level 6 offense (there are 38 levels in all). But if the victims of that fraud lost more than $5 million, that level 6 offense becomes a level 22 offense. Moreover, anything beyond minimal planning to commit the fraud results in an increase of two levels to a level 24 offense. How much difference would this make to the company? As Exhibit 4.2 shows, crimes at or below level 6 incur a base fine of $5,000, whereas the base fine for level 24 is $2.1 million. So the difference is $2.095 million! The base fine for level 38, the top-level offense, is a hefty $72.5 million.

After assessing a *base fine*, the judge computes a culpability score, which is a way of assigning blame to the company. The culpability score can range from a minimum of 0.05 to a maximum of 4.0. The greater the corporate responsibility in conducting, encouraging, or sanctioning illegal or unethical activity, the higher the culpability score. A company that already has a compliance program and voluntarily reports the offense to

© iStockphoto.com/ Terry Hankins

Exhibit 4.2 Offense Levels, Base Fines, Culpability Scores, and Possible Total Fines under the U.S. Sentencing Commission Guidelines for Organizations

Offense Level	Base Fine	Culpability Scores					
		0.05	0.5	1.0	2.0	3.0	4.0
6 or less	$ 5,000	$ 250	$ 2,500	$ 5,000	$ 10,000	$ 15,000	$ 20,000
7	7,500	375	3,750	7,500	15,000	22,500	30,000
8	10,000	500	5,000	10,000	20,000	30,000	40,000
9	15,000	750	7,500	15,000	30,000	45,000	60,000
10	20,000	1,000	10,000	20,000	40,000	60,000	80,000
11	30,000	1,500	15,000	30,000	60,000	90,000	120,000
12	40,000	2,000	20,000	40,000	80,000	120,000	160,000
13	60,000	3,000	30,000	60,000	120,000	180,000	240,000
14	85,000	4,250	42,500	85,000	170,000	255,000	340,000
15	125,000	6,250	62,500	125,000	250,000	375,000	500,000
16	175,000	8,750	87,500	175,000	350,000	525,000	700,000
17	250,000	12,500	125,000	250,000	500,000	750,000	1,000,000
18	350,000	17,500	175,000	350,000	700,000	1,050,000	1,400,000
19	500,000	25,000	250,000	500,000	1,000,000	1,500,000	2,000,000
20	650,000	32,500	325,000	650,000	1,300,000	1,950,000	2,600,000
21	910,000	45,500	455,000	910,000	1,820,000	2,730,000	3,640,000
22	1,200,000	60,000	600,000	1,200,000	2,400,000	3,600,000	4,800,000
23	1,600,000	80,000	800,000	1,600,000	3,200,000	4,800,000	6,400,000
24	2,100,000	105,000	1,050,000	2,100,000	4,200,000	6,300,000	8,400,000
25	2,800,000	140,000	1,400,000	2,800,000	5,600,000	8,400,000	11,200,000
26	3,700,000	185,000	1,850,000	3,700,000	7,400,000	11,100,000	14,800,000
27	4,800,000	240,000	2,400,000	4,800,000	9,600,000	14,400,000	19,200,000
28	6,300,000	315,000	3,150,000	6,300,000	12,600,000	18,900,000	25,200,000
29	8,100,000	405,000	4,050,000	8,100,000	16,200,000	24,300,000	32,400,000
30	10,500,000	525,000	5,250,000	10,500,000	21,000,000	31,500,000	42,000,000
31	13,500,000	675,000	6,750,000	13,500,000	27,000,000	40,500,000	54,000,000
32	17,500,000	875,000	8,750,000	17,500,000	35,000,000	52,500,000	70,000,000
33	22,000,000	1,100,000	11,000,000	22,000,000	44,000,000	66,000,000	88,000,000
34	28,500,000	1,425,000	14,250,000	28,500,000	57,000,000	85,500,000	114,000,000
35	36,000,000	1,800,000	18,000,000	36,000,000	72,000,000	108,000,000	144,000,000
36	45,500,000	2,275,000	22,750,000	45,500,000	91,000,000	136,500,000	182,000,000
37	57,500,000	2,875,000	28,750,000	57,500,000	115,000,000	172,500,000	230,000,000
38 or more	72,500,000	3,625,000	36,250,000	72,500,000	145,000,000	217,500,000	290,000,000

Source: United States Sentencing Commission, *Guidelines Manual*, §3E1.1 (Nov. 2009), 509–531, accessed June 4, 2010, http://www.ussc.gov/2009guid/GL2009.pdf.

authorities will incur a culpability score of 0.05. By contrast, a company whose management secretly plans, approves, and participates in illegal or unethical activity will receive the maximum score of 4.0.

The culpability score is critical because the total fine is computed by multiplying the base fine by the culpability score. Going back to our level 24 fraud of-fense, the left point of the upper arrow in Exhibit 4.2 shows that a company with a compliance program that turns itself in will be fined only $105,000 ($2,100,000 × 0.05). In contrast, a company that secretly planned, approved, and participated in illegal activity will be fined $8.4 million ($2,100,000 × 4.0), as shown by the right point of the upper arrow. The difference is even greater for level 38 offenses. As shown by the left point of the bottom arrow, a company with a compliance program and a 0.05 culpability score is fined only $3.625 million, whereas a company with the maximum 4.0 culpability score is fined a whopping $290 million, as indicated by the right point of the bottom arrow. These differences clearly show the importance of having a compliance program in place. Over the last decade, 1,494 companies have been charged under the U.S. Sentencing Commission Guidelines. Seventy-six percent of those charged were fined, with the average fine exceeding $2 million. Company fines are on average twenty times larger now than before the guidelines were implemented in 1991.[18]

Fortunately for companies that want to avoid paying these stiff fines, the U.S. Sentencing Commission Guidelines clearly spell out the seven necessary components of an effective compliance program to aid companies in their efforts to set up appropriate compliance programs.[19] Exhibit 4.3 lists those components. Caremark International, a managed-care service provider in Delaware, pleaded guilty to criminal charges related to its physician contracts and improper patient referrals. When it was then sued by shareholders for negligence and poor management, the Delaware court dismissed the case, ruling that the company's ethics compliance program, built on the components described in Exhibit 4.3, was a good-faith attempt to monitor employees and that the company did not knowingly allow illegal and unethical behavior to occur. The court went on to rule that a compliance program based on the U.S. Sentencing Commission Guidelines was enough to shield the company from liability.[20]

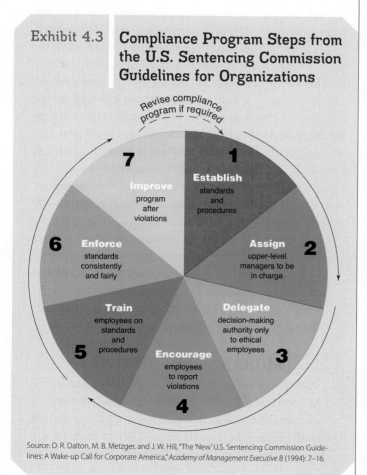

Exhibit 4.3 Compliance Program Steps from the U.S. Sentencing Commission Guidelines for Organizations

Revise compliance program if required

7 **Improve** program after violations

1 **Establish** standards and procedures

2 **Assign** upper-level managers to be in charge

3 **Delegate** decision-making authority only to ethical employees

4 **Encourage** employees to report violations

5 **Train** employees on standards and procedures

6 **Enforce** standards consistently and fairly

Source: D. R. Dalton, M. B. Metzger, and J. W. Hill, "The 'New' U.S. Sentencing Commission Guidelines: A Wake-up Call for Corporate America," *Academy of Management Executive* 8 (1994): 7–16.

How Do You Make Ethical Decisions?

On a cold morning in the midst of a winter storm, schools were closed, and most people had decided to stay home from work. Nevertheless, Richard Addessi had already showered, shaved, and dressed for the office. He kissed his wife Joan goodbye, but before he could get to his car, he fell dead on the garage floor of a sudden heart attack. Addessi was 4 months short of his 30-year anniversary with the company. Having begun work at IBM at the age of 18, he was just 48 years old.[21]

You're the vice president in charge of benefits at IBM. Given that he was only 4 months short of being eligible for full retirement benefits, do you award those benefits to Richard Addessi's wife and daughters? If the answer is yes, they will receive his full retirement benefits of $1,800 a month and free lifetime medical coverage. If you say no, his widow and two daughters will receive only $340 a month. They will also have to pay $473 a month to continue their current medical coverage. As the VP in charge of benefits at IBM, what would be the ethical thing for you to do?

After reading the next two sections, you should be able to

3 **describe what influences ethical decision making.**

4 **explain what practical steps managers can take to improve ethical decision making.**

3 Influences on Ethical Decision Making

Although some ethical issues are easily solved, many do not have clearly right or wrong answers. And, even though the answers are rarely clear, managers do need

Ethical intensity the degree of concern people have about an ethical issue

Magnitude of consequences the total harm or benefit derived from an ethical decision

Social consensus agreement on whether behavior is bad or good

Probability of effect the chance that something will happen and then harm others

Temporal immediacy the time between an act and the consequences the act produces

Proximity of effect the social, psychological, cultural, or physical distance between a decision maker and those affected by his or her decisions

Concentration of effect the total harm or benefit that an act produces on the average person

to have a clear sense of how to arrive at an answer in order to manage this ethical ambiguity well.

*The ethical answers that managers choose depend on **3.1 the ethical intensity of the decision, 3.2 the moral development of the manager,** and **3.3 the ethical principles used to solve the problem.***

3.1 | ETHICAL INTENSITY OF THE DECISION

Managers don't treat all ethical decisions the same. The IBM manager who has to decide whether to deny or extend full benefits to Joan Addessi and her children is going to treat that decision much more seriously than the decision of how to deal with an assistant who has been taking computer paper home for personal use. These decisions differ in their **ethical intensity,** or the degree of concern people have about an ethical issue. When addressing an issue of high ethical intensity, managers are more aware of the impact their decision will have on others. They are more likely to view the decision as an ethical or moral decision rather than as an economic decision. They are also more likely to worry about doing the right thing.

Six factors must be taken into account when determining the ethical intensity of an action, as shown in Exhibit 4.4. **Magnitude of consequences** is the total harm or benefit derived from an ethical decision. The

more people who are harmed or the greater the harm to those people, the larger the magnitude of the consequences. **Social consensus** is agreement on whether behavior is bad or good. **Probability of effect** is the chance that something will happen and then result in harm to others. If we combine these factors, we can see the effect they can have on ethical intensity. For example, if there is *clear agreement* (social consensus) that a managerial decision or action is *certain* (probability of effect) to have *large negative consequences* (magnitude of consequences) in some way, then people will be highly concerned about that managerial decision or action, and ethical intensity will be high. Although Addessi's family will be profoundly affected by IBM's decision, they are one family, and the magnitude of consequences and the probability of effect for others will be quite low if the benefits are denied.

Temporal immediacy is the time between an act and the consequences the act produces. Temporal immediacy is stronger if a manager has to lay off workers next week as opposed to 3 months from now. **Proximity of effect** is the social, psychological, cultural, or physical distance of a decision maker from those affected by his or her decisions. Thus, proximity of effect is greater for the manager who works with employees who are to be laid off than it is for the higher-ups who ordered the layoffs. If the person responsible for the decision were Addessi's direct supervisor, who had known him and his family through his tenure at the company, the ethical intensity would be higher than it would be for an executive who had never met him. Finally, whereas the magnitude of consequences is the total effect across all people, **concentration of effect** is how much an act affects the average person. Temporarily laying off 100 employees for 10 months without pay has a greater concentration of effect than temporarily laying off 1,000 employees for 1 month.

Which of these six factors has the most impact on ethical intensity? Studies indicate that managers are much more likely to view decisions as ethical when the magnitude of consequences (total harm) is high and there is a social consensus (agreement) that a behavior or action is bad.[22]

3.2 | MORAL DEVELOPMENT

A friend of yours has given you the latest version of Microsoft Office. She stuffed the software disks in your backpack with a note saying that you should install it on your computer and get it back to her in a couple of days. You're tempted. No one would find out. Even if someone does, Microsoft probably

Exhibit 4.4	Six Factors That Contribute to Ethical Intensity

Magnitude of consequences
Social consensus
Probability of effect
Temporal immediacy
Proximity of effect
Concentration of effect

Source: Republished with permission of Academy of Management; P.O. Box 3020, Briar Cliff Manor, NY, 10510-8020. T.M. Jones, "Ethical Decision Making by Individuals in Organizations: An Issue Contingent Model," *Academy of Management Review 16* (1991) 366–395; Reproduced by permission of the publisher via Copyright Clearance Center, Inc.

Most people in the workplace need leadership when it comes to ethical decision making.

ishment and obedience stage, your primary concern will be to avoid trouble for yourself. So you won't copy the software because you are afraid of being caught and punished. Yet, in Stage 2, the instrumental exchange stage, you worry less about punishment and more about doing things that directly advance your wants and needs. So you copy the software.

People at the **conventional level of moral development** make decisions that conform to societal expectations. In other words, they look to others for guidance on ethical issues. In Stage 3, the good boy, nice girl stage, you normally do what the other "good boys" and "nice girls" are doing. If everyone else is illegally copying software, you will, too. But if they aren't, you won't either. In the law and order stage, Stage 4, you again look for external guidance but do whatever the *law* permits; so you won't copy the software.

People at the **postconventional level of moral development** use internalized ethical principles to solve ethical dilemmas. In Stage 5, the social contract stage, you will refuse to copy the software because, as a whole, society is better off when the rights of others—in this case, the rights of software authors and manufacturers—are not violated. In Stage 6, the universal principle stage, you might or might not copy the software, depending on your principles of right and wrong. Moreover, you will stick to your principles even if your decision conflicts with the law (Stage 4) or what others believe is best for society (Stage 5). For example, those with socialist or communist beliefs might choose to copy the software because they believe goods and services should be owned by society rather than by individuals and corporations.

Preconventional level of moral development the first level of moral development in which people make decisions based on selfish reasons

Conventional level of moral development the second level of moral development in which people make decisions that conform to societal expectations

Postconventional level of moral development the third level of moral development in which people make decisions based on internalized principles

isn't going to come after you. Microsoft goes after the big fish—companies that illegally copy and distribute software to their workers and pirates that illegally sell cheap unauthorized copies. What would you do?[23]

In part, according to psychologist Lawrence Kohlberg, your decision will be based on your level of moral development. Kohlberg identified three phases of moral development with two stages in each phase (see Exhibit 4.5).[24] At the **preconventional level of moral development**, people decide based on selfish reasons. For example, if you are in Stage 1, the pun-

Exhibit 4.5	**Kohlberg's Stages of Moral Development**				
Stage 1 Punishment and Obedience	**Stage 2** Instrumental Exchange	**Stage 3** Good Boy, Nice Girl	**Stage 4** Law and Order	**Stage 5** Social Contract	**Stage 6** Universal Principle
Preconventional		**Conventional**		**Postconventional**	
Self-Interest		**Societal Expectations**		**Internalized Principles**	

© Cengage Learning 2011

Kohlberg believed that people would progress sequentially from earlier to later stages as they became more educated and mature. But only 20 percent of adults ever reach the postconventional stage of moral development in which internal principles guide their decisions. Most adults are in the conventional stage of moral development and look to others for guidance on ethical issues. This means that most people in the workplace need leadership when it comes to ethical decision making.[25]

3.3 | PRINCIPLES OF ETHICAL DECISION MAKING

Beyond an issue's ethical intensity and a manager's level of moral maturity, the particular ethical principles that managers use will also affect how they solve ethical dilemmas. Unfortunately, there is no one ideal principle to use in making ethical business decisions. According to professor LaRue Hosmer, a number of different ethical principles can be used to make business decisions: long-term self-interest, personal virtue, religious injunctions, government requirements, utilitarian benefits, individual rights, and distributive justice.[26] All of these ethical principles encourage managers and employees to take others' interests into account when making ethical decisions. At the same time, however, these principles can lead to very different ethical actions, as we can see by using these principles to decide whether to award full benefits to Joan Addessi and her children.

According to the **principle of long-term self-interest,** you should never take any action that is not in your or your organization's long-term self-interest. Although this sounds as if the principle promotes selfishness, it doesn't. What we do to maximize our long-term interests (save more, exercise every day, watch what we eat) is often very different from what we do to maximize short-term interests (max out our credit cards, be couch potatoes, eat whatever we want). At any given time, IBM has nearly 1,000 employees who are just months away from retirement. Because of the costs involved, it serves IBM's long-term interest to pay full benefits only after employees have put in their 30 years.

The **principle of personal virtue** holds that you should never do anything that is not honest, open, and truthful and that you would not be glad to see reported in the newspapers or on TV. Using the principle of personal virtue, IBM might have quietly awarded Joan Addessi her husband's full benefits, avoiding the potential for negative media coverage.

The **principle of religious injunctions** holds that you should never take an action that is unkind or that harms a sense of community, such as the positive feelings that come from working together to accomplish a commonly accepted goal. Using this principle, IBM would be concerned foremost with compassion and kindness and would award full benefits to Joan Addessi.

According to the **principle of government requirements,** the law represents the minimal moral standards of society, and so you should never take any action that violates the law. Using this principle, IBM would deny full benefits to Joan Addessi because her husband did not work for the company for 30 years.

The **principle of utilitarian benefits** states that you should never take an action that does not result in greater good for society. In short, you should do whatever creates the greatest good for the greatest number. At first, this principle seems to suggest that IBM should award full benefits to Joan Addessi. If IBM did this with any regularity, however, the costs would be enormous, profits would shrink, and IBM would have to cut its stock dividend, harming countless shareholders, many of whom rely on their dividends for retirement income. In this case, the principle does not lead to a clear choice.

The **principle of individual rights** holds that you should never take an action that infringes on others' agreed-upon rights. Using this principle, IBM would deny Joan Addessi full benefits. If it followed the rules specified in its pension plan and granted her due process, meaning the right to appeal the decision, then IBM would not be violating her rights. In fact, it could be argued that providing full benefits to Joan Addessi would violate the rights of employees who had to wait 30 years to receive full benefits.

Finally, under the **principle of distributive justice,** you should never take any action that harms the least fortunate among us in some way. This principle is designed to protect the poor, the uneducated, and the unemployed. Although Joan Addessi could probably find a job, it's unlikely that after 20 years as a stay-at-home mom, she could easily find one that would support her and her daughters in the manner to which they were accustomed. Using the principle of distributive justice, IBM would award her full benefits.

As mentioned at the beginning of this chapter, one of the practical aspects of ethical decisions is that no matter *what* you decide, someone or some group will be unhappy. This corollary is also true: No matter *how* you decide, someone or some group will be unhappy. Some will argue that you should have used a different principle or weighed concerns differently. Consequently, although all of these ethical principles encourage managers to balance others' needs against their own, they can also lead to very different ethical actions. So even when managers strive to be ethical, there are often no clear answers when it comes to doing the right thing.

So, what did IBM decide to do? Since Richard Addessi had not completed 30 full years with the company, IBM officials felt they had no choice but to give Joan Addessi and her two daughters the smaller, partial retirement benefits. Do you think IBM's decision was ethical? It's likely many of you don't. You may wonder how the company could be so heartless as to deny Richard Addessi's family the full benefits to which you believe they were entitled. Yet others might argue that IBM did the ethical thing by strictly following the rules laid out in its pension benefit plan. Indeed, an IBM spokesperson stated that making exceptions would violate the federal Employee Retirement Income Security Act of 1974. After all, being fair means applying the rules to everyone.

4 | Practical Steps to Ethical Decision Making

*Managers can encourage more ethical decision making in their organizations by **4.1 carefully selecting and hiring ethical employees, 4.2 establishing a specific code of ethics, 4.3 training employees to make ethical decisions,** and **4.4 creating an ethical climate.***

4.1 | SELECTING AND HIRING ETHICAL EMPLOYEES

As an employer, you can increase your chances of hiring an honest person by giving job applicants integrity tests. **Overt integrity tests** estimate job applicants'

honesty by directly asking them what they think or feel about theft or about punishment of unethical behaviors.[27] For example, an employer might ask an applicant, "Don't most people steal from their companies?" Surprisingly, unethical people will usually answer "yes" to such questions, because they believe that the world is basically dishonest and that dishonest behavior is normal.[28]

Personality-based integrity tests indirectly estimate job applicants' honesty by measuring psychological traits such as dependability and conscientiousness. For example, prison inmates serving time for white-collar crimes (counterfeiting, embezzlement, and fraud) scored much lower than a comparison group of middle-level managers on scales measuring reliability, dependability, honesty, conscientiousness, and abiding by rules.[29] These results show that companies can selectively hire and promote people who will be more ethical.[30]

Overt integrity test
a written test that estimates job applicants' honesty by directly asking them what they think or feel about theft or about punishment of unethical behaviors

Personality-based integrity test a written test that indirectly estimates job applicants' honesty by measuring psychological traits such as dependability and conscientiousness

7 Tips for Writing a Code of Ethics

✔ Write in conjunction with the company mission statement and specific conduct policies.

✔ Decide in advance what values are important to the company.

✔ Get input from employees.

✔ Don't agonize over specific ethics scenarios.

✔ Issues may vary depending on the company's size.

✔ Consult an ethicist or human resource specialist if necessary.

✔ Put someone in charge of applying and updating the ethics code.

Source: J. Spiro, "How to Write a Code of Ethics for Business," *Inc.*, February 24, 2010, accessed June 12, 2010, http://www.inc.com/guides/how-to-write-a-code-of-ethics.html

© iStockphoto.com/fredfroese

4.2 | CODES OF ETHICS

Today, almost all large corporations have similar ethics codes in place. Still, two things must happen if those codes are to encourage ethical decision making and behavior.[31] First, a company must communicate its code inside and outside the company. Johnson & Johnson's credo is an example of a well-communicated code of ethics. Anyone inside or outside the company can find the credo on its website and obtain detailed information about the company's specific ethical business practices.

Second, in addition to having an ethics code with general guidelines like "do unto others as you would have others do unto you," management must also develop practical ethical standards and procedures specific to the company's line of business. Nortel has produced a brochure, available to employees and the public on the company website, which lays out the specifics of how employees are expected to act. For example, it helps employees gauge whether an action creates a conflict of interest by laying out specific criteria. A conflict of interest "prevents you from effectively and efficiently performing your regular duties, causes you to compete against the Company, influences your judgment when acting on behalf of Nortel in a way that could hurt the Company, or causes you to misuse Company resources."[32] Specific codes of ethics such as this make it much easier for employees to decide what to do when they want to do the right thing.

4.3 | ETHICS TRAINING

In addition to establishing ethical standards for the company, managers must sponsor and be involved in ethics and compliance training in order to create an ethical company culture.[33] The first objective of ethics training is to develop employees' awareness of ethics.[34] This means helping employees recognize which issues are ethical issues and then avoid rationalizing unethical behavior by thinking, "This isn't really il-

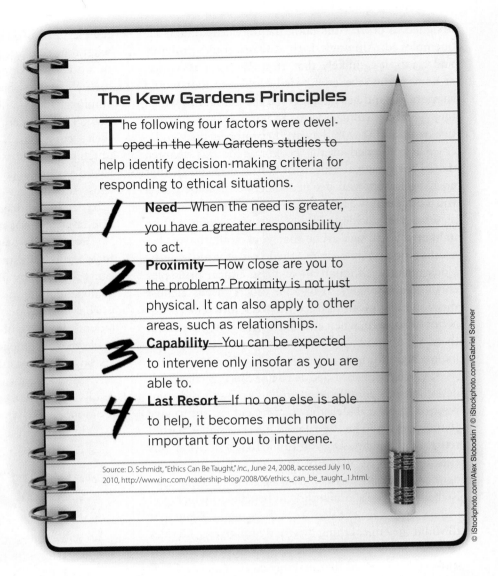

The Kew Gardens Principles

The following four factors were developed in the Kew Gardens studies to help identify decision-making criteria for responding to ethical situations.

1. **Need**—When the need is greater, you have a greater responsibility to act.

2. **Proximity**—How close are you to the problem? Proximity is not just physical. It can also apply to other areas, such as relationships.

3. **Capability**—You can be expected to intervene only insofar as you are able to.

4. **Last Resort**—If no one else is able to help, it becomes much more important for you to intervene.

Source: D. Schmidt, "Ethics Can Be Taught," *Inc.*, June 24, 2008, accessed July 10, 2010, http://www.inc.com/leadership-blog/2008/06/ethics_can_be_taught_1.html.

© iStockphoto.com/Alex Slobodkin / © iStockphoto.com/Gabriel Schroer

legal or immoral" or "No one will ever find out." Several companies have created board games to improve awareness of ethical issues.[35] Other ethics training tools, like the Kew Gardens Principles, examine how ethical decisions can be made in specific scenarios. The Kew Gardens Principles were based on the study of a murder in Kew Gardens, New York, in which witnesses to the attack failed to intervene or seek help. Researchers developed a series of four decision-making factors which could be used to help employees determine how they should respond to problems and ethical situations, even in cases when the problems were not their own doing.[36] These decision-making factors can be applied to other scenarios as well. Specific company-related questions and scenarios make it easier for managers and employees to recognize and be aware of ethical issues and situations.

The second objective for ethics training programs is to achieve credibility with employees. Some companies have hurt the credibility of their ethics programs by having outside instructors and consultants conduct the classes.[37] Employees often complain that outside instructors and consultants are teaching theory that has nothing to do with their jobs and the practical dilemmas they actually face on a daily basis. This is why Lockheed Martin, a defense and aerospace company, frequently has its top managers teach ethics classes. For instance, Manny Zuleuta, a senior vice president of shared services, led seven employees through a DVD-based scenario in which they viewed a worker complaining to his boss's manager that his boss yells at him all of the time. Later, the boss apologizes. But then, according to the employee, the boss retaliates against him by giving him bad assignments. Ethics training becomes even more credible when top managers teach the initial ethics classes to their subordinates, who in turn teach their subordinates.[38] Michael Hoffman, executive director for the Center for Business Ethics at Bentley College, says that having managers teach ethics courses greatly reinforces the seriousness with which employees treat ethics in the workplace.[39] Unfortunately, though, 25 percent of large companies don't require top managers to attend, much less teach, ethics classes.[40]

The third objective of ethics training is to teach employees a practical model of ethical decision making. A basic model should help them think about the consequences their choices will have on others and consider how they will choose between different solutions. Exhibit 4.6 presents a basic model of ethical decision making.

4.4 | ETHICAL CLIMATE

Organizational culture is key to fostering ethical decision making. The 2007 National Business Ethics Survey reported that only 24 percent of employees who work at companies with a strong ethical climate (where core beliefs are widely shared and strongly held) have observed others engaging in unethical behavior, whereas 56 percent of those who work in organizations with a weak ethical climate (where core beliefs are not widely shared or strongly held) have observed others engaging in unethical behavior. In a strong ethical climate, employees are also more likely to report violations because they expect that management wants them to and won't retaliate against them for doing so.[41] We learned in Chapter 3 that leadership is an important factor in creating an organizational culture. So, it's no surprise that in study after study, when researchers ask, "What is the most important influence on your ethical behavior at work?" the answer comes back, "My manager." The first step in establishing an ethical climate is for managers, especially top managers, to act ethically themselves.

A second step in establishing an ethical climate is for top management to be active in and committed to the company ethics program.[42] Business writer Dayton Fandray says, "You can have ethics offices and officers and training programs and reporting systems, but if the CEO doesn't seem to care, it's all just a sham. It's not surprising to find that the companies that really do care about ethics make a point of including senior management in all of their ethics and compliance programs."[43]

Exhibit 4.6 A Basic Model of Ethical Decision Making

1. **Identify the problem.** What makes it an ethical problem? Think in terms of rights, obligations, fairness, relationships, and integrity. How would you define the problem if you stood on the other side of the fence?

2. **Identify the constituents.** Who has been hurt? Who could be hurt? Who could be helped? Are they willing players, or are they victims? Can you negotiate with them?

3. **Diagnose the situation.** How did it happen in the first place? What could have prevented it? Is it going to get worse or better? Can the damage now be undone?

4. **Analyze your options.** Imagine the range of possibilities. Limit yourself to the two or three most manageable. What are the likely outcomes of each? What are the likely costs? Look to the company mission statement or code of ethics for guidance.

5. **Make your choice.** What is your intention in making this decision? How does it compare with the probable results? Can you discuss the problem with the affected parties before you act? Could you disclose without qualm your decision to your boss, the CEO, the board of directors, your family, or society as a whole?

6. **Act.** Do what you have to do. Don't be afraid to admit errors. Be as bold in confronting a problem as you were in causing it.

Source: L. A. Berger, "Train All Employees to Solve Ethical Dilemmas," *Best's Review—Life-Health Insurance Edition* 95 (1995): 70–80.

A Short History of Ethical Lapses

In today's world, it's harder to hide unethical behavior. According to Ronald Sims, a business-ethics professor at the Mason School of Business at The College of William & Mary, "There are so many news

2005

Harry Stonecipher
Boeing

Fired for violating Boeing's personal conduct policy after emails revealed a relationship with a female executive

Thomas M. Coughlin
Wal-Mart

Resigned after allegations of abusing expense accounts and falsifying reimbursement reports

2007

John Browne
BP

Resigned after admitting that he lied to a judge while trying to prevent a British newspaper from exposing details about his personal life

Steven J. Heyer
Starwood

Fired after he was accused of making inappropriate contact with a female employee, a charge he denied

Source: A. Jones and N. Koppel, "Ethical Lapses Felled Long List of Company Executives," *Wall Street Journal*, August 7, 2010, A1.

AP Images/Ted S. Warren / AP Images/Neemah Aaron / © PA Photos/Landov / AP Images/Jennifer Graylock

A third step is to put in place a reporting system that encourages managers and employees to report potential ethics violations. **Whistleblowing,** that is, reporting others' ethics violations, is a difficult step for most people to take.[44] Potential whistleblowers often fear that they, and not the ethics violators, will be punished.[45] Matthew Lee, a former vice president at Lehman Brothers, was troubled when he discovered that the firm was moving $50 billion off its balance sheet in an attempt to hide steep losses, which would eventually lead to the firm's collapse. When Lee raised concerns about the false accounting practices to both the board of directors and to the company that was doing the auditing, Ernst & Young, he was fired.[46]

The factor that does the most to discourage whistleblowers from reporting problems, however, is lack of company action on their complaints.[47] Thus, the final step in developing an ethical climate is for management to fairly and consistently punish those who violate the company's code of ethics. Amazingly, though, not all companies fire ethics violators. In fact, 8 percent of surveyed companies admit that they would promote top performers even if they violated ethical standards.[48]

What Is Social Responsibility?

Social responsibility is a business's obligation to pursue policies, make decisions, and take actions that benefit society.[49] Unfortunately, because there are strong disagreements over to whom and for what in society organizations are responsible, it can be difficult for managers to know what is or will be perceived as socially responsible corporate behavior. In a recent McKinsey & Co. study of 1,144 top executives from around the world, 79 percent predicted that at least some

Whistleblowing
reporting others' ethics violations to management or legal authorities

Social responsibility a business's obligation to pursue policies, make decisions, and take actions that benefit society

outlets that anyone can now pick up a story and run with it. In the past, it was more hush hush." Here's a quick look over some newsworthy ethical lapses on the part of executives from a variety of industries.

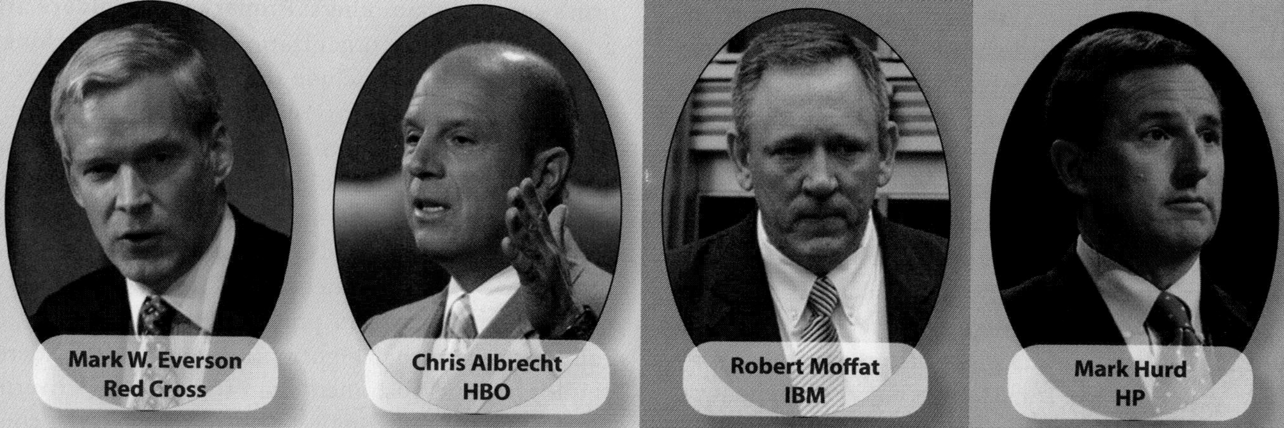

Mark W. Everson, Red Cross (2007): Fired after allegations of having a personal relationship with a subordinate employee

Chris Albrecht, HBO (2007): Resigned after he pleaded no-contest to battery against a girlfriend

Robert Moffat, IBM (2009): Left after being arrested for insider training

Mark Hurd, HP (2010): Fired after a sexual harassment investigation revealed expense-account irregularities

© Roger L. Wollenberg/UPI/Landov / © Chris Pizzello/Reuters/Landov / AP Images/Louis Lanzano / AP Images/Paul Sakuma

responsibility for dealing with future social and political issues would fall on corporations, but only 3 percent said they do a good job of dealing with these issues.[50]

After reading the next four sections, you should be able to

5 **explain to whom organizations are socially responsible.**

6 **explain for what organizations are socially responsible.**

7 **explain how organizations can choose to respond to societal demands for social responsibility.**

8 **explain whether social responsibility hurts or helps an organization's economic performance.**

5 To Whom Are Organizations Socially Responsible?

There are two perspectives concerning whom organizations are socially responsible to: the shareholder model and the stakeholder model. According to the late Nobel Prize–winning economist Milton Friedman, the only social responsibility that organizations have is to satisfy their owners, that is, company shareholders. This view—called the **shareholder model**—holds that the only social responsibility that businesses have is to maximize profits. By maximizing profit, the firm maximizes shareholder wealth and satisfaction. More specifically, as profits rise, the company stock owned by shareholders generally increases in value.

Friedman argued that it is socially irresponsible for companies to divert time, money, and attention from maximizing profits to social causes and charitable organizations. The first problem, he believed, is that organizations cannot act effectively as moral agents for all company shareholders. Although shareholders are likely to agree on investment issues concerning a company, it's highly unlikely that they have common views on what social causes a company should or should not support. Rather than act as moral agents, Friedman

Shareholder model a view of social responsibility that holds that an organization's overriding goal should be to maximize profit for the benefit of shareholders

argued, companies should maximize profits for shareholders. Shareholders can then use their time and increased wealth to contribute to the social causes, charities, or institutions they want rather than those that companies want.

The second major problem, Friedman said, is that the time, money, and attention diverted to social causes undermine market efficiency.[51] In competitive markets, companies compete for raw materials, talented workers, customers, and investment funds. A company that spends money on social causes will have less money to purchase quality materials or to hire talented workers who can produce a valuable product at a good price. If customers find the company's product less desirable, its sales and profits will fall. If profits fall, the company's stock price will decline, and the company will have difficulty attracting investment funds that could be used to fund long-term growth. In the end, Friedman argues, diverting the firm's money, time, and resources to social causes hurts customers, suppliers, employees, and shareholders. Russell Roberts, an economist at George Mason University, agrees, saying, "Doesn't it make more sense to have companies do what they do best, make good products at fair prices, and then let consumers use the savings for the charity of their choice?"[52]

By contrast, under the **stakeholder model**, management's most important responsibility is not just maximizing profits, but the firm's long-term survival, which is achieved by satisfying not just shareholders, but the interests of multiple corporate stakeholders.[53] **Stakeholders** are persons or groups who are interested in and affected by the organization's actions.[54] They are called "stakeholders" because they have a stake in what those actions are. According to PepsiCo CEO Indra Nooyi, because stakeholders are multifaceted, with different interests, a company operating under the stakeholder model has to redefine "profit." She says, "We have to make sure our new P & L (profit & loss statement) actually says revenue, less costs of goods sold, less costs to society—and that's your real profit."[55]

Stakeholder groups may try to influence the firm to act in their own interests. Exhibit 4.7 shows the various stakeholder groups that

the organization must satisfy to ensure its long-term survival. Being responsible to multiple stakeholders raises two basic questions: First, how does a company identify its stakeholders? Second, how does a company balance the needs of different stakeholders? Distinguishing between primary and secondary stakeholders can help answer these questions.[56]

Some stakeholders are more important to the firm's survival than others. **Primary stakeholders** are groups on which the organization depends for its long-term survival. They include shareholders, employees, customers, suppliers, governments, and local communities. When managers are struggling to balance the needs of different stakeholders, the stakeholder model suggests that the needs of primary stakeholders take precedence over the needs of secondary stakeholders. But among primary stakeholders, are some more important than others? In practice, yes, as CEOs typically give somewhat higher priority to shareholders, employees, and customers than to suppliers, governments, and local communities.[57] Addressing the concerns of primary stakeholders is important because if

Real profit = Revenue − Cost of goods sold − Cost to society

Indra Nooyi, PepsiCo CEO

AP Images/Mary Altaffer

a stakeholder group becomes dissatisfied and terminates its relationship with the company, the company could be seriously harmed or go out of business.

Secondary stakeholders, such as the media and special interest groups, can influence or be influenced by a company. Unlike the primary stakeholders, however, they do not engage in regular transactions with the company and are not critical to its long-term survival. Nevertheless, secondary stakeholders are still important because they can affect public perceptions and opinions about a company's socially responsible behavior. For instance, after hundreds of protests by animal-rights activists, including groups such as the People for the Ethical Treatment of Animals (PETA), Smithfield Foods, the nation's largest pork producer, announced that it would phase out small "gestation crates" in which it confined pregnant female pigs at its company-owned farms. In this case, a secondary stakeholder was able to mobilize public opinion and convince Smithfield's primary stakeholders and large customers, such as McDonald's and Wal-Mart, to exert pressure on the company to discontinue the practice.[58]

So, to whom are organizations socially responsible? Many commentators, especially economists and financial analysts, continue to argue that organizations are responsible only to shareholders. Increasingly, however, top managers have come to believe that they and their companies must be socially responsible to their stakeholders. Today, surveys show that as many as 80 percent of top-level managers believe that it is unethical to focus just on shareholders. Twenty-nine states have changed their laws to allow company boards of directors to consider the needs of employees, creditors, suppliers, customers, and local communities as well as those of shareholders.[59] Although there is not complete agreement, a majority of opinion makers would argue that companies must be socially responsible to their stakeholders.

Exhibit 4.7 Stakeholder Model of Corporate Social Responsibility

PRIMARY STAKEHOLDERS:

SECONDARY STAKEHOLDERS:

SECONDARY STAKEHOLDERS

PRIMARY STAKEHOLDERS

Governments

Local Communities

Suppliers

Special Interest Groups

FIRM

Shareholders

Media

Employees

Customers

Trade Associations

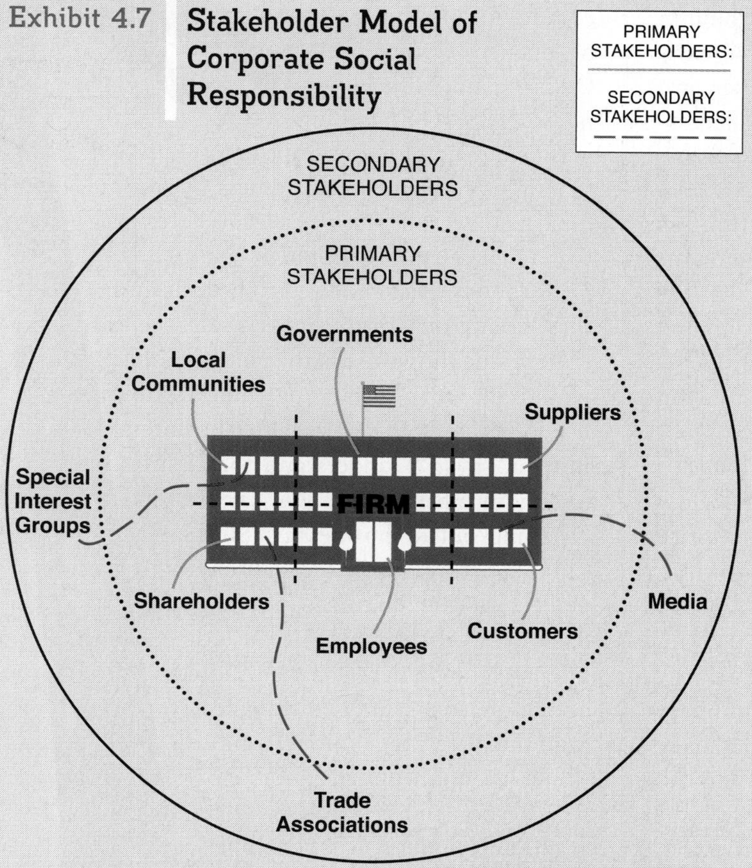

Source: Republished with permission of Academy of Management, P.O. Box 3020, Briar Cliff Manor, NY, 10510-8020. "The Stakeholder Theory of the Corporation: Concepts, Evidence and Implications" (Figure), T. Donaldson and L. E. Preston, *Academy of Management Review* 20 (1995). Reproduced by permission of the publisher via Copyright Clearance Center, Inc.

6 For What Are Organizations Socially Responsible?

If organizations are to be socially responsible to stakeholders, what are they to be socially responsible *for*? Well, companies can best benefit their stakeholders by fulfilling their economic, legal, ethical, and discretionary responsibilities. Economic and legal responsibilities play a larger part in a company's social responsibility than do ethical and discretionary responsibilities. However, the relative importance of these various responsibilities depends on society's expectations of corporate social responsibility at a particular point in time.[60] A century ago, society expected businesses to meet their economic and legal responsibilities and little else. Today, when society judges whether businesses are socially responsible, ethical and discretionary responsibilities are

Economic responsibility the expectation that a company will make a profit by producing a valued product or service

Legal responsibility a company's social responsibility to obey society's laws and regulations

Ethical responsibility a company's social responsibility not to violate accepted principles of right and wrong when conducting business

Discretionary responsibility the expectation that a company will voluntarily serve a social role beyond its economic, legal, and ethical responsibilities

considerably more important than they used to be.

Historically, **economic responsibility,** or the expectation that a company will make a profit by producing a product or service valued by society, has been a business's most basic social responsibility. Organizations that don't meet their financial and economic expectations come under tremendous pressure. For example, company boards are very, very quick these days to fire CEOs. CEOs are three times more likely to be fired today than they were two decades ago. Typically, all it takes is two or three bad quarters in a row. William Rollnick, who became acting chairman of Mattel after the company fired its previous CEO, says, "There's zero forgiveness. You screw up and you're dead."[61] On an annual basis, roughly 4 percent of CEOs of large companies are fired each year.[62] Nearly one-third of all CEOs, however, are eventually fired because of their inability to successfully change their companies.[63]

Legal responsibility is a company's social responsibility to obey society's laws and regulations as it tries to meet its economic responsibilities. For instance, companies award stock options so that managers and employees are rewarded when the company does well. Stock options give you the right to purchase shares of stock at a set price. Let's say that on June 1st, the company awards you the right (or option) to buy 100 shares of stock, which, on that day, sells for $10 a share. If the stock price falls below $10, the options are worthless. But, if the stock price rises to $15 a share, you can exercise your options by paying the company $1,000 (100 shares at $10 a share), and then sell those 100 shares at $15 per share (the current price) for $1,500 and make $500. But if your options had been dated to, say, January 1st when the stock was selling for $5, you'd make $1,000 instead of $500. It would be unethical and illegal, however, to backdate your options to when the stock sold for a lower price. But, that's exactly what the president and COO did at Monster Worldwide (which runs Monster.com). By improperly backdating his options, he earned an additional $24 million.[64] At Monster, however, backdating was condoned by the CEO, who routinely backdated options for members of the management team.[65]

Ethical responsibility is a company's social responsibility to not violate accepted principles of right and wrong when conducting business. Cyrus Hassankola has been "going out of business" for nearly two decades. Swiss-educated, but from Iran, he entered the Oriental rug business in Zurich. Because there were so many shops, he advertised that his was "going out of business." The store stayed open several more months and made a lot of money. He then opened and closed 4 more rug stores after running highly profitable "going out of business" sales. After moving to the United States, Hassankola replicated this strategy in five states, until, weary of moving around, he opened a store in Dallas and officially named it "Going Out of Business," with the hope that it would pull in customers on a regular basis. It's not illegal in Texas to name your store "Going Out of Business," but you are required to get a license for "going out of business" sales. The larger issue, however, is that most people would agree it's the wrong thing to do. David Beasley, of Dallas's Better Business Bureau, says, "I understand the desire to stay in business. But you can't do it by going out of business."[66] So, Hassankola's store is now the "Cyrus Rug Gallery," which has a "Liquidation Sale" banner out front. Because different stakeholders may disagree about what is or is not ethical, meeting ethical responsibilities is more difficult than meeting economic or legal responsibilities.

Discretionary responsibilities pertain to the social roles that businesses play in society beyond their economic, legal, and ethical responsibilities. For example, dozens of companies support the fight against hunger at The Hunger Site (http://www.thehungersite.com). Each time someone clicks on the "donate free food" button (only one click per day per visitor), sponsors of The Hunger Site donate money to pay for food to be sent to Bosnia, Indonesia, Mozambique, or wherever people suffer from hunger. Since it began in 1999, thanks to the corporate sponsors and the clicks of over 300 million, The Hunger Site has generated funding for more than 671 million cups of food.[67] Discretionary responsibilities such as this one are voluntary. Companies are not considered unethical if they don't perform them. Today, however, corporate stakeholders expect companies to do much more than in the past to meet their discretionary responsibilities.

7 Responses to Demands for Social Responsibility

Social responsiveness refers to a company's strategy for responding to stakeholders' expectations concerning economic, legal, ethical, or discretionary responsibility. A social responsibility problem exists whenever company actions do not meet stakeholders' expectations. One model of social responsiveness identifies four strategies for responding to social responsibility problems: reactive, defensive, accommodative, and proactive. These strategies differ in the extent to which the company is willing to act to meet or exceed stakeholders' expectations.

A company using a **reactive strategy** will do less than stakeholders expect. It may deny responsibility for a problem or fight any suggestions that it should solve a problem. By contrast, a company using a **defensive strategy** will admit responsibility for a problem but would do the least required to meet stakeholders' expectations. Documents from a pending lawsuit against Dell computers suggest that the company shipped at least 11.8 million computers that had faulty electrical components and capacitors that broke and leaked fluid. As customer complaints mounted, Dell blamed the problems on the way customers were using the computers, for example, telling the University of Texas that it overworked the computers by having them perform complex math calculations. When an internal study helped Dell identify the problem, instead of alerting customers or initiating a recall (an accommodative strategy), Dell continued to try to cover up the problem. One internal memo to salespeople said, "Don't bring this to customer's attention proactively."[68] And, in many cases, Dell actually repaired the broken computers with more of the same faulty components. Ira Winkler, who was a computer analyst for the National Security Agency, said, "They were fixing bad computers with bad computers and were misleading customers at the same time."[69] While Dell took a $300 million charge to fix the computers and has extended warranties for some customers, it has still not issued a general recall, which means that many customers may not be aware that they had purchased faulty computers. Dell's strategy throughout this process has been defensive.

A company using an **accommodative strategy** will accept responsibility for a problem and take a progressive approach by doing all that could be expected to solve the problem. Unilever, one of the world's largest consumer product companies, annually buys 1.5 million tons of palm oil to be used in margarine, ice cream, soap, and shampoo. Using protests and viral videos to get the message out, Greenpeace claimed that Unilever was responsible for destroying forests in Indonesia and Malaysia to make way for palm oil plantations.[70] Unilever accepted responsibility for the problem, stating, " . . . following a public challenge from Greenpeace, we formalized our commitment to draw all our palm oil from certified sustainable sources by 2015. We also agreed to support a moratorium on any further deforestation in South-East Asia."[71] Unilever also formed a coalition of 50 businesses and nonprofits to influence palm oil growers and began working with Greenpeace to promote change in the industry.

Finally, a company using a **proactive strategy** will anticipate responsibility for a problem before it occurs, do more than expected to address the problem, and lead its industry in its approach. Under current federal tax laws, the health benefits that domestic partners receive from their company are counted as taxable income, which basically means that homosexual couples have to pay an extra tax, an average of $1,069, on health benefits that heterosexual married

Social responsiveness refers to a company's strategy for responding to stakeholders' expectations concerning economic, legal, ethical, or discretionary responsibility

Reactive strategy a social responsiveness strategy in which a company does less than society expects

Defensive strategy a social responsiveness strategy in which a company admits responsibility for a problem but does the least required to meet societal expectations

Accommodative strategy a social responsiveness strategy in which a company accepts responsibility for a problem and does all that society expects to solve that problem

Proactive strategy a social responsiveness strategy in which a company anticipates responsibility for a problem before it occurs and does more than society expects to address the problem

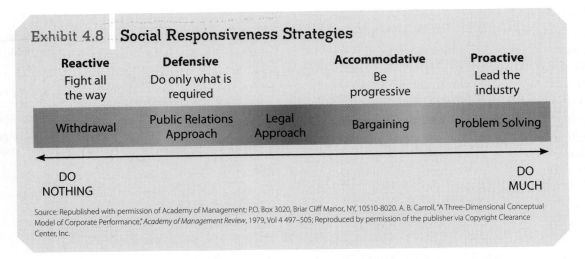

Exhibit 4.8   Social Responsiveness Strategies

Reactive	Defensive		Accommodative	Proactive
Fight all the way	Do only what is required		Be progressive	Lead the industry
Withdrawal	Public Relations Approach	Legal Approach	Bargaining	Problem Solving

DO NOTHING ←——————————————————————→ DO MUCH

Source: Republished with permission of Academy of Management; P.O. Box 3020, Briar Cliff Manor, NY, 10510-8020. A. B. Carroll, "A Three-Dimensional Conceptual Model of Corporate Performance," *Academy of Management Review*, 1979, Vol 4 497–505; Reproduced by permission of the publisher via Copyright Clearance Center, Inc.

couples do not. When Google executives recognized the disparity, its management took radical action and gave every employee with a domestic partner a raise that would cover the tax. But the company didn't stop there. As managers investigated the health benefits issue, they found a number of other areas in which homosexual couples were being treated unequally. Thus, they changed policy so that domestic partners would be included in the family leave policy, and also waived the one-year waiting period for infertility benefits. By going beyond what was legally required, Google set a new standard for the equal treatment of employees.[72] Exhibit 4.8 summarizes the four social responsiveness strategies.

Social Responsibility and Economic Performance

One question that managers often ask is, "Does it pay to be socially responsible?" In previous editions of this textbook, the answer was "no," as early research indicated that there was no inherent relationship between social responsibility and economic performance.[73] Recent research, however, leads to different conclusions. There is no tradeoff between social responsibility and economic performance.[74] And, there is a small, positive relationship between social responsibility and economic performance that strengthens with corporate reputation.[75] Let's explore what each of these results means.

First, there is no tradeoff between being socially responsible and economic performance.[76] Being socially responsible usually won't make a business less profitable. What this suggests is that the costs of being socially responsible—and those costs can be high, especially early on—can be offset by a better product or an improved corporate reputation, which results in stronger sales or higher profit margins. For example, Unilever replaced its laundry detergent All with All Small and Mighty, a concentrated formula that reduces the amount needed to wash a load of clothes by two-thirds. Bringing All Small and Mighty onto the market required Unilever to change its packaging (new bottle molds had to be created), its advertising, and its distribution methods. Unilever incurred significant upfront costs to be more socially responsible with All Small and Mighty detergent, but in the long run, customers will be getting a more efficiently packaged product and retailers will be able to fit more bottles on their shelves.

Second, it usually does pay to be socially responsible, and that relationship becomes stronger particularly when a company or its products have a strong reputation for social responsibility.[77] For example, GE, long one of the most admired and profitable corporations in the world, was one of the first and largest Fortune 500 companies to make a strategic commitment to providing environmentally friendly products and service. CEO Jeffrey Immelt wants GE to "develop and drive the technologies of the future that will protect and clean our environment."[78] GE calls its strategy "ecomagination," which it says is "helping to solve the world's biggest environmental challenges while driving profitable growth for GE."[79] And, in just 5 years, GE has increased the number of ecomagination products and services from 17 to 80, with annual sales of more than $17 billion and annual revenue growth increasing by double digits.[80]

Finally, even if there is generally a small positive relationship between social responsibility and economic performance, which becomes stronger when a company or its products have a positive reputation for social responsibility, and even if there is no tradeoff between social responsibility and economic performance, there is no guarantee that socially responsible companies will be profitable. Simply put, socially responsible companies experience the same ups and downs in economic performance that traditional businesses do. Despite its outstanding reputation as a socially responsible company, Ben & Jerry's consistently had financial trou[ble] going public (selling shares of stock to the [public] years ago. In fact, the financial problems beca[me so se]vere that the founders, Ben Cohen and Jerry Greenfield, sold the company to British-based Unilever.[81] Being socially responsible may be the right thing to do and is usually associated with increased profits, but it doesn't guarantee business success.

STUDENT Study Tools

Located at the back of your book:

- ☐ Rip out and study the Chapter Review Card at the end of the book

Log in to the CourseMate for MGMT at cengagebrain.com to:

- ☐ Review Key Term Flashcards delivered 3 ways (print or online)
- ☐ Complete both Practice Quizzes to prepare for tests
- ☐ Play Beat the Clock and Quizbowl to master concepts
- ☐ Complete the Crossword Puzzle to review key terms
- ☐ Watch the video on the City of Greensburg, Kansas, for a real company example and take the accompanying quiz
- ☐ Watch the Biz Flix clip from *Emperor's Club* and take the quiz
- ☐ Complete the Case Assignment on the San Diego Chargers and the NFL
- ☐ Work through the Management Decision on sustainability
- ☐ Work through the Management Team Decision on paying fines
- ☐ Develop your skills with the Develop Your Career Potential exercise

5 | Planning and Decision Making

© John Wilkes/Photonica/Getty Images

LEARNING OUTCOMES:

1 discuss the benefits and pitfalls of planning.

2 describe how to make a plan that works.

3 discuss how companies can use plans at all management levels, from top to bottom.

4 explain the steps and limits to rational decision making.

5 explain how group decisions and group decision-making techniques can improve decision making.

Chapter 5

Planning

even inexperienced managers know that planning and decision making are central parts of their jobs. They must figure out what the problem is. Generate potential solutions or plans. Pick the best one. Make it work. Experienced managers, however, know how hard it really is to make good plans and decisions. One seasoned manager says: "I think the biggest surprises are the problems. Maybe I had never seen it before. Maybe I was protected by my management when I was in sales. Maybe I had delusions of grandeur, I don't know. I just know how disillusioning and frustrating it is to be hit with problems and conflicts all day and not be able to solve them very cleanly."[1]

Planning is choosing a goal and developing a method or strategy to achieve that goal. In the face of tougher regulations and an industry-wide reputation for selling junk food, General Mills decided that 20 percent of its products must meet more rigorous nutrition standards. To accomplish this goal, the company had to shift its strategy from products that would be popular in the short term to those that would meet longer-range goals. Managers had to adapt old products and develop new ones that were higher in whole grains and lower in sugar and salt and that would encourage people to eat their vegetables. Some products, like single-serving vegetables, were successful. Others, like a version of Go-Gurt (yogurt in a plastic tube) targeted toward adults, were flops. But setting clear standards for nutritional value and tying annual executive bo-

nuses to achievement of those standards helped General Mills meet its goal. The company is now well on its way to its next goal: having 40 percent of its products meet the higher nutrition standards by 2010.[2]

After reading the next three sections, you should be able to

1 **discuss the benefits and pitfalls of planning.**

2 **describe how to make a plan that works.**

3 **discuss how companies can use plans at all management levels, from top to bottom.**

1 Benefits and Pitfalls of Planning

Are you one of those naturally organized people who always make a daily to-do list and never miss a deadline? Or are you one of those flexible, creative, go-with-the-flow people who dislike planning because it restricts their freedom? Some people are natural planners. They love it and can see only its benefits. Others dislike planning and can see only its disadvantages. It turns out that both views have real value.

*Planning has advantages and disadvantages. Let's learn about **1.1 the benefits** and **1.2 the pitfalls of planning.***

1.1 | BENEFITS OF PLANNING

Planning offers four important benefits: intensified effort, persistence, direction, and creation of task strategies.[3] First, managers and employees put forth greater effort when following a plan. Take two workers. Instruct one to "do your best" to increase production, and instruct the other to achieve a 2 percent increase in production each month. Research shows that the one with the specific plan will work harder.[4]

Second, planning leads to persistence, that is, working hard for

Planning choosing a goal and developing a strategy to achieve that goal

long periods. In fact, planning encourages persistence even when there may be little chance of short-term success.[5] McDonald's founder Ray Kroc, a keen believer in the power of persistence, had this quotation from President Calvin Coolidge hung in all of his executives' offices: "Nothing in the world can take the place of persistence. Talent will not; nothing is more common than unsuccessful men with talent. Genius will not; unrewarded genius is almost a proverb. Education will not; the world is full of educated derelicts. Persistence and determination alone are omnipotent."

The third benefit of planning is direction. Plans encourage managers and employees to direct their persistent efforts *toward* activities that help accomplish their goals and *away* from activities that don't.[6]

The fourth benefit of planning is that it encourages the development of task strategies. In other words, planning not only encourages people to work hard for extended periods and to engage in behaviors directly related to goal accomplishment, it also encourages them to think of better ways to do their jobs. Finally, perhaps the most compelling benefit of planning is that it has been proven to work for both companies and individuals. On average, companies with plans have larger profits and grow much faster than companies without plans.[7] The same holds true for individual managers and employees: There is no better way to improve the performance of the people who work in a company than to have them set goals and develop strategies for achieving those goals.

1.2 | PLANNING PITFALLS

Despite the significant benefits associated with planning, planning is not a cure-all. Plans won't fix all organizational problems. In fact, many management authors and consultants believe that planning can harm companies in several ways.[8]

The first pitfall of planning is that it can impede change and prevent or slow needed adaptation. Sometimes companies become so committed to achieving the goals set forth in their plans or following the strategies and tactics spelled out in them that they fail to notice when their plans aren't working or their goals need to change. When it came to producing environmentally sound cars, General Motors missed its initial opportunity because its culture was "wedded to big cars and horsepower." While Toyota formed its "green group" in the mid-1990s—which led to the development of the Prius, its popular electric hybrid—GM didn't begin developing experimental technology for an electric car until 2003. And then it killed the project after deciding

© iStockphoto.com/Mikhail Solovev

to continue selling highly profitable SUVs (sports utility vehicles). GM restarted its work on hybrid cars in 2006, but its new Chevy Volt, a battery-powered car that combines the use of off-peak electricity for overnight recharging of the batteries with daytime recharging by a small gas engine, won't be ready until 2011.[9]

The second pitfall is that planning can create a false sense of certainty. Planners sometimes feel that they know exactly what the future holds for their competitors, their suppliers, and their companies. However, all plans are based on assumptions: "The price of gasoline will increase by 4 percent per year"; "Exports will continue to rise." For plans to work, the assumptions on which they are based must hold true. If the assumptions turn out to be false, then the plans based on them are likely to fail.

The third potential pitfall of planning is the detachment of planners. In theory, strategic planners and top-level managers are supposed to focus on the big picture and not concern themselves with the details of implementation (i.e., carrying out the plan). According to management professor Henry Mintzberg, detachment leads planners to plan for things they don't understand.[10] Plans are meant to be guidelines for action, not abstract theories. Consequently, planners need to be familiar with the daily details of their businesses if they are to produce plans that can work. Andrew Cosslett, CEO of InterContinental Hotels in London, describes one of his earliest experiences working as a sales representative for Unilever subsidiary Wall's Ice Cream. Cosslett's supervisors passed to him a sales plan crafted by upper management that involved making sales calls on roughly 600 shops. Sales quotas and catalogues, however, were the same regardless of the season. The managers who made the plans were disconnected from the work done by the sales force and didn't consider the difficulty salespeople would encounter trying to sell ice cream in the winter.[11]

2 How to Make a Plan That Works

Planning is a double-edged sword. If done correctly, planning brings about tremendous increases in individual and organizational performance. If planning is done incorrectly, however, it can have just the opposite effect and harm individual and organizational performance.

In this section, you will learn how to make a plan that works. As depicted in Exhibit 5.1, planning consists of **2.1 setting goals, 2.2 developing commitment to the goals, 2.3 developing effective action plans, 2.4 tracking progress toward goal achievement,** *and* **2.5 maintaining flexibility in planning.**

2.1 | SETTING GOALS

The first step in planning is to set goals. To direct behavior and increase effort, goals need to be specific and challenging.[12] For example, deciding to "increase sales this year" won't direct and energize workers as much as deciding to "increase North American sales by 4 percent in the next 6 months." Specific, challenging goals provide a target for which to aim and a standard against which to measure success.

One way of writing effective goals for yourself, your job, or your company is to use the S.M.A.R.T. guidelines. **S.M.A.R.T. goals** are Specific, Measurable, Attainable, Realistic, and Timely.[13] Let's take a look at Nissan's zero-emissions program, which is based on Nissan's new "all-electric" cars, such as the Nissan Leaf, to see how it measures up to the S.M.A.R.T. guidelines for goals.

First, is the goal *Specific*? Yes, because "zero-emissions" tells us that Nissan isn't just looking to reduce emissions but to eliminate them. And "all-electric" rules out gas-electric hybrid cars like those produced by Nissan's competitors. In addition to being specific, the goal is also *Measurable* since Nissan has put a number on the emissions—namely zero. Whether the goal is *Attainable* or not depends on whether the technology for an all-electric car performs as expected. Nissan has been researching lithium-ion battery technology for almost twenty years and claims to have developed a battery that can power a car up to 100 miles and recharge overnight. Current trends in government regulation, consumer preferences toward more environmentally friendly vehicles, and increasing gasoline prices suggest that an all-electric car is *Realistic* from a business standpoint, but that can't be determined until the Leaf is available to consumers. Finally, the goal is *Timely* since Nissan's goal was to roll out the Leaf in Japan and the United States in 2010, and then to the rest of the world by 2012.[14]

2.2 | DEVELOPING COMMITMENT TO GOALS

Just because a company sets a goal doesn't mean that people will try to accomplish it. If workers don't care about a goal, that goal won't encourage them to work harder or smarter. Thus, the second step in planning is to develop commitment to goals.[15]

Goal commitment is the determination to achieve a goal. Commitment to achieve a goal is not automatic. Managers and workers must choose to commit

> **S.M.A.R.T. goals**
> goals that are specific, measurable, attainable, realistic, and timely
>
> **Goal commitment**
> the determination to achieve a goal

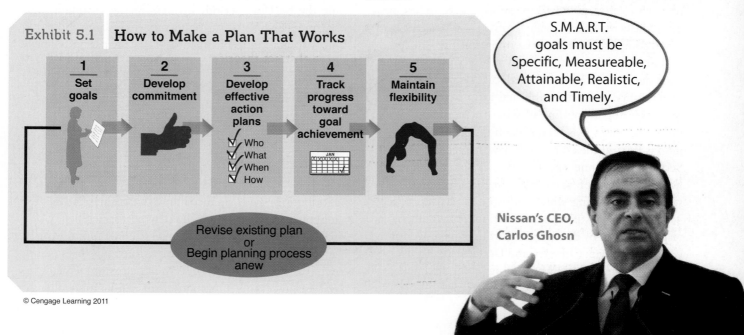

Exhibit 5.1 How to Make a Plan That Works

| 1 Set goals | 2 Develop commitment | 3 Develop effective action plans — Who, What, When, How | 4 Track progress toward goal achievement | 5 Maintain flexibility |

Revise existing plan or Begin planning process anew

S.M.A.R.T. goals must be Specific, Measureable, Attainable, Realistic, and Timely.

Nissan's CEO, Carlos Ghosn

themselves to a goal. Edwin Locke, professor emeritus of management at the University of Maryland and the foremost expert on how, why, and when goals work, tells a story about an overweight friend who finally lost 75 pounds. Locke says, "I asked him how he did it, knowing how hard it was for most people to lose so much weight." His friend responded, "Actually, it was quite simple. I simply decided that I *really wanted* to do it."[16] Put another way, goal commitment is really wanting to achieve a goal.

So how can managers bring about goal commitment? The most popular approach is to set goals collectively, as a team. Rather than assigning goals to workers ("Johnson, you've got until Tuesday of next week to redesign the flux capacitor so it gives us 10 percent more output"), managers and employees choose goals together. The goals are more likely to be realistic and attainable if employees participate in setting them. Another technique for gaining commitment to a goal is to make the goal public by having individuals or work units tell others about their goals. Still another way to increase goal commitment is to obtain top management's support. Top management can show support for a plan or program by providing funds, speaking publicly about the plan, or participating in the plan itself.

2.3 | DEVELOPING EFFECTIVE ACTION PLANS

The third step in planning is to develop effective action plans. An **action plan** lists the specific steps (how), people (who), resources (what), and time period (when) for accomplishing a goal. Coming out of bankruptcy, corporate reorganization, and a government bailout, Chrysler presented a detailed plan for returning to profitability. First, it established a time period (*when*) by presenting an outline of what the company would do for the next five years. Second, it clearly identified *who* is behind the company's new strategic plan. CEO Sergio Machionne spearheaded a "painful and difficult" process of assessing Chrysler's strengths and weaknesses, during which "no stone [was] unturned." Third, Chrysler's plan explained *how* it would return to profitability by detailing a thorough makeover of the core brands Jeep, Chrysler, and Dodge. Under this plan, some older models will be redesigned and repackaged, while other models that did not sell well will be com-

pletely eliminated (such as the Jeep Commander and Chrysler Sebring)—all so that the Chrysler brands will offer cars that appeal to American consumers. As for the resources (*what*), Chrysler's plan calls for extensive collaboration and borrowing from the Italian automaker Fiat (which has a 20 percent stake in Chrysler). Not only will Chrysler sell the Fiat 500, a subcompact city car that has been extremely popular in Europe, but it will borrow Fiat's technological and stylistic innovations to offer fuel-efficient, stylish vehicles that will attract a new segment of U.S. consumers.[17]

2.4 | TRACKING PROGRESS

The fourth step in planning is to track progress toward goal achievement. There are two accepted methods of tracking progress. The first is to set proximal goals and distal goals. **Proximal goals** are short-term goals or subgoals, whereas **distal goals** are long-term or primary goals.[18] The idea behind setting proximal goals is that achieving them may be more motivating and rewarding than waiting to reach far-off distal goals. Proximal goals are less intimidating and more attainable than distal goals, which often feel like biting off more than you can chew. Proximal goals enable you to achieve a distal goal one little piece at a time.

The second method of tracking progress is to gather and provide performance feedback. Regular, frequent performance feedback allows workers and managers to track their progress toward goal achievement and make adjustments in effort, direction, and strategies.[19] Proper action on performance feedback can keep you from failing to adapt, one of the pitfalls of planning. Exhibit 5.2 shows the impact of feedback on safety behavior at a large bakery company. During the baseline period, workers in the wrapping department, who measure and mix ingredients, roll the bread dough, and put it into baking pans, performed their jobs safely about 70 percent of the time (see 1 in Exhibit 5.2). The baseline safety record for workers in the makeup department, who bag and seal baked bread and assemble, pack, and tape cardboard cartons for shipping, was somewhat better at 78 percent (see 2). The company gave workers 30 minutes of safety training, set a goal of 90 percent safe behavior, and then provided daily feedback (such as a chart similar to Exhibit 5.2). Performance improved dramatically. During the intervention period, safely performed behaviors rose to an average of 95.8 percent for wrapping workers (see 3) and 99.3 percent for workers in the makeup department (see 4), and never fell below 83 percent. In this instance, the combination of training, a challenging goal, and feedback led to a dramatic increase in performance.

The importance of feedback can be seen in the reversal stage, when the company quit posting daily feedback on safe behavior. Without daily feedback, the percentage of safely performed behaviors returned to baseline levels—70.8 percent for the wrapping department (see 5) and 72.3 percent for the makeup department (see 6). For planning to be effective, workers need both a specific, challenging goal and regular feedback to track their progress. Indeed, further research indicates that the effectiveness of goal setting can be doubled by the addition of feedback.[20]

2.5 | MAINTAINING FLEXIBILITY

Because action plans are sometimes poorly conceived and goals sometimes turn out not to be achievable, the last step in developing an effective plan is to maintain flexibility. One method of maintaining flexibility while planning is to adopt an options-based approach.[21] The goal of **options-based planning** is to keep options open by making small, simultaneous investments in many alternative plans. Then, when one or a few of the plans emerge as likely winners, you invest even more in those plans while discontinuing or reducing investment in the others. In part, options-based planning is the opposite of traditional planning. Whereas the purpose of an action plan is to commit people and resources to a particular course of action, the purpose of options-based planning is to leave commitments open by maintaining **slack resources**, that is, a cushion of resources, such as extra time, people, money, or production capacity, that can be used to address and adapt to unanticipated changes, problems, or opportunities.[22] For example, in the summer of 2010, still facing uncertainties surrounding the economic recovery, U.S. companies held $1.84 trillion in cash reserves,

Options-based planning maintaining flexibility by making small, simultaneous investments in many alternative plans

Slack resources a cushion of extra resources that can be used with options-based planning to adapt to unanticipated change, problems, or opportunities

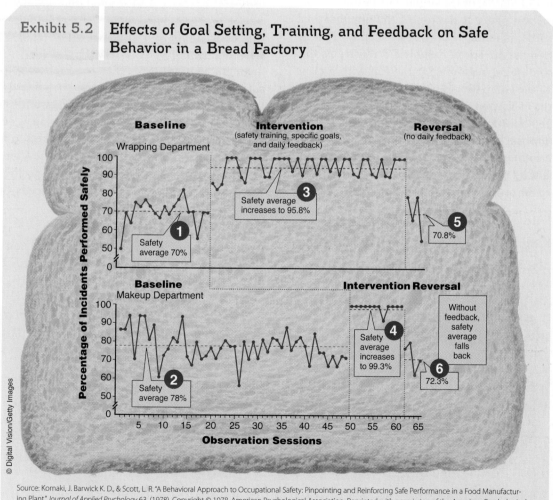

Exhibit 5.2 **Effects of Goal Setting, Training, and Feedback on Safe Behavior in a Bread Factory**

© Digital Vision/Getty Images

Source: Komaki, J. Barwick K. D., & Scott, L. R. "A Behavioral Approach to Occupational Safety: Pinpointing and Reinforcing Safe Performance in a Food Manufacturing Plant." *Journal of Applied Psychology* 63, (1978). Copyright © 1978, American Psychological Association. Reprinted with permission of the American Psychological Association. APA is not responsible for the accuracy of this translation.

up 26 percent from a year earlier. Why did companies have so much cash on hand, much more than they needed to do business? Because when credit markets dried up at the beginning of the recession, most companies could not get the loans they needed to run their businesses.[23] So why keep so much cash on hand? Maintaining substantial cash positions helped those companies keep their options open. And having options, combined with slack resources (i.e., that extra cash), equals flexibility.

3 Planning from Top to Bottom

Planning works best when the goals and action plans at the bottom and middle of the organization support the goals and action plans at the top of the organization. In other words, planning works best when everybody pulls in the same direction. Exhibit 5.3 illustrates this planning continuity, beginning at the top with a clear definition of the company vision and ending at the bottom with the execution of operational plans.

Let's see how **3.1 top managers create the organization's purpose statement and strategic objective, 3.2 middle managers develop tactical plans and use management by objectives to motivate employees' efforts toward the overall purpose and strategic objective,** *and* **3.3 first-level managers use operational, single-use, and standing plans to implement the tactical plans.**

3.1 | STARTING AT THE TOP

Top management is responsible for developing overall **strategic plans** that make clear how the company will serve customers and position itself against competitors in the next 2 to 5 years. Zappos, the online shoe retailer recently purchased by Amazon, is working on a 5-year plan to expand beyond shoes into other markets, particularly into beauty care. Zappos's goal is to grow its beauty section from $1 million in sales last year to $75 million in 5 years.[24]

Strategic planning begins with the creation of an organizational vision or purpose. A **purpose statement**, which is often referred to as an *organizational mission* or *vision*, is a statement of a company's purpose or reason for existing.[25] Purpose statements should be brief—no more than two sentences. They should also be enduring, inspirational, clear, and consistent with widely shared company beliefs and values. An excellent example of a well-crafted purpose statement is that of Avon, the cosmetics company: To be the company that best understands and satisfies the product, service, and self-fulfillment needs of women—globally.[26] That statement guides everyone in the organization and provides a focal point for the delivery of beauty products and services to the customers, women around the world. The purpose is the same whether Avon is selling lipstick to women in India, shampoo packets to women in the Amazon, or jewelry to women in the United States. Despite these regional differences in specific strategy, the overall goal—understanding the needs of women

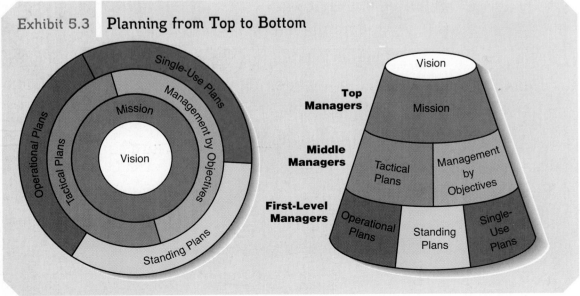

Exhibit 5.3   Planning from Top to Bottom

© Cengage Learning 2011

globally—does not change. Furthermore, Avon's purpose is clear, inspirational, and consistent with Avon's company values and the principles that guide the company. Other examples of organizational purposes that have been particularly effective include Walt Disney Company's "to make people happy" and lock company Schlage's "to make the world more secure."[27]

The **strategic objective,** which flows from the purpose, is a more specific goal that unifies company-wide efforts, stretches and challenges the organization, and possesses a finish line and a time frame. For example, in 1961, President John F. Kennedy established a strategic objective for NASA with this simple statement: "Achieving the goal, before this decade is out, of landing a man on the moon and returning him safely to earth."[28] NASA walked on the moon and safely splashed down in the Pacific Ocean on July 24, 1969. Once the strategic objective has been accomplished, a new one should be chosen. Again, however, the new strategic objective must grow out of the organization's purpose, which does not change significantly over time. For example, NASA hopes to accomplish its latest strategic objective, or what it calls its "exploration systems mission directorate," between 2015 and 2020. NASA's strategic objective is to "return to the moon, where we will build a sustainable long-term human presence." NASA further explains its goal by saying, "As the space shuttle approaches retirement and the International Space Station nears completion, NASA is building the next fleet of vehicles to bring astronauts back to the moon, and possibly to Mars and beyond."[29]

3.2 | BENDING IN THE MIDDLE

Middle management is responsible for developing and carrying out tactical plans to accomplish the organization's strategic objective. **Tactical plans** specify how a company will use resources, budgets, and people to accomplish specific goals related to its strategic objective. Whereas strategic plans and objectives are used to focus company efforts over the next 2 to 5 years, tactical plans are used to direct behavior, efforts, and attention over the next 6 months to 2 years. Several years ago, Clorox, a $4 billion global consumer products company, was not meeting sales goals for 30 percent of its products. So it developed a simple but powerful tactical plan in which the CFO, the director of supply chain, and the vice presidents

> **Strategic objective** a statement of a company's overall goal that unifies company-wide effort toward its vision, stretches and challenges the organization, and possesses a finish line and a time frame
>
> **Tactical plans** plans created and implemented by middle managers that specify how the company will use resources, budgets, and people over the next six months to two years to accomplish specific goals within its strategic objective

Musical Meetings

At Kindermusik International, a music education publisher, all 50 employees attend weekly one-hour sessions to review the company's weekly goals and financial results. Half-day review sessions are held each quarter to review results against quarterly and annual goals and to discuss how to cut costs and increase revenues. Because they regularly review and discuss goal progress, employees are sensitive to reducing costs, so they proposed replacing the company's 5-day sales convention, which costs about $50,000, with a series of year-round virtual meetings with sales managers, sales representatives, and customers. CEO Michael Dougherty said, "If you'd asked me, I would have said, 'We've always done the convention.' But the folks who are closer to the event and closer to the customers know that there were other and better ways to achieve the same goal."

Source: L. Lorberf, "Running the Show—An Open Book: When Companies Share Their Financial Data with Employees, the Results Can Be Dramatic," *Wall Street Journal*, February 23, 2009, R8.

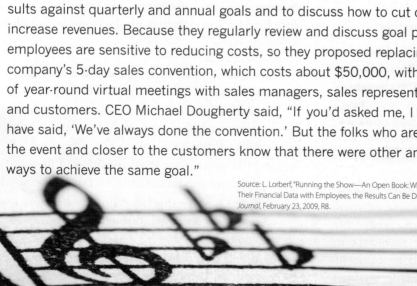

of sales, marketing, and operations met monthly to identify products that were below sales and profit goals. Products exceeding their targets were graded green. Those within 5 percent of target were graded yellow. But products more than 5 percent below target were graded red, and the managers responsible for those product lines were required to develop plans to improve sales or to eliminate product lines whose sales were unlikely to improve. Two years after implementing this tactical plan, more than 90 percent of Clorox's products met sales and profit goals, and the average sales per product increased by 25 percent, giving Clorox the highest sales-per-product figures in its industry.[30]

Management by objectives is a management technique often used to develop and carry out tactical plans. **Management by objectives, or MBO,** is a four-step process in which managers and their employees (1) discuss possible goals; (2) select goals that are challenging, attainable, and consistent with the company's overall goals; (3) develop tactical plans that lead to the accomplishment of tactical goals; and (4) meet regularly to review progress toward accomplishment of goals.

3.3 | FINISHING AT THE BOTTOM

Lower-level managers are responsible for developing and carrying out **operational plans,** which are the day-to-day plans for producing or delivering the organization's products and services. Operational plans direct the behavior, efforts, and priorities of operative employees for periods ranging from 30 days to 6 months. There are three kinds of operational plans: single-use plans, standing plans, and budgets.

Single-use plans deal with unique, one-time-only events. For example, Industrial Motion, Inc., a small international procurement service, relocated from California to North Carolina in order to reduce its operating expenses. The company had to come up with a plan for everything from managing business data, moving key employees and hiring new ones, and buying furniture to improvising in unforeseen situations.[31] Because the move would happen once, it required a single-use plan.

Unlike single-use plans that are created, carried out, and then never used again, **standing plans** can be used repeatedly to handle frequently recurring events. If you encounter a problem that you've seen before, someone in your company has probably written a standing plan that explains how to address it. Using this plan rather than reinventing the wheel will save you time. There are three kinds of standing plans: policies, procedures, and rules and regulations.

Policies indicate the general course of action that company managers should take in response to a particular event or situation. A well-written policy will also specify why the policy exists and what outcome the policy is intended to produce. All companies have travel policies with detailed expense guidelines for airline tickets, hotel rooms, cars, and meals. Many companies utilize new travel software, which can generate automated emails to employees to encourage them to purchase their airline tickets well before their travel dates. Typically, the earlier the purchase, the lower the cost. At American Honda, this early purchase travel policy is reinforced by travel expense tracking software that sends emails to employees and their bosses pointing out that a $1,000 airline ticket purchased by the employee could have been purchased for $800 a week earlier. With American Honda's employees taking 40,000 trips annually, $100 less per trip would save the company $4 million a year.[32]

Procedures are more specific than policies because they indicate the series of steps that should be taken in response to a particular event. A manufacturer's procedure for handling defective products might include the following steps:

1. Rejected material is locked in a secure area with "reject" documentation attached.
2. Material Review Board (MRB) identifies the defect and how far outside the standard the rejected products are.
3. MRB determines the disposition of the defective product as either scrap or as rework.
4. Scrap is either discarded or recycled, and rework is sent back through the production line to be fixed.
5. If delays in delivery will result, MRB member notifies customer.[33]

© Bon Appetit/Alamy

Rules and regulations are even more specific than procedures because they specify what must or must not happen and often describe precisely how a particular action should be performed. For instance, many companies have rules and regulations forbidding managers from writing job reference letters for employees who have worked for them because a negative reference

Budgeting is **quantitative** planning because it forces managers to decide how to allocate available **money** to best **accomplish** company goals.

© iStockphoto.com/fredrose

may prompt a former employee to sue for defamation of character.[34]

Besides single-use plans and standing plans, budgets are the third kind of operational plan. **Budgeting** is quantitative planning because it forces managers to decide how to allocate available money to best accomplish company goals. After organic ice-cream maker PJ Madison's expanded its presence from 200 to 2,000 stores in one year, the company set a goal to triple sales. To achieve this goal, it planned to more than double its marketing budget and spend about 30 percent of the marketing budget on event sponsorship, 15 percent on advertising, and another 25 percent on coupons and direct mailing.[35]

Rules and regulations standing plans that describe how a particular action should be performed or what must happen or not happen in response to a particular event

Budgeting quantitative planning through which managers decide how to allocate available money to best accomplish company goals

Decision making the process of choosing a solution from available alternatives

Rational decision making a systematic process of defining problems, evaluating alternatives, and choosing optimal solutions

What Is Rational Decision Making?

decision making is the process of choosing a solution from available alternatives.[36] **Rational decision making** is a systematic process in which managers define problems, evaluate alternatives, and choose optimal solutions that provide maximum benefits to their organizations.

After reading the next two sections, you should be able to

4 **explain the steps and limits to rational decision making.**

5 **explain how group decisions and group decision-making techniques can improve decision making.**

4 Steps and Limits to Rational Decision Making

There are six steps in the rational decision-making process: 4.1 define the problem, 4.2 identify decision criteria, 4.3 weight the criteria, 4.4 generate alternative courses of action, 4.5 evaluate each alternative, and 4.6 compute the optimal decision. We'll also consider 4.7 limits to rational decision making.

4.1 | DEFINE THE PROBLEM

The first step in decision making is to identify and define the problem. A **problem** exists when there is a gap between a desired state (what is wanted) and an existing state (the situation you are actually facing). Women want to look good and feel comfortable in clothes that fit properly, but sizes are not universal. There are no industry standards, which means it's harder for a woman to know her size than it was in the past. Today's sizes vary from brand to brand and don't take into account body type. As a result, women either leave the store without purchasing anything because they can't find a perfect fit or purchase an imperfectly fitting garment, discard it after wearing it a couple of times, and decide not to buy the brand again. Either way, garment companies lose customers.

The presence of a gap between an existing state (such as selling clothes that should fit, but don't) and a desired state is no guarantee that managers will make a decision to solve the problem. Three things must occur for this to happen.[37] First, managers have to be aware of the gap. But that isn't enough. Managers also have to be motivated to reduce the gap. In other words, managers have to know there is a problem and *want* to solve it. Finally, it's not enough to be aware of a problem and be motivated to solve it. Managers must also have the knowledge, skills, abilities, and resources to fix the problem. Product designer Cricket Lee has tried to solve the sizing problem in the women's clothing industry by developing Fitlogic, a sizing standard that takes account of body types and is not intimidating for larger women. Although relatively unknown, Lee has convinced QVC (a home shopping TV network), Nordstrom, Macy's, and Jones Apparel to license Fitlogic to help women with different body shapes buy better-fitting clothes. With 84 percent of women experiencing fit problems, and poor fit accounting for nearly 40 percent of returned clothes, Lee has clearly identified a widespread problem. Other retailers, such as Banana Republic and Chico's FAS, are taking note and creating their own specialized sizing systems, which Banana Republic has done by assigning different names to pants with different fits.[38]

4.2 | IDENTIFY DECISION CRITERIA

Decision criteria are the standards used to guide judgments and decisions. Typically, the more criteria a potential solution meets, the better that solution will be.

Imagine that your boss asks for suggestions about purchasing new computers for the office. What general factors are important when purchasing the computers? Reliability, price, warranty, on-site service, and compatibility with existing software, printers, and computers are all important, but you must also consider the technical details. What specific factors should the new office computers have? Well, with technology changing so quickly, you'll probably want to buy computers with as much capability and flexibility as you can afford. Today, for the first time, laptops account for more than 50 percent of the market.[39] Business laptops come in four distinct model types. There are budget models that are good for routine office work but are usually saddled with slower processors; workhorse models that are not lightweight but have everything included; slim models for traveling that usually require external drives to read/write to a DVD/CD; and tablet models that include such items as handwriting recognition software.[40] What will the users really need? Will they need to burn CDs and DVDs or just read them? How much memory and hard-drive space will the users need? Should you pay extra for durability, file encryption, and long-life batteries? What about Internet and wireless connectivity? Answering questions like

6 Steps of the Rational Decision-Making Process

1. Define the Problem
2. Identify Decision Criteria
3. Weight the Criteria
4. Generate Alternative Courses of Action
5. Evaluate Each Alternative
6. Compute the Optimal Decision

Problem a gap between a desired state and an existing state

Decision criteria the standards used to guide judgments and decisions

© Verity Smith/Brand X Pictures/Jupiterimages

Exhibit 5.4 Absolute Weighting of Decision Criteria for a Car Purchase

5 critically important
4 important
3 somewhat important
2 not very important
1 completely unimportant

1. Predicted reliability	1	2	3	4	(5)
2. Owner satisfaction	1	(2)	3	4	5
3. Predicted depreciation	(1)	2	3	4	5
4. Avoiding accidents	1	2	3	(4)	5
5. Fuel economy	1	2	3	4	(5)
6. Crash protection	1	2	3	(4)	5
7. Acceleration	(1)	2	3	4	5
8. Ride	1	2	(3)	4	5
9. Front seat comfort	1	2	3	4	(5)

© Cengage Learning 2011

these will help you identify the criteria that will guide the purchase of the new equipment.

4.3 | WEIGHT THE CRITERIA

After identifying decision criteria, the next step is deciding which criteria are more or less important. Although there are numerous mathematical models for weighting decision criteria, all require the decision maker to provide an initial ranking of the criteria. Some use **absolute comparisons,** in which each criterion is compared to a standard or ranked on its own merits. Someone who would like to purchase a new car might consider the following criteria: predicted reliability, previous owners' satisfaction, predicted depreciation (the price you could expect if you sold the car), ability to avoid an accident, fuel economy, crash protection, acceleration, ride, and front seat comfort.

Different individuals will rank these criteria differently, depending on what they value or require in a car. Exhibit 5.4

shows the absolute weights that someone buying a car might use. Because these weights are absolute, each criterion is judged on its own importance, using a five-point scale, with 5 representing "critically important" and 1 representing "completely unimportant." In this instance, predicted reliability, fuel economy, and front seat comfort were rated most important, and acceleration and predicted depreciation were rated least important.

Another method uses **relative comparisons,** in which each criterion is compared directly to every other criterion.[41] Exhibit 5.5 shows six criteria that someone might use when buying a house. Moving down the first column, we see that the time of the daily commute has been rated less important (-1) than school system quality; more important ($+1$) than having an inground pool, sun room, or a quiet street, and just as important as the house being brand new (0). Total weights, which are obtained by summing the scores in each column, indicate that the daily commute and school system quality are the most important factors to this home buyer, while an inground pool, sun room, and a quiet street are the least important.

4.4 | GENERATE ALTERNATIVE COURSES OF ACTION

After identifying and weighting the criteria that will guide the decision-making process, the next step is to identify possible courses of action that could solve the problem. The idea is to generate as many alternatives as possible. Let's assume that you're trying to select a city in Europe to be the location of a major office. After

Absolute comparison a process in which each criterion is compared to a standard or ranked on its own merits

Relative comparison a process in which each criterion is compared directly to every other

Exhibit 5.5 Relative Comparison of Home Characteristics

HOME CHARACTERISTICS	L	SSQ	IP	SR	QS	NBH
Daily commute (L)		+1	–1	–1	–1	0
School system quality (SSQ)	–1		–1	–1	–1	–1
Inground pool (IP)	+1	+1		0	0	+1
Sun room (SR)	+1	+1	0		0	0
Quiet street (QS)	+1	+1	0	0		0
Newly built house (NBH)	0	+1	–1	0	0	
Total weight	(+2)	(+5)	(–3)	(–2)	(–2)	(0)

© Cengage Learning 2011

meeting with your staff, you generate a list of possible alternatives: Amsterdam, the Netherlands; Barcelona or Madrid, Spain; Berlin or Frankfurt, Germany; Brussels, Belgium; London, England; Milan, Italy; Paris, France; and Zurich, Switzerland.

4.5 | EVALUATE EACH ALTERNATIVE

The next step is to systematically evaluate each alternative against each criterion. Because of the amount of information that must be collected, this step can take much longer and be much more expensive than other steps in the decision-making process. When selecting a European city in which to locate an office, you could contact economic development offices in each city, systematically interview businesspeople or executives who operate there, retrieve and use published government data on each location, or rely on published studies such as Cushman & Wakefield's *European Cities Monitor*, which conducts an annual survey of more than 500 senior European executives who rate thirty-four European cities on twelve business-related criteria.[42]

No matter how you gather the information, the key is to use that information to systematically evaluate each alternative against each criterion once you have it. Exhibit 5.6 shows how each of the ten cities on your staff's list fared on each of the twelve criteria (higher scores are better), from qualified staff to freedom from pollution. Although London has the most qualified staff and the best access to markets and telecommunications and is the easiest city to travel to and from, it is also one of the most polluted and expensive cities on the list. Paris offers excellent access to markets, but if your staff is multilingual, Brussels or Amsterdam may be a better choice.

4.6 | COMPUTE THE OPTIMAL DECISION

The final step in the decision-making process is to compute the optimal decision by determining the weighted average for each alternative. This is done by multiplying the rating for each criterion (Step 4.5) by the weight for that criterion (Step 4.3), and then summing those scores for each alternative course of action that you generated (Step 4.4). The executives participating in Cushman & Wakefield's survey of the best European cities for business rated the twelve decision criteria in terms of importance, as shown across the top of Exhibit 5.6. Availability of qualified staff, access to markets and to telecommunications, and easy travel to and from the city were the four most important factors, while quality of life and freedom from pollution were the least important factors. To calculate the weighted average for Paris, its score on each criterion is multiplied by the weight for that criterion ($1.11 \times .59$ for access to markets, for example). Then, all of these scores are added together to produce the weighted average, as follows:

$$(.60 \times .79) + (.59 \times 1.11) + (.54 \times .79) +$$
$$(.53 \times 1.39) + (.40 \times .21) + (.27 \times .26) +$$
$$(.27 \times .57) + (.26 \times .31) + (.25 \times 1.10) +$$
$$(.24 \times .45) + (.21 \times .61) + (.18 \times .16) = 3.22$$

Since London has a weighted average of 4.27 compared to 3.22 for Paris and 2.29 for Frankfurt, London clearly ranks as the best location for your company's new European office because of its large number of qualified staff; easy access to markets; outstanding ease of travel to, from, and within the city; and excellent telecommunications.

4.7 | LIMITS TO RATIONAL DECISION MAKING

In general, managers who diligently complete all six steps of the rational decision-making model will make better decisions than those who don't. So, when they can, managers should try to follow the steps in the rational decision-making model, especially for big decisions with long-range consequences.

To make completely rational decisions, managers would have to operate in a perfect world with no real-world con-

And the winner is . . . London. When all the weighted averages are calculated and compared, London is the best city in Europe for business.

Exhibit 5.6

Criteria Ratings Used to Determine the Best Location for a New Office

Criteria Weights	Qualified Staff 60%	Access to Markets 59%	Telecommunications 54%	Travel to/from City 53%	Cost of Staff 40%	Business Climate 27%	Languages Spoken 27%	Cost & Value of Office Space 26%	Travel within City 25%	Available Office Space 24%	Quality of Life 21%	Freedom from Pollution 18%	Weighted Average	Ranking
Amsterdam	0.45	0.45	0.28	0.64	0.25	0.37	1.13	0.44	0.41	0.29	0.52	0.60	2.03	4
Barcelona	0.31	0.32	0.22	0.21	0.60	0.45	0.30	0.41	0.51	0.42	1.14	0.49	1.71	8
Berlin	0.38	0.29	0.42	0.27	0.46	0.29	0.49	0.67	0.62	0.73	0.31	0.25	1.78	6
Brussels	0.44	0.55	0.31	0.50	0.18	0.44	1.02	0.35	0.34	0.33	0.39	0.30	1.88	5
Frankfurt	0.55	0.72	0.57	1.29	0.11	0.17	0.58	0.28	0.25	0.37	0.22	0.15	2.29	3
London	1.32	1.37	1.21	1.71	0.11	0.52	1.38	0.18	1.11	0.49	0.42	0.11	4.27	(1)
Madrid	0.39	0.40	0.34	0.48	0.48	0.48	0.22	0.37	0.51	0.47	0.50	0.19	1.76	7
Munich	0.51	0.39	0.39	0.41	0.15	0.11	0.29	0.18	0.54	0.36	0.81	0.56	1.67	9
Paris	0.79	1.11	0.79	1.39	0.21	0.26	0.57	0.31	1.10	0.45	0.61	0.16	3.22	2
Zurich	0.28	0.22	0.31	0.26	0.03	0.66	0.54	0.12	0.39	0.16	0.61	0.95	1.41	10

Source: "European Cities Monitor," Cushman & Wakefield, 2008, accessed May 30, 2009, http://www.cushwake.com/cwglobal/docviewer/2008_European_Cities_Monitor.pdf.

straints. Of course, it never actually works like that in the real world. Managers face time and money constraints. They often don't have time to make extensive lists of decision criteria. And they often don't have the resources to test all possible solutions against all possible criteria.

In theory, fully rational decision makers **maximize** decisions by choosing the optimal solution. In practice, however, limited resources along with attention, memory, and expertise problems make it nearly impossible for managers to maximize decisions. Consequently, most managers don't maximize—they satisfice. Whereas maximizing is choosing the best alternative, **satisficing** is choosing a "good enough" alternative. In reality, however, the manager's limited time, money, and expertise mean that only a few alternatives will be assessed against a few decision criteria. In practice, the manager who is purchasing new office computers will visit two or three computer or electronic stores, read a few recent computer reviews, and get bids from Dell, Lenovo, Gateway, and Hewlett-Packard, as well as some online superstores like CDW and PC Connection. The decision will be complete when the manager finds a good enough laptop computer that meets a few decision criteria.

5 Using Groups to Improve Decision Making

According to a study reported in *Fortune* magazine, 91 percent of U.S. companies use teams and groups to solve specific problems (i.e., make decisions).[43] Why so many? When done properly, group decision making can lead to much better decisions than those typically made by individuals. In fact, numerous studies show that groups consistently outperform individuals on complex tasks.

Let's explore the **5.1 advantages and pitfalls of group decision making** and learn about the following group decision-making methods: **5.2 structured conflict, 5.3 the nominal group technique, 5.4 the Delphi technique,** and **5.5 electronic brainstorming.**

Maximizing choosing the best alternative

Satisficing choosing a "good enough" alternative

5.1 | ADVANTAGES AND PITFALLS OF GROUP DECISION MAKING

Groups can do a much better job than can individuals in two important steps of the decision-making process: defining the problem and generating alternative solutions.

Still, group decision making is subject to some pitfalls that can quickly erase these gains. One possible pitfall is groupthink. **Groupthink** occurs in highly cohesive groups of which members feel intense pressure to agree with each other so that the group can approve a proposed solution.[44] Because groupthink leads to consideration of a limited number of solutions and restricts discussion of any of the considered solutions, it usually results in poor decisions. Groupthink is most likely to occur under the following conditions:

- The group is insulated from others who might have different perspectives.
- The group leader begins by expressing a strong preference for a particular decision.
- The group has no established procedure for systematically defining problems and exploring alternatives.
- Group members have similar backgrounds and experiences.[45]

Groupthink may be one of the reasons why Merck's prescription drug Vioxx stayed on the market for over 5 years despite potentially fatal side effects. Merck, one of the largest drug makers in the world, viewed Vioxx as a miracle pain reliever, and over 100 million prescriptions for the drug were written in the 5 years it was on the market. The *New England Journal of Medicine*, however, had reported almost from the start that Vioxx users suffered from significant heart problems, and the drug was eventually withdrawn from the market. Court documents revealed that Merck's internal studies showed an association between Vioxx usage and an elevated incidence of heart attacks. Litigants allege that because the drug generated a substantial profit, managers chose to listen to positive feedback about how well the drug worked as a painkiller rather than act on the information about the serious side effects. After several years in court, Merck agreed to a $4.85 billion settlement with 45,000 eligible claimants.[46]

A second potential problem with group decision making is that it takes considerable time. Reconciling schedules so that group members can meet is time consuming. Furthermore, it's a rare group that consistently holds productive task-oriented meetings to work through the decision process effectively. Some of the most common complaints about meetings (and thus decision making) are that the meeting's purpose is unclear, participants are unprepared, critical people are absent or late, conversation doesn't stay focused on the problem, and no one follows up on the decisions that were made. Teresa Taylor, the chief operations officer at Qwest, avoids many of these problems by opening every meeting with the question "Do we all know why we're here?" Surprisingly, she often finds that many people can't answer the question—they just show up to a meeting because they've been invited. Taylor will clarify the purpose of the meeting even further by asking, "Are we making decisions? Are you going to ask me for something at the end?" In doing so, she helps participants focus their attention. Once the purpose is identified, Taylor will even allow people to leave the meeting if they feel like they don't need to be there.[47]

Strong-willed group members can constitute a third possible pitfall to group decision making. Such an individual, whether the boss or a vocal group member, can dominate group discussions and put limits on how the problem is defined and what the solutions can be. Another potential problem is that group members may not feel accountable for the decisions made and actions taken by the group unless they are personally responsible for some aspect of carrying out those decisions.

Although these pitfalls can lead to poor decision making, this doesn't mean that managers should avoid using groups to make decisions. When done properly, group decision making can lead to much better decisions. The pitfalls of group decision making are not inevitable. Managers can overcome most of them by using the various techniques described next.

5.2 | STRUCTURED CONFLICT

Most people view conflict negatively. Yet the right kind of conflict can lead to much better group decision making. **C-type conflict**, or **cognitive conflict**, focuses on problem- and issue-related differences of opinion.[48] In c-type conflict, group members disagree because their different experiences and areas of expertise lead them to view the problem and its potential solutions differently. C-type conflict is also characterized by a willingness to examine, compare, and reconcile those differences to produce the best possible solution. Alteon WebSystems, now a division of Nortel Networks, makes critical use of c-type conflict. Top manager Dominic Orr described Alteon's use of c-type conflict this way:

Why groups are better than individuals at defining problems and generating possible solutions

1 Group members usually possess different knowledge, skills, abilities, and experiences, so groups are able to view problems from multiple perspectives. Being able to view problems from different perspectives can help groups perform better on complex tasks and make better decisions than can individuals.

2 Groups can find and access much more information than can individuals alone.

3 The increased knowledge and information available to groups make it easier for them to generate more alternative solutions. Studies show that generating lots of alternative solutions is critical to improving the quality of decisions.

4 If groups are involved in the decision-making process, group members will be more committed to making chosen solutions work.

Source: L. Pelled, K. Eisenhardt, and K. Xin, "Exploring the Black Box: An Analysis of Work Group Diversity, Conflict, and Performance," *Administrative Science Quarterly* 44, no. 1 (1 March 1999): 1.

After an idea is presented, we open the floor to objective, and often withering, critiques. And if the idea collapses under scrutiny, we move on to another: no hard feelings. We're judging the idea, not the person. At the same time, we don't really try to regulate emotions. Passionate conflict means that we're getting somewhere, not that the discussion is out of control. But one person does act as referee—by asking basic questions like "Is this good for the customer?" or "Does it keep our time-to-market advantage intact?" By focusing relentlessly on the facts, we're able to see the strengths and weaknesses of an idea clearly and quickly.[49]

By contrast, **a-type conflict,** or **affective conflict,** refers to the emotional reactions that can occur when disagreements become personal rather than professional. A-type conflict often results in hostility, anger, resentment, distrust, cynicism, and apathy. Unlike c-type conflict, a-type conflict undermines team effectiveness. Examples of a-type conflict statements are "your idea," "our idea," "my department," "you don't know what you are talking about," and "you don't understand our situation." Rather than focusing on issues and ideas, these statements focus on individuals.[50]

The **devil's advocacy** approach can be used to create c-type conflict by assigning an individual or a subgroup the role of critic. The following are the five steps of the devil's advocacy approach:

1. Generate a potential solution.

2. Assign a devil's advocate to criticize and question the solution.

3. Present the critique of the potential solution to key decision makers.

4. Gather additional relevant information.

5. Decide whether to use, change, or not use the originally proposed solution.[51]

When properly used, the devil's advocacy approach introduces c-type conflict into the decision-making process. Contrary to the common belief that conflict is bad, studies show that structured conflict leads not only to less a-type conflict, but also to improved decision quality and greater acceptance of decisions once they have been made.[52]

5.3 | NOMINAL GROUP TECHNIQUE

Nominal means "in name only." Accordingly, the **nominal group technique** received its name because it begins with a quiet time in which group members independently write down as many problem definitions and alternative solutions as possible. In other words, the nominal group technique begins by having group members act as individuals. After the quiet time, the group leader asks each group member to share

A-type conflict (affective conflict) disagreement that focuses on individual or personal issues

Devil's advocacy a decision-making method in which an individual or a subgroup is assigned the role of critic

Nominal group technique a decision-making method that begins and ends by having group members quietly write down and evaluate ideas to be shared with the group

Delphi technique
a decision-making method in which members of a panel of experts respond to questions and to each other until reaching agreement on an issue

Brainstorming a decision-making method in which group members build on each others' ideas to generate as many alternative solutions as possible

Electronic brainstorming a decision-making method in which group members use computers to build on each others' ideas and generate many alternative solutions

Production blocking a disadvantage of face-to-face brainstorming in which a group member must wait to share an idea because another member is presenting an idea

Evaluation apprehension fear of what others will think of your ideas

one idea at a time with the group. As they are read aloud, ideas are posted on a flipchart or wallboard for all to see. This step continues until all ideas have been shared. In the next step, the group discusses the advantages and disadvantages of the ideas. The nominal group technique closes with a second quiet time in which group members independently rank the ideas presented. Group members then read their rankings aloud, and the idea with the highest average rank is selected.[53]

The nominal group technique improves group decision making by decreasing a-type conflict. But it also restricts c-type conflict. Consequently, the nominal group technique typically produces poorer decisions than does the devil's advocacy approach. Nonetheless, more than 80 studies have found that nominal groups produce better ideas than those produced by traditional groups.[54]

5.4 | DELPHI TECHNIQUE

In the **Delphi technique,** the members of a panel of experts respond to questions and to each other until reaching agreement on an issue. The first step is to assemble a panel of experts. Unlike other approaches to group decision making, however, the Delphi technique does not require bringing the panel members together in one place. Because this technique does not require the experts to leave their offices or disrupt their schedules, they are more likely to participate.

The second step is to create a questionnaire consisting of a series of open-ended questions for the group. In the third step, the group members' written responses are analyzed, summarized,

and fed back to the panel for reactions until the members reach agreement. Asking the members why they agree or disagree is important because it helps uncover their unstated assumptions and beliefs. Again, this process of summarizing panel feedback and obtaining reactions to that feedback continues until the panel members reach agreement.

5.5 | ELECTRONIC BRAINSTORMING

Brainstorming, in which group members build on others' ideas, is a technique for generating a large number of alternative solutions. Brainstorming has four rules:

1. The more ideas, the better.
2. All ideas are acceptable, no matter how wild or crazy they might seem.
3. Other group members' ideas should be used to come up with even more ideas.
4. Criticism or evaluation of ideas is not allowed.

Although brainstorming is great fun and can help managers generate a large number of alternative solutions, it does have a number of disadvantages. Fortunately, **electronic brainstorming,** in which group members use computers to communicate and generate alternative solutions, overcomes the disadvantages associated with face-to-face brainstorming.[55]

The first disadvantage that electronic brainstorming overcomes is **production blocking,** which occurs when you have an idea but have to wait to share it because someone else is already presenting an idea to the group. During this short delay, you may forget your idea or decide that it really wasn't worth sharing. Production blocking doesn't happen with electronic brainstorming. All group members are seated at computers, so everyone can type in ideas whenever they occur. There's no waiting your turn to be heard by the group.

The second disadvantage that electronic brainstorming overcomes is **evaluation apprehension,** that is, being afraid of what others will think of your ideas. With electronic brainstorming, all ideas are anonymous. When you type in an idea and hit the Enter key to share it with the group, group members see only the idea. Furthermore,

© iStockphoto.com/alengo

many brainstorming software programs also protect anonymity by displaying ideas in random order. So, if you laugh maniacally when you type "Cut top management's pay by 50 percent!" and then hit the Enter key, it won't show up immediately on everyone's screen. This makes it doubly difficult to determine who is responsible for which comments.

In the typical layout for electronic brainstorming, all participants sit in front of computers around a U-shaped table. This configuration allows them to see their computer screens, the other participants, a large main screen, and a meeting leader or facilitator. Step 1 in electronic brainstorming is the anonymous generation of as many ideas as possible. Groups commonly generate 100 ideas in a half-hour period. Step 2 is to edit the generated ideas, categorize them, and eliminate redundancies. Step 3 involves ranking the categorized ideas in terms of quality. Step 4, the last step, has three parts: generate a series of action steps, decide the best order for accomplishing these steps, and identify who is responsible for each step. All four steps are accomplished with computers and electronic brainstorming software.[56]

Studies show that electronic brainstorming is much more productive than face-to-face brainstorming. Four-person electronic brainstorming groups produce 25 to 50 percent more ideas than four-person regular brainstorming groups, and twelve-person electronic brainstorming groups produce 200 percent more ideas than regular groups of the same size! In fact, because production blocking (i.e., waiting your turn) is not a problem for electronic brainstorming, the number and quality of ideas generally increase with group size.[57]

Even though it works much better than traditional brainstorming, electronic brainstorming has disadvantages, too. An obvious problem is the expense of computers, networking, software, and other equipment. As these costs continue to drop, however, electronic brainstorming will become a viable option for more groups.

Another problem is that the anonymity of ideas may bother people who are used to having their ideas accepted by virtue of their position (i.e., the boss). On the other hand, one CEO said, "Because the process is anonymous, the sky's the limit in terms of what you can say, and as a result it is more thought-provoking. As a CEO, you'll probably discover things you might not want to hear but need to be aware of."[58]

A third disadvantage is that outgoing individuals who are more comfortable expressing themselves verbally may find it difficult to express themselves in writing. Finally, the most obvious problem is that participants have to be able to type. Those who can't type and those who type slowly may be easily frustrated and find themselves at a disadvantage relative to experienced typists.

6 Organizational Strategy

LEARNING OUTCOMES:

1 specify the components of sustainable competitive advantage and explain why it is important.

2 describe the steps involved in the strategy-making process.

3 explain the different kinds of corporate-level strategies.

4 describe the different kinds of industry-level strategies.

5 explain the components and kinds of firm-level strategies.

Chapter 6

Basics of Organizational Strategy

less than a decade ago, Apple Computer was not in the music business. And then it released the iPod, which quickly set the standard for all other digital music devices. Designed around a 1.8-inch-diameter hard drive, the iPod boasted low battery consumption and enough storage to hold literally thousands of songs in an easy-to-use product smaller than a deck of cards. Because Apple used existing technology to make the iPod, Sony, Samsung, Dell, Creative, and Microsoft moved quickly to produce their own MP3 players.

which allows you to download and watch HD TV shows and movies on your Zune, which can then be hooked to an HD TV (something you can also do with iTunes and select iPods). Apple still holds a commanding 71 percent of the market for digital music players. SanDisk, its nearest competitor, has 11 percent, and Microsoft's Zune has 4 percent.[1]

How can a company like Apple, which dominates a particular industry, maintain its competitive advantage as strong, well-financed competitors enter the market? What steps can Apple and other companies take to better manage their strategy-making processes? How does strategy relate to sustainable competitive advantage?

After reading the next two sections, you should be able to

1 **specify the components of sustainable competitive advantage and explain why it is important.**

2 **describe the steps involved in the strategy-making process.**

As the market has matured, competitors have tried to steal—or at least minimize—Apple's competitive advantage by adding unique features to their MP3 players in hopes of catching up to the iPod. Sony's new X Series Walkman includes, like the latest touch screen devices, the ability to surf the Internet via Wi-Fi, to view pictures and videos, and to store—and listen to at your convenience—web-based radio shows. SanDisk, best known as a maker of basic flash drive memory, has been competing with the iPod for about 5 years and sells the Sansa View, which is similar to the iPod in terms of audio and video capabilities. However, the Sansa View lacks touch screen controls and the 35,000 apps that can be downloaded onto the iPod Touch or iPhone. Microsoft's Zune player has touch screen control, HD radio (similar in quality to satellite radio) and HD video, the latter of

1 Sustainable Competitive Advantage

Resources are the assets, capabilities, processes, employee time, information, and knowledge that an organization controls. Firms use their resources to improve organizational effectiveness and efficiency. Resources are critical to organizational strategy because they can help companies create and sustain an advantage over competitors.[2]

Organizations can achieve a **competitive advantage** by using

> **Resources** the assets, capabilities, processes, information, and knowledge that an organization uses to improve its effectiveness and efficiency, create and sustain competitive advantage, and fulfill a need or solve a problem
>
> **Competitive advantage** providing greater value for customers than competitors can

**Sustainable com-
petitive advantage**
a competitive advantage
that other companies have
tried unsuccessfully to
duplicate and have, for the
moment, stopped trying to
duplicate

Valuable resources
resources that allow com-
panies to improve efficiency
and effectiveness

Rare resources
resources that are not
controlled or possessed by
many competing firms

their resources to provide greater value for customers than competitors can. For example, the iPod's competitive advantage came from its simple, attractive design relative to its price. But Apple's most important advantage was being the first company to make it easy to use MP3 players to legally buy and download music from iTunes.com. (Prior to the iTunes store at iTunes.com, the only means of acquiring digital music was illegal file swapping.) Apple negotiated agreements with nearly all of the major record labels to sell their music, and iTunes.com quickly became the premier platform for music downloading. The easy-to-understand site offered free downloadable software customers could use to organize and manage their digital music libraries.[3]

The goal of most organizational strategies is to create and then sustain a competitive advantage. A competitive advantage becomes a **sustainable competitive advantage** when other companies cannot duplicate the value a firm is providing to customers. Sustainable competitive advantage is *not* the same as a long-lasting competitive advantage, though companies obviously want a competitive advantage to last a long time. Rather, a competitive advantage is *sustained* if competitors have tried unsuccessfully to duplicate the advantage and have, for the moment, stopped trying to duplicate it. It's the corporate equivalent of your competitors saying, "We give up. You win. We can't do what you do, and we're not even going to try to do it anymore." Four conditions must be met if a firm's resources are to be used to achieve a sustainable competitive advantage. The resources must be valuable, rare, imperfectly imitable, *and* nonsubstitutable.

Valuable resources allow companies to improve their efficiency and effectiveness. Unfortunately, changes in customer demand and preferences, competitors' actions, and tech-

nology can make once-valuable resources much less valuable. Throughout the 1980s, Sony controlled the portable music market with its Sony Walkman, which has sold over 230 million units worldwide since its introduction in 1979. Sony leveraged the capabilities of its engineers and inventors (more resources) to make incremental changes to the Walkman that were not matched by the competition, that is, until the MP3 player came along. With the introduction of Apple's iPod to the market, Sony's Walkman lost nearly all its market share. Sony finally changed the Walkman to a portable digital device and created its own online music store (Connect), which did not match iTunes in simplicity of use or availability of songs.[4] When Connect soon proved unprofitable, Sony shut it down.[5]

For a sustainable competitive advantage, valuable resources must also be rare resources. Think about it: How can a company sustain a competitive advantage if all of its competitors have similar resources and capabilities? Consequently, **rare resources,** resources that are not controlled or possessed by many competing firms, are necessary to sustain a competitive advantage. When Apple introduced the iPod, no other portable music players on the market used existing hard drive technology in their design. The iPod gained an immediate advantage over competitors because it was able to satisfy the desire of consumers to carry large numbers of songs in a portable device, something the newer MP3 systems and older individual CD players could not do. The technology that powered the iPod, however, was readily available, so competitors were able to quickly imitate

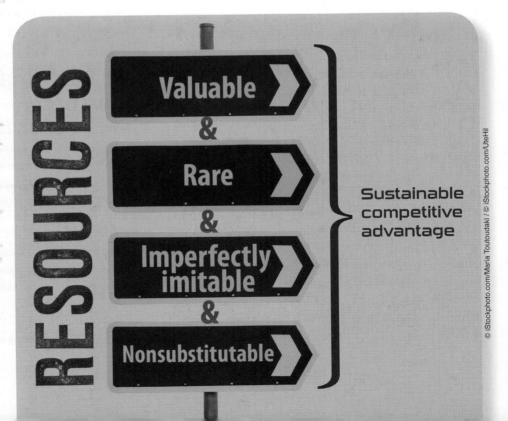

RESOURCES

Valuable
&
Rare
&
Imperfectly imitable
&
Nonsubstitutable

Sustainable competitive advantage

and, for short periods, exceed the iPod's basic storage capacity. As competitors began introducing iPod look-alikes, Apple responded by replacing the original mechanical control wheel with an easier-to-use solid-state touch wheel and then doubling the hard drive storage so that it was larger than that of its competitors. Once again, Apple used its design talents (resources) to gain an advantage over the competition.

As this shows, valuable and rare resources can create temporary competitive advantage. For a sustainable competitive advantage, however, other firms must be unable to imitate or find substitutes for those valuable, rare resources. **Imperfectly imitable resources** are those resources that are impossible or extremely costly or difficult to duplicate. For example, despite numerous attempts by competitors to imitate it, iTunes has retained its competitive lock on the music download business. Because it has capitalized on Apple's reputation for developing customer-friendly software, iTunes has a library of music, movies, and podcasts that is still two to three times larger than those of other music download sites. Because Apple initially developed a closed system for its iTunes and iPod, it was difficult for consumers to download music from sources other than the iTunes store. But most consumers don't seem to mind. Kelly Moore, a sales representative for a Texas software company, takes her pink iPod Mini everywhere she goes and keeps it synchronized with her iBook laptop. She says, "Once I find something I like, I don't switch brands."[6] She's not alone: Total sales at the iTunes store have climbed to more than 6 billion songs, 200 million videos, and 1 billion applications.[7] No other competitor comes close to those numbers.

Valuable, rare, imperfectly imitable resources can produce sustainable competitive advantage only if they are also **nonsubstitutable resources**, meaning that no other resources can replace them and produce similar value or competitive advantage. The industry has tried to produce equivalent substitutes for iTunes, but competitors have had to experiment with different business models in order to get customers to accept them. Napster founders Shawn Fanning and Wayne Rosso created a subscription-based service called Mashboxx that charged $15 a month for unlimited downloads, and Zune Marketplace has established a similar system with unlimited downloads of music, videos (TV shows and movies), podcasts, and audiobooks.[8] In addition to straight subscription models, some companies experimented with price. Whereas iTunes now charges 69 cents, 99 cents, or $1.29 per song, period, Amazon's new online store charges between 89 and 99 cents per song, and generally prices album collections between $5.99 and $9.99. At Amie Street, a newly posted track can be downloaded for free, but as the number of downloads increases, so does the song's price, until it reaches the maximum of 98 cents.[9] In response to competitors' experimentation, Apple adopted variable pricing (69 cents, 99 cents, or $1.29 per song) and also removed digital rights management, which restricted the extent to which users could copy their music from one device to another.[10] It will take years to find out whether any competing music download site will be an effective substitute for iTunes.[11]

In summary, Apple has reaped the rewards of a first-mover advantage from its interdependent iPod and iTunes. The company's history of developing customer-friendly software, the innovative capabilities of the iPod, the simple pay-as-you-go sales model of iTunes, and the unmatched list of music and movies available for download have proven to be valuable, rare, relatively nonsubstitutable, and, in the past, imperfectly imitable resources. Past success is, however, no guarantee of future success: Apple needs to continually change and develop its offerings or risk being unseated by a more nimble competitor whose products are more relevant and have higher perceived value to consumers.

2 | Strategy-Making Process

In order to create a sustainable competitive advantage, a company must have a strategy.[12]

*Exhibit 6.1 on the next page displays the three steps of the strategy-making process: **2.1 assess the need for strategic change, 2.2 conduct a situational analysis,** and then **2.3 choose strategic alternatives.** Let's examine each of these steps in more detail.*

2.1 | ASSESSING THE NEED FOR STRATEGIC CHANGE

The external business environment is much more turbulent than it used to be. With customers' needs constantly growing and changing, and with competitors working harder, faster, and smarter to meet those needs, the first step in creating a strategy is determining the need for strategic change. In other words, the company should determine whether it needs to change

Imperfectly imitable resources resources that are impossible or extremely costly or difficult for other firms to duplicate

Nonsubstitutable resources resources that produce value or competitive advantage and have no equivalent substitutes or replacements

its strategy to sustain a competitive advantage.[13]

Determining the need for strategic change might seem easy to do, but it's really not. There's a great deal of uncertainty in strategic business environments. Furthermore, top-level managers are often slow to recognize the need for strategic change, especially at successful companies that have created and sustained competitive advantages. Because they are acutely aware of the strategies that made their companies successful, they continue to rely on those strategies even as the competition changes. In other words, success often leads to **competitive inertia**—a reluctance to change strategies or competitive practices that have been successful in the past.

Sheraton Hotels, which are a unit of Starwood Hotels and Resorts Worldwide, Inc., are a prime example of competitive inertia. Sheraton, once one of the largest and best recognized hotel chains in the world, is now viewed by many customers as having convenient locations, but old decor, variable quality, and unexceptional service. Sheraton's Hoyt Harper admitted, "The gap between our good Sheraton hotels and our underperforming hotels ... was quite alarming." Those problems show up in prices that people are willing to pay. For example, the average Sheraton room goes for $100.72 compared to $112.62 at Marriott. Starwood, which manages Sheraton, neglected Sheraton for years as it put money and effort into its other hotel brands, such as W and Westin, which are trendier and more upscale. Hoyt Harper, who is in charge of the new strategy, said "Sheraton for eight years has been the ugly stepchild . . . ." Realizing that what worked in the past won't work anymore, Harper has developed an aggressive plan to close 33 poor-performing Sheraton hotels and then spend $4 billion to redo the remaining Sheratons' hotel lobbies, workout facilities, and hotel rooms, all the way down to the coffee in the rooms and the sheets on the beds.[14]

Besides being aware of the dangers of competitive inertia, what can managers do to improve the speed and accuracy with which they determine the need for strategic change? One method is to actively look for signs of strategic dissonance. **Strategic dissonance** is a discrepancy between a company's intended strategy and the strategic actions managers take when implementing that strategy.[15] For example, when Edgar Bronfman Jr. bought the struggling Warner Music Group, his intended strategy was to cut costs and stop excessive spending. Ironically, after laying off 1,200 employees to save $250 million and cutting remaining salaries by as much as 50 percent, he approved a $13,000 bill to charter a private jet to fly top company managers to the Grammy awards in Los Angeles and then quietly restored the salary cuts he had made after top executives complained.[16]

Note, however, that strategic dissonance is not the same thing as failure of a strategy to produce the results that it's supposed to. For instance, after trying to compete in online retailing, eBay is abandoning this approach and returning to selling only used and overstock goods via online auctions.[17] As sales for its main competitor, Amazon, rose and eBay's sales fell, it became clear that eBay was executing a strategy that didn't work.

2.2 | SITUATIONAL ANALYSIS

A situational analysis can also help managers determine the need for strategic change. A

Exhibit 6.1 Three Steps of the Strategy-Making Process

Step 1	Step 2	Step 3
Assess Need for Strategic Change	Conduct Situational Analysis	Choose Strategic Alternatives

- Avoid Competitive Inertia
- Look for Strategic Dissonance (Are strategic actions consistent with the company's strategic intent?)

INTERNAL ENVIRONMENT
Strengths
- Distinctive Competence
- Core Capability
Weaknesses

EXTERNAL ENVIRONMENT
Opportunities
- Environmental Scanning
- Strategic Groups
- Shadow-Strategy Task Force
Threats

Risk-Avoiding Strategies
Strategic Reference Points
Risk-Seeking Strategies

© Cengage Learning 2011

situational analysis, also called a **SWOT analysis** for *strengths, weaknesses, opportunities,* and *threats,* is an assessment of the strengths and weaknesses in an organization's internal environment and the opportunities and threats in its external environment.[18] Ideally, as shown in Step 2 of Exhibit 6.1, a SWOT analysis helps a company determine how to increase internal strengths and minimize internal weaknesses while maximizing external opportunities and minimizing external threats.

An analysis of an organization's internal environment (that is, a company's strengths and weaknesses) often begins with an assessment of its distinctive competencies and core capabilities. A **distinctive competence** is something that a company can make, do, or perform better than its competitors can. For example, *Consumer Reports* magazine consistently ranks Honda and Toyota cars either number one or two in quality and reliability.[19] Similarly, *PC Magazine* readers ranked Garmin's GPS devices best in terms of service and reliability.[20]

Whereas distinctive competencies are tangible—for example, a product or service is faster, cheaper, or better—the core capabilities that produce distinctive competencies are not. **Core capabilities** are the less visible, internal decision-making routines, problem-solving processes, and organizational cultures that determine how efficiently inputs can be turned into outputs.[21] Distinctive competencies cannot be sustained for long without superior core capabilities. Offering gourmet, environmentally conscious food products at a low cost is the distinctive competence at Trader Joe's. One can find ten kinds of hummus and every kind of dried fruit imaginable. Most of the products sold at Trader Joe's have no artificial colors, artificial flavors, or preservatives. The core capability the company uses to execute this strategy is its ability to buy in large quantities and bargain directly with producers. Trader Joe's also offers 80 percent of its products as house brands, compared to 16 percent industry-wide, and does not carry any mass-market brands such as Crest or Pepsi. These capabilities allow Trader Joe's to offer similar products at lower prices than competitors like Whole Foods Market. One customer said, "I love Trader Joe's because they let me eat like a yuppie without taking all my money." Stores also feature 15 or more new products each week, bringing the curious customer back to find out what's new.[22]

After examining internal strengths and weaknesses, the second part of a situational analysis is to look outside the company and assess the opportunities and threats in the external environment. In Chapter 3, you learned that *environmental scanning* involves searching the environment for important events or issues that might affect the organization, such as pricing trends or new products and technology. In a situational analysis, however, managers use environmental scanning to identify specific opportunities and threats that can either improve or harm the company's ability to sustain its competitive advantage. They can do this by identifying strategic groups.

A **strategic group** is a group of other companies within an industry that top managers choose in order to compare, evaluate, and benchmark their company's strategic threats and opportunities.[23] (*Benchmarking* involves identifying outstanding practices, processes, and standards at other companies and adapting them to your own company.) Typically, managers include a company as part of their strategic group if they compete directly with it for customers or if it uses strategies similar to theirs. It's likely that the managers at Hewlett-Packard, one of the most profitable U.S.

Garmin's Distinctive Competence?

It Ranked Best for Service and Reliability

Situational (SWOT) analysis an assessment of the strengths and weaknesses in an organization's internal environment and the opportunities and threats in its external environment

Distinctive competence what a company can make, do, or perform better than its competitors

Core capabilities the internal decision-making routines, problem-solving processes, and organizational cultures that determine how efficiently inputs can be turned into outputs

Strategic group a group of companies within an industry that top managers choose to compare, evaluate, and benchmark strategic threats and opportunities

firms in the infotech sector, assess strategic threats and opportunities by comparing their company to a strategic group consisting of other infotech firms, as illustrated in Exhibit 6.2.

When scanning the environment for strategic threats and opportunities, managers tend to categorize the different companies in their industries as core or secondary firms.[24] **Core firms** are the central companies in a strategic group. For example, the five areas of software, network gear, servers, PCs, and services account for about 75 percent of IT spending. While HP is probably best known for its PCs, where it competes with Dell, it remains a strong competitor in other areas. IBM's biggest business is in the area of services, where it holds the greatest market share. Dell's recent acquisition of Perot Systems makes it a bigger competitor in that space as well. IBM also holds the greatest market share in the server space, and Dell holds the third. Hewlett-Packard has the second largest market share in both of those spaces.[25] Therefore, although IBM does not have a PC division, it still would be considered a core firm in HP's strategic group, as would Dell.

Secondary firms are firms that use strategies related to but somewhat different from those of core firms. For instance, Oracle, Cisco, and Acer are likely

Exhibit 6.2 Core and Secondary Firms in the Information Technology Industry

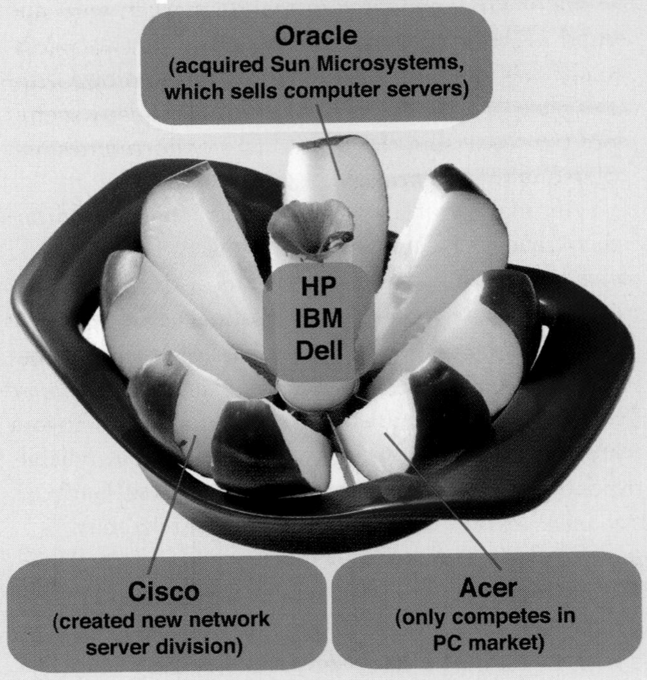

Oracle
(acquired Sun Microsystems, which sells computer servers)

HP
IBM
Dell

Cisco
(created new network server division)

Acer
(only competes in PC market)

secondary firms in HP's strategic group. Oracle, a long-time leader in corporate software, became a secondary firm in HP's strategic group when it acquired Sun Microsystems, which sells high-end computer servers, just like HP. Cisco, the leading provider of network

Do You Really Know Who Your Core Competitors Are? (They Might Not Be Who You Think)

Pay-TV service providers like DIRECTV, DISH Network, and Comcast are getting competition from unexpected sources. By signing content distribution deals with Netflix, Major League Baseball, and the major film studios, video game console makers Sony, Microsoft, and Nintendo now have the ability to use broadband Internet service to deliver TV, movies, music, and major sporting events to households. Sony has even introduced on-demand access to certain HBO shows through its PlayStation 3 game console. As consumers become accustomed to using video game consoles for games and managing home media, some analysts think it may only be a matter of time before consumers begin dropping cable- or satellite-TV services for broadband-only packages. As these examples illustrate, competitive threats sometimes emerge from unexpected places, particularly in rapidly changing environments. The lesson is that firms must be vigilant in monitoring for *potential* competitors before they become *actual* competitive threats.

Source: N. Worden, "Game Consoles to Challenge Pay TV," *Wall Street Journal*, May 26, 2010, B4.

and Internet routers and communication equipment, likewise became one of HP's secondary firms when it decided to begin making network servers. Finally, Acer is a major HP competitor in the PC market, with the second highest market share behind HP.[26] Managers need to be aware of the potential threats and opportunities posed by secondary firms, but they usually spend more time assessing the threats and opportunities associated with core firms.

2.3 | CHOOSING STRATEGIC ALTERNATIVES

After determining the need for strategic change and conducting a situational analysis, the last step in the strategy-making process is to choose strategic alternatives that will help the company create or maintain a sustainable competitive advantage. According to strategic reference point theory, managers choose between two basic alternative strategies: they can choose a conservative *risk-avoiding strategy* that aims to protect an existing competitive advantage, or they can choose an aggressive *risk-seeking strategy* that aims to extend or create a sustainable competitive advantage.

The choice to seek risk or avoid risk typically depends on whether top management views the company as falling above or below strategic reference points. **Strategic reference points** are the targets that manag-

ers use to measure whether their firm has developed the core competencies that it needs to achieve a sustainable competitive advantage. If a hotel chain decides to compete by providing superior quality and service, then top management will track the success of this strategy through customer surveys or published hotel ratings such as those provided by the prestigious *Mobil Travel Guide*. By contrast, if a hotel chain decides to compete on price, it will regularly conduct market surveys to check the prices of other hotels. The competitors' prices are the hotel managers' strategic reference points against which to compare their own pricing strategy. If competitors can consistently underprice them, then the managers need to determine whether their staff and resources have the core competencies to compete on price.

As shown in Exhibit 6.3, when a company is performing above or better than its strategic reference points, top management will typically be satisfied with the company's strategy. Ironically, this satisfaction tends to make top management conservative and risk-averse. Since the company already has a sustainable competitive advantage, the worst thing that could happen would be to lose it, so new issues or changes in the company's external environments are viewed as threats. By contrast, when a company is performing below or worse than its strategic reference points, top management will typically be dissatisfied with the company's strategy. In this instance, managers are much more likely to choose a daring, risk-taking strategy. If the current strategy is producing substandard results, the company has nothing to lose by switching to a risky new strategy in the hopes that it can create a sustainable competitive advantage. Managers of companies in this situation view new issues or changes in external environments as opportunities for potential gain.

> **Strategic reference points** the strategic targets managers use to measure whether a firm has developed the core competencies it needs to achieve a sustainable competitive advantage

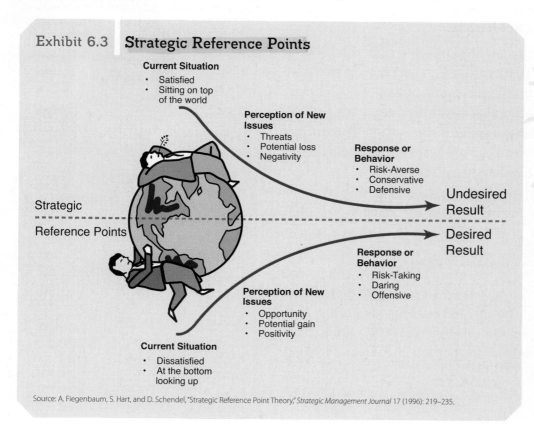

Exhibit 6.3   Strategic Reference Points

Current Situation
- Satisfied
- Sitting on top of the world

Perception of New Issues
- Threats
- Potential loss
- Negativity

Response or Behavior
- Risk-Averse
- Conservative
- Defensive

Strategic Reference Points

Undesired Result

Desired Result

Response or Behavior
- Risk-Taking
- Daring
- Offensive

Perception of New Issues
- Opportunity
- Potential gain
- Positivity

Current Situation
- Dissatisfied
- At the bottom looking up

Source: A. Fiegenbaum, S. Hart, and D. Schendel, "Strategic Reference Point Theory," *Strategic Management Journal* 17 (1996): 219–235.

Strategic reference point theory is not deterministic, however. Managers are not predestined to choose risk-averse or risk-seeking strategies for their companies depending solely on their current situation. Indeed, one of the most important elements of the theory is that managers can influence the strategies chosen by their company by *actively changing and adjusting* the strategic reference points they use to judge strategic performance. If a company has become complacent after consistently surpassing its strategic reference points, then top management can change from a risk-averse to a risk-taking orientation by raising the standards of performance (i.e., strategic reference points). This is just what happened at Menards.

Menards is a hardware store chain with 170 locations throughout the Midwest. Instead of being satisfied with protecting its existing stores (a risk-averse strategy), founder John Menard changed the strategic reference points the company had been using to assess strategic performance. To encourage a daring, offensive-minded strategy, he determined that Menards would have to beat Home Depot on four strategic reference points: price, products, sales per square foot, and "friendly accessibility." The strategy appears to be succeeding. In terms of price, market research indicates that a 100-item shopping cart of goods is consistently cheaper at Menards. In terms of products, Menards sells 50,000 products per store, the same as Home Depot. In terms of sales per square foot, Menards ($407 per square foot) outsells Home Depot ($300 per square foot). Finally, unlike Home Depot's warehouse-like stores, Menards' stores are built to resemble grocery stores. Shiny tiled floors, wide aisles, and easy-to-reach products all make Menards a "friendlier" place for shoppers. And now with Lowe's, the second-largest hardware store chain in the nation, also entering its markets, Menards has added a fifth strategic reference point: store size. At 225,000 square feet, most new Menards stores are more than double the size of Home Depot's stores and 100,000 square feet larger than Lowe's biggest stores.[27]

So even when (perhaps *especially* when) companies have achieved a sustainable competitive advantage, top managers must adjust or change strategic reference points to challenge themselves and their employees to develop new core competencies for the future. In the long run, effective organizations will frequently revise their strategic reference points to better focus managers' attention on the new challenges and opportunities that occur in their ever-changing business environments.

© mm-images/Alamy

Charge It—To My Cell Phone

For decades, paying with credit has mostly meant using Visa or MasterCard. In 2009, 79 percent of all consumer transactions, a total of $2.45 trillion, were spent using those iconic credit cards, putting Visa and MasterCard in the top-of-the-world position according to strategic reference points theory. That could be about to change, however, as AT&T, Verizon Wireless, and T-Mobile are working together to develop a payment system that would replace credit cards with smartphones. According to industry consultant Richard K. Crone, "This is definitely a game changer. Mobile carriers are the biggest recurring billers in every market. They are experts at processing payments." And according to Mercatus, a consulting firm in Boston, more than half of U.S. consumers, and almost 80 percent of those ages 18 to 34, will use mobile financial service within five years. Consumers aren't the only ones willing to shift away from credit cards. Retailers have long tussled with Visa and MasterCard over transaction fees and would likely be very interested in supporting a rival network. If mobile payment systems take hold, card issuers may very well find themselves at the bottom of the world looking up for the first time in ages.

Source: P. Eichenbaum and M. Collins, "We Take Cash, Plastic, and . . . Smartphones," *Bloomberg BusinessWeek*, August 9–15, 2010, 37–38.

Corporate-, Industry-, and Firm-Level Strategies

to formulate effective strategies, companies must be able to answer these three basic questions:

- What business or businesses are we in or should we be in?
- How should we compete in this industry?
- Who are our competitors, and how should we respond to them?

These simple but powerful questions are at the heart of corporate-, industry-, and firm-level strategies.

After reading the next three sections, you should be able to

3 explain the different kinds of corporate-level strategies.

4 describe the different kinds of industry-level strategies.

5 explain the components and kinds of firm-level strategies.

3 Corporate-Level Strategies

Corporate-level strategy is the overall organizational strategy that addresses the question "What business or businesses are we in or should we be in?"

Corporate-Level Strategies

Portfolio Strategies	Grand Strategies
Acquisitions, unrelated diversification, related diversification, single businesses	Growth
	Stability
	Retrenchment/recovery
Boston Consulting Group matrix • Stars • Question marks • Cash cows • Dogs	

© Cengage Learning 2011

There are two major approaches to corporate-level strategy that companies use to decide which businesses they should be in: 3.1 portfolio strategy and 3.2 grand strategies.

3.1 | PORTFOLIO STRATEGY

One of the standard strategies for stock market investors is **diversification,** or owning stocks in a variety of companies in different industries. The purpose of this strategy is to reduce risk in the overall stock portfolio (the entire collection of stocks). The basic idea is simple. If you invest in ten companies in ten different industries, you won't lose your entire investment if one company performs poorly. Furthermore, because they're in different industries, one company's losses are likely to be offset by another company's gains. Portfolio strategy is based on these same ideas. We'll start by taking a look at the theory and ideas behind portfolio strategy and then proceed with a critical review that suggests that some of the key ideas behind portfolio strategy are *not* supported.

Portfolio strategy is a corporate-level strategy that minimizes risk by diversifying investment among various businesses or product lines.[28] Just as a diversification strategy guides an investor who invests in a variety of stocks, portfolio strategy guides the strategic decisions of corporations that compete in a variety of businesses. For example, portfolio strategy could be used to guide the strategy of a company like 3M, which makes 55,000 products for six different business sectors: consumers and offices (Post-its, Scotch tape, etc.); display and graphics (for computers, cell phones, PDAs, and TVs); electronics and communications (flexible circuits used in printers and electronic displays); health care (medical and oral care products, and drug delivery and health information systems); industrial and transportation (tapes, adhesives, abrasives, and specialty materials for markets such as automotive, aerospace, renewable energy, and electronics); and safety, security, and protection services (personal protective equipment, safety and security products, and track and trace solutions).[29] Furthermore, just as investors consider the mix of stocks in their stock portfolios when deciding which stocks to buy or sell, managers following portfolio strategy try to acquire companies that fit well with the

Corporate-level strategy the overall organizational strategy that addresses the question "What business or businesses are we in or should we be in?"

Diversification a strategy for reducing risk by owning a variety of items (stocks or, in the case of a corporation, types of businesses) so that the failure of one stock or one business does not doom the entire portfolio

Portfolio strategy a corporate-level strategy that minimizes risk by diversifying investment among various businesses or product lines

rest of their corporate portfolios and sell those that don't. Portfolio strategy provides the following guidelines to help companies make these difficult decisions.

First, according to portfolio strategy, the more businesses in which a corporation competes, the smaller its overall chances of failing. Think of a corporation as a stool and its businesses as the legs of the stool. The more legs or businesses added to the stool, the less likely it is to tip over. Using this analogy, portfolio strategy reduces 3M's risk of failing because the corporation's survival depends on essentially six different business sectors. Managers employing portfolio strategy can either develop new businesses internally or look for **acquisitions,** that is, other companies to buy. Either way, the goal is to add legs to the stool.

Second, beyond adding new businesses to the corporate portfolio, portfolio strategy predicts that companies can reduce risk even more through **unrelated diversification**—creating or acquiring companies in completely unrelated businesses (more on the accuracy of this prediction later). According to portfolio strategy, when businesses are unrelated, losses in one business or industry should have minimal effect on the performance of other companies in the corporate portfolio. Berkshire Hathaway, owned by billionaire Warren Buffett, is an example of unrelated diversification. Berkshire Hathaway paid $44 billion to acquire Burlington Northern Santa Fe Corp (BNSF), a railroad company, which was added to Berkshire's stable of unrelated businesses, which includes insurers Gen Re and GEICO, confectionery product maker See's Candies, private aircraft contractor NetJets, manufactured housing company Clayton Homes, and many others.[30] Because most internally grown businesses tend to be related to existing products or services, portfolio strategy suggests that acquiring new businesses is the preferred method of unrelated diversification.

Third, investing the profits and cash flows from mature, slow-growth businesses into newer, faster-growing businesses can reduce long-term risk. The best-known portfolio strategy for guiding investment in a corporations' businesses is the Boston Consulting Group (BCG) matrix.[31] The **BCG matrix** is a portfolio strategy that managers use to categorize their corporations' businesses by growth rate and relative market share, helping them decide how to invest corporate funds.

The matrix, shown in Exhibit 6.4, separates businesses into four categories based on how fast the market is growing (high growth or low growth) and the size of the business's share of that market (small or large). A **star** is a company that has a large share of a fast-growing market. To take advantage of a star's fast-growing market and its strength in that market (large share), the corporation must invest substantially in it. The investment is usually worthwhile, however, because many stars produce sizable future profits. A **question mark** is a company that has a small share of a fast-growing market. If the corporation invests in these companies, they may eventually become stars, but their relative weakness in the market (small share) makes investing in question marks more risky than investing in stars. A **cash cow** is a company that has a large share of a slow-growing market. Companies in this situation are often highly profitable, hence the name "cash cow." Finally, a **dog** is a company that has a small share of a slow-growing market. As the name suggests, having a small share of a slow-growth market is often not profitable.

Since the idea is to redirect investment from slow-growing to fast-growing companies, the BCG matrix starts by recommending that the substantial cash flows from cash cows should be reinvested in stars while the cash lasts (see 1 in Exhibit 6.4) to help them grow even faster and obtain even more market share. Using this strategy allows current profits to help produce future profits. As their market growth slows over time, some stars may turn into cash cows (see 2).

Cash flows should also be directed to some question marks (see 3). Though riskier than stars, question marks have great potential because of their fast-growing markets. Managers must decide which question marks are most likely to turn into stars (and therefore warrant further investment) and which ones are too risky and should be sold. Over time, managers hope some question marks will become stars as their small market shares become large ones (see 4). Finally, because dogs lose money, the corporation should "find them new owners" or "take them to the pound." In other words, dogs should either be sold to other companies or be closed down and liquidated for their assets (see 5).

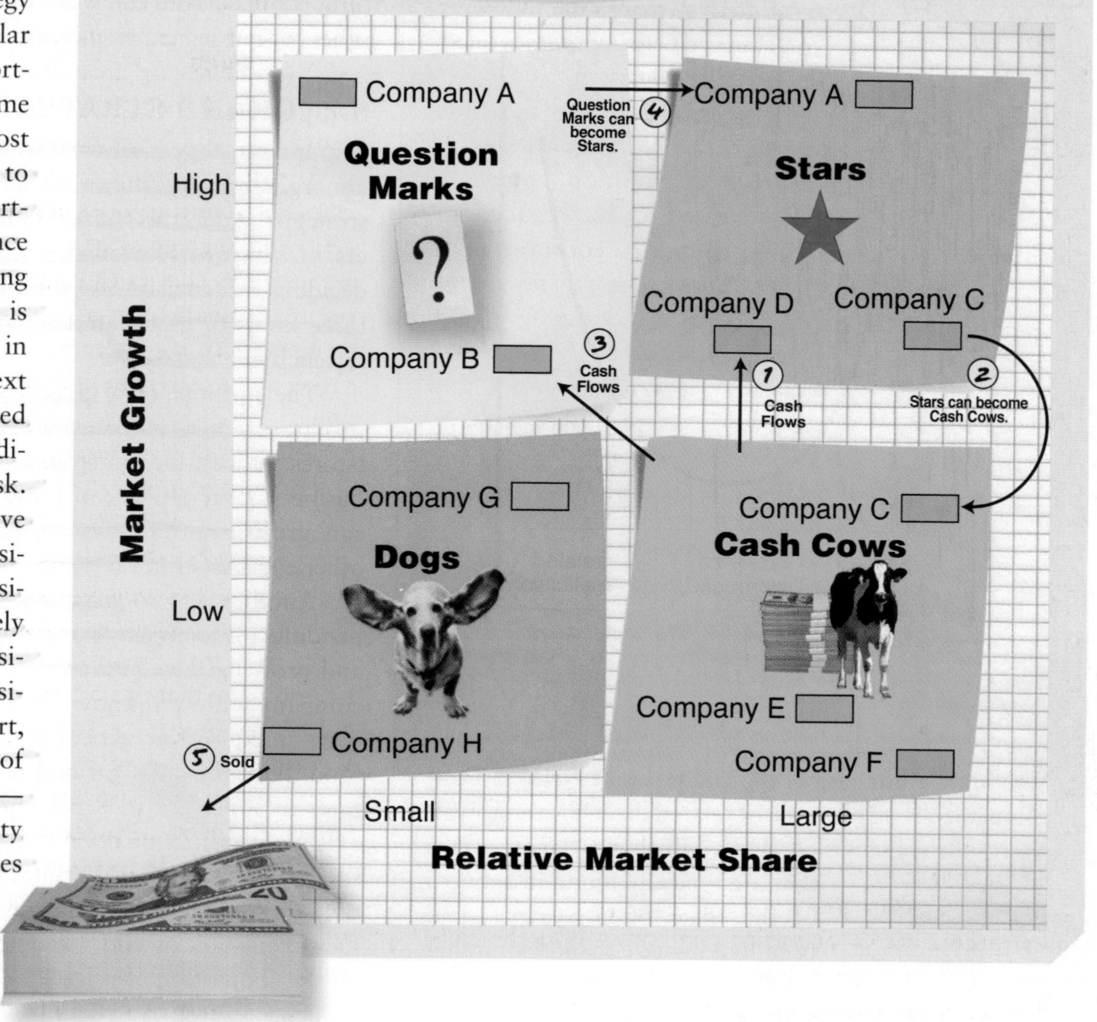

Although the BCG matrix and other forms of portfolio strategy are relatively popular among managers, portfolio strategy has some drawbacks. The most significant? Contrary to the predictions of portfolio strategy, evidence suggests that acquiring unrelated businesses is not useful. As shown in Exhibit 6.5 on the next page, there is a U-shaped relationship between diversification and risk. The left side of the curve shows that single businesses with no diversification are extremely risky (if the single business fails, the entire business fails). So, in part, the portfolio strategy of diversifying is correct—competing in a variety of different businesses can lower risk. However, portfolio strategy is partly wrong, too—the right side of the curve shows that conglomerates composed of completely unrelated businesses are even riskier than single, undiversified businesses.

A second set of problems with portfolio strategy has to do with the dysfunctional consequences that occur when companies are categorized as stars, cash cows, question marks, or dogs. Contrary to expectations, the BCG matrix often yields incorrect judgments about a company's potential. This is because it relies on past performance (i.e., previous market share and previous market growth), which is a notoriously poor predictor of future company performance.

Furthermore, using the BCG matrix can also weaken the strongest performer in the corporate portfolio, the cash cow. As funds are redirected from cash cows to stars, corporate managers essentially take away the resources needed to take advantage of the cash cow's new business opportunities. As a result, the

Exhibit 6.4 Boston Consulting Group Matrix

cash cow becomes less aggressive in seeking new business or in defending its present business. Finally, labeling a top performer as a cash cow can harm employee morale. Cash cow employees realize that they have inferior status and that they are now working to fund the growth of stars and question marks instead of working for themselves.

So, what kind of portfolio strategy does the best job of helping managers decide which companies to buy or sell? The U-shaped curve in Exhibit 6.5 indicates that the best approach is probably **related diversification**, in which the different business units have similar products, manufacturing, marketing, technology, and/or cultures. The key to related diversification is to acquire or create new companies with core capabilities that complement the core capabilities of businesses already in the corporate portfolio.

Related diversification creating or acquiring companies that share similar products, manufacturing, marketing, technology, or cultures

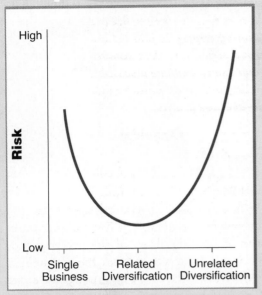

Exhibit 6.5 U-Shaped Relationship between Diversification and Risk

Source: Republished by The Academy of Management, P.O. Box 3020, Briar Cliff Manor, NY, 10510-8020. M. Lubatkin & P.J. Lane, "Psst! . . . The Merger Mavens Still Have It Wrong" *Academy of Management Executive* 10 (1996) 21–39; Reproduced with the permission of the publisher via Copyright Clearance Center, Inc.

to a single, undiversified business or unrelated diversification, related diversification reduces risk because the different businesses can work as a team, relying on each other for needed experience, expertise, and support.

3.2 | GRAND STRATEGIES

A **grand strategy** is a broad strategic plan used to help an organization achieve its strategic goals.[33] Grand strategies guide the strategic alternatives that managers of individual businesses or subunits may use in deciding what businesses they should be in. There are three kinds of grand strategies: growth, stability, and retrenchment/recovery.

The purpose of a **growth strategy** is to increase profits, revenues, market share, or the number of places (stores, offices, locations) in which the company does business. Companies can grow in several ways. They can grow externally by merging with or acquiring other companies in the same or different businesses.

Another way to grow is internally, by directly expanding the company's existing business or creating and growing new businesses. Nestlé, the global food company with well-known brands like Nesquick chocolate milk, KitKat chocolate bars, and Gerber baby food, typically aims for and achieves internal growth rates of 7 percent to 8 percent by increasing sales of existing products or developing new products. For instance, because of rising sales of its products, Nestlé didn't have to cut prices during an economic recession. CEO Paul Bulcke said, "People go for value. It is not always a question of price."[34]

The purpose of a **stability strategy** is to continue doing what the company has been doing, just doing it better. Companies following a stability strategy try to improve the way in which they sell the same products or services to the same customers. Companies often choose a stability strategy when their external environment doesn't change much or after they have struggled with periods of explosive growth.

The purpose of a **retrenchment strategy** is to turn around very poor company performance by shrinking the size or scope of the business or, if a company is in multiple businesses, by closing or shutting down different lines of the business. The first step of a typical retrenchment strategy might include making significant cost reductions; laying off employees; closing poorly performing stores, offices, or

Wal-Mart's purchase of the UK stores of Netto, a Danish retailer, is an example of related diversification. Wal-Mart's British division Asda, which has larger stores that are typically found in suburbs or the edges of large cities, had been looking to expand by putting smaller supermarkets in central locations. Acquiring these stores accomplishes that goal for Asda and complements its larger out-of-town Asda stores.[32]

We began this section with the example of 3M and its 55,000 products sold in six different business sectors. While seemingly different, most of 3M's product divisions are based in some fashion on its distinctive competencies in adhesives and tape (e.g., wet or dry sandpaper, Post-it notes, Scotchgard fabric protector, transdermal skin patches, reflective material used in traffic signs, etc.). Furthermore, all of 3M's divisions share its strong corporate culture that promotes and encourages risk taking and innovation. In sum, in contrast

Grand strategy
a broad corporate-level strategic plan used to achieve strategic goals and guide the strategic alternatives that managers of individual businesses or subunits may use

Growth strategy
a strategy that focuses on increasing profits, revenues, market share, or the number of places in which the company does business

Stability strategy
a strategy that focuses on improving the way in which the company sells the same products or services to the same customers

Retrenchment strategy a strategy that focuses on turning around very poor company performance by shrinking the size or scope of the business

manufacturing plants; or cutting or selling entire lines of products or services.[35] After Sears saw its earnings drop from $800 million to a loss of $50 million over the course of 18 months, it reduced administrative expenses by $168 million by cutting jobs at headquarters and distribution centers and by consolidating its Kenmore, Craftsman, and Diehard brands into one division. It also closed some stores and reduced inventory (particularly in appliances) by substantially cutting prices, decreasing the value of on-hand inventory from $10.3 billion to $9.5 billion. So, despite a 7 percent drop in sales, Sears's retrenchment strategy returned it to profitability a year later.[36]

After cutting costs and reducing a business's size or scope, the second step in a retrenchment strategy is recovery. **Recovery** consists of the strategic actions that a company takes to return to a growth strategy. This two-step process of cutting and recovery is analogous to pruning roses. Prior to each growing season, roses should be cut back to two-thirds their normal size. Pruning doesn't damage the roses; it makes them stronger and more likely to produce beautiful, fragrant flowers. The retrenchment-and-recovery process is similar. Cost reductions, layoffs, and plant closings are sometimes necessary to restore companies to good health. After billions in losses and 10 years of unsuccessfully trying to make its merger with Chrysler work, Daimler AG sold its 80 percent stake in Chrysler to Cerebus Capital Management for $6 billion. Even then, Daimler's remaining 20 percent stake in Chrysler resulted in an additional $2.8 billion in losses. To restore profitability, Daimler cut labor costs by $2.8 billion in Germany by delaying a pay raise of 2.1 percent and postponing a $392 million profit-sharing payout to employees. In North America, it cut costs by $900 million by eliminating its Sterling truck brand.[37] Like pruning, such cuts are intended to allow companies to eventually return to a successful growth strategy (i.e., recovery). When company performance drops significantly, a strategy of retrenchment and recovery may help the company improve performance relatively quickly.

4 Industry-Level Strategies

Industry-level strategy addresses the question "How should we compete in this industry?"

Let's find out more about industry-level strategies by discussing **4.1 the five industry forces that determine overall levels of competition in an industry** and **4.2 the positioning strategies** and **4.3 the adaptive strategies that companies can use to achieve a sustainable competitive advantage and above-average profits.**

4.1 | FIVE INDUSTRY FORCES

According to Harvard professor Michael Porter, five industry forces determine an industry's overall attractiveness and potential for long-term profitability. These include the character of the rivalry, the threat of new entrants, the threat of substitute products or services, the bargaining power of suppliers, and the bargaining power of buyers and are illustrated in Exhibit 6.6. The stronger these forces, the less attractive the industry becomes to corporate investors because it is more difficult for companies to be profitable. Let's examine how these industry forces are bringing changes to several kinds of industries.

Character of the rivalry is a measure of the intensity of competitive behavior between companies in an industry. Is the competition among firms aggressive and cutthroat, or do competitors focus more on serving customers than on attacking each other? Both industry attractiveness and profitability decrease when rivalry is cutthroat.

Exhibit 6.6   Porter's Five Industry Forces

The **threat of new entrants** is a measure of the degree to which barriers to entry make it easy or difficult for new companies to get started in an industry. If new companies can easily enter the industry, then competition will increase and prices and profits will fall. On the other hand, if there are sufficient barriers to entry, such as large capital requirements to buy expensive equipment or plant facilities or the need for specialized knowledge, then competition will be weaker and prices and profits will generally be higher. For several years, lobbyists in the banking industry have fought hard to block the entry of one major new competitor, namely Wal-Mart. Three years ago, fierce opposition from industry insiders caused Wal-Mart to withdraw its application for a banking license, and now banks are seeking a three-year freeze on applications for industrial loan corporations, the type of bank charter for which Wal-Mart would be applying. Wal-Mart has already opened bank branches in Mexico and Canada, offering credit cards and loans such as mortgages.[38]

The **threat of substitute products or services** is a measure of the ease with which customers can find substitutes for an industry's products or services. If customers can easily find substitute products or services, the competition will be greater and profits will be lower. If there are few or no substitutes, competition will be weaker and profits will be higher. Generic medicines are some of the best-known examples of substitute products. Under U.S. patent law, a company that develops a drug has exclusive rights to produce and market that drug for 20 years. Price and profits are generally high during this period if the drug sells well. After 20 years, however, the patent will expire, and any pharmaceutical company can manufacture and sell the same drug. When this happens, the drug's price drops substantially, and the company that developed the drug typically sees its revenues drop sharply.

Bargaining power of suppliers is a measure of the influence that suppliers of parts, materials, and services to firms in an industry have on the prices of these inputs. When companies can buy parts, materials, and services from numerous suppliers, the companies will be able to bargain with the suppliers to keep prices low. Today, there are so many suppliers of inexpensive, standardized parts, computer chips, and video screens that dozens of new companies are beginning to manufacture flat-screen TVs. In other words, the weak bargaining power of suppliers has made it easier for new firms to enter the HDTV business. On the other hand, if there are few suppliers, or if a company is dependent on a supplier with specialized skills and knowledge, then the suppliers will have the bargaining power to dictate price levels. When the global economy fell into a recession, there was a dramatic shift in the bargaining power between retailers and manufacturers. Traditionally, retailers controlled how much a manufacturer would produce based on the popularity of a particular garment or look. But because of the recession, apparel manufacturers shut down their factories and cut down on production to lower their costs. They even declined to take orders from retailers with whom they had enjoyed decades-long relationships and from whom they had received multimillion dollar orders in the past.[39]

Bargaining power of buyers is a measure of the influence that customers have on a firm's prices. If a company sells a popular product or service to multiple buyers, then the company has more power to set prices. By contrast, if a company is dependent on just a few

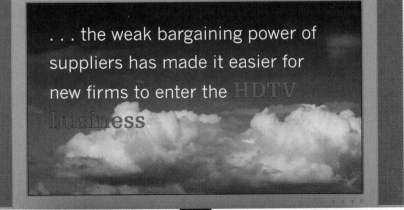

. . . the weak bargaining power of suppliers has made it easier for new firms to enter the HDTV business.

© iStockphoto.com/evirgen

high-volume buyers, those buyers will typically have enough bargaining power to dictate prices. Costco, a membership warehouse chain, and the third largest retailer in the United States, focuses on offering extremely low prices. Often times, when the company feels that a supplier is charging too much for a product, it will simply stop carrying it, even if the product is as iconic as Coca-Cola. The soft-drink maker wanted to raise the prices that retail chains would have to pay for its products. Costco felt the move would force it to raise prices for consumers, and so, simply decided to stop ordering Coca-Cola products. According to a message on Costco's website, "At this time, Coca-Cola has not provided Costco with competitive pricing so that we may pass along the value our members deserve." After three weeks of negotiations, just days before the crucial holiday shopping season began, Costco and Coca-Cola reached a settlement and Coca-Cola products were back on the shelves.[40]

4.2 | POSITIONING STRATEGIES

After analyzing industry forces, the next step in industry-level strategy is to protect your company from the negative effects of industry-wide competition and to create a sustainable competitive advantage. According to Michael Porter, there are three positioning strategies: cost leadership, differentiation, and focus.

Cost leadership means producing a product or service of acceptable quality at consistently lower production costs than those of competitors so that the firm can offer the product or service at the lowest price in the industry. Cost leadership protects companies from industry forces by deterring new entrants, who will have to match low costs and prices. Cost leadership also forces down the prices of substitute products or services, attracts bargain-seeking buyers, and increases bargaining power with suppliers, which have to keep their prices low if they want to do business with the cost leader.

Differentiation means making your product or service sufficiently different from competitors' offerings so that customers are willing to pay a premium price for the extra value or performance that it provides. Differentiation protects companies from industry forces by reducing the threat of substitute products. It also protects companies by making it easier to retain customers and more difficult for new entrants trying to attract new customers. Apple's iPod, iPhone, and iPad are perfect examples of how differentiation can enable a company to command a higher price and dominate the market.

With a **focus strategy**, a company uses either cost leadership or differentiation to produce a specialized product or service for a limited, specially targeted group of customers in a particular geographic region or market segment. Focus strategies typically work in market niches that competitors have overlooked or have difficulty serving. While eBay dominates the online auction business, smaller, more focused auction sites serve select groups of online buyers and sellers. Craftspeople who sell jewelry and handmade goods are attracted to Silkfair because it has larger pictures (which is important when you sell small items like jewelry) and lets sellers use video, customer forums, and blogs to promote their products and interact with customers.[41]

4.3 | ADAPTIVE STRATEGIES

Adaptive strategies are another set of industry-level strategies. Whereas the aim of positioning strategies is to minimize the effects of industry competition and build a sustainable competitive advantage, the purpose of adaptive strategies is to choose an industry-level strategy that is best suited to changes in the organization's external environment. There are four kinds of adaptive strategies: defending, prospecting, analyzing, and reacting.[42]

Defenders seek moderate, steady growth by offering a limited range of products and services to a well-defined set of customers. In other words, defenders aggressively "defend" their current strategic position by doing the best job they can to hold on to customers in a particular market segment.

Prospectors seek fast growth by searching for new market opportunities, encouraging risk taking, and being the first to bring innovative new products to market. Prospectors are analogous to gold miners who "prospect" for gold nuggets (i.e., new products) in hopes that the nuggets will lead them to a rich deposit of gold (i.e., fast growth).

Cost leadership the positioning strategy of producing a product or service of acceptable quality at consistently lower production costs than competitors can, so that the firm can offer the product or service at the lowest price in the industry

Differentiation the positioning strategy of providing a product or service that is sufficiently different from competitors' offerings so that customers are willing to pay a premium price for it

Focus strategy the positioning strategy of using cost leadership or differentiation to produce a specialized product or service for a limited, specially targeted group of customers in a particular geographic region or market segment

Defenders firms that adopt an adaptive strategy aimed at defending strategic positions by seeking moderate, steady growth and by offering a limited range of high-quality products and services to a well-defined set of customers

Prospectors firms that adopt an adaptive strategy that seeks fast growth by searching for new market opportunities, encouraging risk taking, and being the first to bring innovative new products to market

Analyzers firms that adopt an adaptive strategy that seeks to minimize risk and maximize profits by following or imitating the proven successes of prospectors

Reactors firms that take an adaptive strategy of not following a consistent strategy, but instead reacting to changes in the external environment after they occur

Firm-level strategy a corporate strategy that addresses the question "How should we compete against a particular firm?"

Direct competition the rivalry between two companies that offer similar products and services, acknowledge each other as rivals, and react to each other's strategic actions

Market commonality the degree to which two companies have overlapping products, services, or customers in multiple markets

Resource similarity the extent to which a competitor has similar amounts and kinds of resources

Analyzers blend the defending and prospecting strategies. They seek moderate, steady growth *and* limited opportunities for fast growth. Analyzers are rarely first to market with new products or services. Instead, they try to simultaneously minimize risk and maximize profits by following or imitating the proven successes of prospectors. Several years ago Ford introduced SYNC, an in-car communication device that drivers can use to control digital music players, cell phones, and GPS devices with voice commands. SYNC will even allow voice messages to be sent to drivers' phones. Seeing SYNC's success, a number of companies have sought to follow in its footsteps. Kia, for example, will include UVO, a system similar to SYNC, in its 2011 Sorrento models. Continental Automotive Systems, meanwhile, has developed the AutoLinQ, an infotainment system that will also let drivers download smartphone-like applications.[43]

Finally, unlike defenders, prospectors, or analyzers, **reactors** do not follow a consistent strategy. Rather than anticipating and preparing for external opportunities and threats, reactors tend to react to changes in their external environments after they occur. Not surprisingly, reactors tend to be poorer performers than defenders, prospectors, or analyzers. A reacting approach is inherently unstable, and firms that fall into this mode of operation must change their approach or face almost certain failure.

5 Firm-Level Strategies

Microsoft brings out its Xbox 360 video game console; Sony counters with its PlayStation 3. Sprint Nextel drops prices and increases monthly cell phone minutes; Verizon strikes back with better reception and even lower prices and more minutes. Attack and respond, respond and attack. **Firm-level strategy** addresses the question "How should we compete against a particular firm?"

Let's find out more about the firm-level strategies (i.e., direct competition between companies) by considering **5.1 the basics of direct competition** *and* **5.2 the strategic moves involved in direct competition between companies.**

5.1 | DIRECT COMPETITION

Although Porter's five industry forces indicate the overall level of competition in an industry, most companies do not compete directly with all the others in their industry. For example, McDonald's and Red Lobster are both in the restaurant business, but no one would characterize them as competitors. McDonald's offers low-cost, convenient fast food in a seat-yourself restaurant, while Red Lobster offers mid-priced, sit-down seafood dinners complete with servers and a bar.

Instead of competing with an entire industry, most firms compete directly with just a few other firms within it. **Direct competition** is the rivalry between two companies offering similar products or services that acknowledge each other as rivals and take offensive and defensive positions as they act and react to each other's strategic actions.[44] Two factors determine the extent to which firms will be in direct competition with each other: market commonality and resource similarity. **Market commonality** is the degree to which two companies have overlapping products, services, or customers in multiple markets. The more markets in which there is product, service, or customer overlap, the more intense the direct competition between the two companies. **Resource similarity** is the extent to which a competitor has similar amounts and kinds of resources, that is, similar assets, capabilities, processes, information, and knowledge used to create and sustain an advantage over competitors. From a competitive standpoint, resource similarity means that your direct competitors can probably match the strategic actions that your company takes.

Exhibit 6.7 shows how market commonality and resource similarity interact to determine when and where companies are in direct competition.[45] The overlapping area in each quadrant (between the triangle and the rectangle or between the differently colored rectangles) depicts market commonality. The larger the overlap, the greater the market commonality. Shapes depict resource similarity, with rectangles representing one set of competitive resources and triangles representing another.

Quadrant I shows two companies in direct competition because they have similar resources at their disposal and a high degree of market commonality. These companies try to sell similar products and services to

Exhibit 6.7 A Framework of Direct Competition

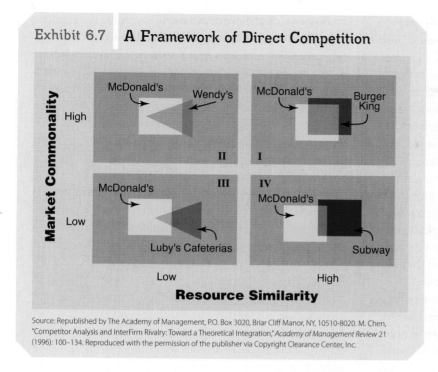

Source: Republished by The Academy of Management, P.O. Box 3020, Briar Cliff Manor, NY, 10510-8020. M. Chen, "Competitor Analysis and InterFirm Rivalry: Toward a Theoretical Integration," *Academy of Management Review* 21 (1996): 100–134. Reproduced with the permission of the publisher via Copyright Clearance Center, Inc.

Finally, in Quadrant IV, the small overlap between the two rectangles shows that McDonald's and Subway compete with similar resources but with little market commonality. In terms of resources, McDonald's sales are much larger, but Subway has grown substantially in the last decade and now has almost 33,000 stores worldwide, compared to 32,000 worldwide for McDonald's.[49] Though Subway and McDonald's compete, they aren't direct competitors in terms of market commonality in the way that McDonald's and Burger King are, because Subway, unlike McDonald's, sells itself as a provider of healthy fast food. Thus, the overlap is much smaller in Quadrant IV than in Quadrant I.

5.2 | STRATEGIC MOVES OF DIRECT COMPETITION

Whereas corporate-level strategies help managers decide what business to be in and industry-level strategies help them determine how to compete within an industry, firm-level strategies help managers determine when, where, and what strategic actions should be taken against a direct competitor. Firms in direct competition can make two basic strategic moves: attacks and responses. These moves occur all the time in virtually every industry, but they are most noticeable in industries where multiple large competitors are pursuing customers in the same market space.

An **attack** is a competitive move designed to reduce a rival's market share or profits. For example, the two leaders in the e-reader market, Amazon and Barnes & Noble, had both priced their devices at $259. However, Barnes & Noble attacked Amazon's Kindle e-reader by aggressively cutting the price on its own Nook e-reader to $199.[50] A **response** is a countermove, prompted by a rival's attack, that is designed to defend or improve a company's market share or profit. There are two kinds of responses.[51] The first is to match or mirror your competitor's move. This is what Amazon did when it cut the price of its Kindle e-reader to $189, undercutting the price of Barnes & Noble's Nook by $10.[52] The second kind of response, however, is to respond along a different dimension from your competitor's move or attack. For example, instead of cutting the price of its

similar customers. McDonald's and Burger King clearly fit here as direct competitors.

In Quadrant II, the overlapping triangle and rectangle show two companies going after similar customers with some similar products or services, but doing so with different competitive resources. McDonald's and Wendy's restaurants fit here. Wendy's is after the same lunchtime and dinner crowds that McDonald's is. Nevertheless, with its more expensive hamburgers, fries, shakes, and salads, Wendy's is less of a direct competitor to McDonald's than Burger King is. For example, Wendy's focuses on its fresh ingredients and its promise of quality food, which might attract customers who would have eaten at more expensive casual dining restaurants such as Applebee's.[46] A representative from Wendy's says, "Our brand is built on the quality of our food as opposed to other fast-food restaurants."[47]

In Quadrant III, the very small overlap shows two companies with different competitive resources and little market commonality. McDonald's and Luby's Cafeterias fit here. Although both are in the fast-food business, there's almost no overlap in terms of products and customers. Luby's sells baked chicken, turkey, roasts, meat loaf, and vegetables, none of which are available at McDonald's. Furthermore, Luby's customers aren't likely to eat at McDonald's. In fact, Luby's is not really competing with other fast-food restaurants, but with eating at home. Company surveys show that close to half of the customers would have eaten at home, not at another restaurant, if they hadn't come to Luby's.[48]

Kobo e-reader, Borders responded to its two competitors' price cuts by offering a $20 Borders gift card with the purchase of each Kobo.[53]

Market commonality and resource similarity determine the likelihood of an attack or response, that is, whether a company is likely to attack a direct competitor or to strike back with a strong response when attacked. When market commonality is large and companies have overlapping products, services, or customers in multiple markets, there is less motivation to attack and more motivation to respond to an attack. The reason for this is straightforward: When firms are direct competitors in a large number of markets, they have a great deal at stake. So when Barnes & Noble launched an aggressive price war, Amazon had no choice but to respond by cutting its own prices. With competing products like the Kobo and new e-readers from Acer and Sony, the e-reader space was already becoming crowded before an outside threat (Apple's iPad) may have forced Amazon and Barnes & Noble to quickly cut prices. While the Nook and Kindle are dedicated e-readers, the iPad is a multi-purpose tablet, with more advanced touch features, color display, and much broader functional capabilities. The iPad's threat to Barnes & Noble's Nook and Amazon's Kindle became clear when Apple CEO Steve Jobs announced that iPad users had purchased more than 5 million e-books in the two months since its release (that's roughly 2.5 books per iPad). Indeed, soon after the introduction of the iPad, Amazon introduced a lighter, thinner, faster, and cheaper ($139) Kindle with a better screen and twice as much storage capability (up to 3,500 books).[54]

Whereas market commonality affects the likelihood of an attack or a response to an attack, resource similarity largely affects response capability, that is, how quickly and forcefully a company can respond to an attack. When resource similarity is high, the responding firm will generally be able to match the strategic moves of the attacking firm. Consequently, a firm is less likely to attack firms with similar levels of resources because it is unlikely to gain a sustainable advantage when the responding firms strike back. On the other hand, if one firm is substantially stronger than another (i.e., low resource similarity), then a competitive attack is more likely to produce a sustainable competitive advantage.

In general, the more moves (i.e., attacks) a company initiates against direct competitors and the greater a company's tendency to respond when attacked, the better its performance. More specifically, attackers and early responders (companies that are quick to launch a retaliatory attack) tend to gain market share and profits at the expense of late responders. This is not to suggest that a "full-attack" strategy always works best. In fact, attacks can provoke harsh retaliatory responses. When it first came on the market, Sony's PlayStation 3 (PS3) cost $599, but it came with an 80-GB

RED OCEAN, BLUE OCEAN

Using the ocean as a metaphor, Professors Renée Mauborgne and W. Chan Kim describe highly competitive markets as shark-infested waters. The water is red with blood from continual attacks and responses, and any gains made by one company are incremental at best and bound to be ceded in the next shark fight.

The only hope for survival is to pursue innovations that take you out of the red ocean and into the deep blue ocean, where there are no competitors. If it sounds hard, it is; but it's not impossible. Cirque du Soleil created a whole new category of entertainment; Gmail lets you store almost unlimited amounts of email for free; and Nintendo's Wii has redefined videogaming with simple games that combine elements of virtual reality.

Reprinted from Omega 36 (August 2008), C. Kim, K. Yang, and J. Kim, "A Strategy for Third-Party Logistics Systems: A Case Analysis Using the Blue Ocean Strategy, pp. 522–534. Copyright © 2007, with permission from Elsevier.

hard drive and a then-rare Blu-ray disc player. Sales lagged. However, Nintendo's Wii game console cost $249 and Microsoft's Xbox 360 game console cost $400. So Sony cut the price of the 80-GB PS3 to $499 and introduced a 40-GB PS3 for $399.90. Microsoft responded over the next 4 years with a combination of price cuts from which Sony has yet to recover, cutting the Xbox 360 with a 20-GB hard drive from $349 to $299, then cutting the price of an Xbox 360 with a 60-GB hard drive from $349 to $299, and cutting a 120-GB Xbox 360 from $399 to $299.[55] Sony's PS3 sales have continued to slow, running at about 20 percent of Wii sales and 40 percent of Xbox 360 sales.[56] Consequently, when deciding when, where, and what strategic actions to take against a direct competitor, managers should always consider the possibility of retaliation.

STUDENT Study Tools

Located at the back of your book:

☐ Rip out and study the Chapter Review Card at the end of the book

Log in to the CourseMate for MGMT at cengagebrain.com to:

☐ Review Key Term Flashcards delivered 3 ways (print or online)

☐ Complete both Practice Quizzes to prepare for tests

☐ Play Beat the Clock and Quizbowl to master concepts

☐ Complete the Crossword Puzzle to review key terms

☐ Watch the video on Numi Organic Tea for a real company example and take the accompanying quiz

☐ Watch the Biz Flix clip from *Field of Dreams* and take the quiz

☐ Complete the Case Assignment on Starbucks

☐ Work through the Management Decision on dealing with competitors

☐ Work through the Management Team Decision on video games

☐ Develop your skills with the Develop Your Career Potential exercise

7 | Innovation and Change

© iStockphoto.com/Marcello Bortolino

LEARNING OUTCOMES:

1. explain why innovation matters to companies.

2. discuss the different methods that managers can use to manage innovation in their organizations effectively.

3. discuss why not changing can lead to organizational decline.

4. discuss the different methods that managers can use to better manage change as it occurs.

Chapter 7

Organizational Innovation

Sometimes the solution to a problem causes another problem. Jernhusen AB, a Swedish property-administration firm, is building a new office and retail building near Stockholm's Central Station. Problem number one: How should they heat it? Problem number two: How should they get rid of excess heat in the train station, generated by the 250,000 people who pass through it every day? As Karl Sundholm, a representative of Jernhusen, puts it, "All people produce heat, and that heat is in fact fairly difficult to get rid of. Instead of opening windows and letting all that heat go to waste we want to harness it through the ventilation system." The innovative solution to both problems: Convert the heat in the station to hot water and pump it through the heating system of the new building using pipes that connect the building to the station. Sundholm estimates the system will cost about 300,000 kronor (32,000 Euros; US$47,000) to install, and it is likely to reduce energy consumption by 15 percent. Per Berggren, Jernhusen's managing director, notes, "It's more like thinking out of the box, being environmentally smart."[1]

Organizational innovation is the successful implementation of creative ideas in an organization.[2] **Creativity,** which is a form of organizational innovation, is the production of novel and useful ideas.[3] In the first part of this chapter, you will learn why innovation matters and how to manage innovation to create and sustain a competitive advantage. In the second part, you will learn about **organizational change,** which is a difference in the form, quality, or condition of an organization over time.[4] You will also learn about the risk of not changing and the ways in which companies can manage change. But first, let's deal with organizational innovations such as using body heat to warm buildings.[5]

After reading the next two sections, you should be able to

1 explain why innovation matters to companies.

2 discuss the different methods that managers can use to manage innovation in their organizations effectively.

1 Why Innovation Matters

We can only guess what changes technological innovations will bring in the next twenty years. Will we carry computers in our pockets? Will solar power and wind power get cheap and efficient enough so that your home has a standalone power source off the main electrical grid? And will HD TVs, now the standard, be replaced by HD holographic pictures (think of R2D2 projecting Princess Leia in *Star*

Organizational innovation the successful implementation of creative ideas in organizations

Creativity the production of novel and useful ideas

Organizational change a difference in the form, quality, or condition of an organization over time

Wars) that project lifelike 3-D images?[6] Who knows? The only thing we do know for sure about the next 20 years is that innovation will continue to change our lives.

Let's begin our discussion of innovation by learning about: 1.1 technology cycles and 1.2 innovation streams.

1.1 | TECHNOLOGY CYCLES

In Chapter 3, you learned that *technology* consists of the knowledge, tools, and techniques used to transform inputs (raw materials, information, etc.) into outputs (products and services). A **technology cycle** begins with the birth of a new technology and ends when that technology reaches its limits and dies as it is replaced by a newer, substantially better technology.[7] For example, technology cycles occurred when air-conditioning supplanted fans, when Henry Ford's Model T replaced horse-drawn carriages, and when planes replaced trains as a means of cross-country travel.

From Gutenberg's invention of the printing press in the 1400s to the rapid advance of the Internet, studies of hundreds of technological innovations have shown that nearly all technology cycles follow the typical **S-curve pattern of innovation** shown in Exhibit 7.1.[8] Early in a technology cycle, there is still much to learn, so progress is slow, as depicted by point A on the S-curve. The flat slope indicates that increased effort (i.e., money, research and development) brings only small improvements in technological performance. Fortunately, as the new technology matures, researchers figure out how to get better performance from it. This is represented by point B of the S-curve in Exhibit 7.1. The steeper slope indicates that small amounts of effort will result in significant increases in performance. At point C, the flat slope again indicates that further efforts to develop this particular technology will result in only small increases in performance. More importantly, how-ever, point C indicates that the performance limits of that particular technology are being reached. In other words, additional significant improvements in performance are highly unlikely.

Intel's technology cycles have followed this pattern. Intel spends billions to develop new computer chips and to build new facilities to produce them. Intel has found that the technology cycle for its integrated circuits is about three years. In each three-year cycle, Intel spends billions to introduce a new chip, improves the chip by making it a little bit faster each year, and then replaces that chip at the end of the cycle with a brand new, different chip that is substantially faster than the old chip. At first, though (point A), the billions Intel spends typically produce only small improvements in performance. But after six months to a year with a new chip design, Intel's engineering and production people typically figure out how to make the new chips much faster than they were initially (point B). Yet, despite impressive gains in performance, Intel is unable to make a particular computer chip run any faster because the chip reaches its design limits.

After a technology has reached its limits at the top of the S-curve, significant improvements in performance usually come from radical new designs or new performance-enhancing materials (point C). In Exhibit 7.1, that new technology is represented by the second S-curve. The changeover or discontinuity between the old and new technologies is represented by the dotted line. At first, the old and new technologies will likely coexist. Eventually, however, the new technology will replace the old technology. When that happens, the old technology cycle will be complete, and a new one will have started. The changeover between Intel's newer and older computer chip designs typically takes about one year. Over time, improving existing technology (tweaking the performance of the current technology cycle), combined with replacing old technology with new technology cycles (i.e., new, faster computer chip designs replacing older ones), has increased the speed of Intel's computer processors by a factor of 70 in just nineteen years.

Though the evolution of Intel's chips has been used to illustrate S-curves and technology cycles, it's

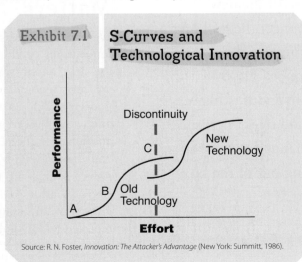

Exhibit 7.1 | **S-Curves and Technological Innovation**

Source: R. N. Foster, *Innovation: The Attacker's Advantage* (New York: Summitt, 1986).

important to note that technology cycles and technological innovation don't necessarily involve faster computer chips or cleaner-burning automobile engines. Remember, *technology* is simply the knowledge, tools, and techniques used to transform inputs into outputs. So a technology cycle occurs whenever there are major advances or changes in the *knowledge, tools,* and *techniques* of a field or discipline, whatever they may be. For example, one of the most important technology cycles in the history of civilization occurred in 1859, when 1,300 miles of central sewer line were constructed throughout London to carry human waste to the sea more than eleven miles away. This sewer system replaced the practice of dumping raw sewage into streets, where it drained into public wells that supplied drinking water. Preventing waste runoff from contaminating water supplies stopped the spread of cholera, which had killed millions of people for centuries in cities throughout the world.[9] Indeed, the water you drink today is safe thanks to this technological breakthrough. So, when you think about technology cycles, don't automatically think "high technology." Instead, broaden your perspective by considering advances or changes in any kind of knowledge, tools, and techniques.

1.2 | INNOVATION STREAMS

In Chapter 6, you learned that organizations can create *competitive advantage* for themselves if they have a *distinctive competence* that allows them to make, do, or perform something better than their competitors can. A competitive advantage becomes sustainable if other companies cannot duplicate the benefits obtained from that distinctive competence. Technological innovation can enable competitors to duplicate the benefits obtained from a company's distinctive advantage. It can also quickly turn a company's competitive advantage into a competitive disadvantage. For more than 110 years, Eastman Kodak was the dominant producer of photographic film worldwide. That is, until Kodak invented the digital camera (patent 4,131,919). But Kodak itself was unprepared for the rapid acceptance of its new technology, and its managers watched film quickly become obsolete for the majority of camera users. Technological innovation turned Kodak's competitive advantage into a competitive disadvantage.[10]

As the Kodak example shows, companies that want to sustain a competitive advantage must understand and protect themselves from the strategic threats of innovation. Over the long run, the best way for a company to do that is to create a stream of its own innovative ideas and products year after year. Consequently, we define **innovation streams** as patterns of innovation over time that can create sustainable competitive advantage.[11] Exhibit 7.2 on the next page shows a typical innovation consisting of a series of technology cycles. Recall that a technology cycle begins with a new technology and ends when that technology is replaced by a newer, substantially better technology. The innovation stream in Exhibit 7.2 shows three such technology cycles.

An innovation stream begins with a **technological discontinuity**, in which a scientific advance or a unique combination of existing technologies creates a significant breakthrough in performance or function. Technological discontinuities are followed by a **discontinuous change**, which is characterized by technological

Innovation streams patterns of innovation over time that can create sustainable competitive advantage

Technological discontinuity when a scientific advance or a unique combination of existing technologies creates a significant breakthrough in performance or function

Discontinuous change the phase of a technology cycle characterized by technological substitution and design competition

For more than a century, Kodak was a pioneer in photographic film. But with the exploding popularity of digital photography, Kodak found itself struggling to remain competitive. For that reason, the firm decided to abandon the declining film market, choosing instead to focus on three areas: digital cameras, the supplies used by retail photo printers, and inkjet photo printers for consumers and businesses.

Sources: R. Tomsho, "Kodak to Take Kodachrome Away," *Wall Street Journal*, June 23, 2009, B1; "Industry Snapshot," *Time*, December 5, 2005, 110; W. Symonds, "Kodak: Is This the Darkest Hour?" *BusinessWeek Online*, August 8, 2006, 3; W. Bulkeley, "Kodak CEO Bets Big on Printers—Perez Says Cash Is Sufficient As Camera Icon Tries to Crack Inkjet Market," *Wall Street Journal*, July 8, 2009, B6.

Technological substitution the purchase of new technologies to replace older ones

Design competition competition between old and new technologies to establish a new technological standard or dominant design

Dominant design a new technological design or process that becomes the accepted market standard

substitution and design competition. **Technological substitution** occurs when customers then purchase new technologies to replace older technologies.

Discontinuous change is also characterized by **design competition,** in which the old technology and several different new technologies compete to establish a new technological standard or dominant design. For example, Toshiba and Sony competed for dominance in a new standard format for home video, Toshiba with its HD DVD technology and Sony with Blu-ray. Because of large investments in old technology, and because the new and old technologies are often incompatible with each other, companies and consumers are reluctant to switch to a different technology during a design competition. Toshiba lost the competition because Warner Bros., which had been using both

technologies, decided to go exclusively with Blu-ray. Retailers followed suit, announcing intentions to focus on Blu-ray equipment and videos. Some "early adopters" of HD DVD will continue to use the technology for their collections, but most people will eventually use Blu-ray because it will dominate the market.[12] In addition, during design competition, the older technology usually improves significantly in response to the competitive threat from the new technologies; this response also slows the changeover from older to newer technologies.

Discontinuous change is followed by the emergence of a **dominant design,** which becomes the new accepted market standard for technology.[13] Dominant designs emerge in several ways. One is critical mass, meaning that a particular technology can become the dominant design simply because most people use it. At the time of Warner Bros.' exclusive adoption of Blu-ray, Blu-ray held 64 percent of the market compared to 36 percent for HD DVD.[14] Toshiba dropped HD DVD in part because, with a critical mass of Blu-ray adopters, Blu-ray had become the dominant design.

The best technology doesn't always become the dominant design, because a number of other factors come into play. For instance, a design can also become dominant if it solves a practical problem. For example, the QWERTY keyboard (named for the top left line of letters) became the dominant design for typewriters because it slowed typists who caused mechanical typewriter keys to jam because they typed too fast. Though computers can easily be switched to the DVORAK keyboard layout, which doubles typing speed and cuts typing errors by half, QWERTY lives on as the standard keyboard. In this instance, the QWERTY keyboard solved a problem that, with computers, is no longer relevant. Yet it remains the dominant technology because most people learned to type that way and continue to use it.

Dominant designs can also emerge through independent standards bodies. The International Telecommunications Union (ITU; http://www.itu.ch) is an independent organization that establishes standards for the communications industry. The ITU was founded in Paris in 1865 because European countries all had different telegraph systems that could not communicate with each other. After three months of negotiations, 20 countries signed the International Telegraph Con-

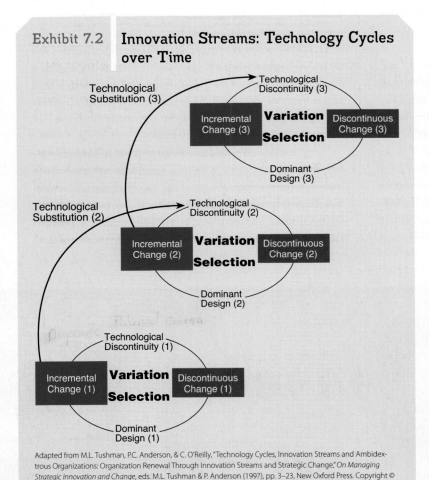

Exhibit 7.2   Innovation Streams: Technology Cycles over Time

Technological Substitution (3)

Technological Discontinuity (3)

Incremental Change (3)   **Variation**   Discontinuous Change (3)

Selection

Dominant Design (3)

Technological Substitution (2)

Technological Discontinuity (2)

Incremental Change (2)   **Variation**   Discontinuous Change (2)

Selection

Dominant Design (2)

Technological Discontinuity (1)

Incremental Change (1)   **Variation**   Discontinuous Change (1)

Selection

Dominant Design (1)

Adapted from M.L. Tushman, P.C. Anderson, & C. O'Reilly, "Technology Cycles, Innovation Streams and Ambidextrous Organizations: Organization Renewal Through Innovation Streams and Strategic Change," *On Managing Strategic Innovation and Change*, eds. M.L. Tushman & P. Anderson (1997), pp. 3–23, New Oxford Press. Copyright © by Oxford University Press, Inc. Used by permission of Oxford University Press, Inc.

Toshiba experienced a technological lockout when consumers adopted Blu-ray technology over its HD DVD technology. Blu-ray became the dominant design, and eventually Toshiba stopped producing its HD DVD players.

AP Images/Paul Sakuma

vention, which standardized equipment and instructions, enabling telegraph messages to flow seamlessly from country to country. Today, as in 1865, various standards are proposed, discussed, negotiated, and changed until an agreement is reached on a final set of standards that communication industries (i.e., Internet, telephone, satellites, radio, etc.) will follow worldwide.

For example, because most cell phones have different charger interfaces (i.e., plugs) and electrical requirements, you've probably had to buy new chargers—one for home, one for work, and one for your car—each time you got a new cell phone. That's now a thing of the past as the ITU has adopted a micro-USB standard (look at the connector that plugs into your digital camera) that could be used with any phone. This new standard will not only make it easy to borrow someone else's charger when you leave yours at home, it will also prevent consumers from throwing away 51,000 tons of obsolete chargers each year. The new chargers are also much more energy efficient.[15]

No matter how it happens, the emergence of a dominant design is a key event in an innovation stream. First, the emergence of a dominant design indicates that there are winners and losers. Technological innovation both enhances and destroys competence. Companies that bet on the now-dominant design usually prosper. By contrast, when companies bet on the wrong design or the old technology, they may experience **technological lockout**, which occurs when a new dominant design (i.e., a significantly better technology) prevents a company from competitively selling its products or makes it difficult to do so.[16] For example, Toshiba stopped producing HD DVD players because a critical mass of consumers adopted Blu-ray technology, which became the dominant design. Toshiba will continue to make spare parts for existing machines and may apply the technol-

ogy to downloading online videos. But it will shift its business strategy to other sectors, such as flash drives, which are beginning to replace hard drives in computers.[17] In fact, more companies are likely to go out of business in a time of discontinuous change and changing standards than in an economic recession or slowdown.

Second, the emergence of a dominant design signals a shift from design experimentation and competition to **incremental change**, a phase in which companies innovate by lowering the cost and improving the functioning and performance of the dominant design. For example, manufacturing efficiencies enable Intel to cut the cost of its chips by one-half to two-thirds during a technology cycle, while doubling or tripling their speeds. This focus on improving the dominant design continues until the next technological discontinuity occurs.

2   Managing Innovation

One consequence of technology cycles and innovation streams is that managers must be equally good at managing innovation in two very different circumstances. First, during discontinuous change, companies must find a way to anticipate and survive the technological changes that can suddenly transform industry leaders into losers and industry unknowns into powerhouses. Companies that can't manage innovation following technological discontinuities risk quick organizational decline and dissolution. Second, after a new dominant design emerges following discontinuous change, companies must manage the very different process of incremental improvement and innovation. Companies that can't manage incremental innovation slowly deteriorate as they fall farther behind industry leaders.

Unfortunately, what works well when managing innovation during discontinuous change doesn't work well when managing innovation during periods of incremental change (and vice versa). *Consequently, to successfully manage innovation streams, companies need to be good at three things: 2.1 managing sources of*

Technological lockout when a new dominant design (i.e., a significantly better technology) prevents a company from competitively selling its products or makes it difficult to do so

Incremental change the phase of a technology cycle in which companies innovate by lowering costs and improving the functioning and performance of the dominant technological design

Creative work environments workplace cultures in which workers perceive that new ideas are welcomed, valued, and encouraged

Flow a psychological state of effortlessness, in which you become completely absorbed in what you're doing and time seems to pass quickly

innovation, 2.2 managing innovation during discontinuous change, and 2.3 managing innovation during incremental change.

2.1 | MANAGING SOURCES OF INNOVATION

Innovation comes from great ideas. So a starting point for managing innovation is to manage the sources of innovation, that is, where new ideas come from. One place that new ideas originate is brilliant inventors. But only a few companies have the likes of an Edison, Marconi, or Graham Bell working for them. Given that great thinkers and inventors are in short supply, what might companies do to ensure a steady flow of good ideas?

Well, when we say that innovation begins with great ideas, we're really saying that innovation begins with creativity. As we defined it at the beginning of this chapter, creativity is the production of novel and useful ideas.[18] Although companies can't command employees to be creative ("You *will* be more creative!"), they can jump-start innovation by building **creative work environments** in which workers perceive that creative thoughts and ideas are welcomed and valued. As Exhibit 7.3 shows, creative work environments have six components that encourage creativity: challenging work, organizational encouragement, supervisory encouragement, work group encouragement, freedom, and a lack of organizational impediments.[19] Leaders at the Tata Group, a conglomerate based in India that produces everything from coffee to cars, encourage every employee to think and act like an innovator. The company allows every employee to use 10 percent of the work week for personal projects, whether it's to learn a new skill, develop an idea, or pursue a personal interest. The company also launched IdeaMax, a social-networking site on which employees can submit their creative ideas and critique others'. Through this support, Tata leaders hope to create an innovative environment by encouraging employees at all levels to share ideas and by fostering "a culture of creative dissatisfaction with the status quo."[20]

Work is *challenging* when it requires effort, demands attention and focus, and is perceived as important to others in the organization. According to researcher Mihaly Csikszentmihalyi (pronounced ME-high-lee CHICK-sent-me-high-ee), challenging work promotes creativity because it creates a rewarding psychological experience known as "flow." **Flow** is a psychological state of effortlessness, in which you become completely absorbed in what you're doing and time seems to fly.[21] A key part of creating flow experiences, and thus creative work environments, is to achieve a balance between skills and task challenge. Workers become bored when they can do more than is required of them and anxious when their skills aren't sufficient to accomplish a task. When skills and task challenge are balanced, however, flow and creativity can occur.

A creative work environment requires three kinds of encouragement: organizational, supervisory, and work group encouragement. *Organizational encouragement* of creativity occurs when management encourages risk taking and new ideas, supports and fairly evaluates new ideas, rewards and recognizes creativity, and encourages the sharing of new ideas throughout different parts of the company. Many companies keep technology on a tight leash. But Douglas Merrill, chief information officer at Google, allows employees to use whatever hardware, operating systems, and software help them be creative and get the job done efficiently, whether Google or another company designed them.[22] *Supervisory encouragement* of creativity occurs when supervisors provide clear goals, encourage open interaction with subordinates, and actively support development teams' work and ideas. *Work group encouragement* occurs when group members have diverse experience, education, and backgrounds and the group fosters mutual openness to ideas; positive, constructive challenge to ideas; and shared commitment to ideas.

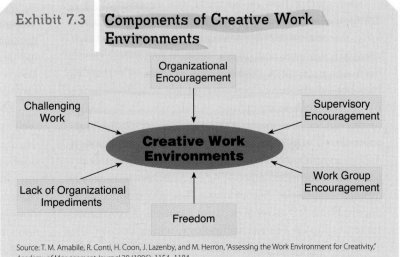

Exhibit 7.3 Components of Creative Work Environments

Source: T. M. Amabile, R. Conti, H. Coon, J. Lazenby, and M. Herron, "Assessing the Work Environment for Creativity," *Academy of Management Journal* 39 (1996): 1154–1184.

A great example of organizational and supervisory encouragement is found in Philip A. Newbold, the CEO of Memorial Hospital in South Bend, Indiana, who goes to unconventional lengths to spur innovation. His hospital was the first in the United States to establish an innovation research and development (R&D) budget, and Newbold encourages collaboration with other, innovative firms. He also created the Innovation Café, a refurbished deli that serves as an inviting place where colleagues can come and share ideas and learn how to innovate. Finally, Newbold emphasizes the value of creativity by giving out the "good try" award, a prize that is focused solely on a project's creativity, rather than its feasibility.[23]

Freedom means having autonomy over one's day-to-day work and a sense of ownership and control over one's ideas. Numerous studies have indicated that creative ideas thrive under conditions of freedom. At Dunkin' Donuts, members of the Culinary Innovation Team are given the freedom to explore new areas, whether it's testing 28 varieties of shortening or spending three months researching new potato products.[24]

To foster creativity, companies may also have to *remove impediments* to creativity from their work environments. Internal conflict and power struggles, rigid management structures, and a conservative bias toward the status quo can all discourage creativity. They create the perception that others in the organization will decide which ideas are acceptable and deserve support.

2.2 | EXPERIENTIAL APPROACH: MANAGING INNOVATION DURING DISCONTINUOUS CHANGE

A study of 72 product-development projects (i.e., innovation) in 36 computer companies across the United States, Europe, and Asia sheds light on how to manage innovation. Companies that succeeded in periods of discontinuous change (characterized by technological substitution and design competition, as described earlier) typically followed an experiential approach to

Reverse Innovation

For most companies involved in global business, innovation flows "downward." That is, a product or service is created in a developed economy, such as in the United States, and then adapted for sale in emerging economies. For example, Kentucky Fried Chicken first established itself as a fast-food chain in the United States and then expanded internationally. General Electric, however, has created an innovation in innovation, so to speak. In what the company calls "reverse innovation," new products are first developed in emerging economies and then adapted for and distributed to developed countries. For example, GE's researchers in India created a handheld electrocardiogram device (a machine that records heart activity), while GE teams in China came up with a portable ultrasound scanner that is slightly larger than an iPod. Both devices were developed to meet the needs of local doctors who needed affordable, lightweight, and portable diagnostic tools that they could take to service patients in rural areas, but both devices also help GE offer lower prices than its competitors in the United States and other developed markets. According to Vijay Govindarajan and Chris Trimble, professors at Dartmouth University, reverse innovation allows GE to expand into emerging economies and prevent competitors from selling similar products. Rethinking the direction of innovation has allowed GE to be more competitive at home and abroad.

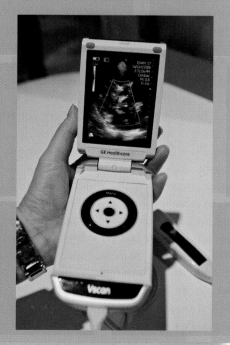

Source: K. Shwiff, "GE CEO Touts 'Reverse Innovation' Model," *Wall Street Journal*, September 23, 2009, accessed on December 1, 2009, http://online.wsj.com/article/NA_WSJ_PUB:SB125364544835231531.html.

innovation.[25] The **experiential approach to innovation** assumes that innovation is occurring within a highly uncertain environment and that the key to fast product innovation is to use intuition, flexible options, and hands-on experience to reduce uncertainty and accelerate learning and understanding. The experiential approach to innovation has five aspects: design iterations, testing, milestones, multifunctional teams, and powerful leaders.[26]

An iteration is a repetition. So a **design iteration** is a cycle of repetition in which a company tests a prototype of a new product or service, improves on the design, and then builds and tests the improved product or service prototype. A **product prototype** is a full-scale working model that is being tested for design, function, and reliability. **Testing** is a systematic comparison of different product designs or design iterations. Companies that want to create a new dominant design following a technological discontinuity quickly build, test, improve, and retest a series of different product prototypes. Many software companies check the quality of new products through a beta test, in which users are given free access to software in exchange for feedback. Before Microsoft released its Office 2010 package, it was downloaded, tested, and evaluated in real-world settings by more than 9 million people.[27]

By trying a number of very different designs or making successive improvements and changes in the same design, frequent design iterations reduce uncertainty and improve understanding. Simply put, the more prototypes you build, the more likely you are to learn what works and what doesn't. Also, when designers and engineers build a number of prototypes, they are less likely to fall in love with a particular prototype. Instead, they'll be more concerned with improving the product or technology as much as they can. Testing speeds up and improves the innovation process, too. When two very different design prototypes are tested against each other or the new design iteration is tested against the previous iteration, product design strengths and weaknesses quickly become apparent. Likewise, testing uncovers errors early in the design process, when they are easiest to correct. Finally, testing accelerates learning and understanding by forcing engineers and product designers to examine hard data about product performance. When there's hard evidence that prototypes are testing well, the confidence of the design team grows. Also, personal conflict between design team members is less likely when testing focuses on hard measurements and facts rather than personal hunches and preferences.

Milestones are formal project review points used to assess progress and performance. For example, a company that has put itself on a 12-month schedule to complete a project might schedule milestones at the 3-month, 6-month, and 9-month points on the schedule. By making people regularly assess what they're doing, how well they're performing, and whether they need to take corrective action, milestones provide structure to the general chaos that follows technological discontinuities. Milestones also shorten the innovation process by creating a sense of urgency that keeps everyone on task.

Multifunctional teams are work teams composed of people from different departments. Multifunctional teams accelerate learning and understanding by mixing and integrating technical, marketing, and manufacturing activities. By involving all key departments in development from the start, multifunctional teams speed innovation through early identification of new ideas or problems that would typically not have been generated or addressed until much later.

Powerful leaders provide the vision, discipline, and motivation to keep the innovation process focused, on time, and on target. Powerful leaders are able to get resources when they are needed, are typically more experienced, have high status in the company, and are held directly responsible for the product's success or failure. On average, powerful leaders can get innovation-related projects done nine months faster than leaders with little power or influence.

2.3 | COMPRESSION APPROACH: MANAGING INNOVATION DURING INCREMENTAL CHANGE

Whereas the experiential approach is used to manage innovation in highly uncertain environments during periods of discontinuous change, the compression approach is used to manage innovation in more certain environments during periods of incremental change. Whereas the goals of the experiential approach are significant improvements in performance and the establishment of a *new* dominant design, the goals of the compression approach are lower costs and incremental improvements in the performance and function of the *existing* dominant design.

The general strategies in each approach are different, too. With the experiential approach, the general strategy is to build something new, different, and substantially better. Because there's so much uncertainty—no one knows which technology will become the market leader—companies adopt a winner-take-all approach by trying to create the market-leading, dominant design. With the compression approach, the general strategy is to compress the time and steps needed to bring about small, consistent improvements in performance and functionality. Because a dominant technology design already exists, the general strategy is to continue improving the existing technology as rapidly as possible.

In short, a **compression approach to innovation** assumes that innovation is a predictable process, that incremental innovation can be planned using a series of steps, and that compressing the time it takes to complete those steps can speed up innovation. The compression approach to innovation has five aspects: planning, supplier involvement, shortening the time of individual steps, overlapping steps, and multifunctional teams.[28]

In Chapter 5, *planning* was defined as choosing a goal and a method or strategy to achieve that goal. When *planning for incremental innovation*, the goal is to squeeze or compress development time as much as possible, and the general strategy is to create a series of planned steps to accomplish that goal. Planning for incremental innovation helps avoid unnecessary steps and enables developers to sequence steps in the right order to avoid wasted time and delays between steps. Planning also reduces misunderstandings and improves coordination.

Most planning for incremental innovation is based on the idea of generational change. **Generational change** occurs when incremental improvements are made to a dominant technological design such that the improved version of the technology is fully backward compatible with the older version.[29] Software is backward compatible if a new version of the software will work with files created by older versions. A key feature of Windows 7 is its XP Mode, which allows users to access older applications in the new operating system. This was a feature that was completely missing from Microsoft's much-criticized Windows Vista, which was Windows 7's predecessor.

Because the compression approach assumes that innovation can follow a series of preplanned steps, one of the ways to shorten development time is through *supplier involvement*. Delegating some of the preplanned steps in the innovation process to outside suppliers reduces the amount of work that internal development teams must do. Plus, suppliers provide an alternative source of ideas and expertise that can lead to better designs. Sysco, the largest foodservice distributor in North America, not only supplies restaurants and chefs with the ingredients they need, but also helps them find ways to improve their businesses through a free consulting business called Business Review. In this program, Sysco employees help restaurateurs select and use ingredients to maximize profitability, design menus so that the most profitable items catch customers' attentions, and train waitstaff to provide excellent customer service. For example, Everett Sanderson, a Houston restaurateur, approached Sysco with a problem—his cooks were throwing away 25 percent of salmon fillets because they kept sticking to the pans. Sysco chef Neil Doherty solved Sanderson's problem by recommending that he use a vegetable/olive oil mix. Not only did the product prevent salmon from sticking, preventing

Compression approach to innovation an approach to innovation that assumes that incremental innovation can be planned using a series of steps and that compressing those steps can speed innovation

Generational change change based on incremental improvements to a dominant technological design such that the improved technology is fully backward compatible with the older technology

> With the **experiential approach**, the general strategy is to build something new, different, and substantially better. . . . With the **compression approach**, . . . the general strategy is to continue improving the existing technology as rapidly as possible.

huge amounts of loss, it was also cheaper than other cooking oils that Sanderson had previously used.[30]

In general, the earlier suppliers are involved, the quicker they catch and prevent future problems, such as unrealistic designs or mismatched product specifications.

Another way to shorten development time is simply to *shorten the time of individual steps* in the innovation process. A common way to do that is through computer-aided design (CAD). CAD speeds up the design process by allowing designers and engineers to make and test design changes using computer models rather than expensive prototypes. CAD also speeds innovation by making it easy to see how design changes affect engineering, purchasing, and production.

In a sequential design process, each step must be completed before the next step begins. But sometimes multiple development steps can be performed at the same time. *Overlapping steps* shorten the development process by reducing delays or waiting time between steps. Summit Entertainment used overlapping steps to great success in producing the *Twilight* franchise. Using new directors and production crews, Summit began production on each film while the previous film was in post-production. This allowed the studio to release films at regular intervals in order to capitalize on the surprising success of the first film.[31]

Pine Chips to Fuel

The unending search for alternative fuels has led one Pennsylvania company to wood chips. Coskata operates a facility that converts pine chips into ethanol for use as a motor fuel. Using a high-temperature (8,000 degrees) plasma torch, the company transforms wood chips into hydrogen and carbon monoxide, which is fed to a tank of bacteria, which, in turn, excretes ethanol. Coskata claims it will be able to produce 100 gallons of ethanol from one ton of chips, at a cost of about $1 per gallon. For now, Coskata's facility only produces 50,000 gallons of ethanol per year, or about 1 percent of what most ethanol plants can produce. However, company executives and investors are optimistic that the firm will soon be able to produce fuel that is ecologically friendly and economically successful.

Source: M. L. Wald, "Industry Built from Scratch," *New York Times*, October 15, 2009, accessed July 22, 2010, http://www.nytimes.com/2009/10/15/business/energy -environment/15biofuel.html?_r=1&hp=&pagewanted=print.

Organizational Change

Companies that fail to change run the risk of organizational decline. Since its earliest days, Hershey was known for its innovative products, whether it was the first chocolate-covered caramels (1894) or the famous Hershey Kiss (1907). In more recent times, Hershey's innovation pipeline has become clogged. Earlier this decade, Hershey released more than 200 new products a year; in the first three quarters of 2009, it released just 40. Though Hershey's earnings rose 15.6 percent during the first half of 2009, that increase was due entirely to a rise in costs for ingredients (milk, sugar, etc.); actual sales declined 3 percent. With the lack of potential breakthrough products, Hershey runs the risk of alienating customers by charging more for the same products. What is more, experts fear that Hershey will not be able to respond once the economy recovers and demand for new, exciting products increases. In the long run, Hershey must reverse its declining interest in innovation, or face significant losses.[32]

After reading the next two sections, you should be able to

3 **discuss why not changing can lead to organizational decline.**

4 **discuss the different methods that managers can use to better manage change as it occurs.**

3 Organizational Decline: The Risk of Not Changing

Businesses operate in a constantly changing environment. Recognizing and adapting to internal and external changes can mean the difference between continued success and going out of business. Companies that fail to change run the risk of organizational decline.[33]

Organizational decline occurs when companies don't anticipate, recognize, neutralize, or adapt to the internal or external pressures that threaten their survival.[34] In other words, decline occurs when organizations don't recognize the need for change. General Motors' loss of market share in the automobile industry (from 52 to 22 percent) is an example of organizational decline.[35] There are five stages of organizational decline: blinded, inaction, faulty action, crisis, and dissolution.[36]

In the *blinded stage*, decline begins because key managers fail to recognize the internal or external changes that will harm their organizations. This blindness may be due to a simple lack of awareness about changes or an inability to understand their significance. It may also come from the overconfidence that can develop when a company has been successful.

In the *inaction stage*, as organizational performance problems become more visible, management may recognize the need to change but still take no action. The managers may be waiting to see if the problems will correct themselves, or they may find it difficult to change the practices and policies that previously led to success. Another possibility is that they wrongly assume that they can easily correct the problems, so they don't feel the situation is urgent.

In the *faulty action stage*, faced with rising costs and decreasing profits and market share, management will announce belt-tightening plans designed to cut costs, increase efficiency, and restore profits. In other words, rather than recognizing the need for fundamental changes, managers assume that if they just run a tighter ship, company performance will return to previous levels.

In the *crisis stage*, bankruptcy or dissolution (i.e., breaking up the company and selling its parts) is likely to occur unless the company completely reorganizes the way it does business. At this point, however, companies typically lack the resources to fully change how they run their businesses. Cutbacks and layoffs will have reduced the level of talent among employees. Furthermore, talented managers who were savvy enough to see the crisis coming will have found jobs with other companies, often with competitors.

In the *dissolution stage*, after failing to make the changes needed to sustain the organization, the company is dissolved through bankruptcy proceedings or by selling assets in order to pay suppliers, banks, and creditors. At this point, a new CEO may be brought in to oversee the closing of stores, offices, and manufacturing facilities, the final layoff of managers and employees, and the sale of assets.

It is important to note that decline is reversible at each of the first four stages, and that not all companies in decline reach final dissolution. After coming out of bankruptcy, GM tried to reverse decades of decline by closing dealerships, cutting labor costs, selling and discontinuing brands (Pontiac, Saab, and Saturn), and introducing innovative models, such as the electric-hybrid Chevrolet Volt. As a result of aggressive cost cutting and improvements in global sales, GM posted an $863 million profit a year after filing bankruptcy—its first quarterly profit in 3 years.[37]

4 Managing Change

According to social psychologist Kurt Lewin, change is a function of the forces that promote change and the opposing forces that slow or resist change.[38] **Change forces** lead to differences in the form, quality, or condition of an organization over time.

By contrast, **resistance forces** support the status quo, that is, the existing conditions in an organization. Change is difficult under any circumstances. In a study of heart bypass patients, doctors told participants straight forwardly to change their eating and health habits or they would die. Unbelievably, a full 90 percent of participants did *not* change their habits at all![39] This fierce resistance to change also applies to organizations.

Resistance to change is caused by self-interest, misunderstanding and distrust, and a general intolerance for change.[40] People resist change out of *self-interest* because they fear that change will cost or deprive them of something they value. For example, resistance might stem from a fear that the changes will result in a loss of

Organizational decline a large decrease in organizational performance that occurs when companies don't anticipate, recognize, neutralize, or adapt to the internal or external pressures that threaten their survival

Change forces forces that produce differences in the form, quality, or condition of an organization over time

Resistance forces forces that support the existing state of conditions in organizations

Resistance to change opposition to change resulting from self-interest, misunderstanding and distrust, and a general intolerance for change

Unfreezing getting the people affected by change to believe that change is needed

Change intervention the process used to get workers and managers to change their behavior and work practices

Refreezing supporting and reinforcing new changes so that they stick

pay, power, responsibility, or even perhaps one's job. The Associated Press (AP), a news agency employing more than 10,000 journalists all over the world, recently changed its policy on employees' use of social media. According to the policy, any material on an employee's Facebook site, even messages from friends, must conform to AP standards concerning decency and political neutrality. AP reporters resisted the change in policy not only because of the potential violation of free speech rights, but also because they could be suspended or fired for what other people post on their Facebook pages.[41]

People also resist change because of *misunderstanding and distrust;* they don't understand the change or the reasons for it, or they distrust the people—typically management—behind the change. Resistance isn't always visible at first, however. Some of the strongest resisters may initially support the changes in public, nodding and smiling their agreement, but then ignore the changes in private and do their jobs as they always have. Management consultant Michael Hammer calls this deadly form of resistance the "Kiss of Yes."[42]

Resistance may also come from a generally low tolerance for change. Some people are simply less capable of handling change than others are. People with a *low tolerance for change* feel threatened by the uncertainty associated with change and worry that they won't be able to learn the new skills and behaviors needed to successfully negotiate change in their companies.

Because resistance to change is inevitable, successful change efforts require careful management. In this section you will learn about **4.1 managing resistance to change, 4.2 what not to do when leading organizational change,** and **4.3 different change tools and techniques.**

4.1 | MANAGING RESISTANCE TO CHANGE

According to Kurt Lewin, managing organizational change is a basic process of unfreezing, change intervention, and refreezing. **Unfreezing** is getting the people affected by change to believe that change is needed. During the **change intervention** itself, workers and managers change their behavior and work practices. **Refreezing** is supporting and reinforcing the new changes so that they stick.

Resistance to change is an example of frozen behavior. Given the choice between changing and not changing, most people would rather not change. Because resistance to change is natural and inevitable, managers need to unfreeze resistance to change to create successful change programs. The following methods can be used to manage resistance to change: education and communication, participation, negotiation, top management support, and coercion.[43]

When resistance to change is based on insufficient, incorrect, or misleading information, managers should *educate* employees about the need for change and *communicate* change-related information to them. Managers must also supply the information and funding or other

---

A Change in Direction Needed at Toyota

For years, Toyota produced the highest-quality, most reliable cars in the world, but a series of highly publicized recalls, such as for faulty accelerators, damaged that reputation. Toyota, however, compounded its troubles through its slow response to these problems. With operations centrally located in Toyota City, Japan, and its chief engineers overseeing projects out of Toyota's headquarters, some speculate that top management was insulated and disconnected from customer complaints, ironically, just as the company began aggressively expanding into global markets. Add Toyota's famously inflexible culture, and the result is a major corporation that was incredibly slow to change.

While Toyota has since admitted to declines in the quality of its vehicles and has appointed a chief quality officer, Toyota president Akio Toyoda has shown little inclination to restructure the company, advocating instead a return to focusing on the basics. The question is whether that will be enough to solve Toyota's quality problems and to restore the company's reputation for reliable, high-quality cars.

Source: A. Taylor III, "How Toyota Lost Its Way," *Fortune,* July 26, 2010, 108–118.

iStockphoto.com/Robyn Mackenzie

support employees need to make changes. Executives at Novartis, a pharmaceutical company, were skeptical when CEO Dan Vasella enacted a new strategy. Rather than directing R&D based on what diseases were prevalent, Novartis would focus on drugs with proven scientific grounding, even if they were intended for rare conditions. To address fears, Vasella demonstrated that a focus on a smaller group of patients would lead to more effective therapies with fewer side effects and thus quicker regulatory approval and increased sales.[44]

Another way to reduce resistance to change is to have those affected by the change *participate in planning and implementing the change process.* Employees who participate have a better understanding of the change and the need for it. Furthermore, employee concerns about change can be addressed as they occur if employees participate in the planning and implementation process. The San Diego Zoo and Wild Animal Park took innovative steps in order to reposition itself as a leader in conservation. A core element of the plan was input from the zoo's staff, as the strategy team invited employees from all departments to provide insights on what they felt the zoo did well and what it could do better. Through this process, the zoo enacted a plan that would highlight its internal resources and capabilities through an expansion of its consulting business, through the use of facilities to display sustainable technology and products, and by hosting events that would highlight the knowledge of zoo scientists.[45]

Employees are also less likely to resist change if they are allowed to discuss and agree on who will do what after change occurs. Resistance to change also decreases when change efforts receive *significant managerial support.* Managers must do more than talk about the importance of change, however. They must provide the training, resources, and autonomy needed to make change happen. For example, with a distinguished 70-year history of hand-drawing Hollywood's most successful animated films (including *Snow White, Bambi, The Little Mermaid,* and *Beauty and the Beast*), animators at Walt Disney Company naturally resisted the move to computer-generated (CG) animation. So Disney supported the difficult change by putting all of its animators through a 6-month "CG Boot Camp," where they learned how to draw animated characters with computers.[46]

Finally, resistance to change can be managed through **coercion,** or the use of formal power and authority to force others to change. Because of the intense negative reactions it can create (e.g., fear, stress, resentment, sabotage of company products), coercion should be used only when a crisis exists or when all other attempts to reduce resistance to change have failed.

Coercion using formal power and authority to force others to change

4.2 | WHAT *NOT* TO DO WHEN LEADING CHANGE

So far, you've learned how to execute a basic change process (unfreezing, change, refreezing) and how to manage resistance to change. Harvard Business School professor John Kotter argues that knowing what *not* to do is just as important as knowing what to do when it comes to achieving successful organizational change.[47]

Managers commonly make certain errors when they lead change. The first two errors occur during the unfreezing phase, when managers try to get the people affected by change to believe that change is really needed. The first and potentially most serious error is *not establishing a great enough sense of urgency.* Indeed, Kotter estimates that more than half of all change efforts fail because the people affected are not convinced that change is necessary. People will feel a greater sense of urgency if a leader in the company makes a public, candid assessment of the company's problems and weaknesses.

The second mistake that occurs in the unfreezing process is *not creating a powerful enough coalition.* Change often starts with one or two people. But change has to be supported by a critical and growing group of people to build enough momentum to change an entire department, division, or company. Besides top management, Kotter recommends that key employees, managers, board members, customers, and even union leaders be members of a *core change coalition* that guides and supports organizational change. "In a turnaround, there are three kinds of employees," says Craig Muhlhauser, CEO of the electronics manufacturing services firm Celestica—those on your side, those on the fence, and those who will never buy in. The latter have to be let go and those on the fence should be persuaded to contribute or leave. Says Muhlhauser, "We have to make change, change is difficult and as we make change, it is important to realize that there are people who are going to resist that change. In talking to those people, the objective is to move everybody into the column of supporters. But that is probably unachievable."[48]

The next four errors that managers make occur during the change phase, when a change intervention is used to try to get workers and managers to change their behavior and work practices. *Lacking a vision*

© iStockphoto.com/Eric Isselée

MGMT SUCCESS

What to Do When Employees Resist Change

Unfreezing

- **Share reasons** for change with employees.
- **Empathize** with employees and managers for whom change is difficult.
- **Communicate** the details simply, clearly, extensively, verbally, and in writing.

Change

- **Explain** the benefits, "what's in it for them."
- **Champion** by identifying a respected manager to manage the change effort.
- **Create opportunities for feedback** from the people who will be affected by change.
- **Time it right** so that you don't begin change at a bad time, for example, during the busiest part of the year or month.
- **Offer security** for employees' jobs, if possible, to minimize fear of change.
- **Educate** employees to ensure they are both confident and competent to handle new requirements.
- **Don't rush** change. Proceed at a manageable pace.

Source: G. J. Iskat and J. Liebowitz, "What to Do When Employees Resist Change," *Supervision*, August 1, 1996.

for change is a significant error at this point. As you learned in Chapter 5, a *vision* is a statement of a company's purpose or reason for existing. A vision for change makes clear where a company or department is headed and why the change is occurring. Change efforts that lack vision tend to be confused, chaotic, and contradictory. By contrast, change efforts guided by visions are clear and easy to understand and can be effectively explained in five minutes or less.

Undercommunicating the vision by a factor of ten is another mistake in the change phase. According to Kotter, companies mistakenly hold just one meeting to announce the vision. Or, if the new vision receives heavy emphasis in executive speeches or company newsletters, senior management then undercuts the vision by behaving in ways contrary to it. Successful communication of the vision requires that top managers link everything the company does to the new vision and that they "walk the talk" by behaving in ways consistent with the vision.

Furthermore, even companies that begin change with a clear vision sometimes make the mistake of *not removing obstacles to the new vision.* They leave formidable barriers to change in place by failing to redesign jobs, pay plans, and technology to support the new way of doing things.

Another error in the change phase is *not systematically planning for and creating short-term wins.* Most people don't have the discipline and patience to wait two years to see if the new change effort works. Change is threatening and uncomfortable, so people need to see an immediate payoff if they are to continue to support it. Kotter recommends that managers create short-term wins by actively picking people and projects that are likely to work extremely well early in the change process.

The last two errors that managers make occur during the refreezing phase, when attempts are made to support and reinforce changes so that they stick. *Declaring victory too soon* is a tempting mistake in the refreezing phase. Managers typically declare victory right after the first large-scale success in the change process. Declaring success too early has the same effect as draining the gasoline out of a car: it stops change efforts dead in their tracks. With success declared, supporters of the change process stop pushing to make change happen. After all, why push when success has been achieved? Rather than declaring victory, managers should use the momentum from short-term wins to push for even bigger or faster changes. This maintains urgency and prevents change supporters from slacking off before the changes are frozen into the company's culture.

The last mistake that managers make is *not anchoring changes in the corporation's culture.* An organization's culture is the set of key values, beliefs, and attitudes shared by organizational members that determines the accepted way of doing things in a company. As you learned in Chapter 3, changing cultures is extremely difficult and slow. According to Kotter, two things help anchor changes in a corporation's culture. The first is directly showing people that the changes have actually improved performance. The second is to make sure that the people who get

MGMT SUCCESS

Errors Managers Make When Leading Change

Unfreezing

1. Not establishing a great enough sense of urgency.
2. Not creating a powerful enough guiding coalition.

Change

3. Lacking a vision.
4. Undercommunicating the vision by a factor of ten.
5. Not removing obstacles to the new vision.
6. Not systematically planning for and creating short-term wins.

Refreezing

7. Declaring victory too soon.
8. Not anchoring changes in the corporation's culture.

Source: J. P. Kotter, "Leading Change: Why Transformation Efforts Fail," *Harvard Business Review* 73, no. 2 (March–April 1995): 59.

promoted fit the new culture. If they don't, it's a clear sign that the changes were only temporary.

4.3 | CHANGE TOOLS AND TECHNIQUES

Imagine your boss came to you and said, "All right, genius, you wanted it. You're in charge of turning around the division." Where would you begin? How would you encourage change-resistant managers to change? What would you do to include others in the change process? How would you get the change process off to a quick start? Finally, what approach would you use to promote long-term effectiveness and performance? Results-driven change, the General Electric workout, and organizational development are three change tools and techniques that can be used to address these issues.

One of the reasons that organizational change efforts fail is that they are activity oriented rather than results oriented. In other words, they focus primarily on changing company procedures, management philosophy, or employee behavior. Typically, there is much buildup and preparation as consultants are brought in, presentations are made, books are read, and employees and managers are trained. There's a tremendous emphasis on doing things the new way. But, with all the focus on "doing," almost no attention is paid to *results*, to seeing if all this activity has actually made a difference.

By contrast, **results-driven change** supplants the emphasis on activity with a laser-like focus on quickly measuring and improving results.[49] Top managers at Hyundai knew that if they were to compete successfully against the likes of Honda and Toyota, they would have to improve the quality of their cars substantially. So top managers guided the company's results-driven change process by increasing the number of quality teams from 100 to 865. Then, all employees were required to attend seminars on quality improvement and use the results of industry quality studies as their benchmark. The results have been dramatic. According to J. D. Power and Associates, Hyundai ranked seventh among all auto manufacturers in initial quality, outpacing such brands as Toyota, BMW, and Infiniti, which have strong reputations for vehicle quality.[50]

Another advantage of results-driven change is that managers introduce changes in procedures, philosophy, or behavior only if they are likely to improve measured performance. In other words, changes are tested to see whether they actually make a difference. Consistent with this approach, Hyundai invested $30 million in a test center where cars were subjected to a sequence of extremely harsh conditions to allow engineers to pinpoint defects and fix problems.[51]

A third advantage of results-driven change is that quick, visible improvements motivate employees to continue to make additional changes to improve measured performance. Exhibit 7.4 on the next page describes the basic steps of results-driven change.

The **General Electric workout** is a special kind of results-driven change. The "workout" involves a three-day meeting that brings together managers and employees from different levels and parts of an organization to quickly generate and act on solutions to specific business problems.[52] On the first morning, the

Results-driven change change created quickly by focusing on the measurement and improvement of results

General Electric workout a three-day meeting in which managers and employees from different levels and parts of an organization quickly generate and act on solutions to specific business problems

Exhibit 7.4 How to Create a Results-Driven Change Program

1. Set measurable, short-term goals to improve performance.

2. Make sure your action steps are likely to improve measured performance.

3. Stress the importance of immediate improvements.

4. Solicit help from consultants and staffers to achieve quick improvements in performance.

5. Test action steps to see if they actually yield improvements. If they don't, discard them and establish new ones.

6. Use resources you have or that can be easily required. It doesn't take much.

Source: R. H. Schaffer and H. A. Thomson, "Successful Change Programs Begin with Results," *Harvard Business Review on Change* (Boston: Harvard Business School Press, 1998), 189–213.

Exhibit 7.5 General Steps for Organizational Development Interventions

1. Entry	A problem is discovered and the need for change becomes apparent. A search begins for someone to deal with the problem and facilitate change.
2. Startup	A change agent enters the picture and works to clarify the problem and gain commitment to a change effort.
3. Assessment & feedback	The change agent gathers information about the problem and provides feedback about it to decision makers and those affected by it.
4. Action planning	The change agent works with decision makers to develop an action plan.
5. Intervention	The action plan, or organizational development intervention, is carried out.
6. Evaluation	The change agent helps decision makers assess the effectiveness of the intervention.
7. Adoption	Organizational members accept ownership and responsibility for the change, which is then carried out through the entire organization.
8. Separation	The change agent leaves the organization after first ensuring that the change intervention will continue to work.

Source: W. J. Rothwell, R. Sullivan, and G. M. McLean, *Practicing Organizational Development: A Guide for Consultants* (San Diego: Pfeiffer & Co., 1995).

boss discusses the agenda and targets specific business problems that the group will solve. The boss then leaves, and an outside facilitator breaks the group (typically 30 to 40 people) into five or six teams and helps them spend the next day and a half discussing and debating solutions. On day three, in what GE calls a "town meeting," the teams present specific solutions to their boss, who has been gone since day one. As each team's spokesperson makes specific suggestions, the boss has only three options: agree on the spot, say no, or ask for more information so that a decision can be made by a specific, agreed-upon date.[53]

Organizational development a philosophy and collection of planned change interventions designed to improve an organization's long-term health and performance

Change agent the person formally in charge of guiding a change effort

Organizational development is a philosophy and collection of planned change interventions designed to improve an organization's long-term health and performance. Organizational development takes a long-range approach to change; assumes that top management support is necessary for change to succeed; creates change by educating workers and managers to change ideas, beliefs, and behaviors so that problems can be solved in new ways; and emphasizes employee participation in diagnosing, solving, and evaluating problems.[54] As shown in Exhibit 7.5, organizational development interventions begin with the recognition of a problem. Then, the company designates a **change agent** to be formally in charge of guiding the change effort. This person can be someone from the company or a professional consultant. The change agent clarifies

Exhibit 7.6 Different Kinds of Organizational Development Interventions

LARGE SYSTEM INTERVENTIONS

Sociotechnical systems	An intervention designed to improve how well employees use and adjust to the work technology used in an organization.
Survey feedback	An intervention that uses surveys to collect information from the members, reports the results of that survey to the members, and then uses those results to develop action plans for improvement.

SMALL GROUP INTERVENTIONS

Team building	An intervention designed to increase the cohesion and cooperation of work group members.
Unit goal setting	An intervention designed to help a work group establish short- and long-term goals.

PERSON-FOCUSED INTERVENTIONS

Counseling/ coaching	An intervention designed so that a formal helper or coach listens to managers or employees and advises them on how to deal with work or interpersonal problems.
Training	An intervention designed to provide individuals with the knowledge, skills, or attitudes they need to become more effective at their jobs.

Source: W. J. Rothwell, R. Sullivan, and G. M. McLean, *Practicing Organizational Development: A Guide for Consultants* (San Diego: Pfeiffer & Co., 1995).

the problem, gathers information, works with decision makers to create and implement an action plan, helps to evaluate the plan's effectiveness, implements the plan throughout the company, and then leaves (if from outside the company) after making sure the change intervention will continue to work.

Organizational development interventions are aimed at changing large systems, small groups, or people.[55] More specifically, the purpose of *large system interventions* is to change the character and performance of an organization, business unit, or department. *Small group intervention* focuses on assessing how a group functions and helping it work more effectively to accomplish its goals. *Person-focused intervention* is intended to increase interpersonal effectiveness by helping people become aware of their attitudes and behaviors and acquire new skills and knowledge. Exhibit 7.6 describes the most frequently used organizational development interventions for large systems, small groups, and people.

STUDENT Study Tools

Located at the back of your book:

☐ Rip out and study the Chapter Review Card at the end of the book

Log in to the CourseMate for MGMT at cengagebrain.com to:

☐ Review Key Term Flashcards delivered 3 ways (print or online)

☐ Complete both Practice Quizzes to prepare for tests

☐ Play Beat the Clock and Quizbowl to master concepts

☐ Complete the Crossword Puzzle to review key terms

☐ Watch the video on Scholfield Honda for a real company example and take the accompanying quiz

☐ Watch the Biz Flix clip from *Field of Dreams* and take the quiz

☐ Complete the Case Assignment on Starbucks

☐ Work through the Management Decision on dealing with competitors

☐ Work through the Management Team Decision on video games

☐ Develop your skills with the Develop Your Career Potential exercise

8 | Global Management

LEARNING OUTCOMES:

1 discuss the impact of global business and the trade rules and agreements that govern it.

2 explain why companies choose to standardize or adapt their business procedures.

3 explain the different ways that companies can organize to do business globally.

4 explain how to find a favorable business climate.

5 discuss the importance of identifying and adapting to cultural differences.

6 explain how to successfully prepare workers for international assignments.

Chapter 8

What Is Global Business?

global business is the buying and selling of goods and services by people from different countries. The Timex watch on my wrist as I write this chapter was purchased at a Wal-Mart in Texas. But since it was made in the Philippines, I participated in global business when I wrote Wal-Mart a check. Wal-Mart, for its part, had already paid Timex, which had paid the company that employs the Filipino managers and workers who made my watch.

Global business presents its own set of challenges for managers. How can you be sure that the way you run your business in one country is the right way to run that business in another? This chapter discusses how organizations answer that question. We will start by examining global business in two ways: first exploring its impact on U.S. businesses and then reviewing the basic rules and agreements that govern global trade. Next, we will examine how and when companies go global by examining the tradeoff between consistency and adaptation and discussing how to organize a global company. Finally, we will look at how companies decide where to expand globally, including finding the best business climate, adapting to cultural differences, and better preparing employees for international assignments. Of course, there is more to global business than buying imported products at Wal-Mart.

After reading the next section, you should be able to

1 **discuss the impact of global business and the trade rules and agreements that govern it.**

1 Global Business, Trade Rules, and Trade Agreements

If you want a simple demonstration of the impact of global business, look at the tag on your shirt, the inside of your shoes, and the inside of your cell phone (take your battery out). Chances are, all of these items were made in different places around the world. As I write this, my shirt, shoes, and cell phone were made in Thailand, China, and Korea, respectively. Where were yours made?

*Let's learn more about **1.1 the impact of global business, 1.2 how tariff and nontariff trade barriers have historically restricted global business, 1.3 how global and regional trade agreements today are reducing those trade barriers worldwide, and 1.4 how consumers are responding to those changes in trade rules and agreements.***

1.1 | THE IMPACT OF GLOBAL BUSINESS

Multinational corporations are corporations that own businesses in two or more countries. In 1970, more than half of the world's 7,000 multinational corporations were headquartered in only the United States and the United Kingdom. Today, there are 79,000 multinational corporations, more than 11 times as many as in 1970, and only 2,418, or 3.1 percent, are based in the United States.[1] Today, 56,448 multinationals, or 71.5 percent, are based in other developed countries (e.g., Germany, Italy, Canada, and Japan), and 20,586, or 26.1 percent, are based in developing countries (e.g., Colombia and South Africa). So, today, multinational companies can be found by the thousands all over the world!

Global business the buying and selling of goods and services by people from different countries

Multinational corporation a corporation that owns businesses in two or more countries

Another way to appreciate the impact of global business is by considering direct foreign investment. **Direct foreign investment** occurs when a company builds a new business or buys an existing business in a foreign country. Nokia Siemens Networks, operated jointly by Finland-based Nokia and Germany-based Siemens, made a direct foreign investment in the United States when it purchased Motorola's network equipment business for $1.2 billion.[2] Many other companies from other countries own businesses in the United States. Companies from the United Kingdom, Japan, the Netherlands, Canada, Germany, Switzerland, France, and Luxembourg have the largest direct foreign investment in the United States. Overall, foreign companies invest more than $2.3 trillion a year to do business in the United States.

Direct Foreign Investment in the United States

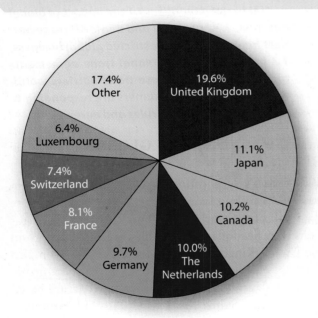

Source: M. Ibarra and J. Koncz, "Direct Investment Positions for 2007: Country and Industry Detail," accessed June 12, 2009, http://www.bea.gov/scb/pdf/2008/07%20July/0708_dip.pdf.

But direct foreign investment in the United States is only half the picture. U.S. companies also have made large direct foreign investments in countries throughout the world. For example, Hershey Co., a Pennsylvania-based candy company, purchased Barry Callebaut AG's Van Houten consumer chocolate business in Asia, allowing Hershey, which gets most of its growth from North America, to expand internationally.[3] U.S. companies have made their largest direct foreign investments in the United Kingdom, Japan, and the Netherlands. Overall, U.S. companies invest more than $3.5 trillion a year to do business in other countries.

U.S. Direct Foreign Investment Abroad

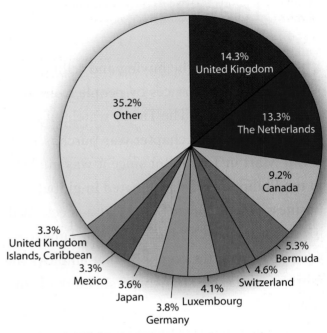

Source: M. Ibarra and J. Koncz, "Direct Investment Positions for 2007: Country and Industry Detail," accessed June 12, 2009, http://www.bea.gov/scb/pdf/2008/07%20July/0708_dip.pdf.

So, whether foreign companies invest in the United States or U.S. companies invest abroad, direct foreign investment is an increasingly important and common method of conducting global business.

1.2 | TRADE BARRIERS

Although today's consumers usually don't care where the products they buy come from (more on this in Section 1.4), national governments have traditionally preferred that consumers buy domestically made products in the hope that such purchases would increase the number of domestic businesses and workers. Indeed, governments have done much more than hope that people will buy from domestic companies. Historically, governments have actively used **trade barriers** to make it much more expensive or difficult (or sometimes impossible) for consumers to buy or consume imported goods. For example, the Chinese government adds a 105 percent tariff to the price of American chickens.[4] The U.S. government imposes a 35 percent tariff on imported Chinese tires.[5] By establishing these restrictions and taxes, the governments of the European Union, China, and the United States are engaging in **protectionism**, which is the use of trade barriers to protect domestic companies and their workers from foreign competition.

Governments have used two general kinds of barriers to trade: tariffs and nontariff barriers. A **tariff** is a direct tax on imported goods. Tariffs increase the costs of imported goods relative to those of domestic goods. **Nontariff barriers** are nontax methods of increasing the cost or reducing the volume of imported goods. There are five types of nontariff barriers: quotas, voluntary export restraints, government import standards, government subsidies, and customs classification. Because there are so many different kinds of nontariff barriers, they can be more potent than tariffs for shielding domestic industries from foreign competition.

Quotas are specific limits on the number or volume of imported products. For example, China has an annual limit of 20 foreign films that are allowed to be released in Chinese movie theaters.[6] Like quotas, **voluntary export restraints** limit the amount of a product that can be exported annually. The difference is that the exporting country rather than the importing country imposes restraints. Countries still impose such restrictions from time to time, however. For example, after a poor cotton crop created a shortage, both India and Pakistan imposed temporary export quotas on cotton and yarn to protect their textile industries.[7] Usually, however, the "voluntary" offer to limit exports occurs because the importing country has implicitly threatened to impose quotas. According to the World Trade Organization (see the discussion in Section 1.3), however, voluntary export restraints are illegal and should not be used to restrict imports.[8]

In theory, **government import standards** are established to protect the health and safety of citizens. In reality, such standards are often used to restrict or ban imported goods. For example, Taiwan restricts both the age and type of beef that can be imported from the United States. According to Taiwanese government and health officials, the restriction is intended to prevent the spread of mad cow disease among native cows, and protect human consumers from developing Creutzfeldt-Jackob disease. However, the ban, which essentially blocks any U.S. beef from entering Taiwan, is also heavily motivated by nationalistic groups, who resent the global influence of the United States and want to reassert Taiwan's political and economic independence.[9]

Many nations also use **subsidies**, such as long-term, low-interest loans, cash grants, and tax deferments, to develop and protect companies in special industries. Not surprisingly, businesses complain about unfair trade practices when foreign companies receive government subsidies. Indeed, the World Trade Organization has ruled what Boeing had been arguing for years, namely, that Airbus, the largest airplane manufacturer in the world, illegally benefited from European government subsidies in the form of no- or low-interest loans. According to the WTO, if Airbus had not received

Protectionism a government's use of trade barriers to shield domestic companies and their workers from foreign competition

Tariff a direct tax on imported goods

Nontariff barriers nontax methods of increasing the cost or reducing the volume of imported goods

Quota a limit on the number or volume of imported products

Voluntary export restraints voluntarily imposed limits on the number or volume of products exported to a particular country

Government import standard a standard ostensibly established to protect the health and safety of citizens but, in reality, often used to restrict or ban imports

Subsidies government loans, grants, and tax deferments given to domestic companies to protect them from foreign competition

After severe drought and fires destroyed much of the Russian grain crop in 2010, Russia, traditionally a major grain exporter, imposed an export ban on grain amidst fears that the remaining crop would not even be able to meet domestic consumption levels.

© Rogulin Dmitry/ITAR-TASS/Landov

European government subsidies, it would have been a much weaker company and probably could not have introduced its A380 superjumbo jet.[10]

The last type of nontariff barrier is **customs classification**. As products are imported into a country, they are examined by customs agents, who must decide into which of nearly 9,000 categories they should classify a product (see the Official Harmonized Tariff Schedule of the United States at http://www.usitc.gov/tata/hts/index.htm for more information). Classification is important because the category assigned by customs agents can greatly affect the size of the tariff and whether the item is subject to import quotas. For example, the U.S. Customs Service has several customs classifications for imported shoes. Tariffs on imported leather or "nonrubber" shoes are about 10 percent, whereas tariffs on imported rubber shoes, such as athletic footwear or waterproof shoes, range from 20 to 84 percent. (See www.usitc.gov for full information on tariffs.) The difference is large enough that some importers try to make their rubber shoes look like leather in hopes of receiving the nonrubber customs classification and lower tariff.

1.3 | TRADE AGREEMENTS

Thanks to the trade barriers described above, buying imported goods has often been much more expensive and difficult than buying domestic goods. During the 1990s, however, the regulations governing global trade were transformed. The most significant change was that 124 countries agreed to adopt the Uruguay Round of the **General Agreement on Tariffs and Trade (GATT).** GATT, which existed from 1947 to 1995, was an agreement to regulate trade among (eventually) more than 120 countries, the purpose of which was "substantial reduction of tariffs and other trade barriers and the elimination of preferences...."[11] GATT members engaged in eight rounds of trade negotiations, with the

Uruguay Round signed in 1994 and going into effect in 1995. Although GATT itself was replaced by the **World Trade Organization (WTO)** in 1995, the changes that it made continue to encourage international trade.

The WTO, headquartered in Geneva, Switzerland, administers trade agreements, provides a forum for trade negotiations, handles trade disputes, monitors national trade policies, and offers technical assistance and training for developing countries for its 150 member countries. Through tremendous decreases in tariff and nontariff barriers, the Uruguay Round of GATT made it much easier and cheaper for consumers in all countries to buy foreign products. First, tariffs were cut 40 percent on average worldwide by 2005. Second, tariffs were eliminated in ten specific industries: beer, alcohol, construction equipment, farm machinery, furniture, medical equipment, paper, pharmaceuticals, steel, and toys. Third, stricter limits were put on government subsidies. Fourth, the Uruguay Round of GATT established protections for intellectual property, such as trademarks, patents, and copyrights. Protection of intellectual property has become an increasingly important issue in global trade because of widespread product piracy. For example, according to music industry association IFPI, 95 percent of global music downloads violate copyright.[12] Finally, trade disputes between countries are now fully settled by arbitration panels from the WTO. In the past, countries could use their veto power to cancel a panel's decision, but now WTO rulings are complete and final.

The second major development that has reduced trade barriers has been the creation of **regional trading zones,** or zones in which tariff and nontariff barriers

World Trade Organization

☑ **FACT FILE**

WORLD TRADE ORGANIZATION

Location: Geneva, Switzerland
Established: January 1, 1995
Created by: Uruguay Round negotiations (1986–1994)
Membership: 153 countries (on July 23, 2008)
Budget: 189 million Swiss francs for 2008
Secretariat staff: 625
Head: Pascal Lamy (Director-General)

Functions:
- Administering WTO trade agreements
- Forum for trade negotiations
- Handling trade disputes
- Monitoring national trade policies
- Technical assistance and training for developing countries
- Cooperation with other international organizations

Source: "What is the WTO?," accessed October 2, 2008, www.wto.org/english/thewto_e/whatis_e/whatis_e.htm.

are reduced or eliminated by treaties or agreements among countries within the trading zone. The largest and most important trading zones are in Europe (the Maastricht Treaty), North America (the North American Free Trade Agreement, or NAFTA), Central America (Central America Free Trade Agreement, or CAFTA-DR), South America (Union of South American Nations, or UNASUR), and Asia (the Association of Southeast Asian Nations, or ASEAN, and the Asia-Pacific Economic Cooperation, or APEC). The maps in Exhibit 8.1 show the extent to which free trade agreements govern global trade.

In 1992, Belgium, Denmark, France, Germany, Greece, Ireland, Italy, Luxembourg, the Netherlands, Portugal, Spain, and the United Kingdom implemented the **Maastricht Treaty of Europe.** The purpose of this treaty was to transform their twelve different economies and twelve currencies into one common economic market, called the European Union (EU), with one common currency. Austria, Finland, and Sweden joined the EU in 1995, followed by Cyprus, the Czech Republic, Estonia, Hungary, Latvia, Lithuania, Malta, Poland, Slovakia, and Slovenia in 2004, and Bulgaria and Romania in 2007, bringing the total membership to twenty-seven countries.[13] Croatia, Macedonia, and Turkey have applied and are being considered for membership.[14] On January 1, 2002, a single common currency, the euro, went into circulation in twelve of the EU's member countries (Austria, Belgium, Finland, France, Germany, Greece, Ireland, Italy, Luxembourg, the Netherlands, Portugal, and Spain).

Prior to the treaty, trucks carrying products around Europe were stopped and inspected by customs agents

Exhibit 8.1 Global Map of Regional Trade Agreements

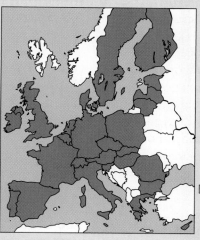
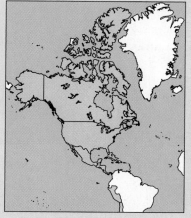
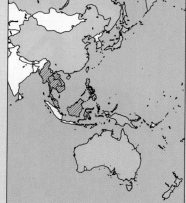

Maastricht Treaty of Europe Austria, Belgium, Bulgaria, Cyprus, the Czech Republic, Denmark, Estonia, Finland, France, Germany, Greece, Hungary, Ireland, Italy, Latvia, Lithuania, Luxembourg, Malta, the Netherlands, Poland, Portugal, Romania, Slovakia, Slovenia, Spain, Sweden, and the United Kingdom.

ASEAN (Association of Southeast Asian Nations) Brunei Darussalam, Cambodia, Indonesia, Lao PDR, Malaysia, Myanmar, the Philippines, Singapore, Thailand, and Vietnam.

APEC (Asia-Pacific Economic Cooperation) Australia, Canada, Chile, the People's Republic of China, Hong Kong (China), Japan, Mexico, New Zealand, Papua New Guinea, Peru, Russia, South Korea, Taiwan, the United States, and all members of ASEAN except Cambodia, Lao PDR, and Myanmar.

NAFTA (North American Free Trade Agreement) United States, Canada, and Mexico.

CAFTA-DR (Dominican Republic-Central American Free Trade Agreement) Costa Rica, the Dominican Republic, El Salvador, Guatemala, Honduras, Nicaragua, and the United States.

UNASUR (Union of South American Nations) Argentina, Brazil, Paraguay, Uruguay, Venezuela, Bolivia, Colombia, Ecuador, Peru, Guyana, Suriname, and Chile.

at each border. Furthermore, since the required paperwork, tariffs, and government product specifications could be radically different in each country, companies often had to file twelve different sets of paperwork, pay twelve different tariffs, produce twelve different versions of their basic product to meet various government specifications, and exchange money in twelve different currencies. Likewise, open business travel from state to state, which we take for granted in the United States, was complicated by inspections at each border crossing. If you lived in Germany but worked in Luxembourg, your car was stopped and your passport was inspected twice every day as you traveled to and from work. Also, every business transaction required a currency exchange, for example, from German deutsche marks to Italian lira, or from French francs to Dutch guilders. Imagine all of this happening to millions of trucks, cars, and businesspeople, and you can begin to appreciate the difficulty and cost of conducting business across Europe before the Maastricht Treaty. (For more information about the Maastricht Treaty, the EU, and Europe's new common currency, the euro, see http://europa.eu /abc/12lessons/index_en.htm.)

The Ambassador Bridge in Detroit is the busiest border crossing between Canada and the United States, carrying 25 percent of all trade between the two countries, or roughly $100 billion in annual trade going in both directions.[15]

NAFTA, the **North American Free Trade Agreement** between the United States, Canada, and Mexico, went into effect on January 1, 1994. More than any other regional trade agreement, NAFTA has liberalized trade between its member countries so that businesses can plan for one market (North America) rather than for three separate markets (the United States, Canada, and Mexico). One of NAFTA's most important achievements was to eliminate most product tariffs *and* prevent Canada, the United States, and Mexico from increasing existing tariffs or introducing new ones. Overall, Mexican and Canadian exports to the United States are up 247 percent since NAFTA went into effect. U.S. exports to Mexico and Canada are up 171 percent, too, growing twice as fast as U.S. exports to any other part of the world.[16] In fact, Mexico and Canada now account for one-third of all U.S. exports.[17]

CAFTA-DR, the **Central America Free Trade Agreement** between the United States, the Dominican Republic, and the Central American countries of Costa Rica, El

Salvador, Guatemala, Honduras, and Nicaragua, went into effect in August 2005. With a combined population close to 50 million, the other CAFTA-DR countries are the tenth-largest U.S. export market in the world and the third-largest U.S. export market in Latin America, after Mexico and Brazil. U.S. companies export more than $26.3 billion in goods each year to the CAFTA-DR countries.[18] Furthermore, U.S. exports to CAFTA-DR countries are increasing at a rate of 16 percent per year, making those countries by far the fastest-growing export market for U.S. companies.[19]

On May 23, 2008, twelve South American countries signed a treaty to form the **Union of South American Nations (UNASUR)**, which united the former Mercosur (Argentina, Brazil, Paraguay, Uruguay, and Venezuela) and Andean Community (Bolivia, Colombia, Ecuador, and Peru) alliances with Guyana, Suriname, and Chile. UNASUR aims to create a unified South America by permitting free movement between nations, creating a common infrastructure that includes an inter-oceanic highway, and establishing the region as a single market by eliminating tariffs by 2019. UNASUR is one of the largest trading zones in the world, encompassing 361 million people in South American countries that have a combined gross domestic product of nearly $1 trillion.[20]

ASEAN, the **Association of Southeast Asian Nations**, and **APEC**, the **Asia-Pacific Economic Cooperation**, are the two largest and most important regional trading groups in Asia. ASEAN is a trade agreement between Brunei Darussalam, Cambodia, Indonesia, Lao PDR, Malaysia, Myanmar, the Philippines, Singapore, Thailand, and Vietnam, which form a market of more than 575 million people. U.S. trade with ASEAN countries exceeds $161 billion a year.[21] In fact, the United States is ASEAN's second-largest trading partner (Japan is its largest), and ASEAN's member nations constitute the fifth-largest trading partner of the United States. An ASEAN free trade area will begin in 2015 for the six original countries (Brunei Darussalam, Indonesia, Malaysia, the Philippines, Singapore, and Thailand) and in 2018 for the newer member countries (Cambodia, Lao PDR, Myanmar, and Vietnam).[22]

APEC is a broader agreement that includes Australia, Canada, Chile, the People's Republic of China, Hong Kong (China), Japan, Mexico, New Zealand, Papua New Guinea, Peru, Russia, South Korea, Taiwan, the United States, and all the members of ASEAN except Cambodia, Lao PDR, and Myanmar. APEC's twenty-one member countries contain 2.6 billion people, account for 47 percent of all global trade, and have a combined gross domestic product of more than $19 trillion. APEC countries began reducing trade barriers in 2000, though the reductions will not be completely phased in until 2020.[23]

1.4 | CONSUMERS, TRADE BARRIERS, AND TRADE AGREEMENTS

The average worker earns nearly $60,820 a year in Switzerland, $77,370 in Norway, $37,790 in Japan, and $46,040 in the United States. Yet, after adjusting these incomes for how much they can buy, the Swiss income is equivalent to just $44,410, the Norwegian income to $53,650, and the Japanese income to $34,750![24] This is the same as saying that $1 of income can buy you only 73 cents' worth of goods in Switzerland, 69 cents' worth in Norway, and 92 cents' worth in Japan. In other words, Americans can buy much more with their incomes than those in other countries can.

One reason that Americans get more for their money is that the U.S. marketplace is the most competitive in the world and has been one of the easiest for foreign companies to enter. Although some U.S. industries, such as textiles, have been heavily protected from foreign competition by trade barriers, for the most part, American consumers (and businesses) have had plentiful choices among American-made and foreign-made products. More important, the high level of competition between foreign and domestic companies that creates these choices helps to keep prices low in the United States. Furthermore, it is precisely the lack of choice and the low level of competition that keep prices higher in countries that have not been as open to foreign companies and products. For example, some estimates suggest that import restrictions cost U.K. consumers an additional £500 million per year on clothing purchases.[25]

So why do trade barriers and free trade agreements matter to consumers? They're important because free trade agreements increase choices, competition, and purchasing power and thus decrease what people pay for food, clothing, other necessities, and luxuries.

Union of South American Nations (UNASUR) a regional trade agreement between Argentina, Brazil, Paraguay, Uruguay, Venezuela, Bolivia, Colombia, Ecuador, Peru, Guyana, Suriname, and Chile

Association of Southeast Asian Nations (ASEAN) a regional trade agreement between Brunei Darussalam, Cambodia, Indonesia, Lao PDR, Malaysia, Myanmar, the Philippines, Singapore, Thailand, and Vietnam

Asia-Pacific Economic Cooperation (APEC) a regional trade agreement between Australia, Canada, Chile, the People's Republic of China, Hong Kong, Japan, Mexico, New Zealand, Papua New Guinea, Peru, Russia, South Korea, Taiwan, the United States, and all members of ASEAN, except Cambodia, Lao PDR, and Myanmar

Accordingly, today's consumers rarely care where their products and services originate. From diapers to diamonds, people don't care where products are from—they just want to know which brand or kind is cheaper.

And why do trade barriers and free trade agreements matter to managers? The reason, as you're about to read, is that while free trade agreements create new business opportunities, they also intensify competition, and addressing that competition is a manager's job.

How to Go Global?

O nce a company has decided that it *will* go global, it must decide *how* to go global. For example, if you decide to sell in Singapore, should you try to find a local business partner who speaks the language, knows the laws, and understands the customs and norms of Singapore's culture? Or should you simply export your products from your home country? What do you do if you are also entering Eastern Europe, perhaps starting in Hungary? Should you use the same approach in Hungary that you used in Singapore?

After reading the next two sections, you should be able to

2 **explain why companies choose to standardize or adapt their business procedures.**

3 **explain the different ways that companies can organize to do business globally.**

2 Consistency or Adaptation?

In this section, we return to a key issue: How can you be sure that the way you run your business in one country is the right way to run that business in another? In other words, how can you strike the right balance between global consistency and local adaptation?

Global consistency means that a multinational company with offices, manufacturing plants, and distribution facilities in different countries uses the same rules, guidelines, policies, and procedures to run those offices, plants, and facilities. Managers at company headquarters value global consistency because it simplifies decisions. By contrast, a company following a policy of **local adaptation** modifies its standard operating procedures to adapt to differences in foreign customers, governments, and regulatory agencies. Local adaptation is typically preferred by local managers who are charged with making the international business successful in their countries. If companies lean too much toward global consistency, they run the risk of using management procedures poorly suited to particular countries' markets, cultures, and employees (i.e., a lack of local adaptation). For instance, Swedish-based H&M is the third largest clothing retailer, with stores in 37 countries. Much of its success is due to the fact that all of its stores carry the same products all over the world. However, this also limits the areas in which H&M can do business. Because most of its clothes are designed for climates that are similar to Sweden (in other words, long, cold winters and short summers) H&M has been unable to enter markets that have drastically different climates. Thus, while H&M has stores in Toledo, Ohio, it has only a minimal presence in Los Angeles, and no presence at all in Dallas, Texas. If it is to continue to grow, H&M must adapt its products to warmer climates.[26]

If, however, companies focus too much on local adaptation, they run the risk of losing the cost effectiveness and productivity that result from using standardized rules and procedures throughout the world. Consider the case of Tupperware in India. Since it first entered India in 1996, Tupperware has grown by nearly 30 percent each year. In fact, Tupperware is acknowledged as a major factor in the doubling of the Indian kitchenware market between 2003 and 2008. Much of the company's success is due to its strategy of adapting and even changing its product line to suit local food habits. While Tupperware sees great potential in India, after all, it has 1 billion people, local adaptation of its products has come at considerable cost. First, Indian households have traditionally stored their leftovers in metal, rather than plastic containers. As a result, Tupperware had to create a new market for itself by convincing consumers that plastic containers would be better. Second, Tupperware had to create many new products. Around the world, one of Tupperware's best-selling products is a square bread container, perfect for storing slices from bread loaves. In India, however, Tupperware had to create, from scratch, a round bread container that could store *roti* and *chapati*, round flatbreads that are integral to Indian cuisine. Finally, in order to reduce prices and compete effectively with local businesses, Tupperware built a new factory in the city of Dehradun, India, at significant cost.[27]

3 Forms for Global Business

Historically, companies have generally followed the *phase model of globalization,* in which a company makes the transition from a domestic company to a global company in the following sequential phases: *3.1 exporting, 3.2 cooperative contracts, 3.3 strategic alliances, and 3.4 wholly owned affiliates.* At each step, the company grows much larger, uses those resources to enter more global markets, is less dependent on home country sales, and is more committed in its orientation to global business. Some companies, however, do not follow the phase model of globalization.[28] Some skip phases on their way to becoming more global and less domestic. Others don't follow the phase model at all. These are known as *3.5 global new ventures.* This section reviews these forms of global business.[29]

3.1 | EXPORTING

When companies produce products in their home countries and sell those products to customers in foreign countries, they are **exporting.** Located about 90 minutes from Shanghai, the city of Honghe is one of China's largest sweater producers. Half of its 100,000 citizens work in more than 100 factories that generate $650 million a year by producing and exporting 200 million sweaters annually.[30]

Exporting as a form of global business offers many advantages. It makes the company less dependent on sales in its home market and provides a greater degree of control over research, design, and production decisions. Though advantageous in a number of ways, exporting also has its disadvantages. The primary disadvantage is that many exported goods are subject to tariff and nontariff barriers that can substantially increase their final cost to consumers. A second disadvantage is that transportation costs can significantly increase the price of an exported product. Yet another disadvantage is that companies that export depend on foreign importers for product distribution. If, for example, the foreign importer makes a mistake on the paperwork that accompanies a shipment of imported goods, those goods can be returned to the foreign manufacturer at the manufacturer's expense.

The United States used to be the most expensive place in the world to produce cars. But the weaker U.S. dollar and new contracts with workers are making production cheaper, prompting companies in a number of industries to rethink their strategies. For example, A-Power Energy Generation Systems, a Chinese alternative energy company, opened a new production and assembly plant in Nevada. The facility will produce wind turbines that will be sold in the United States and exported to Mexico and Canada, as well as Central and South America.[31]

Exporting selling domestically produced products to customers in foreign countries

Cooperative contract an agreement in which a foreign business owner pays a company a fee for the right to conduct that business in his or her country

Licensing an agreement in which a domestic company, the licensor, receives royalty payments for allowing another company, the licensee, to produce the licensor's product, sell its service, or use its brand name in a specified foreign market

Franchise a collection of networked firms in which the manufacturer or marketer of a product or service, the franchisor, licenses the entire business to another person or organization, the franchisee

Strategic alliance an agreement in which companies combine key resources, costs, risk, technology, and people

Joint venture a strategic alliance in which two existing companies collaborate to form a third, independent company

3.2 | COOPERATIVE CONTRACTS

When an organization wants to expand its business globally without making a large financial commitment to do so, it may sign a **cooperative contract** with a foreign business owner who pays the company a fee for the right to conduct its business in his or her country. There are two kinds of cooperative contracts: licensing and franchising.

Under a **licensing** agreement, a domestic company, the *licensor*, receives royalty payments for allowing another company, the *licensee*, to produce its product, sell its service, or use its brand name in a particular foreign market. Abbott Laboratories, a leading pharmaceuticals company based in Illinois, found an efficient and effective way to enter emerging markets by reaching a licensing agreement with Zydus Cadila, based in Ahmedabad, India. Under the terms of the agreement, Abbott will gain the rights to sell 24 of Zydus Cadila's products in 15 emerging markets in South America, Africa, and Asia, with the option to add 40 more products in the future. By partnering with Zydus Cadila instead of going at it alone, Abbott can take advantage of Zydus's expertise in selling pharmaceuticals in emerging markets while also minimizing its financial risk.[32]

One of the most important advantages of licensing is that it allows companies to earn additional profits without investing more money. As foreign sales increase, the royalties paid to the licensor by the foreign licensee increase. Moreover, the licensee, not the licensor, invests in production equipment and facilities to produce the licensed product. Licensing also helps companies avoid tariffs and nontariff barriers. Since the licensee manufactures the product within the foreign country, those kinds of trade barriers don't arise.

The biggest disadvantage associated with licensing is that the licensor gives up control over the quality of the product or service sold by the foreign licensee. Unless the licensing agreement contains specific restrictions, the licensee controls the entire business from production to marketing to final sales. Many licensors include inspection clauses in their license contracts, but closely monitoring product or service quality from thousands of miles away can be difficult. An additional disadvantage is that licensees can eventually become competitors, especially when a licensing agreement includes access to important technology or proprietary business knowledge.

A **franchise** is a collection of networked firms in which the manufacturer or marketer of a product or service, the *franchisor*, licenses the entire business to another person or organization, the *franchisee*. For the price of an initial franchise fee plus royalties, franchisors provide franchisees with training, assistance with marketing and advertising, and an exclusive right to conduct business in a particular location. More than 400 U.S. companies franchise their businesses to foreign franchise partners. Overall, franchising is a fast way to enter foreign markets. Over the last 20 years, U.S. franchisors have more than doubled their global franchise units, to a total of more than 100,000.

Despite franchising's many advantages, franchisors face a loss of control when they sell businesses to franchisees who are thousands of miles away. And, while there are exceptions, franchising success may be somewhat culture-bound. In other words, because most global franchisors begin by franchising their businesses in similar countries or regions (Canada is by far the top choice for American companies taking their first step into global franchising), and because 65 percent of those franchisors make absolutely no change in their business for overseas franchisees, the domestic success of a franchise may not generalize to cultures with different lifestyles, values, preferences, and technological infrastructures.

3.3 | STRATEGIC ALLIANCES

Companies forming **strategic alliances** combine key resources, costs, risks, technology, and people. The most common strategic alliance is a **joint venture**, which occurs when two existing companies collaborate to form a third company. The two founding companies remain intact and unchanged except that together they now own the newly created joint venture. One of the oldest and most successful global joint ventures is Fuji-Xerox, a joint venture between Fuji Film of Japan and U.S.-based Xerox Corporation, which makes copiers and automated office systems. More than 45 years after its creation, Fuji Xerox employs over 42,000 people and has close to $12 billion in revenues.[33]

One of the advantages of global joint ventures is that, like licensing and franchising, they help companies avoid tariffs and nontariff barriers to entry. Another advantage is that companies participating in a joint venture bear only part of the costs and the risks of that business. Many companies find this attractive because it is expensive to enter foreign markets and develop new products. For example, Italian automaker Fiat set up a joint venture with Russian automaker OAO Sollers. Under the agreement, OAO Sollers will produce nine Fiat models including Jeep SUVs (Jeep is owned by Fiat), and market them in Russia and other countries. For Fiat, which has struggled in many foreign markets, the joint venture provides an excellent opportunity to establish a larger presence in the growing global auto market.[34] Global joint ventures can be especially advantageous to local partners who link up with larger, more experienced foreign firms that can bring advanced management, resources, and business skills to the joint venture. For example, Arrow Energy, Ltd., is an oil and natural gas exploration and production company based in Calgary, Canada. Arrow is partnering with Royal Dutch Shell PLC in a global joint venture to mine natural gas from coal seams in Australia and export it.[35]

Global joint ventures are not without problems, though. Because companies share costs and risks with their joint venture partners, they must also share profits. Managing global joint ventures can also be difficult because they represent a merging of four cultures: the country and organizational cultures of the first partner and the country and organizational cultures of the second partner. Often, to be fair to all involved, each partner in the global joint venture will have equal ownership and power. But this can result in power struggles and a lack of leadership. Because of these problems,

companies forming global joint ventures should carefully develop detailed contracts that specify the obligations of each party. Such care is important because some estimate the rate of failure for global joint ventures to be as high as 70 percent.[36]

3.4 | WHOLLY OWNED AFFILIATES (BUILD OR BUY)

Approximately one-third of multinational companies enter foreign markets through wholly owned affiliates. Unlike licensing arrangements, franchises, or joint ventures, **wholly owned affiliates** are 100 percent owned by the parent company. For example, in 2009 Chinese companies announced nearly $5 billion in new direct investments in the United States and the acquisition or startup of 50 U.S. companies. Haier America, which sells and markets a wide range of household goods, from refrigerators to air conditioners to MP3 players, built a refrigerator factory in Camden, South Carolina. Haier America is a wholly owned affiliate of the Haier Group, which is based in Qingdao, China.[37]

The primary advantage of wholly owned affiliates is that the parent company receives all of the profits and has complete control over the foreign facilities. The biggest disadvantage is the expense of building new operations or buying existing businesses. Although the payoff can be enormous if wholly owned affiliates succeed, the losses can be immense if they fail, because the parent company assumes all of the risk.

3.5 | GLOBAL NEW VENTURES

Companies used to evolve slowly from small operations selling in their home markets to large businesses selling to foreign markets. Furthermore, as companies went global, they usually followed the phases of globalization. Recently, however, three trends have combined to allow companies to skip the phase models when going global. First, quick, reliable air travel can transport people nearly anywhere in the world within one day. Second, low-cost communication technologies, such as international email, teleconferencing, phone conferencing, and the Internet, make it easier to communicate with global customers, suppliers, managers, and employees.

© eVox Productions LLC/Drive Images/Photolibrary

Third, there is now a critical mass of businesspeople with extensive personal experience in all aspects of global business.[38] This combination of developments has made it possible to start companies that are global from inception. With sales, employees, and financing in different countries, **global new ventures** are companies that are founded with an active global strategy.[39]

Although there are several different kinds of global new ventures, all share two characteristics. First, the company founders successfully develop and communicate the company's global vision from inception. Second, rather than going global one country at a time, new global ventures bring a product or service to market in several foreign markets at the same time. Founded by longtime airline executives Steven Udvar-Hazy and John L. Plueger, Air Lease Corporation is a new aircraft leasing company that provides aircraft to commercial airlines through lease agreements. Although based in Los Angeles, its mission is to provide equipment and financing to airlines all over the world. CEO Udvar-Hazy says, "We look forward to working with the leading global airlines as they modernize their fleets." Within a year of startup, Air Lease expects to have a fleet of more than 100 commercial jets leased to airlines throughout the world."[40]

Where to Go Global?

deciding where to go global is just as important as deciding how your company will go global.

After reading the next three sections, you should be able to

4 **explain how to find a favorable business climate.**

5 **discuss the importance of identifying and adapting to cultural differences.**

6 **explain how to successfully prepare workers for international assignments.**

4 Finding the Best Business Climate

When deciding where to go global, companies try to find countries or regions with promising business climates.

An attractive foreign business climate 4.1 positions the company for easy access to growing markets, 4.2 is an effective but cost-efficient place to locate an office or manufacturing facility, and 4.3 minimizes the political risk to the company.

4.1 | GROWING MARKETS

The most important factor in an attractive business climate is access to a growing market. Two factors help companies determine the growth potential of foreign markets: purchasing power and foreign competitors. **Purchasing power** is measured by comparing the relative cost of a standard set of goods and services in different countries. Purchasing power is strong in countries such as Mexico, India, and China, which have low average levels of income. This is because basic living expenses, such as food, shelter, and transportation, are very inexpensive in those countries, so consumers still have money to spend after paying for necessities. Because basic living expenses are so low in China, Mexico, and India, purchasing power is strong, and millions of Chinese, Mexican, and Indian consumers increasingly have extra money to spend on what they want in addition to what they need.[41]

Consequently, countries with high or growing levels of purchasing power are good choices for companies looking for attractive global markets. As Exhibit 8.2 shows, Coke has found that the per capita consumption of Coca-Cola, or the number of Cokes a person drinks per year, rises directly with purchasing power. The more purchasing power people have, the more likely they are to purchase soft drinks.

The second part of assessing the growth potential of a foreign market involves analyzing the degree of global competition, which is determined by the number and quality of companies that already compete in the market. One of the trends in global growth potential is increases in trade in and among emerging markets. Rather than put all their efforts into selling products and services to developed nations, firms in emerging market countries are selling to customers in other emerging market countries. For example, Marcopolo is Brazil's biggest bus maker with $1.1 billion in annual sales—none of which comes from U.S. customers. Rather, Marcopolo focuses on selling buses in emerging-market countries such as Argentina, Mexico, Colombia, and South Africa, where it sold 460 buses for the 2010 World Cup. Similarly, by 2010, 33 percent of Brazilian airplane manufacturer Embraer's revenue came from emerging-market customers (in 2005, the figure was 1 percent). According to the World Trade Organization, intra-emerging-market trade

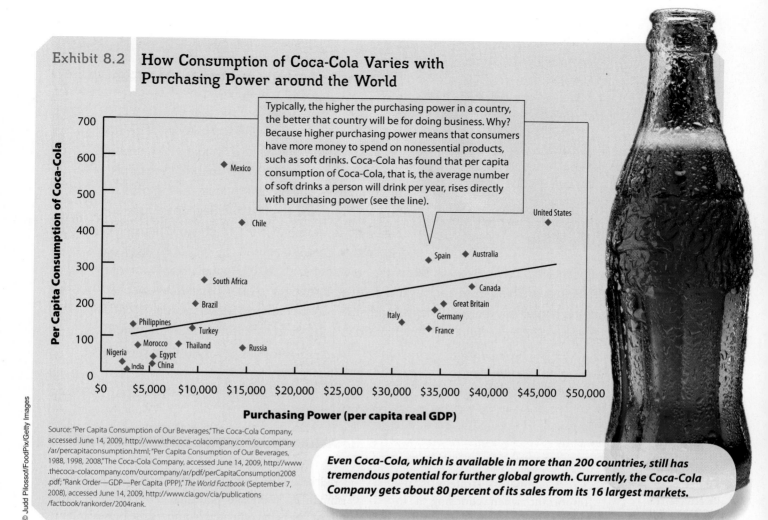

Exhibit 8.2 | How Consumption of Coca-Cola Varies with Purchasing Power around the World

Typically, the higher the purchasing power in a country, the better that country will be for doing business. Why? Because higher purchasing power means that consumers have more money to spend on nonessential products, such as soft drinks. Coca-Cola has found that per capita consumption of Coca-Cola, that is, the average number of soft drinks a person will drink per year, rises directly with purchasing power (see the line).

Per Capita Consumption of Coca-Cola (y-axis)

Purchasing Power (per capita real GDP) (x-axis)

Source: "Per Capita Consumption of Our Beverages," The Coca-Cola Company, accessed June 14, 2009, http://www.thecoca-colacompany.com/ourcompany /ar/percapitaconsumption.html; "Per Capita Consumption of Our Beverages, 1988, 1998, 2008," The Coca-Cola Company, accessed June 14, 2009, http://www .thecoca-colacompany.com/ourcompany/ar/pdf/perCapitaConsumption2008 .pdf; "Rank Order—GDP—Per Capita (PPP)," *The World Factbook* (September 7, 2008), accessed June 14, 2009, http://www.cia.gov/cia/publications /factbook/rankorder/2004rank.

Even Coca-Cola, which is available in more than 200 countries, still has tremendous potential for further global growth. Currently, the Coca-Cola Company gets about 80 percent of its sales from its 16 largest markets.

grew 18 percent per year between 2000 and 2008, and now accounts for roughly $2.8 trillion in trade among companies and consumers across Latin America, the Mideast, Asia, and Africa.[42]

4.2 | CHOOSING AN OFFICE OR MANUFACTURING LOCATION

Companies do not have to establish an office or manufacturing location in each country they enter. They can license, franchise, or export to foreign markets, or they can serve a larger region from one country. But there are many reasons why a company might choose to establish a location in a foreign country. Some foreign offices are established through global mergers and acquisitions, such as the acquisition of IBM's ThinkPad brand, headquartered in Raleigh, North Carolina, by Beijing-based computer maker Lenovo. In fact, while Lenovo maintains offices in both places, top executives hold their monthly meetings at a different location each time—a strategy Bill Amelio, CEO of Lenovo, calls "worldsourcing." Other companies seek a tax haven (although federal laws and regulations make this

more difficult for U.S. companies), want to reflect their customer base, or strive to create a global brand. Although a company must be legally incorporated in one place, some companies have anywhere from nine to twenty-three global hubs and don't regard any one as more central than another.[43]

Thus, the criteria for choosing an office or manufacturing location are different from the criteria for entering a foreign market. Rather than focusing on costs alone, companies should consider both qualitative and quantitative factors. Two key qualitative factors are work force quality and company strategy. Work force quality is important because it is often difficult to find workers with the specific skills, abilities, and experience that a company needs to run its business. Work force quality is one reason that many companies doing business in Europe locate their customer call centers in the Netherlands. Workers in the Netherlands are some of the most multilingual in the world, with 73 percent speaking two languages. They also offer extensive training programs and language courses.[44]

Do we need a new place to outsource?

With a seemingly unlimited number of people willing to work 10 to 12 hours a day, six days per week, for about $100 per month, thousands of companies outsourced manufacturing production to China over the last two decades. There are signs, however, that the era of cheap Chinese labor is about to come to an end. Since 2008, labor costs in China have risen 15 percent a year. And during the summer of 2010, thousands of workers in factories making everything from car parts to iPad components to pharmaceuticals went on strike, demanding higher pay, better benefits, and fewer work hours. Honda responded by raising wages 24 percent to $330 per month, more than double the government-mandated minimum wage. Other companies have followed suit, and it is now estimated that it is now more expensive to outsource to China than to Mexico, India, Vietnam, Russia, and Romania.

Sources: E. Kurtenbach, "Cheap-Labor Era in China Is Disappearing," *Philadelphia Inquirer*, July 10, 2010, accessed July 23, 2010, http://www.philly.com/philly/business/98157269 .html?cmpid=15585797; N. Shirozu, "Honda Offers Strikers in China 24% Pay Boost," *Wall Street Journal*, June 1, 2010, accessed July 23, 2010, http://online.wsj.com/article/SB1000 14240527487034066045752785019163513546.html.

Political uncertainty the risk of major changes in political regimes that can result from war, revolution, death of political leaders, social unrest, or other influential events

A company's strategy is also important when choosing a location. For example, a company pursuing a low-cost strategy may need plentiful raw materials, low-cost transportation, and low-cost labor. A company pursuing a differentiation strategy (typically by providing a higher-priced, better product or service) may need access to high-quality materials and a highly skilled and educated work force.

Quantitative factors such as the kind of facility being built, tariffs and nontariff barriers, exchange rates, and transportation and labor costs should also be considered when choosing a foreign location. Each year, Cushman & Wakefield publishes its "European Cities Monitor" to help companies compare the pluses and minuses of the business climate in various cities, and similar information is available for other parts of the world. Exhibit 8.3 offers a quick overview of the best cities for business based on a variety of criteria. This information is a good starting point if your company is trying to decide where to put an international office or manufacturing plant.

4.3 | MINIMIZING POLITICAL RISK

When managers think about political risk in global business, they envision burning factories and riots in the streets. Although political events such as these receive dramatic and extended coverage from the media, the political risks that most companies face usually are not covered as breaking stories on FOX News and CNN. Nonetheless, the negative consequences of ordinary political risk can be just as devastating to companies that fail to identify and minimize that risk.[45]

When conducting global business, companies should attempt to identify two types of political risk: political uncertainty and policy uncertainty.[46] **Political uncertainty** is the risk of major changes in political regimes that can result from war, revolution, death of

Exhibit 8.3 World's Best Cities for Business

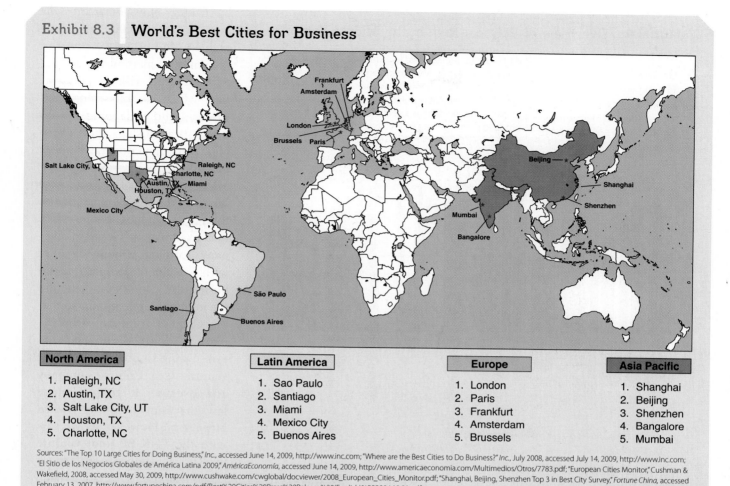

North America	Latin America	Europe	Asia Pacific
1. Raleigh, NC	1. Sao Paulo	1. London	1. Shanghai
2. Austin, TX	2. Santiago	2. Paris	2. Beijing
3. Salt Lake City, UT	3. Miami	3. Frankfurt	3. Shenzhen
4. Houston, TX	4. Mexico City	4. Amsterdam	4. Bangalore
5. Charlotte, NC	5. Buenos Aires	5. Brussels	5. Mumbai

Sources: "The Top 10 Large Cities for Doing Business," *Inc.*, accessed June 14, 2009, http://www.inc.com; "Where are the Best Cities to Do Business?" *Inc.*, July 2008, accessed July 14, 2009, http://www.inc.com; "El Sitio de los Negocios Globales de América Latina 2009," *AméricaEconomía*, accessed June 14, 2009, http://www.americaeconomia.com/Multimedios/Otros/7783.pdf; "European Cities Monitor," Cushman & Wakefield, 2008, accessed May 30, 2009, http://www.cushwake.com/cwglobal/docviewer/2008_European_Cities_Monitor.pdf; "Shanghai, Beijing, Shenzhen Top 3 in Best City Survey," *Fortune China*, accessed February 13, 2007, http://www.fortunechina.com/pdf/Best%20Cities%20Press%20Release%20(English)%202004.12.01.pdf.

political leaders, social unrest, or other influential events. **Policy uncertainty** refers to the risk associated with changes in laws and government policies that directly affect the way foreign companies conduct business.

Policy uncertainty is the most common—and perhaps most frustrating—form of political risk in global business. For example, the Kremlin has cleaned up Russia's once-inefficient auto industry, making it attractive to Western investors. Growth-starved auto companies like Renault have taken the bait. In fact, $80 million of private capital entered Russia in 2007. But such investment is a risk because 40 percent of the industry is owned by the Kremlin, making foreign investors subject to government policy. An example of what can happen as policy winds change is in February 2007, the Kremlin raided BP PLC and TNK-BP, its joint venture, and accused the foreign investor of industrial espionage.[47]

Several strategies can be used to minimize or adapt to the political risk inherent in global business. An *avoidance strategy* is used when the political risks associated with a foreign country or region are viewed as too great.

If firms are already invested in high-risk areas, they may divest or sell their businesses. If they have not yet invested, they will likely postpone their investment until the risk shrinks. Exhibit 8.4 on the next page shows the long-term political risk for various countries in the Middle East (higher scores indicate less political risk). The following factors, which were used to compile the ratings, indicate greater political risk: government instability, poor socioeconomic conditions, internal or external conflict, military involvement in politics, religious and ethnic tensions, high foreign debt as a percentage of gross domestic product, exchange rate instability, and high inflation.[48] An avoidance strategy would likely be used for the riskiest countries shown in Exhibit 8.4 on the next page, such as Iran, Saudi Arabia, and Lebanon, but might not be needed for the less risky countries, such as Israel, Kuwait, and Oman. Risk conditions and factors change, so managers should be sure to make risk

Policy uncertainty
the risk associated with changes in laws and government policies that directly affect the way foreign companies conduct business

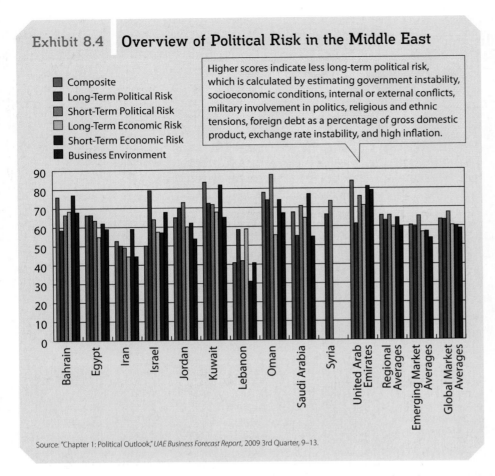

Exhibit 8.4   Overview of Political Risk in the Middle East

Legend:
- Composite
- Long-Term Political Risk
- Short-Term Political Risk
- Long-Term Economic Risk
- Short-Term Economic Risk
- Business Environment

Higher scores indicate less long-term political risk, which is calculated by estimating government instability, socioeconomic conditions, internal or external conflicts, military involvement in politics, religious and ethnic tensions, foreign debt as a percentage of gross domestic product, exchange rate instability, and high inflation.

Countries: Bahrain, Egypt, Iran, Israel, Jordan, Kuwait, Lebanon, Oman, Saudi Arabia, Syria, United Arab Emirates, Regional Averages, Emerging Market Averages, Global Market Averages

Source: "Chapter 1: Political Outlook," *UAE Business Forecast Report*, 2009 3rd Quarter, 9–13.

decisions with the latest available information from resources such as the PRS Group (http://www.prsgroup.com), which supplies information about political risk to 80 percent of the *Fortune* 500 companies.

Control is an active strategy to prevent or reduce political risks. Firms using a control strategy lobby foreign governments or international trade agencies to change laws, regulations, or trade barriers that hurt their business in that country. Emerson Electric Co. had virtually no business for its InSinkErator garbage disposals in Europe during the 1990s. The company lobbied European governments to convince them of the environmentally-friendly impact of a waste disposer compared to other methods of getting rid of food waste, such as composting (which involves a lot of garbage trucks) and landfills (which emit poisonous methane gas). By contrast, garbage disposals are the cheapest way to dispose of food waste because they enable water-treatment plants to turn methane (which comes through the sewer system) into power and decrease the carbon footprint by reducing the amount of waste transported by trucks. Now Emerson sells more than 100,000 disposals each year in Europe.[49]

Another method for dealing with political risk is *cooperation*, which involves using joint ventures and collaborative contracts (franchising and licensing). Although cooperation does not eliminate the political risk of doing business in a country, it can limit the risk associated with foreign ownership of a business. For example, a German company forming a joint venture with a Chinese company to do business in China may structure the joint venture contract so that the Chinese company owns 51 percent or more of the joint venture. Doing so qualifies the joint venture as a Chinese company and exempts it from Chinese laws that apply to foreign-owned businesses. However, as we saw with the TNK-BP joint venture in Russia, cooperation cannot always protect against *policy uncertainty* if a foreign government changes its laws and policies to directly affect the way foreign companies conduct business.

5 Becoming Aware of Cultural Differences

National culture is the set of shared values and beliefs that affects the perceptions, decisions, and behavior of the people from a particular country. The first step in dealing with culture is to recognize that there are meaningful differences. Professor Geert Hofstede spent 20 years studying cultural differences in fifty-three different countries. His research shows that there are five consistent cultural dimensions across countries: power distance, individualism, masculinity, uncertainty avoidance, and short-term versus long-term orientation.[50]

Power distance is the extent to which people in a country tolerate unequal distribution of power in society and organizations. In countries where power distance is weak, such as Denmark and Sweden, employees don't like their organization or their boss to have power over them or tell them what to do. They want to have a say in

National culture
the set of shared values and beliefs that affects the perceptions, decisions, and behavior of the people from a particular country

Exhibit 8.5

Hofstede's Five Cultural Dimensions

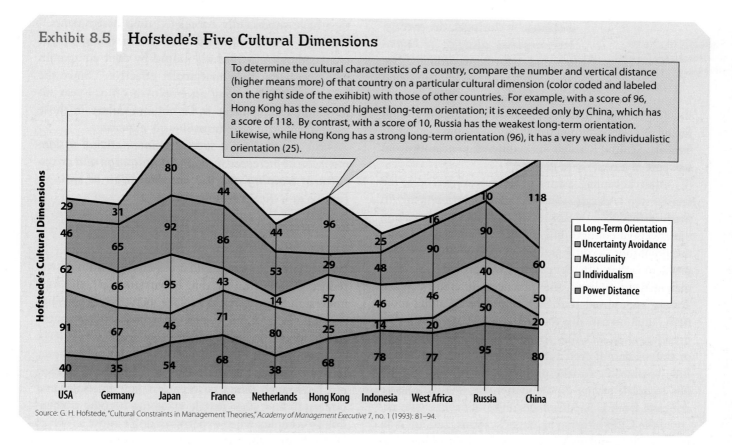

To determine the cultural characteristics of a country, compare the number and vertical distance (higher means more) of that country on a particular cultural dimension (color coded and labeled on the right side of the exihibit) with those of other countries. For example, with a score of 96, Hong Kong has the second highest long-term orientation; it is exceeded only by China, which has a score of 118. By contrast, with a score of 10, Russia has the weakest long-term orientation. Likewise, while Hong Kong has a strong long-term orientation (96), it has a very weak individualistic orientation (25).

- Long-Term Orientation
- Uncertainty Avoidance
- Masculinity
- Individualism
- Power Distance

Source: G. H. Hofstede, "Cultural Constraints in Management Theories," *Academy of Management Executive* 7, no. 1 (1993): 81–94.

decisions that affect them. As Exhibit 8.5 shows, Russia and China, with scores of 95 and 80, respectively, are much stronger in power distance than Germany (35), the Netherlands (38), and the United States (40).

Individualism is the degree to which societies believe that individuals should be self-sufficient. In individualistic societies, employees put loyalty to themselves first and loyalty to their company and work group second. In Exhibit 8.5, the United States (91), the Netherlands (80), France (71), and Germany (67) are the strongest in individualism, while Indonesia (14), West Africa (20), and China (20) are the weakest.

Masculinity and *femininity* capture the differences between highly assertive and highly nurturing cultures. Masculine cultures emphasize assertiveness, competition, material success, and achievement, whereas feminine cultures emphasize the importance of relationships, modesty, caring for the weak, and quality of life. In Exhibit 8.5, Japan (95), Germany (66), and the United States (62) have the most masculine orientations, while the Netherlands (14) has the most feminine orientation.

The cultural difference of *uncertainty avoidance* is the degree to which people in a country are uncomfortable with unstructured, ambiguous, unpredictable situations. In countries with strong uncertainty avoidance

such as Greece and Portugal, people tend to be aggressive and emotional and seek security (rather than uncertainty). In Exhibit 8.5, Japan (92), France (86), West Africa (90), and Russia (90) are strongest in uncertainty avoidance, while Hong Kong (29) is the weakest.

Short-term/long-term orientation addresses whether cultures are oriented to the present and seek immediate gratification or to the future and defer gratification. Not surprisingly, countries with short-term orientations are consumer driven, whereas countries with long-term orientations are savings driven. In Exhibit 8.5, China (118) and Hong Kong (96) have very strong long-term orientations, whereas Russia (10), West Africa (16), Indonesia (25), the United States (29), and Germany (31) have weak long-term orientations. To generate a graphical comparison of two different countries' cultures, go to http://www.geert-hofstede.com/hofstede_dimensions.php. Select a "home culture." Then select a "host culture." A graph comparing the countries on each of Hofstede's five cultural differences will automatically be generated.

Cultural differences affect perceptions, understanding, and behavior. Recognizing cultural differences is critical to succeeding in global business. Nevertheless, as Hofstede pointed out, descriptions of cultural differences are based on averages—the average level of uncertainty avoidance in Portugal, the average level of power distance in Argentina, and so forth. Accordingly, says Hofstede, "If you are going to spend time with a Japanese colleague, you shouldn't assume that overall cultural statements about Japanese society automatically apply to this person."[51] Similarly, cultural beliefs may differ significantly from one part of a country to another.[52]

After becoming aware of cultural differences, the second step is deciding how to adapt your company to those differences. Unfortunately, studies investigating the effects of cultural differences on management practice point more to difficulties than to easy solutions. One problem is that different cultures will probably perceive management policies and practices differently. When Toyota announced that they would be recalling more than 7 million cars due to sudden acceleration issues, its president and CEO Akio Toyoda made no public apology or statement, not even a pledge that as the CEO he was fully responsible for the problems, for several months. His complete silence on the matter was met with heavy criticism from U.S. consumers and politicians, who accused the CEO of being apathetic, callous, and not confident in the company's ability to solve the problem. And because of the CEO's silence, the company was accused of not knowing what the real cause of the problem was. Why was Toyota's CEO so silent? Because he responded in a Japanese fashion. U.S. consumers expect CEOs and company spokesmen to make bold, public statements, filled with promises of how the CEO will personally take charge, when a crisis occurs. Japanese culture, however, emphasizes consensus building and unity, while placing little value on individualism. In this sense, Toyoda's long silence on the recall issue was a typically Japanese response to an urgent situation. Because of this culture clash, what could have been a product recall turned into a larger public relations crisis.[53]

6 Preparing for an International Assignment

An **expatriate** is someone who lives and works outside his or her native country. The difficulty of adjusting to linguistic, cultural, and social differences is the primary reason for expatriate failure in overseas assignments. For example, although there have recently been disagreements among researchers about these numbers, 5 to 20 percent of American expatriates sent abroad by their companies will return to the United States before they have successfully completed their assignments.[54] Of those who do complete their international assignments, about one-third are judged by their companies to be no better than marginally effective.[55] Since the average cost of sending an employee on a 3-year international assignment is $1 million, failure in those assignments can be extraordinarily expensive.[56]

The chances for a successful international assignment can be increased through **6.1 language and cross-cultural training** *and* **6.2 consideration of spouse, family, and dual-career issues.**

6.1 | LANGUAGE AND CROSS-CULTURAL TRAINING

Pre-departure language and cross-cultural training can reduce the uncertainty that expatriates feel, the misunderstandings that take place between expatriates and natives, and the inappropriate ways that expatriates unknowingly behave when they travel to a foreign country. Indeed, simple things such as using a phone, locating a public toilet, asking for directions, finding out how much things cost, exchanging greetings, and understanding what people want can become tremendously complex when expatriates don't know a foreign language or a country's customs and cultures.

Expatriates who receive pre-departure language and cross-cultural training make faster adjustments to foreign cultures and perform better on their international assignments.[57] Unfortunately, only a third of the managers who go on international assignments are offered any kind of pre-departure training, and only half of those actually participate in the training![58] This is somewhat surprising given the failure rates for expatriates and the high cost of those failures. Furthermore, with the exception of some language courses, pre-departure training is not particularly expensive or difficult to provide. Three methods can be used to prepare workers for international assignments: documentary training, cultural simulations, and field simulation training.

Documentary training focuses on identifying specific critical differences between cultures. For example, when sixty workers at Axcelis Technologies in Beverly, Massachusetts, were preparing to do business in India, they learned that whereas Americans make eye contact and shake hands firmly when greeting others, Indians, as a sign of respect, do just the opposite, avoiding eye contact and shaking hands limply.[59]

After learning specific critical differences through documentary training, trainees can then participate in *cultural simulations,* in which they practice adapting

© Red Chopsticks/Glow Asia/Photolibrary

A New Tool for Globalization

A new application might make it easier for managers looking to do business in foreign countries. Google recently announced that it added a translation service to the Google Goggles app. Smartphone users can take a picture of a piece of text, highlight a particular phrase or sentence, and Google will provide a basic translation. Initially, the service will be available in English, French, Italian, German, and Spanish, with plans to include Chinese, Arabic, and numerous other languages as well.

Source: P. Ha, "*Sprechen Sie* Google? A New Web Translator," *Time*, May 6, 2010, accessed July 23, 2010, http://www.time.com/time/business/article/0,8599,1987492,00.html.

said, "At first, I was skeptical and wondered what I'd get out of the class. But it was enlightening for me. Not everyone operates like we do in America."[60]

Finally, *field simulation* training, a technique made popular by the U.S. Peace Corps, places trainees in an ethnic U.S. neighborhood for 3 to 4 hours to talk to residents about cultural differences. For example, a U.S. electronics manufacturer prepared workers for assignments in South Korea by having trainees explore a South Korean neighborhood near their offices to talk to shopkeepers and people on the street about South Korean politics, family orientation, and day-to-day living practices.

6.2 | SPOUSE, FAMILY, AND DUAL-CAREER ISSUES

Not all international assignments are difficult for expatriates and their families, but the evidence clearly shows that how well an expatriate's spouse and family adjust to the foreign culture is the most important factor in determining the success or failure of an international assignment.[61] Barry Kozloff of Selection Research International says, "The cost of sending a family on a foreign assignment is around $1 million and their failure to adjust is an enormous loss."[62] Unfortunately, despite its importance, there has been little systematic research on what does and does not help expatriates' families successfully adapt. A number of companies, however, have found that adaptability screening and intercultural training for families can lead to more successful overseas adjustment.

Adaptability screening is used to assess how well managers and their families are likely to adjust to foreign cultures. For example, Prudential Relocation Management's international division has developed an "Overseas Assignment Inventory" to assess the open-mindedness of a spouse and family, respect for others' beliefs, sense of humor, and marital communication.[63] Likewise, Pennsylvania-based AMP, a worldwide producer of electrical connectors, conducts extensive psychological screening of potential expatriates and their spouses when making international assignments.

Only 40 percent of expatriates' families receive language and cross-cultural training, yet such training is just as important for the families of expatriates as it is for the expatriates themselves.[64] In fact, it may be more important because, unlike expatriates, whose professional jobs often shield them from the full force of a country's culture, spouses and children are fully immersed in foreign neighborhoods and schools. Households must be run, shopping must be done, and

to cultural differences. After the workers at Axcelis Technologies learned about key differences between their culture and Indian culture, they practiced adapting to those differences by role playing. Some Axcelis workers would take the roles of Indian workers, while other Axcelis workers would play themselves and try to behave in a way consistent with Indian culture. As they role-played, Indian music played loudly in the background, and they were coached on what to do or not do. Axcelis human resources director Randy Longo

Who Are the "Small People?"

Pre-departure language training helps expatriates adapt more quickly to foreign cultures and reduces misunderstandings between expatriates and natives. It is not, however, a guarantee of success, particularly if a non-native speaker is placed in the incredibly challenging role of public spokesperson. For example, in the early days of BP's Gulf of Mexico oil spill crisis, the company was roundly accused of not caring about the hundreds of thousands of local businesses and people who were affected by the polluted waters. In response, BP Chairman Carl-Henric Svanberg, a native of Sweden, made this statement: "We care about the small people. I hear comments sometimes that large oil companies, or greedy companies, don't care. But that is not the case in BP. We care about the small people." His statement outraged those affected by the spill, and reinforced perceptions that BP viewed local businesses and people as less important. As a resident of New Orleans put it, "We're not small people. We're human beings. They're no greater than us."

Source: A. Gerhard, "BP Chairman Talks about 'Small People,' Further Angering Gulf," *Washington Post*, June 17, 2010, accessed July 23, 2010, http://www.washingtonpost.com/wp-dyn/content/article/2010/06/16/AR2010061605528.html.

bills must be paid. When William Hines was sent by his employer, Lincoln Electric Company, to Torreon, Mexico, the company had only one other employee there at the time, so there was no one to help Hines and his wife, Meg Sondey, make the adjustment to the local community. As a result, Meg found herself dealing with all sorts of issues on her own—finding housing, taking care of immigration issues, and getting a driver's license. She describes the experience "like jumping into a cold lake. It's uncomfortable, frightening, everything is on hyper alert because it is so different."[65]

A chef serves up a plate of grubs in a Mexican restaurant.

STUDENT Study Tools

Located at the back of your book:

☐ Rip out and study the Chapter Review Card at the end of the book

Log in to the CourseMate for MGMT at cengagebrain.com to:

☐ Review Key Term Flashcards delivered 3 ways (print or online)

☐ Complete both Practice Quizzes to prepare for tests

☐ Play Beat the Clock and Quizbowl to master concepts

☐ Complete the Crossword Puzzle to review key terms

☐ Watch the video on Evo for a real company example and take the accompanying quiz

☐ Watch the Biz Flix clip from *Lost in Translation* and take the quiz

☐ Complete the Case Assignment on Caterpillar

☐ Work through the Management Decision on onshoring

☐ Work through the Management Team Decision on social entrepreneurship

☐ Develop your skills with the Develop Your Career Potential exercise

"The podcasts are the best thing in the world! If one week I don't have enough time to read the chapter for the lesson, it is so easy to listen to it on my way to University on the train, so I can at least have a basic knowledge of that chapter before the lecture, and I can catch up with my reading later."

– Sandra DeWitt, Student at University of Notre Dame Fremantle, Australia

LISTEN UP!

SHE DID

MGMT4 was designed for students just like you—busy people who want choices, flexibility, and multiple learning options.

MGMT4 delivers concise, focused information in a fresh and contemporary format. And…

MGMT4 gives you a variety of online learning materials designed with you in mind.

Through CourseMate for **MGMT4**, you'll find electronic resources such as **video podcasts, audio downloads,** and **interactive quizzes** for each chapter.

These resources will help supplement your understanding of core management concepts in a format that fits your busy lifestyle. Visit CourseMate for **MGMT4** to learn more about the multiple resources available to help you succeed!
Access at **www.cengagebrain.com**.

9 Designing Adaptive Organizations

© Raygun/Cultura/Jupiterimages

LEARNING OUTCOMES:

1 describe the departmentalization approach to organizational structure.

2 explain organizational authority.

3 discuss the different methods for job design.

4 explain the methods that companies are using to redesign internal organizational processes (i.e., intraorganizational processes).

5 describe the methods that companies are using to redesign external organizational processes (i.e., interorganizational processes).

Structure and Process

Organizational structure is the vertical and horizontal configuration of departments, authority, and jobs within a company. Organizational structure is concerned with vertical questions such as "Who reports to whom?" and "Who does what?" and "Where is the work done?" For example, Sony Corporation of America is headed by Chairman and CEO Howard Stringer, who is based in New York City. But Sony has a number of divisions to handle different sectors of the company's business, each headed by its own President or CEO. PlayStations are developed and managed in Foster City, California, by Sony Computer Entertainment. Sony camcorders, home theater equipment, LCD screens, VAIO computers, Blu-ray disc players, and the Walkman are handled in San Diego by Sony Electronics. The *Spider-Man* films and *Seinfeld* were brought to you by Sony Pictures Entertainment in Culver City, California, while the music of Alicia Keyes and AC/DC comes courtesy of Sony Music Entertainment in New York City.[1] Companies like Sony use organizational structure to set up departments and relationships among employees in order to make business happen. You can see Sony's organizational structure in Exhibit 9.1.

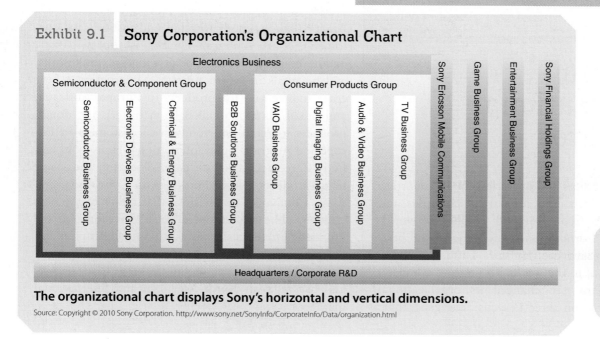

Exhibit 9.1   Sony Corporation's Organizational Chart

Electronics Business

Semiconductor & Component Group

- Semiconductor Business Group
- Electronic Devices Business Group
- Chemical & Energy Business Group

B2B Solutions Business Group

Consumer Products Group

- VAIO Business Group
- Digital Imaging Business Group
- Audio & Video Business Group
- TV Business Group

Sony Ericsson Mobile Communications

Game Business Group

Entertainment Business Group

Sony Financial Holdings Group

Headquarters / Corporate R&D

The organizational chart displays Sony's horizontal and vertical dimensions.

Source: Copyright © 2010 Sony Corporation. http://www.sony.net/SonyInfo/CorporateInfo/Data/organization.html

Organizational structure the vertical and horizontal configuration of departments, authority, and jobs within a company

Organizational process the collection of activities that transform inputs into outputs that customers value

An **organizational process** is the collection of activities that transform inputs into outputs that customers value.[2] Organizational process asks, "How do things get done?" For example, to write computer software, Microsoft uses basic internal and external processes, shown in Exhibit 9.2. The process starts when Microsoft gets external feedback from customers through Internet newsgroups, email, phone calls, or letters. This information helps Microsoft understand customers' needs and problems and identify important software issues and needed changes and functions. Microsoft then rewrites the software, testing it internally at the company and then externally through its beta testing process in which customers who volunteer or are selected by Microsoft give the company extensive feedback which is then used to make improvements. After final corrections are made to the software, the company distributes and sells it to customers. They start the process again by giving Microsoft more feedback. Indeed, Microsoft's advertising campaign for the kickoff of Windows 7, which was developed through extensive beta testing, was, "I'm a PC, and Windows 7 was my idea."

Organizational process is just as important as organizational structure, and you'll learn about both in this chapter.

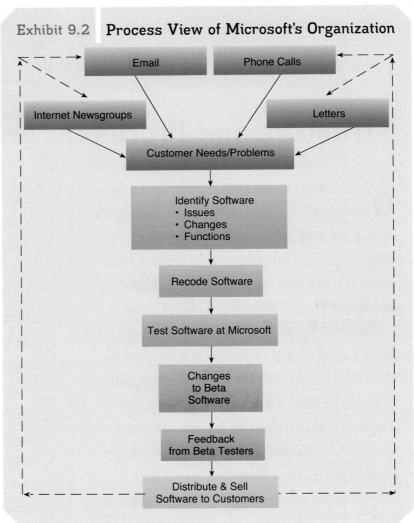

Exhibit 9.2   **Process View of Microsoft's Organization**

© Cengage Learning 2011

Designing Organizational Structures

With offices and operations in 58 countries, products in more than 200 countries, and more than 150,000 employees worldwide, Sara Lee Corporation owns some of the best-known brands (Sara Lee, Hillshire Farm, Ball Park, and Jimmy Dean) in the world. To improve company performance, Sara Lee changed its organizational structure to focus on three key customer/geographic markets: North American Retail (packaged meats such as Hillshire Farm, Ball Park, or Jimmy Dean brands, and Senseo coffee), North American Fresh Bakery (bakery goods to retail and institutional customers), North American Foodservice (meat, bakery, and beverages to foodservice distributors, restaurants, and hospitals in North America), International Beverage (coffee and tea products to Europe, Australia, and Brazil), International Bakery (bakery and dough products to retail and foodservice customers in Europe and Australia), and International Household and Body Care (body care, air care, shoe care, and insecticide products sold in Europe, Africa, Australia, and Asia). Companies or divisions that didn't fit the new structure, like the European meats division and the branded apparel businesses (including Champion and Playtex) were sold. As a result, Sara Lee is now focused on its core businesses—retail, bakery, food service, and beverages in North American and International markets.[3]

Why would a large company like Sara Lee completely restructure its organizational design? What can be gained from such a change?

After reading the next three sections, you should be able to

1 describe the departmentalization approach to organizational structure.

2 explain organizational authority.

3 discuss the different methods for job design.

1 Departmentalization

Traditionally, organizational structures have been based on some form of departmentalization. **Departmentalization** is a method of subdividing work and workers into separate organizational units that take responsibility for completing particular tasks.[4]

Traditionally, organizational structures have been created by departmentalizing work according to five methods: 1.1 functional, 1.2 product, 1.3 customer, 1.4 geographic, and 1.5 matrix.

1.1 | FUNCTIONAL DEPARTMENTALIZATION

The most common organizational structure is functional departmentalization. Companies tend to use this structure when they are small or just starting out. **Functional departmentalization** organizes work and workers into separate units responsible for particular business functions or areas of expertise. A common functional structure might have individuals organized into accounting, sales, marketing, production, and human resources departments.

Not all functionally departmentalized companies have the same functions. The insurance company and the advertising agency shown in Exhibit 9.3 both have sales, accounting, human resources, and information systems departments, as indicated by the orange boxes. The purple and green boxes indicate the functions that are different. As would be expected, the insurance company has separate departments for life, auto, home, and health insurance. The advertising agency has departments for artwork, creative work, print advertising, and radio advertising. So the functional departments in a company that uses functional structure depend in part on the business or industry the company is in.

Functional departmentalization has some advantages. First, it allows work to be done by highly qualified specialists. While the accountants in the accounting department take responsibility for producing accurate revenue and expense figures, the engineers in research and development can focus their efforts on designing a product that is reliable and simple to manufacture. Second, it lowers costs by reducing duplication. When the engineers in research and development come up with that fantastic new product, they don't have to worry about creating an aggressive advertising campaign to sell it. That task belongs to the advertising experts and sales representatives in marketing. Third, with everyone in the same department having similar work experience or training, communication and coordination are less problematic for departmental managers.

At the same time, functional departmentalization has a number of disadvantages. To start, cross-department coordination can be difficult. Managers

Departmentalization subdividing work and workers into separate organizational units responsible for completing particular tasks

Functional departmentalization organizing work and workers into separate units responsible for particular business functions or areas of expertise

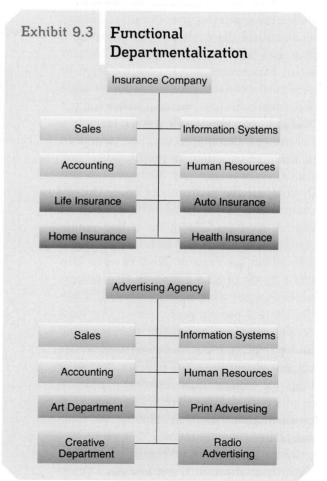

Exhibit 9.3 **Functional Departmentalization**

© Cengage Learning 2011

and employees are often more interested in doing what's right for their function than in doing what's right for the entire organization. As companies grow, functional departmentalization may also lead to slower decision making and produce managers and workers with narrow experience and expertise.

1.2 | PRODUCT DEPARTMENTALIZATION

Product departmentalization organizes work and workers into separate units responsible for producing particular products or services. Exhibit 9.4 shows the product departmentalization structure used by United Technologies (UTC), which is organized along seven different product lines: Carrier, Chubb, Hamilton Sundstrand, Otis, Pratt & Whitney, Sikorsky, UTC Fire & Security, and UTC Power.[5]

One of the advantages of product departmentalization is that, like functional departmentalization, it allows managers and workers to specialize in one area of expertise. Unlike the narrow expertise and experiences in functional departmentalization, however, managers and workers develop a broader set of experiences and expertise related to an entire product line. Likewise, product departmentalization makes it easier for top managers to assess work-unit performance. For example, because of the clear separation of their seven different product divisions, United Technologies' top managers can easily compare the performance of its Otis elevators and its Pratt & Whitney aircraft engines divisions. The divisions had similar revenues—almost $12.9 billion for Otis and $13 billion for Pratt & Whitney—but Otis had a profit of $2.5 billion (a 19.4 percent profit margin) compared with just $2.1 billion (a 16.2 percent profit margin) for Pratt & Whitney.[6] Finally, decision making should be faster because managers and workers are responsible for the entire product line rather than for separate functional departments; in other words, there are fewer conflicts in product departmentalization than in functional departmentalization.

The primary disadvantage of product departmentalization is duplication. For ex-

ample, you can see in Exhibit 9.4 that UTC's Otis elevators and Pratt & Whitney divisions both have customer service, engineering, human resources, legal, manufacturing, and procurement (similar to sourcing and logistics) departments. By contrast, if United Technologies were instead organized by function, one lawyer could handle matters related to both elevators and aircraft engines rather than working only on one or the other. Duplication like this often results in higher costs.

A second disadvantage is the challenge of coordinating across the different product departments. United Technologies would probably have difficulty standardizing its policies and procedures in product departments as different as the Carrier (heating, ventilating, and air-conditioning) and Sikorsky (military and commercial helicopters) divisions.

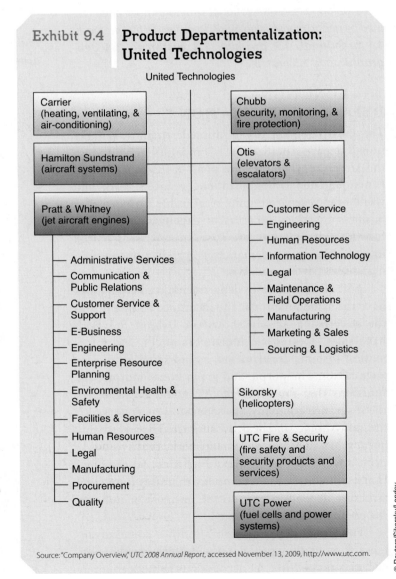

Exhibit 9.4 | Product Departmentalization: United Technologies

United Technologies

Carrier (heating, ventilating, & air-conditioning)

Chubb (security, monitoring, & fire protection)

Hamilton Sundstrand (aircraft systems)

Otis (elevators & escalators)

Pratt & Whitney (jet aircraft engines)
- Administrative Services
- Communication & Public Relations
- Customer Service & Support
- E-Business
- Engineering
- Enterprise Resource Planning
- Environmental Health & Safety
- Facilities & Services
- Human Resources
- Legal
- Manufacturing
- Procurement
- Quality

Otis:
- Customer Service
- Engineering
- Human Resources
- Information Technology
- Legal
- Maintenance & Field Operations
- Manufacturing
- Marketing & Sales
- Sourcing & Logistics

Sikorsky (helicopters)

UTC Fire & Security (fire safety and security products and services)

UTC Power (fuel cells and power systems)

Source: "Company Overview," *UTC 2008 Annual Report*, accessed November 13, 2009, http://www.utc.com.

© Reuters/Sikorsky/Landov

Exhibit 9.5 Customer Departmentalization: Swisscom AG

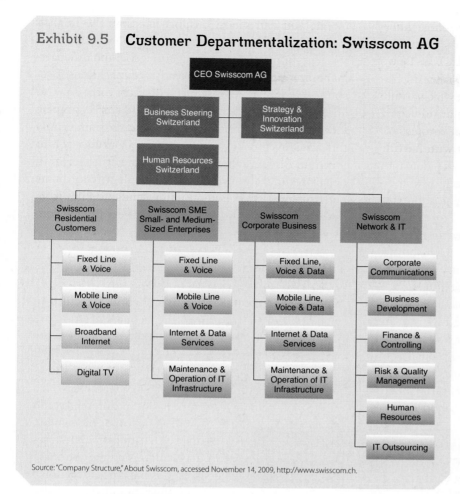

Source: "Company Structure," About Swisscom, accessed November 14, 2009, http://www.swisscom.ch.

1.3 | CUSTOMER DEPARTMENTALIZATION

Customer departmentalization organizes work and workers into separate units responsible for particular kinds of customers. For example, as Exhibit 9.5 shows, Swisscom AG, Switzerland's leading telecommunications provider, is organized into departments by type of customer: residential customers (fixed line and voice, mobile line and voice, broadband Internet, and digital TV), small- and medium-sized businesses (fixed line and voice, mobile line and voice, Internet and data services, and maintenance and operation of IT infrastructure), larger corporations (fixed line, voice and data; mobile line, voice and data; Internet and data services; and maintenance and operation of IT infrastructure), and network and IT customers (corporate communications, business development, finance and controlling, risk and quality management, human resources, and IT outsourcing).[7]

The primary advantage of customer departmentalization is that it focuses the organization

on customer needs rather than on products or business functions. Furthermore, creating separate departments to serve specific kinds of customers allows companies to specialize and adapt their products and services to customer needs and problems.

> **Customer departmentalization** organizing work and workers into separate units responsible for particular kinds of customers
>
> **Geographic departmentalization** organizing work and workers into separate units responsible for doing business in particular geographic areas

The primary disadvantage of customer departmentalization is that, like product departmentalization, it leads to duplication of resources. It can also be difficult to achieve coordination across different customer departments. Finally, the emphasis on meeting customers' needs may lead workers to make decisions that please customers but hurt the business.

1.4 | GEOGRAPHIC DEPARTMENTALIZATION

Geographic departmentalization organizes work and workers into separate units responsible for doing business in particular geographic areas. For example, Exhibit 9.6 shows the geographic departmentalization used by Coca-Cola

Exhibit 9.6 Geographic Departmentalization: Coca-Cola Enterprises

Source: "Our Business at a Glance," Coca-Cola Enterprises, accessed November 14, 2009, http://www.cokecce.com.

Enterprises (CCE), the largest bottler and distributor of Coca-Cola products in the world. CCE has two regional groups: North America and Europe, each of which would be a sizable company by itself.

The primary advantage of geographic departmentalization is that it helps companies respond to the demands of different markets. This can be especially important when the company sells in different countries, as cultural preferences can vary widely. For example, CCE's geographic divisions sell products suited to taste preferences in different countries. CCE bottles and distributes the following products in Europe but not in the United States: Aquarius, Bonaqua, Burn, Coca-Cola Light (which is somewhat different from Diet Coke), Cresta flavors, Five Alive, Kia-Ora, Kinley, Lilt, Malvern, and Oasis.[8] Another advantage is that geographic departmentalization can reduce costs by locating unique organizational resources closer to customers. For instance, it is much cheaper for CCE to build bottling plants in Belgium than to bottle Coke in England and then transport it across the English Channel to Belgium.

The primary disadvantage of geographic departmentalization is that it can lead to duplication of resources. For example, while it may be necessary to adapt products and marketing to different geographic locations, it's doubtful that CCE needs significantly different inventory tracking systems from location to location. Also, even more than with the other forms of departmentalization, it can be difficult to coordinate departments that are literally thousands of miles from each other and whose managers have very limited contact with each other.

1.5 | MATRIX DEPARTMENTALIZATION

Matrix departmentalization is a hybrid structure in which two or more forms of departmentalization are used together. The most common matrix combines the product and functional forms of departmentalization, but other forms may also be used. Exhibit 9.7 shows the matrix structure used by Procter & Gamble, which has 138,000 employees working in 80 different countries.[9] Across the top of the exhibit, you can see that the company uses a product unit structure with managers responsible for the global efforts of their branded products. The left side of the figure, however, shows that the company is also using a functional structure based on three functions—market development, which makes sure that a product is adapted to and sells well within a particular region in the world (market development regions include North America, Asia/India/Australia, Northeast Asia, Greater China, Central-Eastern Europe/Middle East/Africa, Western Europe, and Latin America); global business services, which enable the company to operate efficiently, work effectively with business partners, and increase employee productivity; and corporate functions, which provide global business units with the functional business assistance they need (i.e., finance, accounting, human resources, information technology, etc.).[10]

Fast Facts: Geographic Departmentalization— GM South America

In an effort to rebuild its North American operations, GM relied on geographic departmentalization to create a new South American unit to better take advantage of the region's expanding auto market. Automakers are well known for using geographic departmentalization, and a division dedicated to the region will help GM capitalize on its favorable positioning in many of those countries, where it holds a 20.2 percent overall market share.

Established: June 2010

President: Jaime Ardila (former general manager of GM Mercosur)

Countries: Brazil, Argentina, Colombia, Ecuador, Venezuela, Bolivia, Chile, Paraguay, Peru, Uruguay

Employees: 29,000

South American Vehicle Sales Growth: 20 percent (first quarter 2010, all auto makers)

Sources: T. Murphy and S. Terlep, "GM Creates South America Unit," *Wall Street Journal*, June 23, 2010, accessed July 20, 2010, http://online.wsj.com/article/SB10001424052748704853404575322831559648988.html?KEYWORDS=gm+creates+unit+for+south+america; GM News," GM Announces South America Region," General Motors, June 22, 2010, accessed August 12, 2010, http://media.gm.com/content/media/us/en/news/news_detail.brand_gm.html/content/Pages/news/us/en/2010/Jun/0622_southafrica.

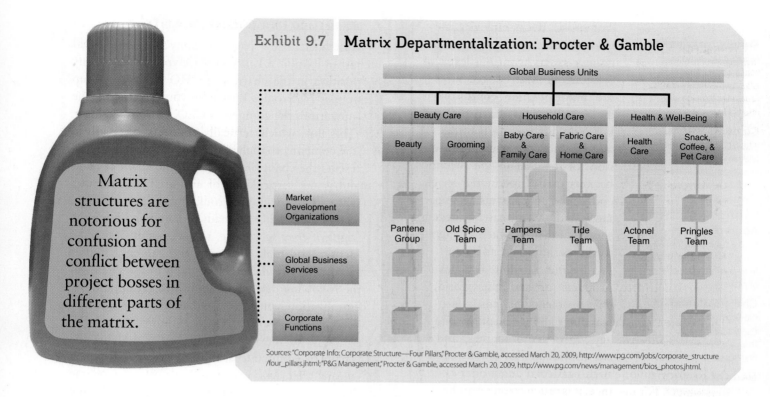

Exhibit 9.7 **Matrix Departmentalization: Procter & Gamble**

Global Business Units

Beauty Care | Household Care | Health & Well-Being

Beauty | Grooming | Baby Care & Family Care | Fabric Care & Home Care | Health Care | Snack, Coffee, & Pet Care

Market Development Organizations

Global Business Services

Corporate Functions

Pantene Group | Old Spice Team | Pampers Team | Tide Team | Actonel Team | Pringles Team

Matrix structures are notorious for confusion and conflict between project bosses in different parts of the matrix.

Sources: "Corporate Info: Corporate Structure—Four Pillars," Procter & Gamble, accessed March 20, 2009, http://www.pg.com/jobs/corporate_structure /four_pillars.jhtml; "P&G Management," Procter & Gamble, accessed March 20, 2009, http://www.pg.com/news/management/bios_photos.jhtml.

© iStockphoto.com/subjug

The boxes in the figure represent the matrix structure, created by combining the product and functional structures. For example, the Pantene Team (Pantene is a set of hair care products within the beauty segment of the beauty care global business unit) would work with market development to adapt and sell Pantene products worldwide, use global business services to work with suppliers and keep costs down, and then rely on corporate functions for assistance in hiring employees, billing customers, and paying suppliers. Similar matrix combinations are shown for P&G's Old Spice, Pampers, Tide, Actonel, and Pringles teams within each of the six segments found under its three global business units.

Several things distinguish matrix departmentalization from the other traditional forms of departmentalization.[11] First, most employees report to two bosses, one from each core part of the matrix. For example, in Exhibit 9.7, managers on the Pampers team responsible for marketing would report to a boss in the baby care and family care segment of the household care global business unit as well as a manager in the market development function. Second, by virtue of their hybrid design, matrix structures lead to much more cross-functional interaction than other forms of departmentalization. In fact, although matrix workers are typically members of only one functional department (based on their work experience and expertise), they are also commonly members of several ongoing project, product, or customer groups. Third, because

of the high level of cross-functional interaction, matrix departmentalization requires significant coordination between managers in the different parts of the matrix. In particular, managers have the complex job of tracking and managing the multiple demands (project, product, customer, or functional) on employees' time.

The primary advantage of matrix departmentalization is that it allows companies to efficiently manage large, complex tasks like researching, developing, and marketing pharmaceuticals or carrying out complex global businesses. Efficiency comes from avoiding duplication. For example, rather than having an entire marketing function for each project, the company simply assigns and reassigns workers from the marketing department (or market development at P&G) as they are needed at various stages of product completion. More specifically, an employee from a department may simultaneously be part of five different ongoing projects, but may be actively completing work on only a few projects at a time.

Another advantage is the pool of resources available to carry out large, complex tasks. Because of the ability to quickly pull in expert help from all the functional areas of the company, matrix project managers have a much more diverse bank of expertise and experience at their disposal than do managers in the other forms of departmentalization.

The primary disadvantage of matrix departmentalization is the high level of coordination required

Simple matrix a form of matrix departmentalization in which managers in different parts of the matrix negotiate conflicts and resources

Complex matrix a form of matrix departmentalization in which managers in different parts of the matrix report to matrix managers, who help them sort out conflicts and problems

Authority the right to give commands, take action, and make decisions to achieve organizational objectives

Chain of command the vertical line of authority that clarifies who reports to whom throughout the organization

Unity of command a management principle that workers should report to just one boss

Line authority the right to command immediate subordinates in the chain of command

Staff authority the right to advise, but not command, others who are not subordinates in the chain of command

to manage the complexity involved with running large, ongoing projects at various levels of completion. Matrix structures are notorious for confusion and conflict between project bosses in different parts of the matrix. At P&G, such confusion or conflict might occur between managers in the snack, coffee, and pet care business segment and the global business services function when trying to decide how best to manufacture and distribute Pringles products around the world. Disagreements or misunderstandings about schedules, budgets, available resources, and the availability of employees with particular functional expertise are common. Another disadvantage is that matrix structures require much more management skill than the other forms of departmentalization.

Because of these problems, many matrix structures evolve from a **simple matrix,** in which managers in different parts of the matrix negotiate conflicts and resources directly, to a **complex matrix,** in which specialized matrix managers and departments are added to the organizational structure. In a complex matrix, managers from different parts of the matrix might report to the same matrix manager, who helps them sort out conflicts and problems.

⊇ Organizational Authority

The second part of traditional organizational structures is authority. **Authority** is the right to give commands, take action, and make decisions to achieve organizational objectives.[12]

Traditionally, organizational authority has been characterized by the following dimensions: 2.1 chain of command, 2.2 line versus staff authority, 2.3 delegation of authority, and 2.4 degree of centralization.

2.1 | CHAIN OF COMMAND

Turn back a few pages to Sony's organizational chart in Exhibit 9.1. If you place your finger on any position in the chart, say, VAIO Business Group (under Electronics Business), you can trace a line upward to the company's CEO, Howard Stringer. This line, which vertically connects every job in the company to higher levels of management, represents the chain of command. The **chain of command** is the vertical line of authority that clarifies who reports to whom throughout the organization. People higher in the chain of command have the right, *if they so choose,* to give commands, take action, and make decisions concerning activities occurring anywhere below them in the chain. In the following discussion about delegation and decentralization, you will learn that managers don't always choose to exercise their authority directly.[13]

One of the key assumptions underlying the chain of command is **unity of command,** which means that workers should report to just one boss.[14] In practical terms, this means that only one person can be in charge at a time. Matrix organizations, in which employees have two bosses, automatically violate this principle. This is one of the primary reasons that matrix organizations are difficult to manage. Unity of command serves an important purpose: to prevent the confusion that might arise when an employee receives conflicting commands from two different bosses.

2.2 | LINE VERSUS STAFF AUTHORITY

A second dimension of authority is the distinction between line and staff authority. **Line authority** is the right to command immediate subordinates in the chain of command. For example, Sony CEO Howard Stringer has line authority over the head of Sony Entertainment Business Group, which contains Sony Pictures. Stringer can issue orders to that division president and expect them to be carried out. In turn, the head of Sony Entertainment Business Group can issue orders to his subordinates and expect them to be carried out.

Staff authority is the right to *advise* but not command others who are not subordinates in the chain of command. For example, a manager in human resources at Sony might advise the manager in charge of Sony's TV Business Group on a hiring decision but cannot order him or her to hire a certain applicant.

The terms *line* and *staff* are also used to describe different functions within the organization. A **line function** is an activity that contributes directly to creating or selling the company's products. So, for example, activities that take place within the manufacturing and marketing departments would be considered line functions. A **staff function**, such as accounting, human resources, or legal services, does not contribute directly to creating or selling the company's products but instead supports line activities. For example, marketing managers might consult with the legal staff to make sure the wording of a particular advertisement is legal.

2.3 | DELEGATION OF AUTHORITY

Managers can exercise their authority directly by completing the tasks themselves, or they can choose to pass on some of their authority to subordinates. **Delegation of authority** is the assignment of direct authority and responsibility to a subordinate to complete tasks for which the manager is normally responsible.

When a manager delegates work, three transfers occur, as illustrated in Exhibit 9.8. First, the manager transfers full responsibility for the assignment to the

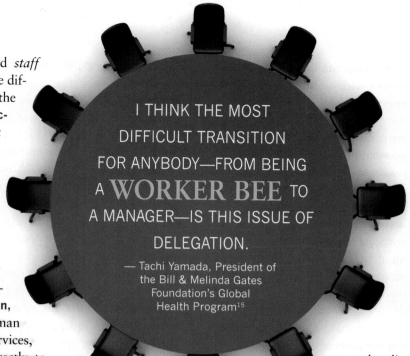

I THINK THE MOST DIFFICULT TRANSITION FOR ANYBODY—FROM BEING A **WORKER BEE** TO A MANAGER—IS THIS ISSUE OF DELEGATION.

— Tachi Yamada, President of the Bill & Melinda Gates Foundation's Global Health Program[15]

Line function an activity that contributes directly to creating or selling the company's products

Staff function an activity that does not contribute directly to creating or selling the company's products, but instead supports line activities

Delegation of authority the assignment of direct authority and responsibility to a subordinate to complete tasks for which the manager is normally responsible

subordinate. Many managers find giving up full responsibility somewhat difficult. For example, when Microsoft's Bill Gates became chairman and chief software architect after being CEO, he found it difficult to relinquish authority to his long-time partner, new CEO Steve Ballmer. Consultant David Nadler says, "There is a savior complex that says, 'I'm the only one' who can lead this company effectively."[16]

As the Gates-Ballmer example illustrates, one reason it is difficult for some managers to delegate is that they often fear the task won't be done as well as if they did it themselves. However, one CEO says, "If you can delegate a task to somebody who can do it 75 percent to 80 percent as well as you can today, you delegate it immediately."[17] Why? Many tasks don't need to be done perfectly; they just need to be *done*. And delegating tasks that someone else can do frees managers to assume other important responsibilities.

Delegating authority can generate a related problem: micromanaging. Sometimes managers delegate only to later interfere with how the employee is performing the task. "Why are you doing it that way? That's not the way I do it." But delegating full responsibility means that the employee—not the manager—is now completely responsible for task completion. Good managers need to trust their subordinates to do the job.

The second transfer that occurs with delegation is that the manager gives the subordinate full authority over the budget, resources, and personnel needed to do the job. To do the job effectively, subordinates must have the same tools and information at their disposal that managers had when they were responsible for the same task. In other words, for delegation to

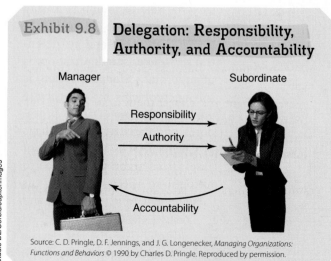

| Exhibit 9.8 | **Delegation: Responsibility, Authority, and Accountability** |

Manager   Subordinate

Responsibility →

Authority →

Accountability

Source: C. D. Pringle, D. F. Jennings, and J. G. Longenecker, *Managing Organizations: Functions and Behaviors* © 1990 by Charles D. Pringle. Reproduced by permission.

Centralization of authority the location of most authority at the upper levels of the organization

Decentralization the location of a significant amount of authority in the lower levels of the organization

Standardization solving problems by consistently applying the same rules, procedures, and processes

work, delegated authority must be commensurate with delegated responsibility.

The third transfer that occurs with delegation is the transfer of accountability. The subordinate now has the authority and responsibility to do the job and in return is accountable for getting the job done. In other words, managers delegate their authority and responsibility to subordinates in exchange for results.

2.4 | DEGREE OF CENTRALIZATION

If you've ever called a company's toll-free number with a complaint or a special request and been told by the customer service representative, "I'll have to ask my manager," or "I'm not authorized to do that," you know that centralization of authority exists in that company. **Centralization of authority** is the location of most authority at the upper levels of the organization. In a centralized organization, managers make most decisions, even the relatively small ones. That's why the customer service representative you called couldn't make a decision without first asking the manager.

If you are lucky, however, you may have talked to a customer service representative at another company who said, "I can take care of that for you right now." In other words, the person was able to handle your problem without any input from or consultation with company management. **Decentralization** is the location of a significant amount of authority in the lower levels of the organization. An organization is decentralized if it has a high degree of delegation at all levels. In a decentralized organization, workers closest to problems are authorized to make the decisions necessary to solve the problems on their own.

Decentralization has a number of advantages. It develops employee capabilities throughout the company and leads to faster decision making and more satisfied customers and employees. Furthermore, a study of 1,000 large companies found that those with a high degree of decentralization outperformed those with a low degree of decentralization in terms of return on assets (6.9 percent versus 4.7 percent), return on investment (14.6 percent versus 9.0 percent), return on equity (22.8 percent versus 16.6 percent), and return on sales (10.3 percent versus 6.3 percent). Surprisingly, the same study found that few large companies actually are decentralized. Specifically, only 31 percent of employees in these 1,000 companies were responsible for recommending improvements to management. Overall, just 10 percent of employees received the training and information needed to support a truly decentralized approach to management.[18]

With results like these, the key question is no longer *whether* companies should decentralize, but *where* they should decentralize. One rule of thumb is to stay centralized where standardization is important and to decentralize where standardization is unimportant. **Standardization** is solving problems by consistently applying the same rules, procedures, and processes. Air Products & Chemicals sells a wide range of gases (from argon to hydrogen to nitrogen to specialty gases), gas equipment and services, and related chemical products. As it grew over the last decade through acquisitions, its information technology (IT)

Delegation Means Hands Off, Not Brains Off

According to Tachi Yamada, President of the Bill & Melinda Gates Foundation's Global Health Program, when it comes to delegation, managers are torn between letting go and still making sure the work gets done. For Yamada, delegation means letting others make decisions, it doesn't mean ignoring delegated tasks and responsibilities. Yamada still takes an interest in the details of delegated projects. For him, that means figuring out what is most critical about a project and where problems are most likely to occur. The key, says Yamada, "I don't micromanage, but I have microinterest."

Source: T. Yamada, "Corner Office: Talk to Me. I'll Turn Off My Phone," interview by A. Bryant, *New York Times*, February 27, 2010, accessed July 20, 2010, http://www.nytimes.com/2010/02/28/business/28corner.html.

department inherited 14 different databases, five different corporate networks, and, of course, different kinds of servers, personal computers, and handheld devices. Supporting so many different platforms was causing IT costs to rise dramatically, so senior IT managers devised a "standardization index" to track and reduce the number of IT platforms in the company. After five years of planning and tracking via the standardization index, Air Products & Chemicals now has only two kinds of databases, one company network, one family of servers, and just four PC options. Instead of rising, IT costs have been reduced by $3 million to $5 million a year.[19]

3 Job Design

1. "Welcome to McDonald's. May I have your order please?"

2. Listen to the order. Repeat it for accuracy. State the total cost. "Please drive to the second window."

3. Take the money. Make change.

4. Give customers drinks, straws, and napkins.

5. Give customers food.

6. "Thank you for coming to McDonald's."

Could you stand to do the same simple tasks an average of 50 times per hour, 400 times per day, 2,000 times per week, 8,000 times per month? Few can. Fast-food workers rarely stay on the job more than 6 months. Indeed, McDonald's and other fast-food restaurants have well over 100 percent employee turnover each year.[20]

The shape of a job is closely related to how happy and fulfilled an employee feels doing it. In this next section, you will learn about **job design**—the number, kind, and variety of tasks that individual workers perform in doing their jobs.

You will learn **3.1 why companies continue to use specialized jobs like the McDonald's drive-through job** and **3.2 how job rotation, job enlargement, job enrichment, and 3.3 the job characteristics model are being used to overcome the problems associated with job specialization.**

3.1 | JOB SPECIALIZATION

ex: McDonald's worker

Job specialization occurs when a job is composed of a small part of a larger task or process. Specialized jobs are characterized by simple, easy-to-learn steps, low variety, and high repetition, like the McDonald's drive-through window job just described. One of the clear disadvantages of specialized jobs is that, being so easy to learn,

they quickly become boring. This, in turn, can lead to low job satisfaction and high absenteeism and employee turnover, all of which are very costly to organizations.

Why, then, do companies continue to create and use specialized jobs? The primary reason is that specialized jobs are very economical. As we learned from Taylor and the Gilbreths in Chapter 2, economy is a key reason why the pioneers of scientific management sought to standardize tasks. Once a job has been specialized, it takes little time to learn and master. Consequently, when experienced workers quit or are absent, the company can replace them with new employees and lose little productivity. For example, next time you're at McDonald's, notice the pictures of the food on the cash registers. These pictures make it easy for McDonald's trainees to quickly learn to take orders. Likewise, to simplify and speed operations, the drink dispensers behind the counter are set to automatically fill drink cups. Put a medium cup below the dispenser. Punch the medium drink button. The soft-drink machine then fills the cup to within a half-inch of the top while that same worker goes to get your fries. At McDonald's, every task has been simplified in this way. Because the work is designed to be simple, wages can remain low since it isn't necessary to pay high salaries to attract highly experienced, educated, or trained workers.

3.2 | JOB ROTATION, ENLARGEMENT, AND ENRICHMENT

Because of the efficiency of specialized jobs, companies are often reluctant to eliminate them. Consequently, job redesign efforts have focused on modifying jobs to keep the benefits of specialized jobs while reducing their obvious costs and disadvantages. Three methods—job rotation, job enlargement, and job enrichment—have been used to try to improve specialized jobs.[21]

Job rotation attempts to overcome the disadvantages of job specialization by periodically moving workers from one specialized job to another to give them more variety and the opportunity to use different skills. For example, an office receptionist who does nothing but answer phones could be systematically rotated to a different job, such as typing, filing, or data entry, every day or two. Likewise, a "mirror attacher" in an automobile plant might attach mirrors in the first half of the day's work shift and then install bumpers during the

Job design the number, kind, and variety of tasks that individual workers perform in doing their jobs

Job specialization a job composed of a small part of a larger task or process

Job rotation periodically moving workers from one specialized job to another to give them more variety and the opportunity to use different skills

Job enlargement

increasing the number of different tasks that a worker performs within one particular job

Job enrichment

increasing the number of tasks in a particular job and giving workers the authority and control to make meaningful decisions about their work

Job characteristics model (JCM)

an approach to job redesign that seeks to formulate jobs in ways that motivate workers and lead to positive work outcomes

Internal motivation

motivation that comes from the job itself rather than from outside rewards

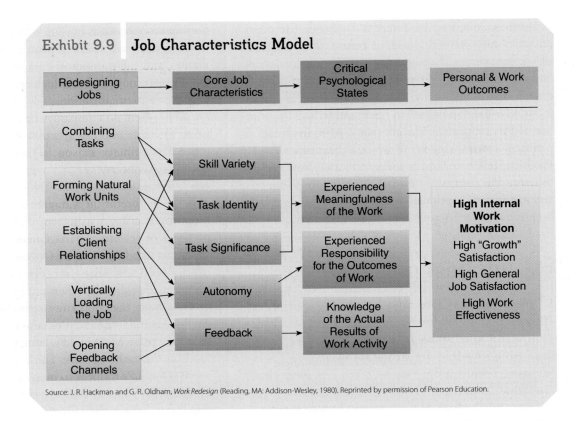

Exhibit 9.9   Job Characteristics Model

Source: J. R. Hackman and G. R. Oldham, *Work Redesign* (Reading, MA: Addison-Wesley, 1980). Reprinted by permission of Pearson Education.

second half. Because employees simply switch from one specialized job to another, job rotation allows companies to retain the economic benefits of specialized work. At the same time, the greater variety of tasks makes the work less boring and more satisfying for workers.

Another way to counter the disadvantages of specialization is to enlarge the job. **Job enlargement** increases the number of different tasks that a worker performs within one particular job. So, instead of being assigned just one task, workers with enlarged jobs are given several tasks to perform. For example, an enlarged "mirror attacher" job might include attaching the mirror, checking to see that the mirror's power adjustment controls work, and then cleaning the mirror's surface. Though job enlargement increases variety, many workers report feeling more stress when their jobs are enlarged. Consequently, many workers view enlarged jobs as simply more work, especially if they are not given additional time to complete the additional tasks. In comparison, **job enrichment** attempts to overcome the deficiencies in specialized work by increasing the number of tasks and by giving workers the authority and control to make meaningful decisions about their work.[22]

3.3 | JOB CHARACTERISTICS MODEL

In contrast to job rotation, job enlargement, and job enrichment, which focus on providing variety in job tasks, the **job characteristics model (JCM)** is an approach to

job redesign that seeks to formulate jobs in ways that motivate workers and lead to positive work outcomes.[23] As shown in the far right column of Exhibit 9.9, the primary goal of the model is to create jobs that result in positive personal and work outcomes such as internal work motivation, satisfaction with one's job, and work effectiveness. Of these, the central concern of the JCM is **internal motivation**, motivation that comes from the job itself rather than from outside rewards, such as a raise or praise from the boss. If workers feel that performing the job well is itself rewarding, then the job has internal motivation. Statements such as "I get a nice sense of accomplishment" or "I feel good about myself and what I'm producing" are examples of internal motivation.

Moving to the left in Exhibit 9.9, you can see that the JCM specifies three critical psychological states that must occur for work to be internally motivating. First, workers must *experience the work as meaningful;* that is, they must view their job as being important. Second, they must *experience responsibility for work outcomes*—they must feel personally responsible for the work being done well. Third, workers must have *knowledge of results;* that is, they must know how well they are performing their jobs. All three critical psychological states must occur for work to be internally motivating.

For example, grocery store cashiers usually have knowledge of results. When you're slow, your checkout line grows long. If you make a mistake, customers point it out: "No, I think that's on sale for $2.99, not $3.99." Likewise, cashiers experience responsibility for work outcomes. At the end of the day, the register is totaled and the money is counted. Ideally, the money matches the total sales in the register. If the money in the till is less than what's recorded in the register, most stores make the cashier pay the difference. Consequently, most cashiers are very careful to avoid being caught short at the end of the day. Nonetheless, despite knowing the results and experiencing responsibility for work outcomes, most grocery store cashiers (at least where I shop) aren't internally motivated because they don't experience the work as meaningful. With scanners, it takes little skill to learn or do the job. Anyone can do it. In addition, cashiers have few decisions to make, and the job is highly repetitive.

What kinds of jobs produce the three critical psychological states? Moving another step to the left in Exhibit 9.9, you can see that these psychological states arise from jobs that are strong on five core job characteristics: skill variety, task identity, task significance, autonomy, and feedback. **Skill variety** is the number of different activities performed in a job. **Task identity** is the degree to which a job, from beginning to end, requires completion of a whole and identifiable piece of work. **Task significance** is the degree to which a job is perceived to have a substantial impact on others inside or outside the organization. **Autonomy** is the degree to which a job gives workers the discretion, freedom, and independence to decide how and when to accomplish the work. Finally, **feedback** is the amount of information the job provides to workers about their work performance.

To illustrate how the core job characteristics work together, let's use them to more thoroughly assess why the McDonald's drive-through window job is not particularly satisfying or motivating. To start, skill variety is low. Except for the size of an order or special requests ("no onions"), the process is the same for each customer. At best, task identity is moderate. Although you take the order, handle the money, and deliver the food, others are responsible for a larger part of the process—preparing the food. Task identity will be even lower if the McDonald's has two drive-through windows, because each drive-through window worker will have an even more specialized task. The first is limited to taking the order and making change, and the second just delivers the food. Task significance, the impact you have on others, is probably low. Autonomy is also very low: McDonald's has strict rules about dress, cleanliness, and procedures. But the job does provide immediate feedback, such as positive and negative customer

comments, car horns honking, the amount of time it takes to process orders, and the number of cars in the drive-through. With the exception of feedback, the low levels of the core job characteristics show why the drive-through window job is not internally motivating for many workers.

What can managers do when jobs aren't internally motivating? The far left column of Exhibit 9.9 lists five job redesign techniques that managers can use to strengthen a job's core characteristics. *Combining tasks* increases skill variety and task identity by joining separate, specialized tasks into larger work modules. For example, some trucking firms are now requiring truck drivers to load their rigs as well as drive them. The hope is that involving drivers in loading will ensure that trucks are properly loaded, thus reducing damage claims.

Work can be formed into *natural work units* by arranging tasks according to logical or meaningful groups. Although many trucking companies randomly assign drivers to trucks, some have begun assigning drivers to particular geographic locations (e.g., the Northeast or Southwest) or to truckloads that require special driving skills when being transported (e.g., oversized loads, chemicals, etc.). Forming natural work units increases task identity and task significance.

Establishing client relationships increases skill variety, autonomy, and feedback by giving employees direct contact with clients and customers. In some companies, truck drivers are expected to establish business relationships with their regular customers. When something goes wrong with a shipment, customers are told to call drivers directly.

Vertical loading means pushing some managerial authority down to workers. For truck drivers, this means that they have the same authority as managers to resolve customer problems. In some companies, if a late shipment causes problems for a customer, the driver has the authority to fully refund the cost of that shipment (without first obtaining management's approval).

The last job redesign technique offered by the model, *opening feedback channels,* means finding additional ways to give employees direct, frequent feedback about their job performance.

Skill variety the number of different activities performed in a job

Task identity the degree to which a job, from beginning to end, requires the completion of a whole and identifiable piece of work

Task significance the degree to which a job is perceived to have a substantial impact on others inside or outside the organization

Autonomy the degree to which a job gives workers the discretion, freedom, and independence to decide how and when to accomplish the job

Feedback the amount of information the job provides to workers about their work performance

Designing Organizational Processes

almost a half century ago, Tom Burns and G. M. Stalker described how two kinds of organizational designs, mechanistic and organic, are appropriate for different kinds of organizational environments.[24] **Mechanistic organizations** are characterized by specialized jobs and responsibilities; precisely defined, unchanging roles; and a rigid chain of command based on centralized authority and vertical communication. This type of organization works best in stable, unchanging business environments. By contrast, **organic organizations** are characterized by broadly defined jobs and responsibility; loosely defined, frequently changing roles; and decentralized authority and horizontal communication based on task knowledge. This type of organization works best in dynamic, changing business environments.

The organizational design techniques described in the first part of this chapter—departmentalization, authority, and job design—are better suited for mechanistic organizations and the stable business environments that were more prevalent before 1980. In contrast, the organizational design techniques discussed next, in the second part of the chapter, are more appropriate for organic organizations and the increasingly dynamic environments in which today's businesses compete.

The key difference between these approaches is that mechanistic organizational designs focus on organizational structure, whereas organic organizational designs are concerned with organizational process, or the collection of activities that transform inputs into outputs valued by customers.

After reading the next two sections, you should be able to

4 explain the methods that companies are using to

redesign internal organizational processes (i.e., intraorganizational processes).

5 describe the methods that companies are using to redesign external organizational processes (i.e., interorganizational processes).

4 Intraorganizational Processes

An **intraorganizational process** is the collection of activities that take place within an organization to transform inputs into outputs that customers value.

Let's take a look at how companies are using 4.1 reengineering and 4.2 empowerment to redesign intraorganizational processes.

4.1 | REENGINEERING

In their best-selling book *Reengineering the Corporation*, Michael Hammer and James Champy define **reengineering** as "the *fundamental* rethinking and *radical* redesign of business *processes* to achieve *dramatic* improvements in critical, contemporary measures of performance, such as cost, quality, service and speed."[25] Hammer and Champy further explained the four key words shown in italics in this definition. The first key word is *fundamental*. When reengineering organizational designs, managers must ask themselves, "Why do we do what we do?" and "Why do we do it the way we do?" The usual answer is, "Because that's the way we've always done it." Fundamental rethinking involves getting behind "that's the way we've always done it" and pursuing answers to these questions down to the foundations so that processes are actually achieving business goals. The second key word is *radical*. Reengineering is about significant change—starting over by throwing out the old ways of getting work done. The third key word is *processes*. Hammer and Champy noted that "most business people are not process oriented; they are focused on tasks, on jobs, on people, on structures, but not on processes." The fourth key word is *dramatic*. Reengineering is about achieving quantum improvements in company performance.

An example from IBM Credit's operation illustrates how work can be reengineered.[26] IBM Credit lends businesses money to pay for IBM's IT and consulting services. Previously, the loan process began when an IBM salesperson called the home office to obtain credit approval for a customer's purchase. The first department involved in the process took the credit information over the phone from the salesperson and recorded it on the credit form. The credit form was sent to the

---

Mechanistic organization an organization characterized by specialized jobs and responsibilities; precisely defined, unchanging roles; and a rigid chain of command based on centralized authority and vertical communication

Organic organization an organization characterized by broadly defined jobs and responsibility; loosely defined, frequently changing roles; and decentralized authority and horizontal communication based on task knowledge

Intraorganizational process the collection of activities that take place within an organization to transform inputs into outputs that customers value

Reengineering fundamental rethinking and radical redesign of business processes to achieve dramatic improvements in critical measures of performance, such as cost, quality, service, and speed

credit checking department, then to the pricing department (where the interest rate was determined), and on through a total of five departments. In all, it took the five departments six days to approve or deny the customer's loan. Of course, this delay cost IBM business. Some customers got their loans elsewhere. Others, frustrated by the wait, simply canceled their orders.

Finally, two IBM managers decided to walk a loan straight through each of the departments involved in the process. At each step, they asked the workers to stop what they were doing and immediately process their loan applications. They were shocked by what they found. From start to finish, the entire process took just 90 minutes! The six-day turnaround time was almost entirely due to delays in handing off the work from one department to another. The solution: IBM redesigned the process so that one person, not five people in five separate departments, now handles the entire loan approval process without any handoffs. Approval time dropped from six days to four hours and allowed IBM Credit to increase the number of loans it handled by a factor of 100!

Reengineering changes an organization's orientation from vertical to horizontal. Instead of taking orders from upper management, lower- and middle-level managers and workers take orders from a customer who is at the beginning and end of each process. Instead of running independent functional departments, managers and workers in different departments take ownership of cross-functional processes. Instead of simplifying work so that it becomes increasingly specialized, reengineering complicates work by giving workers increased autonomy and responsibility for complete processes.

In essence, reengineering changes work by changing **task interdependence**, the extent to which collective action is required to complete an entire piece of work. As shown in Exhibit 9.10, there are three kinds of task interdependence.[27] In **pooled interdependence**, each job or department independently contributes to the whole. In **sequential interdependence**, work must be performed in succession, as one group's or job's outputs become the inputs for the next group or job. Finally, in **reciprocal interdependence**, different jobs or groups work together in a back-and-forth manner to complete the process. By reducing the handoffs between different jobs or groups, reengineering decreases sequential interdependence. Likewise, reengineering decreases pooled interdependence by redesigning work so that formerly independent jobs or departments now work together to complete processes. Finally, reengineering increases reciprocal interdependence by making groups or individuals responsible for larger, more complete processes in which several steps may be accomplished at the same time.

As an organizational design tool, reengineering promises big rewards, but it has also come under severe criticism. The most serious complaint is that because it allows a few workers to do the work formerly done by many, reengineering is simply a corporate code word for cost cutting and worker layoffs.[28] Likewise, for that reason, detractors claim

> **Task interdependence** the extent to which collective action is required to complete an entire piece of work
>
> **Pooled interdependence** work completed by having each job or department independently contribute to the whole
>
> **Sequential interdependence** work completed in succession, with one group's or job's outputs becoming the inputs for the next group or job
>
> **Reciprocal interdependence** work completed by different jobs or groups working together in a back-and-forth manner

Get Out the Red Pen!

While working as the CFO of KPN NV, a Dutch telecommunications company, Marcel Smits was known for his discernment and for disentangling knotty, costly problems. During his tenure at KPN, Smits was faced with making sure the firm complied with the complex Sarbanes-Oxley Act. He noticed that KPN staff completed 13,000 different procedures each month to ensure the firm's financial statements were accurate. In a massive reengineering effort, Smits directed managers to identify which procedures were essential for complying with the law and which weren't providing useful information. The result was a dramatic streamlining of the procedures. Within two years, the number of compliance procedures dropped to about 3,000!

Source: I. Brat and J. Lublin, "Sara Lee CEO Resigns Amid Health Problems," *Wall Street Journal*, August 9, 2010.

© Robert Kneschke/Shutterstock.com

that reengineering hurts morale and performance. Today, even reengineering gurus Hammer and Champy admit that roughly 70 percent of all reengineering projects fail because of the effects on people in the workplace. Says Hammer, "I wasn't smart enough about that [the people issues]. I was reflecting my engineering background and was insufficiently appreciative of the human dimension. I've [now] learned that's critical."[29]

4.2 | EMPOWERMENT

Another way of redesigning intra-organizational processes is through empowerment. **Empowering workers** means permanently passing decision-making authority and responsibility from managers to workers. For workers to be fully empowered, companies must give them the information and resources they need to make and carry out good decisions and then reward them for taking individual initiative.[30] For example, after outgrowing the firm's existing phone systems several times, the receptionist at Zynga, which makes Internet games, came to CEO Mark Pincus and told him that they needed to buy an entirely new phone system. Pincus told her, "Just buy it. Go figure it out."[31] After two weeks meeting with vendors and comparing options, the receptionist made the purchase. By authorizing the receptionist to make the purchase based on her best judgment, Pincus was empowering her with the authority and resources to get the job done.

Unfortunately, this doesn't happen often enough. As Michael Schrage, author and MIT researcher, wrote:

A warehouse employee can see on the intranet that a shipment is late but has no authority to accelerate its delivery. A project manager knows—and can mathematically demonstrate—that a seemingly minor spec change will bust both her budget and her schedule. The spec must be changed anyway. An airline reservations agent tells the Executive Platinum Premier frequent flier that first class appears wide open for an upgrade. However, the airline's yield management software won't permit any upgrades until just four hours before the flight, frequent fliers (and reservations) be damned. In all these cases, the employee has access to valuable information. Each one pos-

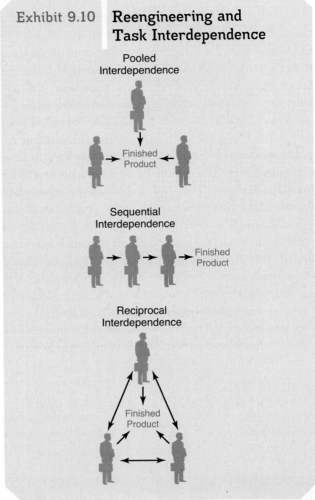

Exhibit 9.10 | Reengineering and Task Interdependence

Pooled Interdependence

Finished Product

Sequential Interdependence

Finished Product

Reciprocal Interdependence

Finished Product

© Cengage Learning 2011

sesses the "knowledge" to do the job better. But the knowledge and information are irrelevant and useless. Knowledge isn't power; the ability to act on knowledge is power.[32]

When workers are given the proper information and resources and are allowed to make good decisions, they experience strong feelings of empowerment. **Empowerment** is a feeling of intrinsic motivation in which workers perceive their work to have meaning and perceive themselves to be competent, having an impact, and capable of self-determination.[33] Work has meaning when it is consistent with personal standards and beliefs. Workers feel competent when they believe they can perform an activity with skill. The belief that they are having an impact comes from a feeling that they can affect work outcomes. A feeling of self-determination arises from workers' belief that they have the autonomy to choose how best to do their work.

Empowerment can lead to changes in organizational processes because meaning, competence, impact, and

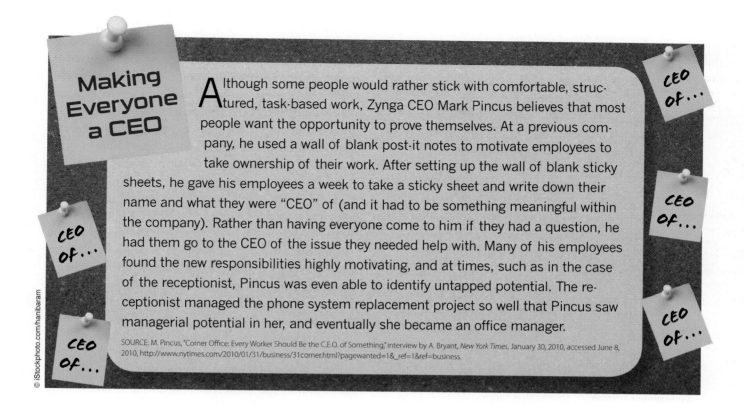

Although some people would rather stick with comfortable, structured, task-based work, Zynga CEO Mark Pincus believes that most people want the opportunity to prove themselves. At a previous company, he used a wall of blank post-it notes to motivate employees to take ownership of their work. After setting up the wall of blank sticky sheets, he gave his employees a week to take a sticky sheet and write down their name and what they were "CEO" of (and it had to be something meaningful within the company). Rather than having everyone come to him if they had a question, he had them go to the CEO of the issue they needed help with. Many of his employees found the new responsibilities highly motivating, and at times, such as in the case of the receptionist, Pincus was even able to identify untapped potential. The receptionist managed the phone system replacement project so well that Pincus saw managerial potential in her, and eventually she became an office manager.

SOURCE: M. Pincus, "Corner Office: Every Worker Should Be the C.E.O. of Something," interview by A. Bryant, *New York Times*, January 30, 2010, accessed June 8, 2010, http://www.nytimes.com/2010/01/31/business/31corner.html?pagewanted=1&_ref=1&ref=business.

self-determination produce empowered employees who take active, rather than passive, roles in their work.

5 Interorganizational Processes

An **interorganizational process** is a collection of activities that occur *among companies* to transform inputs into outputs that customers value. In other words, many companies work together to create a product or service that keeps customers happy. For example, when you purchase a Liz Claiborne outfit, you're not just buying from Liz Claiborne; you're also buying from a network of 250 suppliers in 35 countries and a sourcing team in Hong Kong that produces the right fabrics and the entire line of clothing. Those companies then manufacture the first product prototypes and send them back to the New York designers for final inspection and possibly last-minute changes.[34]

*In this section, you'll explore interorganizational processes by learning about **5.1 modular organizations** and **5.2 virtual organizations**.[35]*

5.1 | MODULAR ORGANIZATIONS

Except for the core business activities that they can perform better, faster, and cheaper than others, **modular organizations** outsource all remaining business activities to outside companies, suppliers, specialists, or consultants. The term *modular* is used because the business activities purchased from outside companies can be added and dropped as needed, much like adding pieces to a three-dimensional puzzle. Exhibit 9.11 depicts a modular organization in which the company has chosen to keep training, human resources, sales, product design, manufacturing, customer service, research and development, and information technology as core business activities, but has outsourced the noncore activities of product distribution, website design, advertising, payroll, accounting, and packaging.

Modular organizations have several advantages. First, because modular organizations pay for outsourced labor, expertise, or manufacturing capabilities only when needed, they can cost significantly less to run than traditional organizations. For example, when Apple came up with its iPod digital music player, it outsourced the audio chip design and manufacture to SigmaTel in Austin, Texas, and final assembly to ASUTeK Computer in Taiwan. Doing so not only reduced costs and sped up production, but also allowed Apple to do what it does best—design innovative products with easy-to-use software.[36] To obtain these advantages, however, modular organizations need reliable

Interorganizational process a collection of activities that take place among companies to transform inputs into outputs that customers value

Modular organization an organization that outsources noncore business activities to outside companies, suppliers, specialists, or consultants

Exhibit 9.11 Modular Organization

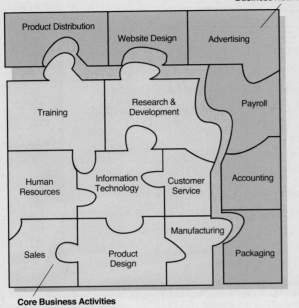

Outsourced Noncore Business Activities

Product Distribution · Website Design · Advertising · Training · Research & Development · Payroll · Human Resources · Information Technology · Customer Service · Accounting · Sales · Product Design · Manufacturing · Packaging

Core Business Activities

© Cengage Learning 2011

partners—vendors and suppliers that they can work closely with and trust.

Modular organizations have disadvantages, too. The primary disadvantage is the loss of control that occurs when key business activities are outsourced to other companies. Also, companies may reduce their competitive advantage in two ways if they mistakenly outsource a core business activity. First, as a result of competitive and technological change, the noncore business activities a company has outsourced may suddenly become the basis for competitive advantage. Second, related to that point, suppliers to whom work is outsourced can sometimes become competitors.

5.2 | VIRTUAL ORGANIZATIONS

In contrast to modular organizations in which the interorganizational process revolves around a central company, a **virtual organization** is part of a network in which many companies share skills, costs, capabilities, markets, and customers with each other. Exhibit 9.12 shows a virtual organization in which, for "today," the parts of a virtual company consist of product design, purchasing, manufacturing, advertising, and information technology. Unlike

Virtual organization an organization that is part of a network in which many companies share skills, costs, capabilities, markets, and customers to collectively solve customer problems or provide specific products or services

modular organizations, in which the outside organizations are tightly linked to one central company, virtual organizations work with some companies in the network alliance but not with all. So, whereas a puzzle with various pieces is a fitting metaphor for a modular organization, a potluck dinner is an appropriate metaphor for a virtual organization. All participants bring their finest dish but eat only what they want.

Another difference is that the working relationships between modular organizations and outside companies tend to be more stable and longer lasting than the shorter, often temporary relationships found among the virtual companies in a network alliance. The composition of a virtual organization is always changing. The combination of network partners that a virtual corporation has at any one time depends on the expertise needed to solve a particular problem or provide a specific product or service. For instance, today the business might need to focus on advertising and product design, as shown in the virtual organization's photo, but tomorrow, the business could want something completely different. In this sense, the term *virtual organization* means the organization that exists "at the moment." Virtual organizations have a number of advantages. They let companies share costs. And, because members can quickly combine their efforts to meet customers' needs, they are fast and flexible.

As with modular organizations, a disadvantage of virtual organizations is that once work has been outsourced, it can be difficult to control the quality of work done by network partners. The greatest disadvantage, however, is that tremendous managerial skills are required to make a network of independent organi-

Exhibit 9.12 Virtual Organizations

Today, I'll have...

Purchasing · Product Design · Information Technology · Manufacturing · Advertising

© Mike Powell/Lifesize/Getty Images

Even Big Corporations Can Steal a Page from the Modular Playbook

While consumer products giant Procter & Gamble uses a more traditional organizational structure, it has still found areas in which modular organizational techniques can be used to its benefit. For example, by outsourcing many traditional IT tasks, like server maintenance, P&G has been acting like a modular organization by reallocating its IT staff to focus on core strategic goals, such as increasing revenue through sales and not just improving worker efficiency. Many of P&G's IT managers and employees now work as business-unit consultants, analyzing data and thinking of ways to improve products and sales. Furthermore, P&G has found a reliable partner in Hewlett-Packard, which now handles many of P&G's basic IT needs, like server maintenance. As a result, P&G has saved $800 million over the last seven years and repurposed its IT staff to work on projects, such as P&G's "Proud Sponsor of Moms" marketing campaign, where they developed tools for tracking advertising data on a daily basis, as well as monitoring P&G's buzz in the media and on Twitter.

Source: J. Fortt, "Tech Executives Stop Cutting and Get Strategic," *Fortune*, June 14, 2010.

zations work well together, especially since their relationships tend to be short and based on a single task or project. Virtual organizations use two methods to solve this problem. The first is to use a *broker*. In traditional, hierarchical organizations, managers plan, organize, and control. But with the horizontal, interorganizational processes that characterize virtual organizations, the job of a broker is to create and assemble the knowledge, skills, and resources from different companies for outside parties, such as customers.[37] The second way to make networks of virtual organizations more manageable is to use a *virtual organization agreement* that, somewhat like a contract, specifies the schedules, responsibilities, costs, payouts, and liabilities for participating organizations.

STUDENT Study Tools

Located at the back of your book:

☐ Rip out and study the Chapter Review Card at the end of the book

Log in to the CourseMate for MGMT at cengagebrain.com to:

☐ Review Key Term Flashcards delivered 3 ways (print or online)

☐ Complete both Practice Quizzes to prepare for tests

☐ Play Beat the Clock and Quizbowl to master concepts

☐ Complete the Crossword Puzzle to review key terms

☐ Watch the video on Evo for a real company example and take the accompanying quiz

☐ Watch the Biz Flix clip from *Rendition* and take the quiz

☐ Complete the Case Assignment on Yahoo!

☐ Work through the Management Decision on garbage jobs

☐ Work through the Management Team Decision on expanding overseas

☐ Develop your skills with the Develop Your Career Potential exercise

10 | Managing Teams

© iStockphoto.com/DNY59

LEARNING OUTCOMES:

1 explain the good and bad of using teams.

2 recognize and understand the different kinds of teams.

3 understand the general characteristics of work teams.

4 explain how to enhance work-team effectiveness.

Why Use Work Teams?

Ninety-one percent of organizations are significantly improving their effectiveness by using work teams.[1] Procter & Gamble and Cummins Engine began using teams in 1962 and 1973, respectively. Boeing, Caterpillar, Champion International, Ford Motor Company, 3M, and General Electric established work teams in the mid to late 1980s. Today, most companies use teams to tackle a variety of issues.[2] "Teams are ubiquitous. Whether we are talking about software development, Olympic hockey, disease outbreak response, or urban warfare, teams represent the critical unit that 'gets things done' in today's world."[3]

Work teams consist of a small number of people with complementary skills who hold themselves mutually accountable for pursuing a common purpose, achieving performance goals, and improving interdependent work processes.[4] Though work teams are not the answer for every situation or organization, if the right teams are used properly and in the right settings, teams can dramatically improve company performance and instill a sense of vitality in the workplace that is otherwise difficult to achieve.

After reading the next two sections, you should be able to

1 **explain the good and bad of using teams.**

2 **recognize and understand the different kinds of teams.**

1 The Good and Bad of Using Teams

Let's begin our discussion of teams by learning about **1.1 the advantages of teams, 1.2 the disadvantages of teams,** *and* **1.3 when to use and not use teams.**

1.1 | THE ADVANTAGES OF TEAMS

Companies are making greater use of teams because they have been shown to improve customer satisfaction, product and service quality, employee job satisfaction, and decision making.[5] Teams help businesses increase *customer satisfaction* in several ways. One way is to create work teams that are trained to meet the needs of specific customers. Hertz, the rental car company, recently created the Gulf Coast Customer Care Center. The customer service teams at the center deal exclusively with private, business, and government customers who need cars and equipment while they help with clean-up efforts after a major oil spill in the Gulf of Mexico. According to Mark Frissoda, Hertz chairman and CEO, "The creation of a one-stop Customer Care Center provides an easy way for organizations and individual customers assisting with clean-up efforts to work with Hertz."[6] Businesses also create problem-solving teams and employee-involvement teams to study ways to improve overall customer satisfaction and make recommendations for improvements. Teams like these typically meet on a weekly or monthly basis.

Teams also help firms improve *product and service quality* in several ways.[7] In contrast to traditional organizational structures in which management is responsible for organizational outcomes

> **Work team** a small number of people with complementary skills who hold themselves mutually accountable for pursuing a common purpose, achieving performance goals, and improving interdependent work processes

Cross-training
training team members to
do all or most of the jobs
performed by the other team
members

and performance, teams take direct responsibility for the quality of the products and services they produce. At Whole Foods, a supermarket chain that sells groceries and health foods, the ten teams that manage each store are responsible for store quality and performance; they are also directly accountable because the size of their team bonus depends on the store's performance. Productive teams get an extra $1.50 to $2.00 per hour in every other paycheck.[8]

Another reason for using teams is that teamwork often leads to increased *job satisfaction.*[9] One reason that teamwork can be more satisfying than traditional work is that it gives workers a chance to improve their skills. This is often accomplished through **cross-training,** in which team members are taught how to do all or most of the jobs performed by the other team members. The advantage for the organization is that cross-training allows a team to function normally when one member is absent, quits, or is transferred. The advantage for workers is that cross-training broadens their skills and increases their capabilities while also making their work more varied and interesting. A second reason that teamwork is satisfying is that work teams often receive proprietary business information that is available only to managers at most companies. For example, Whole Foods has an "open books, open door, open people" philosophy.[10] Each team member is given full access to his or her store's financial information and everyone's salaries, including those of the store manager and the CEO.[11] Team members also gain job satisfaction from unique leadership responsibilities that are not typically available in traditional organizations. For example, rotating leadership among team members can lead to more participation and cooperation in team decision making and improved team performance.[12]

Finally, teams share many of the advantages of group decision making discussed in Chapter 5. For instance, because team members possess different knowledge, skills, abilities, and experiences, a team is able to view problems from multiple perspectives. This diversity of viewpoints increases the odds that team decisions will solve the underlying causes of problems and not just address the symptoms. The increased knowledge and information available to teams also make it easier for them to generate more alternative solutions, a critical part of improving the quality of decisions. Because team members are involved in decision-making processes, they are also likely to be more committed to making those decisions work. In short, teams can do a much better job than individuals in two important steps of the decision-making process: defining the problem and generating alternative solutions.

1.2 | THE DISADVANTAGES OF TEAMS

Although teams can significantly improve customer satisfaction, product and service quality, speed and efficiency in product development, employee job satisfaction, and decision making, using teams does not guarantee these positive outcomes. In fact, if you've ever participated in team projects in your classes, you're probably already aware of some of the problems inherent in work teams. Despite all of their promise, teams and teamwork are also prone to these significant disadvantages: initially high turnover, social loafing, and the problems associated with group decision making.

The first disadvantage of work teams is *initially high turnover.* Teams aren't for everyone, and some workers balk at the responsibility, effort, and learning required in team settings.

© Hugh Sitton/Photographer's Choice RF/Getty Images

Social loafing is another disadvantage of work teams. **Social loafing** occurs when workers withhold their efforts and fail to perform their share of the work.[13] A 19th-century French engineer named Maximilian Ringelmann first documented social loafing when he found that one person pulling on a rope alone exerted an average of 63 kilograms of force on the rope. In groups of three, the average force dropped to 53 kilograms per person. In groups of eight, the average dropped to just 31 kilograms per person. Ringelmann concluded that the larger the team, the smaller the individual effort. In fact, social loafing is more likely to occur in larger groups, where identifying and monitoring the efforts of individual team members can be difficult.[14] In other words, social loafers count on being able to blend into the background where their lack of effort isn't easily spotted. From team-based class projects, most students already know about social loafers or "slackers," who contribute poor, little, or no work whatsoever. Not surprisingly, a study of 250 student teams found that the most talented students are typically the least satisfied with teamwork because they have to carry slackers and do a disproportionate share of their team's work.[15] Perceptions of fairness are negatively related to the extent of social loafing within teams.[16]

> **Social loafing** behavior in which team members withhold their efforts and fail to perform their share of the work

Finally, teams share many of the *disadvantages of group decision making* discussed in Chapter 5, such as groupthink. In *groupthink,* members of highly cohesive groups feel intense pressure not to disagree with each other so that the group can approve a proposed solution. Because groupthink restricts discussion and leads to consideration of a limited number of alternative solutions, it usually results in poor decisions. Also, team decision making takes considerable time, and team meetings can often be unproductive and inefficient. Dan Rosensweig, CEO of Chegg, a company that rents textbooks online and by mail, has some basic strategies for keeping team meetings productive. First, he sticks to the clock, which means starting on time and ending on time. Second, no technology. That means BlackBerrys and iPhones are off, and there's no Twitter, no Facebook, and no email to distract those at the meeting. These simple strategies keep Rosensweig's meetings focused and more productive. As Rosensweig puts it, "Wherever you are, be all in."[17]

Another possible pitfall is *minority domination,* wherein just one or two people dominate team discussions, restricting consideration of different problem definitions and alternative solutions. Finally, team members may not feel accountable for the decisions and actions taken by the team.

MGMT SUCCESS

Factors That Encourage People to Withhold Effort in Teams

1. **The presence of someone with expertise.** Team members will withhold effort when another team member is highly qualified to make a decision or comment on an issue.

2. **The presentation of a compelling argument.** Team members will withhold effort if the arguments for a course of action are very persuasive or similar to their own thinking.

3. **Lacking confidence in one's ability to contribute.** Team members will withhold effort if they are unsure about their ability to contribute to discussions, activities, or decisions. This is especially so for high-profile decisions.

4. **An unimportant or meaningless decision.** Team members will withhold effort by mentally withdrawing or adopting a "who cares" attitude if decisions don't affect them or their units, or if they don't see a connection between their efforts and their team's successes or failures.

5. **A dysfunctional decision-making climate.** Team members will withhold effort if other team members are frustrated or indifferent or if a team is floundering or disorganized.

Source: P. W. Mulvey, J. F. Veiga, and P. M. Elsass, "When Teammates Raise a White Flag," *Academy of Management Executive* 10, no. 1 (1996): 40–79.

Exhibit 10.1 | When to Use and When Not to Use Teams

USE TEAMS WHEN . . .

✓ there is a clear, engaging reason or purpose.

✓ the job can't be done unless people work together.

✓ rewards can be provided for teamwork and team performance.

✓ ample resources are available.

DON'T USE TEAMS WHEN . . .

✗ there isn't a clear, engaging reason or purpose.

✗ the job can be done by people working independently.

✗ rewards are provided for individual effort and performance.

✗ the necessary resources are not available.

Source: R. Wageman, "Critical Success Factors for Creating Superb Self-Managing Teams," *Organizational Dynamics* 26, no. 1 (1997): 49–61.

© iStockphoto.com/Serdar Yagci

1.3 | WHEN TO USE TEAMS

As the two previous subsections made clear, teams have significant advantages *and* disadvantages. Therefore, the question is not *whether* to use teams, but *when* and *where* to use teams for maximum benefit and minimum cost. As Doug Johnson, associate director at the Center for Collaborative Organizations at the University of North Texas, puts it, "Teams are a means to an end, not an end in themselves."[18] Exhibit 10.1 provides some additional guidelines on when to use or not use teams.[19]

First, teams should be used when there is a clear, engaging reason or purpose for doing so. Too many companies use teams because they're popular or because the companies assume that teams can fix all problems. Teams are much more likely to succeed if they know why they exist and what they are supposed to accomplish and more likely to fail if they don't.

Second, teams should be used when the job can't be done unless people work together. This typically means that teams are needed when tasks are complex, require multiple perspectives, or require repeated interaction with others to complete. If tasks are simple and don't require multiple perspectives or repeated interaction with others, however, teams should not be used.[20] For example, Microsoft uses teams to write computer code; software simply has too many options and features for one person (or even one team) to complete it all. Microsoft ensures interaction between teams by having them "check in" their computer code every few days. Once the different pieces of code are compiled to create a prototype, the teams begin testing and debugging the new build.[21] When developing Vista, its widely criticized operating system, Microsoft's development teams didn't share their plans with each other.

While each team's code might test cleanly on its own, conflicts and failure would occur when the different codes were combined. So when developing and testing Windows 7, Vista's replacement, Microsoft development teams shared their plans with each other and spent time listening and collaborating with engineers at computer manufacturers such as Hewlett-Packard and Dell, resulting in Windows 7 being faster, more reliable, and flexible.[22]

Third, teams should be used when rewards can be provided for teamwork and team performance. Rewards that depend on team performance rather than individual performance are the key to rewarding team behaviors and efforts. You'll read more about team rewards later in the chapter, but for now it's enough to know that if the type of reward (individual versus team) is not matched to the type of performance (individual versus team), teams won't work.

2 Kinds of Teams

Let's continue our discussion of teams by learning about the different kinds of teams that companies use to make themselves more competitive. *We look first at* **2.1 how teams differ in terms of autonomy, which is the key dimension that makes one team different from another,** *and then at* **2.2 some special kinds of teams.**

2.1 | AUTONOMY, THE KEY DIMENSION

Teams can be classified in a number of ways, such as permanent or temporary, functional or cross-functional. However, studies indicate that the amount of autonomy possessed by a team is the key difference among teams.[23]

Autonomy is the degree to which workers have the discretion, freedom, and independence to decide how and when to accomplish their jobs. Exhibit 10.2 shows how five kinds of teams differ in terms of autonomy. Moving left to right across the autonomy continuum at the top of the exhibit, traditional work groups and employee involvement groups have the least autonomy, semi-autonomous work groups have more autonomy, and, finally, self-managing teams and self-designing teams have the most autonomy. Moving from bottom to top along the left side of the exhibit, note that the number of responsibilities given to each kind of team increases directly with its autonomy. Let's review each of these kinds of teams and their autonomy and responsibilities in more detail.

The smallest amount of autonomy is found in **traditional work groups,** where two or more people work together to achieve a shared goal. In these groups, workers are responsible for doing the work or executing the task, but they do not have direct responsibility or control over their work. Workers report to managers who are responsible for their performance and have the authority to hire and fire them, make job assignments, and control resources.

Employee involvement teams, which have somewhat more autonomy, meet on company time on a weekly or monthly basis to provide advice or make suggestions to management concerning specific issues such as plant safety, customer relations, or product quality.[24] Though they offer advice and suggestions, they do not have the authority to make decisions. Membership on these teams is often voluntary, but members may be selected because of their expertise. The idea behind employee involvement teams is that the people closest to the problem or situation are best able to recommend solutions.

Traditional work group a group composed of two or more people who work together to achieve a shared goal

Employee involvement team a team that provides advice or makes suggestions to management concerning specific issues

Exhibit 10.2 Team Autonomy Continuum

RESPONSIBILITIES	TRADITIONAL WORK GROUPS	EMPLOYEE INVOLVEMENT GROUPS	SEMI-AUTONOMOUS WORK GROUPS	SELF-MANAGING TEAMS	SELF-DESIGNING TEAMS
Control Design of					
Team					✓
Tasks					✓
Membership					✓
Production/Service Tasks					
Make Decisions				✓	✓
Solve Problems				✓	✓
Major Production/Service Tasks					
Make Decisions			✓	✓	✓
Solve Problems			✓	✓	✓
Information			✓	✓	✓
Give Advice/Make Suggestions		✓	✓	✓	✓
Execute Task	✓	✓	✓	✓	✓

Low Team Autonomy — High Team Autonomy

Sources: R. D. Banker, J. M. Field, R. G. Schroeder, and K. K. Sinha, "Impact of Work Teams on Manufacturing Performance: A Longitudinal Field Study," *Academy of Management Journal* 39 (1996): 867–890; J. R. Hackman, "The Psychology of Self-Management in Organizations," in *Psychology and Work: Productivity, Change, and Employment,* ed. M. S. Pallak and R. Perlof (Washington, DC: American Psychological Association), 85–136.

Semi-autonomous work groups not only provide advice and suggestions to management but also have the authority to make decisions and solve problems related to the major tasks required to produce a product or service. Semi-autonomous groups regularly receive information about budgets, work quality and performance, and competitors' products. Furthermore, members of semi-autonomous work groups are typically cross-trained in a number of different skills and tasks. In short, semi-autonomous work groups give employees the authority to make decisions that are typically made by supervisors and managers.

That authority is not complete, however. Managers still play a role, though much reduced compared to traditional work groups, in supporting the work of semi-autonomous work groups. In semi-autonomous work groups, managers ask good questions, provide resources, and facilitate performance of group goals.

Self-managing teams differ from semi-autonomous work groups in that team members manage and control *all* of the major tasks *directly related* to production of a product or service without first getting approval from management. This includes managing and controlling the acquisition of materials, making a product or providing a service, and ensuring timely delivery. **Self-designing teams** have all the characteristics of self-managing teams, but they can also control and change the design of the teams themselves, the tasks they do and how and when they do them, and the membership of the teams.

2.2 | SPECIAL KINDS OF TEAMS

Companies are also increasingly using several other kinds of teams that can't easily be categorized in terms of autonomy: cross-functional teams, virtual teams, and project teams. Depending on how these teams are designed, they can be either low- or high-autonomy teams.

Cross-functional teams are intentionally composed of employees from different functional areas of the organization.[25] Because their members have different functional backgrounds, education, and experience, cross-functional teams usually attack problems from multiple perspectives and generate more ideas and alternative solutions, all of which are especially important when trying to innovate or solve problems creatively.[26] Cross-functional teams can be used almost anywhere in an organization and are often used in conjunction with matrix and product organizational structures (see Chapter 9). They can also be part-time or temporary team assignments or full-time, long-term teams.

General Electric used a cross-functional team to design a set of stainless steel, high-end kitchen appliances called the Café Series. Marketing staffers came up with the concept directed toward serious cooks who love entertaining at home. Industrial and technical designers made the refrigerators, stoves, dishwashers, and ovens resemble restaurant kitchen appliances. Together, the designers and marketing staff studied consumers who tried the prototype appliances in GE's test kitchens.[27]

Virtual teams are groups of geographically and/or organizationally dispersed coworkers who use a combination of telecommunications and information technologies to accomplish an organizational task.[28] Members of virtual teams rarely meet face-to-face; instead, they use email, videoconferencing, and group communication software.[29] Virtual teams can be employee involvement teams, self-managing teams, or nearly any kind of team discussed in this chapter. Virtual teams are often (but not necessarily) temporary teams that are set up to accomplish a specific task.[30]

The principal advantage of virtual teams is their flexibility. Employees can work with each other regardless of physical location, time zone, or organizational affiliation.[31] Because the team members don't meet in a physical location, virtual teams also find it much easier to include other key stakeholders such as suppliers and customers. Plus, virtual teams have certain efficiency advantages over traditional team structures. Because the teammates do not meet face-to-face, a virtual team typically requires a smaller time commitment than a traditional team does.[32] A drawback of virtual teams is that the team members must learn to express themselves in new contexts.[33] The give-and-take that naturally occurs in face-to-face meetings is more difficult to achieve through video conferencing or other methods of virtual teaming. Indeed, several studies have shown that physical proximity enhances information processing in teams.[34] Therefore, some companies bring virtual team members together in offices or on special trips on a regular basis to try to minimize these problems.

Project teams are created to complete specific, one-time projects or tasks within a limited time.[35] Project teams are often used to develop new products, significantly improve existing products, roll out new information systems, or build new factories or offices. For example, BMW, the German automaker, wanted to create an eco-friendly car that would appeal to urban drivers. The car would have to be small and light, but it would also have to have the performance and luxury associated with other BMW products. To meet this goal, BMW created Project i, a special team of fifteen people, including engineers, exterior specialists, and interior designers. The team was in charge of creating prototypes, field testing systems, and designing the final product, the Multi City Vehicle, or MCV, which BMW hopes to release in 2013.[36] The project team is typically led by a project manager who has the overall responsibility of planning, staffing, and managing the team, which usually includes employees from different functional areas. Effective project teams demand both individual and collective responsibility.[37]

One advantage of project teams is that drawing employees from different functional areas can reduce or eliminate communication barriers. In turn, as long as team members feel free to express their ideas, thoughts, and concerns, free-flowing communication encourages cooperation among separate departments and typically speeds up the design process.[38] Another advantage of project teams is their flexibility. When projects are finished, project team members either move on to the next project or return to their functional units. For example, publication of this book required designers, editors, page compositors, and website designers, among others. When the task was finished, these people applied their skills to other textbook projects. Because of this flexibility, project teams are often used with the matrix organizational designs discussed in Chapter 9.

Project team a team created to complete specific, one-time projects or tasks within a limited time

Managing Work Teams

"Why did I ever let you talk me into teams? They're nothing but trouble."[39] Lots of managers have this reaction after making the move to teams. Many don't realize that this reaction is normal, both for them and for workers. In fact, such a reaction is

M G M T SUCCESS

Tips for Managing Successful Virtual Teams

- Select people who are self-starters and strong communicators.
- Keep the team focused by establishing clear, specific goals and by explaining the consequences and importance of meeting these goals.
- Provide frequent feedback so that team members can measure their progress.
- Keep team interactions upbeat and action-oriented by expressing appreciation for good work and completed tasks.
- Personalize the virtual team by periodically bringing team members together and by encouraging team members to share information with each other about their personal lives. This is especially important when the virtual team first forms.
- Improve communication through increased telephone calls, emails, Internet messaging, and videoconference sessions.
- Periodically ask team members how well the team is working and what can be done to improve performance.
- Empower virtual teams so they have the discretion, freedom, and independence to decide how and when to accomplish their jobs.

Sources: W. F. Cascio, "Managing a Virtual Workplace," *Academy of Management Executive* 14 (2000): 81–90; B. Kirkman, B. Rosen, P. Tesluk, and C. Gibson, "The Impact of Team Empowerment on Virtual Team Performance: The Moderating Role of Face-to-Face Interaction," *Academy of Management Journal* 47 (2004): 175–192; S. Furst, M. Reeves, B. Rosen, and R. Blackburn, "Managing the Life Cycle of Virtual Teams," *Academy of Management Executive* (May 2004): 6–20; C. Solomon, "Managing Virtual Teams," *Workforce* 80 (June 2001): 60.

characteristic of the *storming* stage of team development (discussed in Section 3.5). Managers who are familiar with these stages and with the other important characteristics of teams will be better prepared to manage the predictable changes that occur when companies make the switch to team-based structures.

After reading the next two sections, you should be able to

3 **understand the general characteristics of work teams.**

4 **explain how to enhance work-team effectiveness.**

3 Work-Team Characteristics

Understanding the characteristics of work teams is essential for making teams an effective part of an organization. *Therefore, in this section you'll learn about **3.1 team norms, 3.2 team cohesiveness, 3.3 team size, 3.4 team conflict,** and **3.5 the stages of team development.***

3.1 | TEAM NORMS

Over time, teams develop **norms**, which are informally agreed-upon standards that regulate team behavior.[40] Norms are valuable because they let team members know what is expected of them. While leading Orbis International, an organization dedicated to treating eye diseases around the world, Jilly Stephens noticed a problem with punctuality. While preparing to go do field work, there always seemed to be one person who couldn't wake up early enough, leaving the rest of the team waiting around idly. So she simply decided that there would be no more waiting. If team members did not show up by a designated time, they would be left to find their own transportation. Says Stephens, "We saw behaviors change fairly rapidly."[41]

Studies indicate that norms are one of the most powerful influences on work behavior because they regulate the everyday actions that allow teams to function effectively. Effective work teams develop norms about the quality and timeliness of job performance, absenteeism, safety, and honest expression of ideas and opinions. Team norms are often associated with positive outcomes such as stronger organizational commitment, more trust in management, and stronger job and organizational satisfaction.[42]

Norms can also influence team behavior in negative ways. For example, most people would agree that damaging organizational property; saying or doing something to hurt someone at work; intentionally doing one's work badly, incorrectly, or slowly; griping about coworkers; deliberately breaking rules; or doing something to harm the company are negative behaviors. A study of workers from 34 teams in 20 different organizations found that teams with negative norms strongly influenced their team members to engage in these negative behaviors. In fact, the longer individuals were members of a team with negative norms and the more frequently they interacted with their teammates, the more likely they were to perform negative behaviors. Since team norms typically develop early in the life of a team, these results indicate how important it is for teams to establish positive norms from the outset.[43]

3.2 | TEAM COHESIVENESS

Cohesiveness is another important characteristic of work teams. **Cohesiveness** is the extent to which team members are attracted to a team and motivated to remain in it.[44] The level of cohesiveness in a group is important for several reasons. To start, cohesive groups have a better chance of retaining their members. As a result, cohesive groups typically experience lower turnover.[45] In addition, team cohesiveness promotes cooperative behavior, generosity, and a willingness on the part of team members to assist each other.[46] When team cohesiveness is high, team members are more motivated to contribute to the team because they want to gain the approval of other team members. For these reasons and others, studies have clearly established that cohesive teams consistently perform better.[47] Furthermore, cohesive teams quickly achieve high levels of performance. By contrast, teams low in cohesion take much longer to reach the same levels of performance.[48]

What can be done to promote team cohesiveness? First, make sure that all team members are present at team meetings and activities. Team cohesiveness suffers when members are allowed to withdraw from the team and miss team meetings and events.[49] Second, create additional opportunities for teammates to work together by rearranging work schedules and creating common workspaces. When task interdependence is high and team members have lots of chances to work together, team cohesiveness tends to increase.[50] Third, engaging in nonwork activities as a team can help build cohesion.[51] Finally, companies build team cohesiveness by making

When Extreme Times Call for Extreme Team Building

According to Stanford organizational psychologist Robert Sutton, one of the most effective tools for bringing people closer together is shared discomfort and suffering. In the midst of a major turnaround, San Francisco–based Timbuk2, maker of bags and totes, found itself facing many challenges overhauling its infrastructure and operations to meet growing demand. The executive team, most of whom were new hires, needed to build trust quickly, so team members signed up with the National Outdoor Leadership School (NOLS) for a one-week backpacking trip in Wyoming. For seven days, the team went without toilets or showers. Together, team members climbed in weather ranging from 80 degrees to below freezing. Each day, they would spend several hours hiking to a new campsite, which sometimes was nothing more than a granite ledge. They learned how to dig latrines and cook in the outdoors. They worried about blistery, bloody feet, storm clouds on the horizon, and whether those bear paw prints meant that there was actually a bear nearby. Those real challenges and demands forced team members to work together in ways that simulated traditional team-building exercises (e.g., ropes courses) or pampered team retreats might not. Throughout the trip, the executive team was able to relate what they experienced on the camping trip to situations they faced in their business. Further, the team became more cohesive. One employee observed, "I could see...it had been a lot of hard work, but... everyone seems a little more comfortable together, like there's more trust than there was before."

Source: A. S. Wellner, "Into the Wild," *Inc.*, October 1, 2007, accessed July 27, 2010, http://www.inc.com/magazine/20071001/into-the-wild.html.

employees feel that they are part of a special organization.

3.3 | TEAM SIZE

The relationship between team size and performance appears to be curvilinear. Very small or very large teams may not perform as well as moderately sized teams. For most teams, the right size is somewhere between six and nine members.[52] This size is conducive to high team cohesion, which has a positive effect on team performance, as discussed above. A team of this size is small enough for the team members to get to know each other and for each member to have an opportunity to contribute in a meaningful way to the success of the team. At the same time, the team is also large enough to take advantage of team members' diverse skills, knowledge, and perspectives. It is also easier to instill a sense of responsibility and mutual accountability in teams of this size.[53]

By contrast, when teams get too large, team members find it difficult to get to know one another, and the team may splinter into smaller subgroups. When this occurs, subgroups sometimes argue and disagree, weakening overall team cohesion. As teams grow, there is also a greater chance of minority domination. Even if minority domination doesn't occur, larger groups may not have time for all team members to share their input. And when team members feel that their contributions are unimportant or not needed, the result is less involvement, effort, and accountability to the team.[54] Large teams also face logistical problems such as finding an appropriate time or place to meet.

Finally, the incidence of social loafing, discussed earlier in the chapter, is much higher in large teams.

Team performance can also suffer when a team is too small. Teams with just a few people may lack the diversity of skills and knowledge found in larger teams. Also, teams that are too small are unlikely to gain the advantages of team decision making (i.e., multiple perspectives, generating more ideas and alternative solutions, and stronger commitment) found in larger teams.

What signs indicate that a team's size needs to be changed? If decisions are taking too long, if the team has difficulty making decisions or taking action, if a few members dominate the team, or if the commitment or efforts of team members are weak, chances are the team is too big. In contrast, if a team is having difficulty coming up with ideas or generating solutions, or if the team does not have the expertise to address a specific problem, chances are the team is too small.

3.4 | TEAM CONFLICT

Conflict and disagreement are inevitable in most teams. But this shouldn't surprise anyone. From time to time, people who work together are going to disagree about what and how things get done. What causes conflict in teams? Although almost anything can lead to conflict—casual remarks that unintentionally offend a team member or fighting over scarce resources—the primary cause of team conflict is disagreement over team goals and priorities.[55] Other common causes of team conflict include disagreements over task-related issues, interpersonal incompatibilities, and simple fatigue.

Though most people view conflict negatively, the key to dealing with team conflict is not avoiding it, but rather making sure that the team experiences the right kind of conflict. In Chapter 5, you learned about *c-type conflict,* or *cognitive conflict,* which focuses on problem-related differences of opinion, and *a-type conflict,* or *affective conflict,* which refers to the emotional reactions that can occur when disagreements become personal rather than professional.[56] Cognitive conflict is strongly associated with improvements in team performance, whereas affective conflict is strongly associated with decreases in team performance.[57] Why does this happen? With cognitive conflict, team members disagree because their different experiences and expertise lead them to different views of the problem and solutions. Indeed, managers who participated in teams that emphasized cognitive conflict described their teammates as "smart," "team players," and "best in the business." They described their teams as "open," "fun,"

and "productive." One manager summed up the positive attitude that team members had about cognitive conflict by saying, "We scream a lot, then laugh, and then resolve the issue."[58] Thus, cognitive conflict is also characterized by a willingness to examine, compare, and reconcile differences to produce the best possible solution.

By contrast, affective conflict often results in hostility, anger, resentment, distrust, cynicism, and apathy. Managers who participated in teams that emphasized affective conflict described their teammates as "manipulative," "secretive," "burned out," and "political."[59] Not surprisingly, affective conflict can make people uncomfortable and cause them to withdraw and decrease their commitment to a team.[60] Affective conflict can also lower the satisfaction of team members, lead to personal hostility between coworkers, and decrease team cohesiveness.[61] Although cognitive conflict is a benefit, affective conflict undermines team performance by preventing teams from engaging in the kinds of activities that are critical to team effectiveness.

So, what can managers do to manage team conflict? First, they need to realize that emphasizing cognitive conflict alone won't be enough. Studies show that cognitive and affective conflicts often occur together in a given team activity! Sincere attempts to reach agreement on a difficult issue can quickly deteriorate from

© Inmagine/Inspirestock/Jupiterimages

cognitive to affective conflict if the discussion turns personal and tempers and emotions flare. While cognitive conflict is clearly the better approach to take, efforts to engage in cognitive conflict should be managed well and checked before they deteriorate and the team becomes unproductive.

Can teams disagree and still get along? Fortunately, they can. In an attempt to study this issue, researchers examined team conflict in twelve high-tech companies. In four of the companies, work teams used cognitive conflict to address problems but did so in a way that minimized the occurrence of affective conflict.

There are several ways teams can have good, productive fights.[62] First, work with more, rather than less, information. If data are plentiful, objective, and up-to-date, teams will focus on issues, not personalities. Second, develop multiple alternatives to enrich debate. Focusing on multiple solutions diffuses conflict by getting the team to keep searching for a better solution. Positions and opinions are naturally more flexible with five alternatives than with just two. Third, establish common goals. Remember, most team conflict arises from disagreements over team goals and priorities. Therefore, common goals encourage collaboration and minimize conflict over a team's purpose. Fourth, inject humor into the workplace. Humor relieves tension, builds cohesion, and just makes being in teams fun. Fifth, maintain a balance of power by involving as many people as possible in the decision process. And sixth, resolve issues without forcing a consensus. Consensus means that everyone must agree before decisions are finalized. Effectively, requiring consensus gives everyone on the team veto power. Nothing gets done until everyone agrees, which, of course, is nearly impossible. As a result, insisting on consensus usually promotes affective rather than cognitive conflict. If team members can't agree after constructively discussing their options, it's better to have the team leader make the final choice. Most team members can accept the team leader's choice if they've been thoroughly involved in the decision process.

3.5 | STAGES OF TEAM DEVELOPMENT

As teams develop and grow, they pass through four stages of development. As shown in Exhibit 10.3 on the next page, those stages are forming, storming, norming, and performing.[63] Although not every team passes through each of these stages, teams that do tend to be better performers.[64] This holds true even for teams composed of seasoned executives. After a period of time, however, if a team is not managed well, its performance may start to deteriorate as the team begins a process of decline and progresses through the stages of de-norming, de-storming, and de-forming.[65]

Forming is the initial stage of team development. This is the getting-acquainted stage in which team

Forming the first stage of team development, in which team members meet each other, form initial impressions, and begin to establish team norms

© iStockphoto.com/ranplett

The level of autonomy that a team possesses determines how it will respond to an uncooperative member. Suppose that an experienced worker blatantly refuses to do his share of the work. In a team with low autonomy, such as a traditional work group, the responsibility of getting that employee to put forth effort belongs to the supervisor. In a team with a high level of autonomy, such as a self-designing team or self-managing team, it is the entire team's responsibility to get that team member to do his work well.

Storming the second stage of team development, characterized by conflict and disagreement, in which team members disagree over what the team should do and how it should do it

Norming the third stage of team development, in which team members begin to settle into their roles, group cohesion grows, and positive team norms develop

Performing the fourth and final stage of team development, in which performance improves because the team has matured into an effective, fully functioning team

members first meet each other, form initial impressions, and try to get a sense of what it will be like to be part of the team. Some team norms will be established during this stage as team members begin to find out what behaviors will and won't be accepted by the team. During this stage, team leaders should allow time for team members to get to know each other, set early ground rules, and begin to set up a preliminary team structure.

Conflicts and disagreements often characterize the second stage of team development, **storming.** As team members begin working together, different personalities and work styles may clash. Team members become more assertive at this stage and more willing to state opinions. This is also the stage when team members jockey for position and try to establish a favorable role for themselves on the team. In addition, team members are likely to disagree about what the group should do and how it should do it. Team performance is still relatively low, given that team cohesion is weak and team members are still reluctant to support each other. Since teams that get stuck in the storming stage are almost always ineffective, it is important for team leaders to focus the team on team goals and on improving team performance. Team members need to be particularly patient and tolerant with each other in this stage.

During **norming,** the third stage of team development, team members begin to settle into their roles as team members. Positive team norms will have developed by this stage, and teammates should know what to expect from each other. Petty differences should have been resolved, friendships will have developed, and group cohesion will be relatively strong. At this point, team members will have accepted team goals, be operating as a unit, and, as indicated by the increase in performance, be working together effectively. This stage can be very short and is often characterized by someone on the team saying, "I think things are finally coming together." Note, however, that teams may also cycle back and forth between storming and norming several times before finally settling into norming.

In the last stage of team development, **performing,** performance improves because the team has finally matured into an effective, fully functioning team. At this point, members should be fully committed to the team and think of themselves as members of a team and not just employees. Team members often become intensely loyal to one another at this stage and feel mutual accountability for team successes and failures. Trivial disagreements, which can take time and energy away from the work of the team, should be rare. At this stage, teams get a lot of work done, and it is fun to be a team member. But the team should not become complacent. Without effective management, its performance may begin to decline as it passes through the stages of de-norming, de-storming, and de-forming.[66]

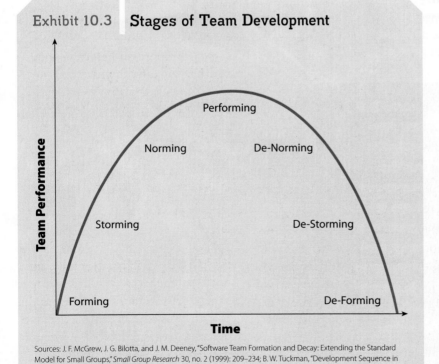

Exhibit 10.3 **Stages of Team Development**

Performing

Norming   De-Norming

Storming   De-Storming

Forming   De-Forming

Team Performance (vertical axis)

Time (horizontal axis)

Sources: J. F. McGrew, J. G. Bilotta, and J. M. Deeney, "Software Team Formation and Decay: Extending the Standard Model for Small Groups," *Small Group Research* 30, no. 2 (1999): 209–234; B. W. Tuckman, "Development Sequence in Small Groups," *Psychological Bulletin* 63, no. 6 (1965): 384–399.

4 Enhancing Work-Team Effectiveness

Making teams work is a challenging and difficult process. *Nonetheless, companies can increase the likelihood that teams will succeed by carefully managing 4.1 the setting of team goals and priorities and*

4.2 how work team members are selected, 4.3 trained, and 4.4 compensated.[67]

4.1 | SETTING TEAM GOALS AND PRIORITIES

In Chapter 5, you learned that having specific, measurable, attainable, realistic, and timely (i.e., S.M.A.R.T.) goals is one of the most effective means for improving individual job performance. Fortunately, team goals also improve team performance, especially when they are *specific* and *challenging*. In fact, team goals lead to much higher team performance 93 percent of the time.[68] For example, steel producer Nucor sets specific, challenging hourly goals for each of its production teams, which consist of first-line supervisors and production and maintenance workers. The average in the steel industry is 10 tons of steel per hour. Nucor production teams have a goal of 8 tons per hour but get a 5 percent bonus for every ton over 8 tons that they produce each hour. With no limit on the bonuses they can receive, Nucor's production teams produce an average of 35 to 40 tons of steel per hour![69]

Why is setting *specific* team goals so critical to team success? One reason is that increasing a team's performance is inherently more complex than just increasing one individual's job performance. For instance, consider that any team is likely to involve at least four different kinds of goals: each member's goal for the team, each member's goal for himself or herself on the team, the team's goal for each member, and the team's goal for itself.[70] In other words, without a specific goal for the team itself (the last of the four goals listed), team members may head off in all directions at once to pursue these other goals. Consequently, setting a specific, challenging goal *for the team* clarifies team priorities by providing a clear focus and purpose.

Challenging team goals affect how hard team members work. In particular, they greatly reduce the incidence of social loafing. When faced with reasonably difficult goals, team members necessarily expect everyone to contribute. Consequently, they are much more likely to notice and complain if a teammate isn't doing his or her share. In fact, when teammates know each other well, when team goals are specific, when team communication is good, and when teams are rewarded for team performance (discussed below), there is only a 1 in 16 chance that teammates will be social loafers.[71]

What can companies and teams do to ensure that team goals lead to superior team performance? One increasingly popular approach is to give teams stretch goals. *Stretch goals* are extremely ambitious goals that workers don't know how to reach.[72] For example, Hyundai recently set a goal of having its entire product line average 50 miles or more per gallon by 2025, an improvement of nearly 60 percent over current ratings. John Krafcik, a spokesmen for Hyundai, recognized the difficulty of the goal, saying, "We don't know precisely how to get there right now." But he also reaffirmed the company's commitment to setting high ambitions, stating "We want to help set the trajectory for the industry."[73] The purpose of stretch goals is to achieve extraordinary improvements in performance by forcing managers and workers to throw away old, comfortable solutions and adopt radical, never-before-used solutions.[74]

Four things must occur for stretch goals to motivate teams effectively.[75] First, teams must have a high degree of autonomy or control over how they achieve their goals. Second, teams must be empowered with control over resources such as budgets, workspaces, computers, or whatever else they need to do their jobs. Third, teams need structural accommodation. **Structural accommodation** means giving teams the ability to change organizational structures, policies, and practices if doing so helps them meet their stretch goals. Finally, teams need bureaucratic immunity. **Bureaucratic immunity** means that teams no longer have to go through the frustratingly slow process of multilevel reviews and sign-offs to get management approval before making changes. Once granted bureaucratic immunity, teams are immune from the influence of various organizational groups and are accountable only to top management. Therefore, teams can act quickly and even experiment with little fear of failure.

4.2 | SELECTING PEOPLE FOR TEAMWORK

University of Southern California management professor Edward Lawler says, "People are very naïve about how easy it is to create a team. Teams are the Ferraris of work design. They're high performance but high maintenance and expensive."[76] It's almost impossible to have an effective work team without carefully selecting people who are suited for teamwork or for working on a particular team. A focus on teamwork (individualism-collectivism), team level, and team diversity can help companies choose the right team members.[77]

Structural accommodation the ability to change organizational structures, policies, and practices in order to meet stretch goals

Bureaucratic immunity the ability to make changes without first getting approval from managers or other parts of an organization

Individualism-collectivism the degree to which a person believes that people should be self-sufficient and that loyalty to oneself is more important than loyalty to one's team or company

Team level the average level of ability, experience, personality, or any other factor of a team

Are you more comfortable working alone or with others? If you strongly prefer to work alone, you may not be well suited for teamwork. Indeed, studies show that job satisfaction is higher in teams when team members prefer working with others.[78] An indirect way to measure someone's *preference for teamwork* is to assess the person's degree of individualism or collectivism. **Individualism-collectivism** is the degree to which a person believes that people should be self-sufficient and that loyalty to oneself is more important than loyalty to one's team or company.[79] *Individualists*, who put their own welfare and interests first, generally prefer independent tasks in which they work alone. In contrast, *collectivists*, who put group or team interests ahead of self-interests, generally prefer interdependent tasks in which they work with others. Collectivists would also rather cooperate than compete and are fearful of disappointing team members or of being ostracized from teams. Given these differences, it makes sense to select team members who are collectivists rather than individualists. Indeed, many companies use individualism-collectivism as an initial screening device for team members. If team diversity is desired, however, individualists may also be appropriate, as discussed below. To determine your preference for teamwork, take the Team Player Inventory shown in Exhibit 10.4.

Team level is the average level of ability, experience, personality, or any other factor on a team. For example, a high level of team experience means that a team has particularly experienced members. This does not mean that every member of the team has considerable experience, but that enough do to significantly raise the average level of experience on the team. Team level is used to guide selection of teammates when teams need a particular set of skills or capabilities to do their jobs well. For example, at GE's Aviation's engines manufacturing plant in Durham, North Carolina, everyone hired had to have an FAA-certified mechanic's license.[80]

One Weak Link

Richard Branson, the founder of the Virgin group of companies (which range from music records to international airlines) strives to provide top-notch customer service in all of his companies, no matter what products or services they provide. Crucial to doing that, he believes, is excellent teamwork. "That's because delivering good customer service requires that a frontline worker receives supportive assistance from an entire network of co-workers. . . . And when it comes to helping a customer, the chain of assistance is only as strong as its weakest link." Branson tells a story of how a Virgin America passenger had missed a limo provided by the airline and, worried that he would miss his flight, took a cab to the airport. Fighting through rush hour, he arrived at the airport late and panicking. The first agent he met assessed the situation, gave him a refund for the taxi fare, and escorted him through security screening so that he could make his flight. Later, when the agent asked her manager for a reimbursement for the taxi fare, she was denied and chastised for not following procedure. By not doing his part to encourage and support the agent's actions, the manager basically told her that regulations were more important than providing excellent service. As Branson describes it, "Any Virgin employee witnessing their supervisor's scornful reaction to their colleague's exemplary deed would be unlikely to display the same resourcefulness. Which means that the customer loses—and so does the entire company."

Source: R. Branson, "Teamwork Is Key to Good Service," Livemint.com, June 19, 2010, http://www.livemint.com/2010/07/19230138/Teamwork-is-key-to-good -servic.html.

AP Images/Jacques Brinon / © iStockphoto.com/ssstep

Whereas team level represents the average level or capability of a team, **team diversity** represents the variances or differences in ability, experience, personality, or any other factor of a team.[81] From a practical perspective, why is team diversity important? Professor John Hollenbeck explains, "Imagine if you put all the extroverts together. Everyone is talking, but nobody is listening. [By contrast,] with a team of [nothing but] introverts, you can hear the clock ticking on the wall."[82] Not only do strong teams have talented members (i.e., team level), but those talented members are also different in terms of ability, experience, or personality. Some interesting research on 700 Nobel Prize winners has implications for team diversity because it indicates that significant, game-changing ideas rarely occur before the age of 30 because of the amount of time it takes to get educated and master the knowledge in a particular discipline, or after the age of 50 when research productivity traditionally drops sharply.[83] For example, Boeing increased the team diversity of its Dreamliner management team by tapping into the wisdom of its top retired engineers and managers. The company has brought together eight retired executives to create a Senior Advisory Group to team up with current Boeing engineers and project managers. One improvement the senior advisors suggested was to reduce Boeing's reliance on outsourcing manufactured plane parts, which had created numerous production delays as suppliers were unable to produce high-quality parts on schedule. Because of the inclusion of the Senior Advisory Group, Boeing brought many of the outsourced jobs back in house and sent Boeing engineers to suppliers to monitor suppliers' quality and progress. Jim Albaugh, chief executive of Boeing Commercial Airplanes says, "I was concerned we had retirees that [sic] were worried about the company, and I wanted to have them inside the [management] tent. They've got some very strong views."[84]

Once the right team has been put together in terms of individualism-collectivism, team level, and team diversity, it's important to keep the team together as long as practically possible. Interesting research by the National Transportation Safety Board shows that 73 percent of the serious mistakes made by jet cockpit crews are made

> **Team diversity** the variances or differences in ability, experience, personality, or any other factor of a team

Exhibit 10.4 The Team Player Inventory

		STRONGLY DISAGREE				STRONGLY AGREE
1.	I enjoy working on team/group projects.	1	2	3	4	5
2.	Team/group project work easily allows others to not pull their weight.	1	2	3	4	5
3.	Work that is done as a team/group is better than work done individually.	1	2	3	4	5
4.	I do my best work alone rather than in a team/group.	1	2	3	4	5
5.	Team/group work is overrated in terms of the actual results produced.	1	2	3	4	5
6.	Working in a team/group gets me to think more creatively.	1	2	3	4	5
7.	Teams/groups are used too often when individual work would be more effective.	1	2	3	4	5
8.	My own work is enhanced when I am in a team/group situation.	1	2	3	4	5
9.	My experiences working in team/group situations have been primarily negative.	1	2	3	4	5
10.	More solutions/ideas are generated when working in a team/group situation than when working alone.	1	2	3	4	5

Reverse score items 2, 4, 5, 7, and 9. Then add the scores for items 1 to 10. Higher scores indicate a preference for teamwork, whereas lower total scores indicate a preference for individual work.

> The more each **team member** knows and can do, the better the **whole team** performs.

on the very first day that a crew flies together; 44 percent of serious mistakes occur on their very first flight together that day (pilot teams fly two to three flights per day). Moreover, research has shown that fatigued pilot crews who have worked together before make significantly fewer errors than rested crews who have never worked together.[85] Their experience working together helps them overcome their fatigue and outperform new teams that have not worked together before. So, once you've created effective teams, keep them together for as long as possible.

4.3 | TEAM TRAINING

After selecting the right people for teamwork, you need to train them. To be successful, teams need significant training, particularly in interpersonal skills, decision-making and problem-solving skills, conflict resolution skills, and technical training. Organizations that create work teams *often underestimate the amount of training* required to make teams effective. This mistake occurs frequently in successful organizations in which managers assume that if employees can work effectively on their own, they can work effectively in teams. In reality, companies that successfully use teams provide thousands of hours of training to make sure that teams work. Stacy Myers, a consultant who helps companies implement teams, says, "When we help companies move to teams, we also require that employees take basic quality and business knowledge classes as well. Teams must know how their work affects the company, and how their success will be measured."[86]

Most commonly, members of work teams receive training in interpersonal skills. **Interpersonal skills,** such as listening, communicating, questioning, and providing feedback, enable people to have effective working relationships with others. Because of teams' autonomy and responsibility, many companies also give team members training in *decision-making and problem-solving skills* to help them do a better job of cutting costs and improving quality and customer service. Many organizations also teach teams *conflict-resolution skills.* "Teams at Delta Faucet have specific protocols for addressing conflict. For example, if an employee's behavior is creating a problem within a team, the team is expected to work it out without involving the team leader. Two team members will meet with the problem team member and work toward a resolution. If this is unsuccessful, the whole team meets to confront the issue. If necessary, the team leader can be brought in to make a decision, but . . . it is a rare occurrence for a team to reach that stage."[87] Firms must also provide team members with the *technical training* they need to do their jobs, particularly if they are being cross-trained to perform all of the different jobs on the team. Cross-training is less appropriate for teams of highly skilled workers. For instance, it is unlikely that a group of engineers, computer programmers, and systems analysts would be cross-trained for each other's jobs.

Team leaders need training, too, as they often feel unprepared for their new duties. New team leaders face myriad problems ranging from confusion about their new roles as team leaders (compared to their old jobs as managers or employees) to not knowing where to go for help when their teams have problems. The solution is extensive training. Overall, does team train-

Interpersonal skills skills, such as listening, communicating, questioning, and providing feedback, that enable people to have effective working relationships with others

ing work? A recent study of 2,650 teams from a wide variety of settings, tasks, and team types found that team training was positively related to team performance outcomes.[88]

4.4 | TEAM COMPENSATION AND RECOGNITION

Compensating teams correctly is very difficult. For instance, one survey found that only 37 percent of companies were satisfied with their team compensation plans and even fewer, just 10 percent, reported their views as being "very positive."[89] One of the problems, according to Susan Mohrman of the Center for Effective Organizations, is that "there is a very strong set of beliefs in most organizations that people should be paid for how well they do. So when people first get put into team-based organizations, they really balk at being paid for how well the team does. It sounds illogical to them. It sounds like their individuality and their sense of self-worth are being threatened."[90] Consequently, companies need to carefully choose a team compensation plan and then fully explain how teams will be rewarded. One basic requirement for team compensation is that the type of reward (individual versus team) must match the type of performance (individual versus team).

Employees can be compensated for team participation and accomplishments in three ways: skill-based pay, gainsharing, and nonfinancial rewards. **Skill-based pay** programs pay employees for acquiring additional skills or knowledge.[91] These programs encourage employees to learn the additional skills they will need to perform multiple jobs within a team and to share knowledge with others within their work groups.[92]

In **gainsharing** programs, companies share the financial value of performance gains, such as productivity increases, cost savings, or quality improvements, with their workers.[93] *Nonfinancial rewards* are another way to reward teams for their performance. These rewards, which can range from vacation trips to T-shirts, plaques, and coffee mugs, are especially effective when coupled with management recognition, such as awards, certificates, and praise.[94] Nonfinancial awards tend to be most effective when teams or team-based interventions, such as total quality management (see Chapter 18), are first introduced.[95]

Which team compensation plan should your company use? In general, skill-based pay is most effective for self-managing and self-directing teams performing complex tasks. In these situations, the more each team member knows and can do, the better the whole team performs. By contrast, gainsharing works best in relatively stable environments where employees can focus on improving productivity, cost savings, or quality.

Skill-based pay compensation system that pays employees for acquiring additional skills or knowledge

Gainsharing a compensation system in which companies share the financial value of performance gains, such as productivity, cost savings, or quality, with their workers

STUDENT Study Tools

Located at the back of your book:

☐ Rip out and study the Chapter Review Card at the end of the book

Log in to the CourseMate for MGMT at cengagebrain.com to:

☐ Review Key Term Flashcards delivered 3 ways (print or online)

☐ Complete both Practice Quizzes to prepare for tests

☐ Play Beat the Clock and Quizbowl to master concepts

☐ Complete the Crossword Puzzle to review key terms

☐ Watch the video on the City of Greensburg, Kansas, for a real company example and take the accompanying quiz

☐ Watch the Biz Flix clip from *Failure to Launch* and take the quiz

☐ Complete the Case Assignment on GE Aircraft Engines

☐ Work through the Management Decision on recruiting teams

☐ Work through the Management Team Decision on avoiding groupthink

☐ Develop your skills with the Develop Your Career Potential exercise

11 | Managing Human Resource Systems

LEARNING OUTCOMES:

1 explain how different employment laws affect human resource practice.

2 explain how companies use recruiting to find qualified job applicants.

3 describe the selection techniques and procedures that companies use when deciding which applicants should receive job offers.

4 describe how to determine training needs and select the appropriate training methods.

5 discuss how to use performance appraisal to give meaningful performance feedback.

6 describe basic compensation strategies and discuss the four kinds of employee separations.

Chapter 11

The Legal Context

human resource management (HRM), or the process of finding, developing, and keeping the right people to form a qualified work force, is one of the most difficult and important of all management tasks. This chapter is organized around the three parts of the human resource management process shown in Exhibit 11.1: attracting, developing, and keeping a qualified work force.

This chapter will walk you through the steps of the HRM process. We explore how companies use recruiting and selection techniques to attract and hire qualified employees to fulfill their personnel needs. Then we discuss how training and performance appraisal can develop the knowledge, skills, and abilities of the work force. The chapter concludes with a review of compensation and employee separation, that is, how companies can keep their best workers through effective compensation practices and how they can manage the separation process when employees leave the organization.

Before we explore how human resource systems work, you need to better understand the complex legal environment in which they exist. So we'll begin the chapter by reviewing the federal laws that govern human resource management decisions.

After reading the next section, you should be able to

1 **explain how different employment laws affect human resource practice.**

1 **Employment Legislation**

Since their inception, Hooters restaurants have hired only female servers. Moreover, consistent with the company's marketing theme, the servers wear short nylon shorts and cutoff T-shirts that show their midriffs. The Equal Employment Opportunity Commission (EEOC) began an investigation of Hooters when a Chicago man filed a sex-based discrimination charge. The man alleged that he had applied for a server's job at a Hooters restaurant and was rejected because of his sex. The dispute between Hooters and the EEOC quickly gained national attention. One sarcastic letter to the EEOC

Exhibit 11.1 **The Human Resource Management Process**

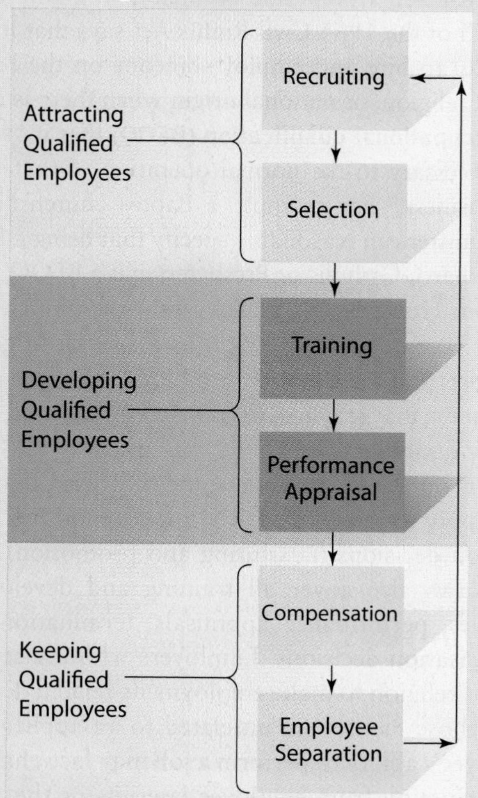

Attracting Qualified Employees
- Recruiting
- Selection

Developing Qualified Employees
- Training
- Performance Appraisal

Keeping Qualified Employees
- Compensation
- Employee Separation

© Cengage Learning 2011

Human resource management (HRM) the process of finding, developing, and keeping the right people to form a qualified work force

Bona fide occupational qualification (BFOQ) an exception in employment law that permits sex, age, religion, and the like to be used when making employment decisions, but only if they are "reasonably necessary to the normal operation of that particular business"; strictly monitored by the Equal Employment Opportunity Commission

printed in *Fortune* magazine read as follows:

Dear EEOC:

Hi! I just wanted to thank you for investigating those Hooters restaurants, where the waitresses wear those shorty shorts and midriffy T-shirts. I think it's a great idea that you have decided to make Hooters hire men as—how do you say it?—waitpersons. Gee, I never knew so many men wanted to be waitpersons at Hooters. No reason to let them sue on their own either. You're right, the government needs to take the lead on this one.[1]

This letter characterized public sentiment at the time. Given its backlog of 100,000 job discrimination cases, many wondered if the EEOC didn't have better things to do with its scarce resources.

Three years after the initial complaint, the EEOC ruled that Hooters had violated antidiscrimination laws and offered to settle the case if the company would agree to pay $22 million to the EEOC for distribution to male victims of the "Hooters Girl" hiring policy, establish a scholarship fund to enhance opportunities or education for men, and provide sensitivity training to teach Hooters' employees how to be more sensitive to men's needs. Hooters responded with a $1 million publicity campaign criticizing the EEOC's investigation. Billboards featuring "Vince," a man dressed in a Hooters Girl uniform and blond wig, sprang up all over the country. Hooters customers were given postcards on which to send complaints to the EEOC. Of course, Hooters paid the postage. As a result of the publicity campaign, restaurant sales increased by 10 percent. Soon thereafter, the EEOC announced that it would not pursue discriminatory hiring charges against Hooters.[2] Nonetheless, the company ended up paying $3.75 million to settle a class-action suit brought by seven men who claimed that their inability to get a job at Hooters violated federal law.[3] Under the settlement, Hooters maintained its women-only policy for server jobs but had to create additional support jobs such as hosts and bartenders that would also be open to men. The story doesn't end there, however: A male applicant who wants to be a Hooters waitperson has sued Hooters, seeking to overturn the prior settlement, which would only allow him to be a host or bartender.[4]

As the Hooters example illustrates, the human resource planning process occurs in a very complicated legal environment. *Let's explore employment legislation by reviewing* **1.1 the major federal employment laws that affect human resource practice, 1.2 how the concept of adverse impact is related to employment discrimination,** *and* **1.3 the laws regarding sexual harassment in the workplace.**

1.1 | FEDERAL EMPLOYMENT LAWS

Exhibit 11.2 lists the major federal employment laws and their websites, where you can find more detailed information. Except for the Family and Medical Leave Act and the Uniformed Services Employment and Reemployment Rights Act, which are administered by the Department of Labor, all of these laws are administered by the EEOC. The general effect of this body of law, which is still evolving through court decisions, is that employers may not discriminate in employment decisions on the basis of sex, age, religion, color, national origin, race, or disability. The intent is to make these factors irrelevant in employment decisions. Stated another way, employment decisions should be based on factors that are "job related," "reasonably necessary," or a "business necessity" for successful job performance. The only time that sex, age, religion, and the like can be used to make employment decisions is when they are considered a bona fide occupational qualification.[5] Title VII of the 1964 Civil Rights Act says that it is not unlawful to hire and employ someone on the basis of gender, religion, or national origin when there is a **bona fide occupational qualification (BFOQ)** that is "reasonably necessary to the normal operation of that particular business." For example, a Baptist church hiring a new minister can reasonably specify that being a Baptist rather than a Catholic or Presbyterian is a BFOQ for the position. However, it's unlikely that the church could specify race or national origin as a BFOQ. In general, the courts and the EEOC take a hard look when a business claims that sex, age, religion, color, national origin, race, or disability is a BFOQ.

It is important to understand, however, that these laws apply to the entire HRM process and not just to selection decisions (i.e., hiring and promotion). Thus, these laws also cover all training and development activities, performance appraisals, terminations, and compensation decisions. Employers who use sex, age, race, or religion to make employment-related decisions when those factors are unrelated to an applicant's or employee's ability to perform a job may face charges of discrimination from employee lawsuits or the EEOC.

Massey Energy Company, an operator of coal mines, bought a shuttered mine from Horizon Natural Resources and reopened it. As they were hiring workers who had worked at the mine before, they refused to hire 229 people who were over 40 years old. The group of miners sued the company and were awarded a settlement of $8.75 million.[6]

In addition to the laws presented in Exhibit 11.2, there are two other important sets of federal laws: labor laws and laws and regulations governing safety standards. Labor laws regulate the interaction between management and labor unions that represent groups of employees. These laws guarantee employees the right to form and join unions of their own choosing. The Occupational Safety and Health Act (OSHA) requires that employers provide employees with a workplace that is "free from recognized hazards that are causing or are likely to cause death or serious physical harm." This law is administered by the Occupational Safety and Health Administration (which, like the act, is referred to as OSHA). OSHA sets safety and health standards for employers and conducts inspections to determine whether those standards are being met. Employers who do not meet OSHA standards may be fined.[7]

1.2 | ADVERSE IMPACT AND EMPLOYMENT DISCRIMINATION

The EEOC has investigatory, enforcement, and informational responsibilities. Therefore, it investigates charges of discrimination, enforces the employment discrimination laws in federal court, and publishes guidelines that organizations can use to ensure they are in compliance with the law. One of the most important guidelines jointly issued by the EEOC, the Department of Labor, the U.S. Justice Department, and the federal Office of Personnel Management is the *Uniform*

Exhibit 11.2 Summary of Major Federal Employment Laws

■ Equal Pay Act of 1963	http://www.eeoc.gov/laws/statutes/epa.cfm	Prohibits unequal pay for males and females doing substantially similar work.
■ Title VII of the Civil Rights Act of 1964	http://www.eeoc.gov/laws/statutes/titlevii.cfm	Prohibits employment discrimination on the basis of race, color, religion, gender, or national origin.
■ Age Discrimination in Employment Act of 1967	http://www.eeoc.gov/laws/statutes/adea.cfm	Prohibits discrimination in employment decisions against persons age 40 and older.
■ Pregnancy Discrimination Act of 1978	http://www.eeoc.gov/laws/statutes/pregnancy.cfm	Prohibits discrimination in employment against pregnant women.
■ Americans with Disabilities Act of 1990	http://www.eeoc.gov/laws/statutes/ada.cfm	Prohibits discrimination on the basis of physical or mental disabilities.
■ Civil Rights Act of 1991	http://www.eeoc.gov/laws/statutes/cra-1991.cfm	Strengthened the provisions of the Civil Rights Act of 1964 by providing for jury trials and punitive damages.
■ Family and Medical Leave Act of 1993	http://www.dol.gov/whd/fmla/index.htm	Permits workers to take up to 12 weeks of unpaid leave for pregnancy and/or birth of a new child, adoption or foster care of a new child, illness of an immediate family member, or personal medical leave.
■ Uniformed Services Employment and Reemployment Rights Act of 1994	http://www.osc.gov/userra.htm	Prohibits discrimination against those serving in the Armed Forces Reserve, the National Guard, or other uniformed services; guarantees that civilian employers will hold and then restore civilian jobs and benefits for those who have completed uniformed service.

Disparate treatment intentional discrimination that occurs when people are purposely not given the same hiring, promotion, or membership opportunities because of their race, color, sex, age, ethnic group, national origin, or religious beliefs

Adverse impact unintentional discrimination that occurs when members of a particular race, sex, or ethnic group are unintentionally harmed or disadvantaged because they are hired, promoted, or trained (or any other employment decision) at substantially lower rates than others

Four-fifths (or 80 percent) rule a rule of thumb used by the courts and the EEOC to determine whether there is evidence of adverse impact; a violation of this rule occurs when the selection rate for a protected group is less than 80 percent or four-fifths of the selection rate for a nonprotected group

Sexual harassment a form of discrimination in which unwelcome sexual advances, requests for sexual favors, or other verbal or physical conduct of a sexual nature occurs while performing one's job

Quid pro quo sexual harassment a form of sexual harassment in which employment outcomes, such as hiring, promotion, or simply keeping one's job, depend on whether an individual submits to sexual harassment

Hostile work environment a form of sexual harassment in which unwelcome and demeaning sexually related behavior creates an intimidating and offensive work environment

Guidelines on Employee Selection Procedures. These guidelines define two important criteria, disparate treatment and adverse impact, that are used in determining whether companies have engaged in discriminatory hiring and promotion practices.

Disparate treatment, which is *intentional* discrimination, occurs when people are *intentionally* not given the same hiring, promotion, or membership opportunities as other employees because of their race, color, age, sex, ethnic group, national origin, or religious beliefs despite the fact that they are qualified.[8] Legally, a key element of discrimination lawsuits is establishing motive, meaning evidence that the employer intended to discriminate. If no motive can be established, then a claim of disparate treatment may actually be a case of adverse impact.

Adverse impact, which is *unintentional* discrimination, occurs when members of a particular race, sex, or ethnic group are *unintentionally* harmed or disadvantaged because they are hired, promoted,

or trained (or benefit from any other employment decision) at substantially lower rates than others. The courts and federal agencies use the **four-fifths (or 80 percent) rule** to determine if adverse impact has occurred. Adverse impact occurs if the decision rate for a protected group of people is less than four-fifths (or 80 percent) of the decision rate for a nonprotected group (usually white males). So, if 100 white applicants and 100 black applicants apply for entry-level jobs, and 60 white applicants are hired (60/100 = 60%), but only 20 black applicants are hired (20/100 = 20%), adverse impact has occurred (0.20/0.60 = 0.33). The criterion for the four-fifths rule in this situation is 0.48 (0.60 × 0.80 = 0.48). Since 0.33 is less than 0.48, the four-fifths rule has been violated.

Violation of the four-fifths rule is not an automatic indication of discrimination, however. If an employer can demonstrate that a selection procedure or test is valid, meaning that the test accurately predicts job performance or that the test is job related because it assesses applicants on specific tasks actually used in the job, then the organization may continue to use the test. If validity cannot be established, however, then a violation of the four-fifths rule will likely result in a lawsuit brought by employees, job applicants, or the EEOC itself.

1.3 | SEXUAL HARASSMENT

According to the EEOC, **sexual harassment** is a form of discrimination in which unwelcome sexual advances, requests for sexual favors, or other verbal or physical conduct of a sexual nature occurs. From a legal perspective, there are two kinds of sexual harassment: quid pro quo and hostile work environment.[9]

Quid pro quo sexual harassment occurs when employment outcomes, such as hiring, promotion, or simply keeping one's job, depend on whether an individual submits to being sexually harassed. In quid pro quo cases, requests for sexual acts are linked to economic outcomes (that is, keeping a job). A **hostile work environment** occurs when unwelcome and demeaning sexually related behavior creates an intimidating, hostile, and offensive work environment. Twenty-one Hispanic female workers sued ABM Industries, a building-maintenance company, for failing to address their complaints about a hostile work environment. In their suit, they alleged that male co-workers groped them, made unwelcome sexual advances, offered promotion for sex, and exposed themselves to the women, and that when the women complained to management, they were ignored, or even fired. As one woman described it, "I asked for help and they wouldn't help me, and instead my supervisor would laugh at me even more." The case was settled when ABM agreed to pay the 21 women $5.8 million.[10] There may be no economic injury—that is, requests for sexual acts aren't tied to economic outcomes. However, they can lead to psychological injury from a stressful work environment.

What should companies do to make sure that sexual harassment laws are followed and not violated?[11] First, respond immediately when sexual harassment is reported. A quick response encourages victims of sexual harassment to report problems to management rather than to lawyers or the EEOC. Furthermore, a quick and fair investigation may serve as a deterrent to future harassment. Next, take the time to write a clear, understandable sexual harassment policy that is strongly worded, gives specific examples of what constitutes sexual harassment, spells out sanctions and punishments, and is widely publicized within the company. This lets potential harassers and victims know what will not be tolerated and how the firm will deal with harassment should it occur.

Next, establish clear reporting procedures that indicate how, where, and to whom incidents of sexual harassment can be reported. The best procedures ensure that a complaint will receive a quick response, that impartial parties will handle the complaint, and that the privacy of the accused and accuser will be protected. At DuPont, Avon, and Texas Industries, employees can call a confidential hotline 24 hours a day, 365 days a year.[12]

Finally, managers should also be aware that most states and many cities or local governments have their own employment-related laws and enforcement agencies. So compliance with federal law is often not enough. In fact, organizations can be in full compliance with federal law and at the same time be in violation of state or local sexual harassment laws.

Finding Qualified Workers

a s Gail Hyland-Savage, the CEO of real estate and marketing firm Michaelson, Connor & Boul, says, "Staffing is absolutely critical to the success of every company. To be competitive in today's economy, companies need the best people to create ideas and execute them for the organization. Without a competent and talented workforce, organizations will stagnate and eventually perish. The right employees are the most important resources of companies today."[13]

After reading the next two sections, you should be able to

2 **explain how companies use recruiting to find qualified job applicants.**

3 **describe the selection techniques and procedures that companies use when deciding which applicants should receive job offers.**

2 Recruiting

Recruiting is the process of developing a pool of qualified job applicants. *Let's examine 2.1 what job analysis is and how it is used in recruiting and 2.2 how companies use internal recruiting and 2.3 external recruiting to find qualified job applicants.*

2.1 | JOB ANALYSIS AND RECRUITING

Job analysis is a "purposeful, systematic process for collecting information on the important work-related aspects of a job."[14] Typically, a job analysis collects four kinds of information:

- work activities, such as what workers do and how, when, and why they do it;
- the tools and equipment used to do the job;
- the context in which the job is performed, such as the actual working conditions or schedule;
- the personnel requirements for performing the job, meaning the knowledge, skills, and abilities needed to do the job well.[15]

Job analysis information can be collected by having job incumbents or supervisors (or both) complete questionnaires about their jobs, by direct observation, by interviews, or by filming employees as they perform their jobs.

Job descriptions and job specifications are two of the most important results of a job analysis. A **job description** is a written description of the basic tasks, duties, and responsibilities required of an employee

Recruiting the process of developing a pool of qualified job applicants

Job analysis a purposeful, systematic process for collecting information on the important work-related aspects of a job

Job description a written description of the basic tasks, duties, and responsibilities required of an employee holding a particular job

holding a particular job. **Job specifications,** which are often included as a separate section of a job description, are a summary of the qualifications needed to successfully perform the job. Exhibit 11.3 shows a job description for a firefighter in the city of Portland, Oregon.

Because a job analysis specifies what a job entails as well as the knowledge, skills, and abilities that are needed to do the job well, companies must complete a job analysis *before* beginning to recruit job applicants.

Job analysis, job descriptions, and job specifications are the foundation on which all critical human resource activities are built. They are used during recruiting and selection to match applicant qualifications with the requirements of the job. Therefore, it is critically important that job descriptions be accurate.

Sioux Logan, of RedStream Technology, an IT staffing company, uses job descriptions to sort through the hundreds of applications she receives for each job opening. To identify the three applicants that she will bring in for interviews, Logan emails the job applicants the description of the job and asks them to indicate

---

Exhibit 11.3   Job Description for a Firefighter for the City of Portland, Oregon

Yes, as a Firefighter you will fight fire and provide emergency medical services to your community. But it doesn't end there: your firefighting career offers you the opportunity to expand your skills to include Hazardous Materials Response, Specialty Response Teams (dive, rope rescue, confined space, etc.), Paramedic Care, Public Education and Information, Fire Investigation, and Fire Code Enforcement.

Teamwork

Professional Firefighters work as a team at emergency scenes. The work day also includes training, fire station and equipment maintenance, fire prevention activities, and public education. As a Firefighter, you must be in excellent physical condition to meet the demands of the job; this means you must work quickly, handling heavy equipment for long periods of time while wearing special protective gear in hot and hazardous environments. If you can meet the challenge of strenuous work and like the idea of helping people, consider applying for the position of Firefighter.

Work Schedule

Portland Fire & Rescue Firefighters work a 24-on/48-off shift. This means that Firefighters report to work at 8:00 a.m. the day of their shift and continue working until 8:00 a.m. the following morning. Our Firefighters then have the following two days (48 hours) off. Firefighters are required to work shifts on holidays and weekends. Portland Fire & Rescue also has 40-hour-a-week firefighters who work in Training, Inspections/Investigations, Public Education, Logistics, and Emergency Management. These positions are usually filled after a Firefighter has met the minimum requirements for these positions.

Source: Portland Fire and Rescue, accessed August 13, 2008, http://www.portlandonline.com/fire/index.cfm?a=haea&c=cgbil.

© iStockphoto.com/ Kendall Griffin

whether they really want this job or not. Says Logan, "A lot of times people apply for . . . jobs without reading the whole job description." By having applicants read and respond to the job description, Logan gives them an opportunity to determine whether they really would be a good fit for the job. The exchange of emails also allows her to evaluate the applicants' writing skills and professionalism, giving her one more way to find the right person for the job.[16]

Job descriptions are also used throughout the staffing process to ensure that selection devices and the decisions based on these devices are job-related. For example, the questions asked in an interview should be based on the most important work activities identified by a job analysis. Likewise, during performance appraisals, employees should be evaluated in areas that a job analysis has identified as the most important in a job.

Job analyses, job descriptions, and job specifications also help companies meet the legal requirement that their human-resource decisions be job-related. To be judged *job-related*, recruitment, selection, training, performance appraisals, and employee separations must be valid and be directly related to the important aspects of the job as identified by a careful job analysis. In fact, in *Griggs v. Duke Power Co.* and *Albemarle Paper Co. v. Moody*, the U.S. Supreme Court stated that companies should use job analyses to help establish the job-relatedness of their human resource procedures.[17] The federal government's *Uniform Guidelines on Employee Selection Procedures* also recommend that companies base their human-resource procedures on job analysis.

2.2 | INTERNAL RECRUITING

Internal recruiting is the process of developing a pool of qualified job applicants from people who already work in the company. Internal recruiting, sometimes called "promotion from within," improves employee commitment, morale, and motivation. Recruiting current employees also reduces recruitment startup time and costs, and because employees are already familiar with the company's culture and procedures, they are more likely to succeed in new jobs. Job posting and career paths are two methods of internal recruiting.

Job posting is a procedure for advertising job openings within the company to existing employees. A job description and requirements are typically posted on a bulletin board, in a company newsletter, or in an internal computerized job bank that is accessible only to employees.

A *career path* is a planned sequence of jobs through which employees may advance within an organization. For example, Procter & Gamble CEO Bob McDonald worked for the company for almost 30 years before becoming CEO. McDonald started out as a brand assistant, then moved up to assistant brand manager and brand manager. From there he became an associate advertising manager, then a product manager before taking on various regional management positions. McDonald eventually rose to vice president and then president of P&G's Northeast Asia division. He served as Vice Chairman of Global Operations and COO before finally stepping in as CEO of the world's largest consumer-products company.[18]

Career paths help employees focus on long-term goals and development while also helping companies increase employee retention. As you can see in Bob McDonald's case, career paths can also help employees gain a broad range of experience, which is especially useful at higher levels of management.

2.3 | EXTERNAL RECRUITING

Wal-Mart's success around the globe and continued growth has, surprisingly, caused some HR problems, as the company struggles to find enough talented applicants for its store manager positions. Traditionally, it had found store managers by promoting from within its employee ranks. Now, however, internal recruiting isn't producing enough talent to manage Wal-Mart's stores.

Wal-Mart created an external program dedicated to recruiting junior military officers (JMOs)—captains and lieutenants returning from tours in Iraq

Internal recruiting the process of developing a pool of qualified job applicants from people who already work in the company

© Brendan Hoffman/Getty Images

and Afghanistan who had typically been responsible for leading 30 to 40 soldiers. According to Jennifer Seidner, senior recruiting manager at Wal-Mart, this allowed the company to, "bring in world-class leadership talent that was already trained and ready to go. And then we could teach them retail, because we know that pretty well." After several years, the focus on veterans—company outsiders—is now a critical part of Wal-Mart's recruiting strategy.[19]

External recruiting, like that used in Wal-Mart's JMO program, is the process of developing a pool of qualified job applicants from outside the company. External recruitment methods include advertising (newspapers, magazines, direct mail, radio, or television), employee referrals (asking current employees to recommend possible job applicants), walk-ins (people who apply on their own), outside organizations (universities, technical/trade schools, and professional societies), employment services (state or private employment agencies, temporary help agencies, and professional search firms), special events (career conferences or job fairs), and Internet job sites. Which external recruiting method should you use? Studies show that employee referrals, walk-ins, newspaper advertisements, and state employment agencies tend to be used most frequently for office/clerical and production/service employees. By contrast, newspaper advertisements and college/university recruiting are used most frequently for professional/technical employees. When recruiting managers, organizations tend to rely most heavily on newspaper advertisements, employee referrals, and search firms.[20]

In the last decade, the biggest change in external recruiting has been the increased use of the Internet. Some companies now recruit applicants through Internet job sites such as Monster.com, HotJobs.com, Hire.com, and CareerBuilder.com. Companies can post job openings for 30 days on one of these sites for about half of the cost of running an advertisement just once in a Sunday newspaper. Plus, Internet job listings generate nine times as many résumés as one ad in the Sunday newspaper.[21] And because these sites attract so many applicants and offer so many services, companies can find qualified applicants without having to resort to more expensive recruitment and search

firms, which typically charge one-third or more of a new hire's salary.[22]

Some companies have even begun using search-engine ads, for example, placing a recruiting advertisement on websites that are the result of a search based on a key word such as "accountant" or "nurse." These ads can be restricted by zip codes so that a company looking for an accountant in Indianapolis doesn't have ads shown to potential applicants in Los Angeles. Because the companies only pay when the recruiting ads are clicked on, such ads can be even cheaper than job websites. And for some companies, they also attract more applicants. Baylor Health Care System, a large medical system in Dallas, found that search-engine ads generated 5,250 applicants at a cost of $4 per applicant. Job websites generated 3,125 applicants at a cost of $30 each. And newspaper and magazine ads generated just 215 applicants at a cost of $750 per applicant. Eileen Bouthillet, Baylor's director of human resources communications, said, "Before we were throwing darts at a dart board trying to see what might stick. Now we have a very targeted strategy and a point of comparison so we can make wise decisions on where we spend our money."[23]

3 Selection

Once the recruitment process has produced a pool of qualified applicants, the selection process is used to determine which applicants have the best chance of performing well on the job. More specifically, **selection** is the process of gathering information about job applicants to decide who should be offered a job. To make sure that selection decisions are accurate and legally defendable, the federal government's *Uniform Guidelines on Employee Selection Procedures* recommend that all selection procedures be validated. **Validation** is the process of determining how well a selection test or procedure predicts future job performance. The better or more accurate the prediction of future job performance, the more valid a test is said to be.

*Let's examine common selection procedures: **3.1 application forms and résumés, 3.2 references and background checks, 3.3 selection tests,** and **3.4 interviews.***

3.1 | APPLICATION FORMS AND RÉSUMÉS

The first selection devices that most job applicants encounter when they seek a job are application forms and résumés. Both contain similar information about an applicant, such as name, address, job and educa-

Don't Ask!
(Topics to Avoid in an Interview)

1. **Children.** Don't ask applicants if they have children, plan to have them, or have or need child care. Questions about children can unintentionally single out women.

2. **Age.** Because of the Age Discrimination in Employment Act, employers cannot ask job applicants their age during the hiring process. Since most people graduate high school at the age of eighteen, even asking for high school graduation dates could violate the law.

3. **Disabilities.** Don't ask if applicants have physical or mental disabilities. According to the Americans with Disabilities Act, disabilities (and reasonable accommodations for them) cannot be discussed until a job offer has been made.

4. **Physical characteristics.** Don't ask for information about height, weight, or other physical characteristics. Questions about weight could be construed as leading to discrimination toward overweight people, and studies show that they are less likely to be hired in general.

5. **Name.** Yes, you can ask an applicant's name, but you cannot ask a female applicant for her maiden name because it indicates marital status. Asking for a maiden name could

also lead to charges that the organization was trying to establish a candidate's ethnic background.

6. **Citizenship.** Asking applicants about citizenship could lead to claims of discrimination on the basis of national origin. However, according to the Immigration Reform and Control Act, companies may ask applicants if they have a legal right to work in the United States.

7. **Lawsuits.** Applicants may not be asked if they have ever filed a lawsuit against an employer. Federal and state laws prevent this to protect whistleblowers from retaliation by future employers.

8. **Arrest records.** Applicants cannot be asked about their arrest records. Arrests don't have legal standing. However, applicants can be asked whether they have been convicted of a crime.

9. **Smoking.** Applicants cannot be asked if they smoke. Smokers might be able to claim that they weren't hired because of fears of higher absenteeism and medical costs. However, they can be asked if they are aware of company policies that restrict smoking at work.

10. **AIDS/HIV.** Applicants can't be asked about AIDS, HIV, or any other medical condition. Questions of this nature would violate the Americans with Disabilities Act, as well as federal and state civil rights laws.

Source: J. S. Pouliot, "Topics to Avoid with Applicants," *Nation's Business* 80, no. 7 (1992): 57.

tional history, and so forth. Though an organization's application form often asks for information already provided by the applicant's résumé, most organizations prefer to collect this information in their own format for entry into a human resource information system.

Employment laws apply to application forms just as they do to all selection devices. Application forms may ask applicants for only valid, job-related information. Nonetheless, application forms commonly ask applicants for non–job-related information such as marital status, maiden name, age, or date of high school graduation. Indeed, one study found that 73 percent of organizations had application forms that violated at least one federal or state law.[24] There's quite a bit of information that companies may not request in application forms, during job interviews, or in any other part of the selection process. Courts will assume that you consider all of the information you request

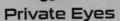

Employment references sources such as previous employers or coworkers who can provide job-related information about job candidates

Background checks procedures used to verify the truthfulness and accuracy of information that applicants provide about themselves and to uncover negative, job-related background information not provided by applicants

of applicants, even if you don't. Be sure to ask only those questions that directly relate to the candidate's ability and motivation to perform the job.

Résumés also pose problems for companies but in a different way. Accu-Screen, Inc., has gathered data for 14 years on résumé falsification and reports that approximately 43 percent of résumés and job applications contain false information. According to a study conducted by J. J. Keller & Associates, Inc., the nation's leading provider of risk and regulatory management solutions, 55 percent of human resource professionals have discovered lies on résumés or applications when conducting pre-employment background or reference checks.[25] Therefore, managers should verify the information collected via résumés and application forms by comparing it with additional information collected during interviews and other stages of the selection process, such as references and background checks, which are discussed next.

3.2 | REFERENCES AND BACKGROUND CHECKS

Nearly all companies ask an applicant to provide **employment references**, such as previous employers or coworkers, that they can contact to learn more about the candidate. **Background checks** are used to verify the truthfulness and accuracy of information that applicants provide about themselves and to uncover negative, job-related background information not provided by applicants. Background checks are conducted by contacting "educational institutions, prior employers, court records, police and governmental agencies, and other informational sources either by telephone, mail, remote computer access, or through in-person investigations."[26]

Unfortunately, previous employers are increasingly reluctant to provide references or background check information for fear of being sued by previous employees for defamation. If former employers provide potential employers with unsubstantiated information that damages applicants' chances of being hired, applicants can (and do) sue for defamation. As a result, 54 percent of employers will not provide information about previous employees.[27] Many provide only dates of employment, positions held, and date of separation.

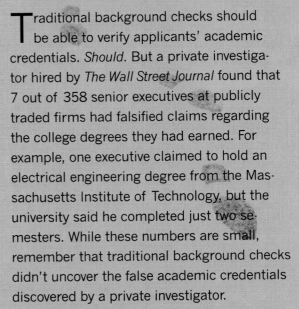

Private Eyes

Traditional background checks should be able to verify applicants' academic credentials. *Should.* But a private investigator hired by *The Wall Street Journal* found that 7 out of 358 senior executives at publicly traded firms had falsified claims regarding the college degrees they had earned. For example, one executive claimed to hold an electrical engineering degree from the Massachusetts Institute of Technology, but the university said he completed just two semesters. While these numbers are small, remember that traditional background checks didn't uncover the false academic credentials discovered by a private investigator.

Source: C. Tuna and K. Winstein, "Economy Promises to Fuel Résumé Fraud—Practices Vary for Vetting Prospective Employees, but Executives Usually Face Tougher Background Checks," *Wall Street Journal*, November 17, 2008, B4.

When previous employers decline to provide meaningful references or background information, they put other employers at risk of *negligent hiring* lawsuits, in which an employer is held liable for the actions of an employee who would not have been hired if the employer had conducted a thorough reference search and background check.[28]

With previous employers generally unwilling to give full, candid references and with negligent hiring lawsuits awaiting companies that don't get such references and background information, what can companies do? They can conduct criminal record checks, especially if the job for which the person is applying involves money, drugs, control over valuable goods, or access to the elderly, children with disabilities, or people's homes.[29] According to the Society for Human Resource Management, 96 percent of companies conduct background checks and 80 percent of companies go further and conduct criminal record checks.[30] Another option is to use social networking sites like Facebook, LinkedIn, and Twitter to research potential employees. A recent survey by CareerBuilder found that 45 percent of prospective employers use social networks to gather information about their applicants. Eighteen percent of those companies reported that they hired a candidate based on what they found on the applicant's profile, such as the applicant's personality, professional qualifications, creativity, and communication skills. However, 35 percent of the companies reported that they rejected a candidate because of what they found on their profile, such as inappropriate photographs, negative talk about previous employers, poor communication skills, and lying about qualifications.[31]

Next, ask applicants to sign a waiver that permits you to check references, run a background check, or contact anyone else with knowledge of their work performance or history. Likewise, ask applicants if there is anything they would like the company to know or if they expect you to hear anything unusual when contacting references.[32] This in itself is often enough to get applicants to share information that they typically withhold. When you've finished checking, keep the findings confidential to minimize the chances of a defamation charge.

Finally, consider hiring private investigators to conduct background checks. They can often uncover surprising information not revealed by traditional background checks.[33]

3.3 | SELECTION TESTS

Selection tests give organizational decision makers a chance to know who will likely do well in a job and who won't. The basic idea behind selection testing is to have applicants take a test that measures something directly or indirectly related to doing well on the job. The selection tests discussed here are specific ability tests, cognitive ability tests, biographical data, personality tests, work sample tests, and assessment centers.

Specific ability tests measure the extent to which an applicant possesses the particular kind of ability needed to do a job well. Specific ability tests are also called **aptitude tests** because they measure aptitude for doing a particular task well. For example, if you took the SAT to get into college, then you've taken the aptly named Scholastic Aptitude Test, which is one of the best predictors of how well students will do in college (i.e., scholastic performance). Specific ability tests also exist for mechanical, clerical, sales, and physical work. For example, clerical workers have to be good at accurately reading and scanning numbers as they type or enter data. Exhibit 11.4 shows items similar to those found on the Minnesota Clerical Test, in which applicants have only a short time to determine if the two columns of numbers and letters are identical. Applicants who are good at this are likely to do well as clerical or data-entry workers.

Cognitive ability tests measure the extent to which applicants have abilities in perceptual speed, verbal comprehension, numerical aptitude, general reasoning, and spatial aptitude. In other words, these tests indicate how quickly and how well people understand words, numbers, logic, and spatial dimensions. Whereas specific ability tests predict job performance in only particular types of jobs, cognitive ability tests accurately predict job performance in almost all kinds of jobs.[34] Why is this so? The reason is that people with strong cognitive or mental abilities are usually good at learning new things, processing complex information, solving problems, and making decisions, and these abilities are important in almost all jobs.[35] In fact, cognitive ability tests are almost always the best predictors of job performance. Consequently, if you were allowed to use just one selection test, a cognitive ability test would be the one to use.[36] (In practice, though, companies use a battery of different tests because doing so leads to much more accurate selection decisions.)

Specific ability tests (aptitude tests) tests that measure the extent to which an applicant possesses the particular kind of ability needed to do a job well

Cognitive ability tests tests that measure the extent to which applicants have abilities in perceptual speed, verbal comprehension, numerical aptitude, general reasoning, and spatial aptitude

Exhibit 11.4	Clerical Test Items Similar to Those Found on the Minnesota Clerical Test			
	NUMBERS/LETTERS		**SAME**	
1.	3468251	3467251	Yes	No
			O	O
2.	4681371	4681371	Yes	No
			O	O
3.	7218510	7218520	Yes	No
			O	O
4.	ZXYAZAB	ZXYAZAB	Yes	No
			O	O
5.	ALZYXMN	ALZYXNM	Yes	No
			O	O
6.	PRQZYMN	PRQZYMN	Yes	No
			O	O

Source: N. W. Schmitt and R. J. Klimoski, *Research Methods in Human Resource Management* (Mason, OH: South-Western, 1991). Used with permission.

Biographical data (biodata) extensive surveys that ask applicants questions about their personal backgrounds and life experiences

Work sample tests tests that require applicants to perform tasks that are actually done on the job

Assessment center a series of managerial simulations, graded by trained observers, that is used to determine applicants' capability for managerial work

Biographical data, or **biodata,** are extensive surveys that ask applicants questions about their personal backgrounds and life experiences. The basic idea behind biodata is that past behavior (personal background and life experience) is the best predictor of future behavior. Most biodata questionnaires have over 100 items that gather information about habits and attitudes, health, interpersonal relations, money, what it was like growing up in your family (parents, siblings, childhood years, teen years), personal habits, current home (spouse, children), hobbies, education and training, values, preferences, and work.[37] In general, biodata are very good predictors of future job performance, especially in entry-level jobs.

You may have noticed that some of the information requested in biodata surveys is related to those topics employers should avoid in applications, interviews, or other parts of the selection process. This information can be requested in biodata questionnaires provided that the company can demonstrate that the information is job-related (i.e., valid) and does not result in adverse impact against protected groups of job applicants. Biodata surveys should be validated and tested for adverse impact before they are used to make selection decisions.[38]

Work sample tests, also called *performance tests,* require applicants to perform tasks that are actually done on the job. So, unlike specific ability, cognitive ability, biographical data, and personality tests, which are indirect predictors of job performance, work sample tests directly measure a job applicant's capability to do the job. For example, a computer-based work sample test has applicants assume the role of a real estate agent who must decide how to interact with virtual clients in a gamelike scenario. And, as in real life, the clients can be frustrating, confusing, demanding, or indecisive. In one situation, the wife loves the house but the husband hates it. The applicants, just like actual real estate agents, must demonstrate what they would do in these realistic situations.[39] This work sample simulation gives real estate companies direct evidence of whether applicants can do the job if they are hired. Work sample tests are generally very good

at predicting future job performance; however, they can be expensive to administer and can be used for only one kind of job. For example, an auto dealership could not use a work sample test for mechanics as a selection test for sales representatives.

Assessment centers use a series of job-specific simulations that are graded by multiple trained observers to determine applicants' ability to perform managerial work. Unlike the previously described selection tests that are commonly used for specific jobs or entry-level jobs, assessment centers are most often used to select applicants who have high potential to be good managers. Assessment centers often last two to five days and require participants to complete a number of tests and exercises that simulate managerial work.

Some of the more common assessment center exercises are in-basket exercises, role-play exercises, small-group presentations, and leaderless group discussions. An *in-basket exercise* is a paper-and-pencil test in which an applicant is given a manager's in-basket containing memos, phone messages, organizational policies, and other communications normally received by and available to managers. Applicants have a limited time to read through the in-basket, prioritize the items, and decide how to deal with each item. Experienced managers then score the applicants' decisions and recommendations. Exhibit 11.5 shows an item that could be used in an assessment center for evaluating applicants for a job as a store manager.

Exhibit 11.5   In-Basket Item for an Assessment Center for Store Managers

```
February 28
Sam & Dave's Discount Warehouse
Orange, California

Dear Store Manager,

Last week, my children and I were shopping in your store.
After doing our grocery shopping, we stopped in the
electronics department and asked the clerk, whose name
is Donald Block, to help us find a copy of the latest
version of the Madden NFL video game. Mr. Block was rude,
unhelpful, and told us to find it for ourselves as he
was busy.

I've been a loyal customer for over six years and expect
you to immediately do something about Mr. Block's
behavior. If you don't, I'll start doing my shopping
somewhere else.

Sincerely,
Margaret Quinlan
```

Source: Adapted from N. W. Schmitt and R. J. Klimoski, *Research Methods in Human Resource Management* (Mason, OH: South-Western 1991).

In a *leaderless group discussion*, another common assessment center exercise, a group of six applicants is given approximately two hours to solve a problem, but no one is put in charge (hence the name "leaderless" group discussion). Trained observers watch and score each participant on the extent to which he or she facilitates discussion, listens, leads, persuades, and works well with others.

Are tests perfect predictors of job performance? No, they aren't. Some people who do well on selection tests will do poorly in their jobs. Likewise, some people who do poorly on selection tests (and therefore weren't hired) would have been very good performers. Nonetheless, valid tests will minimize these selection errors (hiring people who should not have been hired and not hiring people who should have been hired) while maximizing correct selection decisions (hiring people who should have been hired and not hiring people who should not have been hired). In short, tests increase the chances that you'll hire the right person for the job, that is, someone who turns out to be a good performer. So, although tests aren't perfect, almost nothing predicts future job performance as well as the selection tests discussed here.

3.4 | INTERVIEWS

In **interviews,** company representatives ask job applicants job-related questions to determine whether they are qualified for the job. Interviews are probably the most frequently used and relied-upon selection device. There are several basic kinds of interviews: unstructured, structured, and semistructured.

In **unstructured interviews,** interviewers are free to ask applicants anything they want, and studies show that they do. Because interviewers often disagree about which questions should be asked during interviews, different interviewers tend to ask applicants very different questions.[40] Furthermore, individual interviewers even seem to have a tough time asking the same questions from one interview to the next. This high level of inconsistency lowers the validity of unstructured interviews as a selection device because comparing applicant responses can be difficult. As a result, even though unstructured interviews do predict job performance with some success, they are about half as accurate as structured interviews at predicting which job applicants should be hired.[41]

By contrast, for **structured interviews,** standardized interview questions are prepared ahead of time so that all applicants are asked the same job-related questions.[42] Structuring interviews also ensures that interviewers ask only for important, job-related information. Not only are the accuracy, usefulness, and validity of the interview improved, but the chances that interviewers will ask questions about topics that violate employment laws (the "Don't Ask!" box on page 205 has a list of these topics) are reduced.

The primary advantage of structured interviews is that comparing applicants is much easier because they are all asked the same questions. Structured interviews typically contain four types of questions: situational, behavioral, background, and job-knowledge. *Situational questions* ask applicants how they would respond in a hypothetical situation (e.g., "What would you do if . . . ?"). These questions are more appropriate for hiring new graduates, as they are unlikely to have encountered real work situations because of their limited experience. *Behavioral questions* ask applicants what they did in previous jobs that is similar to what is required for the job for which they are applying (e.g., "In your previous jobs, tell me about . . . "). These questions are more appropriate for hiring experienced individuals. *Background questions* ask applicants about their work experience, education, and other qualifications (e.g., "Tell me about the training you received at . . . "). Finally, *job-knowledge questions* ask applicants to demonstrate their job knowledge (e.g., for nurses, "Give me an example of a time when one of your patients had a severe reaction to a medication. How did you handle it?").[43]

Semistructured interviews are hybrids of structured and unstructured interviews. A major part of the semistructured interview (perhaps as much as 80 percent) is based on structured questions, but some time is set aside for unstructured interviewing to allow the interviewer to probe into ambiguous or missing information uncovered during the structured portion of the interview.

How well do interviews predict future job performance? Contrary to what you've probably heard, recent evidence indicates that even unstructured interviews do a fairly good job.[44] When conducted properly, however, structured interviews can lead to much more accurate hiring decisions than can unstructured interviews. In some cases, the validity of structured interviews can rival that of cognitive ability tests. But even more important, because interviews are especially

Interview a selection tool in which company representatives ask job applicants job-related questions to determine whether they are qualified for the job

Unstructured interviews interviews in which interviewers are free to ask the applicants anything they want

Structured interviews interviews in which all applicants are asked the same set of standardized questions, usually including situational, behavioral, background, and job-knowledge questions

Exhibit 11.6   Guidelines for Conducting Effective Structured Interviews

Interview Stage	What to Do

Planning the Interview

- Identify and define the knowledge, skills, abilities, and other (KSAO) characteristics needed for successful job performance.
- For each essential KSAO, develop key behavioral questions that will elicit examples of past accomplishments, activities, and performance.
- For each KSAO, develop a list of things to look for in the applicant's responses to key questions.

Conducting the Interview

- Create a relaxed, nonstressful interview atmosphere.
- Review the applicant's application form, résumé, and other information.
- Allocate enough time to complete the interview without interruption.
- Put the applicant at ease; don't jump right into heavy questioning.
- Tell the applicant what to expect. Explain the interview process.
- Obtain job-related information from the applicant by asking those questions prepared for each KSAO.
- Describe the job and the organization to the applicant. Applicants need adequate information to make a selection decision about the organization.

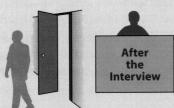

After the Interview

- Immediately after the interview, review your notes and make sure they are complete.
- Evaluate the applicant on each essential KSAO.
- Determine each applicant's probability of success and make a hiring decision.

Source: B. M. Farrell, "The Art and Science of Employment Interviews," *Personnel Journal* 65 (1986): 91–94.

Training developing the skills, experience, and knowledge employees need to perform their jobs or improve their performance

good at assessing applicants' interpersonal skills, they work particularly well with cognitive ability tests. Combining the two—using structured interviews together with cognitive ability tests to identify smart people who work well in conjunction with others—leads to even better selection decisions than using either alone.[45] Exhibit 11.6 provides a set of guidelines for conducting effective structured employment interviews.

Developing Qualified Workers

ccording to the American Society for Training and Development, a typical investment in employee training increases productivity by an average of 17 percent, reduces employee turnover, and makes companies more profitable.[46] Giving employees the knowledge and skills they need to improve their performance is just the first step in developing employees, however. The second step—and not enough companies do this—is giving employees formal feedback about their actual job performance.

After reading the next two sections, you should be able to

4   **describe how to determine training needs and select the appropriate training methods.**

5   **discuss how to use performance appraisal to give meaningful performance feedback.**

4   Training

Training means providing opportunities for employees to develop the job-specific skills, experience, and knowledge they need to do their jobs or improve their performance. American companies spend more than

$60 billion a year on training. *To make sure those training dollars are well spent, companies need to **4.1 determine specific training needs, 4.2 select appropriate training methods,** and **4.3 evaluate training.***

4.1 | DETERMINING TRAINING NEEDS

Needs assessment is the process of identifying and prioritizing the learning needs of employees. Needs assessments can be conducted by identifying performance deficiencies, listening to customer complaints, surveying employees and managers, or formally testing employees' skills and knowledge.

Note that training should never be conducted without first performing a needs assessment. Sometimes training isn't needed at all or isn't needed for all employees. Unfortunately, however, many organizations simply require all employees to attend training whether they need to or not. As a result, employees who aren't interested or don't need the training may react negatively during or after training. Likewise, employees who need training but aren't required to attend may also react negatively. Consequently, a needs assessment is an important tool for deciding who should or should not attend training. In fact, employment law restricts employers from discriminating on the basis of age, sex, race, color, religion, national origin, or disability when selecting training participants. Just as in making hiring decisions, the selection of training participants should be based on job-related information.

4.2 | TRAINING METHODS

Assume that you're a training director for a major oil company and that you're in charge of making sure all employees know how to respond effectively in the event of an oil spill.[47] Exhibit 11.7 on the next page lists a number of training methods you could use: films and videos, lectures, planned readings, case studies, coaching and mentoring, group discussions, on-the-job training, role-playing, simulations and games, vestibule training, and computer-based learning. Which method would be best?

To choose the best method, you should consider a number of factors, such as the number of people to be trained, the cost of training, and the objectives of the training. For instance, if the training objective is to impart information or knowledge to trainees, then you should use films and videos, lectures, and planned readings. In our example, trainees might read a manual or attend a lecture about how to seal a shoreline to keep it from being affected by the spill.

If developing analytical and problem-solving skills is the objective, then use case studies, coaching and mentoring, and group discussions. In our example, trainees might view a video documenting how a team handled exposure to hazardous substances, talk with first responders, and discuss what they would do in a similar situation.

If practicing, learning, or changing job behaviors is the objective, then use on-the-job training, role-playing, simulations and games, and vestibule training. In our example, trainees might participate in a mock shoreline cleanup to learn what to do in the event oil comes to shore. This simulation could take place on an actual shoreline or on a video game-like virtual shoreline.

If training is supposed to meet more than one of these objectives, then your best choice may be to combine one of the previous methods with computer-based training.

These days, many companies are adopting computer-based training, or *e-learning*. E-learning can offer several advantages. Because employees don't need to leave their jobs, travel costs are greatly reduced. Also, because employees can take training modules when it is convenient (in other words, they don't have to fall behind at their jobs to attend week-long training courses), workplace productivity should increase and employee stress should decrease. For example, Golden Harvest Seeds, a producer of agricultural seeds such as hybrid corn, soybeans, grain sorghum, and alfalfa, now has 120 training courses on its website for 250 employees and 2,000 independent crop-seed dealers. The company found that employees typically watched the sales videos and training programs on Saturdays and Monday mornings. As more people took the online courses, sales increased and costs fell to less than $100 per person per course. Says head of sales development David Dam, "We're getting more done with less money."[48] Finally, if the company's technology infrastructure can support it, e-learning can be much faster than traditional training methods.

There are, however, several disadvantages to e-learning. First, despite its increasing popularity, it's not always the appropriate training method. E-learning can be a good way to impart information, but it isn't always as effective for changing job behaviors or developing problem-solving and analytical skills. Second, e-learning requires a significant investment in computers and high-speed Internet and network connections for all employees. Finally, though e-learning can be faster, many employees find it so boring and unengaging that they may choose to do their jobs

Needs assessment
the process of identifying and prioritizing the learning needs of employees

Exhibit 11.7 Training Objectives and Methods

TRAINING OBJECTIVE	TRAINING METHODS
Impart Information and Knowledge	• *Films and videos.* Films and videos share information, illustrate problems and solutions, and effectively hold trainees' attention.
	• *Lectures.* Trainees listen to instructors' oral presentations.
	• *Planned readings.* Trainees read about concepts or ideas before attending training.
Develop Analytical and Problem-Solving Skills	• *Case studies.* Cases are analyzed and discussed in small groups. The cases present a specific problem or decision, and trainees develop methods for solving the problem or making the decision.
	• *Coaching and mentoring.* Coaching and mentoring of trainees by managers involves informal advice, suggestions, and guidance. This method is helpful for reinforcing other kinds of training and for trainees who benefit from support and personal encouragement.
	• *Group discussions.* Small groups of trainees actively discuss specific topics. The instructor may perform the role of discussion leader.
Practice, Learn, or Change Job Behaviors	• *On-the-job training (OJT).* New employees are assigned to experienced employees. The trainee learns by watching the experienced employee perform the job and eventually by working alongside the experienced employee. Gradually, the trainee is left on his or her own to perform the job.
	• *Role-playing.* Trainees assume job-related roles and practice new behaviors by acting out what they would do in job-related situations.
	• *Simulations and games.* Experiential exercises place trainees in realistic job-related situations and give them the opportunity to experience a job-related condition in a relatively low-cost setting. The trainee benefits from hands-on experience before actually performing the job, where mistakes may be more costly.
	• *Vestibule training.* Procedures and equipment similar to those used in the actual job are set up in a special area called a "vestibule." The trainee is then taught how to perform the job at his or her own pace without disrupting the actual flow of work, making costly mistakes, or exposing the trainee and others to dangerous conditions.
Impart Information and Knowledge; Develop Analytical and Problem-Solving Skills; and Practice, Learn, or Change Job Behaviors	• *Computer-based learning.* Interactive videos, software, CD-ROMs, personal computers, teleconferencing, and the Internet may be combined to present multimedia-based training.

Source: A. Fowler, "How to Decide on Training Methods," *People Management* 25, no. 1 (1995): 36.

rather than complete e-learning courses when sitting alone at their desks. E-learning may become more interesting, however, as more companies incorporate game-like features such as avatars and competition into their e-learning courses.

At Silicon Image, employees learn how to make silicon computer chips in a virtual world that simulates the company's corporate campus. Employees interact with their coworkers using three-dimensional charac-ters that they create and control, similar to the popular online world *Second Life.* Workers "walk" through this virtual world just like they would through Silicon Im-age's real buildings. Each time they enter a department, there are videos, information slides, and tasks to be completed. Office Director Andrew Turnbull says that the virtual world adds a "wow factor" to the training. He says, "We wanted to provide the content in a com-pelling way for adults to learn."[49]

4.3 | EVALUATING TRAINING

After selecting a training method and conducting the training, the last step is to evaluate the training. Training can be evaluated in four ways: on *reactions* (how satisfied trainees were with the program), on *learning* (how much employees improved their knowledge or skills), on *behavior* (how much employees actually changed their on-the-job behavior because of training), or on *results* (how much training improved job performance, such as increased sales or quality, or decreased costs).[50] In general, if done well, training provides meaningful benefits for most companies. For example, a study by the American Society for Training and Development shows that a training budget as small as $680 per employee can increase a company's total return on investment by 6 percent.[51]

5 Performance Appraisal

Performance appraisal is the process of assessing how well employees are doing their jobs. Most employees and managers intensely dislike the performance appraisal process. Among them is Yahoo! CEO Carol Bartz. Bartz says, "If I had my way, I wouldn't do annual reviews. I think the annual review process is so antiquated. I almost would rather ask each employee to tell us if they've had a meaningful conversation with their manager this quarter. Yes or no. And if they say no, they ought to have one."[52] Unfortunately, attitudes like this are all too common. Whether it's because, like Bartz, they don't feel like performance appraisals accomplish much or they just find the prospect of appraisals painful to think about, 70 percent of employees are dissatisfied with the performance appraisal process in their companies. Likewise, according to the Society for Human Resource Management, 90 percent of human resource managers are dissatisfied with the performance appraisal systems used by their companies.[53]

Let's explore how companies can improve performance appraisal by 5.1 accurately measuring job performance and 5.2 effectively sharing performance feedback with employees.

5.1 | ACCURATELY MEASURING JOB PERFORMANCE

Workers often have strong doubts about the accuracy of their performance appraisals—and they may be right. It's widely known that assessors are prone to errors when rating worker performance. One of the reasons that managers make these errors is that they often don't spend enough time gathering or reviewing performance data. What can be done to minimize rating errors and improve the accuracy with which job performance is measured? In general, two approaches have been used: improving performance appraisal measures themselves and training performance raters to be more accurate.

One of the ways companies try to improve performance appraisal measures is to use as many objective performance measures as possible. **Objective performance measures** are measures of performance that are easily and directly counted or quantified. Common objective performance measures include output, scrap or waste, sales, customer complaints, and rejection rates.

But when objective performance measures aren't available, and frequently they aren't, subjective performance measures have to be used instead. Subjective performance measures require that someone judge or assess a worker's performance. The most common kind of subjective performance measure is the Graphic Rating Scale (GRS) shown in Exhibit 11.8 on the next page. Graphic rating scales are most widely used because they are easy to construct, but they are very susceptible to rating errors.

A popular alternative to graphic rating scales is the **Behavior Observation Scale (BOS).** The BOS requires raters to rate the frequency with which workers perform specific behaviors representative of the job dimensions that are critical to successful job performance. Exhibit 11.8 shows a BOS for two important job dimensions for a retail salesperson: customer service and money handling. Notice that each dimension lists several specific behaviors characteristic of a worker who excels in that dimension of job performance. (Normally, the scale would list seven to twelve items per dimension, not three as in the exhibit.) Notice also that the behaviors are good behaviors, meaning they indicate good performance, and the rater is asked to judge how frequently an employee engaged in those good behaviors. The logic behind the BOS is that better performers engage in good behaviors more often.

Not only do BOSs work well for rating critical dimensions of performance, but studies also show that managers strongly prefer BOSs for giving performance feedback; accurately differentiating between poor, average, and good workers; identifying training needs;

Performance appraisal the process of assessing how well employees are doing their jobs

Objective performance measures measures of job performance that are easily and directly counted or quantified

Behavioral Observation Scale (BOS) a rating scale that indicates the frequency with which workers perform specific behaviors that are representative of the job dimensions critical to successful job performance

and accurately measuring performance. And in response to the statement, "If I were defending a company, this rating format would be an asset to my case," attorneys strongly preferred BOSs over other kinds of subjective performance appraisal scales.[54]

The second approach to improving the measurement of workers' job performance is **rater training**. The most effective is frame-of-reference training in which a group of trainees learns how to do performance appraisals by watching a video of an employee at work and then evaluating the performance of the person in the video. A trainer (i.e., subject matter expert) then shares his or her evaluations, and trainees' evaluations are compared with the expert's. The expert then explains rationales behind his or her evaluations. This process is repeated until the difference in evaluations given by trainees and evaluations by the expert are minimized. The underlying logic behind the frame-of-reference training is that by adopting the frame of reference used by an expert, trainees will be able to accurately observe, judge, and use the scale to evaluate the performance of others.[55]

Exhibit 11.8 **Subjective Performance Appraisal Scales**

Graphic Rating Scale

	Very poor	Poor	Average	Good	Very good
Example 1: Quality of work performed is …	1	2	3	4	5

	Very poor (20% errors)	Poor (15% errors)	Average (10% errors)	Good (5% errors)	Very good (less than 5% errors)
Example 2: Quality of work performed is …	1	2	3	4	5

Behavioral Observation Scale

Dimension: Customer Service

	Almost Never				Almost Always
1. Greets customers with a smile and a "hello."	1	2	3	4	5
2. Calls other stores to help customers find merchandise that is not in stock.	1	2	3	4	5
3. Promptly handles customer concerns and complaints.	1	2	3	4	5

Dimension: Money Handling

	Almost Never				Almost Always
1. Accurately makes change from customer transactions.	1	2	3	4	5
2. Accounts balance at the end of the day, no shortages or surpluses.	1	2	3	4	5
3. Accurately records transactions in computer system.	1	2	3	4	5

© Cengage Learning 2011

Rater training training performance appraisal raters in how to avoid rating errors and increase rating accuracy

360-degree feedback a performance appraisal process in which feedback is obtained from the boss, subordinates, peers and coworkers, and the employees themselves

5.2 | SHARING PERFORMANCE FEEDBACK

After gathering accurate performance data, the next step is to share performance feedback with employees. Unfortunately, even when performance appraisal ratings are accurate, the appraisal process often breaks down at the feedback stage. Employees become defensive and dislike hearing any negative assessments of their work, no matter how small. Managers become defensive, too, and dislike giving appraisal feedback as much as employees dislike receiving it.

What can be done to overcome the inherent difficulties in performance appraisal feedback sessions? Since performance appraisal ratings have traditionally been the judgments of just one person (the boss) one possibility is to use **360-degree feedback.** In this approach, feedback comes from four sources: the boss, subordinates, peers and coworkers, and the employees themselves. The data, which are obtained anonymously (except for the feedback from the boss), are compiled into a report comparing the employee's self-ratings with those of the boss, subordinates, and peers and coworkers. Usually, a consultant or human resource specialist discusses the results with the employee. The advantage of 360-degree programs is that negative feedback ("You don't listen") is often more credible when it comes from several people.

Herbert Meyer, who has been studying performance appraisal feedback for more than 30 years, recommends a list of topics for discussion in performance appraisal feedback sessions, shown in Exhibit 11.9.[56] How these topics are discussed in a review session is important for its success. Managers can do three different things to make performance reviews as comfortable and productive as possible. First, managers should separate developmental feedback, which is designed to improve future performance, from administrative feedback, which is used to evaluate past performance, often for determining rewards such as raises. When managers give developmental feedback, they're acting as coaches, but when they give administrative feedback, they're acting as judges. These roles, coach and judge, are clearly incompatible. As coaches, managers are encouraging, pointing out opportunities for growth and improvement, and employees are typically open and receptive to feedback. But as judges, managers are evaluative, and employees are typically defensive and closed to feedback.

Second, Meyer suggests that performance appraisal feedback sessions be based on self-appraisals, in which employees carefully assess their own strengths, weaknesses, successes, and failures in writing. Because employees play an active role in the review of their performance, managers can be coaches rather than judges. Also, because the focus is on future goals and development, both employees and managers are likely to be more satisfied with the process and more committed to future plans and changes. And, because the focus is on development and not administrative assessment, studies show that self-appraisals lead to more candid self-assessments than traditional supervisory reviews do.[57]

Finally, what people do with the performance feedback they receive really matters. A study of 1,361 senior managers found that managers who reviewed their 360-degree feedback with an executive coach hired by the company were more likely to set specific goals for improvement, ask their bosses for ways to improve, and subsequently improve their performance.[58]

A 5-year study of 252 managers found that their performance improved dramatically if they met with their subordinates to discuss their 360-degree feedback ("You don't listen") and how they were going to address it ("I'll restate what others have said before stating my opinion"). Performance was dramatically lower for managers who never discussed their 360-degree feedback with subordinates and for managers who did not routinely do so (some managers did not review their 360-degree feedback with subordinates each year of the study). Why is discussing 360-degree feedback with subordinates so effective? These discussions help managers better understand their weaknesses, force them to develop a plan to improve, and demonstrate to the subordinates the managers' public commitment to improving.[59] In short, it helps if people discuss their performance feedback with others, but it is particularly helpful to discuss the feedback with the people who provided it.

| Exhibit 11.9 | What to Discuss in a Performance Appraisal Feedback Session |

✔ Overall progress—an analysis of accomplishments and shortcomings.

✔ Problems encountered in meeting job requirements.

✔ Opportunities to improve performance.

✔ Long-range plans and opportunities—for the job and for the individual's career.

✔ General discussion of possible plans and goals for the coming year.

Source: H. H. Meyer, "A Solution to the Performance Appraisal Feedback Enigma," *Academy of Management Executive* 5, no. 1 (1991): 68–76.

Keeping Qualified Workers

a t Penske Automotive Group, which has 300 car dealerships worldwide, 8 percent of CEO Roger Penske's bonus is tied to keeping employee turnover below 31 percent. Pep Boys, a car parts retail chain, does the same, making 10 percent of its middle managers' pay contingent on low employee turnover. Likewise, ExlService Holdings, an Indian-based offshore outsourcing company, links 30 percent of its lower level managers' pay to employee turnover. Why link managers' pay to employee turnover? According to Tony Pordon, senior vice president at Penske Automotive, "We believe that employee turnover is a symptom of bigger problems at the dealership level."[60] Mark Royal, a consultant for the Hay Group, which specializes in employee compensation, further explains that linking managers' pay to turnover, ". . . is a recognition, on the one hand, of people as a driver of business success. It also reflects a recognition that turnover is costly."[61]

After reading the next section, you should be able to

┗ **describe basic compensation strategies and discuss the four kinds of employee separations.**

┗ Compensation and Employee Separation

Compensation includes both the financial and the nonfinancial rewards that organizations give employees in exchange for their work. **Employee separation** is a broad term covering the loss of an employee for any reason. *Involuntary separation* occurs when employers decide to terminate or lay off employees. *Voluntary separation* occurs when employees decide to quit or retire. Because employee separations affect recruiting, selection, training, and compensation, organizations should include in their human-resource planning a forecast of the number of employees they expect to lose through termination, layoff, turnover, and/or retirement.

*Let's learn more about compensation and employee separation by examining the **6.1 compensation decisions that managers must make** as well as **6.2 termination, 6.3 downsizing, 6.4 retirement,** and **6.5 turnover.***

6.1 | COMPENSATION DECISIONS

There are three basic kinds of compensation decisions: pay level, pay variability, and pay structure.[62]

Pay-level decisions are decisions about whether to pay workers at a level that is below, above, or at current market wages. Companies use job evaluation to set their pay structures. **Job evaluation** determines the worth of each job by determining the market value of the knowledge, skills, and requirements needed to perform it. After conducting a job evaluation, most companies try to pay the going rate, meaning the current market wage. There are always companies, however, whose financial situations cause them to pay considerably less than current market wages. While a director of a child-care center in Vermont may make up to $25 an hour, teachers or caretakers in such a center make only $9 to $11 an hour.[63] According to the American Federation of Teachers, the average annual wage for early childcare workers is $18,820, and hourly wages have increased only 39 cents in the last 25 years.[64]

Some companies choose to pay above-average wages to attract and keep employees. *Above-market wages* can attract a larger, more qualified pool of job applicants, increase the rate of job acceptance, decrease the time it takes to fill positions, and increase the time that employees stay.[65]

Pay-variability decisions concern the extent to which employees' pay varies with individual and organizational performance. Linking pay to performance is intended to increase employee motivation, effort, and job performance. Piecework, sales commissions, profit sharing, employee stock ownership plans, and stock options are common pay-variability options. For instance, under **piecework** pay plans, employees are paid a set rate for each item produced up to some standard (e.g., 35 cents per item produced for output up to 100 units per day). Once productivity exceeds the standard, employees are paid a set amount for each unit of output over the standard (e.g., 45 cents for each unit above 100 units). Under a sales **commission** plan, salespeople are paid a percentage of the purchase price of items they sell. The more they sell, the more they earn. At Installation & Service Technologies, which sells point-of-sales systems, a salesperson's pay is determined in large part by how much they sell. Each member of the sales staff receives a small base salary (about 35 percent of total pay) and a commission based on how much gross profit they make on sales—17 percent for $1 to $50,000, 24 percent for $50,001 to $100,000, and 30 percent over $100,000. Plus, every time a salesperson reaches a new profit level, they receive an extra $1,000.[66]

Because pay plans such as piecework and commissions are based on individual performance, they can reduce the incentive that people have to work together. Therefore, companies also use group incentives (discussed in Chapter 10) and organizational incentives such as profit sharing, employee stock ownership plans, and stock options to encourage teamwork and cooperation.

With **profit sharing**, employees receive a portion of the organization's profits over and above their regular compensation. After posting a surprise $2.7 billion profit for 2009—its first in four years—Ford announced it would be issuing profit-sharing checks of about $450 to each of its hourly workers.[67]

Employee stock ownership plans (ESOPs) compensate employees by awarding them shares of the company stock in addition to their regular compensation. By contrast, **stock options** give employees the right to purchase shares of stock at a set price. Proponents of stock options argue that this gives employees and managers a strong incentive to work hard to make the company successful. If they do, the company's profits and stock price increase, and their stock options increase in value. If they don't, profits stagnate or turn into losses, and their stock options decrease in value or become worthless.

The incentive has to be more than just a piece of paper, however. At Van Meter Industrial, based in Cedar Rapids, Iowa, some employees didn't understand or care about their ESOP program. One even said, "Why don't you just give me a couple hundred bucks for beer and cigarettes [instead]?"[68] So the company created an employee committee to educate coworkers about how the ESOP program works. The committee meets with employees in small groups, where it feels safe to ask questions, and emphasizes, for example, that the company contributes

Profit sharing a compensation system in which a company pays a percentage of its profits to employees in addition to their regular compensation

Employee stock ownership plan (ESOP) a compensation system that awards employees shares of company stock in addition to their regular compensation

Stock options a compensation system that gives employees the right to purchase shares of stock at a set price, even if the value of the stock increases above that price

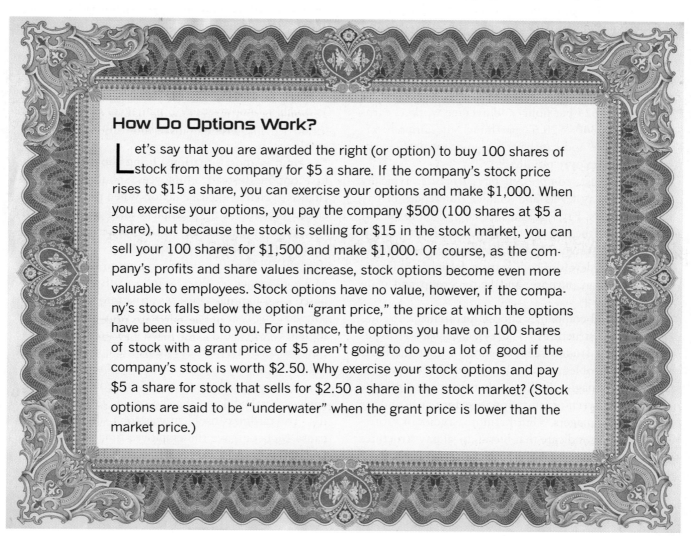

How Do Options Work?

Let's say that you are awarded the right (or option) to buy 100 shares of stock from the company for $5 a share. If the company's stock price rises to $15 a share, you can exercise your options and make $1,000. When you exercise your options, you pay the company $500 (100 shares at $5 a share), but because the stock is selling for $15 in the stock market, you can sell your 100 shares for $1,500 and make $1,000. Of course, as the company's profits and share values increase, stock options become even more valuable to employees. Stock options have no value, however, if the company's stock falls below the option "grant price," the price at which the options have been issued to you. For instance, the options you have on 100 shares of stock with a grant price of $5 aren't going to do you a lot of good if the company's stock is worth $2.50. Why exercise your stock options and pay $5 a share for stock that sells for $2.50 a share in the stock market? (Stock options are said to be "underwater" when the grant price is lower than the market price.)

the equivalent of 9.5 weeks of each employee's pay into the ESOP each year. Also, employees reaching their 6-month anniversaries are given jackets with the words "I am in" on them to emphasize that they're now part of the ESOP. Van Meter Industrial's workers now take a strong interest in what they can do to save the company money on a daily basis because, as the company becomes more profitable, the value of their ESOP shares rises. Although Van Meter's stock value was barely keeping up with inflation before this program, it increased by 78 percent after the program was implemented.[69]

Pay-structure decisions are concerned with internal pay distributions, meaning the extent to which people in the company receive very different levels of pay.[70] With *hierarchical pay structures,* there are big differences from one pay level to another. The highest pay levels are for people near the top of the pay distribution. The basic idea behind hierarchical pay structures is that large differences in pay between jobs or organizational levels should motivate people to work harder to obtain those higher-paying jobs. Many publicly owned companies have hierarchical pay structures, paying huge salaries to their top managers and CEOs. For example, the average CEO now makes 319 times as much as the average worker, down from 525 times the pay of the average worker just 10 years ago. But with CEO pay packages averaging $9.25 million per year ($4,625 per hour) and average workers earning just $41,340 ($20.67 per hour), the difference is still incredible and can have a significant detrimental impact on employee morale.[71]

By contrast, *compressed pay structures* typically have fewer pay levels and smaller differences in pay between levels. Pay is less dispersed and more similar across jobs in the company. The basic idea behind compressed pay structures is that similar pay levels should lead to higher levels of cooperation, feelings of fairness and a common purpose, and better group and team performance.

So should companies choose hierarchical or compressed pay structures? The evidence isn't straightforward, but studies seem to indicate that there are significant problems with the hierarchical approach. The most damaging finding is that there appears to be little link between organizational performance and the pay of top managers.[72] Furthermore, studies of professional athletes indicate that hierarchical pay structures (e.g., paying superstars 40 to 50 times more than the lowest-paid athlete on the team) hurt the performance of teams and individual players.[73] Likewise, managers

are twice as likely to quit their jobs when their companies have very strong hierarchical pay structures (i.e., when they're paid dramatically less than the people above them).[74] For now, it seems that hierarchical pay structures work best for independent work, where it's easy to determine the contributions of individual performers and little coordination with others is needed to get the job done. In other words, hierarchical pay structures work best when clear links can be drawn between individual performance and individual rewards. By contrast, compressed pay structures, in which everyone receives similar pay, seem to work best for interdependent work, which requires employees to work together. Some companies are pursuing a middle ground: combining hierarchical and compressed pay structures by giving ordinary workers the chance to earn more through ESOPs, stock options, and profit sharing.

6.2 | TERMINATING EMPLOYEES

Hopefully, the words "You're fired!" have never been directed at you. Lots of people hear them, however, as more than 400,000 people a year get fired from their jobs. Getting fired is a terrible thing, but many managers make it even worse by bungling the firing process, needlessly provoking the person who was fired and unintentionally inviting lawsuits. Though firing is never pleasant (and managers hate firings nearly as much as employees do), managers can do several things to minimize the problems inherent in firing employees.

First, in most situations, firing should not be the first option. Instead, employees should be given a chance to change their behavior. When problems arise, employees should have ample warning and must be specifically informed as to the nature and seriousness of the trouble they're in. After being notified, they should be given sufficient time to change. Mitch McLeod, owner of ARCOS, Inc., a software company based in Columbus, Ohio, was frustrated with the best software engineer in the company, who always showed up late to work and always had a bizarre excuse. One time, he told McLeod that he was late because his cat hid his car keys. McLeod could have fired the always-late employee, but instead, he decided to switch the engineer's schedule so that he could start later in the day. The tardiness problem was soon solved. And, because McLeod gave the employee time to change, he was able to keep a top performer.[75]

If the problems continue, however, the employees should again be counseled about his or her job performance, what could be done to improve it, and the possible consequences if things don't change (e.g., written reprimand, suspension without pay, or firing). Sometimes this is enough to solve the problem. If the problem isn't corrected after several rounds of warnings and discussions, however, the employee may be terminated.[76]

Second, employees should be fired only with good reason. Employers used to hire and fire employees under the legal principle of employment at will, which allowed them to fire employees for good reasons, bad reasons, or no reason at all. (Employees could also quit for good reasons, bad reasons, or no reason whenever they desired.) As employees began contesting their firings in court, however, the principle of wrongful discharge emerged. **Wrongful discharge** is a legal doctrine that requires an employer to have a job-related reason to terminate an employee. In other words, like other major human resource decisions, termination decisions should be made on the basis of job-related factors, such as violating company rules or consistently poor performance.

6.3 | DOWNSIZING

Downsizing is the planned elimination of jobs in a company. Whether it's because of cost cutting, declining market share, previous overaggressive hiring and growth, or outsourcing, 1 million to 1.9 million jobs are eliminated each year.[77] Two-thirds of companies that downsize will downsize a second time within a year. For example, after laying off 1,520 employees in December 2008 and almost 1,000 employees 10 months earlier, Yahoo!, which saw its profits drop by 78 percent, announced in April 2009 plans to cut 5 percent of its remaining workforce.[78] General Motors announced in June 2009 it would cut 4,000 white-collar jobs, with an overall goal of eliminating 10,000 of its 73,000 salaried positions worldwide. When the downsizing is complete, GM will employ 23,500 white-collar workers, half the number it had a decade ago.[79]

Does downsizing work? In theory, downsizing is supposed to lead to higher productivity and profits, better stock performance, and increased organizational flexibility. However, numerous studies demonstrate that it doesn't. For instance, a 15-year study of downsizing found that eliminating 10 percent of a company's work force produced only a 1.5 percent decrease in costs; that firms that downsized increased their stock price by only 4.7 percent over 3 years, compared with 34.3 percent for firms that didn't; and that profitability and productivity were generally not improved by downsizing.[80] Downsizing can also result in the loss

> **Wrongful discharge** a legal doctrine that requires employers to have job-related reasons to terminate employees
>
> **Downsizing** the planned elimination of jobs in a company

MGMT SUCCESS

Guidelines for Conducting Layoffs

1. Provide clear reasons and explanations for the layoffs.
2. To avoid laying off employees with critical or irreplaceable skills, knowledge, and expertise, get input from human resources, the legal department, and several levels of management.
3. Train managers in how to tell employees that they are being laid off (i.e., stay calm; make the meeting short; explain why, but don't be personal; and provide information about immediate concerns such as benefits, finding a new job, and collecting personal goods).
4. Give employees the bad news early in the day, and try to avoid laying off employees before holidays.
5. Provide outplacement services and counseling to help laid-off employees find new jobs.
6. Communicate with employees who have not been laid off to explain how the company and their jobs will change.

Source: M. Boyle, "The Not-So-Fine Art of the Layoff," *Fortune*, March 19, 2001, 209.

You are about to be unemployed.

of skilled workers who will be expensive to replace when the company grows again.[81] Since the end of 2007, U.S. manufacturers have laid off more than 2 million employees. As the economy started picking up again, manufacturers slowly began hiring again, but many have had surprising trouble filling positions. Job descriptions for many of the new position openings require workers who can operate complex computerized machinery, interpret detailed technical blueprints, and demonstrate higher math proficiency. Looking to fill 100 positions, one drug maker in Cleveland, Ohio, found only 47 qualified applicants in a pool of 3,600. Many potential candidates failed its skills aptitude screening test, which required that applicants demonstrate ninth-grade reading and math levels.[82] These results make it clear that the best strategy is to conduct effective human resource planning and avoid downsizing altogether. Indeed, downsizing should always be a last resort.

If companies do find themselves in financial or strategic situations in which downsizing is required for survival, however, they should train managers in how to break the news to downsized employees, have senior managers explain in detail why downsizing is necessary, and time the announcement so that employees hear it from the company and not from other sources such as TV or newspaper reports.[83] Finally, companies should do everything they can to help downsized employees find other jobs. One of the best ways to do this is to use **outplacement services** that provide employment-counseling services for employees faced with downsizing. Outplacement services often include advice and training in preparing résumés and getting ready for job interviews, and may even identify job opportunities in other companies.

6.4 | RETIREMENT

Early retirement incentive programs (ERIPs) offer financial benefits to employees to encourage them to retire early. Companies use ERIPs to reduce the number of employees in the organization, to lower costs by eliminating positions after employees retire, to lower costs by replacing high-paid retirees with lower-paid, less-experienced employees, or to create openings and job opportunities for people inside the company.

Although ERIPs can save companies money, they can pose a big problem for managers if they fail to accurately predict which employees—the good performers or the poor performers—and how many will retire early. Consultant Ron Nicol says, "The thing that doesn't work is just asking for volunteers. You get the wrong volunteers. Some of your best people will feel they can get a job anywhere. Or you have people who are close to retirement and are a real asset to the company."[84] When Progress Energy, in Raleigh, North Carolina, identified 450 jobs it wanted to eliminate with an ERIP, managers shared the list of jobs with employees, indicated that layoffs would follow if not enough people took early retirement, and then held 80 meetings with employees to answer questions. Despite this carefulness, an extra 1,000 employees, for a total of 1,450, took the ERIP offer and applied for early retirement![85]

Because of the problems associated with ERIPs, many companies are now offering **phased retirement,** in which employees transition to retirement by working reduced hours over a period of time before completely retiring. The advantage for employees is that they have more free time but continue to earn salaries and benefits without changing companies or careers. The advantage for companies is that it allows them to reduce salaries as well as hiring and training costs and retain experienced, valuable workers.[86]

6.5 | EMPLOYEE TURNOVER

Employee turnover is the loss of employees who voluntarily choose to leave the company. In general, most companies try to keep the rate of employee turnover low to reduce recruiting, hiring, training, and replacement costs. Engage Direct Mail, a direct mail marketing firm based in Ontario, has an amazing retention rate of 95 percent, meaning just 5 percent of employees leave the company each year. How is it able to prevent turnover so well? First, the company prefers to hire people who live near its office, since those who have to deal with long commutes have a less healthy work-life balance. Second, it provides great perks. Instead of giving traditional vacation days, Engage employees have a leave bank, in which they can store up to 60 days off, to use however they want. This policy has been especially attractive to female employees looking to start families. Engage also creates a team environment by giving each employee a personality test, and by giving work teams rewards for meeting quarterly goals.[87]

Not all kinds of employee turnover are bad for organizations, however. In fact, some turnover can actually be good. For instance, **functional turnover** is the loss of poor-performing employees who choose to leave the organization.[88] Functional turnover gives the organization a chance to replace poor performers with better workers. In fact, one study found that simply replacing poor-performing leavers with average workers would increase the revenues produced by retail salespeople in an upscale department store by $112,000 per person per year.[89] By contrast, **dysfunctional turnover,** the loss of high performers who choose to leave, is a costly loss to the organization.

Employee turnover should be carefully analyzed to determine whether good or poor performers are choosing to leave the organization. If the company is losing too many high performers, managers should determine the reasons and find ways to reduce the loss of valuable employees. The company may have to raise salary levels, offer enhanced benefits, or improve working conditions to retain skilled workers. One of the best ways to influence functional and dysfunctional turnover is to link pay directly to performance. A study of four sales forces found that when pay was strongly linked to performance via sales commissions and bonuses, poor performers were much more likely to leave (i.e., functional turnover). By contrast, poor performers were much more likely to stay when paid large, guaranteed monthly salaries and small sales commissions and bonuses.[90]

Functional turnover loss of poor-performing employees who voluntarily choose to leave a company

Dysfunctional turnover loss of high-performing employees who voluntarily choose to leave a company

STUDENT Study Tools

Located at the back of your book:
- ☐ Rip out and study the Chapter Review Card at the end of the book

Log in to the CourseMate for MGMT at cengagebrain.com to:
- ☐ Review Key Term Flashcards delivered 3 ways (print or online)
- ☐ Complete both Practice Quizzes to prepare for tests
- ☐ Play Beat the Clock and Quizbowl to master concepts
- ☐ Complete the Crossword Puzzle to review key terms
- ☐ Watch the video on the Maine Media Workshops for a real company example and take the accompanying quiz
- ☐ Watch the Biz Flix clip from *Played* and take the quiz
- ☐ Complete the Case Assignment on Burgerville
- ☐ Work through the Management Decision on managing HR in a recession
- ☐ Work through the Management Team Decision on customer service training
- ☐ Develop your skills with the Develop Your Career Potential exercise

12 | Managing Individuals and a Diverse Work Force

© Flying Colours Ltd/Digital Vision/Jupiterimages

LEARNING OUTCOMES:

1 describe diversity and explain why it matters.

2 understand the special challenges that the dimensions of surface-level diversity pose for managers.

3 explain how the dimensions of deep-level diversity affect individual behavior and interactions in the workplace.

4 explain the basic principles and practices that can be used to manage diversity.

Diversity and Why It Matters

Workplace diversity as we know it today is changing. Exhibit 12.1 on the next page shows predictions from the U.S. Census Bureau concerning how the U.S. population will change over the next 40 years. The percentage of white, non-Hispanic Americans in the general population is expected to decline from 64.7 percent in 2010 to 46.3 percent by the year 2050. By contrast, the percentage of Asian Americans will increase from 4.7 percent to 7.8 percent. Meanwhile, the proportion of Native Americans will hold fairly steady (increasing from 1.0 to 1.2 percent), as will the percentage of black Americans (increasing from 12.9 percent to 13.0 percent). The fastest-growing group by far, though, is Hispanics, who are expected to increase from 16 percent of the total population in 2010 to 30.3 percent by 2050.[1]

Other significant changes have already occurred. For example, today women hold 46.5 percent of the jobs in the United States, up from 38.2 percent in 1970. Furthermore, white males, who composed 63.9 percent of the work force in 1950, hold just 38.2 percent of today's jobs.[2]

These rather dramatic changes have taken place in a relatively short time. And, as these trends clearly show, the work force of the near future will be increasingly Hispanic, Asian American, black American, and female. It will also be older, as the average baby boomer approaches the age of 70 around 2020. Since many boomers are likely to postpone retirement and work well into their 70s to offset predicted reductions in Social Security and Medicare benefits, the work force may become even older than expected.[3]

Diversity means variety. Therefore, **diversity exists in an organization when there are a variety of demographic, cultural, and personal differences among the people who work there and the customers who do business there.** For example, Kayak.com is a travel search engine that gives users data on the prices of airline tickets, rental cars, and hotels from hundreds of providers. The company fields phone calls and email from customers all over the world, so CEO Paul English assembled German, Greek, Russian, Italian, French, and Indian personnel to address the different needs, cultures, and languages represented in its customer base. As English puts it, "One of my missions is that we will be able to answer every customer call, in any language."[4]

After reading the next section, you should be able to

1 describe diversity and explain why it matters.

1 Diversity: Differences That Matter

You'll begin your exploration of diversity by learning 1.1 that diversity is not affirmative action and 1.2 how to build a business case for diversity.

1.1 | DIVERSITY IS NOT AFFIRMATIVE ACTION

A common misconception is that workplace diversity and affirmative action are the same, yet these concepts differ in several critical ways, including their purpose, how they are practiced, and the

Diversity a variety of demographic, cultural, and personal differences among an organization's employees and customers

Exhibit 12.1

Percent of the Projected Population by Race and Hispanic Origin for the United States: 2010 to 2050

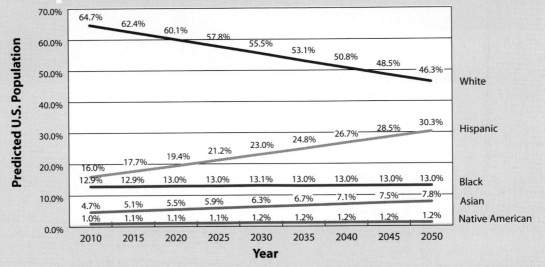

Predicted U.S. Population (vertical axis)

White: 64.7% (2010), 62.4% (2015), 60.1% (2020), 57.8% (2025), 55.5% (2030), 53.1% (2035), 50.8% (2040), 48.5% (2045), 46.3% (2050)

Hispanic: 16.0% (2010), 17.7% (2015), 19.4% (2020), 21.2% (2025), 23.0% (2030), 24.8% (2035), 26.7% (2040), 28.5% (2045), 30.3% (2050)

Black: 12.9% (2010), 12.9% (2015), 13.0% (2020), 13.0% (2025), 13.1% (2030), 13.0% (2035), 13.0% (2040), 13.0% (2045), 13.0% (2050)

Asian: 4.7% (2010), 5.1% (2015), 5.5% (2020), 5.9% (2025), 6.3% (2030), 6.7% (2035), 7.1% (2040), 7.5% (2045), 7.8% (2050)

Native American: 1.0% (2010), 1.1% (2015), 1.1% (2020), 1.1% (2025), 1.2% (2030), 1.2% (2035), 1.2% (2040), 1.2% (2045), 1.2% (2050)

Year (horizontal axis): 2010, 2015, 2020, 2025, 2030, 2035, 2040, 2045, 2050

Note: The original race data from Census 2000 are modified to eliminate the "some other race" category. This modification is used for all Census Bureau projections products and is explained in the document entitled "Modified Race Data Summary File Technical Documentation and ASCII Layout" that can be found on the Census Bureau website at http://www.census.gov/popest/archives/files/MRSF-01-US1.html.

Sources: Population Division, U.S. Census Bureau, "Percent of the Projected Population by Race and Hispanic Origin for the United States: 2008 to 2050," U.S. Census Bureau, August 14, 2008, accessed November 4, 2009, http://www.census.gov/population/www/projections/tablesandcharts/table_4.xls.

reactions they produce. To start with, **affirmative action** refers to purposeful steps taken by an organization to create employment opportunities for minorities and women.[5] By contrast, diversity exists in organizations when there is a variety of demographic, cultural, and personal differences among the people who work there and the customers who do business there. So, one key difference is that affirmative action is more narrowly focused on demographics such as sex and race, while diversity has a broader focus that includes demographic, cultural, and personal differences. A second difference is that affirmative action is a policy for actively creating diversity, but diversity can exist even if organizations don't take purposeful steps to create it. For example, Kayak.com achieved a high level of diversity without having a formal affirmative action program. Likewise, a local restaurant located near a university in a major city is likely to have a more diverse group of employees than one located in a small town. Affirmative action does not guarantee diversity. An organization can create employment opportunities for women and minorities yet not have a diverse work force.

A third important difference is that affirmative action is required by law for private employers with 50 or more employees, whereas diversity is not. Affirmative action originated with Executive Order 11246

(https://www.dol.gov/ofccp/regs/compliance/aa.htm) but is also related to the 1964 Civil Rights Act, which bans discrimination in voting, public places, federal government programs, federally supported public education, and employment. Title VII of the Civil Rights Act (http://www.eeoc.gov/laws/statutes/titlevii.cfm) requires that workers have equal employment opportunities when being hired or promoted. More specifically, Title VII prohibits companies from discriminating in their employment practices on the basis of race, color, religion, sex, or national origin. Title VII also created the Equal Employment Opportunity Commission, or EEOC (http://www.eeoc.gov), to administer these laws. By contrast, there is no federal law or agency to oversee diversity. Organizations that pursue diversity goals do so voluntarily.

Fourth, affirmative action programs and diversity programs also have different purposes. The purpose of

Affirmative action
purposeful steps taken by an organization to create employment opportunities for minorities and women

A business located near a university in a major city is likely to have a more diverse group of employees than one located in a small town.

© iStockphoto.com/Lawrence Sawyer

affirmative action programs is to compensate for past discrimination, which was widespread when legislation was introduced in the 1960s; to prevent ongoing discrimination; and to provide equal opportunities to all regardless of race, color, religion, sex, or national origin. Organizations that fail to uphold these laws may be required to

- hire, promote, or give back pay to those not hired or promoted;
- reinstate those who were wrongly terminated;
- pay attorneys' fees and court costs for those who bring charges against them; or
- take other actions that make individuals whole by returning them to the condition or place they would have been had it not been for discrimination.[6]

Consequently, affirmative action is basically a punitive approach.[7] By contrast, the general purpose of diversity programs is to create a positive work environment where no one is advantaged or disadvantaged, where "we" is everyone, where everyone can do his or her best work, where differences are respected and not ignored, and where everyone feels comfortable.[8] So, unlike affirmative action, which punishes companies for not achieving specific sex and race ratios in their work forces, diversity programs seek to benefit both organizations and their employees by encouraging organizations to value all kinds of differences.

Despite the overall success of affirmative action in making workplaces much fairer than they used to be, many people argue that some affirmative action programs unconstitutionally offer preferential treatment to females and minorities at the expense of other employees, a view accepted by some courts.[9] The American Civil Rights Institute successfully campaigned to ban race- and sex-based affirmative action in college admissions, government hiring, and government contracting programs in California (1996), Washington (1998), and Michigan (2006). Led by Ward Connerly, the Institute backed similar efforts in Arizona, Colorado, Missouri, Nebraska, and Oklahoma in 2008. Opponents like Connerly believe that affirmative action policies establish only surface-level diversity and, ironically, promote preferential treatment.[10]

Furthermore, research shows that people who have gotten a job or promotion as a result of affirmative action are frequently viewed as unqualified, even when clear evidence of their qualifications exists.[11] So, while affirmative action programs have created opportunities for minorities and women, those same minorities and women are frequently presumed to be unqualified when others believe they obtained their jobs as a result of affirmative action.

1.2 | DIVERSITY MAKES GOOD BUSINESS SENSE

Those who support the idea of diversity in organizations often ignore its business aspects altogether, claiming instead that diversity is simply the right thing to do. Yet diversity actually makes good business sense in several ways: it reduces costs, attracts and retains talent, and drives business growth.[12]

Diversity helps companies *reduce costs* by decreasing turnover and absenteeism and enabling them to avoid expensive lawsuits.[13] In fact, turnover costs typically amount to more than 90 percent of employees' salaries. So, if an executive who makes $200,000 a year leaves an organization, it can cost approximately $180,000 to find a replacement; even the lowest-paid hourly workers can cost companies as much as $10,000 when they quit. Since turnover rates for black Americans average 40 percent higher than for whites, and since women quit their jobs at twice the rate men do, companies that manage diverse work forces well can cut costs by reducing the turnover rates of their employees.[14] And, with women absent from work 60 percent more often than men, primarily because of family responsibilities, diversity programs that address the needs of female workers can also reduce the substantial costs of absenteeism.[15]

Diversity programs also save companies money by helping them avoid discrimination lawsuits, which have increased by a factor of 20 since 1970 and quadrupled just since 1995. In one survey conducted by the Society for Human Resource Management, 78 percent of respondents reported that diversity efforts helped them avoid lawsuits and litigation costs.[16] Indeed, because companies lose two-thirds of all discrimination cases that go to trial, the best strategy from a business perspective is not to be sued for discrimination at all. When companies lose such lawsuits, the average

> **Diversity** actually makes **good business sense** in several ways: it reduces costs, attracts and retains talent, and drives business growth.

individual settlement amounts to more than $600,000.[17] And settlement costs can be substantially higher in class-action lawsuits, in which individuals join together to sue a company as a group. In fact, the average class-action lawsuit costs companies $58.9 million for racial discrimination and $24.9 million for gender discrimination.[18]

Diversity also makes business sense by helping companies *attract and retain talented workers.*[19] Indeed, diversity-friendly companies tend to attract better and more diverse job applicants. Very simply, diversity begets more diversity. Companies that make *Fortune* magazine's list of the 50 best companies for minorities or are recognized by *Working Women* or *DiversityInc.* magazines have already attracted a diverse and talented pool of job applicants. But after being recognized for their efforts, they subsequently experience even bigger increases in both the quality and the diversity of people who apply for jobs. Research shows that companies with acclaimed diversity programs not only attract more talented workers but also have higher stock market performance.[20]

The third way that diversity makes business sense is by *driving business growth.* Diversity helps companies grow by improving their understanding of the marketplace. When companies have diverse work forces, they are better able to understand the needs of their increasingly diverse customer bases. A recent survey conducted by the Society for Human Resource Management found that tapping into "diverse customers and markets" was the number one reason managers gave for implementing diversity programs.[21] Turner Broadcasting, which operates cable networks such as CNN, TNT, and the Cartoon Network, operates its business with diversity as a core principle. The company sponsors nine Business Resource Groups (BRGs)—support and resource groups that help integrate minority employees into the organization. The BRGs also influence the company's programming by shedding light on their unique cultures and sharing information about the viewing habits of their specific groups. This has helped Turner gain numerous new sponsors, and reach a new segment of viewers, through critically acclaimed documentaries such as *Black in America,* and *Latino in America* and minority-driven programming such as *Are We There Yet?, Tyler Perry's House of Pain,* and *Lopez Tonight.* In fact, TBS is currently the only network—broadcast or cable—with an African American comedy show.[22]

Diversity also helps companies grow through higher-quality problem solving. Though diverse groups initially have more difficulty working together than do homogeneous groups, diverse groups eventually establish a rapport and do a better job of identifying problems and generating alternative solutions, the two most important steps in problem solving.[23]

Diversity and Individual Differences

a survey that asked managers, "What is meant by diversity to decision makers in your organization?" found that they most frequently mentioned race, culture, sex, national origin, age, religion, and regional origin.[24] When managers describe workers this way, they are focusing on surface-level diversity. **Surface-level diversity** consists of differences that are immediately observable, typically unchangeable, and easy to measure.[25] In other words, independent observers can usually agree on dimensions of surface-level diversity, such as another person's age, sex, race/ethnicity, or physical capabilities.

Most people start by using surface-level diversity to categorize or stereotype other people. But those initial categorizations typically give way to deeper impressions formed from knowledge of others' behavior and psychological characteristics such as personality and attitudes.[26] When you think of others this way, you are focusing on deep-level diversity. **Deep-level diversity**

SURFACE-LEVEL DIVERSITY
Age, Gender, Race/Ethnicity, Physical Capabilities

DEEP-LEVEL DIVERSITY
Personality, Attitudes, Values/Beliefs

consists of differences that are communicated through verbal and nonverbal behaviors and are recognized only through extended interaction with others.[27] Examples of deep-level diversity include personality differences, attitudes, beliefs, and values. In other words, as people in diverse workplaces get to know each other, the initial focus on surface-level differences such as age, race/ethnicity, sex, and physical capabilities is replaced by deeper, more complex knowledge of co-workers.

If managed properly, the shift from surface- to deep-level diversity can accomplish two things.[28] First, coming to know and understand co-workers better can result in reduced prejudice and conflict. Second, it can lead to stronger social integration. **Social integration** is the degree to which group members are psychologically attracted to working with each other to accomplish a common objective, or, as one manager put it, "working together to get the job done."

After reading the next two sections, you should be able to

2 understand the special challenges that the dimensions of surface-level diversity pose for managers.

3 explain how the dimensions of deep-level diversity affect individual behavior and interactions in the workplace.

---

2 Surface-Level Diversity

Because age, sex, race/ethnicity, and physical disabilities are usually immediately observable, many managers and workers use these dimensions of surface-level diversity to form initial impressions and categorizations of coworkers, bosses, customers, or job applicants. Whether intentionally or not, sometimes those initial categorizations and impressions lead to decisions or behaviors that discriminate. Consequently, these dimensions of surface-level diversity pose special challenges for managers who are trying to create positive work environments where everyone feels comfortable and no one is advantaged or disadvantaged.

Let's learn more about those challenges and the ways that 2.1 age, 2.2 sex, 2.3 race/ethnicity, and 2.4 mental or physical disabilities can affect decisions and behaviors in organizations.

2.1 | AGE

Age discrimination is treating people differently (e.g., in hiring and firing, promotion, and compensation decisions) because of their age. According to the Society for

Human Resource Management, 53 percent of 428 surveyed managers believed that older workers "didn't keep up with technology," and 28 percent said that older workers were "less flexible." When 57-year-old Sam Horgan, a former chief financial officer, was interviewing for a job, he was asked by a 30-something job interviewer, "Would you have trouble working with young bright people?"[29] It is also commonly assumed that older workers cost more, and some companies fear that older workers will require higher salaries and more health-care benefits.[30]

So, what's reality and what's myth? Do older employees actually cost more? In some ways, they do. The older people are and the longer they stay with a company, the more the company pays for salaries, pension plans, and vacation time. But older workers cost companies less, too, because they tend to show better judgment and care more about the quality of their work, and they are less likely to quit, show up late, or be absent, the cost of which can be substantial.[31] A survey by Chicago outplacement firm Challenger, Gray & Christmas found that only 3 percent of employees age 50 and older changed jobs in any given year, compared to 10 percent of the entire U.S. work force and 12 percent of workers ages 25 to 34. The study also found that while older workers make up about 14 percent of the work force, they suffer only 10 percent of all workplace injuries and use fewer health-care benefits than younger workers with school-age children.[32] As for the widespread belief that job performance declines with age, the scientific evidence clearly refutes this stereotype. Performance does not decline with age regardless of the type of job.[33]

What can companies do to reduce age discrimination?[34] To start with, managers need to recognize that age discrimination is much more pervasive than they probably think. Whereas "old" used to mean mid-50s, in today's workplace, "old" is closer to 40. When 773 CEOs were asked "At what age does a worker's productivity peak?" the average age they gave was 43. Thus, age discrimination may be affecting more workers because perceptions about age have changed. In addition, age discrimination is more likely to occur with the aging of baby boomers simply because there are millions more older workers than there used to be. And, because studies show that interviewers rate younger job candidates as more qualified (even when

Social integration
the degree to which group members are psychologically attracted to working with each other to accomplish a common objective

Age discrimination
treating people differently (e.g., in hiring and firing, promotion, and compensation decisions) because of their age

Older Workers Facing Greater Odds in Recessionary Job Market

According to the Bureau of Labor Statistics, on average unemployed workers aged 55 years and older were out of work 35.5 weeks in 2010, compared to 23.3 weeks for those aged 16 to 24 years and 30.3 weeks for those 25 to 54 years old. Furthermore, older workers generally have to take significantly greater pay cuts than their younger counterparts when they do finally find jobs. Age discrimination lawsuits rose 30 percent in 2008 compared to those from the prior year. However, the majority of those complaints involved layoffs—age discrimination in hiring is much more difficult to prove.

Sources: E. Sok, "Record Unemployment among Older Workers Does Not Keep Them out of the Job Market," *Issues in Labor Statistics—Summary 10-04*, U.S. Bureau of Labor Statistics, March 2010, accessed July 30, 2010, http://www.bls.gov/opub/ils/summary_10_04/older_workers.htm; M. Luo, "Longer Unemployment for Those 45 and Older," *New York Times*, April 12, 2009, accessed July 30, 2010, http://www.nytimes.com/2009/04/13/us/13age.html?scp=13&sq=age%20discrimination&st=Search.

Sex discrimination treating people differently because of their sex

Glass ceiling the invisible barrier that prevents women and minorities from advancing to the top jobs in organizations

they aren't), companies need to train managers and recruiters to make hiring and promotion decisions on the basis of qualifications, not age. Companies also need to monitor the extent to which older workers receive training. The Bureau of Labor Statistics found that the number of training courses and number of hours spent in training drops dramatically after employees reach the age of 44.[35] Finally, companies need to ensure that younger and older workers interact with each other. One study found that younger workers generally hold positive views of older workers and that the more time they spent working with older co-workers, the more positive their attitudes became.[36]

2.2 | SEX

Sex discrimination occurs when people are treated differently because of their sex. Sex discrimination and racial/ethnic discrimination (discussed in the next section) are often associated with the so-called **glass ceiling,** the invisible barrier that prevents women and minorities from advancing to the top jobs in organizations.

To what extent do women face sex discrimination in the workplace? In some ways, there is much less sex discrimination than there used to be. For example, whereas women held only 17 percent of managerial jobs in 1972, they now outnumber men, with 50.6 percent of managerial jobs, a percentage that surpasses their current representation in the work force (46.3 percent). Also, women own 40 percent of all U.S. businesses. Whereas women owned 700,000 businesses in 1977 and 4.1 million businesses in 1987, today they own 10 million! Finally, though women still earn less than men on average, the differential is narrowing, as shown in Exhibit 12.2. Women earned 79.9 percent of what men did in 2008, up from 63 percent in 1979.[37]

Although progress is being made, the glass ceiling is still in place, creating sex discrimination at higher levels in organizations, as shown in Exhibit 12.3. For instance, while the trends are upward, women were the top earners in their companies in just 6.3 percent of *Fortune* 500 companies in 2009. Likewise, while there has been progress, only 13.5 percent of corporate officers (i.e., top management) at *Fortune* 500 companies are women, and the number is even lower for women of color. Indra K. Nooyi, PepsiCo's CEO, Andrea Jung, Avon's CEO, and Ursula Burns, Xerox's CEO, are the only women of color heading *Fortune* 500 companies.[38] Indeed, only 15 of the 500 largest companies in the United States have women CEOs. Women CEOs run three *Fortune* 50 companies, including Nooyi,

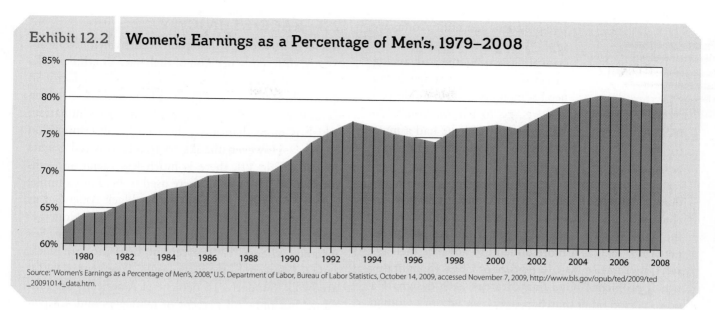

Exhibit 12.2 **Women's Earnings as a Percentage of Men's, 1979–2008**

Source: "Women's Earnings as a Percentage of Men's, 2008," U.S. Department of Labor, Bureau of Labor Statistics, October 14, 2009, accessed November 7, 2009, http://www.bls.gov/opub/ted/2009/ted_20091014_data.htm.

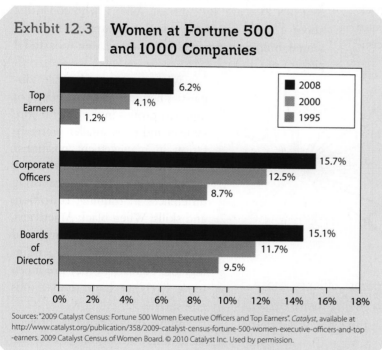

Exhibit 12.3 **Women at Fortune 500 and 1000 Companies**

Sources: "2009 Catalyst Census: Fortune 500 Women Executive Officers and Top Earners." *Catalyst*, available at http://www.catalyst.org/publication/358/2009-catalyst-census-fortune-500-women-executive-officers-and-top-earners. 2009 Catalyst Census of Women Board. © 2010 Catalyst Inc. Used by permission.

jobs or careers that also give them a greater sense of accomplishment, more control over their work schedules, and easier movement in and out of the workplace.[42] Furthermore, women are historically much more likely than men to prioritize family over work at some time in their careers. For example, 96 percent of 600 female Harvard MBAs held jobs while they were in their 20s. That dropped to 71 percent in their late 30s when they had children, but then increased to 82.5 percent in their late 40s as their children became older.[43]

Beyond these reasons, however, it's likely that sex discrimination does play a role in women's slow progress into the higher levels of management. And even if you don't think so, many of the women you work with probably do. Indeed, one study found that more than 90 percent of executive women believed that the glass ceiling had hurt their careers.[44] In another study, 80 percent of women said they left their last organization because the glass ceiling had limited their chances for advancement.[45] A third study indicated that the glass ceiling is prompting more and more women to leave companies to start their own businesses.[46] In fact, discrimination is believed to be the most significant factor to explain the infrequency of women at top levels of management.[47]

So, what can companies do to make sure that women have the same opportunities for development and advancement as men? One strategy is *mentoring*, or pairing promising female executives with senior executives from whom they can seek advice and support. A

Patricia Woertz of Archer Daniels Midland, and Angela Braly of WellPoint.[39] Similarly, only 15.2 percent of the members of corporate boards of directors are women.[40]

Is sex discrimination the sole reason for the slow rate at which women have been promoted to middle and upper levels of management and seated on corporate boards? Some studies indicate that it's not.[41] In some instances, the slow progress appears to be due to career and job choices. Whereas men's career and job choices are often driven by the search for higher pay and advancement, women are more likely to choose

vice president at a utility company says, "I think it's the single most critical piece to women advancing career-wise. In my experience you need somebody to help guide you and . . . go to bat for you."[48] In fact, 91 percent of female executives have had a mentor at some point and believe that their mentors were critical to their advancement.

Another strategy is to make sure that male-dominated social activities don't unintentionally exclude women. Nearly half (47 percent) of women in the work force believe that "exclusion from informal networks" makes it more difficult to advance their careers. By contrast, just 18 percent of CEOs thought this was a problem.[49] One final strategy is to designate a go-to person other than her supervisor whom a woman can talk to if she believes that she is being held back or discriminated against because of her sex. Make sure this person has the knowledge and authority to conduct a fair, confidential internal investigation.[50]

2.3 | RACE/ETHNICITY

Racial or ethnic discrimination occurs when people are treated differently because of their race or ethnicity. To what extent is racial/ethnic discrimination a factor in the workplace? Every year, the EEOC receives between 26,000 and 35,000 charges of race discrimination, which is more than any other type of discrimination charge.[51] However, thanks to the 1964 Civil Rights Act and Title VII, there is much less racial and ethnic discrimination than there used to be. For example, eighteen *Fortune* 500 firms had a black American as CEO in 2007, whereas none did in 1988.[52] Nonetheless, strong racial and ethnic disparities still exist. For instance, whereas 12.9 percent of Americans are black, only 6.4 percent of managers and 3.9 percent of CEOs are black. Similarly, 16 percent of Americans are Hispanic, but only 7.3 percent of managers and 4.8 percent of CEOs are. By contrast, Asians, who constitute about 4.7 percent of the population, are better represented, holding 4.6 percent of management jobs and 4 percent of CEO jobs.[53]

What accounts for the disparities between the percentages of minority groups in the general population and their smaller representation in management positions? Some studies have found that the disparities are due to preexisting differences in training, education, and skills. When black Americans, Hispanics, Asian Americans, and whites have similar skills, training, and education, they are much more likely to have similar jobs and salaries.[54]

Other studies, however, provide increasingly strong direct evidence of racial or ethnic discrimination in the workplace. For example, one study directly tested hiring discrimination by sending pairs of black and white males and pairs of Hispanic and non-Hispanic males to apply for the same jobs. Each pair had résumés with identical qualifications, and all were trained to present themselves in similar ways to minimize differences during interviews. The researchers found that the white males got three times as many job offers as the black

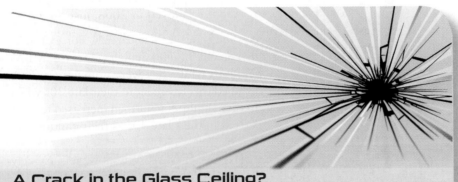

A Crack in the Glass Ceiling?

Although women may be the minority of corporate officers, those who have made it to that level may finally be seeing their payday. Of 16 women CEOs at the head of companies in the S&P 500 index, average earnings came out 43 percent higher than that of their male counterparts. Furthermore, of those who had also been CEOs in 2008, women received on average a raise of 19 percent. In contrast, the men took a 5 percent pay cut. Yahoo! CEO Carol Bartz received compensation of $47.2 million in 2009, and Irene Rosenfeld, CEO of Kraft Foods Inc., received $26.3 million.

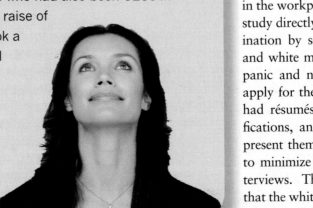

Source: A. Leondis, "CEO Pay Breaks Glass Ceiling: Yahoo's Bartz Gets $47.2 Million," *Bloomberg*, May 12, 2010, accessed July 27, 2010, http://www.bloomberg.com/news/2010-05-12/ceo-pay-breaks-glass-ceiling-as-bartz-gets-42-7-million-with-09-bonanza.html.

males and that the non-Hispanic males got three times as many offers as the Hispanic males.[55]

Another study, which used similar methods to test hiring procedures at 149 different companies, found that whites received 10 percent more interviews than blacks. Half of the whites interviewed received job offers, but only 11 percent of the blacks did. And when job offers were made, blacks were much more likely to be offered lower-level positions, whereas whites were more likely to be offered jobs at higher levels than the jobs they had applied for.[56]

Critics of these studies point out that it's nearly impossible to train different applicants to give identical responses in job interviews and that differences in interviewing skills may have somehow accounted for the results. However, British researchers found similar kinds of discrimination when they sent letters of inquiry to prospective employers. As in the other studies, differences were minimized by making the letters identical except for the applicant's race. Employers frequently responded to letters from Afro-Caribbean, Indian, or Pakistani applicants by indicating that the positions had been filled. By contrast, they often responded to white, Anglo-Saxon applicants by inviting them to face-to-face interviews. Similar results were found with Vietnamese and Greek applicants in Australia.[57] In short, the evidence indicates that there is strong and persistent racial and ethnic discrimination in the hiring processes of many organizations.

What can companies do to make sure that people of all racial and ethnic backgrounds have the same opportunities?[58] Start by looking at the numbers. Compare the hiring rates of whites to the hiring rates for racial and ethnic applicants. Do the same thing for promotions within the company. See if nonwhite workers quit the company at higher rates than white workers. Also, survey employees to compare white and nonwhite employees' satisfaction with jobs, bosses, and the company, as well as their perceptions concerning equal treatment. Next, if the numbers indicate racial or ethnic disparities, consider employing a private firm to test your hiring system by having applicants of different races with identical qualifications apply for jobs in your company.[59] Although disparities aren't proof of discrimination, it's much better to investigate hiring and promotion disparities yourself than to have the EEOC or a plaintiff's lawyer do it for you.

Another step companies can take is to eliminate unclear selection and promotion criteria. Vague criteria allow decision makers to focus on characteristics unrelated to the job, which may unintentionally lead to employment discrimination. Instead, selection and promotion criteria should spell out the specific knowledge, skills, abilities, education, and experience needed to perform a job well. Finally, as explained in Chapter 11 on human resources management, it is also important to train managers and others who make hiring and promotion decisions.

Disability a mental or physical impairment that substantially limits one or more major life activities

Disability discrimination treating people differently because of their disabilities

2.4 | MENTAL OR PHYSICAL DISABILITIES

According to the Americans with Disabilities Act (http://www.ada.gov), a **disability** is a mental or physical impairment that substantially limits one or more major life activities.[60] One in every five Americans, or more than 54 million people, have a disability.[61] **Disability discrimination** occurs when people are treated differently because of their disabilities.

To what extent is disability discrimination a factor in the workplace? Although 79.7 percent of the overall U.S. population was employed in 2006, just 36.9 percent of people with disabilities had jobs. Individuals with sensory disabilities, such as blindness or deafness, had the highest employment rate (46.4 percent), while those with self-care disabilities, which inhibit their motor skills and their ability to care for their grooming needs, were the least well-represented in the work force (at 16.7 percent).[62] Furthermore, people with disabilities are disproportionately employed in low-status or part-time jobs, have little chance for advancement, and, on average, are twice as likely to live in poverty as people without disabilities.[63] Numerous studies also indicate that managers and the general public believe that discrimination against people with disabilities is common and widespread.[64]

What accounts for the disparities between the employment and income levels of people with and without disabilities? Contrary to popular opinion, it has nothing to do with how well people with disabilities can do their jobs. Studies show that as long as companies make reasonable accommodations for disabilities (e.g., changing procedures or equipment), people with disabilities perform their jobs just as well as other employees do. They also have better safety records and are no more likely to be absent or quit their jobs.[65]

What can companies do to make sure that people with disabilities have the same opportunities as everyone else? Beyond educational efforts to address incorrect stereotypes and expectations, a good place to start is to

Disposition the tendency to respond to situations and events in a predetermined manner

Personality the relatively stable set of behaviors, attitudes, and emotions displayed over time that makes people different from each other

commit to reasonable workplace accommodations such as changing work schedules, reassigning jobs, acquiring or modifying equipment, or providing assistance when needed. IBM recently received top ranking in *DiversityInc*'s survey of the Top 10 Companies for People with Disabilities. In addition to education and recruitment programs, IBM provides a wide range of accommodations for its disabled workers. Ramps and power doors are installed for employees who use wheelchairs. Captioning devices, sign language interpreters, and note takers are available for deaf employees. Software programs that read text on a computer screen and audio transcripts of company publications are available for the blind. IBM has also formed Accommodation Assessment Teams to consult with employees to continue to identify and resolve unmet accommodations.[66]

Accommodations for disabilities needn't be expensive, either. According to the Job Accommodation Network, 56 percent of accommodations don't cost anything at all, while the average cost of the rest is about $600.[67] Finally, companies should actively recruit qualified workers with disabilities. Numerous organizations such as Mainstream, Kidder Resources, the American Council of the Blind (http://www.acb.org), the National Federation of the Blind (http://www.nfb.org), the National Association of the Deaf (http://www.nad.org), the Epilepsy Foundation of America (http://www.epilepsyfoundation.org), and the National Amputation Foundation (http://www.nationalamputation.org) actively work with employers to find jobs for qualified people with disabilities. Companies can also place advertisements in publications such as *CAREERS and the disABLED* that specifically target workers with disabilities.[68]

3 Deep-Level Diversity

As you learned in Section 2, people often use the dimensions of surface-level diversity to form initial impressions about others. Over time, however, as people have a chance to get to know each other, initial impressions based on age, sex, race/ethnicity, and mental or physical disabilities give way to deeper impressions based on behavior and psychological characteristics. When we think of others this way, we are focusing on deep-level diversity. *Deep-level diversity* is reflected in differences that can be recognized only through extended interaction with others. Examples include differences in personality, attitudes, beliefs, and values. In short, recognizing deep-level diversity requires getting to know and understand co-workers better. And that matters because it can result in less prejudice, discrimination, and conflict in the workplace. These changes can then lead to better *social integration*, the degree to which organizational or group members are psychologically attracted to working with each other to accomplish a common objective.

Stop for a second and think about your boss (or the boss you had in your last job). What words would you use to describe him or her? Is your boss introverted or extraverted? Emotionally stable or unstable? Agreeable or disagreeable? Organized or disorganized? Open or closed to new experiences? When you describe your boss or others in this way, what you're really doing is describing dispositions and personality.

A **disposition** is the tendency to respond to situations and events in a predetermined manner. **Personality** is the

TECHNOLOGY = ABILITY

Individuals with disabilities face unique challenges in the workplace. Richard Saab became paralyzed from an aneurysm and was forced to leave his job as a cook because he could no longer stand. Following his recovery, he wanted to cook again. The Florida Department of Vocational Rehabilitation was able to assist him by acquiring a standing wheelchair, which enabled him to assume a position as a line chef again.

Source: "Standing Wheelchair for a Chef," accessed June 26, 2008, http://www.workrerc.org.

EasyStand Evolv Mobile, by Altimate Medical www.easystand.com

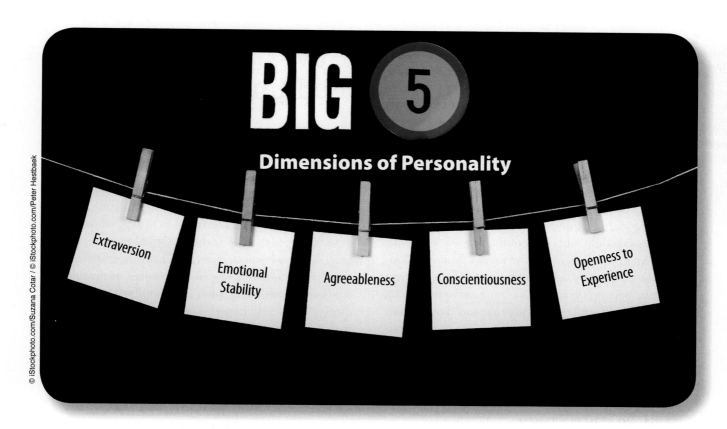

BIG 5
Dimensions of Personality

Extraversion

Emotional Stability

Agreeableness

Conscientiousness

Openness to Experience

relatively stable set of behaviors, attitudes, and emotions displayed over time that makes people different from each other.[69] For example, which of your aunts or uncles is a little offbeat, a little out of the ordinary? What was that aunt or uncle like when you were small? What is she or he like now? Chances are she or he is pretty much the same wacky person. In other words, the person's core personality hasn't changed. For years, personality researchers studied thousands of different ways to describe people's personalities. In the last decade, however, personality research conducted in different cultures, different settings, and different languages has shown that five basic dimensions of personality account for most of the differences in people's behaviors, attitudes, and emotions. The *Big Five Personality Dimensions* are extraversion, emotional stability, agreeableness, conscientiousness, and openness to experience.[70]

Extraversion is the degree to which someone is active, assertive, gregarious, sociable, talkative, and energized by others. In contrast to extraverts, introverts are less active, prefer to be alone, and are shy, quiet, and reserved. For the best results in the workplace, introverts and extraverts should be correctly matched to their jobs.

Emotional stability is the degree to which someone is not angry, depressed, anxious, emotional, insecure, or excitable. People who are emotionally

stable respond well to stress. In other words, they can maintain a calm, problem-solving attitude in even the toughest situations (e.g., conflict, hostility, dangerous conditions, or extreme time pressures). By contrast, emotionally unstable people find it difficult to handle the most basic demands of their jobs under only moderately stressful situations and become distraught, tearful, self-doubting, and anxious. Emotional stability is particularly important for high-stress jobs such as police work, fire fighting, emergency medical treatment, piloting planes, or commanding rockets.

Agreeableness is the degree to which someone is cooperative, polite, flexible, forgiving, good-natured, tolerant, and trusting. Basically, agreeable people are easy to work with and be around, whereas disagreeable people are distrusting and difficult to work with and be around.

Conscientiousness is the degree to which someone is organized, hardworking, responsible, persevering, thorough, and achievement oriented. One management consultant wrote about his experiences

Extraversion the degree to which someone is active, assertive, gregarious, sociable, talkative, and energized by others

Emotional stability the degree to which someone is not angry, depressed, anxious, emotional, insecure, or excitable

Agreeableness the degree to which someone is cooperative, polite, flexible, forgiving, good-natured, tolerant, and trusting

Conscientiousness the degree to which someone is organized, hardworking, responsible, persevering, thorough, and achievement oriented with a conscientious employee: "He arrived at our first meeting with a typed copy of his daily schedule, a sheet bearing his home and office phone numbers, addresses, and his email address. At his request, we established a timetable for meetings for the next 4 months. He showed up on time every time, day planner in hand, and carefully listed tasks and due dates. He questioned me exhaustively if he didn't understand an assignment and returned on schedule with the completed work or with a clear explanation as to why it wasn't done."[71] Conscientious employees are also more likely to engage in positive behaviors, such as helping new employees, co-workers, and supervisors, and are less likely to engage in negative behaviors, such as verbally or physically abusing co-workers and stealing.[72]

Openness to experience is the degree to which someone is curious, broad-minded, and open to new ideas, things, and experiences; is spontaneous; and has a high tolerance for ambiguity. People in marketing, advertising, research, and other creative fields need to be curious, open to new ideas, and spontaneous. By contrast, openness to experience is not particularly important to accountants, who need to consistently apply stringent rules and formulas to make sense out of complex financial information.

Which of the Big Five Personality Dimensions has the largest impact on behavior in organizations? The cumulative results indicate that conscientiousness is related to job performance across five different occupational groups (professionals, police, managers, sales, and skilled or semiskilled jobs).[73] In short, people "who are dependable, persistent, goal directed, and organized tend to be higher performers on virtually any job; viewed negatively, those who are careless, irresponsible, low-achievement striving, and impulsive tend to be lower performers on virtually any job."[74] The results also indicate that extraversion is related to performance in jobs in areas such as sales and management, which involve significant interaction with others. In people-intensive jobs such as these, it helps to be sociable, assertive, and talkative and to have energy and be able to energize others. Finally, people who are extraverted and open to experience seem to do much better in training. Being curious and open to new experiences as well as sociable, assertive, talkative, and full of energy helps people perform better in learning situations.[75]

How Can Diversity Be Managed?

how much should companies change their standard business practices to accommodate the diversity of their workers? What do you do when a talented top executive has a drinking problem that seems to affect his behavior only at company business parties (for entertaining clients), where he has made inappropriate advances toward female employees? What do you do when, despite aggressive company policies against racial discrimination, employees continue to tell racial jokes and publicly post cartoons displaying racial humor? And, since many people confuse diversity with affirmative action, what do you do to make sure that your company's diversity practices and policies are viewed as benefiting all workers and not just some workers?

No doubt about it, questions like these make managing diversity one of the toughest challenges that managers face. Nonetheless, there are steps companies can take to begin to address these issues.

After reading the next section, you should be able to

4 **explain the basic principles and practices that can be used to manage diversity.**

4 Managing Diversity

As discussed earlier, diversity programs try to create a positive work environment where no one is advantaged or disadvantaged, where "we" is everyone, where everyone can do his or her best work, where differences are respected and not ignored, and where everyone feels comfortable. *Let's see how companies can move toward those goals by learning about 4.1 different diversity paradigms, 4.2 diversity principles, and 4.3 diversity training and practices.*

4.1 | DIVERSITY PARADIGMS

There are several different methods or paradigms for managing diversity: the discrimination and fairness paradigm, the access and legitimacy paradigm, and the learning and effectiveness paradigm.[76] The *discrimination and fairness paradigm*, which is the most common method of approaching diversity, focuses on equal opportunity, fair treatment, recruitment of minorities,

What Do You Think?

In Canada, McGregory Jackman, a bus driver for the York Region's VIVA public transportation system, was sent home for violating the organization's dress code by refusing to take off his kufi, a brimless cap often worn by Muslims as part of their religious observance. Said Jackman, "I just want to go back to work and take care of my family. I just want to be a Muslim and do my job."

Source: N. Keung, "Bus Driver in Headgear Battle," *Toronto Star*, March 25, 2008, A07.

Should Jackman be allowed to wear his kufi as prescribed by his religious beliefs, or is his employer correct for insisting that all bus drivers follow the dress code?

© iStockphoto.com/ Jurjen Draaijer / © iStockphoto.com/ Daniel Loiselle

and strict compliance with the equal employment opportunity laws. Under this approach, success is usually measured by how well companies achieve recruitment, promotion, and retention goals for women, people of different racial/ethnic backgrounds, and other underrepresented groups. According to a recent workplace diversity practices survey conducted by the Society for Human Resource Management, 77 percent of companies with more than 500 employees systematically collect measurements on diversity-related practices.[77] For example, one manager says, "If you don't measure something, it doesn't count. You measure your market share. You measure your profitability. The same should

be true for diversity. There has to be some way of measuring whether you did, in fact, cast your net widely, and whether the company is better off today in terms of the experience of people of color than it was a few years ago. I measure my market share and my profitability. Why not this?"[78] The primary benefit of the discrimination and fairness paradigm is that it generally brings about fairer treatment of employees and increases demographic diversity. The primary limitation is that the focus of diversity remains on the surface-level dimensions of sex, race, and ethnicity.[79]

The *access and legitimacy paradigm* focuses on the acceptance and celebration of differences to ensure that the diversity within the company matches the diversity found among primary stakeholders such as customers, suppliers, and local communities. This is related to the *business growth* advantage of diversity discussed earlier in the chapter. The basic idea behind this approach is to create a demographically diverse work force in order to attract a broader customer base. Consistent with this goal, Ed Adams, vice president of human resources for Enterprise Rent-a-Car, says, "We want people who speak the same language, literally and figuratively, as our customers. We don't set quotas. We say [to our managers], 'Reflect your local market.'"[80] The primary benefit of this approach is that it establishes a clear business reason for diversity. Like the discrimination and fairness paradigm, however, it focuses only on the surface-level diversity dimensions of sex, race, and ethnicity. Furthermore, employees who are assigned responsibility for customers and stakeholders on the basis of their sex, race, or ethnicity may eventually feel frustrated and exploited.

Whereas the discrimination and fairness paradigm focuses on assimilation (having a demographically representative work force), and the access and legitimacy paradigm focuses on differentiation (having demographic differences inside the company match those of key customers and stakeholders), the *learning and effectiveness paradigm* focuses on integrating deep-level diversity differences, such as personality, attitudes, beliefs, and values, into the actual work of the organization. Aetna's 28,000 employees are diverse not only in terms of sex, ethnicity and race, but also age, sexual orientation, work style, perspective, education, skills, and other characteristics. Raymond Arroyo, head of diversity at Aetna, says, "Diversity at Aetna means treating individuals individually, leveraging everyone's best, and maximizing the powerful potential of our workforce." He adds, "Part of a top diversity executive's role in any organization is to integrate diversity into every aspect of a business, including the workforce, customers, suppliers, products, services, and even into the community a business serves."[81]

The learning and effectiveness paradigm is consistent with achieving organizational plurality. **Organizational plurality** is a work environment in which (1) all members are empowered to contribute in a way that maximizes the benefits to the organization, customers, and themselves, and (2) the individuality of each member is respected by not segmenting or polarizing people on the basis of their membership in a particular group.[82]

The learning and effectiveness diversity paradigm offers four benefits.[83] First, it values common ground.

Dave Thomas of the Harvard Business School explains: "Like the fairness paradigm, it promotes equal opportunity for all individuals. And like the access paradigm, it acknowledges cultural differences among people and recognizes the value in those differences. Yet this new model for managing diversity lets the organization internalize differences among employees so that it learns and grows because of them. Indeed, with the model fully in place, members of the organization can say, 'We are all on the same team, with our differences—not despite them.'"[84]

Second, this paradigm makes a distinction between individual and group differences. When diversity focuses only on differences between groups, such as females versus males, large differences within groups are ignored.[85] For example, think of the women you know at work. Now, think for a second about what they have in common. After that, think about how they're different. If your situation is typical, the list of differences should be just as long as, if not longer than, the list of commonalities. In short, managers can achieve a greater understanding of diversity and their employees by treating them as individuals and by realizing that not all black Americans, Hispanics, women, or white males want the same things at work.[86]

Third, because the focus is on individual differences, the learning and effectiveness paradigm is less likely to lead to the conflict, backlash, and divisiveness sometimes associated with diversity programs that focus only on group differences. Ray Haines, a consultant who has helped companies deal with the aftermath of diversity programs that became divisive, says, "There's a large amount of backlash related to diversity training. It stirs up a lot of hostility, anguish, and resentment but doesn't give people tools to deal with [the backlash]. You have people come in and talk about their specific ax to grind."[87] Not all diversity programs are divisive or lead to conflict. But, by focusing on individual rather than group differences, the learning and effectiveness paradigm helps to minimize these potential problems.

MGMT SUCCESS

How to Create a Learning and Effectiveness Diversity Paradigm

1. Understand that a diverse work force will embody different perspectives and approaches to work. Value variety of opinion and insight.

2. Recognize both the learning opportunities and the challenges that the expression of different perspectives presents for your organization.

3. Set high standards of performance for everyone.

4. Create an organizational culture that stimulates personal development.

5. Encourage openness and a high tolerance for debate. Support constructive conflict on work-related matters.

6. Create an organizational culture in which workers feel valued.

7. Establish a clear mission and make sure it is widely understood. This keeps discussions about work differences from degenerating into debates about the validity of individual perspectives.

8. Create a relatively egalitarian, nonbureaucratic structure.

Source: D. A. Thomas and R. J. Ely, "Making Differences Matter: A New Paradigm for Managing Diversity," *Harvard Business Review* 74 (September–October 1996): 79–90.

Finally, unlike the other diversity paradigms that simply focus on the value of being different (primarily in terms of surface-level diversity), the learning and effectiveness paradigm focuses on bringing different talents and perspectives *together* (i.e., deep-level diversity) to make the best organizational decisions and to produce innovative, competitive products and services. Video game designer Will Wright believes that his teams work best when they consist of diverse individuals. He will try to find older, more experienced veterans and mix them with younger employees who might be highly talented and motivated and less set in their ways. He'll also try to add in some individuals who might be somewhere in between. When he's able to achieve this diverse balance in his teams, Will has found that members work together very well and create significant value.[88]

4.2 | DIVERSITY PRINCIPLES

Diversity paradigms are general approaches or strategies for managing diversity. Whatever diversity paradigm a manager chooses, diversity principles will help managers do a better job of *managing company diversity programs.*[89]

Begin by *carefully and faithfully following and enforcing federal and state laws regarding equal opportunity employment.* Diversity programs can't and won't succeed if the company is being sued for discriminatory actions and behavior. Faithfully following the law will also reduce the time and expense associated with EEOC investigations or lawsuits. Start by learning more at the EEOC website (http://www.eeoc.gov). Following the law also means strictly and fairly enforcing company policies.

Treat group differences as important but not special. Surface-level diversity dimensions such as age, sex, and race/ethnicity should be respected but should not be treated as more important than other kinds of differences (i.e., deep-level diversity). Remember, the shift from surface- to deep-level diversity helps people know and understand each other better, reduces prejudice and conflict, and leads to stronger social integration, as people want to work together and get the job done. Also, *find the common ground.* Respecting differences is important. But it's just as important, especially with diverse work forces, to actively find ways for employees to see and share commonalities.

Tailor opportunities to individuals, not groups. Special programs for training, development, mentoring, or promotions should be based on individual strengths and weaknesses, not on group status. Instead of making mentoring available for just one group of workers, create mentoring opportunities for everyone who wants to be mentored.

Solicit negative as well as positive feedback. Diversity is one of the most difficult management issues. No company or manager gets it right from the start. Consequently, companies should aggressively seek positive and negative feedback about their diversity programs. One way to do that is to use a series of measurements to see if progress is being made.

Set high but realistic goals. Just because diversity is difficult doesn't mean that organizations shouldn't try to accomplish as much as possible. The general purpose of diversity programs is to try to create a positive work environment where no one is advantaged or disadvantaged, where "we" is everyone, where everyone can do his or her best work, where differences are respected and not ignored, and where everyone feels comfortable. Even if progress is slow, companies should not abandon these goals.

4.3 | DIVERSITY TRAINING AND PRACTICES

Organizations use diversity training and several common diversity practices to manage diversity. There are

MGMT SUCCESS

Diversity Principles

1. Carefully and faithfully follow and enforce federal and state laws regarding equal employment opportunity.
2. Treat group differences as important but not special.
3. Find the common ground.
4. Tailor opportunities to individuals, not groups.
5. Reexamine, but maintain, high standards.
6. Solicit negative as well as positive feedback.
7. Set high but realistic goals.

Source: L. S. Gottfredson, "Dilemmas in Developing Diversity Programs," in *Diversity in the Workplace,* ed. S. E. Jackson & Associates (New York: Guildford Press, 1992).

Awareness training training that is designed to raise employees' awareness of diversity issues and to challenge the underlying assumptions or stereotypes they may have about others

Skills-based diversity training training that teaches employees the practical skills they need for managing a diverse work force, such as flexibility and adaptability, negotiation, problem solving, and conflict resolution

Diversity audits formal assessments that measure employee and management attitudes, investigate the extent to which people are advantaged or disadvantaged with respect to hiring and promotions, and review companies' diversity-related policies and procedures

Diversity pairing a mentoring program in which people of different cultural backgrounds, sexes, or races/ethnicities are paired so that they can get to know each other and change any stereotypical beliefs and attitudes

two basic types of diversity training programs. **Awareness training** is designed to raise employees' awareness of diversity issues, such as the Big Five Personality Dimensions discussed in this chapter, and to get employees to challenge underlying assumptions or stereotypes they may have about others. As a starting point in awareness training, some companies have begun using the Implicit Association Test (IAT), which measures the extent to which people associate positive or negative thoughts (i.e., underlying assumptions or stereotypes) with blacks or whites, men or women, homosexuals or heterosexuals, young or old, or other groups. For example, test takers are shown black or white faces that they must instantly pair with various words. Response times (shorter responses generally indicate stronger associations) and the pattern of associations indicates the extent to which people are biased. Most people are, and strongly so. For example, 88 percent of whites have a more positive mental association toward whites than toward blacks, but, surprisingly, 48 percent of blacks also show the same bias. Taking the IAT is a good way to increase awareness of diversity issues. To take the IAT and to learn more about the decade of research behind it, go to http://implicit.harvard.edu.[90] By contrast, **skills-based diversity training** teaches employees the practical skills they need for managing a diverse work force such as flexibility and adaptability, negotiation, problem solving, and conflict resolution.[91]

Companies also use diversity audits, diversity pairing, and minority experiences for top executives to better manage diversity. **Diversity audits** are formal assessments that measure employee and management attitudes, investigate the extent to which people are advantaged or disadvantaged with respect to hiring and promotions, and review companies' diversity-related policies and procedures. For example, the results of a formal diversity audit prompted BRW, an architecture and engineering firm, to increase job advertising in minority publications, set up a diversity committee to make

recommendations to upper management, provide diversity training for all employees, and rewrite the company handbook to make a stronger statement about the company's commitment to a diverse work force.[92]

Earlier in the chapter you learned that *mentoring,* pairing a junior employee with a senior employee, is a common strategy for creating learning and promotional opportunities for women. Diversity pairing is a special kind of mentoring. In **diversity pairing,** people of different cultural backgrounds, sexes, or races/ethnicities are paired for mentoring. The hope is that stereotypical beliefs and attitudes will change as people get to know each other as individuals.[93] For more than 20 years, Xerox has been fostering a culture where women and minorities are prepared and considered for top positions. CEO Ursula Burns, the

first African American woman to lead a major U.S. company, worked as special assistant to Xerox's president of marketing and customer operations, Wayland Hicks, in 1990 and later with former CEO Paul A. Allaire. When Anne Mulcahy took over in 2001, Burns was gradually given control of day-to-day operations while Mulcahy repaired Xerox's financial position and customer service.[94]

Finally, because top managers are still overwhelmingly white and male, a number of companies believe that it is worthwhile to *have top executives experience what it is like to be in the minority*. This can be done by having top managers go to places or events where nearly everyone else is of a different sex or racial/ethnic background. At Hoechst Celanese (which has now split into two companies), top managers joined two organizations in which they were a minority. For instance, the CEO, a white male, joined the boards of Hampton University, a historically African American college, and Jobs for Progress, a Hispanic organization that helps people prepare for jobs. Commenting on his experiences, he said, "The only way to break out of comfort zones is to be exposed to other people. When we are, it becomes clear that all people are similar." A Hoechst vice president who joined three organizations in which he was in the minority said, "Joining these organizations has been more helpful to me than 2 weeks of diversity training."[95]

STUDENT Study Tools

Located at the back of your book:

☐ Rip out and study the Chapter Review Card at the end of the book

Log in to the CourseMate for MGMT at cengagebrain.com to:

☐ Review Key Term Flashcards delivered 3 ways (print or online)

☐ Complete both Practice Quizzes to prepare for tests

☐ Play Beat the Clock and Quizbowl to master concepts

☐ Complete the Crossword Puzzle to review key terms

☐ Watch the video on Mitchell Gold + Bob Williams for a real company example and take the accompanying quiz

☐ Watch the Biz Flix clip from *Because I Said So* and take the quiz

☐ Complete the Case Assignment on City Hall, New Haven, Connecticut

☐ Work through the Management Decision on personality profiles

☐ Work through the Management Team Decision on mentoring

☐ Develop your skills with the Develop Your Career Potential exercise

13 | Motivation

LEVEL

1

© Peter Cade/Photographer's Choice/Getty Images

LEARNING OUTCOMES:

1 explain the basics of motivation.

2 use equity theory to explain how employees' perceptions of fairness affect motivation.

3 use expectancy theory to describe how workers' expectations about rewards, effort, and the link between rewards and performance influence motivation.

4 explain how reinforcement theory works and how it can be used to motivate.

5 describe the components of goal-setting theory and how managers can use them to motivate workers.

6 discuss how the entire motivation model can be used to motivate workers.

Chapter 13

What Is Motivation?

What makes people happiest and most productive at work? Is it money, benefits, opportunities for growth, interesting work, or something else altogether? And if people desire different things, how can a company keep everyone motivated? It takes insight and hard work to motivate workers to join the company, perform well, and then stay with the company. Indeed, when asked to name their biggest management challenge, nearly one-third of executives polled by The Creative Group, a specialized staffing service in Menlo Park, California, cited "motivating employees."[1]

So what is motivation? **Motivation** is the set of forces that initiates, directs, and makes people persist in their efforts to accomplish a goal.[2] *Initiation of effort* is concerned with the choices that people make about how much effort to put forth in their jobs. ("Do I really knock myself out for these performance appraisals or just do a decent job?") *Direction of effort* is concerned with the choices that people make in deciding where to put forth effort in their jobs. ("I should be spending time with my high-dollar accounts instead of learning this new computer system!") *Persistence of effort* is concerned with the choices that people make about how long they will put forth effort in their jobs before reducing or eliminating those efforts. ("I'm only halfway through the project, and I'm exhausted. Do I plow through to the end, or just call it quits?") Initiation, direction, and persistence are at the heart of motivation.

After reading the next section, you should be able to

1 explain the basics of motivation.

1 Basics of Motivation

Nobody gets to determine his or her salary or bonus, right? But what if your boss let you do just that? At San Francisco–based Skyline Construction, vice president Mark Trento and senior project manager Adam Chelini, along with thirteen others, were allowed to choose their salaries, which had to be between $125,000 and $150,000. Choosing a higher salary meant that Trento and Chelini would get a smaller bonus and less overall compensation. By contrast, choosing a smaller salary would give them the opportunity—but no guarantee—to earn a larger bonus and higher overall compensation.[3] If you were in their shoes, which would you choose—a lower bonus but the security of a higher salary, or a smaller salary but the potential for a larger bonus and higher overall compensation? Which would motivate you more? Why? What motivates people to take one option versus another? Answering questions like these is at the heart of figuring out how best to motivate people at work.

*Let's learn more about motivation by building a basic model of motivation out of **1.1 effort and performance, 1.2 need satisfaction**, and **1.3 extrinsic and intrinsic rewards**. Then we'll discuss **1.4 how to motivate people with this basic model of motivation**.*

1.1 | EFFORT AND PERFORMANCE

When most people think of work motivation, they think that working hard (effort) should lead to a good job (performance). Exhibit 13.1 on the next page shows a

Motivation the set of forces that initiates, directs, and makes people persist in their efforts to accomplish a goal

basic model of the relationship of work motivation and performance. The first thing to notice about Exhibit 13.1 is that it displays a basic model of work motivation *and* performance. In practice, it's almost impossible to talk about one without mentioning the other. Not surprisingly, managers often assume motivation to be the only determinant of performance when they say things such as "Your performance was really terrible last quarter. What's the matter? Aren't you as motivated as you used to be?" In fact, motivation is just one of three primary determinants of job performance. In industrial psychology, job performance is frequently represented by this equation:

Job Performance =
Motivation × Ability × Situational Constraints

In this formula, *job performance* is how well someone performs the requirements of the job. *Motivation*, in this formula, is effort, the degree to which someone works hard to do the job well. *Ability* is the degree to which workers possess the knowledge, skills, and talent needed to do a job well. And *situational constraints* are factors beyond the control of individual employees, such as tools, policies, and resources that have an effect on job performance.

Since job performance is a multiplicative function of motivation times ability times situational constraints, it will suffer if any one of these components is weak. Does this mean that motivation doesn't matter? No, not at all. It just means that all the motivation in the world won't translate into high performance when an employee has little ability and high situational constraints. So, even though we will spend this chapter developing a model of work motivation, it is important to remember that ability and situational constraints affect job performance as well.

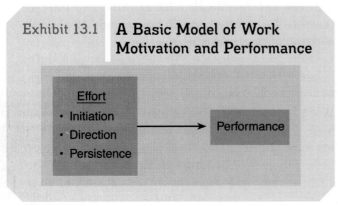

Exhibit 13.1 **A Basic Model of Work Motivation and Performance**

Effort
• Initiation
• Direction
• Persistence
→ Performance

© Cengage Learning 2011

1.2 | NEED SATISFACTION

In Exhibit 13.1, we started with a very basic model of motivation in which effort leads to job performance. But managers want to know, "What leads to effort?" Determining employee needs is the first step to answering that question.

Needs are the physical or psychological requirements that must be met to ensure survival and well-being.[4] As shown on the left side of Exhibit 13.2, a person's unmet need creates an uncomfortable, internal state of tension that must be resolved. For example, if you normally skip breakfast but then have to work through lunch, chances are you'll be so hungry by late afternoon that the only thing you'll be motivated to do is find something to eat. So, according to needs theories, people are motivated by unmet needs. But a need no longer motivates once it is met. When this occurs, people become satisfied, as shown on the right side of Exhibit 13.2.

NOTE: Throughout this chapter, as we build on this basic model, the parts that we've already discussed will be shaded in color in order to make the model easier to understand. Since we've already discussed the effort → performance part of the model, those components are shown with a colored background in Exhibit 13.2. When we add new parts to the model, they will have a white background. Because we're adding need satisfaction to the model at this step, the components of unsatisfied need, tension, energized to take action, and satisfaction are shown with a white background.

Since people are motivated by unmet needs, managers must learn what those unmet needs are and address them. This is not always a straightforward task, however, because different needs theories suggest different needs categories. Consider three well-known needs theories: Maslow's Hierarchy of Needs suggests that people are motivated by *physiological* (food and water), *safety* (physical and economic), *belongingness* (friendship, love, and social interaction), *esteem* (achievement and recognition), and *self-actualization* (realizing your full potential) needs.[5] Alderfer's ERG Theory collapses Maslow's five types of needs into three: *existence* (safety and physiological needs), *relatedness* (belongingness), and *growth* (esteem and self-actualization) needs.[6] McClelland's Learned Needs Theory suggests that people are motivated by the need for *affiliation* (to be liked and accepted), the need for *achievement* (to accomplish challenging goals), or the need for *power* (to influence others).[7]

Exhibit 13.2 A Basic Model of Work Motivation and Performance

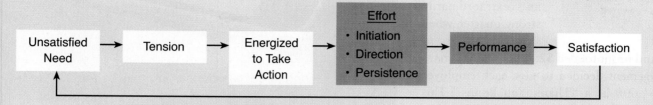

Unsatisfied Need → Tension → Energized to Take Action → **Effort** (• Initiation • Direction • Persistence) → Performance → Satisfaction

As shown on the left side of this exhibit, a person's unsatisfied need creates an uncomfortable, internal state of tension that must be resolved. So, according to needs theories, people are motivated by unmet needs. But once a need is met, it no longer motivates. When this occurs, people become satisfied, as shown on the right side of the exhibit.

© Cengage Learning 2011

Things become even more complicated when we consider the different predictions made by these theories. According to Maslow, needs are arranged in a hierarchy from low (physiological) to high (self-actualization), and people are motivated by their lowest unsatisfied need. As each need is met, they work their way up the hierarchy from physiological to self-actualization needs. By contrast, Alderfer says that people can be motivated by more than one need at a time. Furthermore, he suggests that people are just as likely to move down the needs hierarchy as up, particularly when they are unable to achieve satisfaction at the next higher need level. McClelland argues that the degree to which particular needs motivate varies tremendously from person to person, with some people being motivated primarily by achievement and others by power or affiliation. Moreover, McClelland says that needs are learned, not innate. For instance, studies show that children whose parents own small businesses or hold managerial positions are much more likely to have high needs for achievement.[8]

So, with three different sets of needs and three very different ideas about how needs motivate, how do we provide a practical answer to managers who just want to know, "What leads to effort?" Fortunately, the research simplifies things a bit. To start, studies indicate that there are two basic kinds of needs categories.[9] As you would expect, *lower-order needs* are concerned with safety and with physiological and existence requirements, whereas *higher-order needs* are concerned with relationships (belongingness, relatedness, and affiliation), challenges and accomplishments (esteem, self-actualization, growth, and achievement), and influence (power). Studies generally show that higher-order needs will not motivate people as long as lower-order needs remain unsatisfied.[10]

For example, imagine that you graduated from college 6 months ago and are still looking for your first job. With money running short (you're probably living on your credit cards) and the possibility of having to move back in with your parents looming (if this doesn't motivate you, what will?), your basic needs for food, shelter, and security drive your thoughts, behavior, and choices at this point. But once you land that job, find a great place (of your own!) to live, and put some money in the bank, these basic needs should decrease in importance as you begin to think about making new friends and taking on challenging work assignments. In fact, once lower-order needs are satisfied, it's difficult for managers to predict which higher-order needs will motivate employees' behavior.[11] Some people will be motivated by affiliation, while others will be motivated by growth or esteem. Also, the relative importance of the various needs may change over time but not necessarily in any predictable pattern.

1.3 | EXTRINSIC AND INTRINSIC REWARDS

So, what leads to effort? In part, needs do. But rewards are important, too, and no discussion of motivation would be complete without considering them. Let's add two kinds of rewards—extrinsic and intrinsic—to the work motivation model, as shown in Exhibit 13.3 on page 245.[12]

Extrinsic rewards are tangible and visible to others and are given to employees contingent on the performance of specific tasks or behaviors.[13] External agents (managers, for example) determine and control the distribution, frequency, and amount of extrinsic rewards such

Extrinsic reward a reward that is tangible, visible to others, and given to employees contingent on the performance of specific tasks or behaviors

Doing the Right Thing?

Intrinsic reward a natural reward associated with performing a task or activity for its own sake

as pay, company stock, benefits, and promotions. After an extraordinarily strong quarter, when sales rose 28 percent and profit totaled $2.2 billion, Intel management decided to give each employee $1,000 as a "Thank You Bonus." This was followed by two more rounds of bonuses which, on average, gave employees an extra 23 days of pay, the highest bonus amount at Intel in nearly a decade.[14]

Why do companies provide extrinsic rewards? To get people to do things they wouldn't otherwise do. Companies use extrinsic rewards to motivate people to perform four basic behaviors: join the organization, regularly attend their jobs, perform their jobs well, and stay with the organization.[15] Think about it. Would you show up to work every day to do the best possible job that you could just out of the goodness of your heart? Very few people would. This is why SAS, a statistical software company, offers numerous employee perks, such as on-site day care centers, dry-cleaning services, subsidized cafeterias, on-site fitness centers, and a centrally located free health care center. Typical work weeks at SAS are 35 hours, with flexible work schedules for nearly everyone. Through these great benefits, CEO Jim Goodnight aims to make his workforce happy, healthy, and satisfied with their jobs and the company. It seems to be working. As one employee says, "People do work hard here, because they're motivated to take care of a company that takes care of them."[16]

By contrast, **intrinsic rewards** are the natural rewards associated with performing a task or activity for its own sake. For example, aside from the external rewards management offers for doing something well, employees often find the activities or tasks they perform interesting and enjoyable. Examples of intrinsic rewards include a sense of accomplishment or achievement, a feeling of responsibility, the chance to learn something new or in-

With technological assistance, you may be tempted to engage in "impression management" to try to convince your boss and coworkers that you're working hard when you're really not. For instance, a tech support worker who enjoyed 3-hour lunches used a program on his Palm PDA to remotely control his office computer. He would open, close, and move files so it would look as if he had just stepped away from his desk. Other employees write email before they go home and then "send" them after midnight (we won't tell you how this is done) to make it look as though they are still at work. Some people leave early and, on their way home, send emails via their BlackBerry so it will appear they are still at the office. You may be thinking that these ruses are harmless, but 59 percent of human resources managers and 53 percent of supervisors have caught employees lying about the hours they work. Furthermore, if you're using technology to fake it, you're usually leaving high-tech tracks and footprints along the way. That tech worker who controlled his office computer with his Palm at lunch was fired for habitual lateness. Motivation is all about effort. So, do the right thing. Work hard for your company, your customers, and yourself.

Source: J. Spencer, "Shirk Ethic: How to Fake a Hard Day at the Office—White-Collar Slackers Get Help from New Gadgets: The Faux 4 A.M. E-Mail," *Wall Street Journal*, May 15, 2003, D1.

© iStockphoto.com/Lise Gagne / © iStockphoto.com/Laurent Davoust

Exhibit 13.3 Adding Rewards to the Model

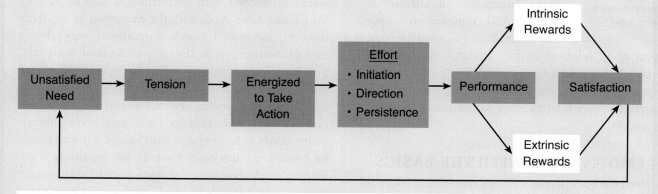

Unsatisfied Need → Tension → Energized to Take Action → Effort (• Initiation • Direction • Persistence) → Performance → Intrinsic Rewards / Extrinsic Rewards → Satisfaction

Performing a job well can be rewarding intrinsically (the job itself is fun, challenging, or interesting) or extrinsically (as you receive better pay, promotions, etc.). Intrinsic and extrinsic rewards lead to satisfaction of various needs.

© Cengage Learning 2011

teract with others, or simply the fun that comes from performing an interesting, challenging, and engaging task. Australian software company Atlassian has found self-direction—giving people the opportunity to work on what they want—to be an effective intrinsic motivator. Once every quarter, Atlassian gives its developers 24 hours to work on any project they want, with whomever they want, in whatever way they want. The only requirement: developers have to show the company their results at the end. The program spawned so many valuable innovations that Atlassian expanded the policy, allowing employees to use 20 percent of the work week on projects of their choice.[17]

Which types of rewards are most important to workers in general? A number of surveys suggest that both extrinsic and intrinsic rewards are important. One survey found that the most important rewards were good benefits and health insurance, job security, a week or more of

The Best Rewards Aren't Expensive

Which reward do you think would be more effective at motivating employees—an all-expenses-paid trip to Europe given out once a year, or a gift certificate to a local restaurant for $100 given out every week or two? It may surprise you, but according to Globoforce, a Boston-based company that helps businesses motivate their staff, it's the smaller reward. Eric Mosley, the CEO of Globoforce, says that the most effective rewards are small, an average of just $110; prizes larger than that are certainly appreciated, but don't motivate employees any better. Mosley says rewards should also be given out weekly, so that employees don't forget about incentives that a company offers. Finally, Mosley says that the majority of a company's staff, 80 percent to 90 percent, should be given rewards. Though people may worry about creating an environment where everyone wins, "when you're trying to reinforce certain behaviors, you need to constantly recognize them."

Source: T. Demos, "Motivate Without Spending Millions," *Bloomberg Businessweek*, April 12, 2010, 37–38.

© iStockphoto.com/Pamela Moore

vacation (all extrinsic rewards), interesting work, the opportunity to learn new skills, and independent work situations (all intrinsic rewards). And employee preferences for intrinsic and extrinsic rewards appear to be relatively stable. Studies conducted over the last three decades have consistently found that employees are twice as likely to indicate that important and meaningful work matters more to them than what they are paid.[18]

1.4 | MOTIVATING WITH THE BASICS

So, given the basic model of work motivation based on needs and rewards that is shown in Exhibit 13.3, what practical steps can managers take to motivate employees to increase their effort?

Well, *start by asking people what their needs are.* If managers don't know what workers' needs are, they won't be able to provide them the opportunities and rewards that can satisfy those needs. Tommy Lee Hayes-Brown, who is in charge of recognition programs at MetLife, points out why it's important to be aware of employees' needs: "Let's say you decide to reward an employee's great performance with a ham. If he doesn't eat ham, it's not going to be all that meaningful."[19]

Next, *satisfy lower-order needs first.* Since higher-order needs will not motivate people as long as lower-order needs remain unsatisfied, companies should satisfy lower-order needs first. In practice, this means providing the equipment, training, and knowledge to create a safe workplace free of physical risks, paying employees well enough to provide financial security, and offering a benefits package that will protect employees and their families through good medical coverage and health and disability insurance.

Third, managers should *expect people's needs to change.* As some needs are satisfied or situations change, what motivated people before may not motivate them now. Likewise, what motivates people to accept a job (pay and benefits) may not necessarily motivate them once they have the job (the job itself, opportunities for advancement). Managers should also expect needs to change as people mature.[20] For older employees, benefits are as important as pay, which is always ranked as more important by younger employees. Older employees also rank job security as more important than personal and family time, which is more important to younger employees.[21]

Finally, *as needs change and lower-order needs are satisfied, create opportunities for employees to satisfy higher-order needs.* Recall that intrinsic rewards such as accomplishment, achievement, learning something new, and interacting with others are the natural rewards associated with performing a task or activity for its own sake. And, with the exception of influence (power), intrinsic rewards correspond very closely to higher-order needs that are concerned with relationships (belongingness, relatedness, and affiliation) and challenges and accomplishments (esteem, self-actualization, growth, and achievement). Therefore, one way for managers to meet employees' higher-order needs is to create opportunities for employees to experience intrinsic rewards by providing challenging work, encouraging employees to take greater responsibility for their work, and giving employees the freedom to pursue tasks and projects they find naturally interesting.

How Perceptions and Expectations Affect Motivation

We've seen that people are motivated to achieve intrinsic and extrinsic rewards. However, if employees don't believe that rewards are fairly awarded or don't believe that they can achieve the performance goals the company has set for them, they won't be very motivated.

After reading the next two sections, you should be able to

2 **use equity theory to explain how employees' perceptions of fairness affect motivation.**

3 **use expectancy theory to describe how workers' expectations about rewards, effort, and the link between rewards and performance influence motivation.**

2 Equity Theory

Fairness, or what people perceive to be fair, is a critical issue in organizations. **Equity theory** says that people will be motivated at work when they *perceive* that they are being treated fairly. In particular, equity theory stresses the importance of perceptions. So, regardless of the actual level of rewards people receive, they must also perceive that they are being treated fairly relative to others. For example, you learned in Chapter 11 that the average CEO now makes 364 times as much as the average worker.[22] Many people believe that CEO pay is obscenely high and unfair. In order to keep CEO salaries in check, companies like Aflac, a Georgia insurance company, have adopted "say-on-pay" policies that allow investors a vote on executive compensation packages.[23] Others believe that CEO pay is fair because if it were easier to find good CEOs, then CEOs would be paid much less. Equity theory doesn't focus on objective equity (i.e., that CEOs make 364 times more than blue-collar workers). Instead, it says that equity, like beauty, is in the eye of the beholder.

Let's learn more about equity theory by examining **2.1 the components of equity theory, 2.2 how people react to perceived inequities,** *and* **2.3 how to motivate people using equity theory.**

2.1 | COMPONENTS OF EQUITY THEORY

The basic components of equity theory are inputs, outcomes, and referents. **Inputs** are the contributions employees make to the organization. Inputs include education and training, intelligence, experience, effort, number of hours worked, and ability. **Outcomes** are the rewards employees receive in exchange for their contributions to the organization. Outcomes include pay, fringe benefits, status symbols, and job titles and assignments. And, since perceptions of equity depend on comparisons, **referents** are others with whom people compare themselves to determine if they have been treated fairly. The referent can be a single person (comparing yourself with a coworker), a generalized other (comparing yourself with "students in general," for example), or even yourself at a previous time ("I was better off last year than I am this year"). Usually, people choose to compare themselves to referents who hold the same or similar jobs or who are otherwise similar in gender, race, age, tenure, or other characteristics.[24]

According to equity theory, employees compare their outcomes (the rewards they receive from the organization) to their inputs (their contributions to the organization). This comparison of outcomes to inputs is called the **outcome/input (O/I) ratio.**

After an internal comparison in which they compare their outcomes to their inputs, employees then make external comparisons in which they compare their O/I ratios with the O/I ratios of referents.[25]

$$\frac{OUTCOMES_{SELF}}{INPUTS_{SELF}} = \frac{OUTCOMES_{REFERENT}}{INPUTS_{REFERENT}}$$

When people perceive that their O/I ratios are equal to the referents' O/I ratios, they conclude that they are being treated fairly. But, when people perceive that their O/I ratios are less than their referents' O/I ratios, they conclude that they have been treated inequitably or unfairly.

Inequity can take two forms, underreward and overreward. **Underreward** occurs when your O/I ratio is less than your referent's O/I ratio. In other words, you are getting fewer outcomes relative to your inputs than your referent is getting. When people perceive that they have been underrewarded, they tend to experience anger or frustration.

By contrast, **overreward** occurs when your O/I ratio is higher than your referent's O/I ratio. In this case, you are getting more outcomes relative to your inputs than your referent is. In theory, when people perceive that they have been overrewarded, they experience guilt. But, not surprisingly, people have a very high tolerance for overreward. It takes a tremendous amount of overpayment before people decide that their pay or benefits are more than they deserve.

2.2 | HOW PEOPLE REACT TO PERCEIVED INEQUITY

So what happens when people perceive that they have been treated inequitably at work? Exhibit 13.4 on the next page shows that perceived inequity affects satisfaction. In the case of underreward, this usually translates into frustration or anger; with overreward, the reaction is guilt. These reactions lead to tension and a strong need to take action to restore equity in some way. At first, a slight inequity may not be strong enough to motivate an employee to take immediate action. If the inequity continues or there are multiple inequities, however, tension may build over time until a point of intolerance is reached and the person is energized to take action.[26]

When people perceive that they have been treated unfairly, they may try to restore equity by reducing inputs, increasing outcomes, rationalizing inputs or outcomes, changing the referent, or simply leaving. We will

Inputs in equity theory, the contributions employees make to the organization

Outcomes in equity theory, the rewards employees receive for their contributions to the organization

Referents in equity theory, others with whom people compare themselves to determine if they have been treated fairly

Outcome/input (O/I) ratio in equity theory, an employee's perception of how the rewards received from an organization compare with the employee's contributions to that organization

Underreward a form of inequity in which you are getting fewer outcomes relative to inputs than your referent is getting

Overreward a form of inequity in which you are getting more outcomes relative to inputs than your referent

Exhibit 13.4 Adding Equity Theory to the Model

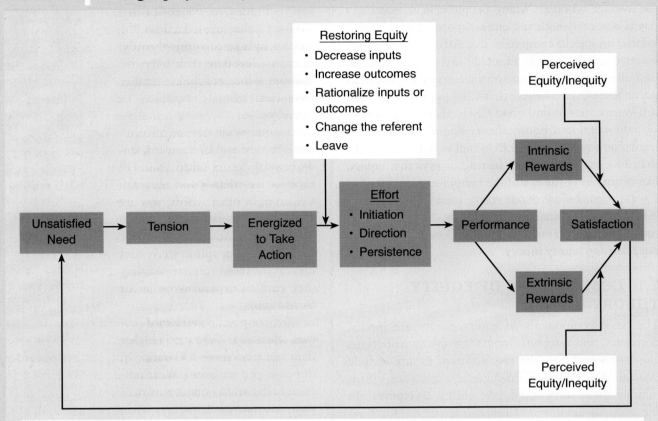

Restoring Equity
- Decrease inputs
- Increase outcomes
- Rationalize inputs or outcomes
- Change the referent
- Leave

Unsatisfied Need → Tension → Energized to Take Action → Effort (Initiation, Direction, Persistence) → Performance → Intrinsic Rewards / Extrinsic Rewards → Satisfaction

Perceived Equity/Inequity

When people perceive that they have been treated inequitably at work because of the intrinsic or extrinsic rewards they receive relative to their efforts, they are dissatisfied (or frustrated or angry), their needs aren't met, and those reactions lead to tension and a strong need to take action to restore equity in some way.

© Cengage Learning 2011

discuss these possible responses in terms of perceived inequity associated with underreward, which occurs much more often than that associated with overreward.

People who perceive that they have been underrewarded may try to restore equity by *decreasing or withholding their inputs (i.e., effort).* Pilots at American Airlines took a 23 percent pay cut after 9/11 to help keep the airline solvent. When American began doing well again and top managers collectively received a quarter-billion dollars in stock, the pilots requested their old salaries back. It is common for airline pilots to protest their employers' inaction in such circumstances by calling in sick or going on strike.[27]

Increasing outcomes is another way people try to restore equity. This might include asking for a raise or pointing out the inequity to the boss and hoping that he or she takes care of it. Sometimes, however, employees may go to external organizations such as labor unions, federal agencies, or the courts for help in increasing outcomes to restore equity. For example, in 2001, employees of Family Dollar Stores sued the company, claiming that it had misclassified hourly employees (who are eligible for overtime pay) as managers (who are not eligible for overtime pay). The case ultimately went to the U.S. Supreme Court, which upheld a lower court's decision in favor of the employees. More than 1,400 employees will divide $35.6 million.[28]

Another method of restoring equity is to *rationalize or distort inputs or outcomes.* Instead of decreasing inputs or increasing outcomes, employees restore equity by making mental or emotional adjustments to their O/I ratios or the O/I ratios of their referents. For example, suppose that a company downsizes 10 percent of its work force. It's likely that the survivors, the people who still have jobs, will be angry or frustrated with company management because of the layoffs. If alternative jobs are difficult to find, however, these survivors may rationalize or distort their O/I ratios and conclude, "Well, things could be worse. At least I still have my job." Rationalizing or distorting outcomes may be used when other ways to restore equity aren't available.

Changing the referent is another way of restoring equity. In this case, people compare themselves to someone other than the referent they had been using for previous O/I ratio comparisons. Since people usually choose to compare themselves to others who hold the same or similar jobs or who are otherwise similar (i.e., friends, family members, neighbors who work at other companies), they may change referents to restore equity when their personal situations change, such as a decrease in job status or pay.[29] Finally, when none of these methods are possible or restore equity, *employees may leave* by quitting their jobs, transferring, or increasing absenteeism.[30]

2.3 | MOTIVATING WITH EQUITY THEORY

What practical steps can managers take to use equity theory to motivate employees? They can *start by looking for and correcting major inequities.* Among other things, equity theory makes us aware that an employee's sense of fairness is based on subjective perceptions. What one employee considers grossly unfair may not affect another employee's perceptions of eq-

uity at all. Although these different perceptions make it difficult for managers to create conditions that satisfy all employees, it's critical that they do their best to take care of major inequities that can energize employees to take disruptive, costly, or harmful actions such as decreasing inputs or leaving. So, whenever possible, managers should look for and correct major inequities.

At Burgerville, a 39-restaurant fast-food chain in Vancouver, Washington, annual employee turnover was 128 percent per year. The key inequity? Employees making $9 an hour couldn't afford health insurance for themselves and their families. Indeed, while Burgerville's health plan was inexpensive at $42 a month for employees and $105 a month for families, it provided limited benefits and came with a $1,000 deductible. As a result, only 3 percent of employees were enrolled in it. Under Burgerville's revised health plan, employees who work at least 20 hours a week get full health insurance at a cost of just $15 a month for themselves and $90 a month for their families—in both instances, there's no deductible. While the new plan was expensive for Burgerville, nearly doubling health care costs from $2.1 million to $4.1 million, the cost was easily offset by lower employee turnover, which dropped from 128 percent per year to 54 percent per year, and higher sales, which rose by 11 percent. Furthermore, 98 percent of Burgerville's hourly employees and 97 percent of its salaried employees enrolled in the new health plan, compared to just 3 percent enrollment in the previous plan.[31]

Second, managers can *reduce employees' inputs.* Increasing outcomes is often the first and only strategy that companies use to restore equity, yet reducing employee inputs is just as viable a strategy. In fact, with dual-career couples working 50-hour weeks, more and more employees are looking for ways to reduce stress and restore a balance between work and family. Consequently, it may make sense to ask employees to do less, not more; to have them identify and eliminate the 20 percent of their jobs that doesn't increase productivity or add value for customers; and

MGMT SUCCESS

Layoffs *vs.* Pay Cuts + Time Off + Honesty

Managers of struggling companies typically use layoffs as a last resort. Why? Because layoffs have long-term negative effects on employee morale (researchers call it the "survivor syndrome"). As a result, more struggling companies are turning to pay cuts as an alternative to layoffs. No one gets fired and no one worries about job security. What lessons have managers learned when cutting management and employee pay? First, across-the-board pay cuts should be avoided at all costs. Second, employees should be given something in exchange for their lost pay, such as time off. Third, there should be clear and honest communication about the timing and amount of pay cuts. Some companies, such as Hewlett-Packard, have even instituted tiered pay cuts, which reflect how people's jobs have changed during the recession.

Source: M. Conlin, "Pay Cuts Made Palatable," *BusinessWeek*, May 4, 2009, 67.

to eliminate company-imposed requirements that really aren't critical to the performance of managers, employees, or the company (e.g., unnecessary meetings and reports).

Finally, managers should *make sure decision-making processes are fair.* Equity theory focuses on **distributive justice,** the degree to which outcomes and rewards are perceived to be fairly distributed or allocated. However, **procedural justice,** the perceived fairness of the procedures used to make reward allocation decisions, is just as important.[32] Procedural justice matters because even when employees are unhappy with their outcomes (i.e., low pay), they're much less likely to be unhappy with company management if they believe that the procedures used to allocate outcomes were fair. For example, employees who are laid off tend to be hostile toward their employers when they perceive that the procedures leading to the layoffs were unfair. By contrast, employees who perceive layoff procedures to be fair tend to continue to support and trust their employers.[33] Also, if employees perceive that their outcomes are unfair (i.e., distributive injustice), but that the decisions and procedures leading to those outcomes were fair (i.e., procedural justice), they are much more likely to seek constructive ways of restoring equity, such as discussing these matters with their managers. In contrast, if employees perceive both distributive and procedural injustice, they may resort to more destructive tactics such as withholding effort, absenteeism, tardiness, or even sabotage and theft.[34]

3 | Expectancy Theory

One of the hardest things about motivating people is that rewards that are attractive to some employees are unattractive to others. **Expectancy theory** says that people will be motivated to the extent to which they believe that their efforts will lead to good performance, that good performance will be rewarded, and that they will be offered attractive rewards.[35]

Let's learn more about expectancy theory by examining 3.1 the components of expectancy theory and 3.2 how to use expectancy theory as a motivational tool.

> One of the hardest things about **motivating people** is that rewards that are **attractive** to some employees are **unattractive** to others.

3.1 | COMPONENTS OF EXPECTANCY THEORY

Expectancy theory holds that people make conscious choices about their motivation. The three factors that affect those choices are valence, expectancy, and instrumentality.

Valence is simply the attractiveness or desirability of various rewards or outcomes. Expectancy theory recognizes that the same reward or outcome—say, a promotion—will be highly attractive to some people, will be highly disliked by others, and will not make much difference one way or the other to still others. Accordingly, when people are deciding how much effort to put forth, expectancy theory says that they will consider the valence of all possible rewards and outcomes that they can receive from their jobs. The greater the sum of those valences, each of which can be positive, negative, or neutral, the more effort people will choose to put forth on the job. Crowd-Flower, an employment agency based in San Francisco, understands that different people are motivated by different rewards. So, when it assigns someone from its workforce to a task, which can range from verifying search engine links to categorizing Twitter posts, it gives the option of receiving payment as cash or virtual cash. Some employees choose real money, while others choose virtual money that can be spent in online games such as Farmville, Mafia Wars, or TinierMe.com. Though the idea of working for virtual money may sound strange, Amanda Dorsey, one of CrowdFlower's workers, says, "Doing work for virtual currency is pretty much like any other form of putting forth an effort for a reward."[36]

Expectancy is the perceived relationship between effort and performance. When expectancies are strong, employees believe that their hard work and efforts will result in good performance, so they work harder. By contrast, when expectancies are weak, employees figure that no matter what they do or how hard they work, they won't be able to perform their jobs successfully, so they don't work as hard.

Instrumentality is the perceived relationship between performance and rewards. When instrumentality is strong, employees believe that improved performance will lead to better and more rewards, so they choose to work harder. When instrumentality is weak, employees don't believe that better performance will result in more or better rewards, so they choose not to work as hard.

Expectancy theory holds that for people to be highly motivated, all three variables—valence, expectancy, and instrumentality—must be high. Thus, expectancy theory can be represented by the following simple equation:

$$\text{Motivation} = \text{Valence} \times \text{Expectancy} \times \text{Instrumentality}$$

If any one of these variables (valence, expectancy, or instrumentality) declines, overall motivation will decline, too.

Exhibit 13.5 incorporates the expectancy theory variables into our motivation model. Valence and instrumentality combine to affect employees' willingness to put forth effort (i.e., the degree to which they are energized to take action), while expectancy transforms intended effort ("I'm really going to work hard in this job") into actual effort. If you're offered rewards that you desire and you believe that you will in fact receive these rewards for good performance, you're highly likely to be energized to take action. However, you're not likely to actually exert effort unless you also believe that you can do the job (i.e., that your efforts will lead to successful performance).

> **Instrumentality**
> the perceived relationship between performance and rewards

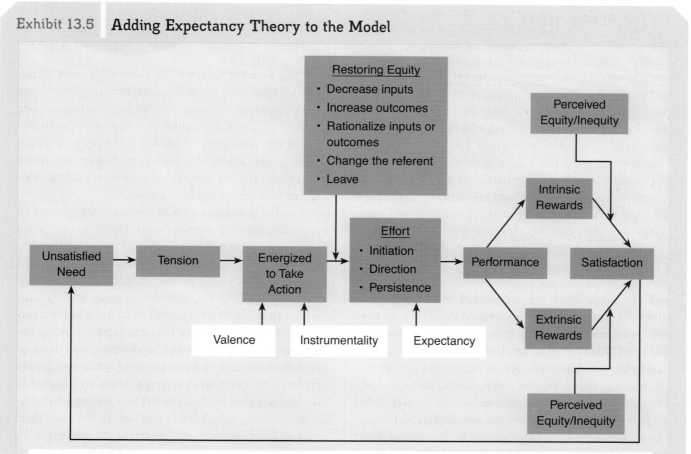

Exhibit 13.5 Adding Expectancy Theory to the Model

If rewards are attractive (valence) and linked to performance (instrumentality), then people are energized to take action. In other words, good performance gets them rewards that they want. Intended effort (i.e., becoming energized to take action) turns into actual effort when people expect that their hard work and efforts will result in good performance. After all, why work hard if that hard work is wasted?

Trashing the Workweek

Giving employees freedom to go to a baseball game on Wednesday afternoon might seem like a risky way to motivate them. But the Results-Only Work Environment (ROWE) approach, pioneered at Best Buy by Cali Ressler and Jody Thompson, taps into employees' need for independence in order to get them to perform at their best. At Best Buy, 80 percent of the corporate staff can come and go as they please (that means there's no such thing as coming in "late" and leaving "early"). Conference calls occur from lakefront cabins and on road trips by employees following their favorite rock bands on tour. With ROWE, employees aren't evaluated on how many hours they spend in their chair but on the quality and quantity of their work.

Source: L. Belkin, "Flexible Work in a Recession," *New York Times*, October 2, 2009, accessed November 10, 2009, http://parenting.blogs.nytimes.com/2009/10/02/flexible-work-in-a-recession/.

3.2 | MOTIVATING WITH EXPECTANCY THEORY

What practical steps can managers take to use expectancy theory to motivate employees? First, they can *systematically gather information to find out what employees want from their jobs.* In addition to individual managers directly asking employees what they want from their jobs (see Section 1.4 of this chapter, "Motivating with the Basics"), companies need to survey their employees regularly to determine their wants, needs, and dissatisfactions. Since people consider the valence of all the possible rewards and outcomes that they can receive from their jobs, regular identification of wants, needs, and dissatisfactions gives companies the chance to turn negatively valent rewards and outcomes into positively valent rewards and outcomes, thus raising overall motivation and effort. Therefore, employers should routinely survey employees to identify not only the range of rewards that are valued by most employees but also to understand the preferences of specific employees.

Second, managers can *take specific steps to link rewards to individual performance in a way that is clear and understandable to employees.* Unfortunately, most employees are extremely dissatisfied with the link between pay and performance in their organizations. In one study, based on a representative sample, 80 percent of the employees surveyed wanted to be paid according to a different kind of pay system! Moreover, only 32 percent of employees were satisfied with how their annual pay raises were determined,

and only 22 percent were happy with the way the starting salaries for their jobs were determined.[37] One way to make sure that employees see the connection between pay and performance (see Chapter 11 for a discussion of compensation strategies) is for managers to publicize the way in which pay decisions are made. This is especially important given that only 41 percent of employees know how their pay increases are determined.[38]

Finally, managers should *empower employees to make decisions if management really wants them to believe that their hard work and effort will lead to good performance.* If valent rewards are linked to good performance, people should be energized to take action. However, this works only if they also believe that their efforts will lead to good performance. One of the ways that managers destroy the expectancy that hard work and effort will lead to good performance is by restricting what employees can do or by ignoring employees' ideas. In Chapter 9, you learned that *empowerment* is a feeling of intrinsic motivation, which leads workers to perceive their work to have meaning and perceive themselves to be competent, to have an impact, and to be capable of self-determination.[39] So, if managers want workers to have strong expectancies, they should empower them to make decisions. Doing so will motivate employees to take active rather than passive roles in their work.

How Rewards and Goals Affect Motivation

When used properly, rewards motivate and energize employees. But when used incorrectly, they can de-motivate, baffle, and even anger them. Goals are also supposed to motivate employees. But leaders who focus blindly on meeting goals at all costs often find that they destroy motivation.

After reading the next three sections, you should be able to

4 explain how reinforcement theory works and how it can be used to motivate.

5 describe the components of goal-setting theory and how managers can use them to motivate workers.

6 discuss how the entire motivation model can be used to motivate workers.

4 Reinforcement Theory

Reinforcement theory says that behavior is a function of its consequences, that behaviors followed by positive consequences (i.e., reinforced) will occur more frequently, and that behaviors followed by negative consequences, or not followed by positive consequences, will occur less frequently.[40] For example, more and more hotels with 100 percent smoke-free policies have increased fines (i.e., negative consequences) for customers who smoke in their rooms. Sheraton Hotels charges a $200 fine, Walt Disney World charges $500, and Swissôtel Chicago raised their fine from $175 to $250. Swissôtel's marketing director, Nicole Jachimiak, says, "$175 wasn't quite enough to get people to stop."[41]

More specifically, **reinforcement** is the process of changing behavior by changing the consequences that follow behavior.[42] Reinforcement has two parts: reinforcement contingencies and schedules of reinforcement. **Reinforcement contingencies** are the cause-and-effect relationships between the performance of specific behaviors and specific consequences. For example, if you get docked an hour's pay for being late to work, then a reinforcement contingency

exists between a behavior (being late to work) and a consequence (losing an hour's pay). A **schedule of reinforcement** is the set of rules regarding reinforcement contingencies that specifies which behaviors will be reinforced, which consequences will follow those behaviors, and the schedule by which those consequences will be delivered.[43]

Exhibit 13.6 on the next page incorporates reinforcement contingencies and reinforcement schedules into our motivation model. First, notice that extrinsic rewards and the schedules of reinforcement used to deliver them are the primary methods for creating reinforcement contingencies in organizations. In turn, those reinforcement contingencies directly affect valences (the attractiveness of rewards), instrumentality (the perceived link between rewards and performance), and effort (how hard employees will work).

Let's learn more about reinforcement theory by examining 4.1 the components of reinforcement theory, 4.2 the different schedules for delivering reinforcement, and 4.3 how to motivate with reinforcement theory.

4.1 | COMPONENTS OF REINFORCEMENT THEORY

As just described, *reinforcement contingencies* are the cause-and-effect relationships between the performance of specific behaviors and specific consequences. There are four kinds of reinforcement contingencies: positive reinforcement, negative reinforcement, punishment, and extinction.

Positive reinforcement strengthens behavior (i.e., increases its frequency) by following behaviors with desirable consequences. Even though most consumers and businesses know that they should recycle beverage cans and plastic bottles, few actually do—only 34 percent of all beverage containers, and only 25 percent of all plastic bottles, are recycled. PepsiCo and Waste Management teamed up to create the "dream machine" point system to encourage consumers to recycle. Each bottle

---

Reinforcement theory a theory that states that behavior is a function of its consequences, that behaviors followed by positive consequences will occur more frequently, and that behaviors followed by negative consequences, or not followed by positive consequences, will occur less frequently

Reinforcement the process of changing behavior by changing the consequences that follow behavior

Reinforcement contingencies cause-and-effect relationships between the performance of specific behaviors and specific consequences

Schedule of reinforcement rules that specify which behaviors will be reinforced, which consequences will follow those behaviors, and the schedule by which those consequences will be delivered

Positive reinforcement reinforcement that strengthens behavior by following behaviors with desirable consequences

Exhibit 13.6 **Adding Reinforcement Theory to the Model**

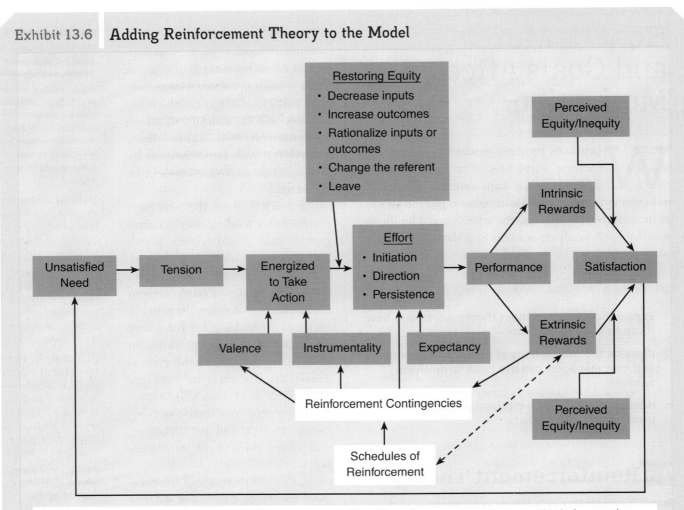

Extrinsic rewards and the schedules of reinforcement used to deliver them are the primary methods for creating reinforcement contingencies in organizations. In turn, those reinforcement contingencies directly affect valences (the attractiveness of rewards), instrumentality (the perceived link between rewards and performance), and effort (how hard employees will work).

© Cengage Learning 2011

Negative reinforcement reinforcement that strengthens behavior by withholding an unpleasant consequence when employees perform a specific behavior

Punishment reinforcement that weakens behavior by following behaviors with undesirable consequences

or can deposited into the dream machine is rewarded with points that can be used on coupons for entertainment, dining, travel, and personal services from vendors such as Marriott, Domino's, and Blockbuster.[44]

In contrast to positive reinforcement, **negative reinforcement** strengthens behavior by withholding an unpleasant consequence when employees perform a specific behavior. Negative reinforcement is also called *avoidance learning* because workers perform a behavior to *avoid* a negative consequence. For example, at the Florist Network, a small business

in Buffalo, New York, management instituted a policy of requiring good attendance for employees to receive their annual bonuses. Employee attendance improved significantly when excessive absenteeism threatened to result in the loss of $1,500 or more.[45]

By contrast, **punishment** weakens behavior (i.e., decreases its frequency) by following behaviors with undesirable consequences. For example, the standard disciplinary or punishment process in most companies is an oral warning ("Don't ever do that again"), followed by a written warning ("This letter is to discuss the serious problem you're having with . . . "), followed by three days off without pay ("While you're at home not being paid, we want you to think hard about . . . "), followed by being fired ("That was your last chance"). Though punishment can weaken behavior, managers have to be careful to avoid the backlash that sometimes occurs when employees are punished at work. For example, Frito-Lay began getting complaints from customers that they were finding potato chips with obscene messages written on them. Frito-Lay eventually traced the problem to a potato chip plant where supervisors had fired 58 out of the 210 workers for disciplinary reasons over a nine-month period. The remaining employees were so angry over what they saw as unfair treatment from management that they began writing the phrases on potato chips with felt-tipped pens.[46]

Extinction is a reinforcement strategy in which a positive consequence is no longer allowed to follow a previously reinforced behavior. By removing the positive consequence, extinction weakens the behavior, making it less likely to occur. Based on the idea of positive reinforcement, most companies give company leaders and managers substantial financial rewards when the company performs well. Based on the idea of extinction, you would then expect that leaders and managers would not be rewarded (i.e., removing the positive consequence) when companies perform poorly. If companies want to use financial rewards to reinforce the right kinds of behaviors, then the rewards have to be removed when management doesn't deliver successful performance.

4.2 | SCHEDULES FOR DELIVERING REINFORCEMENT

As mentioned earlier, a *schedule of reinforcement* is the set of rules regarding reinforcement contingencies such as which behaviors will be reinforced, which consequences will follow those behaviors, and the schedule by which those consequences will be delivered. There are two categories of reinforcement schedules: continuous and intermittent.

With **continuous reinforcement schedules,** a consequence follows every instance of a behavior. For example, employees working on a piece-rate pay system earn money (consequence) for every item they manufacture (behavior). The more they produce, the more they earn. By contrast, with **intermittent reinforcement schedules,** consequences are delivered after a specified or average time has elapsed or after a specified or average number of behaviors has occurred. As Exhibit 13.7 shows, there are four types of intermittent reinforcement schedules. Two of these are based on time and are called *interval reinforcement schedules,* while the other two, known as *ratio reinforcement schedules,* are based on behaviors.

With **fixed interval reinforcement schedules,** consequences follow a behavior only after a fixed time has elapsed. For example, most people receive their paychecks on a fixed interval schedule (e.g., once or twice per month). As long as they work (behavior) during a specified pay period (interval), they get a paycheck (consequence). With **variable interval reinforcement schedules,** consequences follow a

Exhibit 13.7 Intermittent Reinforcement Schedules

INTERMITTENT REINFORCEMENT SCHEDULES		
	FIXED	**VARIABLE**
INTERVAL (TIME)	Consequences follow behavior after a fixed time has elapsed.	Consequences follow behavior after different times, some shorter and some longer, that vary around a specific average time.
RATIO (BEHAVIOR)	Consequences follow a specific number of behaviors.	Consequences follow a different number of behaviors, sometimes more and sometimes less, that vary around a specified average number of behaviors.

© Cengage Learning 2011

Fixed ratio reinforcement schedule an intermittent schedule in which consequences are delivered following a specific number of behaviors

Variable ratio reinforcement schedule an intermittent schedule in which consequences are delivered following a different number of behaviors, sometimes more and sometimes less, that vary around a specified average number of behaviors

behavior after different times, some shorter and some longer, that vary around a specified average time. On a 90-day variable interval reinforcement schedule, you might receive a bonus after 80 days or perhaps after 100 days, but the average interval between performing your job well (behavior) and receiving your bonus (consequence) would be 90 days.

With **fixed ratio reinforcement schedules,** consequences are delivered following a specific number of behaviors. For example, a car salesperson might receive a $1,000 bonus after every 10 sales. Therefore, a salesperson with only 9 sales would not receive the bonus until he or she finally sold a 10th car.

With **variable ratio reinforcement schedules,** consequences are delivered following a different number of behaviors, sometimes more and sometimes less, that vary around a specified average number of behaviors. With a 10-car variable ratio reinforcement schedule, a salesperson might receive the bonus after 7 car sales, or after 12, 11, or 9 sales, but the average number of cars sold before receiving the bonus would be 10 cars.

Which reinforcement schedules work best? In the past, the standard advice was to use continuous reinforcement when employees were learning new behaviors because reinforcement after each success leads to faster learning. Likewise, the standard advice was to use intermittent reinforcement schedules to maintain behavior after it is learned because intermittent rewards are supposed to make behavior much less subject to extinction.[47] Research shows, however, that interval-based schedules usually produce weak results, but that the effectiveness of continuous, fixed ratio, and variable ratio reinforcement schedules differs very little.[48] In organizational settings, all three produce consistently large increases over noncontingent reward schedules. So managers should choose whichever of these three is easiest to use in their companies.

4.3 | MOTIVATING WITH REINFORCEMENT THEORY

What practical steps can managers take to use reinforcement theory to motivate employees? University of Nebraska business professor Fred Luthans, who has been studying the effects of reinforcement theory in organizations for more than a quarter of a century, says that there are five steps to motivating workers with reinforcement theory: *identify, measure, analyze, intervene,* and *evaluate* critical performance-related behaviors.[49]

Identify means identifying critical, observable, performance-related behaviors. These are the behaviors that are most important to successful job performance. In addition, they must also be easily observed so that they can be accurately measured. *Measure* means measuring the baseline frequencies of these behaviors. In other words, find out how often workers perform them. *Analyze* means analyzing the causes and consequences of these behaviors. Analyzing the causes helps managers create the conditions that produce these critical behaviors, and analyzing the consequences helps them determine if these behaviors produce the results that they want. *Intervene* means changing the organization by using positive and negative reinforcement to increase the frequency of these critical behaviors. *Evaluate* means determining the extent to which the intervention actually changed workers' behavior. This is done by comparing behavior after the intervention to the original baseline of behavior before the intervention.

In addition to these five steps, managers should remember three other key elements when motivating with reinforcement theory. *Don't reinforce the wrong behaviors.* Although reinforcement theory sounds simple, it's actually very difficult to put into practice. One of the most common mistakes is accidentally reinforcing the wrong behaviors. Sometimes managers reinforce behaviors that they don't want!

Managers should also *correctly administer punishment at the appropriate time.* Many managers believe that punishment can change workers' behavior and help them improve their job performance. Furthermore, managers believe that fairly punishing workers also lets other workers know what is or isn't acceptable.[50] A danger of using punishment is that it can produce a backlash against managers and companies. But, if administered properly, punishment can weaken the frequency of undesirable behaviors without creating a backlash.[51] To be effective, the punishment must be strong enough to stop the undesired behavior and must be administered objectively (same rules applied to everyone), impersonally (without emotion or anger), consistently and contingently (each time improper behavior occurs), and quickly (as soon as possible following the undesirable behavior). In addition, managers should clearly explain what the appropriate behavior is and why the employee is being punished. Employees typically respond well when punishment is administered this way.[52]

Finally, managers should *choose the simplest and most effective schedule of reinforcement*. When choosing a schedule of reinforcement, managers need to balance effectiveness against simplicity. In fact, the more complex the schedule of reinforcement, the more likely it is to be misunderstood and resisted by managers and employees. Since continuous, fixed ratio, and variable ratio reinforcement schedules are about equally effective, continuous reinforcement schedules may be the best choice in many instances by virtue of their simplicity.

5 Goal-Setting Theory

The basic model of motivation with which we began this chapter shows that individuals feel tension after becoming aware of an unfulfilled need. Once they experience tension, they search for and select courses of action that they believe will eliminate this tension. In other words, they direct their behavior toward something. This something is a goal. A **goal** is a target, objective, or result that someone tries to accomplish. **Goal-setting theory** says that people will be motivated to the extent they accept specific, challenging goals and receive feedback that indicates their progress toward goal achievement.

Let's learn more about goal setting by examining **5.1 the components of goal-setting theory** *and* **5.2 how to motivate with goal-setting theory.**

5.1 | COMPONENTS OF GOAL-SETTING THEORY

The basic components of goal-setting theory are goal specificity, goal difficulty, goal acceptance, and performance feedback.[53] **Goal specificity** is the extent to which goals are detailed, exact, and unambiguous. Specific goals, such as "I'm going to have a 3.0 average this semester," are more motivating than general goals, such as "I'm going to get better grades this semester."

Goal difficulty is the extent to which a goal is hard or challenging to accomplish. Difficult goals, such as "I'm going to have a 3.5 average and make the Dean's List this semester," are more motivating than easy goals, such as "I'm going to have a 2.0 average this semester."

Goal acceptance, which is similar to the idea of goal commitment discussed in Chapter 5, is the extent to which people consciously understand and agree to goals. Accepted goals, such as "I really want to get a 3.5 average this semester to show my parents how much I've improved," are more motivating than unaccepted goals, such as "My parents really want me to get a 3.5 average this semester, but there's so much more I'd rather do on campus than study!"

Performance feedback is information about the quality or quantity of past performance that indicates whether progress is being made toward the accomplishment of a goal. Performance feedback, such as "My prof said I need a 92 percent on the final to get an A in that class," is more motivating than no feedback: "I have no idea what my grade is in that class." In short, goal-setting theory says that people will be motivated to the extent to which they accept specific, challenging goals and receive feedback that indicates their progress toward goal achievement.

How does goal setting work? To start with, challenging goals focus employees' attention (i.e., direction of effort) on the critical aspects of their jobs and away from unimportant areas. Goals also energize behavior. When faced with unaccomplished goals, employees typically develop plans and strategies to reach those goals. Goals also create tension between the goal, which is the desired future state of affairs, and the place where the employee or company is now, meaning the current state of affairs. This tension can be satisfied only by achieving or abandoning the goal. Finally, goals influence persistence. Since goals only go away when they are accomplished, employees are more likely to persist in their efforts in the presence of goals. Exhibit 13.8 on the next page incorporates goals into the motivation model by showing how they directly affect tension, effort, and the extent to which employees are energized to take action.

Goal a target, objective, or result that someone tries to accomplish

Goal-setting theory a theory that states that people will be motivated to the extent to which they accept specific, challenging goals and receive feedback that indicates their progress toward goal achievement

Goal specificity the extent to which goals are detailed, exact, and unambiguous

Goal difficulty the extent to which a goal is hard or challenging to accomplish

Goal acceptance the extent to which people consciously understand and agree to goals

Performance feedback information about the quality or quantity of past performance that indicates whether progress is being made toward the accomplishment of a goal

Exhibit 13.8 **Adding Goal-Setting Theory to the Model**

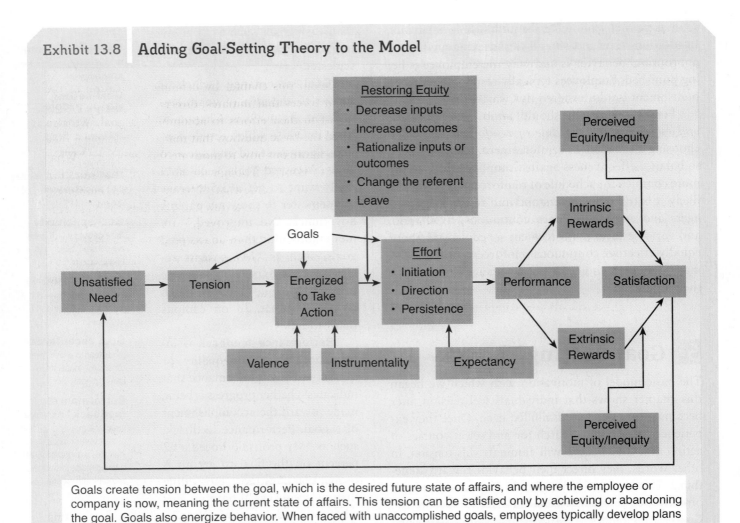

Goals create tension between the goal, which is the desired future state of affairs, and where the employee or company is now, meaning the current state of affairs. This tension can be satisfied only by achieving or abandoning the goal. Goals also energize behavior. When faced with unaccomplished goals, employees typically develop plans and strategies to reach those goals. Finally, goals influence persistence.

© Cengage Learning 2011

5.2 | MOTIVATING WITH GOAL-SETTING THEORY

What practical steps can managers take to use goal-setting theory to motivate employees? One of the simplest, most effective ways to motivate workers is to *assign them specific, challenging goals.* For example, Valpak Direct Marketing Systems is a direct-mailing company that awards regional franchises to people with enough business experience and cash ($43,000 is usually enough for a small region). However, if you work for Valpak and meet the goal of $1.1 million in sales over 3 years, putting you among the top third of its salespeople, the company lets you choose your reward: $50,000 toward the purchase of a small regional territory or $10,000 toward getting an MBA. Joe Bourdow, Valpak's president, said, "Sharp people coming out of school have choices,

and so we're trying to give them a reason to at least consider us."[54]

Second, managers should *make sure workers truly accept organizational goals.* Specific, challenging goals won't motivate workers unless they really accept, understand, and agree to the organization's goals. For this to occur, people must see the goals as fair and reasonable. Plus, they must trust management and believe that managers are using goals to clarify what is expected from them rather than to exploit or threaten them ("If you don't achieve these goals . . ."). Participative goal setting, in which managers and employees generate goals together, can help increase trust and understanding and thus acceptance of goals. Furthermore, providing workers with training can help increase goal acceptance, particularly when workers don't believe they are capable of reaching the organization's goals.[55]

Finally, managers should *provide frequent, specific, performance-related feedback*. Once employees have accepted specific, challenging goals, they should receive frequent performance-related feedback so that they can track their progress toward goal completion. Feedback leads to stronger motivation and effort in three ways.[56] Receiving specific feedback that indicates how well they're performing can encourage employees who don't have specific, challenging goals to set goals to improve their performance. Once people meet goals, performance feedback often encourages them to set higher, more difficult goals. And feedback lets people know whether they need to increase their efforts or change strategies in order to accomplish their goals. So, to motivate employees with goal-setting theory, make sure they receive frequent performance-related feedback so that they can track their progress toward goal completion.

6 Motivating with the Integrated Model

We began this chapter by defining motivation as the set of forces that initiates, directs, and makes people persist in their efforts to accomplish a goal. We also asked the basic question that managers ask when they try to figure out how to motivate their workers: "What leads to effort?" Though the answer to that question is likely to be somewhat different for each employee, the diagram on the Review Card for this chapter helps you begin to answer it by consolidating the practical advice from the theories reviewed in this chapter in one convenient location. So, if you're having difficulty figuring out why people aren't motivated where you work, check your Review Card for a useful, theory-based starting point.

STUDENT Study Tools

Located at the back of your book:

- ☐ Rip out and study the Chapter Review Card at the end of the book

Log in to the CourseMate for MGMT at cengagebrain.com to:

- ☐ Review Key Term Flashcards delivered 3 ways (print or online)
- ☐ Complete both Practice Quizzes to prepare for tests
- ☐ Play Beat the Clock and Quizbowl to master concepts
- ☐ Complete the Crossword Puzzle to review key terms
- ☐ Watch the video on Flight 001 for a real company example and take the accompanying quiz
- ☐ Watch the Biz Flix clip from *Friday Night Lights* and take the quiz
- ☐ Complete the Case Assignment on Ann Taylor
- ☐ Work through the Management Decision on vacation time
- ☐ Work through the Management Team Decision on mining human capital
- ☐ Develop your skills with the Develop Your Career Potential exercise

14 | Leadership

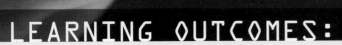

© Comstock/Jupiterimages

LEARNING OUTCOMES:

1. explain what leadership is.

2. describe who leaders are and what effective leaders do.

3. explain Fiedler's contingency theory.

4. describe how path-goal theory works.

5. explain the normative decision theory.

6. explain how visionary leadership (i.e., charismatic or transformational leadership) helps leaders achieve strategic leadership.

Chapter 14

What Is Leadership?

If you've ever been in charge, or even just thought about it, chances are you've considered questions such as: Do I have what it takes to lead? What are the most important things leaders do? How can I transform a poorly performing department, division, or company? Do I need to adjust my leadership depending on the situation and the employee? Why doesn't my leadership inspire people? If you feel overwhelmed at the prospect of being a leader, you're not alone—millions of leaders in organizations across the world struggle with fundamental leadership issues on a daily basis.

How does an ensemble of 100 or more musicians, all playing different parts at different times on different instruments, manage to produce something as beautiful as Beethoven's Fifth Symphony? (Or, if Gustav Mahler's Eighth Symphony, aptly dubbed "Symphony of a Thousand," is on the program, a lot more people might be involved!) The conductor, like a CEO, is responsible for managing all of this complexity and ensuring great performance. But conductors do much more than just keeping the beat with a baton. According to Ramona Wis, author of *The Conductor as Leader: Principles of Leadership Applied to Life on the Podium*, conductors must also build connections between people, inspire them with vision, command their trust, and persuade them to participate in the ensemble at their very best.

Whether the end result is a stirring musical performance, innovation of new products, or increased profits, **leadership** is the process of influencing others to achieve group or organizational goals. The knowledge and skills you'll learn in this chapter won't make the task of leadership less daunting, but they will help you navigate it.

After reading the next two sections, you should be able to

1 **explain what leadership is.**

2 **describe who leaders are and what effective leaders do.**

1 Leaders versus Managers

According to University of Southern California business professor Warren Bennis, the primary difference between leaders and managers is that leaders are concerned with doing the right thing, whereas managers are concerned with doing things right.[1] In other words, leaders begin with the question, "What should we be doing?" while managers start with "How can we do what we're already doing better?" Leaders focus on vision, mission, goals, and objectives, while managers focus on productivity and efficiency. Managers see themselves as preservers of the status quo, while leaders see themselves as promoters of change and challengers of the status quo. Leaders, consequently, encourage creativity and risk taking. At Maddock Douglas, an Elmhurst, Illinois firm that helps companies develop new products, President Louis Viton leads by encouraging creativity and risk-taking with an annual "Fail Forward" award for ambitious ideas that end in disaster—even if they end up costing the company huge amounts of money. Viton says the latest "Fail Forward" winner produced a new product design that "was a total embarrassment. . . . But she was trying to do something new and different and better. She went for it, and she won an award for it."[2]

Leadership the process of influencing others to achieve group or organizational goals

Another difference is that managers have a relatively short-term perspective, while leaders take a long-term view. Managers are also concerned with control and limiting the choices of others, while leaders are more concerned with expanding people's choices and options.[3] Further, managers solve problems so that others can do their work, while leaders inspire and motivate others to find their own solutions. Finally, managers are also more concerned with *means*, how to get things done, while leaders are more concerned with *ends*, what gets done. When Ed Whitacre was named CEO of General Motors, he set two goals—return GM to profitability and repay bailout funds borrowed from the U.S. government. To meet these long-term goals, Whitacre brought wholesale changes to GM's management team, firing many senior-level managers who had been with the company for decades, and replacing them with younger candidates, many of whom were taking their first management jobs in the auto industry. Whitacre then charged the management team to come up with plans to make his goal a reality and evaluated their efforts based on six areas: market share, revenue, operating profit, cash flow, quality, and customer satisfaction.[4]

Though leaders are different from managers, organizations need them both. Managers are critical to getting out the day-to-day work, and leaders are critical to inspiring employees and setting the organization's long-term direction. The key issue for any organization is the extent to which it is properly led and properly managed. As Warren Bennis said in summing up the difference between leaders and managers, "American organizations (and probably those in much of the rest of the industrialized world) are underled and overmanaged. They do not pay enough attention to doing the right thing, while they pay too much attention to doing things right."[5]

2 Who Leaders Are and What Leaders Do

Indra Nooyi, PepsiCo's CEO, talks straight, has a sharp sense of humor, and sings in the hallways wherever she is. Nooyi is an extravert. By contrast, J.C. Penney's CEO, Mike Ullman, who is soft-spoken and easy to approach, is an introvert.[6] Which one is likely to be

The Three Ms

Doctors take the Hippocratic Oath. Lawyers swear to protect and enforce the law. Leaders . . . well, there's no equivalent for business leaders. That's why Harvard professor Howard Gardner says that business leaders can develop personal ethics by focusing on their mission, a mentor, and the mirror.

First, leaders need to develop a personal mission statement by asking themselves these questions: Why am I doing what I'm doing? What do I want from my work? What are my personal goals? Let your personal mission statement, and not the company's, guide your ethical behavior. Second, take care in choosing a mentor. An interesting study compared 20 business leaders selected at random with 20 "good" business leaders nominated by businesspeople, business school professors, and deans. The randomly selected business leaders focused on short-term goals exclusively, worrying only about next quarter's results. By contrast, 18 of the 20 "good" executives focused on the long term, on doing what was right for the company in the long run. So, if you want to be a good leader, choose a "good" mentor. Third, periodically stand in front of the mirror to assess your ethical performance as a business leader. Are you proud or ashamed of what you accomplished and how you accomplished it? Are you proud or ashamed of your company? What needs to change to make you proud? So, do the right thing. Develop a personal mission statement. Choose the right mentor. And look hard at yourself in the mirror.

Source: K. Voigt, "Enron, Andersen Scandals Offer Ethical Lessons—Businesspeople Can Strive to Avoid Common Pitfalls through the 'Three Ms'," *Wall Street Journal Europe*, September 3, 2002, A12.

more successful as a CEO? According to a survey of 1,542 senior managers, it's the extravert. Forty-seven percent of those 1,542 senior managers felt that extraverts make better CEOs, while 65 percent said that being an introvert hurts a CEO's chances of success.[7] So clearly senior managers believe that extraverted CEOs are better leaders. But are they? Not necessarily. In fact, a relatively high percentage of CEOs, 40 percent, are introverts. Sara Lee CEO Brenda Barnes says, "I've always been shy.... People wouldn't call me that [an introvert], but I am."[8] Indeed, Barnes turns down all speaking requests and rarely gives interviews.

So, what makes a good leader? Does leadership success depend on who leaders are, such as introverts or extraverts, or on what leaders do and how they behave? Let's learn more about who leaders are by investigating 2.1 leadership traits and 2.2 leadership behaviors.

2.1 | LEADERSHIP TRAITS

Trait theory is one way to describe who leaders are. **Trait theory** says that effective leaders possess a similar set of traits or characteristics. **Traits** are relatively stable characteristics, such as abilities, psychologi-

cal motives, and consistent patterns of behavior. For example, according to trait theory, leaders are taller and more confident and have greater physical stamina (i.e., higher energy levels) than nonleaders. Indeed, whereas just 14.5 percent of men are 6 feet tall, 58 percent of Fortune 500 CEOs are 6 feet or taller.[9] Trait theory is also known as the "great person" theory because early versions of the theory stated that leaders are born, not made. In other words, you either have the right stuff to be a leader or you don't. And if you don't, there is no way to get it.

For some time it was thought that trait theory was wrong and that there are no consistent trait differences between leaders and nonleaders or between effective and ineffective leaders. However, more recent evidence shows that "successful leaders are not like other people," that successful leaders are indeed different from the rest of us.[10] More specifically, leaders are different from nonleaders in the following traits: drive, the desire to lead, honesty/integrity, self-confidence, emotional stability, cognitive ability, and knowledge of the business.[11]

Drive refers to a high level of effort and is characterized by achievement, motivation, initiative, energy, and tenacity. In terms of achievement and ambition, leaders always try to make improvements or achieve success in what they're doing. Because of their initiative, they have a strong desire to promote change or solve problems. Leaders typically have more energy—they have to, given the long hours they put in and followers' expectations that they be positive and upbeat. Leaders are also more tenacious than nonleaders and are better at overcoming obstacles and problems that would deter most of us.

Successful leaders also have a stronger *desire to lead.* They want to be in charge and think about ways to influence or convince others about what should or shouldn't be done. *Honesty/integrity* is also important to leaders. *Honesty,* being truthful with others, is a cornerstone of leadership. Leaders won't be trusted if they are dishonest. When they are honest, subordinates are willing to overlook other flaws. *Integrity* is the extent to which leaders do what they say they will do. Leaders may be honest and have good intentions, but they also won't be trusted if they don't consistently deliver on what they promise.

Self-confidence, believing in one's abilities, also distinguishes leaders from nonleaders. Self-confident leaders are more decisive and assertive and are more

Trait theory a leadership theory that holds that effective leaders possess a similar set of traits or characteristics

Traits relatively stable characteristics, such as abilities, psychological motives, and consistent patterns of behavior

likely to gain others' confidence. Moreover, self-confident leaders will admit mistakes because they view them as learning opportunities rather than as refutation of their leadership capabilities. This also means that leaders have *emotional stability*. Even when things go wrong, they remain even-tempered and consistent in their outlook and in the way they treat others. Leaders who can't control their emotions, who anger quickly or attack and blame others for mistakes, are unlikely to be trusted.

Leaders are also smart. Leaders typically have strong *cognitive abilities*. This doesn't mean that leaders are necessarily geniuses—far from it. But it does mean that leaders have the capacity to analyze large amounts of seemingly unrelated, complex information and see patterns, opportunities, or threats where others might not see them. Finally, leaders also know their stuff, which means they have superior technical knowledge about the businesses they run. Leaders who have a good *knowledge of the business* understand the key technological decisions and concerns facing their companies. More often than not, studies indicate that effective leaders have long, extensive experience in their industries. Under the leadership of CEO Tim Solso, Cummins Inc., an engine and power-systems manufacturer based in Columbus, Indiana, has become a world leader in diesel-engine technology. Much of Solso's success can be attributed to the fact that he has almost four decades of experience with Cummins. In 1971, he got his first job with the firm, as assistant to the vice president of personnel. Over the next several years, he took on

Keep Your Job? Take Costs Out and Grow Revenue

In the first half of 2010, there were only 709 CEO changes in publicly traded U.S. companies. That amounts to roughly 4 exits per day, down from 6 per day in 2008. According to Gail Meneley, co-founder of an executive search firm, the drop in the CEO churn rate shows that corporate boards are much more likely to fire a CEO during good times and "stick with the devil they know" during tough times. It could also be that a CEO's poor performance is disguised by the general downturn in the economy. But companies are searching for replacements even if they aren't firing current leaders just yet. Meneley is doing an "unusually high number" of confidential CEO searches. She says, "It was easy to look quite capable if all you needed to do was to take costs out of a business. This is all now about growing revenue."

Source: T. Black, "HP, GM, CEO Exits Buck 'C-Suite Churn' Falling to Five-Year Low," *Bloomberg*, August 16, 2010, http://www.bloomberg.com/news/2010-08-16/hp-gm-ceo-exits-buck-c-suite-churn-at-five-year-low-as-boards-stand-pat.html.

" . . . **leaders** have the capacity to **analyze** large amounts of seemingly unrelated, complex **information** and see patterns, opportunities, or threats where others might not see them. "

positions such as director of development and training, executive director of personnel, and executive vice president of operations, before being appointed CEO in 2000.[12]

2.2 | LEADERSHIP BEHAVIORS

Thus far, you've read about who leaders *are*. It's hard to imagine a truly successful leader who lacks all of these qualities. But traits alone are not enough to make a successful leader. Leaders who have all these traits (or many of them) must then take actions that encourage people to achieve group or organizational goals.[13] So we will now examine what leaders *do,* meaning the behaviors they perform or the actions they take to influence others to achieve group or organizational goals.

Researchers at the University of Michigan, Ohio State University, and the University of Texas examined the specific behaviors that leaders use to improve the satisfaction and performance of their subordinates. Hundreds of studies were conducted and hundreds of leader behaviors were examined. At all three universities, two basic leader behaviors emerged as central to successful leadership: initiating structure (called *job-centered leadership* at the University of Michigan and *concern for production* at the University of Texas) and considerate leader behavior (called *employee-centered leadership* at the University of Michigan and *concern for people* at the University of Texas).[14] These two leader behaviors form the basis for many of the leadership theories discussed in this chapter.

Initiating structure is the degree to which a leader structures the roles of followers by setting goals, giving directions, setting deadlines, and assigning tasks. A leader's ability to initiate structure primarily affects subordinates' job performance. Next Media Animation is a Taiwanese media company that specializes in producing computer-animated depictions of current events. When CEO Jimmy Lai told his animation team that he wanted news clips produced in just two hours, most people told him they would need two weeks. However, his team spent several months finding ways to speed up the animation process, such as using stock digital faces and motion-capture technology, which allowed them to meet the two-hour goal.[15]

Consideration is the extent to which a leader is friendly, approachable, and supportive and shows concern for employees. Consideration primarily affects subordinates' job satisfaction. Specific leader consideration behaviors include listening to employees' problems and concerns, consulting with employees before making decisions, and treating employees as equals. When Gamal

Aziz became president of MGM Grand Hotel and Casino in Las Vegas, he set a goal of increasing revenue. But before he changed any programs, he first invited employees at all levels, not just managers, to share with him how the hotel could improve. One survey of employees showed that the staff was given little information about what was happening in the hotel each day. Some employees didn't even know if certain guests had special needs, or if there was a convention meeting in the hotel, making it difficult for them to do their jobs well. Aziz listened and then addressed employee concerns by requiring that each of the hotels' 10,000 employees begin their work shift by attending a brief meeting during which they learn which conferences are at the hotel and what special services are being offered to those guests.[16]

Although researchers at all three universities generally agreed that initiating structure and consideration were basic leader behaviors, their interpretations differed as to how these two behaviors are related to one another and which is necessary for effective leadership. The University of Michigan studies indicated that initiating structure and consideration were mutually exclusive behaviors on opposite ends of the same continuum. In other words, leaders who wanted to be more considerate would have to do less initiating of structure (and vice versa). The University of Michigan studies also indicated that only considerate leader behaviors (i.e., employee-centered behaviors) were associated with successful leadership. By contrast, researchers at Ohio State University and the University of Texas found that initiating structure and consideration were independent behaviors, meaning that leaders can be considerate and initiate structure at the same time. Additional evidence confirms this finding.[17] The same researchers also concluded that the most effective leaders excelled at both initiating structure and considerate leader behaviors.

This "high-high" approach can be seen in the upper-right corner of the Blake/Mouton leadership grid, shown in Exhibit 14.1 on the next page. Blake and Mouton used two leadership behaviors—concern for people (i.e., consideration) and concern for production (i.e., initiating structure)—to categorize five different leadership styles. Both behaviors are rated on a 9-point scale, with 1 representing "low" and 9 representing "high." Blake and Mouton suggest that a "high-high" or 9,9 leadership style is the best. They call this style *team management*

Initiating structure the degree to which a leader structures the roles of followers by setting goals, giving directions, setting deadlines, and assigning tasks

Consideration the extent to which a leader is friendly, approachable, and supportive and shows concern for employees

Leadership style
the way a leader generally
behaves toward followers

because leaders who use it display a high concern for people (9) and a high concern for production (9).

By contrast, leaders use a 9,1 *authority-compliance* leadership style when they have a high concern for production and a low concern for people. A 1,9 *country club* style occurs when leaders care about having a friendly, enjoyable work environment but don't really pay much attention to production or performance. The worst leadership style, according to the grid, is the 1,1 *impoverished* leader, who shows little concern for people or production and does the bare minimum needed to keep his or her job. Finally, the 5,5 *middle-of-the-road* style occurs when leaders show a moderate amount of concern for both people and production.

Is the team management style, with a high concern for production and a high concern for people, really the best leadership style? Logically, it would seem so. Why wouldn't you want to show high concern for both people and production? Nonetheless, nearly 50 years of research indicates that there isn't one best leadership style. The best leadership style depends on the situation. In other words, no one leadership behavior by itself and no one combination of leadership behaviors works well across all situations and types of employees.

Situational Approaches to Leadership

after leader traits and behaviors, the situational approach to leadership is the third major method used in the study of leadership. We'll review three major situational approaches to leadership—Fiedler's contingency theory, path-goal theory, and Vroom and Yetton's normative decision model. All assume that the effectiveness of any **leadership style,**

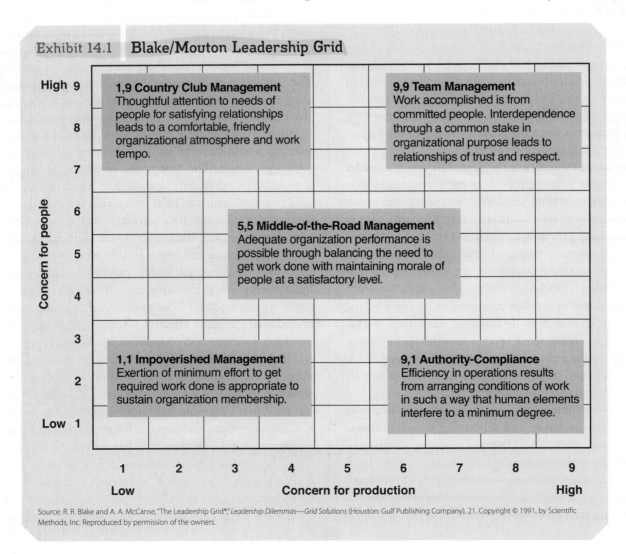

Exhibit 14.1 Blake/Mouton Leadership Grid

High 9

1,9 Country Club Management
Thoughtful attention to needs of people for satisfying relationships leads to a comfortable, friendly organizational atmosphere and work tempo.

9,9 Team Management
Work accomplished is from committed people. Interdependence through a common stake in organizational purpose leads to relationships of trust and respect.

5,5 Middle-of-the-Road Management
Adequate organization performance is possible through balancing the need to get work done with maintaining morale of people at a satisfactory level.

1,1 Impoverished Management
Exertion of minimum effort to get required work done is appropriate to sustain organization membership.

9,1 Authority-Compliance
Efficiency in operations results from arranging conditions of work in such a way that human elements interfere to a minimum degree.

Concern for people (vertical axis, 1 Low to 9 High)

Concern for production (horizontal axis, 1 Low to 9 High)

Source: R. R. Blake and A. A. McCanse, "The Leadership Grid®," *Leadership Dilemmas—Grid Solutions* (Houston: Gulf Publishing Company), 21. Copyright © 1991, by Scientific Methods, Inc. Reproduced by permission of the owners.

the way a leader generally behaves toward followers, depends on the situation.[18]

According to situational leadership theories, there is no one best leadership style. But one of these situational theories differs from the other three in one significant way. Fiedler's contingency theory assumes that leadership styles are consistent and difficult to change. Therefore, leaders must be placed in or "matched" to situations that fit their leadership styles. By contrast, the other situational theories assume that leaders are capable of adapting and adjusting their leadership styles to fit the demands of different situations.

After reading the next three sections, you should be able to

3 **explain Fiedler's contingency theory.**

4 **describe how path-goal theory works.**

5 **explain the normative decision theory.**

3 Putting Leaders in the Right Situations: Fiedler's Contingency Theory

Fiedler's **contingency theory** states that in order to maximize work group performance, leaders must be matched to the right leadership situations.[19] More specifically, the first basic assumption of Fiedler's theory is that leaders are effective when the work groups they lead perform well. So, instead of judging leaders' effectiveness by what they do (i.e., initiating structure and consideration) or who they are (i.e., trait theory), Fiedler assesses leaders by the conduct and performance of the people they supervise. Second, Fiedler assumes that leaders are generally unable to change their leadership styles and that they will be more

effective when their styles are matched to the proper situations. Third, Fiedler assumes that the favorableness of a situation for a leader depends on the degree to which the situation permits the leader to influence the behavior of group members. Fiedler's third assumption is consistent with our definition of leadership as the process of influencing others to achieve group or organizational goals. In other words, in addition to traits, behaviors, and a favorable situation to match, leaders have to be allowed to lead.

Let's learn more about Fiedler's contingency theory by examining **3.1 the least preferred coworker and leadership style,** *3.2 situational favorableness, and* **3.3 how to match leadership styles to situations.**

3.1 | LEADERSHIP STYLE: LEAST PREFERRED COWORKER

When Fiedler refers to *leadership style*, he means the way that leaders generally behave toward their followers. Do the leaders yell and scream and blame others when things go wrong? Or do they correct mistakes by listening and then quietly but directly making their point? Do they let others make their own decisions and hold them accountable for the results? Or do they micromanage, insisting that all decisions be approved first by them? Fiedler also assumes that leadership styles are tied to leaders' underlying needs and personalities. Since personality and needs are relatively stable, he assumes that leaders are generally incapable of changing their leadership styles. In other words, the way that leaders treat people now is probably the way they've always treated others.

> **Contingency theory** a leadership theory that states that in order to maximize work group performance, leaders must be matched to the situations that best fit their leadership styles

How LPC is described	Leadership style
positively	relationship
negatively	task
moderately	flexible

Fiedler uses a questionnaire called the Least Preferred Co-worker (LPC) scale to measure leadership style. When completing the LPC scale, people are instructed to consider all of the people with whom they have ever worked and then to choose the one person with whom they have worked *least* well. Fiedler explains, "This does not have to be the person you liked least well, but should be the one person with whom you have the most trouble getting the job done."[20] How you describe this person is a clue to your own preferred leadership style.

Would you describe your LPC as pleasant, friendly, supportive, interesting, cheerful, and sincere? Or would you describe the person as unpleasant, unfriendly, hostile, boring, gloomy, and insincere? People who describe their LPC in a positive way (scoring 64 and higher on the full inventory of 18 oppositional pairs) have *relationship-oriented* leadership styles. After all, if they can still be positive about their least preferred coworker, they must be people-oriented. By contrast, people who describe their LPC in a negative way (scoring 57 or lower) have *task-oriented* leadership styles. Given a choice, they'll focus first on getting the job done and second on making sure everyone gets along. Finally, those with moderate scores (from 58 to 63) have a more flexible leadership style and can be somewhat relationship-oriented or somewhat task-oriented.

3.2 | SITUATIONAL FAVORABLENESS

Fiedler assumes that leaders will be more effective when their leadership styles are matched to the proper situations. More specifically, Fiedler defines **situational favorableness** as the degree to which a particular situation either permits or denies a leader the chance to influence the behavior of group members.[21] In highly favorable situations, leaders find that their actions influence followers. But in highly unfavorable situations, leaders have little or no success influencing the people they are trying to lead.

Three situational factors determine the favorability of a situation: leader-member relations, task structure, and position power. The most important situational factor is **leader-member relations**, which refers to how well followers respect, trust, and like their leaders. When leader-member relations are good, followers trust the leader and there is a friendly work atmosphere. **Task structure** is the degree to which the requirements of a subordinate's tasks are clearly specified. With highly structured tasks, employees have clear job responsibilities, goals, and procedures. **Position power** is the degree to which leaders are able to hire, fire, reward, and punish workers. The more influence leaders have over hiring, firing, rewards, and punishments, the greater their power.

Exhibit 14.2 shows how leader-member relations, task structure, and position power can be combined into eight situations that differ in their favorability to leaders. In general, Situation I, on the left side of Exhibit 14.2, is the most favorable leader situation. Followers like and trust their leaders and know what to do because their tasks are highly structured. Also, the leaders have the formal power to influence workers through hiring, firing, rewarding, and punishing them. Therefore, in Situation I, it's relatively easy for a leader to influence followers. By contrast, Situation VIII, on the right side of Exhibit 14.2, is the least favorable situation for leaders. Followers don't like or trust their leaders. Plus, followers are not sure what they're supposed to be doing because their tasks or jobs are highly unstructured. Finally, leaders find it difficult to influ-

Exhibit 14.2 Situational Favorableness

Leader-Member Relations	Good	Good	Good	Good	Poor	Poor	Poor	Poor
Task Structure	High	High	Low	Low	High	High	Low	Low
Position Power	Strong	Weak	Strong	Weak	Strong	Weak	Strong	Weak
Situation	I	II	III	IV	V	VI	VII	VIII
	Favorable			Moderately Favorable			Unfavorable	

© Cengage Learning 2011

ence followers without the ability to hire, fire, reward, or punish the people who work for them. In short, it's very difficult to influence followers given the conditions found in Situation VIII.

3.3 | MATCHING LEADERSHIP STYLES TO SITUATIONS

After studying thousands of leaders and followers in hundreds of different situations, Fiedler found that the performance of relationship- and task-oriented leaders followed the pattern displayed in Exhibit 14.3.

Relationship-oriented leaders (those with high LPC scores) were better leaders (i.e., their groups performed more effectively) under moderately favorable situations. In moderately favorable situations, the leader may be liked somewhat, tasks may be somewhat structured, and the leader may have some position power. In this situation, a relationship-oriented leader improves leader-member relations, which is the most important of the three situational factors. In turn, morale and performance improve.

By contrast, as Exhibit 14.3 shows, task-oriented leaders, with low LPC scores, are better leaders in highly favorable and unfavorable situations. Task-oriented leaders do well in favorable situations where leaders are liked, tasks are structured, and the leader has the power to hire, fire, reward, and punish. In these favorable situations, task-oriented leaders effectively step on the gas of a well-tuned car. Their focus on performance sets the goal for the group, which then charges forward to meet it. But task-oriented leaders also do well in unfavorable situations in which leaders are disliked, tasks are unstructured, and the leader doesn't have the power to hire, fire, reward, or punish. In these unfavorable situations, the task-oriented leader sets goals that focus attention on performance and clarify what needs to be done, thus overcoming low task structure. This is enough to jump-start performance even if workers don't like or trust the leader.

Finally, though not shown in Exhibit 14.3, people with moderate LPC scores (who can be somewhat relationship-oriented or somewhat task-oriented) tend to do fairly well in all situations because they can adapt their behavior. Typically, though, they don't perform quite as well as relationship-oriented or task-oriented leaders whose leadership styles are well matched to the situations.

Recall, however, that Fiedler assumes leaders to be incapable of changing their leadership styles. Accordingly, the key to applying Fiedler's contingency theory in the workplace is to accurately measure and match leaders to situations *or* to teach leaders how to change situational favorableness by changing leader-member relations, task structure, or position power. Though matching or placing leaders in appropriate situations works particularly well, practicing managers have had little luck reengineering situations to fit their leadership styles. The primary problem, as you've no doubt realized, is the complexity of the theory. In a study designed to teach leaders how to reengineer their situations to fit their leadership styles, Fiedler found that most of the leaders simply did not understand what they were supposed to do to change their situations. Furthermore, if they didn't like their LPC profiles (perhaps they felt they were more relationship-oriented than their scores indicated), they arbitrarily changed them to better suit their views of themselves. Of course, the theory won't work as well if leaders are attempting to change situational factors to fit their perceived leadership styles rather than their real leadership styles.[22]

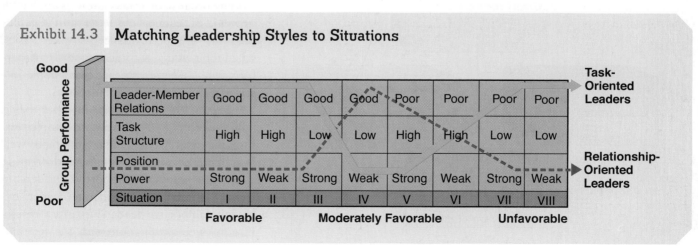

Exhibit 14.3 Matching Leadership Styles to Situations

Leader-Member Relations	Good	Good	Good	Good	Poor	Poor	Poor	Poor	Task-Oriented Leaders
Task Structure	High	High	Low	Low	High	High	Low	Low	
Position Power	Strong	Weak	Strong	Weak	Strong	Weak	Strong	Weak	Relationship-Oriented Leaders
Situation	I	II	III	IV	V	VI	VII	VIII	

Favorable | Moderately Favorable | Unfavorable

(Group Performance: Good to Poor)

4 Adapting Leader Behavior: Path-Goal Theory

Just as its name suggests, **path-goal theory** states that leaders can increase subordinate satisfaction and performance by clarifying and clearing the paths to goals and by increasing the number and kinds of rewards available for goal attainment. Said another way, leaders need to clarify how followers can achieve organizational goals, take care of problems that prevent followers from achieving goals, and then find more and varied rewards to motivate followers to achieve those goals.[23]

Leaders must meet two conditions if path clarification, path clearing, and rewards are to increase followers' motivation and effort. First, leader behavior must be a source of immediate or future satisfaction for followers. The things you do as a leader must please your followers today or lead to activities or rewards that will satisfy them in the future. One of the biggest challenges facing managers today is how to institute cost-saving measures, such as pay cuts, while still motivating employees to do their best. When Matt

Ferguson, CEO of CareerBuilder.com, decided to cut employee pay, he wanted to make sure that every employee heard the news directly from him. So he scheduled a conference call with every single branch office to announce the pay cuts. During the calls, he promised that pay cuts would allow employees to keep their jobs and the company to avoid layoffs. And, to make up for less money, he gave employees Friday afternoons off. As an account manager at CareerBuilder.com says, "I don't think anyone is ever happy about a pay cut. But giving us time off was giving us something back."[24]

Second, while providing the coaching, guidance, support, and rewards necessary for effective work performance, leaders must complement and not duplicate the characteristics of followers' work environments. Thus, leader behaviors must offer something unique and valuable to followers beyond what they're already experiencing as they do their jobs or what they can already do for themselves.

In contrast to Fiedler's contingency theory, path-goal theory assumes that leaders *can* change and adapt their leadership styles. Exhibit 14.4 illustrates this process, showing that leaders change and adapt their leadership styles contingent on their subordinates or the environments in which those subordinates work.

Let's learn more about path-goal theory by examining **4.1 the four kinds of leadership styles that leaders use, 4.2 the subordinate and environmental contingencies that determine when different leader styles are effective, and 4.3 the outcomes of path-goal theory in improving employee satisfaction and performance.**

4.1 | LEADERSHIP STYLES

As illustrated in Exhibit 14.4, the four leadership styles in path-goal theory are directive, supportive, participative, and achievement-oriented.[25] **Directive leadership** involves letting employees know precisely what is expected of them, giving them specific guidelines for the performance of their tasks, scheduling work, setting standards of performance, and making sure that people follow standard rules and regulations.

Supportive leadership involves being approachable and friendly to employees, showing concern for them and their welfare, treating them as equals, and creating a friendly climate. Supportive leadership is very similar to considerate leader behavior. Supportive leadership often results in employee satisfaction with the job and

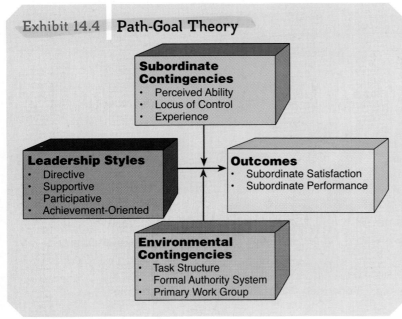

Exhibit 14.4 **Path-Goal Theory**

Subordinate Contingencies
- Perceived Ability
- Locus of Control
- Experience

Leadership Styles
- Directive
- Supportive
- Participative
- Achievement-Oriented

Outcomes
- Subordinate Satisfaction
- Subordinate Performance

Environmental Contingencies
- Task Structure
- Formal Authority System
- Primary Work Group

© Cengage Learning 2011

with leaders. This leadership style may also result in improved performance when it increases employee confidence, lowers employee job stress, or improves relations and trust between employees and leaders.[26] When gas prices surged to over $4 a gallon, commuting costs took a toll on employee budgets and bank accounts. A survey at the time found that one-third of employees would quit to take comparable jobs closer to home. Atlanta-based Lathem Time Corp. responded by changing from a 5-day workweek to a compressed 4-day workweek with 10-hour days. The change saved employees a tank of gas a month (worth $60 to $100 at the time) and greatly reduced commutes (leaving work at 6:30 p.m. reduced 90-minute commutes to 30 minutes). Lathem Time Corp. employee Jason Dupree said, "It's definitely improved my work. My stress level is down. Getting that break in the middle of the week is like a mini-weekend for me."[27]

Participative leadership involves consulting employees for their suggestions and input before making decisions. Participation in decision making should help followers understand which goals are most important and clarify the paths to accomplishing them. Furthermore, when people participate in decisions, they become more committed to making them work. Thomas Walter, the CEO of Tasty Catering in Elk Grove, Illinois, wanted to involve his employees in key company decisions. So he started two councils, one operating in English and the other in Spanish, that would make all of the strategic choices for the company. Each council is made up of eight employees representing the entire workforce—cooks, accountants, office staff, and drivers—and to make sure that every employee has a chance to participate, two employees are picked at random to join the councils for one-month terms. When the owners of the company wanted to provide health care coverage, the councils decided to opt for a less costly package, since most employees already had coverage through spouses. Anna Wollin, an account executive, says the councils "[put] us all on an even playing field. I have been with the company for less than a year, and my opinion was as important as an owner's opinion."[28]

Achievement-oriented leadership means setting challenging goals, having high expectations of employees, and displaying confidence that employees will assume responsibility and put forth extraordinary effort. Simon Cooper, president and COO of the Ritz-Carlton luxury hotel chain, uses the expression "He who says it, does" to describe achievement-oriented leadership. Cooper explains that he says this "whenever some-

one convinces me that they can achieve something I consider to be unachievable."[29]

Whatever leadership style you adopt, the ability to persuade and influence others is key to your success. As business becomes more global, and as the way people work changes, organizational structures are becoming flatter, or less hierarchical. This means that leaders must cross traditional boundaries and work with both peers and subordinates in other divisions or even in other companies. Motivation is thus becoming far more important than direction. Whether you're a directive, supportive, participative, or achievement-oriented leader, your ability to bring others on board with your vision and plan is vital to good leadership.[30]

4.2 | SUBORDINATE AND ENVIRONMENTAL CONTINGENCIES

As we saw in Exhibit 14.4, path-goal theory specifies that leader behaviors should be adapted to subordinate characteristics. The theory identifies three kinds of subordinate contingencies: perceived ability,

MGMT SUCCESS

How to Apply Path-Goal Theory

- Clarify paths to goals.
- Clear paths to goals by solving problems and removing roadblocks.
- Increase the number and kinds of rewards available for goal attainment.
- Do things that satisfy followers today or will lead to future rewards or satisfaction.
- Offer followers something unique and valuable beyond what they're experiencing or can already do for themselves.

Source: R. J. House and T. R. Mitchell, "Path-Goal Theory of Leadership," *Journal of Contemporary Business* 3 (1974): 81–97.

experience, and locus of control. *Perceived ability* is simply how much ability subordinates believe they have for doing their jobs well. Subordinates who perceive that they have a great deal of ability will be dissatisfied with directive leader behaviors. Experienced employees are likely to react in a similar way. Since they already know how to do their jobs (or perceive that they do), they don't need or want close supervision. By contrast, subordinates with little experience or little perceived ability will welcome directive leadership.

Locus of control is a personality measure that indicates the extent to which people believe that they have control over what happens to them in life. *Internals* believe that what happens to them, good or bad, is largely a result of their choices and actions. *Externals,* on the other hand, believe that what happens to them is caused by external forces beyond their control. Accordingly, externals are much more comfortable with a directive leadership style, whereas internals greatly prefer a participative leadership style because they like to have a say in what goes on at work.

Path-goal theory specifies that leader behaviors should complement rather than duplicate the characteristics of followers' work environments. In other words, a leader should use a leadership style that best responds to the characteristics of the environment as well as the characteristics of the people involved. There are three kinds of environmental contingencies: task structure, the formal authority system, and the primary work group. As in Fiedler's contingency theory, *task structure* is the degree to which the requirements of a subordinate's tasks are clearly specified. When task structure is low and tasks are unclear, directive leadership should be used because it complements the work environment. When task structure is high and tasks are clear, however, directive leadership is not needed because it duplicates what task structure provides. Alternatively, when tasks are stressful, frustrating, or dissatisfying, leaders should respond with supportive leadership.

The *formal authority system* is an organization's set of procedures, rules, and policies. When the formal authority system is unclear, directive leadership complements the situation by reducing uncertainty and increasing clarity. But when the formal authority system is clear, directive leadership is redundant and should not be used.

Primary work group refers to the amount of work-oriented participation or emotional support that is provided by an employee's immediate work group. Participative leadership should be used when tasks are complex and there is little existing work-oriented participation in the primary work group. When tasks are stressful, frustrating, or repetitive, supportive leadership is called for.

Finally, since keeping track of all of these subordinate and environmental contingencies can get a bit confusing, Exhibit 14.5 provides a summary of when directive, supportive, participative, and achievement-oriented leadership styles should be used. Above all, using path-goal theory means that a leader must be attuned and responsive to the sometimes changing complexities of his or her environment.

Exhibit 14.5	**Path-Goal Theory: When to Use Directive, Supportive, Participative, or Achievement-Oriented Leadership**		
DIRECTIVE LEADERSHIP	**SUPPORTIVE LEADERSHIP**	**PARTICIPATIVE LEADERSHIP**	**ACHIEVEMENT-ORIENTED LEADERSHIP**
Unstructured tasks	Structured, simple, repetitive tasks; Stressful, frustrating tasks	Complex tasks	Unchallenging tasks
Workers with external locus of control	Workers lack confidence	Workers with internal locus of control	
Unclear formal authority system	Clear formal authority system	Workers not satisfied with rewards	
Inexperienced workers		Experienced workers	
Workers with low perceived ability		Workers with high perceived ability	

© Cengage Learning 2011

4.3 | OUTCOMES

Does following path-goal theory improve subordinate satisfaction and performance? Preliminary evidence suggests that it does.[31] In particular, people who work for supportive leaders are much more satisfied with their jobs and their bosses. Likewise, people who work for directive leaders are more satisfied with their jobs and bosses (but not quite as much as when their bosses are supportive) and perform their jobs better, too. Does adapting one's leadership style to subordinate and environmental characteristics improve subordinate satisfaction and performance? At this point, because it is difficult to completely test this complex theory, it's too early to tell.[32] However, since the data clearly show that it makes sense for leaders to be both supportive *and* directive, it also makes sense that leaders could improve subordinate satisfaction and performance by adding participative and achievement-oriented leadership styles to their capabilities as leaders.

5 Adapting Leader Behavior: Normative Decision Theory

Many people believe that making tough decisions is at the heart of leadership. Yet experienced leaders will tell you that deciding *how* to make decisions is just as important. The **normative decision theory** (also known as the *Vroom-Yetton-Jago model*) helps leaders decide how much employee participation (from none to letting employees make the entire decision) should be used when making decisions.[33]

*Let's learn more about normative decision theory by investigating **5.1 decision styles** and **5.2 decision quality and acceptance**.*

5.1 | DECISION STYLES

Unlike nearly all of the other leadership theories discussed in this chapter, which have specified *leadership* styles, the normative decision theory specifies five different *decision* styles, or ways of making decisions. (Refer back to Chapter 5 for a more complete review of decision making in organizations.) As shown in Exhibit 14.6 on the next page, those styles vary from *autocratic decisions* (AI or AII) on the left, in which leaders make the decisions by themselves, to *consultative decisions* (CI or CII), in which leaders share problems with subordinates but still make the decisions themselves, to *group decisions* (GII) on the right, in which leaders share the problems with subordinates and then have the group make the decisions. GE Aviation in Durham, North Carolina, uses the normative approach to decision making. According to *Fast Company* magazine, "At GE/ Durham, every decision is either an 'A' decision, a 'B' decision, or a 'C' decision. An 'A' decision is one that the plant manager makes herself, without consulting anyone."[34] Plant manager Paula Sims says, "I don't make very many of those, and when I do make one, everyone at the plant knows it. I make maybe 10 or 12 a year."[35] "B" decisions are also made by the plant manager, but with input from the people affected. "C" decisions, the most common type, are made by consensus, by the people directly involved, with plenty of discussion. With "C" decisions, the view of the plant manager doesn't necessarily carry more weight than the views of those affected.[36]

> **Normative decision theory** a theory that suggests how a leader can determine an appropriate amount of employee participation when making decisions

5.2 | DECISION QUALITY AND ACCEPTANCE

According to the normative decision theory, using the right degree of employee participation improves the quality of decisions and the extent to which employees accept and are committed to decisions. Exhibit 14.7 on page 275 lists the decision rules that normative decision theory uses to increase the quality of a decision and the degree to which employees accept and commit to a decision.

The quality, leader information, subordinate information, goal congruence, and problem structure rules are used to increase decision quality. For example, the leader information rule states that if a leader doesn't have enough information to make a decision on his or her own, then the leader should not use an autocratic decision style. The commitment probability, subordinate conflict, and commitment requirement rules shown in Exhibit 14.7 are used to increase employee

© iStockphoto.com/Jacob Hellbach

Exhibit 14.6

Normative Theory, Decision Styles, and Levels of Employee Participation

Leader solves the problem or makes the decision

Leader is willing to accept any decision supported by the entire group

AI	AII	CI	CII	GII
Using information available at the time, the leader solves the problem or makes the decision.	The leader obtains necessary information from employees and then selects a solution to the problem. When asked to share information, employees may or may not be told what the problem is.	The leader shares the problem and gets ideas and suggestions from relevant employees on an individual basis. Individuals are not brought together as a group. Then the leader makes the decision, which may or may not reflect their input.	The leader shares the problem with employees as a group, obtains their ideas and suggestions, and then makes the decision, which may or may not reflect their input.	The leader shares the problem with employees as a group. Together, the leader and employees generate and evaluate alternatives and try to reach an agreement on a solution. The leader acts as a facilitator and does not try to influence the group. The leader is willing to accept and implement any solution that has the support of the entire group.

Source: Table 2.1 Decision Methods for Group and Individual Problems from *Leadership and Decision-Making*, by Victor H. Vroom and Philip W. Yetton, © 1973. Reprinted by permission of the University of Pittsburgh Press.

acceptance and commitment to decisions. For example, the commitment requirement rule says that if decision acceptance and commitment are important and the subordinates share the organization's goals, then you shouldn't use an autocratic or consultative style. In other words, if followers want to do what's best for the company and you need their acceptance and commitment to make a decision work, then use a group decision style and let them make the decision. As you can see, these decision rules help leaders improve decision quality and follower acceptance and commitment by eliminating decision styles that don't fit the particular decision or situation they're facing. Normative decision theory, like path-goal theory, is situational in nature.

The abstract decision rules in Exhibit 14.7 are framed as yes/no questions, which makes the process of applying these rules more concrete. These questions are shown in the decision tree displayed in Exhibit 14.8 on page 276. You start at the left side of the tree and answer the first question, "How important is the technical quality of this decision?" by choosing "high" or "low." Then you continue by answering each question as you

proceed along the decision tree until you get to a recommended decision style.

Let's use the model to make the decision of whether to change from a formal business attire policy to a casual wear policy. The problem sounds simple, but it is actually more complex than you might think. Follow the yellow line in Exhibit 14.8 as we work through the decision in the discussion below.

Problem: Change to Casual Wear?

1. *Quality requirement: How important is the technical quality of this decision?* High. This question has to do with whether there are quality differences in the alternatives and whether those quality differences matter. In other words: Is there a lot at stake in this decision? Although most people would assume that quality isn't an issue here, it really is, given the overall positive changes that generally accompany changes to a casual wear policy.

2. *Commitment requirement: How important is subordinate commitment to the decision?* High.

Exhibit 14.7   Normative Theory Decision Rules

DECISION RULES TO INCREASE DECISION QUALITY

Quality Rule. If the quality of the decision is important, then don't use an autocratic decision style.

Leader Information Rule. If the quality of the decision is important, and if the leader doesn't have enough information to make the decision on his or her own, then don't use an autocratic decision style.

Subordinate Information Rule. If the quality of the decision is important, and if the subordinates don't have enough information to make the decision themselves, then don't use a group decision style.

Goal Congruence Rule. If the quality of the decision is important, and subordinates' goals are different from the organization's goals, then don't use a group decision style.

Problem Structure Rule. If the quality of the decision is important, the leader doesn't have enough information to make the decision on his or her own, and the problem is unstructured, then don't use an autocratic decision style.

DECISION RULES TO INCREASE DECISION ACCEPTANCE

Commitment Probability Rule. If having subordinates accept and commit to the decision is important, then don't use an autocratic decision style.

Subordinate Conflict Rule. If having subordinates accept the decision is important and critical to successful implementation and subordinates are likely to disagree or end up in conflict over the decision, then don't use an autocratic or consultative decision style.

Commitment Requirement Rule. If having subordinates accept the decision is absolutely required for successful implementation and subordinates share the organization's goals, then don't use an autocratic or consultative style.

Sources: Adapted from V. H. Vroom, "Leadership," in *Handbook of Industrial and Organizational Psychology*, ed. M. D. Dunnette (Chicago: Rand McNally, 1976); V. H. Vroom and A. G. Jago, *The New Leadership: Managing Participation in Organizations* (Englewood Cliffs, NJ: Prentice Hall, 1988).

Changes in culture, such as modifying the dress code, require subordinate commitment or they fail.

3. *Leader's information: Do you have sufficient information to make a high-quality decision?* Yes. Let's assume that you've done your homework. Much has been written about casual wear, from how to make the change to the effects it has in companies (almost all positive).

4. *Commitment probability: If you were to make the decision by yourself, are you reasonably certain that your subordinate(s) would be committed to the decision?* No. Studies of casual wear find that employees' reactions are almost uniformly positive. Nonetheless, employees are likely to be angry if you change something as personal as clothing policies without consulting them.

5. *Goal congruence: Do subordinates share the organizational goals to be attained in solving this problem?* Yes. The goals that usually accompany a change to casual dress policies are a more informal culture, better communication, and less money spent on business attire.

6. *Subordinate information: Do subordinates have sufficient information to make a high-quality decision?* No. Most employees know little about casual wear policies or even what constitutes casual wear in most companies. Consequently, most companies have to educate employees about casual wear practices and policies before making a decision.

7. *CII is the answer:* With a CII, or consultative decision process, the leader shares the problem with employees as a group, obtains their ideas and suggestions, and then makes the decision, which may or may not reflect their input. So, given the answers to these questions (remember, different managers won't necessarily answer these questions the same way), the normative decision theory recommends that leaders consult with their subordinates before deciding whether to change to a casual wear policy.

How well does the normative decision theory work? A prominent leadership scholar has described it as the best supported of all leadership theories.[37] In general, the more managers violate the decision rules in Exhibit 14.7, the less effective their decisions are, especially with respect to subordinate acceptance and commitment.[38]

Exhibit 14.8 **Normative Decision Theory Tree for Determining the Level of Participation in Decision Making**

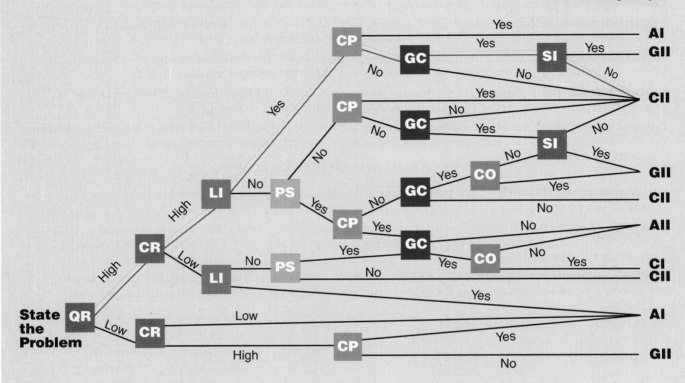

Problem Attributes

QR	Quality requirement:	How important is the technical quality of this decision?
CR	Commitment requirement:	How important is subordinate commitment to the decision?
LI	Leader's information:	Do you have sufficient information to make a high-quality decision?
PS	Problem structure:	Is the problem well structured?
CP	Commitment probability:	If you were to make the decision by yourself, are you reasonably certain that your subordinate(s) would be committed to the decision?
GC	Goal congruence:	Do subordinates share the organizational goals to be attained in solving this problem?
CO	Subordinate conflict:	Is conflict among subordinates over preferred solutions likely?
SI	Subordinate information:	Do subordinates have sufficient information to make a high-quality decision?

Figure 9.3 Decision-Process Flow Chart for Both Individual and Group Problems from *Leadership and Decision-Making*, by Victor H. Vroom and Philip W. Yetton, © 1973. Reprinted by permission of the University of Pittsburgh Press.

Strategic Leadership

Strategic leadership is the ability to anticipate, envision, maintain flexibility, think strategically, and work with others to initiate changes that will create a positive future for an organization.[39] Thus, strategic leadership captures how leaders inspire their companies to change and their followers to give extraordinary effort to accomplish organizational goals.

After reading the next section, you should be able to

6 explain how visionary leadership (i.e., charismatic or transformational leadership) helps leaders achieve strategic leadership.

6 Visionary Leadership

In Chapter 5, we defined a purpose statement, which is often referred to as an organizational mission or vision, as a statement of a company's purpose or reason for existing. Similarly, **visionary leadership** creates a positive image of the future that motivates organizational members and provides direction for future planning and goal setting.[40]

Two kinds of visionary leadership are 6.1 charismatic leadership and 6.2 transformational leadership.

6.1 | CHARISMATIC LEADERSHIP

Charisma is a Greek word meaning "divine gift." The ancient Greeks saw people with charisma as inspired by the gods and capable of incredible accomplishments. German sociologist Max Weber viewed charisma as a special bond between leaders and followers.[41] Weber wrote that the special qualities of charismatic leaders enable them to strongly influence followers. Jose Mourinho, coach of the Spanish soccer team Real Madrid, certainly qualifies as a charismatic leader. He has developed such a deep bond with his players that one of them was even quoted as saying that he would play for Mourinho on a broken leg. How was he able to form such ties? Former players and fellow coaches praise him for being confident, enthusiastic, and meticulous in his attention to detail. Above all, however, he shows his players that he cares for them. In a field where coaches often criticize their players for mistakes, Mourinho encourages them with personalized notes, emails, and text messages. He even does outrageous things to take pressure off of his players. Once, while preparing for a game against an archrival, Mourinho walked out on the pitch (i.e., the field) by himself. "I knew that I would get a thunderous reception in the negative sense, so I decided to go on the pitch alone before the team. There were 80,000 booing me but in off-loading that against me, they spared the team."[42] Weber also noted that charismatic leaders tend to emerge in times of crisis and that the radical solutions they propose enhance the admiration that followers feel for them. Indeed, charismatic leaders tend to have incredible influence over followers who may be inspired by their leaders and become fanatically devoted to them. From this perspective, charismatic leaders are often seen as larger than life or more special than other employees of the company.

Charismatic leaders have strong, confident, dynamic personalities that attract followers and enable the leaders to create strong bonds with their followers.

Strategic leadership the ability to anticipate, envision, maintain flexibility, think strategically, and work with others to initiate changes that will create a positive future for an organization

Visionary leadership leadership that creates a positive image of the future that motivates organizational members and provides direction for future planning and goal setting

A charismatic leader, Jose Mourinho, coach of the Spanish soccer team Real Madrid, is described by former players and fellow coaches as confident, enthusiastic, and caring. His personality and behavior enable Mourinho to attract and create strong bonds with his followers.

AP Images/Francois Mori

Charismatic leadership the behavioral tendencies and personal characteristics of leaders that create exceptionally strong relationships between them and their followers

Ethical charismatics charismatic leaders who provide developmental opportunities for followers, are open to positive and negative feedback, recognize others' contributions, share information, and have moral standards that emphasize the larger interests of the group, organization, or society

Unethical charismatics charismatic leaders who control and manipulate followers, do what is best for themselves instead of their organizations, want to hear only positive feedback, share only information that is beneficial to themselves, and have moral standards that put their interests before everyone else's

Followers trust charismatic leaders, are loyal to them, and are inspired to work toward the accomplishment of the leader's vision. Followers who become devoted to charismatic leaders may go to extraordinary lengths to please them. Therefore, we can define **charismatic leadership** as the behavioral tendencies and personal characteristics of leaders that create exceptionally strong relationships between them and their followers. Charismatic leaders also

- articulate clear visions for the future that are based on strongly held values or morals;
- model those values by acting in ways consistent with their visions;
- communicate high performance expectations to followers;
- display confidence in followers' abilities to achieve the visions.[43]

Does charismatic leadership work? Studies indicate that it often does. In general, the followers of charismatic leaders are more committed and satisfied, are better performers, are more likely to trust their leaders, and simply work harder.[44] Nonetheless, charismatic leadership also has risks that are at least as large as its benefits. The problems are likely to occur with ego-driven charismatic leaders who take advantage of fanatical followers.

In general, there are two kinds of charismatic leaders: ethical charismatics and unethical charismatics.[45] **Ethical charismatics** provide developmental opportunities for followers, are open to positive and negative feedback, recognize others' contributions, share information, and have moral standards that emphasize the larger interests of the group, organization, or society. By contrast, **unethical charismatics** control and manipulate followers, do what

is best for themselves instead of their organizations, want to hear only positive feedback, share only information that is beneficial to themselves, and have moral standards that put their interests before everyone else's. Because followers can become just as committed to unethical as to ethical charismatics, unethical charismatics pose a tremendous risk for companies.

Exhibit 14.9 shows the stark differences between ethical and unethical charismatics on several leader behaviors: exercising power, creating the vision, communicating with followers, accepting feedback, stimulating followers intellectually, developing followers, and living by moral standards. For example, ethical charismatics include followers' concerns and wishes when creating a vision by having them participate in the development of the company vision. By contrast, unethical charismatics develop a vision by themselves solely to meet their personal agendas. One unethical charismatic said, "The key thing is that it is my idea; and I am going to win with it at all costs."[46]

6.2 | TRANSFORMATIONAL LEADERSHIP

Whereas charismatic leadership involves articulating a clear vision, modeling values consistent with that vision, communicating high performance expectations, and

How to Reduce the Risks Associated with Unethical Charismatics

1. Have a clearly written code of conduct that is fairly and consistently enforced for all managers.
2. Recruit, select, and promote managers with high ethical standards.
3. Train leaders to value, seek, and use diverse points of view.
4. Train leaders and subordinates regarding ethical leader behaviors so that abuses can be recognized and corrected.
5. Reward people who exhibit ethical behaviors, especially ethical leader behaviors.

Sources: J. M. Burns, *Leadership* (New York: Harper & Row, 1978); B. M. Bass, "From Transactional to Transformational Leadership: Learning to Share the Vision," *Organizational Dynamics* 18 (1990): 19–36.

Exhibit 14.9 Ethical and Unethical Charismatics

CHARISMATIC LEADER BEHAVIORS	ETHICAL Charismatics . . .	UNETHICAL Charismatics . . .
Exercising power	. . . use power to serve others.	. . . use power to dominate or manipulate others for personal gain.
Creating the vision	. . . allow followers to help develop the vision.	. . . are the sole source of vision, which they use to serve their personal agendas.
Communicating with followers	. . . engage in two-way communication and seek out viewpoints on critical issues.	. . . engage in one-way communication and are not open to suggestions from others.
Accepting feedback	. . . are open to feedback and willing to learn from criticism.	. . . have inflated egos, thrive on attention and admiration of sycophants, and avoid candid feedback.
Stimulating followers intellectually	. . . want followers to think and question status quo as well as leader's views.	. . . don't want followers to think but instead want uncritical acceptance of leader's ideas.
Developing followers	. . . focus on developing people with whom they interact, express confidence in them, and share recognition with others.	. . . are insensitive and unresponsive to followers' needs and aspirations.
Living by moral standards	. . . follow self-guided principles that may go against popular opinion and have three virtues: courage, a sense of fairness or justice, and integrity.	. . . follow standards only if they satisfy immediate self-interests, manipulate impressions so that others think they are doing the right thing, and use communication skills to manipulate others to support their personal agendas.

Source: J. M. Howell and B. J. Avolio, "The Ethics of Charismatic Leadership: Submission or Liberation?" *Academy of Management Executive* 6, no. 2 (1992): 43–54.

establishing very strong relationships with followers, **transformational leadership** goes further by generating awareness and acceptance of a group's purpose and mission and by getting employees to see beyond their own needs and self-interest for the good of the group.[47] Like charismatic leaders, transformational leaders are visionary, but they transform their organizations by getting their followers to accomplish more than they intended and even more than they thought possible.

Transformational leaders make their followers feel that they are vital parts of the organizations and help them see how their jobs fit with the organizations' visions. By linking individual and organizational interests, transformational leaders encourage followers to make sacrifices for the organizations because they know that they will prosper when the organizations prosper. Transformational leadership has four components: charismatic leadership or idealized influence, inspirational motivation, intellectual stimulation, and individualized consideration.[48]

Charismatic leadership or idealized influence means that transformational leaders act as role models for their followers. Because transformational leaders put others' needs ahead of their own and share risks with their followers, they are admired, respected, and trusted, and followers want to emulate them. Thus, in contrast to purely charismatic leaders (especially unethical charismatics), transformational leaders can be counted on to do the right thing and maintain high standards for ethical and personal conduct.

Inspirational motivation means that transformational leaders motivate and inspire followers by providing meaning and challenge to their work. By clearly communicating

Transformational leadership leadership that generates awareness and acceptance of a group's purpose and mission and gets employees to see beyond their own needs and self-interests for the good of the group

expectations and demonstrating commitment to goals, transformational leaders help followers envision the future, as one must do to form the organizational vision or mission. In turn, this leads to greater enthusiasm and optimism about the future.

Intellectual stimulation means that transformational leaders encourage followers to be creative and innovative, to question assumptions, and to look at problems and situations in new ways even if their ideas are different from the leaders'. Carol Bartz, former CEO of AutoDesk, the industry leader in computer-aided design software, and now CEO of Yahoo!, pushes the people who work for her to think beyond their original assumptions by asking questions. Says Bartz, "All you have to do is ask questions. You just have to keep asking questions. You ask questions and guess what, they go, 'Oh, I never thought of that.' Because it unleashes so much power in people by just asking. Why do I [as the CEO] have to be the know-it-all? . . . I'm not that smart. But I'm smart enough to just keep asking questions and say, 'Is that the best you can do? Does that excite you? Will that excite the customer? Does this really have to work this way?'"[49]

Individualized consideration means that transformational leaders pay special attention to followers' individual needs by creating learning opportunities, accepting and tolerating individual differences, encouraging two-way communication, and being good listeners. When Bill Witherspoon founded The Sky Factory, an Iowa company that produces ocean- and sky-scape ceilings and walls that are installed in hospitals, restaurants, and spas, he created an environment that had no hierarchy and that empowered employees. To make everyone feel responsible for the company's financial performance, Witherspoon gives each employee the option of purchasing stock in the company. He also holds a company-wide meeting each week, during which financial numbers, quality issues, the number of clients that visited—is presented and discussed freely. Witherspoon is so committed to empowering the group that when he wanted to expand to Europe, but the group decided against it, he accepted their decision.[50]

Finally, a distinction needs to be drawn between transformational leadership and transactional leadership. While transformational leaders use visionary and inspirational appeals to influence followers, **transactional leadership** is based on an exchange process in which followers are rewarded for good performance and punished for poor performance. When leaders administer rewards fairly and offer followers the rewards that they want, followers will often reciprocate with effort. A problem, however, is that transactional leaders often rely too heavily on discipline or threats to bring performance up to standards. This may work in the short run, but it's much less effective in the long run. Also, as discussed in Chapters 11 and 13, many leaders and organizations have difficulty successfully linking pay practices to individual performance. As

© iStockphoto.com/Jacob Wackerhausen

a result, studies consistently show that transformational leadership is much more effective on average than transactional leadership. In the United States, Canada, Japan, and India and at all organizational levels, from first-level supervisors to upper-level executives, followers view transformational leaders as much better leaders and are much more satisfied when working for them. Furthermore, companies with transformational leaders have significantly better financial performance.[51]

MGMT SUCCESS

Leaderless?

One of the basic assumptions about leadership is that organizations are sure to fail without good leadership. But there are some circumstances when leadership is not likely to make much of a difference. When subordinates have ability, expertise, training, and knowledge about their jobs, their performance is unlikely to improve under a task-related leader. In other circumstances, there are subordinate, task, or organizational characteristics that can make it impossible for a leader to influence followers. This could occur when subordinates are indifferent towards organizational rewards, or are forced to deal with inflexible rewards.

STUDENT Study Tools

Located at the back of your book:

☐ Rip out and study the Chapter Review Card at the end of the book

Log in to the CourseMate for MGMT at cengagebrain.com to:

☐ Review Key Term Flashcards delivered 3 ways (print or online)

☐ Complete both Practice Quizzes to prepare for tests

☐ Play Beat the Clock and Quizbowl to master concepts

☐ Complete the Crossword Puzzle to review key terms

☐ Watch the video on the City of Greenburg, Kansas, for a real company example and take the accompanying quiz

☐ Watch the Biz Flix clip from *Doomsday* and take the quiz

☐ Complete the Case Assignment on PepsiCo

☐ Work through the Management Decision on new offices

☐ Work through the Management Team Decision on executive salaries

☐ Develop your skills with the Develop Your Career Potential exercise

15 Managing Communication

© Hans Neleman/The Image Bank/Getty Images

LEARNING OUTCOMES:

1 explain the role that perception plays in communication and communication problems.

2 describe the communication process and the various kinds of communication in organizations.

3 explain how managers can manage one-on-one communication effectively.

4 describe how managers can manage organization-wide communication effectively.

Chapter 15

What Is Communication?

It's estimated that the average manager spends over 80 percent of his or her day communicating with others.[1] Indeed, much of the basic management process—planning, organizing, leading, and controlling—cannot be performed without effective communication. If this weren't reason enough to study communication, consider that effective oral communication, such as listening, following instructions, conversing, or giving feedback, is the most important skill for college graduates who are entering the work force.[2] Furthermore, across all industries, poor communication skills rank as the single most important reason that people do not advance in their careers.[3]

Communication is the process of transmitting information from one person or place to another. While some bosses sugarcoat bad news, smart managers understand that effective, straightforward communication between managers and employees is essential for success.

After reading the next two sections, you should be able to

1 explain the role that perception plays in communication and communication problems.

2 describe the communication process and the various kinds of communication in organizations.

1 Perception and Communication Problems

One study found that when *employees* were asked whether their supervisors gave recognition for good work, only 13 percent said their supervisors gave pats on the back, and a mere 14 percent said their supervisors gave sincere and thorough praise. But when the *supervisors* of these employees were asked if they gave recognition for good work, 82 percent said they gave pats on the back, and 80 percent said that they gave sincere and thorough praise.[4] How could managers and employees have had such different perceptions of something as simple as praise?

*Let's learn more about perception and communication problems by examining **1.1 the basic perception process, 1.2 perception problems, 1.3 how we perceive others,** and **1.4 how we perceive ourselves.** We'll also consider how all of these factors make it difficult for managers to communicate effectively.*

1.1 | BASIC PERCEPTION PROCESS

As shown in Exhibit 15.1 on the next page, **perception** is the process by which individuals attend to, organize, interpret, and retain information from their environments. And since communication is the process of transmitting information from one person or place to another, perception is obviously a key part of communication. Yet, perception can also be a key obstacle to communication.

As people perform their jobs, they are exposed to a wide variety of informational stimuli such as emails, direct conversations with the boss or coworkers, rumors heard over lunch, stories about the

Communication the process of transmitting information from one person or place to another

Perception the process by which individuals attend to, organize, interpret, and retain information from their environments

Perceptual filters
the personality-, psychology-, or experience-based differences that influence people to ignore or pay attention to particular stimuli

company in the press, or a video broadcast of a speech from the CEO to all employees. Just being exposed to an informational stimulus, however, is no guarantee that an individual will pay attention to that stimulus. People experience stimuli through their own **perceptual filters**—the personality-, psychology-, or experience-based differences that influence them to ignore or pay attention to particular stimuli. Because of filtering, people exposed to the same information will often disagree about what they saw or heard. As shown in Exhibit 15.1, perceptual filters affect each part of the *perception process:* attention, organization, interpretation, and retention.

Attention is the process of noticing or becoming aware of particular stimuli. Because of perceptual filters, we attend to some stimuli and not others. *Organization* is the process of incorporating new information (from the stimuli that you notice) into your existing knowledge. Because of perceptual filters, we are more likely to incorporate new knowledge that is consistent

with what we already know or believe. *Interpretation* is the process of attaching meaning to new knowledge. Because of perceptual filters, our preferences and beliefs strongly influence the meaning we attach to new information (e.g., "This decision must mean that top management supports our project"). Finally, *retention* is the process of remembering interpreted information. In other words, retention is what we recall and commit to memory after we have perceived something. Of course, perceptual filters also affect retention, that is, what we're likely to remember in the end.

For instance, imagine that you miss the first 10 minutes of a TV show and turn on your TV to see two people talking to each other in a living room. As they talk, they walk around the room, picking up and putting down various items. Some items, such as a ring, watch, and credit card, appear to be valuable, while others appear to be drug-related, such as a water pipe for smoking marijuana. In fact, this situation was depicted on videotape in a well-known study that manipulated people's perceptual filters.[5] Before watching the video, one-third of the study participants were told that the people were there to rob the apartment. Another third of the participants were told that police were on their way to conduct a drug raid and that the people in the apartment were getting rid of incriminating evidence. The remaining third of the participants were told that the people were simply waiting for a friend.

After watching the video, participants were asked to list all of the objects from the video that they could remember. Not surprisingly, the different perceptual filters (theft, drug raid, and waiting for a friend) affected what the participants attended to, how they organized the information, how they interpreted it, and ultimately which objects they remembered. Participants who thought a theft was in progress were more likely to remember the valuable objects in the video. Those who thought a drug raid was imminent were more likely to remember the drug-related objects. There was no discernible pattern to the items remembered by those who thought that the people in the video were simply waiting for a friend.

In short, because of perception and perceptual filters, people are likely to pay attention to different things, organize and interpret what they pay attention to differently, and, finally, remember things differently. Consequently, even when people are exposed to the same communications (e.g., organizational memos, discussions with managers or customers), they can end up with very different perceptions and understandings. This is why communication can be so difficult

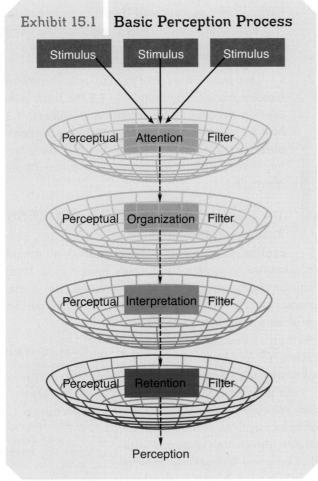

Exhibit 15.1   **Basic Perception Process**

Stimulus   Stimulus   Stimulus

Perceptual   Attention   Filter

Perceptual   Organization   Filter

Perceptual   Interpretation   Filter

Perceptual   Retention   Filter

Perception

© Cengage Learning 2011

and frustrating for managers. Let's review some of the communication problems created by perception and perceptual filters.

1.2 | PERCEPTION PROBLEMS

Perception creates communication problems for organizations because people exposed to the same communication and information can end up with completely different ideas and understandings. Two of the most common perception problems in organizations are selective perception and closure.

At work, we are constantly bombarded with sensory stimuli—phones ringing, people talking in the background, computers dinging as new email arrives, people calling our names, and so forth. As limited processors of information, we cannot possibly notice, receive, and interpret all of this information. As a result, we attend to and accept some stimuli but screen out and reject others. This isn't a random process. **Selective perception** is the tendency to notice and accept stimuli and information consistent with our values, beliefs, and expectations while ignoring, screening out, or not accepting inconsistent stimuli and information. When Dave Sokol took over as the CEO of NetJets, a company that operates partial ownership and rental of private jets, he found a disaster—$1.9 billion in debt, $711 million lost the previous year, and a hangar full of unsold planes. He decided to take immediate action to revive the company, selling old planes (even at a loss) canceling orders for new ones, and laying off employees. He even cut costs by canceling the company's annual poker tournament in Las Vegas and no longer allowing free flights for celebrities. All of these moves were met with severe resistance from senior managers who were used to an organization that was entrepreneurial in spirit and focused on short-term success rather than long-term planning. They were not used to having to think about the company's services and costs or the long-term impact of inflation, fuel prices, inventory, or changing markets.[6]

Once we have initial information about a person, event, or process, **closure** is the tendency to fill in the gaps where information is missing, that is, to assume that what we don't know is consistent with what we already know. If employees are told that budgets must be cut by 10 percent, they may automatically assume that 10 percent of employees will lose their jobs, too, even if that isn't the case. Not surprisingly, when closure occurs, people sometimes fill in the gaps with inaccurate information, which can create problems for organizations.

1.3 | PERCEPTIONS OF OTHERS

Attribution theory says that we all have a basic need to understand and explain the causes of other people's behavior.[7] In other words, we need to know why people do what they do. According to attribution theory, we use two general reasons or attributions to explain people's behavior: an *internal attribution,* in which behavior is thought to be voluntary or under the control of the individual, and an *external attribution,* in which behavior is thought

Selective perception the tendency to notice and accept objects and information consistent with our values, beliefs, and expectations while ignoring, screening out, or not accepting inconsistent stimuli or information

Closure the tendency to fill in gaps of missing information by assuming that what we don't know is consistent with what we already know

Attribution theory a theory that states that we all have a basic need to understand and explain the causes of other people's behavior

Did You See That?

A study at the University of Illinois asked viewers to watch people in black shirts and white shirts toss a basketball back and forth and to count the number of times someone in a black shirt tossed the basketball. Because their perceptual filters had narrowed to track the activities of people in black shirts, half of the viewers did not notice when the experimenters had someone in a gorilla suit walk through the midst of the people tossing the basketball back and forth.

Source: D. Simons and C. Chabris, "Gorillas in Our Midst: Sustained Inattentional Blindness for Dynamic Events," *Perception* 28 (1999): 1059–1074.

© iStockphoto.com/Eric Isselée / © iStockphoto.com/Benjamin Goode

to be involuntary and outside of the control of the individual.

For example, have you ever seen someone changing a flat tire on the side of the road and thought to yourself, "What rotten luck—somebody's having a bad day"? If you did, you perceived the person through an external attribution known as the defensive bias. The **defensive bias** is the tendency for people to perceive themselves as personally and situationally similar to someone who is having difficulty or trouble.[8] And, when we identify with the person in a situation, we tend to use external attributions (i.e., the situation) to explain the person's behavior. For instance, since flat tires are common, it's easy to perceive ourselves in that same situation and put the blame on external causes such as running over a nail.

Now, let's assume a different situation, this time in the workplace:

A utility company worker puts a ladder on a utility pole and then climbs up to do his work. As he's doing his work, he falls from the ladder and seriously injures himself.[9]

Answer this question: Who or what caused the accident? If you thought, "It's not the worker's fault. Anybody could fall from a tall ladder," then you inter-

preted the incident with a defensive bias in which you saw yourself as personally and situationally similar to someone who is having difficulty or trouble. In other words, you made an external attribution by attributing the accident to an external cause or to some feature of the situation.

Most accident investigations, however, initially blame the worker (i.e., an internal attribution) and not the situation (i.e., an external attribution). Typically, 60 to 80 percent of workplace accidents each year are blamed on "operator error," that is, the employees themselves. In reality, more complete investigations usually show that workers are responsible for only 30 to 40 percent of all workplace accidents.[10] Why are accident investigators so quick to blame workers? The reason is that they are committing the **fundamental attribution error,** which is the tendency to ignore external causes of behavior and to attribute other people's actions to internal causes.[11] In other words, when investigators examine the possible causes of an accident, they're much more likely to assume that the accident is a function of the person and not the situation.

Which attribution—the defensive bias or the fundamental attribution error—are workers likely to make when something goes wrong? In general, as shown in Exhibit 15.2, employees and coworkers are more likely to perceive events and explain behavior from a defensive bias. Because they do the work themselves and see themselves as similar to others who make mistakes,

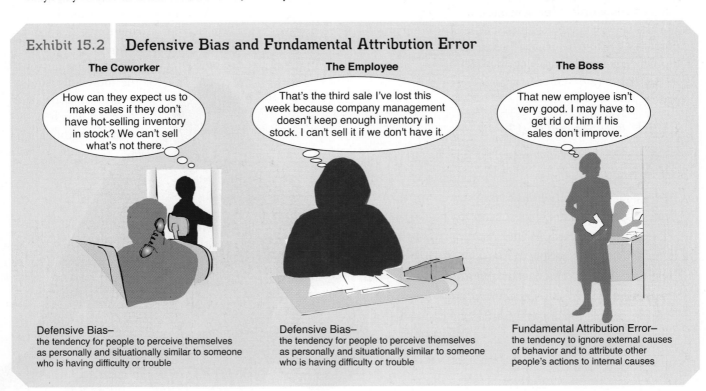

Exhibit 15.2   Defensive Bias and Fundamental Attribution Error

The Coworker

How can they expect us to make sales if they don't have hot-selling inventory in stock? We can't sell what's not there.

Defensive Bias— the tendency for people to perceive themselves as personally and situationally similar to someone who is having difficulty or trouble

The Employee

That's the third sale I've lost this week because company management doesn't keep enough inventory in stock. I can't sell it if we don't have it.

Defensive Bias— the tendency for people to perceive themselves as personally and situationally similar to someone who is having difficulty or trouble

The Boss

That new employee isn't very good. I may have to get rid of him if his sales don't improve.

Fundamental Attribution Error— the tendency to ignore external causes of behavior and to attribute other people's actions to internal causes

© Cengage Learning 2011

have accidents, or are otherwise held responsible for things that go wrong at work, employees and coworkers are likely to attribute problems to external causes such as failed machinery, poor support, or inadequate training. By contrast, because they are typically observers (who don't do the work themselves) and see themselves as situationally and personally different from workers, managers (i.e., the boss) tend to commit the fundamental attribution error and blame mistakes, accidents, and other things that go wrong on workers (i.e., an internal attribution).

Consequently, in most workplaces, when things go wrong, workers and managers can be expected to take opposite views. Therefore, together, the defensive bias (which is typically used by workers) and the fundamental attribution error (which is typically made by managers) present a significant challenge to effective communication and understanding in organizations.

1.4 | SELF-PERCEPTION

The **self-serving bias** is the tendency to overestimate our value by attributing successes to ourselves (internal causes) and attributing failures to others or the environment (external causes).[12] The self-serving bias can make it especially difficult for managers to talk to employees about performance problems. In general, people have a need to maintain a positive self-image. This need is so strong that when people seek feedback at work, they typically want verification of their worth (rather than information about performance deficiencies) or assurance that mistakes or problems weren't their fault.[13] People can become defensive and emotional when managerial communication threatens their positive self-image. They quit listening, and communication becomes ineffective. In the second half of this chapter, which focuses on improving communication, we'll explain ways in which managers can minimize this self-serving bias and improve effective one-on-one communication with employees.

2 Kinds of Communication

There are many kinds of communication—formal, informal, coaching/counseling, and nonverbal—but they all follow the same fundamental process.

Let's learn more about the different kinds of communication by examining 2.1 the communication process, 2.2 formal communication channels, 2.3 informal communication channels, 2.4 coaching and counseling, or one-on-one communication, and 2.5 nonverbal communication.

2.1 | THE COMMUNICATION PROCESS

At the beginning of this chapter, we defined *communication* as the process of transmitting information from one person or place to another. Exhibit 15.3 displays a model of the communication process and its major components: the sender (message to be conveyed, encoding the message, transmitting the message); the receiver (receiving message, decoding the message, and the message that was understood); and noise (interferes with the communication process).

The communication process begins when a *sender* thinks of a message he or she wants to convey to another person. The next step is to encode the message. **Encoding** means putting a message into a verbal (written or spoken) or symbolic form that can be recognized and understood by the receiver. The sender then *transmits the message* via *communication channels*. With some

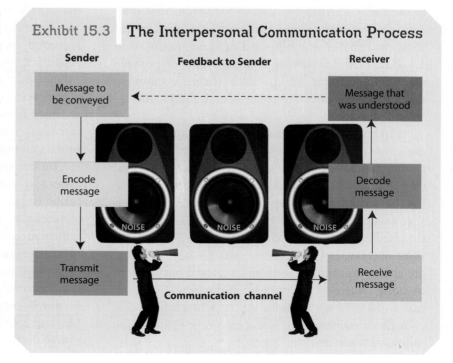

Exhibit 15.3   The Interpersonal Communication Process

Sender — Feedback to Sender — Receiver

Message to be conveyed → Encode message → Transmit message → Communication channel → Receive message → Decode message → Message that was understood

NOISE

Decoding the process by which the receiver translates the written, verbal, or symbolic form of a message into an understood message

Feedback to sender in the communication process, a return message to the sender that indicates the receiver's understanding of the message

Noise anything that interferes with the transmission of the intended message

Jargon vocabulary particular to a profession or group

Formal communication channels the system of official channels that carry organizationally approved messages and information

Downward communication communication that flows from higher to lower levels in an organization

communication channels such as the telephone and face-to-face communication, the sender receives immediate feedback, whereas with others such as email (or text messages and file attachments), faxes, beepers, voice mail, memos, and letters, the sender has to wait for the receiver to respond.

Unfortunately, because of technical difficulties (e.g., fax down, dead battery on the mobile phone, inability to read email attachments) or people-based transmission problems (e.g., forgetting to pass on the message), messages aren't always transmitted. If the message is transmitted and received, however, the next step is for the receiver to decode it. **Decoding** is the process by which the receiver translates the verbal or symbolic form of the message into an understood message. However, the message as understood by the receiver isn't always the same message that was intended by the sender. Because of different experiences or perceptual filters, receivers may attach a completely different meaning to a message than was intended.

The last step of the communication process occurs when the receiver gives the sender feedback. **Feedback to sender** is a return message to the sender that indicates the receiver's understanding of the message (of what the receiver was supposed to know, to do, or to not do). Feedback makes senders aware of possible miscommunications and enables them to continue communicating until the receiver understands the intended message.

Unfortunately, feedback doesn't always occur in the communication process. Complacency and overconfidence about the ease and simplicity of communication can lead senders and receivers to simply assume that they share a common understanding of the message and, consequently, to not use feedback to improve the effectiveness of their communication. This is a serious mistake, especially since messages and feedback are always transmitted with and against a background of noise. **Noise** is anything that interferes with the transmission of the intended message, much like static on a TV or radio station. Noise can occur in any of the following situations:

- The sender isn't sure what message to communicate.
- The message is not clearly encoded.
- The wrong communication channel is chosen.
- The message is not received or decoded properly.
- The receiver doesn't have the experience or time to understand the message.

Jargon, which is vocabulary particular to a profession or group, is another form of noise that interferes with communication in the workplace. Do you have any idea what "rightsizing," "delayering," "unsiloing," and "knowledge acquisition" mean? *Rightsizing* means laying off workers. *Delayering* means firing managers or getting rid of layers of management. *Unsiloing* means getting workers from different parts of the company (i.e., different vertical silos) to work with others outside their own areas. *Knowledge acquisition* means teaching workers new knowledge or skills. Unfortunately, the business world is rife with jargon. According to Carol Hymowitz of the *Wall Street Journal*, "A new crop of buzzwords usually sprouts every 3 to 5 years, or about the same length of time many top executives have to prove themselves. Some can be useful in swiftly communicating, and spreading, new business concepts. Others are less useful, even devious."[14]

2.2 | FORMAL COMMUNICATION CHANNELS

An organization's **formal communication channels** are the official channels that carry organizationally approved messages and information. Organizational objectives, rules, policies, procedures, instructions, commands, and requests for information are all transmitted via this formal communication system. There are three formal communication channels: downward communication, upward communication, and horizontal communication.[15]

Downward communication flows from higher to lower levels in an organization. Downward communication is used to issue orders down the organizational hierarchy, to give organizational members job-related information, to give managers and workers performance reviews from upper managers, and to clarify organizational objectives and goals.[16] Compared to Baby Boomers, born between 1946 and 1964, Generation Y employees, born after 1980, are much more likely to ask their bosses for downward communication in the form of frequent feedback and performance

Common Problems with Downward, Upward, and Horizontal Communication

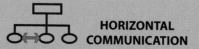

DOWNWARD COMMUNICATION

- Overusing downward communication by sending too many messages
- Issuing contradictory messages
- Hurriedly communicating vague, unclear messages
- Issuing messages that indicate management's low regard for lower-level workers

UPWARD COMMUNICATION

- The risk involved with telling upper management about problems (i.e., fear of retribution)
- Managers reacting angrily and defensively when workers report problems
- Not enough opportunities or channels for lower-level workers to contact upper levels of management

HORIZONTAL COMMUNICATION

- Management discouraging or punishing horizontal communication, viewing it as small talk
- Not giving managers and workers the time or opportunity for horizontal communication
- Not enough opportunities or channels for lower-level workers to engage in horizontal communication

reviews. For example, at Big Four accounting firm Ernst & Young, half of baby boomers indicated that they wanted "frequent and candid performance feedback," compared to 85 percent of gen Y employees. As a result of this gen Y preference, Ernst & Young started the "Feedback Zone," which allows employees to ask for formal feedback any time they want it, rather than waiting for a once-a-year review as at most companies.

Upward communication flows from lower levels to higher levels in an organization. Upward communication is used to give higher-level managers feedback about operations, issues, and problems; to help higher-level managers assess organizational performance and effectiveness; to encourage lower-level managers and employees to participate in organizational decision making; and to give those at lower levels the chance to share their concerns with higher-level authorities. Barry Salzberg, the CEO of professional services firm Deloitte & Touche USA, says that clear communication between employees and leaders is extremely important, especially during economic recessions. He says, "They want to feel part of a caring community with leaders who, when making the hard choices, will balance the health of the organization with the best long-term interests of the workforce." To hear from his employees, Salzberg runs the Straight Talk program. He holds town hall meetings in different offices throughout the company, during which employees are invited to ask the CEO whatever they want. And each of these sessions is archived and accessible to every other employee 24 hours a day. Company surveys show that employees appreciate honesty from the CEO and really like the opportunity to offer feedback on the direction that the company is going. Salzberg, meanwhile, says that the sessions have influenced his leadership of the company as they helped him understand how vulnerable people feel in tough economic times.[17]

Horizontal communication flows among managers and workers who are at the same organizational level, as when a day shift nurse comes in at 7:30 a.m. for a half-hour discussion with the night nurse supervisor, who leaves at 8:00 a.m. Horizontal communication helps facilitate coordination and cooperation between different parts of a company and allows coworkers to share relevant information. It also helps people at the same level

Upward communication communication that flows from lower to higher levels in an organization

Horizontal communication communication that flows among managers and workers who are at the same organizational level

Informal communication channel (grapevine) the transmission of messages from employee to employee outside of formal communication channels

resolve conflicts and solve problems without involving high levels of management. Studies show that communication breakdowns, which occur most often during horizontal communication, such as when patients are handed over from one nurse or doctor to another, are the largest source of medical errors in hospitals.[18]

In general, what can managers do to improve formal communication? First, decrease reliance on downward communication. Second, increase chances for upward communication by increasing personal contact with lower-level managers and workers. Third, encourage much better use of horizontal communication.

2.3 | INFORMAL COMMUNICATION CHANNEL

An organization's **informal communication channel**, sometimes called the **grapevine**, is the transmission of messages from employee to employee outside of formal communication channels. The grapevine arises out of curiosity, that is, the need to know what is going on in an organization and how it might affect you or others. To satisfy this curiosity, employees need a consistent supply of relevant, accurate, in-depth information about "who is doing what and what changes are occurring within the organization."[19] Supervisor Paul McCann of Appleton Papers, Inc., a specialty paper and packaging products manufacturer, agrees that when management doesn't explain what's happening in the company, "people will work together to develop their own reason."[20] Employee Paul Haze supports this view: "If employees don't have a definite explanation from management, they tend to interpret for themselves."[21]

Grapevines arise out of informal communication networks such as the gossip and cluster chains shown in Exhibit 15.4. In a *gossip chain*, one highly connected individual shares information with many other managers and workers. By contrast, in a *cluster chain*, numerous people simply tell a few of their friends. The result in

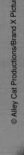

Your Company Stinks!

Did you know there are over 20,000 Internet domain names that end in "sucks.com" and 2,000 that end in "stinks.com"? As a preemptive strategy, 30 percent of Fortune 500 companies have purchased the "sucks.com" domain names that include their company (e.g., Goldmansachssucks.com) or product names (e.g., michelobsucks.com). But buying the domain names isn't the only strategy for dealing with Internet gripe sites. There are seven others on the list of ways to handle angry feedback.

1. Correct misinformation. Put an end to false rumors and set the record straight. Don't be defensive.
2. Don't take angry comments personally.
3. Give your name and contact number to show employees that you're concerned and that they can contact you directly.
4. Hold a town meeting to discuss the issues raised on the gripe site.
5. Set up anonymous discussion forums on the company server. Then encourage employees to gripe anonymously on the internal intranet, rather than on the Web.
6. If a mistake has been made, apologize; explain what happened and how the company will attempt to make it right.
7. Stop the gripes before they start by having clear communication channels, online or via phone or mail, through which employees and others can communicate concerns to management.
8. Purchase "IHateYourCompany.com" domain names and then use them to invite and collect feedback from disgruntled employees and customers.

Sources: C. Martin and N. Bennett, "Business Insight (A Special Report): Corporate Reputation; What to Do About Online Attacks: Step No. 1: Stop Ignoring Them," *Wall Street Journal*, March 10, 2008, R6; J. Simons, "Stop Moaning about Gripe Sites and Log On," *Fortune*, April 2, 2001, 181; E. Steel, "How to Handle 'IHateYourCompany.com': Some Firms Buy Up Negative Domain Names to Avert 'Gripe Sites,'" *Wall Street Journal*, September 5, 2008, B5.

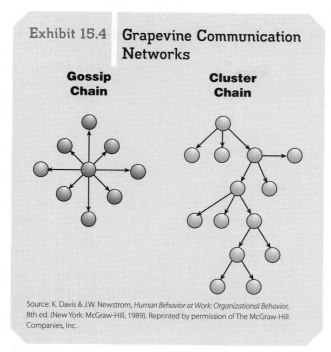

Exhibit 15.4   Grapevine Communication Networks

Gossip Chain

Cluster Chain

Source: K. Davis & J.W. Newstrom, *Human Behavior at Work: Organizational Behavior*, 8th ed. (New York: McGraw-Hill, 1989). Reprinted by permission of The McGraw-Hill Companies, Inc.

both cases is that information flows freely and quickly through the organization. Some believe that grapevines are a waste of employees' time, that they promote gossip and rumors that fuel political speculation, and that they are sources of highly unreliable, inaccurate information. Yet studies clearly show that grapevines are highly accurate sources of information for a number of rea-

sons.[22] First, because grapevines typically carry "juicy" information that is interesting and timely, information spreads rapidly. At Meghan De Goyler Hauser's former company, the word on the grapevine was that her boss drank on the job, the company accountant was robbing the company blind, and one of her coworkers was a nude model. She says, "The rumors all turned out to be true."[23] Second, since information is typically spread by face-to-face conversation, receivers can send feedback to make sure they understand the message that is being communicated. This reduces misunderstandings and increases accuracy. Third, since most of the information in a company moves along the grapevine rather than through formal communication channels, people can usually verify the accuracy of information by checking it out with others.

What can managers do to manage organizational grapevines? The very worst thing they can do is withhold information or try to punish those who share information with others. The grapevine abhors a vacuum, and rumors and anxiety will flourish in the absence of information from company management. Why does this occur? According to workplace psychologist Nicholas DiFonzo, "The main focus of rumor is to figure out the truth. It's the group trying to make sense of something that's important to them."[24] A better strategy is to embrace the grapevine and keep employees

> The main focus of **rumor** is to figure out the truth. It's the group trying to **make sense** of something that's important to them.

informed about possible changes and strategies. Failure to do so will just make things worse. And, in addition to using the grapevine to communicate with others, managers should not overlook the grapevine as a tremendous source of valuable information and feedback. In fact, information flowing through organizational grapevines is estimated to be 75 to 95 percent accurate.[25]

2.4 | COACHING AND COUNSELING: ONE-ON-ONE COMMUNICATION

When the Wyatt Company surveyed 531 U.S. companies undergoing major changes and restructuring, it asked their CEOs, "If you could go back and change one thing, what would it be?" The answer: "The way we communicated with our employees." The CEOs said that instead of flashy videos, printed materials, or formal meetings, they would make greater use of one-on-one communication, especially with employees' immediate supervisors rather than higher-level executives that employees didn't know.[26]

Coaching and counseling are two kinds of one-on-one communication. **Coaching** is communicating with someone for the direct purpose of improving the person's on-the-job performance or behavior.[27] Managers tend to make several mistakes when coaching employees, however. First, they wait for a problem before coaching. Jim Concelman, manager for leadership development at Development Dimensions International, says, "Of course, a boss has to coach an employee if a mistake has been made, but they shouldn't be waiting for the error. While it is a lot easier to see a mistake and correct it, people learn more through success than through failure, so bosses should ensure that employees are experiencing as many successes as possible. Successful employees lead to a more successful organization."[28] Second, when mistakes *are* made, managers wait much too long before talking to the employee about the problem. Management professor Ray Hilgert says, "A manager must respond as soon as possible after an incident of poor performance. Don't bury your head. . . . When employees are told nothing, they assume everything is okay."[29]

By contrast, **counseling** is communicating with someone about non–job-related issues such as stress, child care, health issues, retirement planning, or legal

issues that may be affecting or interfering with the person's performance. But counseling does not mean that managers should try to be clinicians, even though an estimated 20 percent of employees are dealing with personal problems at any one time. Instead, managers should discuss specific performance problems, listen if the employee chooses to share personal issues, and then recommend that the employee call the company's *employee assistance program (EAP)*. EAPs are typically free when provided as part of a company's benefit package. In emergencies or times of crisis, EAPs can offer immediate counseling and support and provide referrals to organizations and professionals who can help employees and their family members address personal issues.

2.5 | NONVERBAL COMMUNICATION

Nonverbal communication is any communication that doesn't involve words. Nonverbal communication almost always accompanies verbal communication and may either support and reinforce the verbal message or contradict it. The importance of nonverbal communication is well established. Researchers have estimated that as much as 93 percent of any message is transmitted nonverbally, with 55 percent coming from body language and facial expressions and 38 percent coming from the tone and pitch of the voice.[30] Since many nonverbal cues are unintentional, receivers often consider nonverbal communication to be a more accurate representation of what senders are thinking and feeling than the words they use.

Kinesics and paralanguage are two kinds of nonverbal communication.[31] **Kinesics** (from the Greek word *kinesis*, meaning "movement") are movements of the body and face.[32] These movements include arm and hand gestures, facial expressions, eye contact, folding arms, crossing legs, and leaning toward or away from another person.

It turns out that kinesics play an incredibly important role in communication. Studies of married couples' kinesic interactions can predict whether they will stay married with 93 percent accuracy.[33] The key is the ratio of positive to negative kinesic interactions that husbands and wives make as they communicate. Negative kinesic expressions such as eye rolling suggest contempt, whereas positive kinesic expressions such as maintaining eye contact and nodding suggest listening and caring. When the ratio of positive to negative interactions drops below 5 to 1, the chances for divorce quickly increase. Kinesics operate similarly in the workplace, providing clues about people's true feelings, over and above what they say (or don't say). For instance, Louis Giuliano, former CEO of ITT, a manufacturing conglomerate that makes heavy use of teams, says, "When you get a team together and say to them we're going to change a process, you always have people who say, 'No, we're not.'" They usually don't say it out loud, but "the body language is there," making it clear that their real answer is "no."[34]

Paralanguage includes the pitch, rate, tone, volume, and speaking pattern (i.e., use of silences, pauses, or hesitations) of one's voice. For example, when people are unsure what to say, they tend to decrease their communication effectiveness by speaking softly. When people are nervous, they tend to talk faster and louder. These characteristics have a tremendous influence on whether listeners are receptive to what speakers are saying.

In short, because nonverbal communication is so informative, especially when it contradicts verbal communication, managers need to learn how to monitor and control their nonverbal behavior.

How to Improve Communication

When it comes to improving communication, managers face two primary tasks, managing one-on-one communication and managing organization-wide communication.

After reading the next two sections, you should be able to

3 explain how managers can manage one-on-one communication effectively.

4 describe how managers can manage organization-wide communication effectively.

3 Managing One-on-One Communication

On average, first-line managers spend 57 percent of their time with people, middle managers spend 63 percent of their time directly with people, and top managers spend as much as 78 percent of their time dealing with people.[35] These numbers make it clear that managers spend a great deal of time in one-on-one communication with others.

*Let's learn more about managing one-on-one communication by exploring how to **3.1 choose the right communication medium, 3.2 be a good listener,** and **3.3 give effective feedback.***

3.1 | CHOOSING THE RIGHT COMMUNICATION MEDIUM

Sometimes messages are poorly communicated simply because they are delivered using the wrong **communication medium**, which is the method used to deliver a message. For example, the wrong communication medium is being used when an employee returns from lunch, picks up the note left on her office chair, and learns she has been fired.

There are two general kinds of communication media: oral and written communication. *Oral communication* takes place in meetings of two or more people conducted face-to-face or through telephone calls, videoconferencing, or any other means of sending and receiving spoken messages. Studies show that managers generally prefer oral communication over written because it provides the opportunity to ask questions about parts of the message that they don't understand. Oral communication is also a rich communication medium because it allows managers to receive and assess the nonverbal communication that accompanies spoken messages (i.e., body language, facial expressions, and the voice characteristics associated with paralanguage). Furthermore, you don't need a personal computer and an Internet connection to conduct oral communication. Oral communication should not be used for all communication, however. In general, when the message is simple, such as a quick request or a presentation of straightforward information, a memo or email is often the better communication medium.

Written communication includes letters, email, and memos. Although most managers still like and use oral communication, email in particular is changing how they communicate with workers, customers, and each other. Email is the fastest growing form of communication in organizations primarily because of its convenience and speed. For instance, because people read six times faster than they can listen, they usually can read 30 email messages in 10 to 15 minutes.[36] By contrast, dealing with voice messages can take a considerable amount of time.

Written communication such as email is well suited for delivering straightforward messages and

Paralanguage the pitch, rate, tone, volume, and speaking pattern (i.e., use of silences, pauses, or hesitations) of one's voice

Communication medium the method used to deliver an oral or written message

information. Furthermore, with email accessible at the office, at home, and on the road (via computer, cell phone, or PDA), managers can use email to stay in touch from anywhere at almost any time. And, since email and other written communications don't have to be sent and received simultaneously, messages can be sent and stored for reading at any time. Consequently, managers can send and receive many more messages using email than using oral communication, which requires people to get together in person or by phone or videoconference.

Email has its drawbacks, however. One is that it lacks the formality of paper memos and letters. It is easy to fire off a rushed email that is not well written or fully thought through. Another drawback to email is that it lacks nonverbal cues, making messages very easy to misinterpret. Kristin Byron, assistant professor of management at Syracuse University, says, "People perceive emails as more negative than they are intended to be, and even emails that are intended to be positive can be misinterpreted as more neutral. You get an email that's really short, with no greeting, no closing; it's probably because they were very rushed, or maybe they're not very good typists. But because of those things, people have a tendency to perceive the message as negative."[37] So, take a minute to reflect before you hit "Reply."

Although written communication is well suited for delivering straightforward messages and information, it is not well suited to complex, ambiguous, or emotionally laden messages, which are better delivered through oral communication.

3.2 | LISTENING

Are you a good listener? You probably think so. But, in fact, most people, including managers, are terrible listeners, retaining only about 25 percent of what they hear.[38] You qualify as a poor listener if you frequently interrupt others, jump to conclusions about what people will say before they've said it, hurry the speaker to finish his or her point, are a passive listener (not actively working at your listening), or simply don't pay attention to what people are saying.[39] On this last point—attentiveness—college students were periodically asked to record their thoughts during a psychology course. On average, 20 percent of the students were paying attention (only 12 percent were actively working at being good listeners), 20 percent were thinking about sex, 20 percent were thinking about things they had done before class, and the remaining 40 percent were thinking about other things unrelated to the class (e.g., worries, religion, lunch, daydreams).[40]

How important is it to be a good listener? In general, about 45 percent of the total time you spend communicating with others is spent listening. Furthermore, listening is important for managerial and business success, even for those at the top of an organization. When Carol

MGMT SUCCESS

Protect Personal, Confidential Information

By virtue of their jobs, managers are privy to information that others aren't. Although much of that information will be about the company, some of it will be personal and confidential information about employees. Managers have a moral and legal obligation to protect employee privacy. Moreover, sharing others' personal, confidential information may dissuade employees from confiding in managers or seeking help from a company's employee assistance program. Does this mean that if employees confide in their managers that the managers can't tell anyone else? No, managers sometimes have to inform their bosses or human resources about a situation. But they should inform only those who have a need to know and who are also obligated to protect employee privacy. Furthermore, not all information that employees disclose to managers should be protected. Information about discrimination, sexual harassment, potential workplace violence, or conflicts of interest between employees and the company may need to be shared with upper management to protect the rights and well-being of others. So, when employees disclose personal, confidential information, do the right thing. Don't discuss it with others unless it falls under one of the exceptions discussed here.

Source: T. Andrews, "E-Mail Empowers, Voice-Mail Enslaves," *PC Week*, April 10, 1995, E11.

Bartz took over as the CEO of Yahoo!, she was charged with turning around a famous but struggling company that was losing market share to Google. The first thing she did was listen—she set up 45-minute meetings with as many people as possible, throughout the organization and asked, "Okay, what do you think needs to be changed here? What's good? What's bad? What would you do if you were sitting in my seat?" Bartz would even ask who else she needed to talk to. Thanks to her willingness to listen, Bartz has been able to reverse Yahoo!'s fortunes. The company's net income rose 51 percent from the previous year and total revenues rose 2 percent, a significant improvement from the previous year, when revenues fell 13 percent.[41]

Listening is a more important skill for managers than ever, since generation X employees (born between 1965 and 1979) tend to expect a high level of interaction with their supervisors. They want feedback on their performance, but they also want to offer feedback and know that it is heard.[42] In fact, managers with good listening skills are rated as better managers by their employees and are much more likely to be promoted.[43]

So, what can you do to improve your listening ability? First, understand the difference between hearing and listening. According to *Webster's New World Dictionary*, **hearing** is the act or process of perceiving sounds, whereas **listening** is making a conscious effort to hear. In other words, we react to sounds, such as bottles breaking or music being played too loud, because hearing is an involuntary physiological process. By contrast, listening is a voluntary behavior. So, if you want to be a good listener, you have to choose to be a good listener. Typically, that means choosing to be an active, empathetic listener.[44]

Active listening means assuming half the responsibility for successful communication by actively giving the speaker nonjudgmental feedback that shows you've accurately heard what he or she said. Active listeners make it clear from their behavior that they are listening carefully to what the speaker has to say. Active listeners put the speaker at ease, maintain eye contact, and show the speaker that they are attentively listening by nodding and making short statements.

Several specific strategies can help you be a better active listener. First, *clarify responses* by asking the speaker to explain confusing or ambiguous statements. Second, when there are natural breaks in the speaker's delivery, use this time to paraphrase or summarize what has been said. *Paraphrasing* is restating in your own words what has been said. *Summarizing* is reviewing the speaker's main points or emotions. Paraphrasing and summarizing give the speaker the

Hearing the act or process of perceiving sounds

Listening making a conscious effort to hear

Active listening assuming half the responsibility for successful communication by actively giving the speaker nonjudgmental feedback that shows you've accurately heard what he or she said

Listen Up!

Communications coach Carmine Gallo offers four tips on how to become a better listener:

1. Fix your gaze. If you're listening to someone, look the person in the eyes.

2. Respond to a question with a question. When someone asks you a question, don't just answer and move on. Ask a meaningful question in return.

3. When people ask for feedback, give it. It shows you were listening and that you take them seriously.

4. Be available for the tough questions. Be attentive, ask questions, and show that you understand (and want to know) the complexities.

Source: C. Gallo, "Why Leadership Means Listening," *BloombergBusinessweek*, January 31, 2008, accessed September 3, 2008, http://www.businessweek.com/smallbiz/content/jan2007/sb20070131_192848.htm.

Empathetic listening understanding the speaker's perspective and personal frame of reference and giving feedback that conveys that understanding to the speaker

chance to correct the message if the active listener has attached the wrong meaning to it. Paraphrasing and summarizing also show the speaker that the active listener is interested in the speaker's message. Exhibit 15.5 lists specific statements that listeners can use to clarify responses, paraphrase, or summarize what has been said.

Active listeners also avoid evaluating the message or being critical until the message is complete. They recognize that their only responsibility during the transmission of a message is to receive it accurately and derive the intended meaning from it. Evaluation and criticism can take place after the message is accurately received. To be a good listener, you should avoid thinking about your response while someone is talking, and turn all of your attention to listening. Finally, active listeners also recognize that a large portion of any message is transmitted nonverbally and thus pay very careful attention to the nonverbal cues transmitted by the speaker.

Empathetic listening means understanding the speaker's perspective and personal frame of reference and giving feedback that conveys that understanding to the speaker. Empathetic listening goes beyond active listening because it depends on our ability to set aside our own attitudes or relationships to be able to see and understand things through someone else's eyes. Empathetic listening is just as important as active listening, especially for managers, because it helps build rapport and trust with others.

The key to being a more empathetic listener is to show your desire to understand and to reflect people's feelings. You can *show your desire to understand* by asking people to talk about what's most important to them and then by giving them sufficient time to talk before responding or interrupting.

Reflecting feelings is also an important part of empathetic listening because it demonstrates that you understand the speaker's emotions. Unlike active listening, in which you restate or summarize the informational content of what has been said, the focus is on the affective part of the message. As an empathetic listener, you can use the following statements to *reflect the speaker's emotions:*

- So, right now it sounds like you're feeling . . .
- You seem as if you're . . .
- Do you feel a bit . . . ?
- I could be wrong, but I'm sensing that you're feeling . . .

In the end, says management consultant Terry Pearce, empathetic listening can be boiled down to these three steps. First, wait 10 seconds before you answer or respond. It will seem an eternity, but waiting prevents you from interrupting others and rushing your response. Second, to be sure you understand what the speaker wants, ask questions to clarify the speaker's intent. Third, only then should you respond first with feelings and then facts (notice that facts *follow* feelings).[45]

This section provides you with important tools to help you become a better listener. Applying them insincerely—or indiscriminately—may make you seem patronizing and derail your attempt to build better working relationships. Not everyone appreciates having what they said repeated back to them—even if you've repeated it in your own words. Manager Candy

Exhibit 15.5 — Clarifying, Paraphrasing, and Summarizing Responses for Active Listeners

CLARIFYING RESPONSES	PARAPHRASING RESPONSES	SUMMARIZING RESPONSES
Could you explain that again?	What you're really saying is	Let me summarize . . . .
I don't understand what you mean.	If I understand you correctly	Okay, your main concerns are . . . .
I'm not sure how	In other words	To recap what you've said . . . .
I'm confused. Would you run through that again?	So your perspective is that	Thus far, you've discussed . . . .
	Tell me if I'm wrong, but what you seem to be saying is	

Source: E. Atwater, *I Hear You*, rev. ed. (New York: Walker, 1992).

Friesen says that whenever she did that, "I seemed to engender animosity or hostility . . . the person to whom you're speaking may not appreciate having his [or her] thoughts paraphrased one little bit."[46] So, when applying these listening techniques, pay attention to the body language and tone of voice of the person you're communicating with to make sure he or she appreciates your attempts to be a better listener.

3.3 | GIVING FEEDBACK

In Chapter 11, you learned that performance appraisal feedback (i.e., judging) should be separated from developmental feedback (i.e., coaching).[47] We can now focus on the steps needed to communicate feedback one-on-one to employees.

To start, managers need to recognize that feedback can be constructive or destructive. **Destructive feedback** is disapproving without any intention of being helpful and almost always causes a negative or defensive reaction in the recipient. Kent Thiry, CEO of DaVita, a corporation that runs dialysis treatment centers, admits that he regularly gets dinged by his senior executives for giving too much negative feedback. Says Thiry, "They say I'm not harder on them than I am on myself, but my negativity isn't constructive." Thiry now gives himself "a daily score about feedback, to remind myself—and change." Avoiding destructive feedback is important. One study found that 98 percent of employees responded to destructive feedback from their bosses with either verbal aggression (two-thirds) or physical aggression (one-third).[48]

By contrast, **constructive feedback** is intended to be helpful, corrective, and/or encouraging. It is aimed at correcting performance deficiencies and motivating employees. For feedback to be constructive rather than destructive, it must be immediate, focused on specific behaviors, and problem oriented. *Immediate feedback* is much more effective than delayed feedback because managers and workers can recall

Destructive feedback feedback that disapproves without any intention of being helpful and almost always causes a negative or defensive reaction in the recipient

Constructive feedback feedback intended to be helpful, corrective, and/or encouraging

"For feedback to be constructive rather than **destructive**, it must be immediate, focused on specific behaviors, and **problem oriented**."

a mistake or incident more accurately and discuss it in detail. For example, if a worker is rude to a customer and the customer immediately reports the incident to management, and if the manager, in turn, immediately discusses the incident with the employee, there should be little disagreement over what was said or done. By contrast, it's unlikely that either the manager or the worker will be able to accurately remember the specifics of what occurred if the manager waits several weeks to discuss the incident. When that happens, it's usually too late to have a meaningful conversation.

Specific feedback focuses on particular acts or incidents that are clearly under the control of the employee. For instance, instead of telling an employee that he or she is "always late for work," it's much more constructive to say, "In the last 3 weeks, you have been 30 minutes late on four occasions and more than an hour late on two others." Furthermore, specific feedback isn't very helpful unless employees have control over the problems that the feedback addresses. Giving negative feedback about behaviors beyond someone's control is likely to be seen as unfair. Similarly, giving positive feedback about behaviors beyond someone's control may be viewed as insincere.

Last, *problem-oriented feedback* focuses on the problems or incidents associated with the poor performance rather than on the worker or the worker's personality. Giving feedback does not give managers the right to personally attack workers. Though managers may be frustrated by a worker's poor performance, the point of problem-oriented feedback is to draw attention to the problem in a nonjudgmental way so that the employee has enough information to correct it.

4 Managing Organization-Wide Communication

Although managing one-on-one communication is important, managers must also know how to communicate effectively with a larger number of people throughout an organization.

*Learn more about organization-wide communication by reading the following sections about **4.1 improving transmission by getting the message out** and **4.2 improving reception by finding ways to hear what others feel and think.***

4.1 | IMPROVING TRANSMISSION: GETTING THE MESSAGE OUT

Several methods of electronic communication—email, collaborative discussion sites, televised/videotaped speeches and conferences, and broadcast voice mail—now make it easier for managers to communicate with people throughout the organization and get the message out.

Although we normally think of *email*, or the transmission of messages via computers, as a means of one-on-one communication, it also plays an important role in organization-wide communication. With the click of a button, managers can send a message to everyone in the company via email distribution lists. Many CEOs now use this capability regularly to keep employees up to date on changes and developments. When Polycom, Inc. CEO Robert Hagerty learned that some employees of his firm had been implicated in a massive insider trading scandal, he sent off a company-wide email reminding employees of the company's strict financial policies and promising that the firm would cooperate with law enforcement agencies. In his email, Hagerty said, "As you know, Polycom has strict rules and policies against employees divulging confidential insider information, and we completely support government action against anyone who breaks these rules."[49] Many CEOs and top executives also make their email addresses public and encourage employees to contact them directly.

Collaborative discussion sites are another electronic means of promoting organization-wide communication. **Collaborative discussion sites** use Web- or software-based discussion tools to allow employees across the company to easily ask questions and share knowledge with each other. The point is to share expertise and not duplicate solutions already discovered by others in the company. Furthermore, because the discussions are archived, they provide a historical database for people who are dealing with particular problems for the first time. Collaborative discussion sites are typically organized by topic, project, or person and can take the form of blogs that allow readers to post comments, wikis that allow collaborative discussions and document sharing and editing, or traditional discussion forums (see Chapter 17 on Managing Information for further explanation). HCL Technologies, an IT services firm located in Noida, India, encourages collaboration through a site it calls U&I. The online forum allows employees to post questions and complaints, and to respond to others' posts. The forum is completely uncensored, and many of the first postings were variants of "Why do you guys [management] suck?" "Why does your strategy suck?" and "Why aren't you living up to your ideals?" Though some managers were tempted to censor posts, employees saw U&I as a commitment to communication transparency and a way to hold management accountable. CEO Vineet Nayar also hosts a "My Problems" section on the U&I site, in which he describes various issues that company leadership is dealing with and ask employees at all levels to give him advice on how to handle them.[50]

Exhibit 15.6 lists the steps companies need to take to establish successful collaborative discussion sites. First, pinpoint your company's top intellectual assets through a knowledge audit; then spread that knowledge throughout the organization. Second, create an online directory detailing the expertise of individual workers and make it available to all employees. Third, set up discussion groups on the intranet so that managers and workers can collaborate on problem solving. Finally, reward information sharing by making the online sharing of knowledge a key part of performance ratings.

Televised/videotaped speeches and meetings are a third electronic method of organization-wide communication. **Televised/videotaped speeches and meetings** are simply speeches and meetings originally made to a smaller audience that are either simultaneously broadcast to other locations in the company or videotaped for subsequent distribution and viewing. Cisco's CEO, John Chambers, tapes ten to fifteen videos a quarter to communicate with his employees and customers.[51]

Voice messaging, or voice mail, is a telephone answering system that records audio messages. In one survey, 89 percent of respondents said that voice messaging is critical to business communication, 78 percent said that it improves productivity, and 58 percent said they would rather leave a message on a voice messaging system than with a receptionist.[52] Nonetheless, most people are unfamiliar with the ability to *broadcast voice mail* by sending a recorded message to everyone in the company. Broadcast voice mail gives top managers a quick, convenient way to address their work forces via oral communication.

Exhibit 15.6 Establishing Collaborative Discussion Sites

Step 1 → Knowledge Audit
Step 2 → Online Directory
Step 3 → Discussion Groups on Intranet
Step 4 → Reward Information Sharing

© Cengage Learning 2011

4.2 | IMPROVING RECEPTION: HEARING WHAT OTHERS FEEL AND THINK

When people think of "organization-wide" communication, they think of the CEO and top managers getting their message out to people in the company. But organization-wide communication also means finding ways to hear what people throughout the organization are thinking and feeling. This is important because most employees and managers are reluctant to share their thoughts and feelings with top managers. Surveys indicate that only 29 percent of first-level managers feel that their companies encourage employees to express their opinions openly. Another study of 22 companies found that 70 percent of the people surveyed were afraid to speak up about problems they knew existed at work.

Withholding information about organizational problems or issues is called **organizational silence.** Organizational silence occurs when employees believe that telling management about problems won't make a difference or that they'll be punished or hurt in some way for sharing such information.[53] Company hotlines, survey feedback, frequent informal meetings, surprise visits, and blogs are ways of overcoming organizational silence.

Company hotlines are phone numbers that anyone in the company can call anonymously to leave information for upper management. For example, Force Protection, which builds vehicles that protect armed forces personnel from explosions and ballistics, has a toll-free hotline for employees to call to report any kind of problem or issue within the company. Force Protection's policy states, "The Company Hotline is available 24 hours a day, 7 days a week and is serviced by an independent contractor. The Hotline will

---

not be answered by an employee of Force Protection. You have the option to remain anonymous. No retaliation or reprisals will be taken against anyone utilizing this confidential service in good faith."[54]

Hotlines are particularly important because without access to one, 44 percent of employees will not report misconduct. Why not? The reason is twofold: They don't believe anything will be done, and they "fear that the report will not be kept confidential."[55] Company hotlines are effective: 47 percent of the calls placed to them result in an investigation and some form of corrective action within the organization. Anonymity is critical, however, because as such investigations proceed, it is found that 54 percent of the callers do not want their identities revealed.[56]

Survey feedback is information that is collected from surveys given to organization members and then compiled, disseminated, and used to develop action plans for improvement. Many organizations make use of survey feedback by surveying their managers and employees several times a year. Guardian News and Media, the publisher of the British newspaper the *Guardian*, conducts an annual survey of its employees to gauge their satisfaction and their confidence in the company. After a recent restructuring of the organization, during which more than 100 journalists, editors, and editorial staff lost their jobs, the survey showed *Guardian* employees still had a lot of confidence in the company. Eighty-six percent of respondents reported that they were still proud to work at the *Guardian*, and 93 percent reported that they did extra work beyond what was required of them.

And perhaps most importantly, 86 percent stated that they understood the need for cost-cutting measures and layoffs given the challenges facing the newspaper and the news industry as a whole.[57]

Frequent *informal meetings* between top managers and lower-level employees are one of the best ways for top managers to hear what others feel and think. Many people assume that top managers are at the center of everything that goes on in organizations, but top managers commonly feel isolated from most of their lower-level managers and employees. Consequently, more and more top managers are scheduling frequent informal meetings with people throughout their companies.

Yogesh Gupta, CEO of Fatwire, which makes software to manage business websites, says that managers must not get defensive during informal meetings. Says Gupta, "I've heard so many executives tell employees to be candid and then jump down their throats if they bring up a problem or ask a critical question."[58] Gupta has spent hundreds of hours in informal meetings with his 200 managers and 9 executives. He meets with each privately because he believes that it encourages people to be candid. And, he asks each these questions: "What am I doing wrong? What would you do differently if you were running the company? What's the biggest thing getting in the way of you doing your job well?"[59] As a result of these meetings, Gupta learned that Fatwire was understaffed in marketing and product development.

Have you ever been around when a supervisor learns that upper management will be paying a visit? First there's panic, as everyone is told to drop what he or she is doing to polish, shine, and spruce up the workplace so that it looks perfect for the visit. Then, of course, top managers don't get a realistic look at

© iStockphoto.com/Amanda Rohde

Someone in the firm has to **actively monitor** what is being said on **websites**, **blogs**, and **Twitter**.

what's going on in the company. Consequently, one of the ways to get an accurate picture is to pay *surprise visits* to various parts of the organization. These visits should not just be surprise inspections but should also be used as an opportunity to encourage meaningful upward communication from those who normally don't get a chance to communicate with upper management.

Blogs are another way to hear what people are thinking and saying both inside and outside the organization. A **blog** is a personal website on which someone can post opinions, recommendations, or news, and readers can answer with comments. At Google, which owns the blog-hosting service Blogger, hundreds of employees are writing *internal blogs.* One employee even set up a blog for posting all the notes from the brainstorming sessions used to redesign the search page used by millions each day.[60] *External blogs* and Twitter sites (microblogs where entries, called *tweets,* are limited to 140 characters), written by people outside the company, can be a good way to find out what others are saying or thinking about your organization or its products or actions. But it means that someone in the firm has to actively monitor what is being said on websites, blogs, and Twitter. The airline Virgin America has a dedicated interactive marketing team that not only tracks what customers say about the airline's service on their Twitter accounts, but also acts to make them satisfied. Since Virgin America offers wireless Internet access on all its flights, customers often tweet about how the flight is going, what is missing from the service, or what they are not happy with. Members of the interactive marketing team can read these tweets and meet the need almost as soon as the customer posts them. When one passenger tweeted about not getting food service, the interactive marketing team alerted the flight staff, who saw to it that a meal was served. When another passenger tweeted about how much he hated his flight and how terrible it was, the interactive marketing team arranged to have customer service agents meet the passenger at his destination airport as soon as he arrived, find out what made the flight so terrible, and resolve the issue quickly.[61]

Blog a personal website that provides personal opinions or recommendations, news summaries, and reader comments

STUDENT
Study
Tools

Located at the back of your book

☐ Rip out and study the Chapter Review Card at the end of the book

Log in to the CourseMate for MGMT at cengagebrain.com to:

☐ Review Key Term Flashcards delivered 3 ways (print or online)

☐ Complete both Practice Quizzes to prepare for tests

☐ Play Beat the Clock and Quizbowl to master concepts

☐ Complete the Crossword Puzzle to review key terms

☐ Watch the video on Greensburg Public Schools for a real company example and take the accompanying quiz

☐ Watch the Biz Flix clip from *Friday Night Lights* and take the quiz

☐ Complete the Case Assignment on Starbucks

☐ Work through the Management Decision on creating a new communication policy

☐ Work through the Management Team Decision on communication dilemmas and decisions

☐ Develop your skills with the Develop Your Career Potential exercise

16 | Control

LEARNING OUTCOMES:

1 describe the basic control process.

2 discuss the various methods that managers can use to maintain control.

3 describe the behaviors, processes, and outcomes that today's managers are choosing to control in their organizations.

Chapter 16

Basics of Control

for all companies, past success is no guarantee of future success. Even successful companies fall short or face challenges and thus have to make changes. **Control** is a regulatory process of establishing standards to achieve organizational goals, comparing actual performance to the standards, and taking corrective action when necessary to restore performance to those standards. Control is achieved when behavior and work procedures conform to standards and company goals are accomplished.[1] Control is not just an after-the-fact process, however. Preventive measures are also a form of control.

In the airline industry, product quality is king. Every single airplane manufacturer must pass rigorous certification tests from governmental agencies (such as the U.S. Federal Aviation Administration) before it can even think about selling equipment to regional and global airlines. In late 2009, Boeing announced that it would begin testing of its newest model, the 787 Dreamliner. Boeing built six aircraft specifically for the tests, at a cost of more than $1 billion. Two of the planes were dedicated to test for how the plane would operate in extreme ice conditions. One plane was built solely to test all interior systems, such as flight controls, climate control, and safety systems. Other tests on the planes included operations at extremely low speeds, operations at extremely high speeds (nearly 50 percent higher than normal cruising speed), takeoffs and landings in virtually every condition imaginable, thorough measurements of the stress and load that the plane's wings and frame could handle, and how long the plane

could operate with one engine. And all these tests were run on a virtually 24-hour schedule that closely mimicked the real-world schedules that airlines maintain.[2] Through all of this testing, Boeing hopes to ensure that it has produced a high-quality, fuel-efficient, and most of all safe airplane that will appeal to cost-conscious airlines all over the world.

After reading the next section, you should be able to

1 describe the basic control process.

1 The Control Process

*The basic control process **1.1 begins with the establishment of clear standards of performance; 1.2 involves a comparison of performance to those standards; 1.3 takes corrective action, if needed, to repair performance deficiencies; 1.4 is a dynamic, cybernetic process;** and **1.5 uses three basic methods—feedback control, concurrent control, and feedforward control.*** However, as much as managers would like, **1.6 control isn't always worthwhile or possible.**

1.1 | STANDARDS

The control process begins when managers set goals, such as satisfying 90 percent of customers or increasing sales by 5 percent. Companies then specify the performance standards that must be met to accomplish those goals. **Standards** are a basis of comparison for measuring the extent to which organizational performance is satisfactory or unsatisfactory. For example, many pizzerias use 30–40 minutes as the standard for delivery time. Since anything

Control a regulatory process of establishing standards to achieve organizational goals, comparing actual performance to the standards, and taking corrective action when necessary

Standards a basis of comparison for measuring the extent to which various kinds of organizational performance are satisfactory or unsatisfactory

longer is viewed as unsatisfactory, they'll typically reduce the price if they can't deliver a hot pizza to you within that time period.

So how do managers set standards? How do they decide which levels of performance are satisfactory and which are unsatisfactory? The first criterion for a good standard is that it must enable goal achievement. If you're meeting the standard but still not achieving company goals, then the standard may have to be changed. In the salmon industry, to maximize productivity, it was standard procedure to grow as many fish as possible in fish farms and deal with diseases (which spread readily because the fish are in such close proximity) through liberal use of antibiotics in the fish food. This was effective until a few years ago, when the ISA (infectious salmon anemia) virus, which is resistant to antibiotics, developed. Norwegian salmon farms, the largest in the world, sharply reduced the incidence of ISA by developing new production standards that included the use of antiviral vaccines and the elimination of overcrowded fish pens.[3]

Companies also determine standards by listening to customers' comments, complaints, and suggestions or by observing competitors. TNT NV is a global delivery company based in the Netherlands. After frequent complaints about how late deliveries were being handled, the company conducted a number of customer discussion forums to better understand the customers' perspective and what TNT NV might do to address the problem. One of the issues that came to light was the company policy of requiring drivers who were running late to call TNT NV's call control center, which would then notify customer services, which would let the customer know that the driver was running late. This overly complicated process was slow and frequently resulted in late notifications, frustrated customers, and embarrassed drivers. The company's new policy is that drivers who are running late are to contact the customer directly. Customers appreciate the personal contact and drivers, who often see their customers on a daily basis, appreciate being given control of the situation.[4]

Standards can also be determined by benchmarking other companies. **Benchmarking** is the process of determining how well other companies (though not just competitors) perform business functions or tasks. In other words, benchmarking is the process of determining other companies' standards. When setting standards by benchmarking, the first step is to determine what to benchmark. Companies can benchmark anything from cycle time (how fast) to quality (how well) to price (how much). The next step is to identify the companies against which to benchmark your standards. The last step is to collect data to determine other companies' performance standards.

1.2 | COMPARISON TO STANDARDS

The next step in the control process is to compare actual performance to performance standards. Although this sounds straightforward, the quality of the comparison largely depends on the measurement and information systems a company uses to keep track of performance. The better the system, the easier it is for a company to track performance and identify problems that need to be fixed. One way for retailers to verify that performance standards are being met is to use secret shoppers, individuals who visit stores pretending to be customers in order to determine whether employees provide helpful customer service. The Communications Consumer Panel, based in England, used secret shoppers to evaluate the quality of customer service of mobile phone service providers. It found that more than half of the shoppers were given false information about minimum contract lengths and cancellation policies.[5]

1.3 | CORRECTIVE ACTION

The next step in the control process is to identify performance deviations, analyze those deviations, and then develop and implement programs to correct them.

Beta versions of software programs are a classic tool that developers use to monitor deviations from the standard and take corrective action *before* the product is released on the market. Prior to releasing *StarCraft II*, the sequel to its hugely popular *StarCraft* video game (more than 11 million units sold), Blizzard Entertainment invited gamers and journalists from all over the world to download a trial version, try it out, and, most importantly, tell them what they liked and didn't like about it. By incorporating their feedback, such as notification of undiscovered software glitches, Blizzard was able to release a highly refined product that had already met the approval of a large number of potential buyers.[6]

1.4 | DYNAMIC, CYBERNETIC PROCESS

As shown in Exhibit 16.1, control is a continuous, dynamic, cybernetic process. Control begins by setting standards and then measuring performance and comparing performance to the standards. If the performance deviates from the standards, managers and employees analyze the deviations and develop and implement cor-

Exhibit 16.1

Cybernetic Control Process

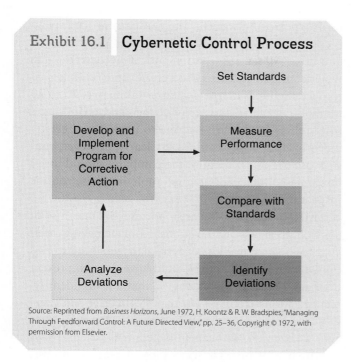

Set Standards

↓

Measure Performance

↓

Compare with Standards

↓

Identify Deviations

→

Analyze Deviations

↑

Develop and Implement Program for Corrective Action

→ (to Measure Performance)

Source: Reprinted from *Business Horizons*, June 1972, H. Koontz & R. W. Bradspies, "Managing Through Feedforward Control: A Future Directed View," pp. 25–36, Copyright © 1972, with permission from Elsevier.

rective programs that (hopefully) achieve the desired performance by meeting the standards. Managers must repeat the entire process again and again in an endless feedback loop (a continuous process). Thus, control is not a one-time achievement or result. It continues over time (i.e., it is dynamic) and requires daily, weekly, and monthly attention from managers to maintain performance levels at the standards. This constant attention is what makes control a cybernetic process. **Cybernetic** derives from the Greek word *kubernetes*, meaning "steersman," that is, one who steers or keeps a craft on course.[7] The control process shown in Exhibit 16.1 is cybernetic because constant attention to the feedback loop is necessary to keep the company's activities on course.

1.5 | FEEDBACK, CONCURRENT, AND FEEDFORWARD CONTROL

The three basic control methods are feedback control, concurrent control, and feedforward control. **Feedback control** is a mechanism for gathering information about performance deficiencies *after* they occur. This information is then used to correct performance deficiencies or prevent future deficiencies. Study after study has clearly shown that feedback improves both individual and organizational performance. In most instances, any feedback is better than no feedback. If feedback has a downside, it's that it always occurs after the fact, after performance deficiencies have already occurred. Control can minimize the effects, but the damage is already done.

Concurrent control addresses the problems inherent in feedback control by gathering information about performance deficiencies as they occur. The Nissan Leaf, an all-electric compact car, features the Intelligent Transportation system, which gives drivers instant information about how much battery power is remaining, how many more miles the car can go before needing a recharge, and the location of the nearest charging station. When the car is plugged in for recharging, the system will even call the driver's mobile phone when charging is complete.[8] Concurrent control is an improvement over feedback because it attempts to eliminate or shorten the delay between performance and feedback about the performance.

Feedforward control is a mechanism for gathering information about performance deficiencies *before* they occur. In contrast to feedback and concurrent control, which provide feedback on the basis of outcomes and results, feedforward control provides information about performance deficiencies by monitoring inputs,

Cybernetic the process of steering or keeping on course

Feedback control a mechanism for gathering information about performance deficiencies after they occur

Concurrent control a mechanism for gathering information about performance deficiencies as they occur, thereby eliminating or shortening the delay between performance and feedback

Feedforward control a mechanism for monitoring performance inputs rather than outputs to prevent or minimize performance deficiencies before they occur

The Nissan Leaf gives drivers instant information about battery power and distance to the next charging station.

AP Images/Mark Humphrey

Control loss the situation in which behavior and work procedures do not conform to standards

Regulation costs the costs associated with implementing or maintaining control

not outputs. Thus, feedforward control seeks to prevent or minimize performance deficiencies before they happen. Microsoft uses feedforward controls to try to prevent software problems before they occur. For example, when developing the latest version of its Windows Server software (for network and Internet computer servers), Microsoft taught 8,500 experienced programmers new methods for writing more reliable software code *before* asking them to develop new features for Windows Server software. Microsoft has also developed new software testing tools that let programmers thoroughly test the code they've written (i.e., the inputs) before passing the code on to others to be used in beta testing of Windows 7. Using feedforward control has shortened development time, and Windows 7 was released earlier than expected.[9]

1.6 | CONTROL ISN'T ALWAYS WORTHWHILE OR POSSIBLE

Control is achieved when behavior and work procedures conform to standards and goals are accomplished. By contrast, **control loss** occurs when behavior and work procedures do not conform to standards.[10] After American Airlines missed a deadline to conduct wiring inspections of its planes, the FAA grounded every plane that had not yet been inspected and certified. With nearly 1,500 American Airlines flights cancelled and thousands of customers stranded, unable to make their connections, CEO Gerard Arpey promised that the company would spend "tens of millions of dollars" to cover overtime pay and costs of the inspections and, if needed, repairs. American also promised to refund and rebook customers' flights. With reinspections taking just 15 to 20 minutes per plane, and repairs, when needed, taking 2 to 6 hours, American was able to inspect and certify its entire fleet within 4 days.[11] Clearly, however, control loss occurred, because the company should never have missed the deadline for completing these routine inspections.

Maintaining control is important because loss of control prevents organizations from achieving their goals. When control loss occurs, managers need to find out what, if anything, they could have done to prevent it. Usually, as discussed above, that means identifying deviations from standard performance, analyzing the causes of those deviations, and taking corrective action. Even so, implementing controls isn't always worthwhile or possible. Let's look at regulation costs and cybernetic feasibility to see why.

To determine whether control is worthwhile, managers need to carefully assess **regulation costs,** or costs associated with implementing or maintaining control. If a control process costs more than an organization gains from its benefits, it may not be worthwhile. For example, the European Union uses the metric system—kilograms and centimeters—to ensure standard pricing throughout its 27 member states. But, since the United Kingdom still relies on the British imperial system (pounds, ounces, inches, miles, etc.), the EU regulation allows businesses to use both metric and imperial measures. When Janet Devers, who runs a vegetable stall at the Ridley Road market in East London, sold vegetables only by the pound and the ounce, she faced 13 criminal charges and fines totaling $130,000 for not also posting prices in metric units. Devers could not believe she was being prosecuted, "We have knifings. We have killings. And they're taking me to court because I'm selling in pounds and ounces."[12] Since everyone in Britain buys fruits and vegetables by the pound or ounce, the British public was outraged by the charges. Clearly, the regulatory costs outweighed the benefits. Innovations Secretary for

MGMT SUCCESS

Guidelines for Using Feedforward Control

1. Plan and analyze thoroughly.
2. Be discriminating as you select input variables.
3. Keep the feedforward system dynamic. Don't let it become a matter of habit.
4. Develop a model of the control system.
5. Collect data on input variables regularly.
6. Assess data on input variables regularly.
7. Take action on what you learn.

Source: Reprinted from *Business Horizons*, June 1972, H. Koontz & R. W. Bradspies, "Managing Through Feedforward Control: A Future Directed View," pp. 25–36, Copyright © 1972, with permission from Elsevier.

Coupon Redemption

Retail stores are struggling to find successful ways to provide discounts via the Web and social media. When Indianapolis-based Marsh Supermarkets used Facebook to give 3,100 "friends" a $10 coupon, the number of people who tried to redeem the coupons spiraled out of control. Marsh had to halt the offer after 4 days and apologized on its website, saying, "We at Marsh recently stuck our toe in the water to try this whole social media thing. Unfortunately, we ended up stubbing it. Our recent $10 coupon offer on Facebook has instead left us red in the face and many of our loyal customers angry. Rightfully so. For that we are truly sorry. Needless to say, we're learning." In this instance, there was no cybernetic feasibility.

Source: E. Smith, "Marsh Gets Clipped by Online Coupon Deal," *Indianapolis Star*, August 5, 2009, A1.

the UK, John Denham, soon indicated that such prosecutions were not in the public interest. And the local government council, which had spent $50,000 pursuing the case in court, eventually dropped all the charges.[13]

Another factor to consider is **cybernetic feasibility,** the extent to which it is possible to implement each of the three steps in the control process. If one or more steps cannot be implemented, then maintaining effective control may be difficult or impossible.

How and What to Control

Skiers and snowboarders who love the thrill of racing down steep mountain slopes may have to start carrying a radar detector. In response to the more than 70,000 accidents each year on Swiss ski slopes, the state-controlled Swiss Accident Insurance (Suva), the country's biggest provider of compulsory insurance, will now be using radar guns on the slopes to track and "pull over" skiers and snowboarders who go faster than 19 mph. Studies using crash test dummies on skis show that going faster than 19 mph is not safe, and that going faster than 30 mph can be fatal. While speeders will only be warned at first, they could eventually be fined and have their ski passes taken away.[14]

If you managed a ski resort, would you use radar guns to "pull over" skiers and snowboarders who were going too fast? Would skiers and snowboarders see this policy as aimed at increasing their safety or at lowering the business's costs and legal risks? Is this a reasonable policy that you should pursue, or is this something that you shouldn't even consider? Should you also require all skiers and snowboarders to wear helmets on the slopes? If you were running a ski resort, what would you do?

After reading the next two sections, you should be able to

2 **discuss the various methods that managers can use to maintain control.**

3 **describe the behaviors, processes, and outcomes that today's managers are choosing to control in their organizations.**

Cybernetic feasibility the extent to which it is possible to implement each step in the control process

" If you managed a ski resort, would you use radar guns to 'pull over' skiers and snowboarders who were going too fast? "

2 Control Methods

Managers can use five different methods to achieve control in their organizations: **2.1 bureaucratic, 2.2 objective, 2.3 normative, 2.4 concertive,** *and* **2.5 self-control.**

2.1 | BUREAUCRATIC CONTROL

When most people think of managerial control, what they have in mind is bureaucratic control. **Bureaucratic control** is top-down control, in which managers try to influence employee behavior by rewarding or punishing employees for compliance or noncompliance with organizational policies, rules, and procedures. Most employees, however, would argue that bureaucratic managers emphasize punishment for noncompliance much more than rewards for compliance. For instance, one manager gave an employee a written reprimand for "leaving work without permission"—after she passed out in the bathroom and was whisked by ambulance to a nearby hospital.[15]

As you learned in Chapter 2, bureaucratic management and control were created to prevent just this type of managerial behavior. By encouraging managers to apply well-thought-out rules, policies, and procedures in an impartial, consistent manner to everyone in the organization, bureaucratic control is supposed to make companies more efficient, effective, and fair. Ironically, it frequently has just the opposite effect. Managers who use bureaucratic control often emphasize following the rules above all else.

Another characteristic of bureaucratically controlled companies is that due to their rule- and policy-driven decision making, they are highly resistant to change and slow to respond to customers and competitors. Recall from Chapter 2 that even Max Weber, the German philosopher who is largely credited with popularizing bureaucratic ideals in the late 19th century, referred to bureaucracy as the "iron cage." He said, "Once fully established, bureaucracy is among those social structures which are the hardest to destroy."[16]

2.2 | OBJECTIVE CONTROL

In many companies, bureaucratic control has evolved into **objective control,** which is the use of observable measures of employee behavior or output to assess performance and influence behavior. Whereas bureaucratic control focuses on whether policies and rules are followed, objective control focuses on observing and mea-

Access Denied?

Facebook, YouTube, ESPN.com, personal email, even news sites—all of these represent a challenge to companies that are trying to maintain employee productivity. To decrease the amount of time lost, many companies have banned non–work-related Internet usage. A recent study in Australia suggests, however, that such bans actually reduce productivity. The study argues that allowing employees time to visit websites of personal interest gives them a mental break and raises productivity by nine percent. Further, many technology experts argue that if employees are blocked from visiting certain sites, they will actually spend more time trying to get around the block instead of getting back to work. An Internet ban may even hurt a company's staffing. A recent study in England showed that 39 percent of 18- to 24-year-olds would quit their jobs if social media access was restricted.

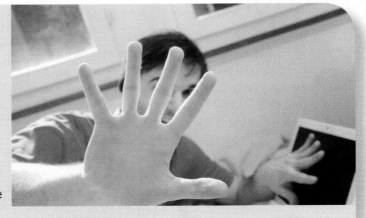

Sources: G. Ferenstein, "Why Banning Social Media Often Backfires," Mashable, April 13, 2010, accessed July 15, 2010, http://mashable.com/2010/04/13/social-media-ban-backfire/; M. Kirkpatrick, "Shocking News: Scientists Say Workplace Social Networking Increases Productivity!" ReadWriteWeb, April 2, 2009, accessed July 15, 2010, http://www.readwriteweb.com/archives/shocking_news_scientists_say_workplace_social_netw.php; I. Thompson, "Facebook Ban Could Lead to Staff Exodus," V3.co.uk, June 5, 2008, accessed July 15, 2010, http://www.v3.co.uk/vnunet/news/2218385/workers-consider-quitting.

suring worker behavior or output. There are two kinds of objective control: behavior control and output control.

Behavior control is regulating behaviors and actions that workers perform on the job. The basic assumption of behavior control is that if you do the right things (i.e., the right behaviors) every day, then those things should lead to goal achievement. Behavior control is still management-based, however, which means that managers are responsible for monitoring and rewarding or punishing workers for exhibiting desired or undesired behaviors. Companies that use global positioning satellite (GPS) technology to track where workers are and what they're doing are using behavior control. JEA, an electric utility company located in Jacksonville, Florida, had a problem with employees who would show up to work, drive off in service vehicles, then goof off for the rest of the day. A local TV station also caught JEA's employees selling company equipment. Now, to monitor employee behavior, JEA has installed GPS tracking devices in its fleet of vehicles, which allows managers to track how and where employees spend their time and make sure that they are completing their assigned projects.[17]

Instead of measuring what managers and workers do, **output control** measures the results of their efforts. Whereas behavior control regulates, guides, and measures how workers behave on the job, output control gives managers and workers the freedom to behave as they see fit as long as they accomplish pre-specified, measurable results. Output control is often coupled with rewards and incentives.

Three things must occur for output control to lead to improved business results. First, output control measures must be reliable, fair, and accurate. Second, employees and managers must believe that they can produce the desired results. If they don't, then the output controls won't affect their behavior. Third, the rewards or incentives tied to output control measures must truly be dependent on achieving established standards of performance. For example, Erik Bedard is a pitcher for the Seattle Mariners. Due to a shoulder injury, he missed most of the 2009 season and was left without a contract at the beginning of the 2010 season. He ended up signing a one-year deal with the Mariners for $1.5 million, nearly $2 million less than the average Major League salary. He can, however, earn up to $7.5 million more if he meets certain performance levels. Bedard will earn an extra $250,000 each time he is injury-free for 30 days (i.e., 60 days means $500,000, 90

days means $750,000, and so on). On the 14th, 17th, 20th, 23rd and 26th games he pitches in, he will make $500,000 each. If he pitches 75 innings, he will make $500,000 and an additional $600,000 for every 25 innings after that.[18] For output control to work with rewards, the rewards must truly be at risk if performance doesn't measure up. This is clearly the case with Erik Bedard's contract.

2.3 | NORMATIVE CONTROL

Rather than monitoring rules, behavior, or output, another way to control what goes on in organizations is to use normative control to shape the beliefs and values of the people who work there. With **normative controls,** a company's widely shared values and beliefs guide workers' behavior and decisions. For example, at Nordstrom, a Seattle-based department store chain, one value permeates the entire work force from top to bottom: extraordinary customer service. On the first day of work at Nordstrom, trainees begin their transformation to the "Nordstrom way" by reading the employee handbook. Sounds boring, doesn't it? But Nordstrom's handbook is printed on *one side* of a 3-by-5-inch note card, shown in its entirety in Exhibit 16.2. That's it. No lengthy rules. No specifics about what behavior is or is not appropriate. Just use your judgment.[19]

Normative controls are created in two ways. First, companies that use normative controls are very careful about whom they hire. While many companies screen potential applicants on the basis of their abilities,

---

Exhibit 16.2 **Nordstrom's Employee Handbook**

Welcome to Nordstrom. We're glad to have you with our company. Our Number One goal is to provide outstanding customer service. Set both your personal and professional goals high. We have great confidence in your ability to achieve them.

Nordstrom Rules:

Rule #1: Use your good judgment in all situations.

There will be no additional rules. Please feel free to ask your department manager, store manager, or division general manager any question at any time.

Source: S. Williford, "Nordstrom Sets the Standard for Customer Service," *Memphis Business Journal* (July 1996) 21. Copyright © 1996 American City Business Journals. All rights reserved. Reproduced by permission.

© iStockphoto/Derya Celik

normatively controlled companies are just as likely to screen potential applicants based on their attitudes and values. For example, before building stores in a new city, Nordstrom sends its human resource team into town to interview prospective applicants. In a few cities, the company canceled its expansion plans when it could not find enough qualified applicants who embodied the service attitudes and values for which Nordstrom is known.[20]

Second, with normative controls, managers and employees learn what they should and should not do by observing experienced employees and by listening to the stories they tell about the company. At Nordstrom, many of these stories, which employees call "heroics," have been inspired by the company motto, "Respond to Unreasonable Customer Requests!"[21] "Nordies," as Nordstrom employees call themselves, like to tell the story about a customer who just had to have a pair of burgundy Donna Karan slacks that had gone on sale, but she could not find her size. The sales associate who was helping her contacted five nearby Nordstrom stores, but none had the customer's size. So rather than leave the customer dissatisfied with her shopping experience, the sales associate went to her manager for petty cash and then went across the street and paid full price for the slacks at a competitor's store. She then resold them to the customer at Nordstrom's lower sale price.[22] Obviously, Nordstrom would quickly go out of business if this were the norm. Nevertheless, this story makes clear the attitude that drives employee performance at Nordstrom in ways that rules, behavioral guidelines, or output controls could not.

2.4 | CONCERTIVE CONTROL

Whereas normative controls are based on beliefs that are strongly held and widely shared throughout a company, **concertive controls** are based on beliefs that are shaped and negotiated by work groups.[23] Whereas normative controls are driven by strong organizational cultures, concertive controls usually arise when companies give work groups complete autonomy and responsibility for task completion. The most autonomous groups operate without managers and are completely responsible for controlling work group processes, outputs, and behavior. Such groups do their own hiring, firing, worker discipline, work schedules, materials ordering, budget making and meeting, and decision making.

Concertive control is not established overnight. Highly autonomous work groups evolve through two phases as they develop concertive control. In phase one, group members learn to work with each other, supervise each other's work, and develop the values and beliefs that will guide and control their behavior. And because they develop these values and beliefs themselves, work group members feel strongly about following them.

In the steel industry, Nucor was long considered an upstart compared to the "biggies," U.S. Steel and Bethlehem Steel. Today, however, not only has Nucor managed to outlast many other mills, but the company has also bought out thirteen other mills in the past 5 years. Nucor has a unique culture that gives real power to employees on the line and fosters teamwork throughout the organization. This type of teamwork can be a difficult thing for a newly acquired group of employees to get used to. For example, at Nucor's first big acquisition in Auburn, New York, David Hutchins is a front-line supervisor, or "lead man," in the rolling mill, where steel from the furnace is spread thin enough to be cut into sheets. When the plant was under the previous ownership, if the guys doing the cutting got backed up, the guys doing the rolling—including Hutchins—would just take a break. He says, "We'd sit back, have a cup of coffee, and complain: 'Those guys stink.'" It took 6 months to convince the employees at the Auburn plant that the Nucor teamwork way was better than the old way. Now, Hutchins says, "At Nucor, we're not 'you guys' and 'us guys.' It's all of us guys. Wherever the bottleneck is, we go there, and everyone works on it."[24]

The second phase in the development of concertive control is the emergence and formalization of objective rules to guide and control behavior. The beliefs and values developed in phase one usually develop into more objective rules as new members join teams. The clearer those rules, the easier it becomes for new members to figure out how and how not to behave.

Ironically, concertive control can lead to even more stress for workers who try to conform to expectations than does bureaucratic control. Under bureaucratic control, most workers only have to worry about pleasing the boss. But with concertive control, their behavior has to satisfy the rest of their team members. For example, one team member says, "I don't have to sit there and look for the boss to be around; and if the boss is not around, I can sit there and talk to my neighbor or do what I want. Now the whole team is around me and the whole team is observing what I'm doing."[25] Plus, with concertive control, team members have a second, much more stressful role to perform—that of making sure that their team members adhere to team values and rules.

2.5 | SELF-CONTROL

Self-control, also known as **self-management,** is a control system in which managers and workers control their own behavior.[26] Self-control does not result in anarchy, or a state in which everyone gets to do whatever he or she wants. In self-control or self-management, leaders and managers provide workers with clear boundaries within which they may guide and control their own goals and behaviors.[27] Leaders and managers also contribute to self-control by teaching others the skills they need to maximize and monitor their own work effectiveness. In turn, individuals who manage and lead themselves establish self-control by setting their own goals, monitoring their own progress, rewarding or punishing themselves for achieving or for not achieving their self-set goals, and constructing positive thought patterns that remind them of the importance of their goals and their ability to accomplish them.[28]

For example, let's assume you need to do a better job of praising and recognizing the good work that your staff does for you. You can use goal setting, self-observation, and self-reward to self-manage this behavior. For self-observation, write "praise/recognition" on a 3-by-5-inch card. Put the card in your pocket. Put a check on the card each time you praise or recognize someone (wait until the person has left before you do this). Keep track for a week. This serves as your baseline or starting point. Simply keeping track will probably increase how often you do this. After a week, assess your baseline or starting point, and then set a specific goal. For instance, if your baseline was twice a day, you might set a specific goal to praise or recognize others' work five times a day. Continue monitoring your performance with your cards. Once you've achieved your goal every day for a week, give yourself a reward (perhaps a CD, a movie, or lunch with a friend at a new restaurant) for achieving your goal.[29]

The components of self-management, self-set goals, self-observation, and self-reward have their

> If you **control** for just one dimension, . . . then other dimensions, like **marketing**, customer service, and quality, are likely to suffer.

roots in the motivation theories you read about in Chapter 13. The key difference, though, is that the goals, feedback, and rewards originate from employees themselves and not from their managers or organizations.

3 What to Control?

In the first section of this chapter, we discussed the basics of the control process and noted that control isn't always worthwhile or possible. In the second section, we looked at the various ways in which control can be achieved. In this third and final section, we address an equally important issue: What should managers control? Costs? Quality? Customer satisfaction? The way managers answer this question has critical implications for most businesses.

If you control for just one dimension, such as costs, as many grocers have done in their meat departments, then other dimensions, like marketing, customer service, and quality, are likely to suffer. But if you try to control for too many things, managers and employees become confused about what's really important. In the end, successful companies find a balance that comes from doing three or four things right, like managing costs, providing value, and keeping customers and employees satisfied.

*After reading this section, you should be able to explain **3.1 the balanced scorecard approach to control and how companies can achieve balanced control of performance by controlling 3.2 budgets, cash flows, and economic value added; 3.3 customer defections; 3.4 quality; and 3.5 waste and pollution.***

3.1 | THE BALANCED SCORECARD

Most companies measure performance using standard financial and accounting measures such as return on capital, return on assets, return on investments, cash flow, net income, and net margins. The **balanced scorecard** encourages managers to look beyond traditional financial measures to four different perspectives on company performance: How do customers see us (the customer perspective)? At what must we excel (the internal perspective)? Can we continue to improve and create value (the innovation and learning perspective)?

Self-control (self-management) a control system in which managers and workers control their own behavior by setting their own goals, monitoring their own progress, and rewarding themselves for goal achievement

Balanced scorecard measurement of organizational performance in four equally important areas: finances, customers, internal operations, and innovation and learning

How do we look to shareholders (the financial perspective)?[30]

The balanced scorecard has several advantages over traditional control processes that rely solely on financial measures. First, it forces managers at each level of the company to set specific goals and measure performance in each of the four areas. For example, Exhibit 16.3 shows that Southwest Airlines uses nine different measures in its balanced scorecard in order to determine whether it is meeting the standards it has set for itself in the control process. Of those, only three—market value, seat revenue, and plane lease costs (at various compounded annual growth rates, or CAGRs)—are standard financial measures of performance. In addition, Southwest measures its FAA on-time arrival rating and the cost of its airfares compared to those of its competitors (customer perspective); how much time each plane spends on the ground after landing and the percent-age of planes that depart on time (internal perspective); and the percentage of its ground crew workers, such as mechanics and luggage handlers, who own company stock and have received job training (innovation and learning perspective).

The second major advantage of the balanced scorecard approach to control is that it minimizes the chances of **suboptimization,** which occurs when performance improves in one area at the expense of decreased performance in others. A recent study published by *Harvard Business Review* found that companies that try to gain a competitive advantage by ramping up production speed actually have lower sales and profits. Conversely, companies that slowed production speed and gave employees time to think and reflect averaged 40 percent higher sales and 52 percent higher profits.[31]

Let's examine some of the ways in which companies are controlling the four basic parts of the balanced scorecard: the financial perspective (budgets, cash

Exhibit 16.3 **Southwest Airlines' Balanced Scorecard**

	GOALS	STANDARDS	MEASURES	INITIATIVES
FINANCIAL	Profitability	30% CAGR	Market Value	
	Increased Revenue	20% CAGR	Seat Revenue	
	Lower Costs	5% CAGR	Plane Lease Cost	
CUSTOMER	On-Time Flights	#1	FAA On-Time Arrival Rating	Quality Management, Customer Loyalty Program
	Lowest Prices	#1	Customer Ranking (Market Survey)	
INTERNAL	Fast Ground Turnaround	30 Minutes	Time on Ground	Cycle Time Optimization Program
		90%	On-Time Departure	
INNOVATION AND LEARNING	Ground Crew Alignment with Company Goals	Year 1: 70%	% Ground Crew Shareholders	Employee Stock Option Plan, Ground Crew Training
		Year 3: 90%		
		Year 5: 100%	% Ground Crew Trained	

Source: G. Anthes, "ROI Guide: Balanced Scorecard," *Computer World,* February 17, 2003, accessed September 5, 2008, http://www.computerworld.com/action/article.do?command=viewArticleBasic&articleId=78512&intsrc=article_pots_bot.

© Image100/Jupiterimages

flows, and economic value added), the customer perspective (customer defections), the internal perspective (total quality management), and the innovation and learning perspective (waste and pollution).

3.2 | THE FINANCIAL PERSPECTIVE: CONTROLLING BUDGETS, CASH FLOWS, AND ECONOMIC VALUE ADDED

The traditional approach to controlling financial performance focuses on accounting tools such as cash flow analysis, balance sheets, income statements, financial ratios, and budgets. **Cash flow analysis** predicts how changes in a business will affect its ability to take in more cash than it pays out. **Balance sheets** provide a snapshot of a company's financial position at a particular time (but not the future). **Income statements**, also called *profit-and-loss statements*, show what has happened to an organization's income, expenses, and net profit (income less expenses) over a period of time. **Financial ratios** are typically used to track a business's liquidity (cash), efficiency, and profitability over time compared to other businesses in its industry. Finally, **budgets** are used to project costs and revenues, prioritize and control spending, and ensure that expenses don't exceed available funds and revenues. The Financial Review Card bound in the back of this book contains tables that (a) show the basic steps or parts for cash flow analyses, balance sheets, and income statements; (b) list a few of the most common financial ratios and explain how they are calculated, what they mean, and when to use them; and (c) review the different kinds of budgets managers can use to track and control company finances.

By themselves, none of these tools—cash-flow analyses, balance sheets, income statements, financial ratios, or budgets—tell the whole financial story of a business. They must be used together when assessing a company's financial performance. Since these tools are reviewed in detail in your accounting and finance classes, only a brief overview is provided here. Still, these are necessary tools for controlling organizational finances and expenses, and they should be part of your business toolbox.

Though no one would dispute the importance of these four accounting tools, accounting research also indicates that the complexity and sheer amount of information contained in them can shut down the brain and glaze over the eyes of even the most experienced manager.[32] Sometimes there's simply too much information to make sense of. The balanced scorecard simplifies things by focusing on one simple question when it comes to finances: How do we look to shareholders? One way to answer that question is through something called economic value added.

Conceptually, **economic value added (EVA)** is not the same thing as profits. It is the amount by which profits exceed the cost of capital in a given year. It is based on the simple idea that capital is necessary to run a business and that capital comes at a cost. Although most people think of capital as cash, once it is invested (i.e., spent), capital is more likely to be found in a business in the form of computers, manufacturing plants, employees, raw materials, and so forth. And just like the interest that a homeowner pays on a mortgage or that a college graduate pays on a student loan, there is a cost to that capital.

The most common costs of capital are the interest paid on long-term bank loans used to buy all those resources, the interest paid to bondholders (who lend organizations their money), and the dividends (cash payments) and growth in stock value that accrue to shareholders. EVA is positive when company profits (revenues minus expenses minus taxes) exceed the cost of capital in a given year. In other words, if a business is to truly grow, its revenues must be large enough to cover both short-term costs (annual expenses and taxes) and long-term costs (the cost of borrowing capital from bondholders and shareholders). If you're a bit confused, the late Roberto Goizueta, the former CEO of Coca-Cola, explained it this way: "You borrow money at a certain rate and invest it at a higher rate and pocket the difference. It is simple. It is the essence of banking."[33]

Exhibit 16.4 on the next page shows how to calculate EVA. First, starting with a company's income statement, you calculate the net operating profit after taxes (NOPAT) by subtracting taxes owed from income from operations. (Remember, a quick review of an income statement is on the Financial Review Card found at

---

Cash flow analysis a type of analysis that predicts how changes in a business will affect its ability to take in more cash than it pays out

Balance sheets accounting statements that provide a snapshot of a company's financial position at a particular time

Income statements accounting statements, also called *profit-and-loss statements*, that show what has happened to an organization's income, expenses, and net profit over a period of time

Financial ratios calculations typically used to track a business's liquidity (cash), efficiency, and profitability over time compared to other businesses in its industry

Budgets quantitative plans through which managers decide how to allocate available money to best accomplish company goals

Economic value added (EVA) the amount by which company profits (revenues, minus expenses, minus taxes) exceed the cost of capital in a given year

Exhibit 16.4   Calculating Economic Value Added (EVA)

1.	Calculate net operating profit after taxes (NOPAT).	$3,500,000
2.	Identify how much capital the company has invested (i.e., spent).	$16,800,000
3.	Determine the cost (i.e., rate) paid for capital (usually between 5 percent and 13 percent).	10%
4.	Multiply capital used (Step 2) times cost of capital (Step 3).	(10% × $16,800,000) = $1,680,000
5.	Subtract the total dollar cost of capital from net profit after taxes.	$3,500,000 NOPAT −$1,680,000 Total cost of capital $1,820,000 Economic value added

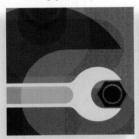

Accounting 101

If you struggle to understand how financial ratios can be used where you work, you might find help in the following books:

Accounting the Easy Way, by Peter J. Eisen

Accounting for Dummies and *How to Read a Financial Report: Wringing Vital Signs Out of the Numbers,* both by John A. Tracy

Schaum's Quick Guide to Business Formulas: 201 Decision-Making Tools for Business, Finance, and Accounting Students, by Joel G. Siegel, Jae K. Shim, and Stephen W. Hartman

The Vest-Pocket Guide to Business Ratios, by Michael R. Tyran

Essential Managers: Managing Budgets, by Stephen Brookson

Forecasting Budgets: 25 Keys to Successful Planning (The New York Times Pocket MBA Series), by Norman Moore and Grover Gardner

And don't forget to check out the special Financial Review Card bound in with your Chapter Review cards.

the back of your book.) The NOPAT shown in Exhibit 16.4 is $3,500,000. Second, identify how much capital the company has invested (i.e., spent). Total liabilities (what the company owes) less accounts payable and less accrued expenses, neither of which you pay interest on, provides a rough approximation of this amount. In Exhibit 16.4, total capital invested is $16,800,000. Third, calculate the cost (i.e., rate) paid for capital by determining the interest paid to bondholders (who lend organizations their money), which is usually somewhere between 5 and 8 percent, and the return that stockholders want in terms of dividends and stock price appreciation, which is historically about 13 percent. Take a weighted average of the two to determine the overall cost of capital. In Exhibit 16.4, the cost of capital is 10 percent. Fourth, multiply the total capital ($16,800,000) from Step 2 by the cost of capital (10 percent) from Step 3. In Exhibit 16.4, this amount is $1,680,000. Fifth, subtract the total dollar cost of capital in Step 4 from the NOPAT in Step 1. In Exhibit 16.4, this value is $1,820,000, which means that our example company has created economic value or wealth this year. If the EVA value had been negative, meaning that the company didn't make enough profit to cover the cost of capital from bondholders and shareholders, then the company would have destroyed economic value or wealth by taking in more money than it returned.[34]

Why is EVA so important? First and most importantly, because it includes the cost of capital, it shows whether a business, division, department, profit center, or product is really paying for itself. The key is to make sure that managers and employees can see how their choices and behavior affect the company's EVA.

Second, because EVA can easily be determined for subsets of a company such as divisions, regional offices, manufacturing plants, and sometimes even departments, it makes managers and workers at all levels pay much closer attention to their segment of the business. When company offices were being refurbished at Genesco, a shoe company, a worker who had EVA training handed CEO Ben Harris $4,000 in cash. The worker explained that he now understood the effect his job had on the company's ability to survive and prosper. Since the company was struggling, he had sold the old doors that had been removed during remodeling so that the company could have the cash.[35] In other words, awareness of EVA motivates managers and workers to think like small-business owners who must scramble to contain costs and generate enough business to meet their bills each month. And, unlike many kinds of financial controls, EVA-based evaluation doesn't specify what should or should not be done to improve performance. Thus, it encourages managers and workers to be creative in looking for ways to improve EVA.

Remember that EVA is the amount by which profits exceed the cost of capital in a given year. So the more that EVA exceeds the total dollar cost of capital, the better a company has used investors' money that year. Market value added (MVA) is simply the cumulative EVA created by a company over time. Thus, MVA indicates how much value or wealth a company has created or destroyed in total during its existence. The top ten U.S. companies in terms of MVA and EVA are listed in Exhibit 16.5.

3.3 | THE CUSTOMER PERSPECTIVE: CONTROLLING CUSTOMER DEFECTIONS

The second aspect of organizational performance that the balanced scorecard helps managers monitor is customers. It does so by forcing managers to address the question, "How do customers see us?" Unfortunately, most companies try to answer this question through customer satisfaction surveys, but these are often misleadingly positive. Most customers are reluctant to talk about problems they perceive because they don't know who to complain to or think that complaining will not do any good. Indeed, a study by the Office of Consumer Affairs for South Australia found that 96 percent of unhappy customers never complain to anyone in the company.[36]

One reason that customer satisfaction surveys can be misleading is that sometimes even very satisfied customers will leave to do business with competitors. Rather than poring over customer satisfaction surveys from current customers, studies indicate that companies may do a better job of answering the question "How do customers see us?" by closely monitoring **customer defections**, that is, by identifying which customers are leaving the company and measuring the rate at which they are leaving. Unlike the results of customer satisfaction surveys, customer defections and retention do have a great effect on profits.

For example, very few managers realize that obtaining a new customer costs ten times as much as keeping a current one. In fact, the cost of replacing old customers with new ones is so great that most companies could double

> **Customer defections** a performance assessment in which companies identify which customers are leaving and measure the rate at which they are leaving

| Exhibit 16.5 | Top Ten U.S. Companies by Market Value Added and Economic Value Added |

Rank	Company	Market value added as of June 30, 2008 ($ millions)	Economic value added in 2007 ($ millions)
1	Microsoft Corp.	$206,995	$12,012
2	Exxon Mobil Corp.	205,448	38,565
3	Wal-Mart Stores, Inc.	166,394	6,771
4	General Electric Co.	161,584	15,873
5	Procter & Gamble Co.	140,013	2,954
6	Apple, Inc.	136,801	2,805
7	Google, Inc.	123,662	2,991
8	Johnson & Johnson	117,908	6,009
9	Intl. Business Machines Corp.	112,519	1,794
10	Cisco Systems, Inc.	101,091	2,386

Source: "2008 1000 EVA/MVA Annual Ranking Database," evaDimensions, June 30, 2008, accessed August 23, 2009, http://evadimensions.com.

their profits by increasing the rate of customer retention by just 5 to 10 percent per year.[37] Retaining customers obviously means having more customers, but how many more? Consider two companies starting with a customer base of 100,000 customers and an acquisition rate of 20 percent (i.e., each company's customer base grows by 20 percent each year). Assuming that Company B has a retention rate that is just 5 percent higher (85 percent retention rate for Company A versus 90 percent retention rate for Company B), Company B will double its customer base around the 9th year, while it will take company A slightly more than 15 years to double its customer base. On average, this means Company B also profits by a higher percentage.[38] And, if a company can keep a customer for life, the benefits are even larger. According to Stew Leonard, owner of the Connecticut-based Stew Leonard's grocery store chain, "The lifetime value of a customer in a supermarket is about $246,000. Every time a customer comes through our front door I see, stamped on their forehead in big red numbers, '$246,000.' I'm never going to make that person unhappy with me. Or lose her to the competition."[39]

Beyond the clear benefits to the bottom line, the second reason to study customer defections is that customers who have left are much more likely than current customers to tell you what you were doing wrong. Finally, companies that understand why customers leave can not only take steps to fix ongoing problems but can also identify which customers are likely to leave and make changes to prevent them from leaving.

3.4 | THE INTERNAL PERSPECTIVE: CONTROLLING QUALITY

The third part of the balanced scorecard, the internal perspective, consists of the processes, decisions, and actions that managers and workers make within the organization. In contrast to the EVA-oriented financial perspective and the outward-looking customer perspective, the internal perspective focuses on internal processes and systems that add value to the organization. Consequently, the internal perspective of the balanced scorecard usually leads managers to a focus on quality.

Quality is typically defined and measured in three ways: excellence, value, and conformance to specifications.[40] When the company defines its quality goal as *excellence,* managers must try to produce a product or service of unsurpassed performance and features. For example, Singapore Airlines is the best airline in the world by almost any standard. It has also received various "best airline" awards from the Pacific Asia Travel Association, *Travel+Leisure, Business Traveller, Condé Nast Traveller,* and *Fortune.*[41] Whereas many airlines try to cram passengers into every available inch on a plane, Singapore Airlines delivers creature comforts to encourage repeat business from customers willing to pay premium prices. On its newer planes, the first-class cabin is divided into eight private mini-rooms, each with an unusually wide leather seat that folds down flat for sleeping, a 23-inch LCD TV that doubles as a computer monitor, and an adjustable table. These amenities and services are common for private jets but truly unique in the commercial airline industry.[42] Singapore Airlines was the first airline, in the 1970s, to introduce a choice of meals, complimentary drinks, and earphones in coach class. It was the first to introduce worldwide video, news, telephone, and fax services and the first to feature personal video monitors for movies, news, and games. Singapore Airlines has had AC power for laptop computers for some time, and recently it became the first airline to introduce on-board high-speed Internet access.

Value is the customer perception that the product quality is excellent for the price offered. At a higher price, for example, customers may perceive the product to be less of a value. When a company emphasizes value as its quality goal, managers must simultaneously control excellence, price, durability, and any other features of a product or service that customers strongly associate with value. One of the ways that Hyundai has succeeded in the U.S. auto market is by emphasizing value in its cars. For example, the 2011 Sonata comes standard with dozens of features that are only optional in competitors' models, such as active head restraints, electronic stability control, and Bluetooth connectivity. The Sonata also has an engine that leads the class in power and fuel-efficiency. The entire package, however, has great value, since a Sonata costs 10-20 percent less than similarly equipped competitors, such as the Honda Accord or Toyota Camry. And to reassure the customer that the Sonata is not only affordable but durable, Hyundai backs the vehicle with a 10-year warranty.[43]

When a company defines its quality goal as conformance to specifications, employees must base decisions and actions on whether services and products measure up to the standards. In contrast to excellence- and value-based definitions of quality, which can be somewhat ambiguous, measuring whether products and services are "in spec" is relatively easy. Although conformance to specifications (e.g., precise tolerances for a part's weight or thickness) is usually associated with manufacturing, it can be used equally well to control quality in nonmanufacturing businesses. Exhibit 16.6 shows a checklist that a cook or restaurant owner would use to ensure quality when buying fresh fish.

The way in which a company defines quality affects the methods and measures that workers use to control quality. Accordingly, Exhibit 16.7 shows the advantages and disadvantages associated with the excellence, value, and conformance to specification definitions of quality.

Exhibit 16.6 Conformance to Specifications Checklist for Buying Fresh Fish

FRESH WHOLE FISH	ACCEPTABLE	NOT ACCEPTABLE
Gills	✓ bright red, free of slime, clear mucus	✗ brown to grayish, thick, yellow mucus
Eyes	✓ clear, bright, bulging, black pupils	✗ dull, sunken, cloudy, gray pupils
Smell	✓ inoffensive, slight ocean smell	✗ ammonia, putrid smell
Skin	✓ opalescent sheen, scales adhere tightly to skin	✗ dull or faded color, scales missing or easily removed
Flesh	✓ firm and elastic to touch, tight to the bone	✗ soft and flabby, separating from the bone
Belly cavity	✓ no viscera or blood visible, lining intact, no bone protruding	✗ incomplete evisceration, cuts or protruding bones, off-odor

Sources: "A Closer Look: Buy It Fresh, Keep It Fresh," *Consumer Reports Online*, accessed June 20, 2005, http://www.seagrant.sunysb.edu/SeafoodTechnology/SeafoodMedia/CR02-2001/CR-SeafoodII020101.htm; "How to Purchase: Buying Fish," AboutSeafood, accessed June 20, 2005, http://www.aboutseafood.com/faqs/purchase1.html.

Exhibit 16.7 Advantages and Disadvantages of Different Measures of Quality

QUALITY MEASURE	ADVANTAGES	DISADVANTAGES
Excellence	Promotes clear organizational vision.	Provides little practical guidance for managers.
	Being/providing the "best" motivates and inspires managers and employees.	Excellence is ambiguous. What is it? Who defines it?
Value	Appeals to customers who know excellence "when they see it."	Difficult to measure and control.
	Customers recognize differences in value.	Can be difficult to determine what factors influence whether a product/service is seen as having value.
	Easier to measure and compare whether products/services differ in value.	Controlling the balance between excellence and cost (i.e., affordable excellence) can be difficult.
Conformance to Specifications	If specifications can be written, conformance to specifications is usually measurable.	Many products/services cannot be easily evaluated in terms of conformance to specifications.
	Should lead to increased efficiency.	Promotes standardization, so may hurt performance when adapting to changes is more important.
	Promotes consistency in quality.	May be less appropriate for services, which are dependent on a high degree of human contact.

Source: Republished by The Academy of Management, P.O. Box 3020, Briar Cliff Manor, NY, 10510-8020; C. A. Reeves and D. A. Bednar, "Defining Quality: Alternatives and Implications," *Academy of Management Review* 19 (1994): 419–445. Reproduced by permission of the publisher via Copyright Clearance Center, Inc.

3.5 | THE INNOVATION AND LEARNING PERSPECTIVE: CONTROLLING WASTE AND POLLUTION

The last part of the balanced scorecard, the innovation and learning perspective, addresses the question, "Can we continue to improve and create value?" Thus, the innovation and learning perspective involves continuous improvement in ongoing operations (discussed in Chapter 18); relearning and redesigning the processes by which products and services are created (discussed in Chapter 7); and even things like waste and pollution minimization, an increasingly important area of innovation.

Exhibit 16.8 shows the four levels of waste minimization ranging from waste disposal, which produces the smallest minimization of waste, to waste prevention and reduction, which produces the greatest minimization.[44] The goals of the top level, *waste prevention and reduction,* are to prevent waste and pollution before they occur or to reduce them when they do occur. For example, United Parcel Service (UPS) uses a software program that helps drivers plan routes with only right turns to save driving time. The strategy also prevents environmental waste, since UPS saves 3 million gallons of fuel each year and reduces emissions of carbon dioxide by 31,000 metric tons.[45] There are three strategies for waste prevention and reduction:

1. *Good housekeeping*—performing regularly scheduled preventive maintenance of offices, plants, and equipment. Examples of good housekeeping include fixing leaky valves quickly to prevent wasted water and making sure machines are running properly so that they don't use more fuel than necessary.

2. *Material/product substitution*—replacing toxic or hazardous materials with less harmful materials. As part of its Pollution Prevention Pays program over the last 30 years, 3M eliminated 2.2 billion pounds of pollutants and saved $1 billion by using benign substitutes for toxic solvents in its manufacturing processes.[46]

3. *Process modification*—changing steps or procedures to eliminate or reduce waste. The Lavergne Group used to recycle HP printer cartridges by shredding the plastic. Recently, though, in conjunction with HP, it created a process by which the cartridges would be dismantled piece-by-piece. This change has allowed Lavergne facilities to recover 50 percent more plastic from each printer cartridge.[47]

At the second level of waste minimization, *recycle and reuse,* wastes are reduced by reusing materials as long as possible or by collecting materials for on- or off-site recycling. A growing trend in recycling is *design for disassembly,* where products are designed from the start for easy disassembly, recycling, and reuse once they are no longer usable. Herman Miller, a manufacturer of office equipment, not only uses recycled material in its award-winning chairs, but also takes steps to make

© iStockphoto.com/Olga Lyubkina

Exhibit 16.8 Four Levels of Waste Minimization

- Waste Prevention & Reduction
- Recycle & Reuse
- Waste Treatment
- Waste Disposal

Source: Reprinted from *Business Horizons*, September-October 1995, D.R. May & B.L. Flannery, "Cutting Waste with Employee Involvement Teams," pp. 28–38, Copyright © 1995, with permission from Elsevier.

recycling them very easy. The company clearly labels which parts are recyclable. It also identifies the type of plastic used in each part and minimizes the different types of plastics used making things that much more convenient for the consumer. Finally, the company designs its chairs so that they are easy to take apart, and even includes detailed instruction on how to disassemble their products safely and easily.[48] While Herman Miller is taking this "green" approach voluntarily, the European Union has required companies to make most of their products and packaging recyclable for some time. And since companies, not consumers, are held responsible for recycling the products they manufacture, they must design their products from the start with recycling in mind.[49] Under the European Union's end-of-life vehicle program, companies will have to be able to recover and recycle 80 percent of parts from cars built in Europe since January 2002. The requirement rises to 85 percent for cars made since 2006, and will be 95 percent for cars made after 2015. Moreover, since 2007, the European Union has required auto manufacturers to recycle all the cars that they made between 1989 and 2002.[50]

At the third level of waste minimization, *waste treatment,* companies use biological, chemical, or other processes to turn potentially harmful waste into harmless compounds or useful by-products. In Africa, slaughterhouses often dump untreated animal waste into rivers and lakes. This spreads disease and generates methane and carbon dioxide—greenhouse gases that contribute to global warming. Instead of traditional treatment processes, Cows to Kilowatts Partnership Limited uses an advanced anaerobic reactor to turn animal blood and waste into biogas, which is then processed and compressed into cooking gas or fuel to run household generators. Even the leftover sludge can be reused as environmentally friendly fertilizer.[51]

The fourth and lowest level of waste minimization is *waste disposal*. Wastes that cannot be prevented, reduced, recycled, reused, or treated should be safely disposed of in processing plants or in environmentally secure landfills that prevent leakage and contamination of soil and underground water supplies. For example, with the average computer lasting just 3 years, approximately 60 million computers come out of service each year.[52] But organizations can't just throw old computers away, because there are lead-containing cathode ray tubes in the monitors, toxic metals in the circuit boards, paint-coated plastic in the casings, and metal coatings that can contaminate ground water.[53] For a fee, companies and consumers can use HP's Planter Partners website to arrange to have their old computer equipment picked up. HP has already diverted from landfills and recycled 1 billion pounds of electronic products and supplies and will recover another billion pounds by the end of 2010.

STUDENT
Study
Tools

Located at the back of your book

☐ Rip out and study the Chapter Review Card at the end of the book

Log in to the CourseMate for MGMT at cengagebrain.com to:

☐ Review Key Term Flashcards delivered 3 ways (print or online)

☐ Complete both Practice Quizzes to prepare for tests

☐ Play Beat the Clock and Quizbowl to master concepts

☐ Complete the Crossword Puzzle to review key terms

☐ Watch the video on Numi Organic Tea for a real company example and take the accompanying quiz

☐ Watch the Biz Flix clip on *Friday Night Lights* and take the quiz

☐ Complete the Case Assignment on Starbucks

☐ Work through the Management Decision on controlling employee theft

☐ Work through the Management Team Decision on making airport security more efficient

☐ Develop your skills with the Develop Your Career Potential exercise

17 Managing Information

© iStockphoto.com/aprott

LEARNING OUTCOMES:

1 explain the strategic importance of information.

2 describe the characteristics of useful information (i.e., its value and costs).

3 explain the basics of capturing, processing, and protecting information.

4 describe how companies can access and share information and knowledge.

Chapter 17

Why Information Matters

a generation ago, computer hardware and software had little to do with managing business information. Rather than storing information on hard drives, managers stored it in filing cabinets. Instead of uploading daily sales and inventory levels to corporate databases, they mailed hard-copy summaries to headquarters at the end of each month. Managers communicated by sticky notes, not email. Phone messages were written down by assistants and coworkers, not left on voice mail. Workers did not use desktop or laptop computers as daily tools to get work done. Instead, they scheduled limited access time to run batch jobs on the mainframe computer (and prayed that the batch job computer code they wrote would work).

Today, a generation later, computer hardware and software are an integral part of managing business information. This is due mainly to something called **Moore's law.** Gordon Moore is one of the founders of Intel Corporation, which makes 75 percent of the integrated processors used in personal computers. In 1965, Moore predicted that computer-processing power would double and its cost would drop by 50 percent about every 2 years.[1] As Exhibit 17.1 on the next page shows, Moore was right. Computer power, as measured by the number of transistors per computer chip, *has* more than doubled every few years. Consequently, the computer sitting in your lap or on your desk is not only smaller but also much cheaper and more powerful than the large mainframe computers used by *Fortune* 500 companies 15 years ago. In fact, if car manufacturers had achieved the same power increases and cost decreases attained by computer manufacturers, a fully outfitted Lexus or Mercedes sedan would cost less than $1,000!

Raw data are facts and figures. For example, 11, $452, 4, and 26,100 are some data that I used the day I wrote this section of the chapter. However, facts and figures aren't particularly useful unless they have meaning. For example, you probably can't guess what these four pieces of raw data represent, can you? And if you can't, these data are useless. That's why researchers make the distinction between raw data and information. Whereas raw data consist of facts and figures, **information** is useful data that can influence someone's choices and behavior. One way to think about the difference between data and information is that information has context.

So what did those four pieces of data mean to me? Well, 11 stands for Channel 11, the local CBS affiliate on which I watched part of the men's PGA golf tournament; $452 is how much it would cost me to rent a minivan for a week if I go skiing over spring break; 4 is for the 4-gigabyte storage card that I want to add to my digital camera (prices are low, so I'll probably buy it); and 26,100 means that it's time to get the oil changed in my car.

After reading the next two sections, you should be able to

1 **explain the strategic importance of information.**

2 **describe the characteristics of useful information (i.e., its value and costs).**

Moore's law the prediction that the cost of computing will drop by 50 percent about every 2 years as computer-processing power doubles

Raw data facts and figures

Information useful data that can influence people's choices and behavior

Exhibit 17.1 Moore's Law

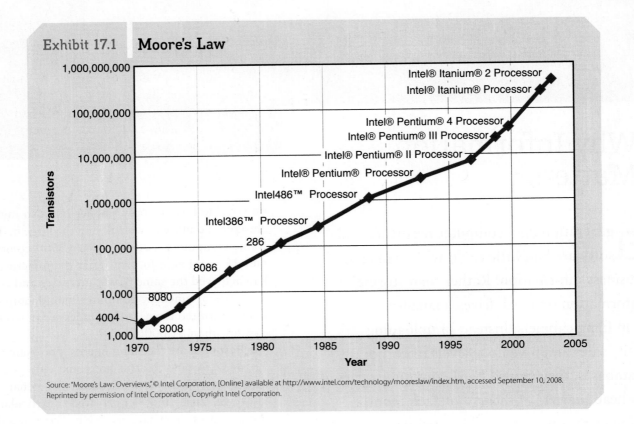

1 | Strategic Importance of Information

In today's hypercompetitive business environments, information is as important as capital (i.e., money) for business success, whether it's about furniture delivery, product inventory, pricing, or costs. It takes money to get businesses started, but businesses can't survive and grow without the right information.

*Information has strategic importance for organizations because it can be used to **1.1 obtain first-mover advantage** and **1.2 sustain a competitive advantage once it has been created.***

1.1 | FIRST-MOVER ADVANTAGE

First-mover advantage is the strategic advantage that companies earn by being the first in an industry to use new information technology to substantially lower costs or to differentiate a product or service from that of competitors. Texas-based DG Fastchannel revolutionized TV marketing when it built its own satellite and Web-based distribution network. While other companies were sending commercials to TV stations on videotapes, DG Fastchannel uses its digital network to make commercials available just a few hours after it produces them. The speed of the network also allows the company to adjust commercials based on near-real-time feedback from consumers. Thanks to its network, DG Fastchannel has been growing at an average of 43 percent over the last three years, and controls almost 65 percent of the ad delivery market in the United States.[2] First-mover advantages like those established by DG Fastchannel can be sizable. On average, first movers earn a 30 percent market share compared to 19 percent for the companies that follow.[3] Likewise, over 70 percent of market leaders started as first movers.[4]

1.2 | SUSTAINING A COMPETITIVE ADVANTAGE

As described above, companies that use information technology to establish a first-mover advantage usually have higher market shares and profits. According to the resource-based view of information technology shown in Exhibit 17.2, companies need to address three critical issues in order to sustain a competitive advantage through information technology. First, does the information technology create value for the firm by lowering costs or providing a better product or service? If an information technology doesn't add value, then investing

First-mover advantage the strategic advantage that companies earn by being the first to use new information technology to substantially lower costs or to make a product or service different from that of competitors

Exhibit 17.2 Using Information Technology to Sustain a Competitive Advantage

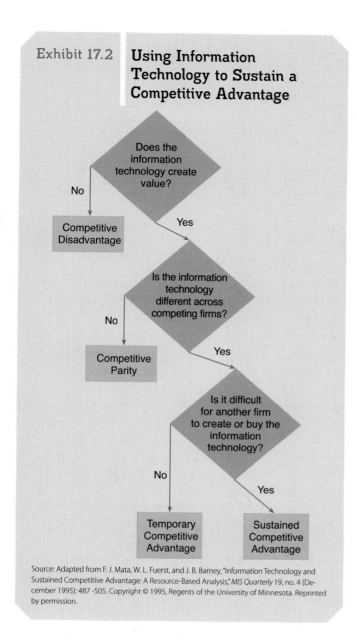

Does the information technology create value?

No → Competitive Disadvantage

Yes → Is the information technology different across competing firms?

No → Competitive Parity

Yes → Is it difficult for another firm to create or buy the information technology?

No → Temporary Competitive Advantage

Yes → Sustained Competitive Advantage

Source: Adapted from F. J. Mata, W. L. Fuerst, and J. B. Barney, "Information Technology and Sustained Competitive Advantage: A Resource-Based Analysis," *MIS Quarterly* 19, no. 4 (December 1995): 487-505. Copyright © 1995, Regents of the University of Minnesota. Reprinted by permission.

in it would put the firm at a competitive disadvantage relative to companies that choose information technologies that do add value.

Second, is the information technology the same or different across competing firms? If all the firms have access to the same information technology and use it in the same way, then no firm has an advantage over another (i.e., competitive parity).

Third, is it difficult for another company to create or buy the information technology used by the firm? If so, then the firm has established a sustainable competitive advantage over competitors through information technology. If not, then the competitive advantage is just temporary, and competitors should eventually be able to duplicate the advantages the leading firm has gained from information technology. For more about sustainable competitive advantage and its sources, see Chapter 6 on organizational strategy.

In short, the key to sustaining a competitive advantage is not faster computers, more memory, and larger hard drives. The key is using information technology to continuously improve and support the core functions of a business. A number of hotels and resorts, such as Marriott, have turned to social media to improve their customer service. Staff members spend hours searching for any mention of their hotel on Twitter, Facebook, blogs, TripAdvisor, and other sites. Whenever they find a complaint about service, they offer an immediate apology and, more often than not, extra perks like room upgrades and free meals to make up for the problem. When Paul Horan tweeted that his room at the Orlando Marriott World Center was "the crappiest room in the hotel," a member of the hotel's staff saw the tweet, immediately sent an apology note, and upgraded his room. By paying attention to social media, tech-savvy hotels have found a way to get near-instantaneous feedback from customers and resolve any potential problems quickly, so developing a reputation for excellent service.[5] Companies like Marriott that achieve a first-mover advantage with information technology and then sustain it with continued investment create a moving target that competitors have difficulty hitting.

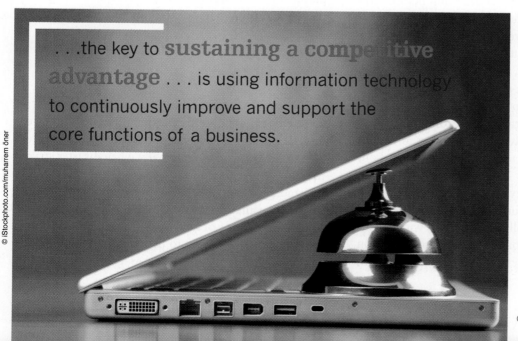

. . .the key to **sustaining a competitive advantage** . . . is using information technology to continuously improve and support the core functions of a business.

© iStockphoto.com/muharrem öner

2 Characteristics and Costs of Useful Information

Komatsu, the second largest producer of heavy machinery (think bulldozers, dump trucks, backhoes, etc.) in the world, installs the KOMTRAX system in nearly all of its products. A combination GPS device and Web application, KOMTRAX provides real-time information that is vital to managing a fleet of huge machines. The system not only shows the location of every machine, helping to prevent theft, but also measures fuel consumption, gauges the load that each machine bears, and provides maintenance alerts. The system even reports how many hours a particular machine was working, idling, or in transport. The information that KOMTRAX provides has helped numerous companies use their heavy machinery more efficiently. The KOMTRAX information is quite beneficial to Komatsu, as well. Because KOMTRAX provides a real-time snapshot of construction activity all over the world, Komatsu has very detailed information about the supply of and demand for its products. As spokeswoman Natsuko Usami says, "If mines and construction sites are operating the equipment full-time, we know there's a chance that market demand will go up, and we can order our factories to ramp up production."[6]

As Komatsu's KOMTRAX demonstrates, information is useful when it is 2.1 accurate, 2.2 complete, 2.3 relevant, and 2.4 timely. However, there can be significant 2.5 acquisition, 2.6 processing, 2.7 storage, 2.8 retrieval, and 2.9 communication costs associated with useful information.

2.1 | ACCURATE INFORMATION

Information is useful when it is accurate. Before relying on information to make decisions, you must know that the information is correct. But what if it isn't? For example, the restaurant business is notoriously difficult for two reasons. First, it's extremely competitive. Customers in any location typically have hundreds of restaurants from which to choose when dining out. Second, 60 percent of restaurants go out of business within three years. Why? Restaurant owners and managers typically have little accurate information about their businesses. Sure, they know whether they're losing money or not, but they don't know why. Restaurants often don't have accurate information regarding how much alcohol they sell (for example, wine versus beer versus hard liquor) nor do they have information regarding which food dishes (lobster versus swordfish)

sell more or are more expensive to prepare. With Avero's Slingshot software, however, restaurants can track this information and more. John Stinson, the head chef at Antonio's in Las Vegas, says, "My bosses keep asking, 'How many did you sell? How many did you sell?' I constantly need to provide the numbers." So Stinson uses Slingshot to examine the data and plan his menus accordingly. For instance, he found out that sea bass sold 196 times in one month, whereas ahi tuna sold 89 times. Since they both cost the same and sell for $29, Stinson reduced costs and eliminated unsold food by cutting his ahi tuna orders from suppliers in half.[7]

2.2 | COMPLETE INFORMATION

Information is useful when it is complete. Incomplete or missing information makes it difficult to recognize problems and identify potential solutions. For example, doctors hate learning new technology, but they hate inaccurate and incomplete information even more. So, the University of Pittsburgh Medical Center (UPMC) set up a computerized medical system called eRecords to replace paper medical charts and test results that were easily lost or misplaced and therefore not available when doctors and nurses needed them. eRecords automatically tracks vital signs, such as pulse, blood pressure, and respiration rate, and gives doctors and nurses immediate bedside access to x-rays, medical test results, and patients' prescriptions. Dr. Ibrahim Ghobrial, UPMC's director of Ambulatory Services, says, "The applications within eRecords also enable the physician to complete clinical documentation, transcription, family histories, procedure histories, and a variety of other tasks online . . . online documentation is organized in clear, concise formats, which eliminates the task of interpreting handwritten notes sometimes placed in the margins of paper records or scattered throughout other parts of the paper forms."[8]

2.3 | RELEVANT INFORMATION

You can have accurate, complete information, but it's not very useful if it doesn't pertain to the problems you're facing. Imagine that an earthquake destroys a large city in Japan or that a hurricane devastates cities and towns in a five-state area in the southeastern part of the United States. Usually when disaster strikes, the power goes out, and the authorities, first responders, and people affected lose access to what they need most—relevant information. Microsoft's Claire Bonilla is a senior director of field operations who coordinates the company's resources to help people affected by disasters around the world (this is part of Microsoft's corporate social responsibility efforts). Bonilla says, "The core to the effectiveness of any disaster response is the ability to share information and coordinate the effort between the many organizations involved. Software can play a huge role in doing that. Whenever we hear about a disaster, the first step is to establish a connection with the lead response organization locally. Then we help with real-time communication and use mapping software to provide partners with situational awareness so that, for example, relief agencies can see the location of a shelter in need of medical supplies. We also give data-sharing capability to first responders and government agencies so they can share relevant information with outside organizations without compromising security."[9]

2.4 | TIMELY INFORMATION

Finally, information is useful when it is timely. News that your bus passed the stop 10 minutes ago is not helpful in getting you where you want to go. To be timely, the information must be available when needed to define a problem or to begin to identify possible solutions. If you've ever thought, "I wish I had known that earlier," then you understand the importance of timely information and the opportunity cost of not having it. If it seems as if airlines are misplacing your bags more often than they used to, they are. The number of mishandled bags is 28 percent higher now than it was 10 years ago. The primary reason for this is a lack of timeliness because of delayed flights. David Castelveter of the Air Transport Association says, "Delays cause missed connections. Missed connections caused mishandled bags."[10] Airlines that do a better job of handling baggage, however, have been using bar code tags and scanners to keep track of luggage and make sure it gets where it's supposed to be at the right time. For example, after having one of the worst baggage handling records, American Airlines purchased mobile scanning units for its gates at Dallas–Fort Worth Airport, which is American's main hub. These scanners are attached to the small tractors that are used to move bags between connecting flights. Importantly, they give baggage handlers timely information on gate changes and allow the company to know precisely where your bag is at any time. That, in turn, helps American figure out where the bottlenecks are in its baggage handling system.

2.5 | ACQUISITION COSTS

Acquisition cost is the cost of obtaining data that you don't have. Every ten years, the United States performs a census of the entire population. Through direct mail,

Internet forms, and door-to-door interviews, employees and volunteers of the Census Bureau aim to produce a comprehensive database of the American population, which includes the total number of residents as well as information about demographics, ethnicities, and the geographic distribution of residents. Compiling such a huge database is costly. The Census Bureau had to prepare and print 360 million paper surveys, a stack of paper that would be 29 miles high. It had to mail these surveys to more than 134 million households. It also had to set up online survey forms on the Internet and hire more than 1.2 million people who would go door-to-door to obtain information. The Bureau also had to set up facilities to process and standardize the data collected, particularly since the survey was available in six languages. What's more, to maximize the response rate, the Census Bureau launched a number

Acquisition cost the cost of obtaining data that you don't have

Airlines that do a **better job** of handling baggage have been using bar code tags and scanners to keep track of luggage and make sure it gets where it's supposed to be at the **right time**.

Processing cost the cost of turning raw data into usable information

Storage cost the cost of physically or electronically archiving information for later use and retrieval

Retrieval cost the cost of accessing already-stored and processed information

Communication cost the cost of transmitting information from one place to another

of marketing campaigns with local organizations and celebrities. The total cost for obtaining all of this information? $14.5 billion.[11]

2.6 | PROCESSING COSTS

Companies often have massive amounts of data but not in the form or combination they need. Consequently, **processing cost** is the cost of turning raw data into usable information. The Large Hadron Collider (LHC), the world's largest particle accelerator, was designed to perform research on sub-atomic particles, with the hope of expanding knowledge on the beginnings of the universe. According to CERN, the agency that operates LHC, the collider will produce 4 gigabytes of data per second, enough to fill 1.7 million DVDs per year. To analyze, process, and distribute this massive amount of data, CERN created the Worldwide LHC Computing Grid (WLCG), a complex computer network connecting 130 research centers in 34 countries. The cost for the WLCG is expected to total €500 million (about $640 million), while CERN expects to spend about €14 million (about $18 million) per year to maintain and purchase computing equipment at the LHC site.[12]

2.7 | STORAGE COSTS

Storage cost is the cost of physically or electronically archiving information for later use and retrieval. For consumers who want to make sure they never lose their computer files, Carbonite offers an online-backup service. For an annual fee, Carbonite gives users unlimited storage space on its servers so that they can back up whatever files they don't want to lose. It's estimated that over 100 million files are added to Carbonite's servers each day. To make room for all those files, Carbonite recently opened a new server facility in Boston, at a cost of more than $46 million, which features multiple AC feeds (necessary for preventing the servers from overheating) and an uninterruptable diesel generator (in case the electricity ever goes out).[13]

2.8 | RETRIEVAL COSTS

Retrieval cost is the cost of accessing already-stored and processed information. One of the most common misunderstandings about information is that it is easy and cheap to retrieve once the company has it. Not so.

First, you have to find the information. Then, you've got to convince whoever has it to share it with you. Then the information has to be processed into a form that is useful for you.

For example, as companies move toward paperless office systems, how will employees quickly and easily retrieve archived emails, file records, website information, word-processing documents, and images? One solution is enterprise content management (ECM), which is a way of storing and providing access to unstructured information. Ulrich Kampffmeyer, former member of the board of directors of the Association for Information and Image Management, summed up the challenge of retrieval costs: "The most important job is to keep in-house information under control. The questions add up: where to put the thousands and thousands of emails, what to do with the electronically signed business correspondence, where to put taxation-relevant data, how to transfer information from the disorganized file system, how to consolidate information in a repository that everybody can use, how to get a single login for all the systems, how to create a uniform in-basket for all incoming information, how to make sure that no information is lost or ignored, etc., etc."[14]

2.9 | COMMUNICATION COSTS

Communication cost is the cost of transmitting information from one place to another. A flight data recorder, also known as a black box, records information about an airplane's flight performance (altitude, speed, climb rate, etc.) that is used for investigating accidents. In some cases, however, such as with Air France Flight 447, which crashed in the Atlantic Ocean in June 2009, the black box cannot be found, leaving investigators very few clues about what caused the accident. To solve this problem, Star Aviation and AeroMechanical Services both market a next-generation "black box" that provides airlines with real-time black box data. This information does not come cheap, though, at $3 to $5 per minute. An airline operating hundreds of flights per day all over the globe would have to spend several hundred million dollars to obtain real-time data.[15] Utility companies are now replacing RF meters with "smart meters," which, besides sending information to the utility companies, also provide consumers with online information about their energy usage and recommendations on how to reduce it.[16] Pacific Gas and Electric, based in San Francisco, is spending $2.2 billion to introduce this new technology.

Getting and Sharing Information

In 1907, Metropolitan Life Insurance built a huge office building in New York City for its brand new, state-of-the-art information technology system. What was this great breakthrough in information management? Card files. That's right, the same card file systems that every library in America used before computers. Metropolitan Life's information technology consisted of 20,000 separate file drawers that sat in hundreds of file cabinets more than 15 feet tall. This filing system held 20 million insurance applications, 700,000 accounting books, and 500,000 death certificates. Metropolitan Life employed 61 workers who did nothing but sort, file, and climb ladders to pull files as needed.[17]

How we get and share information has clearly changed. Today, if a storm, fire, or accident damages a policyholder's property, the insurance company writes a check on the spot to cover the loss. When policyholders buy a car, they call their insurance agent from the dealership to activate their insurance before driving off in their new car. And now, insurance companies are marketing their products and services to customers directly from the Internet. From card files to Internet files in just under a century, the rate of change in information technology is spectacular.

After reading the next two sections, you should be able to

3 explain the basics of capturing, processing, and protecting information.

4 describe how companies can access and share information and knowledge.

3 Capturing, Processing, and Protecting Information

In this section, you will learn about the information technologies that companies use to **3.1 capture, 3.2 process,** and **3.3 protect information.**

3.1 | CAPTURING INFORMATION

There are two basic methods of capturing information: manual and electronic. Manual capture of information is a slow, costly, labor-intensive process that entails recording and entering data by hand into a data storage device. Consequently, companies are relying more on electronic capture. They use electronic devices such as bar codes, radio frequency identification tags, and document scanners to capture and record data electronically.

Bar codes represent numerical data by varying the thickness and pattern of vertical bars. The primary advantage of bar codes is that the data they represent can be read and recorded in an instant with a handheld or pen-type scanner. Bar codes cut checkout times in half, reduce data entry errors by 75 percent, and save stores money because stockers don't have to go through the labor-intensive process of putting a price tag on each item in the store.[18] Consumer product companies, like Unilever, are now partnering with grocery stores and technology companies to test bar code–based coupons that can be scanned directly from consumers' cell phones.[19]

Radio frequency identification (RFID) tags contain minuscule microchips and antennas that transmit information via radio waves.[20] Unlike bar codes, which require direct line-of-sight scanning, RFID tags are read by turning on an RFID reader that, like a radio, tunes to a specific frequency to determine the number *and* location of products, parts, or anything else to which the RFID tags are attached. Turn on an RFID reader, and every RFID tag within the reader's range (from several hundred to several thousand feet) is accounted for. Because they are now so inexpensive, RFID tags and readers are being put to thousands of uses in all kinds of businesses. For example, Blue C Sushi has five restaurants in Seattle where, as is the tradition, plates of food circle the restaurant on a conveyor belt so that diners can pick the food they want. At the end of the meal, your bill is determined by the number of plates you've taken. Blue C uses RFID tags on all its plates to make sure that the food it serves is fresh. Plates are scanned as they leave each chef's workstation and then are periodically scanned on the conveyor belt to determine if the food on them is still fresh. If a plate of food is still on the belt after 90 minutes, the system issues an alert to remove it. The system also keeps track of which plates are selling the fastest and when sales begin to slow. This has helped each of the company's five restaurants, which would typically throw 80 to 100 plates of food each night, cut waste by about 45 percent.[21]

Electronic scanners, which convert printed text and pictures into digital images, have become an

> **Bar code** a visual pattern that represents numerical data by varying the thickness and pattern of vertical bars
>
> **Radio frequency identification (RFID) tags** tags containing minuscule microchips that transmit information via radio waves and can be used to track the number and location of the objects into which the tags have been inserted
>
> **Electronic scanner** an electronic device that converts printed text and pictures into digital images

increasingly popular method of capturing data electronically because they are inexpensive and easy to use. The first requirement for a good scanner is a *document feeder* that automatically feeds document pages into the scanner or turns the pages (often with a puff of air) when scanning books or bound documents.[22] Text that has been digitized cannot be searched or edited like the text you create or work with in word-processing software, however, so the second requirement for a good scanner is **optical character recognition** software to convert digitized documents into ASCII (American Standard Code for Information Interchange) text or Adobe PDF documents. ASCII text can be searched, read, and edited with standard word processing, email, desktop publishing, database management, and spreadsheet software, while PDF documents can be searched and edited with Adobe's Acrobat software.

3.2 | PROCESSING INFORMATION

Processing information means transforming raw data into meaningful information that can be applied to business decision making. Evaluating sales data to determine the best- and worst-selling products, examining repair records to determine product reliability, and monitoring the cost of long-distance phone calls are all examples of processing raw data into meaningful information. And with automated, electronic capture of data, increased processing power, and cheaper and more plentiful ways to store data, managers no longer worry about getting data. Instead, they scratch their heads about how to use the over-

AP Images/Joey Ivansco, AJC

A Radio-Controlled Soda Fountain

Coca-Cola is testing a soft-drink vending machine that it calls the Freestyle. From this one machine, which contains 30 different flavor cartridges, consumers can order over 100 different drinks and even make custom blends. Each of the flavor cartridges is equipped with an RFID chip, which provides Coca-Cola with a wealth of information about sales, quality control, and supply management. For example, the RFID chips provide a daily report of which drinks, and how much of them, are being purchased every day, helping the company understand what is popular and what is not. The RFID chips also provide alerts for when certain cartridges are running low and need to be replaced. In addition, RFID provides Coca-Cola with a security measure. The chips allow the machine to determine whether a cartridge has been installed correctly or whether it is a genuine Coca-Cola product. In the case of a product recall, Coca-Cola can even stop a Freestyle machine from using a cartridge through the RFID chip.

Source: C. Swedberg, "RFID to Revolutionize Coca-Cola's Dispensers," *RFID Journal*, June 10, 2009, http://www.rfidjournal.com/article/view/4967.

whelming amount of data that pours into their businesses every day. Furthermore, most managers know little about statistics and have neither the time nor the inclination to learn how to use them to analyze data.

One promising tool to help managers dig out from under the avalanche of data is data mining. **Data mining** is the process of discovering patterns and relationships in large amounts of data.[23] Data mining works by using complex algorithms such as neural networks, rule induction, and decision trees. If you don't know what those are, that's okay. With data mining, you don't have to. Most managers only need to know that data mining looks for patterns that are already in the data but are too complex for them to spot on their own.

Data mining typically splits a data set in half, finds patterns in one half, and then tests the validity of those patterns by trying to find them again in the second half of the data set. The data typically come from a **data warehouse** that stores huge amounts of data that have been prepared for data mining analysis by being cleaned of errors and redundancy. The data in a data warehouse can then be analyzed using two kinds of data mining. **Supervised data mining** usually begins with the user telling the data mining software to look and test for specific patterns and relationships in a data set. Typically, this is done through a series of "what if?" questions or statements. For instance, a grocery store manager might instruct the data mining software to determine if coupons placed in the Sunday paper increase or decrease sales. By contrast, with **unsupervised data mining**, the user simply tells the data mining software to uncover whatever patterns and relationships it can find in a data set. For example, State Farm Insurance used to have three pricing categories for car insurance, depending on your driving record: preferred for the best drivers, standard for typical drivers, and nonstandard for the worst drivers. Now, however, it has moved to tiered pricing based on the 300 different kinds of driving records that its data mining software was able to discover. This allows State Farm to be much more precise in matching 300 different price levels to 300 different kinds of driving records.[24]

Unsupervised data mining is particularly good at identifying association or affinity patterns, sequence patterns, and predictive patterns. It can also identify what data mining technicians call data clusters.[25] **Association or affinity patterns** occur when two or more database elements tend to occur together in a significant way.

Data mining the process of discovering patterns and relationships in large amounts of data

Data warehouse stores huge amounts of data that have been prepared for data mining analysis by being cleaned of errors and redundancy

Supervised data mining the process when the user tells the data mining software to look and test for specific patterns and relationships in a data set

Unsupervised data mining the process when the user simply tells the data mining software to uncover whatever patterns and relationships it can find in a data set

Association or affinity patterns when two or more database elements tend to occur together in a significant way

Surprisingly, Osco Drug, based in Chicago, found that beer and diapers tended to be bought together between 5 and 7 p.m. The question, of course, was "why?" The answer, on further review, was fairly straightforward: Fathers, who were told by their wives to buy some diapers on their way home, decided to pick up a six-pack for themselves, too.[26]

Sequence patterns occur when two or more database elements occur together in a significant pattern in which one of the elements precedes the other. Most professional baseball teams change the price of a ticket depending on the day of the week and the opponent. For example, the New York Yankees will charge a higher price for a ticket to a weekend game versus the Boston Red Sox, their historical rivals, than for a weekday game versus the Washington Nationals. The San Francisco Giants have taken things one step further by introducing dynamic pricing. The club re-prices tickets on a daily basis by calculating the impact of various factors (i.e., database elements) that only become clear a few days before a game, such as the weather, winning streaks, and pitching matchups, all of which influence how many people will want to attend. During the 2009 season, the Giants lowered and raised prices in a small section of seats using this data and were able to sell an extra 25,000 tickets, increasing revenue by $500,000. At the midway point of the 2010 season, when the Giants switched to dynamic pricing for all seats, ticket revenues increased by 6 percent.[27]

Predictive patterns are just the opposite of association or affinity patterns. Whereas association or affinity patterns identify database elements that seem to go together, **predictive patterns** help identify database elements that are different. Banks and credit card companies use data mining to find predictive patterns that distinguish customers who are good credit risks from those who are poor credit risks and less likely to pay their loans and monthly bills. J. P. Martin, an executive at Canadian Tire, pioneered the use of purchase data to predict consumer behavior. By analyzing what customers were buying, he created a method of forecasting how reliably they would repay. For example, he found that people who bought generic motor oil were more likely to miss payments than those who bought name-brand oil. He also found that people who bought felt furniture pads, which keep wood floors from getting scratched, were very unlikely to miss payments. He even identified the riskiest bar in Canada when he found that 47 percent of all patrons of Sharx Pool Bar in Montreal missed an average of four credit card payments per year.[28]

Data clusters are the last kind of pattern found by data mining. **Data clusters** occur when three or more database elements occur together (i.e., cluster) in a significant way. After analyzing several years' worth of repair and warranty claims, Ford Motor Company might find that, compared with cars built in its Chicago plant, the cars it builds in Kansas City (first element) are more likely to have over-tightened fan belts (second element) that break (third element) and result in overheated engines (fourth element), ruined radiators (fifth element), and payments for tow trucks (sixth element), which are paid for by Ford's 5-year, 60,000-mile power train warranty.

Traditionally, data mining has been very expensive and very complex. Today, however, data mining services and analysis are much more affordable and within reach of most companies' budgets. And, if it follows the path of most technologies, it will become even easier and cheaper to use in the future.

3.3 | PROTECTING INFORMATION

Protecting information is the process of ensuring that data are reliably and consistently retrievable in a usable format for authorized users but no one else. When customers purchase prescription medicine at Drugstore.com, an online drugstore and health-aid retailer, they want to be confident that their medical and credit card information is available only to them, the pharmacists at Drugstore.com, and their doctors. So Drugstore.com has an extensive privacy policy (click "Privacy Policy" at http://www.drugstore.com) to make sure this is the case.

Companies like Drugstore.com find it necessary to protect information because of the numerous security threats to data and data security listed in Exhibit 17.3. People inside and outside companies can steal or destroy company data in various ways including denial-of-service Web server attacks that can bring down some of the busiest and best-run sites on the Internet; viruses and spyware/adware that spread quickly and can result in data loss and business disruption; keystroke monitoring in which every mouse click and keystroke you make is monitored, stored, and sent to unauthorized

Exhibit 17.3 Security Threats to Data and Data Networks

Security Problem	Source	Affects	Severity	The Threat	The Solution
Denial of service; Web server attacks and corporate network attacks	Internet hackers	All servers	High	Loss of data, disruption of service, and theft of service.	Implement firewall, password control, server-side review, threat monitoring, and bug fixes; turn PCs off when not in use.
Password cracking software and unauthorized access to PCs	Local area network, Internet	All users, especially digital subscriber line and cable Internet users	High	Hackers take over PCs. Privacy can be invaded. Corporate users' systems are exposed to other machines on the network.	Close ports and firewalls, disable file and print sharing, and use strong passwords.
Viruses, worms, Trojan horses, and rootkits	Email, downloaded and distributed software	All users	Moderate to high	Monitor activities and cause data loss and file deletion; compromise security by sometimes concealing their presence.	Use antivirus software and firewalls; control Internet access.
Spyware, adware, malicious scripts and applets	Rogue Web pages	All users	Moderate to high	Invade privacy, intercept passwords, and damage files or file system.	Disable browser script support; use security, blocking, and spyware/adware software.
Email snooping	Hackers on your network and the Internet	All users	Moderate to high	People read your email from intermediate servers or packets, or they physically access your machine.	Encrypt messages, ensure strong password protection, and limit physical access to machines.
Keystroke monitoring	Trojan horses, people with direct access to PCs	All users	High	Records everything typed at the keyboard and intercepts keystrokes before password masking or encryption occurs.	Use antivirus software to catch Trojan horses, control Internet access to transmission, and implement system monitoring and physical access control.
Phishing	Hackers on your network and the Internet	All users, including customers	High	Fake but real-looking emails and websites that trick users into sharing personal information on what they wrongly think is a company's website. This leads to unauthorized account access.	Educate and warn users and customers about the dangers. Encourage both not to click on potentially fake URLs, which might take them to phishing websites. Instead, have them type your company's URL into the Web browser.
Spam	Email	All users and corporations	Mild to high	Clogs and overloads email servers and inboxes with junk mail. HTML-based spam may be used for profiling and identifying users.	Filter known spam sources and senders on email servers; have users create further lists of approved and unapproved senders on their personal computers.
Cookies	Websites you visit	Individual users	Mild to moderate	Trace Web usage and permit the creation of personalized Web pages that track behavior and interest profiles.	Use cookie managers to control and edit cookies, and use ad blockers.

Sources: K. Bannan, "Look Out: Watching You, Watching Me," *PC Magazine*, July 2002, 99; A. Dragoon, "Fighting Phish, Fakes, and Frauds," *CIO*, September 1, 2004, 33; B. Glass, "Are You Being Watched?" *PC Magazine*, April 23 2002, 54; K. Karagiannis, "DDoS: Are You Next?" *PC Magazine*, January 2003, 79; B. Machrone, "Protect & Defend," *PC Magazine*, June 27, 2000, 168–181; "Top 10 Security Threats," *PC Magazine*, April 10, 2007, 66; M. Sarrel, "Master End-User Security," *PC Magazine*," May 2008, 101.

Authentication making sure potential users are who they claim to be

Authorization granting authenticated users approved access to data, software, and systems

Two-factor authentication authentication based on what users know, such as a password, and what they have in their possession, such as a secure ID card or key

Biometrics identifying users by unique, measurable body features, such as fingerprint recognition or iris scanning

Firewall a protective hardware or software device that sits between the computers in an internal organizational network and outside networks, such as the Internet

Virus a program or piece of code that, against your wishes, attaches itself to other programs on your computer and can trigger anything from a harmless flashing message to the reformatting of your hard drive to a systemwide network shutdown

users; password cracking software that steals supposedly secure passwords; and *phishing*, using fake but real-looking emails and websites to trick users into sharing personal information (user names, passwords, and account numbers), that leads to unauthorized account access. On average, 19 percent of computers are infected with viruses, 80 percent have spyware, and only one-third are running behind a protected firewall (discussed shortly). Studies show that the threats listed in Exhibit 17.3 are so widespread that automatic attacks will begin on an unprotected computer just 15 seconds after it connects to the Internet.[29]

As shown in the right-hand column of Exhibit 17.3, numerous steps can be taken to secure data and data networks. Some of the most important are authentication and authorization, firewalls, antivirus software for PCs and email servers, data encryption, and virtual private networks.[30] We will discuss those steps and then finish this section with a brief review of the dangers of wireless networks, which are exploding in popularity.

Two critical steps are required to make sure that data can be accessed by authorized users and no one else. One is **authentication,** that is, making sure potential users are who they claim to be.[31] The other is **authorization,** that is, granting authenticated users approved access to data, software, and systems.[32] When an ATM prompts you to enter your personal identification number (PIN), the bank is authenticating that you are you. Once you've been authenticated, you are authorized to access your funds and no one else's. Of course, as anyone who has lost a PIN or password or had one stolen knows, user authentication systems are not foolproof. In particular, users create security risks by not changing their default account passwords (such as birth dates) or by using weak passwords such as names ("Larry") or complete words ("football") that are quickly guessed by password cracker software.[33]

This is why many companies are now turning to **two-factor authentication,** which is based on what users know, such as a password, and what they have, such as a secure ID card. Amazon Web Services, a cloud computing platform, protects data by requiring all users to sign with an account name (usually an email address) and password, as well as a six-digit code that is randomly generated from an Ezio Time Token, a handheld device given to the customer that outputs a new random code periodically.[34] Some companies are moving to three-factor authentication by also including biometrics. With **biometrics** such as fingerprint recognition or iris scanning, users are identified by unique, measurable body features. Of course, since some fingerprint scanners can be fooled by fingerprint molds, some companies take security measures even further by requiring users to simultaneously scan their fingerprint *and* insert a secure smart card containing a digital file of their fingerprint. This is another form of two-factor authentication.

Unfortunately, stolen or cracked passwords are not the only way for hackers and electronic thieves to gain access to an organization's computer resources. Unless special safeguards are put in place, every time corporate users are online there's literally nothing between their personal computers and the Internet (home users with high-speed DSL or cable Internet access face the same risks). Hackers can access files, run programs, and control key parts of computers if precautions aren't taken. To reduce these risks, companies use **firewalls,** hardware or software devices that sit between the computers in an internal organizational network and outside networks, such as the Internet. Firewalls filter and check incoming and outgoing data. They prevent company insiders from accessing unauthorized sites or from sending confidential company information to people outside the company. Firewalls also prevent outsiders from identifying and gaining access to company computers and data. If a firewall is working properly, the computers behind the company firewall literally cannot be seen or accessed by outsiders.

A **virus** is a program or piece of code that, without your knowledge, attaches itself to other programs on your computer and can trigger anything from a harmless flashing message to the reformatting of your hard drive to a systemwide network shutdown. You used to have to do or run something to get a virus, such as double-clicking an infected email attachment. Today's viruses are much more threatening. In fact, with some

Biometrics at the Borders

The U.S. Coast Guard is using biometrics in its efforts to control illegal immigration. In the past, when Coast Guard crews detained people trying to enter the United States illegally, they would just send them back to their native countries because they had no easy way to identify or screen the individuals. Now, thanks to portable fingerprint scanners linked to Department of Homeland Security databases, the Coast Guard can quickly identify people who are repeat offenders, wanted criminals, under deportation orders, or on the terrorist watch list. This system has been particularly effective in identifying the pilots of the boats that ferry people into the United States. This use of biometrics to access information quickly has led to an increase in the arrest of criminals wanted in the United States, as well as a decrease in the number of people who try to make the dangerous ocean crossing into the country.

Source: K. Dalecki, "Coast Guard Biometrics Put Brakes on Illegal Immigration," *Federal Computer Week*, May 20, 2010, accessed May 21, 2010, http://fcw.com /Articles/2010/05/24/FEAT-coast-guard-biometrics.aspx?Page=1.

viruses, just being connected to a network can infect your computer. *Antivirus software for personal computers* scans email, downloaded files, and computer hard drives, disk drives, and memory to detect and stop computer viruses from doing damage. However, this software is effective only to the extent that users of individual computers have and use up-to-date versions. With new viruses appearing all the time, users should update their antivirus software weekly or, even better, configure their virus software to automatically check for, download, and install updates. By contrast, *corporate antivirus software* automatically scans email attachments such as Microsoft Word documents, graphics, and text files as they come across the company email server. It also monitors and scans all file downloads across company databases and network servers. So, while antivirus software for personal computers prevents individual computers from being infected, corporate antivirus software for email servers, databases, and network servers adds another layer of protection by preventing infected files from multiplying and being sent to others.

Another way of protecting information is to encrypt sensitive data. **Data encryption** transforms data into complex, scrambled digital codes that can be unencrypted only by authorized users who possess unique decryption keys. One method of data encryption is to use products by PGP (Pretty Good Privacy) (http:// www.pgp.com) to encrypt the files stored on personal computers or network servers and databases. This is especially important with laptop computers, which are easily stolen. Recently a laptop belonging to a contractor working with the Department of Veterans Affairs containing names, addresses, and social security numbers of 616 veterans was stolen. Though the data does not seem to have been compromised, a subsequent security review found that more than one-third of the contracts between the VA and the contractor did not have any requirements for using data encryption.[35]

With people increasingly gaining unauthorized access to email messages—email snooping—it's also important to encrypt sensitive email messages and file attachments. You can use a system called "public key encryption" to do so. First, give copies of your "public key" to anyone who sends you files or email. Have the

Data encryption the transformation of data into complex, scrambled digital codes that can be unencrypted only by authorized users who possess unique decryption keys

sender use the public key, which is actually a piece of software, to encrypt files before sending them to you. The only way to decrypt the files is with a companion "private key" that you keep to yourself. If you want to learn more or want to begin encrypting your own files, download a free copy of Pretty Good Privacy from http://web.mit.edu/pgp.

Although firewalls can protect personal computers and network servers connected to the corporate network, people away from their offices (e.g., salespeople, business travelers, telecommuters who work at home) who interact with their company networks via the Internet face a security risk. Because Internet data are not encrypted, packet sniffer software easily allows hackers to read everything sent or received except files that have been encrypted before sending. Previously, the only practical solution was to have employees dial into secure company phone lines for direct access to the company network. Of course, with international and long-distance phone calls, the costs quickly added up. Now, **virtual private networks (VPNs)** have solved this problem by using software to encrypt all Internet

Password Dos and Don'ts

Anyone with access to sensitive personal (personnel or medical files), customer (credit cards), or corporate (costs) data has a clear responsibility to protect those data from unauthorized access. Use the following dos and don'ts to maintain a "strong" password system and protect your data.

- Don't use any public information such as part of your name, address, or birthdate to create a password.

- Don't use complete words, English or foreign, that are easily guessed by password software using "dictionary attacks."

- Use eight or more characters and include some unique characteristics such as !@#$ to create passwords, for example cow@#boy.

- The longer the password and the more unique characters, the more difficult it is to guess.

- Consider using "passphrases," such as "My European vacation starts July 8th," instead of shorter passwords. The longer password, including upper- and lower-case letters, spaces, and numbers, is easy to remember and much more difficult to guess using password-cracking software.

- Remember your password and don't write it down on a sticky note attached to your computer.

- Change your password every 6 weeks. Better yet, specify that your computer system force all users to change their passwords this often.

- Don't reuse old passwords.

Together, these basic steps can make it much more difficult to gain unauthorized access to sensitive data.

Sources: K. Karagiannis, "Security Watch: Don't Make It Easy," *PC Magazine*, April 8, 2003, 72; M. Steinhart, "Password Dos and Don'ts," *PC Magazine*, February 12, 2002, 69; L. Seltzer, "Are Pa55.W0rd5 Dead?" *PC Magazine*, December 28, 2004, 86.

data at both ends of the transmission process. Instead of making long-distance calls, employees connect to the Internet. But, unlike typical Internet connections in which Internet data packets are unencrypted, the VPN encrypts the data sent by employees outside the company computer network, decrypts the data when they arrive within the company network, and does the same when data are sent back to the computer outside the network.

Alternatively, many companies are now adopting Web-based **secure sockets layer (SSL) encryption** to provide secure off-site access to data and programs. If you've ever entered your credit card in a Web browser to make an online purchase, you've used SSL technology to encrypt and protect that information. SSL encryption is being used if a gold lock (Internet Explorer) or a gold key (Netscape) appears along the bottom of your Web browser page. SSL encryption works the same way in the workplace. Managers and employees who aren't at the office simply connect to the Internet, open a Web browser, and then enter a user name and password to gain access to SSL-encrypted data and programs.

Finally, many companies now have wireless networks, which make it possible for anybody with a laptop and a wireless card to access the company network from anywhere in the office. Though a wireless network comes equipped with security and encryption capabilities that, in theory, permit only authorized users to access the network, those capabilities are easily bypassed with the right tools. Compounding the problem, many wireless networks are shipped with their security and encryption capabilities turned off for ease of installation.[36] Caution is important even when encryption is turned on because the WEP (Wired Equivalent Privacy) security protocol is easily compromised. If you work at home or are working on the go, extra care is critical because Wi-Fi networks in homes and public places such as hotel lobbies are among the most targeted by hackers.[37] See the Wi-Fi Alliance website at http://www.wi-fi.org for the latest information on wireless security and encryption protocols that provide much stronger protection for your company's wireless network.

4 Accessing and Sharing Information and Knowledge

Today, information technologies allow companies to communicate data, share data, and provide data access to workers, managers, suppliers, and customers in ways that were unthinkable just a few years ago. *After reading this section, you should be able to explain how companies use information technology to improve 4.1 internal access and sharing of information, 4.2 external access and sharing of information, and 4.3 the sharing of knowledge and expertise.*

4.1 | INTERNAL ACCESS AND SHARING

Executives, managers, and workers inside the company use three kinds of information technology to access and share information: executive information systems, intranets, and portals. An **executive information system (EIS)** uses internal and external sources of data to provide managers and executives the information they need to monitor and analyze organizational performance.[38] The goal of an EIS is to provide accurate, complete, relevant, and timely information to managers.

Managers at Lands' End, the retail clothing company, use their EIS, which they call their "dashboard," to see how well the company is running. With just a few mouse clicks and basic commands such as "find," "compare," and "show," the EIS displays costs, sales revenues, and other kinds of data in color-coded charts and graphs. Managers can drill down to view and compare data by region, state, time period, and product. Lands' End's CIO Frank Giannantonio says, "Our dashboards include an early alert system that utilizes key performance metrics to target items selling faster than expected and gives our managers the ability to adjust product levels far earlier than they were able to do in the past."[39]

Intranets are private company networks that allow employees to easily access, share, and publish information using Internet software. Intranet sites are just like external websites, but the firewall separating the internal company network from the Internet permits only authorized internal access.[40] Companies typically use intranets to share information (e.g., about benefits) and to replace paper forms with online forms. Many company intranets are built on the Web model as it existed a decade ago.

Secure sockets layer (SSL) encryption Internet browser–based encryption that provides secure off-site Web access to some data and programs

Executive information system (EIS) a data processing system that uses internal and external data sources to provide the information needed to monitor and analyze organizational performance

Intranets private company networks that allow employees to easily access, share, and publish information using Internet software

Intranets are evolving to include:

- collaboration tools, such as wikis, where team members can post all relevant information for a project they're working on together,

- customizable email accounts,

- presence awareness (whether someone you are looking for on the network is in the office, in a meeting, working from home, etc.),

- instant messaging, and

- simultaneous access to files for virtual team members.

Finally, **corporate portals** are a hybrid of executive information systems and intranets. While an EIS provides managers and executives with the information they need to monitor and analyze organizational performance, and intranets help companies distribute and publish information and forms within the company, corporate portals allow company managers and employees to access customized information *and* complete specialized transactions using a Web browser. Hillman Group is the company that sells the nuts, bolts, fasteners, keys, and key-cutting machines that you find in Home Depot, Lowe's, Ace, and nearly every other hardware store. Hillman's 1,800 employees produce products for 25,000 customers. Hillman's portal contains a real-time revenue report for every product with updated sales and production numbers on a continuous basis. Today, Hillman's portal contains 75 specialized reports that are accessed by 800 managers and employees.[41]

4.2 | EXTERNAL ACCESS AND SHARING

Historically, companies have been unable or reluctant to let outside groups have access to corporate information. Now, however, a number of information technologies—electronic data interchange, extranets, Web services, and the Internet—are making it easier to share company data with external groups like suppliers and customers. They're also reducing costs, increasing productivity by eliminating manual information processing (70 percent of the data output from one company, such as a purchase order, ends up as data input at another company, such as a sales invoice or shipping order), reducing data entry errors, improving customer service, and speeding communications.

With **electronic data interchange,** or **EDI,** two companies convert purchase and ordering information to a standardized format to enable direct electronic transmission of that information from one company's computer system to the other company's system. For example, when a Wal-Mart checkout clerk drags an Apple iPod across the checkout scanner, Wal-Mart's computerized inventory system automatically reorders another iPod through the direct EDI connection that its computer has with Apple's manufacturing and shipping computer. No one at Wal-Mart or Apple fills out paperwork. No one makes phone calls. There are no delays to wait to find out whether Apple has the iPod in stock. The transaction takes place instantly and automatically because the data from both companies were translated into a standardized, shareable, compatible format.

Web services, such as the system used by Food Lion discussed below, are another way for companies to directly and automatically transmit purchase and ordering information from one company's computer system to another company's computer system. **Web services** use standardized protocols to describe and transfer data from one company in such a way that those data can automatically be read, understood, transcribed, and processed by different computer systems in another company.[42] For example, "Vendor Pulse" is a data-sharing program started by grocery store chain Food Lion. Food Lion provides vendors, such as consumer goods company Unilever, with 14 kinds of sales metrics, from point-of-sale statistics (down to each cash register), store inventory (how much of each item is left in each store), distribution center inventory (how much of each item is in the warehouse), shrinkage (how much of each item has been stolen or misplaced), out-of-stocks (the extent to which your product is out of stock in various locations), to reclamations (how much of each item has been returned). Troy Prothero, Food Lion's supply chain manager, says that the data are so rich in information that, "there are no more data requests from suppliers [and the program]. Anything they would have requested comes to them daily."[43] How good is Food Lion's "Vendor Pulse" program? According to Andy Patel, manager of business capabilities for Unilever, " . . . few have the rich and robust data of Food Lion. It's got 14 metrics around each individual UPC [Universal Product Code, which is unique to each product], while some other retailers have only got two."[44]

Now, what's the difference between Web services and EDI? For EDI to work, the data in different companies' computer, database, and network systems must adhere to a particular set of standards for data structure and processing. For example, company X, which has a seven-digit parts numbering system, and company Y, which has an eight-digit parts numbering system, would agree to convert their internal parts numbering systems to identical ten-digit part numbers when their computer systems talk to each other. By contrast, the tools underlying Web services such as extensible markup language (or XML) automatically do the describing and transcribing so that data with different structures can be shared across very different computer systems in different companies. (Don't worry if you don't understand how this works, just appreciate what it does.) As a result, Web services allow organizations to communicate data without having special knowledge of each other's computer information systems by automatically handling those differences.

With EDI, the different purchasing and ordering applications in each company interact automatically without any human input. No one has to lift a finger to click a mouse, enter data, or hit the return key. An **extranet**, by contrast, allows companies to exchange information and conduct transactions by purposely providing outsiders with direct, Web browser–based access to authorized parts of a company's intranet or information system. Typically, user names and passwords are required to access an extranet.[45] For example, General Mills uses an extranet to provide Web-based access to its trucking database to twenty other companies that ship their products over similar distribution routes to make sure that its distribution trucks don't waste money by running half empty (or make late deliveries to customers because it waited to ship until the trucks were full). When other companies are ready to ship products, they log on to General Mills' trucking database, check the availability, and then enter the shipping load, place, and pickup time. By sharing shipping capacity on its trucks, General Mills can run its trucks fully loaded all the time. In several test areas, General Mills saved 7 percent on shipping costs (nearly $2 million) in the first year. Expanding the program company-wide is producing even larger cost savings.[46]

Finally, companies are reducing paperwork and manual information processing by using the Internet to electronically automate transactions with customers; this procedure is similar to the way in which extranets are used to handle transactions with suppliers and distributors. One way companies achieve transaction automation is through self-service kiosks. Blockbuster Express is a self-service kiosk located in supermarkets, gas stations, and convenience stores that customers can use to rent and buy the latest DVDs.[47]

In the long run, the goal is to link customer Internet sites with company intranets (or EDI) and extranets so that everyone—all the employees and managers within a company as well as the suppliers and distributors outside the company—who is involved in providing a service or making a product for a customer is automatically notified when a purchase is made. Companies that use EDI, extranets, and the Internet to share data with customers and suppliers achieve increases in productivity 2.7 times larger than those that don't.[48]

> **Extranets** networks that allow companies to exchange information and conduct transactions with outsiders by providing them direct, Web-based access to authorized parts of a company's intranet or information system

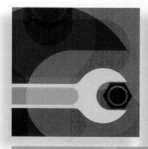

Cloud Sharing

Although it is best known for its Internet search engine—"to google" is even in the Oxford English Dictionary—Google is trying to change the ways people work with information. The Google Docs software suite offers inexpensive, easy access to cloud computing. Rather a single machine, cloud computing allows files to be stored and edited on the Internet, allowing easy and efficient file sharing. A new update to Google Docs even allows for multi-author collaboration; up to 50 people can work on the same file at the same time. All of this allows users of Google Docs to build collaborative work environments in an online setting.

Source: B. Stone, "New Collaborative Google Docs Unveiled," *New York Times*, April 12, 2010, accessed June 27, 2010, http://bits.blogs.nytimes.com/2010/04/12/new-collaborative-google-docs-unveiled/.

Knowledge the understanding that one gains from information

Decision support system (DSS) an information system that helps managers understand specific kinds of problems and potential solutions and analyze the impact of different decision options using "what if" scenarios

4.3 | SHARING KNOWLEDGE AND EXPERTISE

At the beginning of the chapter, we distinguished between raw data, which consist of facts and figures, and information, which consists of useful data that influence someone's choices and behavior. One more important distinction needs to be made: Data and information are not the same as knowledge.

Knowledge is the understanding that one gains from information. Importantly, knowledge does not reside in information. Knowledge resides in people. That's why companies hire consultants and why family doctors refer patients to specialists. Unfortunately, it can be quite expensive to employ consultants, specialists, and experts. So companies have begun using two information technologies to capture and share the knowledge of consultants, specialists, and experts with other managers and workers: decision support systems and expert systems.

Whereas an executive information system speeds up and simplifies the acquisition of information, a **decision support system (DSS)** helps managers understand problems and potential solutions by acquiring and analyzing

information with sophisticated models and tools.[49] Furthermore, whereas EIS programs are broad in scope and permit managers to retrieve all kinds of information about a company, DSS programs are usually narrow in scope and targeted toward helping managers solve specific kinds of problems. DSS programs have been developed to help managers pick the shortest and most efficient routes for delivery trucks, select the best combination of stocks for investors, and schedule the flow of inventory through complex manufacturing facilities.

It's important to understand that DSS programs don't replace managerial decision making; they *improve* it by furthering managers' and workers' understanding of the problems they face and the solutions that might work. Though used by just 2 percent of physicians, medical DSS programs hold the promise of helping doctors make more accurate patient diagnoses. A British study of eighty-eight cases misdiagnosed or initially misdiagnosed (to be correctly diagnosed much later) found that a medical DSS made the right diagnosis 69 percent of the time.[50] With a medical DSS, doctors enter patient data, such as age, gender, weight, and medical symptoms. The medical DSS then produces a list of diseases and conditions, ranked by probability, low or high, or by medical specialty, such as cardiology or oncology. For instance, when emergency room

physician Dr. Harold Cross treated a 10-year-old boy who had been ill with nausea and dizziness for 2 weeks, he wasn't sure what was wrong because the boy had a healthy appetite, no abdominal pain, and just one brief headache. However, when the medical DSS that Dr. Cross used suggested a possible problem in the back of the boy's brain, he ordered an MRI scan that revealed a tumor, which was successfully removed 2 days later. Says Dr. Cross, "My personal knowledge of the literature and physical findings would not have prompted me to suspect a brain tumor."[51]

Expert systems are created by capturing the specialized knowledge and decision rules used by experts and experienced decision makers. They permit nonexpert employees to draw on this expert knowledge base to make decisions. Most expert systems work by using a collection of "if–then" rules to sort through information and recommend a course of action. For example, let's say that you're using your American Express card to help your spouse celebrate a promotion. After dinner and a movie, the two of you stroll by a travel office with a Las Vegas poster in its window. Thirty minutes later, caught up in the moment, you find yourselves at the airport ticket counter trying to purchase last-minute tickets to Vegas. But there's just one problem. American Express didn't approve your purchase. In fact, the ticket counter agent is now on the phone with an American Express customer service agent.

So what put a temporary halt to your weekend escape to Vegas? An expert system that American Express calls "Authorizer's Assistant."[52] The first "if–then" rule that prevented your purchase was the rule "*if* a purchase is much larger than the cardholder's regular spending habits, *then* deny approval of the purchase." This "if–then" rule, just one of 3,000, is built into American Express's transaction-processing system, which handles thousands of purchase requests per second. Now that the American Express customer service agent is on the line, he or she is prompted by the Authorizer's Assistant to ask the ticket counter agent to examine your identification. You hand over your driver's license and another credit card to prove you're you. Then the ticket agent asks for your address, phone number, Social Security number, and your mother's maiden name and relays the information to American Express. Finally, your ticket purchase is approved. Why? Because you met the last series of "if–then" rules. *If* the purchaser can provide proof of identity and *if* the purchaser can provide personal information that isn't common knowledge, *then* approve the purchase.

> **Expert system** an information system that contains the specialized knowledge and decision rules used by experts and experienced decision makers so that nonexperts can draw on this knowledge base to make decisions

18 | Managing Service and Manufacturing Operations

© Chris Gould/Photographer's Choice/Getty Images

LEARNING OUTCOMES:

1 discuss the kinds of productivity and their importance in managing operations.

2 explain the role that quality plays in managing operations.

3 explain the essentials of managing a service business.

4 describe the different kinds of manufacturing operations.

5 explain why and how companies should manage inventory levels.

Chapter 18

Managing for Productivity and Quality

furniture manufacturers, hospitals, restaurants, automakers, airlines, and many other kinds of businesses struggle to find ways to produce quality products and services efficiently and then deliver them in a timely manner. Managing the daily production of goods and services, or *operations management*, is a key part of a manager's job. But an organization's success depends on the quality of its products and services as well as its productivity. Modeled after U.S.-based Southwest Airlines, European airline Ryanair achieves dramatically lower prices through aggressive price cutting, high productivity, and quality customer service.

Want a frequent-flier plan? You won't find one at Ryanair. It's too expensive. Want a meal on your flight? Pack a lunch. Ryanair doesn't even serve peanuts because it takes too much time (i.e., expense) to get them out of the seat cushions. Passengers enter and exit the planes using old-fashioned, rolling stairs because they're quicker and cheaper than extendable boarding gates. As a result of such cost-cutting moves, Ryanair does more with less and thus has higher productivity. For example, most airlines break even on their flights when they're 75 percent full, but Ryanair's productivity allows it to break even when its planes are only half full, even with its incredibly low prices. With this low break-even point, Ryanair attracts plenty of cus-

tomers, who enable it to fill most of its seats (84 percent) and achieve a 20 percent net profit margin. Because of its extremely low prices and high productivity, Ryanair is one of the few airlines in the world that consistently turns a profit, making €319 million (about $400 million) in 2009, a 204 percent increase over the previous year.[1]

After reading the next two sections, you should be able to

1. discuss the kinds of productivity and their importance in managing operations.
2. explain the role that quality plays in managing operations.

1 Productivity

At their core, organizations are production systems. Companies combine inputs such as labor, raw materials, capital, and knowledge to produce outputs in the form of finished products or services. **Productivity** is a measure of performance that indicates how many inputs it takes to produce or create an output.

$$\text{Productivity} = \frac{\text{Outputs}}{\text{Inputs}}$$

The fewer inputs it takes to create an output (or the greater the output from one input), the higher the productivity. For example, a car's gas mileage is a common measure of productivity. A car that gets 35 miles (output) per gallon (input) is more productive and fuel efficient than a car that gets 18 miles per gallon.

Let's examine **1.1 why productivity matters** and **1.2 the different kinds of productivity**.

1.1 | WHY PRODUCTIVITY MATTERS

Why does productivity matter? For companies, higher productivity—

Productivity a measure of performance that indicates how many inputs it takes to produce or create an output that is, doing more with less—results in lower costs for the company, lower prices, faster service, higher market share, and higher profits. For example, every second saved in the drive-through lane at fast-food restaurants increases sales by 1 percent. And with up to 75 percent of all fast-food restaurant sales coming from the drive-through window, it's no wonder that Wendy's (average drive-through time of 131 seconds per vehicle), Burger King (average time of 153 seconds per vehicle), and McDonald's (average time of 167.1 seconds per vehicle) continue to look for ways to shorten the time it takes to process a drive-through order.[2] Productivity matters so much at the drive-through that several fast-food chains have experimented with outsourcing. Franchises at chains like McDonald's, Wendy's, Hardee's, and Jack in the Box have used call centers to take orders from drive-through customers. Companies like Bronco Communications and Exit 41, both of which provide off-site ordering services, can take orders for a restaurant in North Carolina with employees based in, say, Texas. Although Bronco and Exit 41 sell their services as time and money savers, none of the restaurant chains has introduced call-center ordering on a national level. The reason? They haven't been able to prove it actually saves money.[3]

The productivity of businesses within a country matters to that country because it results in a higher standard of living. One way productivity leads to a higher standard of living is through increased wages. When companies can do more with less, they can raise employee wages without increasing prices or sacrificing normal profits. For instance, recent government economic data indicated that companies were paying workers 3.1 percent more than in the previous year. But, since workers were producing 4.3 percent more than they had the year before, real labor costs had actually decreased by 1.2 percent.[4] According to the U.S. Census Bureau, the median income for the American family was approximately $61,521 in 2008. If produc-

> ## Productivity matters because it results in a **higher standard** of living and more affordable (or better) products.

tivity grows 1 percent a year, that family's income will increase to $78,896 in 2033. But if productivity grows 2 percent a year, their annual income in 2033 will be $100,932, nearly $22,000 higher, and that's without working longer hours.[5] Thanks to long-term increases in business productivity, the average American family today earns 37 percent more than the average family in 1980 and 65 percent more than the average family in 1967—and that's after accounting for inflation.[6]

Rising income stemming from increased productivity creates numerous other benefits as well. Productivity increased by an average of 2.7 percent a year between 1995 and 2002, and then the rate of increase slowed to an average of 1.4 percent a year from 2005 to 2007.[7] From 1996 to 2006, the U.S. economy created nearly 17.5 million new jobs.[8] When more people have jobs that pay more, they give more to charity. For example, in 2008 Americans donated over $315 billion to charities, but in 2009, as the economic downturn took hold and millions of people remained unemployed, donations dropped to roughly $304 billion, or a drop of 3.5 percent.[9]

Another benefit of productivity is that it makes products more affordable or better. In 1981, the IBM PC Model 5150, featuring 16 K of memory, a 4.7 Mhz processor, a floppy disk or cassette tape drive, and a monochromatic monitor, sold for $1995, equivalent to about $4800 in 2010. A 10 MB hard drive and a 4-color display were optional add-ons. Today, thanks to increased productivity in the computer industry, you could take $1995 and buy five IdeaPad netbooks from Lenovo, which are more than 300 times faster and nearly 50 pounds lighter than the original IBM PC. You'll even get a hard drive and a color screen.[10]

1.2 | KINDS OF PRODUCTIVITY

Two common measures of productivity are partial productivity and multifactor productivity. **Partial productivity** indicates how much of a particular kind of input it takes to produce an output.

$$\text{Partial Productivity} = \frac{\text{Outputs}}{\text{Single Kind of Input}}$$

Labor is one kind of input that is frequently used when determining partial productivity. *Labor productivity* typically indicates the cost or the number of hours of labor it takes to produce an output. In other words, the lower the cost of the labor to produce a unit of output or the less time it takes to produce a unit of output, the higher the labor productivity. For example, the automobile industry often measures labor productivity by determining the average number of hours of labor needed to completely assemble a car. According to a recent *Harbour Report*, the three Detroit-based automakers have nearly reached parity with their Japanese rivals in manufacturing efficiency. Toyota and Chrysler assemble a car in 30.37 hours, Honda in 31.33 hours, General Motors in 32.29 hours, Nissan in 32.96 hours, and Ford in 33.88 hours. The gap between the most and least productive automakers has narrowed from 10.51 labor hours in 2003 to just 3.5 labor hours in 2008.[11]

Partial productivity assesses how efficiently companies use only one input, such as labor, when creating outputs. Multifactor productivity is an overall measure of productivity that assesses how efficiently companies use all the inputs it takes to make outputs. More specifically, **multifactor productivity** indicates how much labor, capital, materials, and energy it takes to produce an output.[12]

$$\frac{\text{Multifactor}}{\text{Productivity}} = \frac{\text{Outputs}}{(\text{Labor} + \text{Capital} + \text{Materials} + \text{Energy})}$$

Exhibit 18.1 shows the trends in multifactor productivity across a number of U.S. industries since 1987. With a 182 percent increase between 1997 (scaled at 100) and 2006 (when it reached a level of 282) and nearly a tenfold increase since 1987, the growth in multifactor productivity in the computers and electronic products industry far exceeded the productivity growth in retail stores, auto manufacturing, mining, utilities, and air transportation as well as most other industries tracked by the U.S. government.

Should managers use multiple or partial productivity measures? In general, they should use both. Multifactor productivity indicates a company's overall level of productivity relative to its competitors. In the end, that's what counts most. However, multifactor productivity measures don't indicate the specific contributions that labor, capital, materials, or energy make to overall productivity. To analyze the contributions of these individual components, managers need to use partial productivity measures. Doing so can help them determine what factors need to be adjusted or in what areas adjustment can make the most difference in overall productivity.

> **Multifactor productivity** an overall measure of performance that indicates how much labor, capital, materials, and energy it takes to produce an output

2 Quality

With the average car costing about $29,000, car buyers want to make sure that they're getting good quality for their money. Fortunately, as indicated by the number of problems per 100 cars (PP100), today's cars are of much higher quality than earlier models.[13] In 1981, Japanese cars averaged 240 PP100. General Motors'

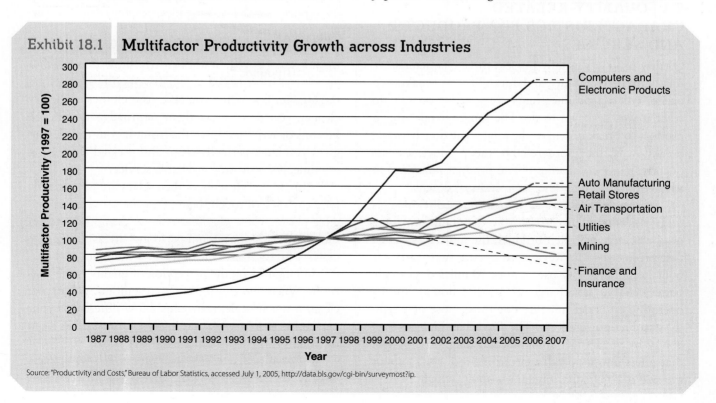

Exhibit 18.1 Multifactor Productivity Growth across Industries

Source: "Productivity and Costs," Bureau of Labor Statistics, accessed July 1, 2005, http://data.bls.gov/cgi-bin/surveymost?ip.

cars averaged 670, Ford's averaged 740, and Chrysler's averaged 870! In other words, measured in PP100, the quality of American cars was two to three times worse than that of Japanese cars. In 2009, even the worst cars on the J.D. Power and Associates Survey of Initial Car quality beat the scores of the Japanese cars of decades ago. And high-quality brands such as Lexus and Porsche came in with scores under 100 (84 and 90 to be exact). That means there's less than one problem per car![14]

The American Society for Quality gives two meanings for **quality**. It can mean a product or service free of deficiencies, for example, having a very low number of problems per 100 cars, or it can mean that the characteristics of a product or service satisfy customer needs.[15] Today's cars are of higher quality than those produced 20 years ago in both senses. Not only do they have fewer problems per 100 cars, they also have a number of additional standard features (power brakes and steering, stereo/CD player, power windows and locks, air bags, cruise control, etc.).

*In this part of the chapter, you will learn about **2.1 quality-related characteristics for products and services, 2.2 ISO 9000 and 14000, 2.3 the Baldrige National Quality Award**, and **2.4 total quality management**.*

2.1 | QUALITY-RELATED CHARACTERISTICS FOR PRODUCTS AND SERVICES

Quality products usually possess three characteristics: reliability, serviceability, and durability.[16] A breakdown occurs when a product quits working or doesn't do what it was designed to do. The longer it takes for a product to break down, or the longer the time between breakdowns, the more reliable the product. Consequently, many companies define product *reliability* in terms of the average time between breakdowns.

Serviceability refers to how easy or difficult it is to fix a product. The easier it is to maintain a working product or fix a broken product, the more serviceable that product is. The Reva is an electric two-seater car built in India for city use. It goes 50 miles on a single battery charge (a recharge takes just 5 hours), and its operating costs per mile are one-third those of a typical gasoline-powered car. The Reva has high serviceability by virtue of a computerized diagnostic system that plugs into a portable electronic tool (PET) about the size of a personal digital assistant, which assesses how well the car is running. Because the PET can be linked to a phone, customers can quickly transmit their Reva's operational history to find out if the car needs work and, if so, what kind.[17]

A product breakdown assumes that a product can be repaired. However, some products don't break down—they fail. *Product failure* means products can't be repaired, only replaced. *Durability* is defined as the mean time to failure. Typically, for example, when an LCD screen "dies," it can't be repaired. Consequently, durability, or the average time before failure, is a key part of LCD quality. Why buy a great-looking LCD if it's only going to last a few years? Indeed, Toshiba is now producing thin film transistor LCDs with a mean time before failure of 100,000 hours, or 11.4 years.[18]

While high-quality products are characterized by reliability, serviceability, and durability, services are different. There's no point in assessing the durability of a service because services don't last—they are consumed the minute they're performed. For example, once a lawn service has mowed your lawn, the job is done until the mowers come back next week to do it again. Services also don't have serviceability. You can't maintain or fix a service. If a service wasn't performed correctly, all you can do is perform it again. Rather than serviceability and durability, the quality of service interactions often depends on how the service provider interacts with the customer. Was the service provider friendly, rude, or helpful? Five characteristics typically distinguish a quality service: reliability, tangibles, responsiveness, assurance, and empathy.[19]

Service reliability is the ability to consistently perform a service well. Studies clearly show that reliability matters more to customers than anything else when buying services. When you take your clothes to the dry cleaner, you don't want them returned with cracked buttons or wrinkles down the front. If your dry cleaner gives you back perfectly clean and pressed clothes every time, it's providing a reliable service.

Also, although services themselves are not tangible (you can't see or touch them), they are provided in tangible places. Thus, *tangibles* refer to the appearance of the offices, equipment, and personnel involved with the delivery of a service. One of the best examples of the effect of tangibles on the perception of quality is the restroom. When you eat at a fancy restaurant, you expect clean, if not upscale, restrooms. How different is your perception of a business, say a gas station, if it has clean restrooms rather than filthy ones?

Responsiveness is the promptness and willingness with which service providers give good service (your

Guilt by Association

In 2008, inspectors found that infant formula was tainted with melamine, a toxic chemical that is often used as a pesticide. Six infants died, and 300,000 others became ill from drinking the formula. Since then, Chinese infant formula manufacturers have faced tremendous difficulties in reassuring the public that their products are safe. For example, Chinese media recently reported that three babies in the city of Wuhan who had been fed formula produced by Synutra had premature breast development. Even though there was no evidence linking the condition to Synutra's product, consumer confidence in the company fell dramatically, and Synutra's stock posted a single-day loss of 27 percent.

Source: B. Einhorn, "Baby Formula Scare Hurts China's Synutra," *BloombergBusinessweek*, August 12, 2010, accessed August 15, 2010, http://www.businessweek.com/blogs/eyeonasia/archives/2010/08/baby_formula_scare_hurts_chinas_synutra.html.

dry cleaner returning your laundry perfectly clean and pressed in a day or an hour). *Assurance* is the confidence that service providers are knowledgeable, courteous, and trustworthy. *Empathy* is the extent to which service providers give individual attention and care to customers' concerns and problems.

2.2 | ISO 9000 AND 14000

ISO, pronounced "eye-so," comes from the Greek word *isos*, meaning "equal, similar, alike, or identical" and is also an acronym for the International Organization for Standardization, which helps set standards for 163 countries. The purpose of this agency is to develop and publish standards that facilitate the international exchange of goods and services.[20] **ISO 9000** is a series of five international standards, from ISO 9000 to ISO 9004, for achieving consistency in quality management and quality assurance in companies throughout the world. **ISO 14000** is a series of international standards for managing, monitoring, and minimizing an organization's harmful effects on the environment.[21] (For more on environmental quality and issues, see Section 3.5 of Chapter 16 on controlling waste and pollution.)

The ISO 9000 and 14000 standards publications, which are available from the American National Standards Institute, are general and can be used for manufacturing any kind of product or delivering any kind of service. Importantly, the ISO 9000 standards don't describe how to make a better-quality car, computer, or widget. Instead, they describe how companies can extensively document (and thus standardize) the steps they take to create and improve the quality of their products. ISO 9000 certification is increasingly becoming a requirement for doing business with many *Fortune* 500 companies.[22]

To become ISO certified, a process that can take months, a company must show that it is following its own procedures for improving production, updating design plans and specifications, keeping machinery in top condition, educating and training workers, and satisfactorily dealing with customer complaints.[23] An accredited third party oversees the ISO certification process, just as a certified public accountant verifies that a company's financial accounts are up-to-date and accurate. Once a company has been certified as ISO 9000 compliant, the accredited third party will issue an ISO 9000 certificate that the company can use in its advertising and publications. This is the quality equivalent of the Good Housekeeping Seal of Approval. But continued ISO 9000 certification is not guaranteed. Accredited third parties typically conduct periodic audits to make sure the company is still following quality procedures. If it is not, its certification is suspended or canceled.

To get additional information on ISO 9000 guidelines and procedures, go to the websites of the American National Standards Institute (http://www.webstore.ansi.org; the ISO 9000 and ISO 14000 standards publications are available at this site for about $400 and $300, respectively), the American Society for Quality (http://www.asq.org), and the International Organization for Standardization (http://www.iso.org).

ISO 9000 a series of five international standards, from ISO 9000 to ISO 9004, for achieving consistency in quality management and quality assurance in companies throughout the world

ISO 14000 a series of international standards for managing, monitoring, and minimizing an organization's harmful effects on the environment

2.3 | BALDRIGE NATIONAL QUALITY AWARD

The Baldrige National Quality Award, which is administered by the U.S. government's National Institute for Standards and Technology, is given "to recognize U.S. companies for their achievements in quality and business performance and to raise awareness about the importance of quality and performance excellence as a competitive edge."[24] Each year, up to three awards may be given in these categories: manufacturing, service, small business, education, and health care.

The costs of applying for the Baldrige Award include a $150 eligibility fee, an application fee of $7,000 for manufacturing firms and $3,500 for small businesses, and a site visitation fee of $20,000 to $35,000 for manufacturing firms and $10,000 to $17,000 for small businesses.[25] Why does it cost so much just to apply? Because you get a great deal of information about your business that will be useful even if you don't win. At a minimum, each company that applies receives an extensive report based on 300 hours of assessment from at least eight business and quality experts. At $10 an hour for small businesses and about $20 an hour for manufacturing and service businesses, the *Journal for Quality and Participation* called the Baldrige feedback report "the best bargain in consulting in America."[26]

Businesses that apply for the Baldrige Award are judged on a 1,000-point scale based on the seven criteria in Exhibit 18.2.[27] "Results" is clearly the most important category, as it accounts for 450 out of 1,000 points. In other words, in addition to the six other criteria, companies must show that they have achieved superior quality when it comes to products and services, customers, financial performance and market share, treatment of employees, work systems and processes, and leadership and social responsibil-

The Baldrige Award indicates the extent to which companies have actually achieved world-class quality.

ity. This emphasis on results is what differentiates the Baldrige Award from the ISO 9000 standards. The Baldrige Award indicates the extent to which companies have actually achieved world-class quality. The ISO 9000 standards simply indicate whether a company is following the management system it put in place to improve quality. In fact, ISO 9000 certification covers less than 10 percent of the requirements for the Baldrige Award.[28] Most companies that apply for the Baldrige Award do it to grow and stay competitive.[29] Furthermore, the companies that have won the Baldrige Award have achieved superior financial returns. Since 1988, an investment in Baldrige Award winners would have outperformed the Standard & Poor's 500 stock index 80 percent of the time.[30]

2.4 | TOTAL QUALITY MANAGEMENT

Total quality management (TQM) is an integrated organization-wide strategy for improving product and service quality.[31] TQM is not a specific tool or technique but a philosophy or overall approach to management that is characterized by three principles: customer focus and satisfaction, continuous improvement, and teamwork.[32]

Although most economists, accountants, and financiers argue that companies exist to earn profits for shareholders, TQM suggests that customer focus and customer satisfaction should be a company's primary goals. **Customer focus** means that the entire organization, from top to bottom, should concentrate on meeting customers' needs. The result of that customer focus should be **customer satisfaction,** which occurs when the company's products or services meet or exceed customers' expectations. At companies where TQM is taken seriously, such as Enterprise Rent-a-Car, paychecks and promotions depend on keeping customers satisfied.[33] Enterprise measures customer satisfaction with a detailed survey called the Enterprise Service Quality index. Enterprise not only ranks each branch office by operating profits and customer satisfaction but also makes promotions to higher-paying jobs contingent on above-average customer satisfaction scores.

Exhibit 18.2 Criteria for the Baldrige National Quality Award

2007 Categories/Items	Point Values
1 LEADERSHIP	**120**
1.1 Senior Leadership	70
1.2 Governance and Social Responsibilities	50
2 STRATEGIC PLANNING	**85**
2.1 Strategy Development	40
2.2 Strategy Deployment	45
3 CUSTOMER FOCUS	**85**
3.1 Customer Engagement	40
3.2 Voice of the Customer	45
4 MEASUREMENT, ANALYSIS, AND KNOWLEDGE MANAGEMENT	**90**
4.1 Measurement, Analysis, and Improvement of Organizational Performance	45
4.2 Management of Information, Information Technology, and Knowledge	45
5 WORKFORCE FOCUS	**85**
5.1 Workforce Engagement	45
5.2 Workforce Environment	40
6 PROCESS MANAGEMENT	**85**
6.1 Work Systems	35
6.2 Work Processes	50
7 RESULTS	**450**
7.1 Product Outcomes	100
7.2 Customer-Focused Outcomes	70
7.3 Financial and Market Outcomes	70
7.4 Workforce-Focused Outcomes	70
7.5 Process Effectiveness Outcomes	70
7.6 Leadership Outcomes	70
TOTAL POINTS 1,000	

Source: "Criteria for Performance Excellence," *Baldrige National Quality Program 2007*, accessed September 15, 2008, http://www.quality.nist.gov/PDF_files/2008_Business_Nonprofit_Criteria.pdf.

Continuous improvement is an ongoing commitment to increase product and service quality by constantly assessing and improving the processes and procedures used to create those products and services. How do companies know whether they're achieving continuous improvement? Besides higher customer satisfaction, continuous improvement is usually associated with reduced variation. **Variation** is a deviation in the form, condition, or appearance of a product from the qual-ity standard for that product. The less a product varies from the quality standard, or the more consistently a company's products meet a quality standard, the higher the quality. McNeil Consumer Healthcare, maker of Tylenol, Motrin, Zyrtec, and Benadryl, was forced to issue two separate recalls, affecting almost 90 of its products, because of a failure to prevent variation in product quality. The first recall occurred because consumers noticed a moldy odor in products and complained of unusual nausea and stomach pains.[34] The second recall occurred because inspectors found problems with purity. They discovered that some products, such as Children's Tylenol, contained too much of the active ingredient, while others were contaminated with mold, bacteria, or other metallic substances.[35]

The third principle of TQM is teamwork. **Teamwork** means collaboration between managers and nonmanagers, across business functions, and between the company and its customers and suppliers. In short, quality improves when everyone in the company is given the incentive to work together and the responsibility and authority to make improvements and solve problems. A recent study by Dr. Beth Lown of Mt. Auburn Hospital and Harvard Medical School showed that giving doctors an opportunity to talk to other medical professionals about job-related and personal issues dramatically reduced their stress levels and improved the level of care they gave to patients. The study also found that collaboration among hospital staff led to a greater appreciation of how patients' lives were affected by their illnesses, a deeper level of trust between doctor and patient, and a significant reduction in the number of malpractice lawsuits.[36]

Customer focus and satisfaction, continuous improvement, and teamwork mutually reinforce each other to improve quality throughout a company. Customer-focused continuous improvement is necessary to increase customer satisfaction. At the same time, continuous improvement depends on teamwork from different functional and hierarchical parts of the company.

Continuous improvement an organization's ongoing commitment to constantly assess and improve the processes and procedures used to create products and services

Variation a deviation in the form, condition, or appearance of a product from the quality standard for that product

Teamwork collaboration between managers and nonmanagers, across business functions, and between companies, customers, and suppliers

Managing Operations

At the start of this chapter, you learned that operations management means managing the daily production of goods and services. Then you learned that to manage production, you must oversee the factors that affect productivity and quality. In this part of the chapter, you will learn about managing operations in service and manufacturing businesses. The chapter ends with a discussion of inventory management, a key factor in a company's profitability.

After reading the next three sections, you should be able to

3 explain the essentials of managing a service business.

4 describe the different kinds of manufacturing operations.

5 explain why and how companies should manage inventory levels.

3 Service Operations

Imagine that your trusty TiVo digital video recorder (DVR) breaks down as you try to record your favorite TV show. You've got two choices. You can run to Wal-Mart and spend $250 to purchase a new DVR, or you can spend less (you hope) to have it fixed at a repair shop. Either way you end up with the same thing, a working DVR. However, the first choice, getting a new DVR, involves buying a physical product (a good), while the second, dealing with a repair shop, involves buying a service.

Services differ from goods in several ways. First, goods are produced or made, but services are performed. In other words, services are almost always labor-intensive: Someone typically has to perform the service for you. A repair shop could give you the parts needed to repair your old DVR, but you're still going to have a broken DVR without the technician to perform the repairs. Second, goods are tangible, but services are intangible. You can touch and see that new DVR, but you can't touch or see the service provided by the technician who fixes your old DVR. All you can "see" is that the DVR works. Third, services are perishable and unstorable. If you don't use them when

they're available, they're wasted. For example, if your DVR repair shop is backlogged on repair jobs, then you'll just have to wait until next week to get your DVR repaired. You can't store an unused service and use it when you like. By contrast, you can purchase a good, such as motor oil, and store it until you're ready to use it. Finally, services account for 59 percent of the U.S. gross national product, whereas manufacturing accounts for 30.8 percent.[37]

Because services are different from goods, managing a service operation is different from managing a manufacturing or production operation. Let's look at 3.1 the service-profit chain and 3.2 service recovery and empowerment.

3.1 | THE SERVICE-PROFIT CHAIN

One of the key assumptions in the service business is that success depends on how well employees—that is, service providers—deliver their services to customers. But success actually begins with how well management treats service employees, as the service-profit chain, depicted in Exhibit 18.3, demonstrates.[38]

The key concept behind the service-profit chain is *internal service quality,* meaning the quality of treatment that employees receive from a company's internal service providers such as management, payroll and benefits, human resources, and so forth. For example, Wegmans, a supermarket chain, allowed employees to buy store gift cards at a 10 percent discount. The biotechnology firm Genentech gives employees who drive

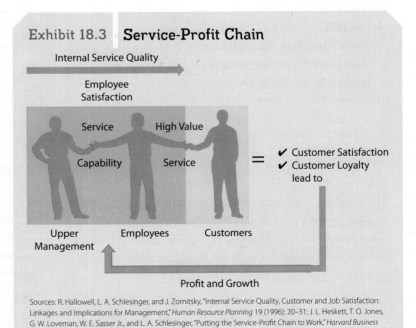

Exhibit 18.3 Service-Profit Chain

Internal Service Quality

Employee Satisfaction

Service Capability

High Value Service

= ✔ Customer Satisfaction ✔ Customer Loyalty lead to

Upper Management   Employees   Customers

Profit and Growth

Sources: R. Hallowell, L. A. Schlesinger, and J. Zornitsky, "Internal Service Quality, Customer and Job Satisfaction: Linkages and Implications for Management," *Human Resource Planning* 19 (1996): 20–31; J. L. Heskett, T. O. Jones, G. W. Loveman, W. E. Sasser Jr., and L. A. Schlesinger, "Putting the Service-Profit Chain to Work," *Harvard Business Review* (March–April 1994): 164–174.

a carpool $4 for each co-worker who rides with them. Workers who take public transportation or ride their bikes also get $4 per day. At the online shoe retailer Zappos, every employee is provided with a free lunch every day, while Baptist Health South Florida, a health care provider, gives employees buying their first house a subsidy ranging from $2,000 to $10,000.[39]

As depicted in Exhibit 18.3, good internal service leads to employee satisfaction and service capability. *Employee satisfaction* occurs when companies treat employees in a way that meets or exceeds their expectations. In other words, the better employees are treated, the more satisfied they are, and the more likely they are to give high-value service that satisfies customers.

How employers treat employees is important because it affects service capability. *Service capability* is an employee's perception of his or her ability to serve customers well. When an organization treats its employees in ways that help them to do their jobs well, employees, in turn, are more likely to believe that they can and ought to provide high-value service to customers.

Finally, according to the service-profit chain shown in Exhibit 18.3, *high-value service* leads to *customer satisfaction* and *customer loyalty,* which, in turn, lead to *long-term profits and growth.* What's the link between customer satisfaction and loyalty, on the one hand, and profits, on the other? To start, the average business keeps only 70 to 90 percent of its existing customers each year. No big deal, you say? Just replace leaving customers with new customers. Well, there's one significant problem with that solution: It costs ten times as much to find a new customer as it does to keep an existing customer. Also, new customers typically buy only 20 percent as much as established customers do. In fact, keeping existing customers is so cost-effective that most businesses could double their profits by simply keeping 5 percent more customers per year![40] How does this work? Imagine that keeping more of your customers turns some of those customers into customers for life. How much of a difference would that make to company profits? Consider that just one lifetime customer spends $8,000 on pizza and over $330,000 on luxury cars![41]

3.2 | SERVICE RECOVERY AND EMPOWERMENT

When mistakes are made, when problems occur, and when customers become dissatisfied with the service they've received, service businesses must switch from the process of service delivery to the process of **service recovery,** or restoring customer satisfaction to strongly dissatisfied customers.[42] Service recovery sometimes requires service employees not only to fix whatever mistake was made but also to perform heroic service acts that delight highly dissatisfied customers by far surpassing their expectations of fair treatment. Passengers on a Southwest Airlines flight from Fort Lauderdale to Denver were quite dismayed when they were told that, due to weather, they would be diverted to another airport. Many, no doubt, feared that they would be part of yet another story of how an airline trapped passengers in a plane for three, four, five hours or more. They were pleased, however, when the flight crew had pizza delivered for the entire plane and made sure that everyone had enough to eat and drink. As James Mino, a passenger on the plane, described it, "The flight crew went out of their way to make sure spirits were high through this ordeal."[43]

MGMT SUCCESS

Rewarding Customer Service

There are several elements that constitute good internal service quality. For employees to do a good job serving customers, management must implement policies and procedures that support good customer service; provide workers the tools and training they need to do their jobs; reward, recognize, and support good customer service; facilitate communication; and encourage people and departments to work together as teams to accomplish company goals with respect to internal service quality and customer service. For example, companies that reward employees for low rates of customer complaints unwittingly encourage those employees to ignore dissatisfied customers so that their problems aren't acknowledged and counted (which would endanger employee bonuses).

Unfortunately, when mistakes occur, service employees often don't have the discretion to resolve customer complaints. Customers who want service employees to correct or make up for poor service are frequently told, "I'm not allowed to do that," "I'm just following company rules," or "I'm sorry, only managers are allowed to make changes of any kind." In other words, company rules prevent them from engaging in acts of service recovery meant to turn dissatisfied customers back into satisfied customers. The result is frustration for customers and service employees and lost customers for the company.

Now, however, many companies are empowering their service employees.[44] In Chapter 9, you learned that *empowering workers* means permanently passing decision-making authority and responsibility from managers to workers. With respect to service recovery, empowering workers means giving service employees the authority and responsibility to make decisions that immediately solve customer problems.[45] At Diapers.com, all customer service agents are empowered to do whatever is necessary to take care of the customer, regardless of cost. As CEO Marc Lore describes it, "The concept is just if Mom calls and there's an issue, do whatever is necessary to make her happy and really wow her." One customer tried to order a car seat for the weekend but wouldn't receive it in time because of UPS's delivery schedule. So the customer service representative had it shipped to her own home (since UPS came to her house in the morning), and then drove it over to the customer's house.[46] Empowering service workers does entail some costs, although they are usually less than the company's savings from retaining customers.

4 | Manufacturing Operations

Ford makes cars, and Dell makes computers. Shell produces gasoline, whereas Sherwin-Williams makes paint. Boeing makes jet planes, but Budweiser makes beer. Maxtor makes hard drives, and Maytag makes appliances. The *manufacturing operations* of these companies all produce physical goods. But not all manufacturing operations, especially these, are the same. *Let's learn how various manufacturing operations differ in terms of 4.1 the* *amount of processing that is done to produce and assemble a product* and *4.2 the flexibility to change the number, kind, and characteristics of products that are produced.*

4.1 | AMOUNT OF PROCESSING IN MANUFACTURING OPERATIONS

Manufacturing operations can be classified according to the amount of processing or assembly that occurs after a customer order is received. The highest degree of processing occurs in **make-to-order operations**. A make-to-order operation does not start processing or assembling products until it receives a customer order. In fact, some make-to-order operations may not even order parts until a customer order is received. Not surprisingly, make-to-order operations produce or assemble highly specialized or customized products for customers.

For example, Dell has one of the most advanced make-to-order operations in the computer business. Because Dell has no finished goods inventory and no component parts inventory, its computers always have the latest, most advanced components, and Dell can pass on price cuts to customers. Plus, Dell can customize all of its orders, big and small. So whether you're ordering 5,000 personal computers for your company or just one personal computer for your home, Dell doesn't make the product until it has an order for it.

A moderate degree of processing occurs in **assemble-to-order operations**. A company using an assemble-to-order operation divides its manufacturing or assembly process into separate parts or modules. The company orders parts and assembles modules ahead of customer orders. Then, based on actual customer orders or on research forecasting what customers will want,

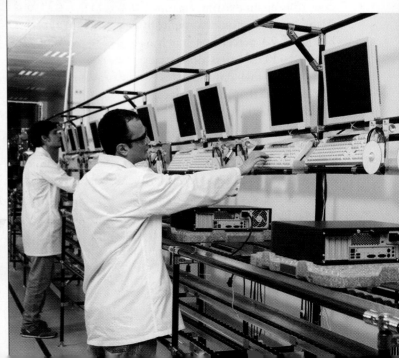

© iStockphoto.com/gerenme

those modules are combined to create semicustomized products. For example, when a customer orders a new car, General Motors may have already ordered the basic parts or modules it needs from suppliers. Based on sales forecasts, GM may already have ordered enough tires, air-conditioning compressors, brake systems, and seats from suppliers to accommodate nearly all customer orders on a particular day. Special orders from customers and car dealers are then used to determine the final assembly checklist for particular cars as they move down the assembly line.

The lowest degree of processing occurs in **make-to-stock operations** (also called *build-to-stock*). Because the products are standardized, meaning each product is exactly the same as the next, a company using a make-to-stock operation starts ordering parts and assembling finished products before receiving customer orders. Customers then purchase these standardized products—such as Rubbermaid storage containers, microwave ovens, and vacuum cleaners—at retail stores or directly from the manufacturer. Because parts are ordered and products are assembled before customers order the products, make-to-stock operations are highly dependent on the accuracy of sales forecasts. If sales forecasts are incorrect, make-to-stock operations could end up building too many or too few products, or they could make products with the wrong features or without the features that customers want. These disadvantages are leading many companies to move from make-to-stock to assemble-to-order systems.

4.2 | FLEXIBILITY OF MANUFACTURING OPERATIONS

A second way to categorize manufacturing operations is by **manufacturing flexibility,** meaning the degree to which manufacturing operations can easily and quickly change the number, kind, and characteristics of products they produce. Flexibility allows companies to respond quickly to changes in the marketplace (i.e., competitors and customers) and to reduce the lead time between ordering and final delivery of products. There is often a tradeoff between flexibility and cost, however, with the most flexible manufacturing operations frequently having higher costs per unit and the least flexible operations having lower costs per unit.[47] Some common manufacturing operations, arranged in order from the least flexible to the most flexible, are continuous-flow production, line-flow production, batch production, and job shops.

Most production processes generate finished products at a discrete rate. A product is completed, and

then—perhaps a few seconds, minutes, or hours later—another is completed, and so on. By contrast, in **continuous-flow production,** products are produced continuously rather than at a discrete rate. Like a water hose that is never turned off and just keeps on flowing, production of the final product never stops. Liquid chemicals and petroleum products are examples of continuous-flow production. Because of their complexity, continuous-flow production processes are the most standardized and least flexible manufacturing operations.

Line-flow production processes are preestablished, occur in a serial or linear manner, and are dedicated to making one type of product. Line-flow production processes are therefore inflexible. For example, nearly every city has a local bottling plant for soft drinks or beer. The processes or steps in bottling plants are serial, meaning they must occur in a particular order: sterilize; fill with soft drink or beer; crown or cap bottles; check for underfilling and missing caps; apply label; inspect a final time; and then place bottles in cases, cases on pallets, and pallets on delivery trucks.[48]

Batch production involves the manufacture of large batches of products in standard lot sizes. This production method is finding increasing use among restaurant chains. To ensure consistency in the taste and quality of their products, many restaurants have central kitchens, or commissaries, that produce batches of food such as mashed potatoes, stuffing, macaroni and cheese, rice, quiche filling, and chili, in volumes ranging from 10 to 200 gallons. These batches are then delivered to restaurants, which serve the food to customers.

Finally, **job shops** are typically small manufacturing operations that handle special manufacturing processes or jobs. In contrast to batch production, which handles large batches of different products, job shops typically handle very small batches, some as small as one product or process per batch. Basically, each job in a job shop is different, and once a job is done, the job shop

Make-to-stock operation a manufacturing operation that orders parts and assembles standardized products before receiving customer orders

Manufacturing flexibility the degree to which manufacturing operations can easily and quickly change the number, kind, and characteristics of products they produce

Continuous-flow production a manufacturing operation that produces goods at a continuous, rather than a discrete, rate

Line-flow production manufacturing processes that are preestablished, occur in a serial or linear manner, and are dedicated to making one type of product

Batch production a manufacturing operation that produces goods in large batches in standard lot sizes

Job shops manufacturing operations that handle custom orders or small batch jobs

Inventory the amount and number of raw materials, parts, and finished products that a company has in its possession

Raw material inventories the basic inputs in a manufacturing process

Component parts inventories the basic parts used in manufacturing that are fabricated from raw materials

Work-in-process inventories partially finished goods consisting of assembled component parts

moves on to a completely different job or manufacturing process for, most likely, a different customer. Grauch Enterprises in Philipsburg, Pennsylvania, is a job shop that mills, turns, drills, paints, and finishes everything from plastics (such as nylon, polycarbonates, and laminates) to metals (such as brass, aluminum, stainless and alloy steels, titanium, and cast iron). It makes 650 different parts for one customer alone and received one order to make 5,000 units out of 20,000 individual parts. When it comes to making different parts for different customers, owner Fred Grauch says, "There's very little we won't try. . . ."[49]

5 | Inventory

Inventory is the amount and number of raw materials, parts, and finished products a company has in its possession. No matter how efficient or productive a company is, it can't do business (and can't make money!) if it doesn't have enough inventory. During the global recession that began in 2008, manufacturers, such as Apple, Nissan, and HTC, reduced costs by carrying less of the inventory they needed to make their products. However, as the economy recovered and consumer demand for products increased, they found themselves unable to meet demand because they didn't have enough inventory. For example, Apple has been unable to meet the demand for its very popular iPad due to a shortage of touch-screen displays, while Nissan has had to shut down some of its factories because it doesn't have enough computer chips for an engine control unit.[50]

*In this section, you will learn about **5.1 the different types of inventory, 5.2 how to measure inventory levels, 5.3 the costs of maintaining an inventory, and 5.4 the different systems for managing inventory.***

5.1 | TYPES OF INVENTORY

Exhibit 18.4 shows the four kinds of inventory a manufacturer has: raw materials, component parts, work-in-process, and finished goods. The flow of inventory through a manufacturing plant begins when the purchasing department buys raw materials from vendors. **Raw material inventories** are the basic inputs in the

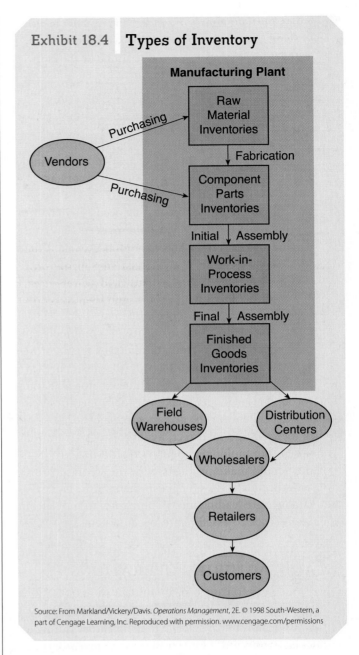

Exhibit 18.4 Types of Inventory

Source: From Markland/Vickery/Davis. *Operations Management*, 2E. © 1998 South-Western, a part of Cengage Learning, Inc. Reproduced with permission. www.cengage.com/permissions

manufacturing process. For example, to begin making a car, automobile manufacturers purchase raw materials such as steel, iron, aluminum, copper, rubber, and unprocessed plastic.

Next, raw materials are fabricated or processed into **component parts inventories**, meaning the basic parts used in manufacturing a product. For example, in an automobile plant, steel is fabricated or processed into a car's body panels, and steel and iron are melted and shaped into engine parts like pistons or engine blocks. Some component parts are purchased from vendors rather than fabricated in-house.

The component parts are then assembled to make unfinished **work-in-process inventories**, which are also known as *partially finished goods*. This process is also called *initial assembly*. For example, steel body panels are welded to each other and to the frame of the car to make a "unibody," which comprises the unpainted interior frame and exterior structure of the car. Likewise, pistons, camshafts, and other engine parts are inserted into the engine block to create a working engine.

Next, all the work-in-process inventories are assembled to create **finished goods inventories,** which are the final outputs of the manufacturing process. This process is also called *final assembly*. For a car, the engine, wheels, brake system, suspension, interior, and electrical system are assembled into a car's painted unibody to make the working automobile, which is the factory's finished product. In the last step in the process, the finished goods are sent to field warehouses, distribution centers, or wholesalers, and then to retailers for final sale to customers.

5.2 | MEASURING INVENTORY

As you'll learn below, uncontrolled inventory can lead to huge costs for a manufacturing operation. Consequently, managers need good measures of inventory to prevent inventory costs from becoming too large. Three basic measures of inventory are average aggregate inventory, weeks of supply, and inventory turnover.

If you've ever worked in a retail store and had to take inventory, you probably weren't too excited about the process of counting every item in the store and storeroom. It's an extensive task that's a bit easier today because of bar codes that mark items and computers that can count and track them. Nonetheless, inventories still differ from day to day depending on when in the month or week they're taken. Because of such differences, companies often measure **average aggregate inventory,** which is the average overall inventory during a particular time period. Average aggregate inventory for a month can be determined by simply averaging the inventory counts at the end of each business day for that month. One way companies know whether they're carrying too much or too little inventory is to compare their average aggregate inventory to the industry average for such inventory. For example, 72 days of inventory is the average for the automobile industry. Thus, Ford's inventory of SUVs is about average, whereas Toyota's is quite low and Chrysler's quite high.

Inventory is also measured in terms of *weeks of supply*, meaning the number of weeks it would take for a company to run out of its current supply of inventory. In general, there is an acceptable number of weeks of inventory for a particular kind of business. Too few

weeks of inventory on hand puts a company at risk for a **stockout**—running out of inventory. When Burger King introduced a limited-time offer of pork-barbeque ribs, many of its stores began to run out of supplies of ribs and packaging. Test markets showed customers favoring three-piece servings, but when they released nationally, many customers were willing to indulge in larger six- and eight-piece portions.[51] On the other hand, a business that has too many weeks of inventory on hand incurs high costs (discussed below). Excess inventory can be reduced only by cutting prices or temporarily stopping production.

Another common inventory measure, **inventory turnover,** is the number of times per year that a company sells or "turns over" its average inventory. For example, if a company keeps an average of 100 finished widgets in inventory each month, and it sold 1,000 widgets this year, then it turned its inventory 10 times this year.

In general, the higher the number of inventory turns, the better. In practice, a high turnover means that a company can continue its daily operations with just a small amount of inventory on hand. For example, let's take two companies, A and B, that have identical inventory levels (520,000 widget parts and raw materials) over the course of a year. If company A turns its inventories twenty-six times a year, it will completely replenish its inventory every 2 weeks and have an average inventory of 20,000 widget parts and raw materials. By contrast, if company B turns its inventories only two times a year, it will completely replenish its inventory every 26 weeks and have an average inventory of 260,000 widget parts and raw materials. So, by turning its inventory more often, company A has 92 percent less inventory on hand at any one time than company B.

The average number of inventory turns across all kinds of manufacturing plants is approximately 8 per year, although the average can be higher or lower for different industries.[52] For example, whereas the average auto company turns its entire inventory 13 times per year, some of the best auto companies more than double that rate, turning their inventory 27.8 times per year, or once every 2 weeks.[53] Turning inventory more frequently than the industry average can cut an auto

Finished goods inventories the final outputs of manufacturing operations

Average aggregate inventory average overall inventory during a particular time period

Stockout the situation when a company runs out of finished product

Inventory turnover the number of times per year that a company sells or "turns over" its average inventory

Ordering cost the costs associated with ordering inventory, including the cost of data entry, phone calls, obtaining bids, correcting mistakes, and determining when and how much inventory to order

Setup cost the costs of downtime and lost efficiency that occur when a machine is changed or adjusted to produce a different kind of inventory

Holding cost the cost of keeping inventory until it is used or sold, including storage, insurance, taxes, obsolescence, and opportunity costs

Stockout costs the costs incurred when a company runs out of a product, including transaction costs to replace inventory and the loss of customers' goodwill

company's costs by several hundred million dollars per year. Finally, it should be pointed out that even make-to-order companies like Dell turn their inventory. In theory, make-to-order companies have no inventory. In fact, they've got inventory, but you have to measure it in hours. For example, Dell turns its inventory 500 times a year in its factories, which means that on average it has 17 hours—that's hours and not days—of inventory on hand in its factories.[54]

5.3 | COSTS OF MAINTAINING AN INVENTORY

Maintaining an inventory results in four kinds of costs: ordering, setup, holding, and stockout. **Ordering cost** is not the cost of the inventory itself but the costs associated with ordering the inventory. It includes the costs of completing paperwork, manually entering data into a computer, making phone calls, getting competing bids, correcting mistakes, and simply determining when and how much new inventory should be reordered. For example, ordering costs are relatively high in the restaurant business because 80 percent of food-service orders (by which restaurants reorder food supplies) are processed manually. A report, *Enabling Profitable Growth in the Food-Prepared-Away-From-Home Industries*, estimated that the food industry could save $14.3 billion a year if all restaurants converted to electronic data interchange (see Chapter 17), in which purchase and ordering information from one company's computer system is automatically relayed to another company's computer system.[55]

Setup cost is the cost of changing or adjusting a machine so that it can produce a different kind of inventory.[56] For example, 3M uses the same production machinery to make several kinds of industrial tape, but it must adjust the machines whenever it switches from one kind of tape to another. There are two kinds of setup costs: downtime and lost efficiency. *Downtime* occurs whenever a machine is not being used to process inventory. If it takes 5 hours to switch a machine from processing one kind of inventory to another, then 5 hours of downtime have occurred. Downtime is costly because companies earn an economic return only when

Uncontrolled inventory can lead to **huge** costs for a manufacturing operation.

© iStockphoto.com/Peeter Viisimaa / © iStockphoto.com/U.P.images

machines are actively turning raw materials into parts or parts into finished products. The second setup cost is *lost efficiency*. Recalibrating a machine to its optimal settings after a switchover typically takes some time. It may take several days of fine-tuning before a machine finally produces the number of high-quality parts that it is supposed to. So, each time a machine has to be changed to handle a different kind of inventory, setup costs (downtime and lost efficiency) rise.

Holding cost, also known as *carrying* or *storage cost,* is the cost of keeping inventory until it is used or sold. Holding cost includes the cost of storage facilities, insurance to protect inventory from damage or theft, inventory taxes, the cost of obsolescence (holding inventory that is no longer useful to the company), and the opportunity cost of spending money on inventory that could have been spent elsewhere in the company. For example, it's estimated that U.S. airlines have a total of $44 billion worth of airplane parts in stock for maintenance, repair, and overhauling their planes at any one time. The holding cost for managing, storing, and purchasing these parts is nearly $11 billion—or roughly one-quarter of the cost of the parts themselves.[57]

Stockout costs are the costs incurred when a company runs out of a product. There are two basic kinds of stockout costs. First, the company incurs the transaction costs of overtime work, shipping, and the like

© iStockphoto.com/Luis Carlos Torres

in trying to quickly replace out-of-stock products with new inventories. The second and perhaps more damaging cost is the loss of customers' goodwill when a company cannot deliver the desired products.

5.4 | MANAGING INVENTORY

Inventory management has two basic goals. The first is to avoid running out of stock and thus angering and dissatisfying customers. This goal calls for increasing inventory to a safe level that won't risk stockouts. The second is to efficiently reduce inventory levels and costs as much as possible without impairing daily operations. This goal calls for a minimum level of inventory. The following inventory management techniques—economic order quantity (EOQ), just-in-time inventory (JIT), and materials requirement planning (MRP)—are different ways of balancing these competing goals.

Economic order quantity (EOQ) is a system of formulas that helps determine how much and how often inventory should be ordered. EOQ takes into account the overall demand (D) for a product while trying to minimize ordering costs (O) and holding costs (H). The formula for EOQ is

$$EOQ = \sqrt{\frac{2DO}{H}}$$

For example, if a factory uses 40,000 gallons of paint a year (D), ordering costs (O) are $75 per order, and holding costs (H) are $4 per gallon, then the optimal quantity to order is 1,225 gallons:

$$EOQ = \sqrt{\frac{2(40,000)(75)}{4}} = 1,225$$

With 40,000 gallons of paint being used per year, the factory uses approximately 110 gallons per day:

$$\frac{40,000 \text{ gallons}}{365 \text{ days}} = 110$$

Consequently, the factory would order 1,225 new gallons of paint approximately every 11 days:

$$\frac{1,225 \text{ gallons}}{110 \text{ gallons per day}} = 11.1 \text{ days}$$

While EOQ formulas try to minimize holding and ordering costs, the just-in-time (JIT) approach to inventory management attempts to eliminate holding costs by reducing inventory levels to near zero. With a **just-in-time (JIT) inventory system**, component parts arrive from suppliers just as they are needed at each stage of production. By having parts arrive just in time, the manufacturer has little inventory on hand and thus avoids the costs associated with holding inventory.

To have just the right amount of inventory arrive at just the right time requires a tremendous amount of coordination between manufacturing operations and suppliers. One way to promote tight coordination under a JIT system is close proximity. Most parts suppliers for Toyota's plant at Georgetown, Kentucky, are located within 200 miles of the plant. Furthermore, parts are picked up from suppliers and delivered to Toyota as often as 16 times a day.[58] A second way to promote close coordination under a JIT system is to have a shared information system that allows a manufacturer and its suppliers to know the quantity and kinds of parts inventory the other has in stock. Generally, factories and suppliers facilitate information sharing by using the same part numbers and names. Ford's seat supplier accomplishes this by sticking a bar code on each seat, and Ford then uses the sticker to route the seat through its factory.

Manufacturing operations and their parts suppliers can also facilitate close coordination by using the Japanese system of kanban. **Kanban**, which is Japanese for "sign," is a simple ticket-based system that indicates when it is time to reorder inventory. Suppliers attach kanban cards to batches of parts. Then, when an assembly-line worker uses the first part out of a batch, the kanban card is removed. The cards are then collected, sorted, and quickly returned to the supplier, who begins resupplying the factory with parts that match the order information on the kanban cards. Because prices and batch sizes are typically agreed to ahead of time, kanban tickets greatly reduce paperwork and ordering costs.[59]

A third method for managing inventory is **materials requirement planning (MRP)**. MRP is a production and

Economic order quantity (EOQ) a system of formulas that minimizes ordering and holding costs and helps determine how much and how often inventory should be ordered

Just-in-time (JIT) inventory system an inventory system in which component parts arrive from suppliers just as they are needed at each stage of production

Kanban a ticket-based system that indicates when to reorder inventory

Materials requirement planning (MRP) a production and inventory system that determines the production schedule, production batch sizes, and inventory needed to complete final products

inventory system that, from beginning to end, precisely determines the production schedule, production batch sizes, and inventories needed to complete final products. The three key parts of MRP systems are the master production schedule, the bill of materials, and inventory records. The *master production schedule* is a detailed schedule that indicates the quantity of each item to be produced, the planned delivery dates for those items, and the time by which each step of the production process must be completed in order to meet those delivery dates. Based on the quantity and kind of products set forth in the master production schedule, the *bill of materials* identifies all the necessary parts and inventory, the quantity or volume of inventory to be ordered, and the order in which the parts and inventory should be assembled. *Inventory records* indicate the kind, quantity, and location of inventory that is on hand or that has been or-

dered. When inventory records are combined with the bill of materials, the resulting report indicates what to buy, when to buy it, and what it will cost to order. Today, nearly all MRP systems are available in the form of powerful, flexible computer software.[60]

Which inventory management system should you use? EOQ formulas are intended for use with **independent demand systems,** in which the level of one kind of inventory does not depend on another. For example, because inventory levels for automobile tires are unrelated to the inventory levels of women's dresses, Sears could use EOQ formulas to calculate separate optimal order quantities for dresses and tires. By contrast, JIT and MRP are used with **dependent demand systems,** in which the level of inventory depends on the number of finished units to be produced. For example, if Yamaha makes 1,000 motorcycles a day, then it will need 1,000 seats, 1,000 gas tanks, and 2,000 wheels and tires each day. So, when optimal inventory levels depend on the number of products to be produced, use a JIT or MRP inventory management system.

STUDENT Study Tools

Located at the back of your book

☐ Rip out and study the Chapter Review Card at the end of the book

Log in to the CourseMate for MGMT at cengagebrain.com to:

☐ Review Key Term Flashcards delivered 3 ways (print or online)

☐ Complete both Practice Quizzes to prepare for tests

☐ Play Beat the Clock and Quizbowl to master concepts

☐ Complete the Crossword Puzzle to review key terms

☐ Watch the video on Preserve for a real company example and take the accompanying quiz

☐ Watch the Biz Flix clip from *In Bruges* and take the quiz

☐ Complete the Case Assignment on Starbucks

☐ Work through the Management Decision on dealing with oversupply

☐ Work through the Management Team Decision on lean production

☐ Develop your skills with the Develop Your Career Potential exercise

Endnotes

Chapter 1

1. S. Prasso, "American Made . . .Chinese Owned," *Fortune*, May 24, 2010, 92.
2. M. Herper and R. Langreth, "Dangerous Devices," *Forbes*, November 27, 2006, 94.
3. "Business Services: Global Industry Guide," *Data Monitor*, October 7, 2009, accessed April 18, 2009, http://www.marketresearch.com.
4. V. Nayar, "Corner Office: He's Not Bill Gates, or Fred Astaire," interview by A. Bryant, *New York Times*, February 13, 2010, accessed June 22, 2010, http://www.nytimes.com/2010/02/14/business/14cornerweb.html.
5. M. Gottfredson, S. Schaubert, and E. Babcock, "Achieving Breakthrough Performance," *Stanford Social Initiative Review* (Summer 2008): 35.
6. S. McCartney, "At JFK, More Flying, Less Waiting on the Tarmac," *Wall Street Journal*, July 29, 2010, D3.
7. D. A. Wren, A. G. Bedeian, and J. D. Breeze, "The Foundations of Henri Fayol's Administrative Theory," *Management Decision* 40 (2002): 906–918.
8. H. Fayol, *General and Industrial Management* (London: Pittman & Sons, 1949).
9. R. Stagner, "Corporate Decision Making," *Journal of Applied Psychology* 53 (1969): 1–13.
10. D. W. Bray, R. J. Campbell, and D. L. Grant, *Formative Years in Business: A Long-Term AT&T Study of Managerial Lives* (New York: Wiley, 1993).
11. G. Fowler, "EBay to Unload Skype in IPO, Citing Poor Fit," *Wall Street Journal*, April 15, 2009, B1; G. Fowler and E. Ramstad, "EBay Looks Abroad for Growth—Online Auctioneer to Buy Korean Site as It Refocuses on E-Commerce, PayPal," *Wall Street Journal*, April 16, 2009, B2.
12. P. Burrows, "Innovator: Marthin De Beer," *Bloomberg Businessweek*, May 17–23, 2010, 38.
13. A. Johnson, "Pfizer Outlines Post-Wyeth R&D Structure—Company Splits Research on Traditional Drugs from Biologics and Strives to Retain Scientists," *Wall Street Journal*, April 8, 2009, B4.
14. A. Taylor III, "Fixing Up Ford," *Fortune*, May 25, 2009, 44–51.
15. Ibid.
16. N. Bunkley, "Ford Profit Comes as Toyota Hits a Bump," *New York Times*, January 28, 2010, accessed June 23, 2010, http://www.nytimes.com/2010/01/29/business/29ford.html; A. Taylor III, "Fixing Up Ford."
17. J. Lunsford, "Get into Hot Water to Save Fuel," *Wall Street Journal*, June 11, 2008, B1.
18. H. S. Jonas III, R. E. Fry, and S. Srivastva, "The Office of the CEO: Understanding the Executive Experience," *Academy of Management Executive* 4 (1990): 36–47.
19. P. Dvorak, "Companies Cut Holes in CEOs' Golden Parachutes," *Wall Street Journal*, September 15, 2008, B4; P. Sellers, "Lessons of the Fall," *Fortune*, June 9, 2008, 70–80.
20. M. Porter, J. Lorsch, and N. Nohria, "Seven Surprises for New CEOs," *Harvard Business Review* (October 2004): 62.
21. B. O'Keefe, "Battle-Tested: How a Decade of War Has Created a New Generation of Elite Business Leaders," *Fortune*, March 22, 2010, 114.
22. E. Byron, "P & G's Lafley Sees CEOs As Link to World," *Wall Street Journal*, March 23, 2009, B6.
23. Q. Huy, "In Praise of Middle Managers," *Harvard Business Review* (September 2001): 72–79.
24. I. Barat, "Rebuilding after a Catastrophe: How Caterpillar is Responding to Tornado's Lesson," *Wall Street Journal*, May 19, 2008, B1–2.
25. N. Heintz, "Building a Culture of Employee Appreciation," *Inc.*, September 1, 2009, accessed August 3, 2009, http://www.inc.com/magazine/20090901/building-a-culture-of-employee-appreciation.html.
26. S. Tully, "What Team Leaders Need to Know," *Fortune*, February 20, 1995, 93.
27. B. Francella, "In a Day's Work," *Convenience Store News*, September 25, 2001, 7.
28. L. Liu and A. McMurray, "Frontline Leaders: The Entry Point for Leadership Development in the Manufacturing Industry," *Journal of European Industrial Training* 28, no. 2–4 (2004): 339–352.
29. "What Makes Teams Work?" *Fast Company*, November 1, 2000, 109.
30. K. Hultman, "The 10 Commandments of Team Leadership," *Training & Development,* February 1, 1998, 12–13.
31. L. Landro, "The Informed Patient: Bringing Surgeons Down to Earth—New Programs Aim to Curb Fear that Prevents Nurses from Flagging Problems," *Wall Street Journal*, November 16, 2005, D1.
32. Ibid.
33. N. Steckler and N. Fondas, "Building Team Leader Effectiveness: A Diagnostic Tool," *Organizational Dynamics* (Winter 1995): 20–34.
34. S. Tully, "What Team Leaders Need to Know."
35. H. Mintzberg, *The Nature of Managerial Work* (New York: Harper & Row, 1973).
36. P. Hales, "What Do Managers Do? A Critical Review of the Evidence," *Journal of Management Studies* 23, no. 1 (1986): 88–115.
37. "Cessna CEO Joins Mesa Mayor to Open New Jet Center," *Business Wire*, for February 2009, http://www.Reuters.com.
38. C. Penttila, "Employee Benefits in Today's Economy," *Entrepreneur* 37, no. 1 (January 2009): 51–55.
39. B. Francella, "In a Day's Work."
40. K. Clark and R. Sidel, "Gang Green Meets Wall Street," *Wall Street Journal*, May 5, 2010, accessed June 22, 2010, http://online.wsj.com/article/SB100014240527487038667045752244807793420098.html.
41. S. Holtz, "Bring Your Intranet into the 21st Century," *Communication World* 25 (January–February 2008): 14–19.
42. S. Humphries, "Grapevine Goes High-Tech," *Courier Mail*, January 10, 2009.
43. A. Lashinsky, "The Decade of Steve," *Fortune*, November 23, 2009, 114; Y. Iwatani Kane and I. Sherr, "Apple Unveils iPhone 4," *Wall Street Journal*, June 8, 2010, accessed June 8, 2010, http://online.wsj.com/article/SB1000142405274870330390457529270349181 5956.html?mod=WSJ_hps_MIDDLE TopStories.
44. J. Levitz, "UPS Thinks Out of the Box on Driver Training," *Wall Street Journal*, April 6, 2010, accessed June 22, 2010, http://online.wsj.com/article/SB1000142405270230391 2104575164573823418844.html?mod=WSJ_hp_editorsPicks.
45. C. Cosh, "In Wal-Mart We Trust," *National Post*, March 28, 2008, A15.
46. J. Scheck, "R&D Spending Holds Steady in Slump—Big Companies Invest to Grab Sales in Recovery; The iPod Lesson," *Wall Street Journal*, April 6, 2009, A1.
47. L. A. Hill, *Becoming a Manager: Mastery of a New Identity* (Boston: Harvard Business School Press, 1992).
48. R. L. Katz, "Skills of an Effective Administrator," *Harvard Business Review* (September–October 1974): 90–102.
49. A. Bartlett and S. Ghoshal, "Changing the Role of Top Management: Beyond Systems to People," *Harvard Business Review* (May–June 1995): 132–142.

50. S. I. Sadove, "Corner Office: For the Chief of Saks, It's Culture That Drives Results," interview by A. Bryant, *Wall Street Journal*, May 28, 2010, accessed August 12, 2010, http://www.nytimes.com/2010/05/30/business/30corner.html?_r=1.

51. L. Schmidt and J. E. Hunter, "Development of a Causal Model of Process Determining Job Performance," *Current Directions in Psychological Science* 1 (1992): 89–92.

52. J. B. Miner, "Sentence Completion Measures in Personnel Research: The Development and Validation of the Miner Sentence Completion Scales," in *Personality Assessment in Organizations,* ed. H. J. Bernardin and D. A. Bownas (New York: Praeger, 1986), 147–146.

53. M. W. McCall, Jr., and M. M. Lombardo, "What Makes a Top Executive?" *Psychology Today*, February 1983, 26–31; E. van Velsor and J. Brittain, "Why Executives Derail: Perspectives across Time and Cultures," *Academy of Management Executive* (November 1995): 62–72.

54. M. W. McCall, Jr., and M. M. Lombardo "What Makes a Top Executive?"

55. K. Naj, "Corporate Therapy: The Latest Addition to Executive Suite Is Psychologist's Couch," *Wall Street Journal*, August 29, 1994, A1.

56. M. Mathieu, "Corner Office: Want the Job? Tell Him the Meaning of Life," interview by A. Bryant, *New York Times*, June 18, 2010, accessed June 22, 2010, http://www.nytimes.com/2010/06/20/business/20corner.html.

57. L. A. Hill, *Becoming a Manager: Mastery of a New Identity* (Boston, MA: Harvard Business School Press, 1992), 55.

58. Ibid., 57.

59. Ibid., 67.

60. Ibid., 103.

61. Ibid., 161.

62. J. Pfeffer, *The Human Equation: Building Profits by Putting People First* (Boston: Harvard Business School Press, 1996); J. Pfeffer, *Competitive Advantage through People: Unleashing the Power of the Work Force* (Boston: Harvard Business School Press, 1994).

63. M. A. Huselid, "The Impact of Human Resource Management Practices on Turnover, Productivity, and Corporate Financial Performance," *Academy of Management Journal* 38 (1995): 635–672.

64. Ibid.

65. D. McDonald and A. Smith, "A Proven Connection: Performance Management and Business Results," *Compensation & Benefits Review* 27, no. 6 (1 January 1995): 59.

66. I. Fulmer, B. Gerhart, and K. Scott, "Are the 100 Best Better? An Empirical Investigation of the Relationship between Being a 'Great Place to Work' and Firm Performance," *Personnel Psychology* (Winter 2003): 965–993.

67. B. Schneider and D. E. Bowen, "Employee and Customer Perceptions of Service in Banks: Replication and Extension," *Journal of Applied Psychology* 70 (1985): 423–433; B. Schneider, J. J. Parkington, and V. M. Buxton, "Employee and Customer Perceptions of Service in Banks," *Administrative Science Quarterly* 25 (1980): 252–267.

68. D. Simon and J. DeVaro, "Do the Best Companies to Work for Provide Better Customer Satisfaction?" *Managerial and Decision Economics*, 27 (2006): 667–683.

Chapter 2

1. C. S. George, Jr., *The History of Management Thought* (Englewood Cliffs, NJ: Prentice Hall, 1972).

2. A. Erman, *Life in Ancient Egypt* (London: Macmillan & Co., 1984).

3. S. A. Epstein, *Wage Labor and Guilds in Medieval Europe* (Chapel Hill: University of North Carolina Press, 1991).

4. R. Braun, *Industrialization and Everyday Life*, trans. S. Hanbury-Tenison (Cambridge: Cambridge University Press, 1990).

5. J. B. White, "The Line Starts Here: Mass-Production Techniques Changed the Way People Work and Live throughout the World," *Wall Street Journal*, January 11, 1999, R25.

6. R. B. Reich, *The Next American Frontier* (New York: Times Books, 1983).

7. J. Mickelwait and A. Wooldridge, *The Company: A Short History of a Revolutionary Idea* (New York: Modern Library, 2003).

8. H. Kendall, "Unsystematized, Systematized, and Scientific Management," in *Scientific Management: A Collection of the More Significant Articles Describing the Taylor System of Management*, ed. C. Thompson (Easton, PA: Hive Publishing, 1972), 103–131.

9. United States Congress, House, Special Committee, *Hearings to Investigate the Taylor and Other Systems of Shop Management*, vol. 3 (Washington, D.C.: Government Printing Office, 1912).

10. Ibid.

11. A. Derickson, "Physiological Science and Scientific Management in the Progressive Era: Frederic S. Lee and the Committee on Industrial Fatigue," *Business History Review* 68 (1994): 483–514.

12. United States Congress, House, Special Committee, *Hearings to Investigate the Taylor and Other Systems of Shop Management*.

13. F. W. Taylor, *The Principles of Scientific Management* (Elibron Classics, 1911) 26.

14. C. D. Wrege and R. M. Hodgetts, "Frederick W. Taylor's 1899 Pig Iron Observations," *Academy of Management Journal* 43 (2000): 1283–1291; J. R. Hough and M. A. White, "Using Stories to Create Change: The Object Lesson of Frederick Taylor's 'Pig-Tale,'" *Journal of Management* 27, no. 5 (2001) 585.

15. E. Locke, "The Ideas of Frederick W. Taylor: An Evaluation," *Academy of Management Review* 7 (1982): 14–24.

16. C. S. George, Jr., *The History of Management Thought*.

17. F. Gilbreth and L. Gilbreth, "Applied Motion Study," in *The Writings of the Gilbreths*, ed. W. R. Spriegel and C. E. Myers (1917; reprint, Homewood, IL: Richard D. Irwin, 1953), 207–274.

18. D. Ferguson, "Don't Call It 'Time and Motion Study,'" *IIE Solutions* 29, no. 5 (1997): 22–23.

19. P. Peterson, "Training and Development: The View of Henry L. Gantt (1861–1919)," *SAM Advanced Management Journal* (Winter 1987): 20–23.

20. H. Gantt, "Industrial Efficiency," *National Civic Federation Report of the 11th Annual Meeting*, New York, January 12, 1991, 103.

21. Ibid.

22. M. Weber, *The Theory of Economic and Social Organization*, trans. A. Henderson and T. Parsons (New York: The Free Press, 1947).

23. M. Weber, *Economy and Society: An Outline of Interpretive Sociology* (University of California Press, 1978).

24. C. S. George, Jr., *The History of Management Thought*.

25. D. Wren, "Henri Fayol as Strategist: A Nineteenth Century Corporate Turnaround," *Management Decision* 39 (2001): 475–487.

26. Ibid.

27. F. Blancpain, "Les cahiers inédits d'Henri Fayol," trans. D. Wren, *Extrait du bulletin de l'institut international d'administration publique* 28–29 (1974): 1–48.

28. D. A. Wren, A. G. Bedeian, and J. D. Breeze, "The Foundations of Henri Fayol's Administrative Theory," *Management Decision* 40 (2002): 906–918.

29. H. Fayol, *General and Industrial Management* (London: Pittman & Sons, 1949); D. A. Wren, A. G. Bedeian, and J. D. Breeze, "The Foundations of Henri Fayol's Administrative Theory."

30. Mary Parker Follett, *Mary Parker Follett—Prophet of Management: A Celebration of Writings from the 1920s*, ed. P. Graham (Boston: Harvard Business School Press, 1995).

31. Ibid.

32. Ibid.

33. D. Linden, "The Mother of Them All," *Forbes*, January 16, 1995, 75.

34. J. H. Smith, "The Enduring Legacy of Elton Mayo," *Human Relations* 51, no. 3 (1998): 221–249.

35. E. Mayo, *The Human Problems of an Industrial Civilization* (New York: Macmillan, 1933).

36. Ibid.

37. "Hawthorne Revisited: The Legend and the Legacy," *Organizational Dynamics* (Winter 1975): 66–80.

38. E. Mayo, *The Social Problems of an Industrial Civilization* (Boston: Harvard Graduate School of Business Administration, 1945) 65–67.

39. "Hawthorne Revisited: The Legend and the Legacy."

40. C. S. George, Jr., *History of Management Thought*.

41. C. I. Barnard, *The Functions of the Executive* (Cambridge, MA: Harvard University Press, 1938), 4.

42. E. Mayo, *The Social Problems of an Industrial Civilization*, 45.

43. J. Fuller and A. Mansour, "Operations Management and Operations Research:

A Historical and Relational Perspective," *Management Decision* 41 (2003): 422–426.

44. D. Wren and R. Greenwood, "Business Leaders: A Historical Sketch of Eli Whitney," *Journal of Leadership and Organizational Studies* 6 (1999): 131.

45. "Monge, Gaspard, comte de Péluse," *Britannica Online,* accessed January 9, 2005, http://www.eb.com.

46. M. Schwartz and A. Fish, "Just-in-Time Inventories in Old Detroit," *Business History* 40, no. 3 (July 1998): 48.

47. D. Ashmos and G. Huber, "The Systems Paradigm in Organization Theory: Correcting the Record and Suggesting the Future," *Academy of Management Review* 12 (1987): 607–621; F. Kast and J. Rosenzweig, "General Systems Theory: Applications for Organizations and Management," *Academy of Management Journal* 15 (1972): 447–465; D. Katz and R. Kahn, *The Social Psychology of Organizations* (New York: Wiley, 1966).

48. R. Mockler, "The Systems Approach to Business Organization and Decision Making," *California Management Review* 11, no. 2 (1968): 53–58.

49. F. Luthans and T. Stewart, "A General Contingency Theory of Management," *Academy of Management Review* 2, no. 2 (1977): 181–195.

Chapter 3

1. Y. I. Kane, "Sony's Newest Display is a Culture Shift," *Wall Street Journal,* May 8, 2008, B1.

2. Y. I. Kane and D. Wakabayashi, "Microsoft Puts Gaming Plans in Motion," *Wall Street Journal,* June 13, 2010, accessed June 15, 2010, http://online.wsj.com /article/SB100014240527487036854045753070824434894 89528.html; C. Morris, "Video Games Under the Gun as Big Changes Loom," *CNBC.com,* June 14, 2010, accessed June 15, 2010, http:// www.cnbc.com/id/37685274/.

3. E. Romanelli and M. L. Tushman, "Organizational Transformation as Punctuated Equilibrium: An Empirical Test," *Academy of Management Journal* 37 (1994): 1141–1166.

4. H. Banks, "A Sixties Industry in a Nineties Economy," *Forbes,* May 9, 1994, 107–112.

5. L. Cowan, "Cheap Fuel Should Carry Many Airlines to More Record Profits for 1st Quarter," *Wall Street Journal,* April 4, 1998, B17A.

6. C. Isidore, "Airlines Still in Upheaval, 5 Years after 9/11," *CNNMoney.com,* September 8, 2006, accessed July 25, 2008, http://money.cnn.com/2006/09/08 /news/companies/airlines_sept11 /?postversion=2006090813&eref=yahoo.

7. B. Jones, "The Changing Dairy Industry," Department of Agricultural and Applied Economics and Center for Dairy Profitability, accessed July 25, 2008, http:// www.aae.wisc.edu/jones/Presentations /Wisc&TotalDairyTrends.pdf.

8. B. Stone, "Revenue at Craigslist is said to Top $100 Million," *New York Times,* June 9, 2009, accessed August 1, 2010, http://www.nytimes.com/2009/06/10 /technology/internet/10craig.html?_r =1&ref=craigslist.

9. J. Falls, "What the Wall Street Journal Has, Few Will Match," *Social Media Explorer,* October 30, 2009, accessed August 1, 2010, http://www .socialmediaexplorer.com/2009/10/30 /what-the-wall-street-journal-has-few -will-match/.

10. "Samsung Invests $2.1B in LCD Line," *Electronic News,* March 7, 2005; "LG Phillips Develops World's Largest LCD Panel Measuring 100 Inches," *NewLaunches.com,* March 7, 2006, accessed July 25, 2008, http://www.newlaunches .com/archives/lgphilips_develops_worlds _largest_lcd_panel_measuring_100 _inches.php; H. Ryoo, "Samsung to Invest $1 Billion in New LCD Production Line," *eWeek,* April 1, 2003, accessed July 25, 2008, http://www.eweek .com/c/a/Past-News/Samsung-to-Invest -1-Billion-in-New-LCD-Production-Line; "Samsung Develops World's Largest (820) Full HDTV TFT-LCD," accessed July 25, 2008, http://www.samsung.com /us/business/semiconductor/newsView .do?news_id=638; E. Ramstad, "I Want My Flat TV Now!" *Wall Street Journal,* May 27, 2004, B1; P. Watt, "LCD Factories Expand," *PC World,* accessed July 24, 2008, http://blogs.pcworld.com/staffblog /archives/003369.html.

11. E. Fyrwald, "The King of Water," interview by G. Colvin, *Fortune,* July 5, 2010, 52–59.

12. N. Casey, "Tainted Toys Get Another Turn: After Last Year's Recalls, Spin Master and Mega Brands Try Again with New Look," *Wall Street Journal,* October 31, 2008, B1.

13. "CEO Confidence Survey," *The Conference Board,* April 9, 2009, accessed April 27, 2009, http://www.conference-board .org.

14. "Despite Recession, U.S. Small Business Confidence Index Increases Six Points; Small Business Research Board Study Finds Increase in Key Indicators," *U.S. Business Confidence,* February 23, 2009, accessed April 27, 2009, http:// www.ipasrb.net.

15. J. Cuneo, "10 Perks We Love," *Inc.,* June 2010, 94–95.

16. "The Civil Rights Act of 1991," U.S. Equal Employment Opportunity Commission, accessed July 25, 2008, http:// www.eeoc.gov/policy/cra91.html.

17. "Compliance Assistance—Family and Medical Leave Act (FMLA)," U.S. Department of Labor: Employment Standards Administration Wage and Hour Division, accessed July 25, 2005, http:// www.dol.gov/.

18. R. J. Bies and T. R. Tyler, "The Litigation Mentality in Organizations: A Test of Alternative Psychological Explanations," *Organization Science* 4 (1993): 352–366.

19. S. Gardner, G. Gomes, and J. Morgan, "Wrongful Termination and the Expanding Public Policy Exception: Implications and Advice," *SAM Advanced Management Journal* 65 (2000): 38.

20. M. Orey, "Fear of Firing," *Business Week,* April 23, 2007, 52–62.

21. R. Johnston and S. Mehra, "Best-Practice Complaint Management," *Academy of Management Experience* 16 (November 2002): 145–154.

22. D. Smart and C. Martin, "Manufacturer Responsiveness to Consumer Correspondence: An Empirical Investigation of Consumer Perceptions," *Journal of Consumer Affairs* 26 (1992): 104.

23. S. Morrison, "Companies Have a Treasure Trove of Customer Intelligence; Now They also Have the Tools to Make Sense of It," *Wall Street Journal,* January 28, 2008, R6.

24. S. A. Zahra and S. S. Chaples, "Blind Spots in Competitive Analysis," *Academy of Management Executive* 7 (1993): 7–28.

25. K. G. Provan, "Embeddedness, Interdependence, and Opportunism in Organizational Supplier-Buyer Networks," *Journal of Management* 19 (1993): 841–856.

26. M. Dalton, "AB InBev Suppliers Feel Squeeze," *Wall Street Journal,* April 17, 2009, B2.

27. S. Parker and C. Axtell, "Seeing Another Viewpoint: Antecedents and Outcomes of Employee Perspective Taking," *Academy of Management Journal* 44 (2001): 1085–1100; B. K. Pilling, L. A. Crosby, and D. W. Jackson, "Relational Bonds in Industrial Exchange: An Experimental Test of the Transaction Cost Economic Framework," *Journal of Business Research* 30 (1994): 237–251.

28. "Carmakers Eye Economy with Unease," *USA Today,* May 24, 2004, B.06.

29. R. McGill Murphy, "Why Doing Good Is Good for Business," *Fortune,* February 8, 2010, 93.

30. N. Casey and M. Trottman, "Toys Containing Banned Plastics Still on Market; Restrictions on Phthalates Don't Take Effect Until '09; Fears of Reproductive Defects," *Wall Street Journal,* October 23, 2008, D1.

31. M. Hughlett, "PETA Targets McDonald's over Slaughter of Chickens," *Chicago Tribune,* February 16, 2009, accessed May 10, 2009, http://www .Chicagotribune.com.

32. S. Simon and J. Jargon, "PETA Ads to Target McDonald's," *Wall Street Journal,* May 1, 2009, B7.

33. J. Berr, "Boycott BP? That Hurts Station Owners—Not the Company," *Daily Finance,* June 2, 2010, accessed June 3, 2010, http://www.dailyfinance.com/story /media/boycott-bp-that-hurts-station -owners-not-the-company/19499350/.

34. "2009 AHA Environmental Scan," *Hospitals and Health Networks* 9 (2008): 35–42.

35. Ibid.

36. B. Bold, "Gatorade Takes Social Media Seriously with 'Mission Control Center'," *The Wall,* June 17, 2010, accessed August 5, 2010, http://www.wallblog .co.uk/2010/06/17/gatorade-takes-social -media-seriously-with-mission-control -center/.

37. D. F. Jennings and J. R. Lumpkin, "Insights between Environmental Scanning Activities and Porter's Generic Strategies: An Empirical Analysis," *Journal of Management* 4 (1992): 791–803.

38. S. Greenhouse, "Factory Defines Sweatshop Label, but Can It Thrive?" *New York Times*, July 18, 2010, BU1.

39. S. E. Jackson and J. E. Dutton, "Discerning Threats and Opportunities," *Administrative Science Quarterly* 33 (1988): 370–387.

40. B. Thomas, S. M. Clark, and D. A. Gioia, "Strategic Sensemaking and Organizational Performance: Linkages among Scanning, Interpretation, Action, and Outcomes," *Academy of Management Journal* 36 (1993): 239–270.

41. R. Daft, J. Sormunen, and D. Parks, "Chief Executive Scanning, Environmental Characteristics, and Company Performance: An Empirical Study," *Strategic Management Journal* 9 (1988): 123–139; V. Garg, B. Walters, and R. Priem, "Chief Executive Scanning Emphases, Environmental Dynamism, and Manufacturing Firm Performance," *Strategic Management Journal* 24 (2003): 725–744; D. Miller and P. H. Friesen, "Strategy-Making and Environment: The Third Link," *Strategic Management Journal* 4 (1983): 221–235.

42. A. Sharma, "AT&T, Verizon Make Different Calls," *Wall Street Journal*, January 28, 2009, B1; N. Worden and V. Kumar, "Earnings: Comcast Feels the Strain of Economic Slump," *Wall Street Journal*, February 19, 2009, B7.

43. Ibid.

44. D. Ionescu, "Update: Apple Hits 1 Billion App Store Downloads," *PC World*, April 24, 2009, accessed May 10, 2009, http://www.pcworld.com.

45. D. Wakabayashi and C. Lawton, "Sony Turns Focus to Low-Cost Video Camera," *Wall Street Journal*, April 16, 2009, B9; Y. Kane, "Sony's Newest Display Is a Culture Shift," *The Wall Street Journal*, May 8, 2008, B1.

46. P. Elmer-DeWitt, "Mine, All Mine; Bill Gates Wants a Piece of Everybody's Action, but Can He Get It?" *Time*, June 5, 1995.

47. D. M. Boje, "The Storytelling Organization: A Study of Story Performance in an Office-Supply Firm," *Administrative Science Quarterly* 36 (1991): 106–126.

48. S. Walton and J. Huey, *Sam Walton: Made in America* (New York: Doubleday, 1992).

49. M. Hayes, "Bowa Builders: NRS Excellence in Class, 50—Plus," *HousingZone.com*, accessed January 19, 2005, http://www.housingzone.com/topics/pr/nrs/pr03ia009.asp.

50. D. R. Denison and A. K. Mishra, "Toward a Theory of Organizational Culture and Effectiveness," *Organization Science* 6 (1995): 204–223.

51. S. Rosenbaum, "The Happiness Culture: Zappos Isn't a Company—It's a Mission," *Fast Company*, June 6, 2010, accessed August 5, 2010, http://www.fastcompany.com/1657030/the-happiness-culture-zappos-isn-t-a-company-it-s-a-mission.

52. M. Moskowitz, R. Levering, and C. Tkaczyk, "100 Best Companies: The List," *Fortune*, February 8, 2010, 79; "Changing Diabetes," Norvo Nordisk, accessed August 4, 2010, http://www.novonordisk-us.com/documents/promotion_page/document/ch_diab_home2.asp.

53. J. Sorenson, "The Strength of Corporate Culture and the Reliability of Firm Performance," *Administrative Science Quarterly* 47 (2002): 70–91.

54. T. Hsieh, "Corner Office: On a Scale of 1 to 10, How Weird Are You?" interview by A. Bryant, *New York Times*, January 9, 2010, accessed June 1, 2010, http://www.nytimes.com/2010/01/10/business/10corner.html.

55. A. Zuckerman, "Strong Corporate Cultures and Firm Performance: Are There Tradeoffs?" *Academy of Management Executive* (November 2002): 158.

56. E. Schein, *Organizational Culture and Leadership*, 2d ed. (San Francisco: Jossey-Bass, 1992).

57. E. Byron, "'Call Me Mike!'—To Attract and Keep Talent, JCPenney CEO Loosens Up Once-Formal Workplace," *Wall Street Journal*, March 27, 2006, B1.

58. J. Vatner, "Changing a Culture by Removing Walls," *New York Times*, February 9, 2010, accessed August 10, 2010, http://www.nytimes.com/2010/02/10/realestate/commercial/10grey.html?_r=1.

59. S. Napier, "Corner Office: On Her Team, It's All About Bench Strength," interview by A. Bryant, *New York Times*, May 7, 2010, accessed May 25, 2010, http://www.nytimes.com/2010/05/09/business/09corner.html.

Chapter 4

1. J. Schramm, "Perceptions on Ethics," *HR Magazine* 49 (November 2004) 176.

2. M. Jackson, "Workplace Cheating Rampant, Half of Employees Surveyed Admit They Take Unethical Actions," *Peoria Journal Star*, April 5, 1997.

3. C. Smith, "The Ethical Workplace," *Association Management* 52 (2000): 70–73.

4. E. Castro-Wright, "Corner Office: In a Word, He Wants Simplicity," interview by A. Bryant, *New York Times*, May 23, 2009, accessed June 4, 2010, http://www.nytimes.com/2009/05/24/business/24corner.html.

5. "2008 Report to the Nation on Occupational Fraud and Abuse, Association of Certified Fraud Examiners," accessed July 15, 2008, http://www.acfe.com/resources/publications.asp?copy=rttn.

6. S. L. Robinson and R. J. Bennett, "A Typology of Deviant Workplace Behaviors: A Multidimensional Scaling Study," *Academy of Management Journal* 38 (1995): 555–572.

7. S. Covel, "Building Your Business: Today's Topic: Dealing with Dishonesty," *Wall Street Journal*, February 19, 2009, B5.

8. S. Needleman, "Businesses Say Theft by Their Workers Is Up—Companies Find That Trusted Employees Often Commit the Crimes, and They Believe the Recession Is to Blame," *Wall Street Journal*, December 11, 2008, B8.

9. K. Grannis, "Retail Losses Hit $41.6 Billion Last Year, According to National Retail Security Survey," National Retail Federation, June 11, 2007, accessed July 12, 2010, http://www.nrf.com/modules.php?name=News&op=viewlive&sp_id=318.

10. M. Pressler, "Cost and Robbers: Shoplifting and Employee Thievery Add Dollars to Price Tag," *Washington Post*, February 16, 2003, H05.

11. L. Middlebrooks and P. C. Vreeland, "Many U.S. Employers Aren't Doing Enough to Address Workplace Violence," *Alabama Employment Law Letter*, December 2006.

12. J. Merchant and J. Lundell, "Workplace Violence: A Report to the Nation," University of Iowa Injury Prevention Center, February 2001, accessed June 4, 2010, http://www.public-health.uiowa.edu/iprc/resources/workplace-violence-report.pdf.

13. D. Palmer and A. Zakhem, "Bridging the Gap between Theory and Practice: Using the 1991 Federal Sentencing Guidelines as a Paradigm for Ethics Training," *Journal of Business Ethics* 29, no. 1/2 (2001): 77–84.

14. K. Tyler, "Do the Right Thing: Ethics Training Programs Help Employees Deal with Ethical Dilemmas," *HR Magazine* 50 (February 2005), http://www.shrm.org/hrmagazine/articles/0205/0205tyler.asp.

15. D. R. Dalton, M. B. Metzger, and J. W. Hill, "The 'New' U.S. Sentencing Commission Guidelines: A Wake-Up Call for Corporate America," *Academy of Management Executive* 8 (1994): 7–16.

16. B. Ettore, "Crime and Punishment: A Hard Look at White-Collar Crime," *Management Review* 83 (1994): 10–16.

17. F. Robinson and C. C. Pauze, "What Is a Board's Liability for Not Adopting a Compliance Program?" *Healthcare Financial Management* 51, no. 9 (1997): 64.

18. D. Murphy, "The Federal Sentencing Guidelines for Organizations: A Decade of Promoting Compliance and Ethics," *Iowa Law Review* 87 (2002): 697–719.

19. F. Robinson and C. C. Pauze, "What Is a Board's Liability for Not Adopting a Compliance Program?"

20. B. Schwartz, "The Nuts and Bolts of an Effective Compliance Program," *HR Focus* 74, no. 8 (1997): 13–15.

21. L. A. Hays, "A Matter of Time: Widow Sues IBM over Death Benefits," *Wall Street Journal*, July 6, 1995.

22. S. Morris and R. McDonald, "The Role of Moral Intensity in Moral Judgments: An Empirical Investigation," *Journal of Business Ethics* 14 (1995): 715–726; B. Flannery and D. May, "Environmental Ethical Decision Making in the U.S. Metal-Finishing Industry," *Academy of Management Journal* 43 (2000): 642–662.

23. S. Sparks, "Federal Agents Seize Computers in 27 Cities as Part of Crackdown on Software Piracy," *Wall Street Journal*, December 12, 2001, B4.

24. L. Kohlberg, "Stage and Sequence: The Cognitive-Developmental Approach to Socialization," in *Handbook of Socialization Theory and Research*, ed. D. A. Goslin (Chicago: Rand McNally, 1969); L. Trevino, "Moral Reasoning and Business Ethics: Implications for Research,

Education, and Management," *Journal of Business Ethics* 11 (1992): 445–459.

25. L. Trevino and M. Brown, "Managing to be Ethical: Debunking Five Business Ethics Myths," *Academy of Management Executive* 18 (May 2004): 69–81.

26. L. T. Hosmer, "Trust: The Connecting Link between Organizational Theory and Philosophical Ethics," *Academy of Management Review* 20 (1995): 379–403.

27. M. R. Cunningham, D. T. Wong, and A. P. Barbee, "Self-Presentation Dynamics on Overt Integrity Tests: Experimental Studies of the Reid Report," *Journal of Applied Psychology* 79 (1994): 643–658; J. Wanek, P. Sackett and D. Ones, "Toward an Understanding of Integrity Test Similarities and Differences: An Item-Level Analysis of Seven Tests," *Personnel Psychology* 56 (Winter 2003): 873–894.

28. H. J. Bernardin, "Validity of an Honesty Test in Predicting Theft among Convenience Store Employees," *Academy of Management Journal* 36 (1993): 1097–1108.

29. J. M. Collins and F. L. Schmidt, "Personality, Integrity, and White Collar Crime: A Construct Validity Study," *Personnel Psychology* (1993): 295–311.

30. W. C. Borman, M. A. Hanson, and J. W. Hedge, "Personnel Selection," *Annual Review of Psychology* 48 (1997): 299–337.

31. Ibid.

32. Nortel, "Code of Business Conduct," accessed June 12, 2010, http://www.nortel .com/corporate/community/ethics /collateral/english_code_2007.pdf.

33. "More Corporate Boards Involved in Ethics Programs; Ethics Training Becoming Standard Practice," *PR Newswire*, October 16, 2006.

34. S. J. Harrington, "What Corporate America Is Teaching about Ethics," *Academy of Management Executive* 5 (1991): 21–30.

35. L. A. Berger, "Train All Employees to Solve Ethical Dilemmas," *Best's Review—Life-Health Insurance Edition* 95 (1995): 70–80.

36. D. Schmidt, "Ethics Can Be Taught," *Inc.*, June 24, 2008, accessed July 10, 2010, http://www.inc.com/leadership -blog/2008/06/ethics_can_be_taught_1 .html.

37. L. Trevino, G. Weaver, D. Gibson, and B. Toffler, "Managing Ethics and Legal Compliance: What Works and What Hurts," *California Management Review* 41, no. 2 (1999): 131–151.

38. "Leader's Guide: A Culture of Trust 2008," Lockheed Martin, accessed July 17, 2008, http://www.lockheedmartin .com/data/assets/corporate/documents /ethics/2008_EAT_Leaders_Guide.pdf.

39. E. White, "Theory and Practice: What Would You Do? Ethics Courses Get Context; Beyond Checking Boxes, Some Firms Start Talking about Handling Gray Areas," *Wall Street Journal*, June 12, 2006, B3.

40. A. Countryman, "Leadership Key Ingredient in Ethics Recipe, Experts Say," *Chicago Tribune*, December 1, 2002, Business 1.

41. "2007 National Business Ethics Survey," accessed July 17, 2008, http://www .ethics.org.

42. G. Weaver and L. Trevino, "Integrated and Decoupled Corporate Social Performance: Management Commitments, External Pressures, and Corporate Ethics Practices," *Academy of Management Journal* 42 (1999): 539–552; G. Weaver, L. Trevino, and P. Cochran, "Corporate Ethics Programs as Control Systems: Influences of Executive Commitment and Environmental Factors," *Academy of Management Journal* 42 (1999): 41–57.

43. J. Salopek, "Do the Right Thing," *Training & Development* 55 (July 2001): 38–44.

44. L. Whitney, "iPhone 4 Sales Hurt More by Carriers than Antennas," *cNet*, September 9, 2009, accessed November 7, 2010, http://news.cnet.com/8301 -13579_3-20015950-37.html?tag =contentMain;contentBody;2n; S. Gustin, "Apple Reports Profit of $4.3 Billion on Record Sales," *Daily Finance*, October 18, 2010, accessed November 7, 2010, http://www.dailyfinance.com/story /apple-reports-profit-of-4-3-billion-on -record-sales/19678995/.

46. M. Corkery, "Lehman Whistle-Blower's Fate: Fired," *Wall Street Journal*, March 15, 2010, accessed August 5, 2010, http:// online.wsj.com/article/NA_WSJ_PUB:SB1 0001424052748704588404575124134271085018.html.

47. M. P. Miceli and J. P. Near, "Whistleblowing: Reaping the Benefits," *Academy of Management Executive* 8 (1994): 65–72.

48. M. Master and E. Heresniak. "The Disconnect in Ethics Training," *Across the Board* 39 (September 2002): 51–52.

49. H. R. Bower, *Social Responsibilities of the Businessman* (New York: Harper & Row, 1953).

50. "Beyond the Green Corporation," *BusinessWeek*, January 29, 2007.

51. S. L. Wartick and P. L. Cochran, "The Evolution of the Corporate Social Performance Model," *Academy of Management Review* 10 (1985): 758–769.

52. J. Nocera, "The Paradox of Businesses as Do-Gooders," *New York Times,* February 3, 2007, C1.

53. S. Waddock, C. Bodwell, and S. Graves. "Responsibility: The New Business Imperative," *Academy of Management Executive* 16 (2002): 132–148.

54. T. Donaldson and L. E. Preston, "The Stakeholder Theory of the Corporation: Concepts, Evidence, and Implications," *Academy of Management Review* 20 (1995): 65–91.

55. I. Nooyi, "PepsiCo CEO: Redefine Profit and Loss," interview by K. Ryssdal, *Marketplace*, American Public Radio, January 29, 2010, accessed July 15, 2010, http://marketplace.publicradio.org /display/web/2010/01/29/pm-davos -pepsi-ceo-q#.

56. M. B. E. Clarkson, "A Stakeholder Framework for Analyzing and Evaluating Corporate Social Performance," *Academy of Management Review* 20 (1995): 92–117.

57. B. Agle, R. Mitchell, and J. Sonnenfeld, "Who Matters to CEOs? An Investigation of Stakeholder Attributes and Salience, Corporate Performance, and CEO Values," *Academy of Management Journal* 42 (1999): 507–525.

58. L. Etter, "Smithfield to Phase Out Crates: Big Pork Producer Yields to Activists, Customers on Animal-Welfare Issue," *Wall Street Journal*, January 25, 2007, A14.

59. E. W. Orts, "Beyond Shareholders: Interpreting Corporate Constituency Statutes," *George Washington Law Review* 61 (1992): 14–135.

60. A. B. Carroll, "A Three-Dimensional Conceptual Model of Corporate Performance," *Academy of Management Review* 4 (1979): 497–505.

61. J. Lublin and M. Murrary, "CEOs Leave Faster Than Ever Before as Boards, Investors Lose Patience," *Wall Street Journal Interactive*, October 27, 2000.

62. J. Lublin, "CEO Firings On the Rise As Downturn Gains Steam," *Wall Street Journal*, January 13, 2009, B1.

63. D. Woodruff, "Europe Shows More CEOs the Door," *Wall Street Journal,* July 1, 2002.

64. C. Bray, "Ex-Monster President Found Guilty in Backdating Case," *Wall Street Journal*, May 13, 2009, C4.

65. J. Bandler, "McKelvey Admits Monster Backdating; Ex-CEO to Repay Millions but Avoids Jail Due to Illness," *Wall Street Journal*, January 24, 2008, B4.

66. B. Newman, "In Texas, There's No Business Like 'Going Out of Business'— Owner Alters Rug Shop's Controversial Name but the Haggling Goes On and On," *Wall Street Journal*, June 24, 2009, A1.

67. "How You're Helping," The Hunger Site, accessed June 4, 2010, http://www .thehungersite.com.

68. A. Vance, "In Faulty-Computer Suit, Window to Dell Decline," *Wall Street Journal*, June 28, 2010, accessed June 28, 2010, http://www.nytimes .com/2010/06/29/technology/29dell .html?pagewanted=1&hp.

69. Ibid.

70. A. Patrick, "After Protests, Unilever Does About-Face on Palm Oil," *Wall Street Journal*, May 2, 2008, B1.

71. "Sustainable Palm Oil," Unilever, accessed August 30, 2009, http://www .unilever.com.

72. T.S. Bernard, "Google to Add Pay to Cover a Tax for Same-Sex Benefits," *New York Times*, July 1, 2010, B1.

73. A. McWilliams and D. Siegel, "Corporate Social Responsibility: A Theory of the Firm Perspective," *Academy of Management Review* 26, no. 1 (2001): 117–127; H. Haines, "Noah Joins Ranks of Socially Responsible Funds," *Dow Jones News Service*, October 13, 1995. A meta-analysis of 41 different studies also found no relationship between corporate social responsibility and profitability. Though not reported in the meta-analysis, when confidence intervals are placed around its average sample-weighted correlation of .06, the lower confidence interval includes zero, leading to the conclusion that there is no relationship between corporate social responsibility and

profitability. See M. Orlitzky, "Does Firm Size Confound the Relationship between Corporate Social Responsibility and Firm Performance?" *Journal of Business Ethics* 33 (2001): 167–180; S. Ambec and P. Lanoie, "Does it Pay to Be Green? A Systematic Overview," *Academy of Management Perspectives* 22 (2008): 45–62.

74. M. Orlitzky, "Payoffs to Social and Environmental Performance," *Journal of Investing* 14 (2005): 48–51.

75. M. Orlitzky, F. Schmidt, and S. Rynes, "Corporate Social and Financial Performance: A Meta-analysis," *Organization Studies* 24 (2003): 403–441.

76. M. Orlitzky, "Payoffs to Social and Environmental Performance," *Journal of Investing* 14 (2005): 48–51.

77. M. Orlitzky, F. Schmidt, and S. Rynes, "Corporate Social and Financial Performance: A Meta-analysis."

78. A. Murray and A. Strassel, "Environment (A Special Report); Ahead of the Pack: GE's Jeffrey Immelt on Why It's Business, Not Personal," *Wall Street Journal*, March 24, 2008, R3.

79. K. Kranhold, "Greener Postures: GE's Environment Push Hits Business Realities; CEO's Quest to Reduce Emissions Irks Clients; The Battle of the Bulbs," *Wall Street Journal*, September 14, 2007, A1.

80. "Ecomagination is GE," *2008 Ecomagination Annual Report*, accessed August 30, 2009, http://ge.ecomagination.com.

81. K. Brown, "Chilling at Ben & Jerry's: Cleaner, Greener," *Wall Street Journal*, April 15, 2004, B1.

Chapter 5

1. L. A. Hill, *Becoming a Manager: Master a New Identity* (Boston: Harvard Business School Press, 1992).

2. J. Jargon, "General Mills Sees Wealth via Health," *Wall Street Journal*, February 25, 2008, A9.

3. E. A. Locke and G. P. Latham, *A Theory of Goal Setting and Task Performance* (Englewood Cliffs, NJ: Prentice Hall, 1990).

4. M. E. Tubbs, "Goal-Setting: A Meta-Analytic Examination of the Empirical Evidence," *Journal of Applied Psychology* 71 (1986): 474–483.

5. J. Bavelas and E. S. Lee, "Effect of Goal Level on Performance: A Trade-Off of Quantity and Quality," *Canadian Journal of Psychology* 32 (1978): 219–240.

6. Harvard Management Update, "Learn by 'Failing Forward,'" *Globe & Mail*, October 31, 2000, B17.

7. C. C. Miller, "Strategic Planning and Firm Performance: A Synthesis of More Than Two Decades of Research," *Academy of Management Performance* 37 (1994): 1649–1665.

8. H. Mintzberg, "Rethinking Strategic Planning," *Long Range Planning* 27 (1994): 12–30; H. Mintzberg, "The Pitfalls of Strategic Planning," *California Management Review* 36 (1993): 32–47.

9. J. D. Stoll, "GM Sees Brighter Future," *Wall Street Journal*, January 18, 2008, A3; D. Welch, "Live Green or Die," *BusinessWeek*, May 26, 2008, 36–41;

L. Greenemeier, "GM's Chevy Volt to hit the streets of San Francisco and Washington, D.C." *60-Second Science Blog*, February 5, 2009, accessed May 29, 2009, http://www.scientificamerican.com.

10. H. Mintzberg, "Pitfalls of Strategic Planning," *California Management Review* 36 (1993): 32–47.

11. A. Cosslett, "Corner Office: Where Are You When the Going Gets Tough?" interview by A. Bryant, *New York Times*, April 2, 2010, accessed August 11, 2010, http://www.nytimes.com/2010/04/04/business/04corner.html?_r=1.

12. E. A. Locke and G. P. Latham, *A Theory of Goal Setting and Task Performance*.

13. A. King, B. Oliver, B. Sloop, and K. Vaverek, *Planning and Goal Setting for Improved Performance: Participant's Guide* (Cincinnati, OH: Thomson Executive Press, 1995).

14. A. Taylor III, "Here Comes the Electric Nissan," *Fortune*, March 1, 2010. 90–98.

15. H. Klein and M. Wesson, "Goal and Commitment and the Goal-Setting Process: Conceptual Clarification and Empirical Synthesis," *Journal of Applied Psychology* 84 (1999): 885–886.

16. E. A. Locke and G. P. Latham, *A Theory of Goal Setting and Task Performance*.

17. K. Linbaugh and N.E. Boudette, "Fiat Models to Drive Chrysler," *Wall Street Journal*, October 27, 2009, accessed August 10, 2010, http://online.wsj.com/article/SB125659536562909009.html?mg=com-wsj; B. Vlasic and N. Bunkley, "Party's Over: A New Tone for Chrysler," *New York Times*, November 4, 2009, accessed August 10, 2010, http://www.nytimes.com/2009/11/05/business/05auto.html.

18. A. Bandura and D. H. Schunk, "Cultivating Competence, Self-Efficacy, and Intrinsic Interest through Proximal Self-Motivation," *Journal of Personality & Social Psychology* 41 (1981): 586–598.

19. E. A. Locke and G. P. Latham, *A Theory of Goal Setting and Task Performance*.

20. M. J. Neubert, "The Value of Feedback and Goal Setting over Goal Setting Alone and Potential Moderators of This Effect: A Meta-Analysis," *Human Performance* 11 (1998): 321–335.

21. E. H. Bowman and D. Hurry, "Strategy through the Option Lens: An Integrated View of Resource Investments and the Incremental-Choice Process," *Academy of Management Review* 18 (1993): 760–782.

22. M. Lawson, "In Praise of Slack: Time Is of the Essence," *Academy of Management Executive* 15 (2000): 125–135.

23. J. Lahart, "U.S. Firms Build Up Record Cash Piles," *Wall Street Journal*, June 10, 2010, accessed June 11, 2010, http://online.wsj.com/article/SB10001424052748704312104575298652567988246.html.

24. R. Brown, "Zappos Eyes 5-Year Goal of $75M Beauty Biz," *Women's Wear Daily*, April 9, 2010, 10.

25. J. C. Collins and J. I. Porras, "Organizational Vision and Visionary Organiza-

tions," *California Management Review* (Fall 1991): 30–52.

26. "What We Stand For," Avon, accessed November 14, 2010, http://responsibility.avoncompany.com/page-13-our-vision-and-mission.

27. J. C. Collins and J. I. Porras, "Organizational Vision and Visionary Organizations," *California Management Review* (Fall 1991): 30–52.

28. "NASA's Exploration Systems Mission Directorate," Exploration: NASA's Plans to Explore the Moon, Mars, and Beyond, accessed May 29, 2009, http://www.nasa.gov.

29. Ibid.

30. R. Van Hoek and K. Pegels, "Growing by Cutting SKUs at Clorox," *Harvard Business Review* (April 2006): 22.

31. S. Covel, "Moving Across Country to Cut Costs," *Wall Street Journal*, January 10, 2008, B4.

32. S. McCartney, "Is Your Boss Spying on Your Upgrades?" *Wall Street Journal*, August 12, 2008, D1.

33. Adapted from quality procedure at G & G Manufacturing, Cincinnati, Ohio.

34. N. Humphrey, "References a Tricky Issue for Both Sides," *Nashville Business Journal* 11 (May 8, 1995): 1A.

35. J. Del Rey, "One Company's Budget: A Nice Consistency," *Inc.*, January 1, 2010, accessed July 16, 2010, http://www.inc.com/magazine/20090101/one-companys-budget-a-nice-consistency.html.

36. K. R. MacCrimmon, R. N. Taylor, and E. A. Locke, "Decision Making and Problem Solving," in *Handbook of Industrial and Organizational Psychology*, ed. M. D. Dunnette (Chicago: Rand McNally, 1976), 1397–1453.

37. Ibid.

38. A. Zimmerman, "Cricket Lee Takes on the Fashion Industry," *Wall Street Journal*, March 17, 2008, R1.

39. "Notebook Shipments Surpass Desktops in the U.S. Market for the First Time, According to IDC," IDC, October 28, 2008, accessed May 30, 2009, http://www.idc.com.

40. *Consumer Reports Buying Guide: 2006*, 129–131.

41. P. Djang, "Selecting Personal Computers," *Journal of Research on Computing in Education* 25 (1993): 327.

42. "European Cities Monitor," Cushman & Wakefield, 2009, accessed July 19, 2010, http://www.europeancitiesmonitor.eu/.

43. B. Dumaine, "The Trouble with Teams," *Fortune*, September 5, 1994, 86–92.

44. I. L. Janis, *Groupthink* (Boston: Houghton Mifflin, 1983).

45. C. P. Neck and C. C. Manz, "From Groupthink to Teamthink: Toward the Creation of Constructive Thought Patterns in Self-Managing Work Teams," *Human Relations* 47 (1994): 929–952; J. Schwartz and M. L. Wald, "'Groupthink' Is 30 Years Old, and Still Going Strong," *New York Times,* March 9, 2003, 5.

46. "Merck Wins Suit on Vioxx Monitoring," *Wall Street Journal*, June 5, 2008, D8.

47. T. Taylor, "Corner Office: Everything on One Calender, Please," interview by A. Bryant, *New York*

Times, December 26, 2009, accessed July 12, 2010, http://www.nytimes.com/2009/12/27/business/27corner.html?pagewanted=1&_r=1.

48. A. Mason, W. A. Hochwarter, and K. R. Thompson, "Conflict: An Important Dimension in Successful Management Teams," *Organizational Dynamics* 24 (1995): 20.

49. C. Olofson, "So Many Decisions, So Little Time: What's Your Problem?" *Fast Company*, October 1, 1999, 62.

50. Ibid.

51. R. Cosier and C. R. Schwenk, "Agreement and Thinking Alike: Ingredients for Poor Decisions," *Academy of Management Executive* 4 (1990): 69–74.

52. K. Jenn and E. Mannix, "The Dynamic Nature of Conflict: A Longitudinal Study of Intragroup Conflict and Group Performance," *Academy of Management Journal* 44, no. 2 (2001): 238–251; R. L. Priem, D. A. Harrison, and N. K. Muir, "Structured Conflict and Consensus Outcomes in Group Decision Making," *Journal of Management* 21 (1995): 691–710.

53. A. Van De Ven and A. L. Delbecq, "Nominal versus Interacting Group Processes for Committee Decision Making Effectiveness," *Academy of Management Journal* 14 (1971): 203–212.

54. A. R. Dennis and J. S. Valicich, "Group, Sub-Group, and Nominal Group Idea Generation: New Rules for a New Media?" *Journal of Management* 20 (1994): 723–736.

55. R. B. Gallupe, W. H. Cooper, M. L. Grise, and L. M. Bastianutti, "Blocking Electronic Brainstorms," *Journal of Applied Psychology* 79 (1994): 77–86.

56. R. B. Gallupe and W. H. Cooper, "Brainstorming Electronically," *Sloan Management Review*, Fall 1993, 27–36.

57. Ibid.

58. G. Kay, "Effective Meetings through Electronic Brainstorming," *Management Quarterly* 35 (1995): 15.

Chapter 6

1. L. Kahney, "Inside Look at the Birth of the iPod," *Wired*, July 21, 2004, http://www.wired.com/news/culture/0,64286-0.html; K. Hall, "Sony's iPod Assault Is No Threat to Apple," *BusinessWeek*, March 13, 2006, 53; N. Wingfield, "SanDisk Raises Music-Player Stakes," *Wall Street Journal*, August 21, 2006, B4; "Growing Louder: Microsoft Plods after iPod Like a Giant—Powerful, Determined, Untiring," *Winston-Salem Journal*, November 15, 2006, D1–D2; A. Athavaley and R. A. Guth, "How the Zune Is Faring So Far with Consumers," *Wall Street Journal*, December 12, 2006, D1, D7; P. Cruz, "U.S. Top Selling Computer Hardware for January 2007," Bloomberg.com, accessed July 29, 2008, http://www.bloomberg.com/apps/news?pid=conewsstory&refer=conews&tkr=AAPL:US&sid=ap0bqJw2VpwI.

2. J. Barney, "Firm Resources and Sustained Competitive Advantage," *Journal of Management* 17 (1991): 99–120; J. Barney, "Looking Inside for Competitive Advantage," *Academy of Management Executive* 9 (1995): 49–61.

3. J. Snell, "Apple's Home Run," *Macworld*, November 2006, 7.

4. J. D'Arcy and T. Davies, "The Walkman at 20," *Maclean's*, August 30, 1999, 10; K. Hall, "Sony's iPod Assault Is No Threat to Apple."

5. E. Smith, "Sony to Take Over Music Partnership; Firm Raises Its Bet on Ailing Industry; Bertelsmann Exits," *Wall Street Journal*, August 6, 2008, B1.

6. A. Athavaley and R. A. Guth, "How the Zune Is Faring So Far with Consumers," D7.

7. "iTunes Tops 200 Million TV Episodes Sold, Including over One Million HD Episodes," Apple.com, October 16, 2008, accessed June 4, 2009, http://www.apple.com; "Thanks a Billion," Apple.com, accessed June 4, 2009, http://www.apple.com; E. Schonfeld, "iTunes Sells 6 Billion Songs, and Other Fun Stats from the Philnote," *TechCrunch*, January 6, 2009, accessed June 4, 2009, http://www.techcrunch.com.

8. S. H. Wildstrom, "Zune 2.0: Playing Tomorrow's Tune?," *BusinessWeek*, December 10, 2007, 87.

9. J. Warren, "At New Web Store, Many Songs Sell for a Few Cents," *Wall Street Journal*, October 14, 2006, P2; "Amazon.com MP3 Music Downloads: Getting Started," Amazon.com, accessed July 22, 2010, http://www.amazon.com/gp/dmusic/help/faq.html/ref=sv_dmusic_0.

10. E. Smith and Y. Kane, "Apple Changes Tune on Music Pricing," *Wall Street Journal*, January 7, 2009, B1.

11. R. Levine, "Napster's Ghost Rises," *Fortune*, March 6, 2006, 30; "30 Products for 30 Years," *MacWorld*, June 2006, 15–16.

12. S. Hart and C. Banbury, "How Strategy-Making Processes Can Make a Difference," *Strategic Management Journal* 15 (1994): 251–269.

13. R. A. Burgelman, "Fading Memories: A Process Theory of Strategic Business Exit in Dynamic Environments," *Administrative Science Quarterly* 39 (1994): 24–56; R. A. Burgelman and A. S. Grove, "Strategic Dissonance," *California Management Review* 38 (1996): 8–28.

14. T. Audi, "Last Resort: Ailing Sheraton Shoots for a Room Upgrade; Starwood to Tackle Biggest Hotel Brand; The 'Ugly Stepchild,'" *Wall Street Journal*, March 25, 2008, A1.

15. R. Burgelman and A. Grove, "Strategic Dissonance," *California Management Review* (Winter 1996): 8–28.

16. E. Smith and M. Peers, "Cost Cutting Is an Uphill Fight at Warner Music," *Wall Street Journal*, May 24, 2004, B1.

17. G. Fowler, "eBay Retreats in Web Retailing—Company Will Return to Its Roots as Internet Flea Market, Put Focus on PayPal," *Wall Street Journal*, March 12, 2009, A1.

18. A. Fiegenbaum, S. Hart, and D. Schendel, "Strategic Reference Point Theory," *Strategic Management Journal* 17 (1996): 219–235.

19. "Most Reliable Cars," *Consumer Reports*, April 2010, accessed June 30, 2010, http://www.consumerreports.org/cro/cars/new-cars/cr-recommended/best-worst-in-car-reliability-1005/reliability-findings/reliability-findings.htm.

20. "Readers' Choice Service and Reliability Survey 2009 Winners," *PC Magazine*, September 15, 2009, accessed June 30, 2010, http://www.pcmag.com/article2/0,2817,2352863,00.asp.

21. D. J. Collis, "Research Note: How Valuable Are Organizational Capabilities?," *Strategic Management Journal* 15 (1994): 143–152.

22. C. Palmieri, "Inside Tesco's New U.S. Stores," *BusinessWeek Online*, December 4, 2007; "Unique Products, Reasonable Prices Spell Success for Trader Joe's," *The Food Institute Report* 81 (March 3, 2008) 4; "Trader Joe's: Why the Hype?," *Bulletin*, March 27, 2008.

23. A. Fiegenbaum and H. Thomas, "Strategic Groups as Reference Groups: Theory, Modeling and Empirical Examination of Industry and Competitive Strategy," *Strategic Management Journal* 16 (1995): 461–476.

24. R. K. Reger and A. S. Huff, "Strategic Groups: A Cognitive Perspective," *Strategic Management Journal* 14 (1993): 103–124.

25. J. Hempel, "Clash of the Technology Titans," *Fortune*, January 18, 2010, 33–38.

26. Ibid.

27. H. Murphy, "Menard's Tool in Retail Battle: Gigantic Stores," *Crain's Chicago Business*, August 12, 2002, 3.

28. M. Lubatkin, "Value-Creating Mergers: Fact or Folklore?" *Academy of Management Executive* 2 (1988): 295–302; M. Lubatkin and S. Chatterjee, "Extending Modern Portfolio Theory into the Domain of Corporate Diversification: Does It Apply?" *Academy of Management Journal* 37 (1994): 109–136; M. H. Lubatkin and P. J. Lane, "Psst . . . The Merger Mavens Still Have It Wrong!" *Academy of Management Executive* 10 (1996): 21–39.

29. "3M Businesses," 3M, accessed June 1, 2010, http://solutions.3m.com/wps/portal/3M/en_US/about-3M/information/about/businesses/.

30. A. Frye, "Berkshire Buys Burlington in Buffet's Biggest Deal," Bloomberg, November 3, 2009, accessed June 1, 2010, http://www.bloomberg.com/apps/news?pid=20601103&sid=asfU7Dluabw4; "Berkshire Subsidiary Companies," Berkshire Hathaway, accessed June 1, 2010, http://www.berkshirehathaway.com/.

31. B. Henderson, "The Experience Curve—Reviewed: IV The Growth Share Matrix or the Product Portfolio," *The Boston Consulting Group*, 1973, accessed June 6, 2009, http://www.bcg.com/documents/file13904.pdf.

32. C. Rohwedder, "Wal-Mart U.K. Deal Fits Goal: Go Small," *Wall Street Journal*, May 28, 2010, B1.

33. J. A. Pearce II, "Selecting among Alternative Grand Strategies," *California Management Review* (Spring 1982): 23–31.

34. A. Patrick, "Nestlé Sales Outpace Forecasts," *Wall Street Journal*, October 24, 2008.

35. J. A. Pearce II, "Retrenchment Remains the Foundation of Business Turnaround," *Strategic Management Journal* 15 (1994): 407–417.

36. M. Bustillo, "Corporate News: Sears Swings to a Profit and Secures New Credit," *Wall Street Journal*, May 22, 2009, B3; G. McWilliams, "Corporate News: Sears, Like Consumers, Cuts Back; Jobs, Budgets Pared as Retailer Preserves Financial Strength," *Wall Street Journal*, May 6, 2008 B5; K. Talley and D. Kardos, "Corporate News: Sears Turns in Loss as Sales Drop 5.8%; Costco's Net Rises 32% as Consumers Shop For Bulk Bargains," *Wall Street Journal*, May 30, 2008, B3; P. Eavis, "Sears Looks in Dire Shape," *Wall Street Journal*, May 30, 2008, C14.

37. C. Rauwald, "Corporate News: Daimler to Close Truck Plants, Drop Sterling Brand," *Wall Street Journal*, October 15, 2008, B3; C. Rauwald, "Corporate News: Daimler Posts Loss Due to Chrysler—Impairment from U.S. Foray Saps $2 Billion; Mercedes-Benz Sales Slow," *Wall Street Journal*, February 18, 2009, B2; C. Rauwald, "Corporate News: Daimler to Deepen Its Cost Cuts Auto Maker Intends to Pare $2.66 Billion in Labor Expenses in Germany," *Wall Street Journal*, April 2, 2009, B2.

38. R. Winkler, R. Cox, and M. Hutchinson, "The Halls of Finance Fear Wal-Mart," *New York Times*, June 23, 2010, accessed July 2, 2010, http://www.nytimes.com/2010/06/24/business/economy/24views.html?_r=1&src=busln.

39. E. Holmes, "Tug-of-War in Apparel World," *Wall Street Journal*, July 16, 2010, B1.

40. E. Fredrix and S. Skidmore, "Costco Nixes Coke Products Over Pricing Dispute," ABCNews.com, November 17, 2009, accessed August 10, 2010, http://abcnews.go.com/Business/wireStory?id=9103485; "Update1-Costco to Resume Stocking Coca-Cola drinks," Reuters.com, December 10, 2009, accessed August 10, 2010, http://www.reuters.com/article/idUSN1020190520091210.

41. M. Mangalindan, "Irked by eBay, Some Sellers Trade Elsewhere; Niche Sites Tout Lower Fees, Tutorials, More Photos; Buyers Still Face Fraud Risks," August 12, 2008, D1.

42. R. E. Miles and C. C. Snow, *Organizational Strategy, Structure, and Process* (New York: McGraw Hill, 1978); S. Zahra and J. A. Pearce, "Research Evidence on the Miles-Snow Typology," *Journal of Management* 16 (1990): 751–768; W. L. James and K. J. Hatten, "Further Evidence on the Validity of the Self Typing Paragraph Approach: Miles and Snow Strategic Archetypes in Banking," *Strategic Management Journal* 16 (1995): 161–168.

43. R. Beene, "Continental Automotive to Market AutoLinQ Infotainment System," *Crain's Detroit Business*, June 8, 2010, accessed August 10, 2010, http://www.crainsdetroit.com/article/20100608

/FREE/100609862#; D. Lavrinc, "KIA UVO Details Released, like SYNC Circa 2008," Autoblog.com, January 5, 2010, accessed August 10, 2010, http://www.autoblog.com/2010/01/05/kia-uvo-details-released-virtually-same-as-sync/.

44. M. Chen, "Competitor Analysis and Interfirm Rivalry: Toward a Theoretical Integration," *Academy of Management Review* 21 (1996): 100–134; J. C. Baum and H. J. Korn, "Competitive Dynamics of Interfirm Rivalry," *Academy of Management Journal* 39 (1996): 255–291.

45. Ibid.

46. Ibid.

47. D. Quenqua, "In a Weak Economy, Quirky Restaurant Ads Yield to Tried and True," *New York Times*, May 9, 2008, accessed June 8, 2010, http://www.nytimes.com/2008/05/09/business/media/09adco.html?_r=1.

48. L. Lavelle, "The Chickens Come Home to Roost, and Boston Market Is Prepared to Expand," *The Record*, 6 October 1996.

49. Subway, accessed June 8, 2010, http://www.subway.com; N. Torres, "Full Speed Ahead," Entrepreneur.com, accessed June 8, 2010, http://www.entrepreneur.com/magazine/entrepreneur/2007/january/172060.html.

50. B. Stone, "In Price War, E-Readers Go Below $200," *New York Times*, June 21, 2010, accessed July 2, 2010, http://www.nytimes.com/2010/06/22/technology/22reader.html?_r=2.

51. D. Ketchen Jr., C. Snow, and V. Street, "Improving Firm Performance by Matching Strategic Decision-Making Processes to Competitive Dynamics," *Academy of Management Executive* 18 (2004): 29–43.

52. B. Stone, "In Price War, E-Readers Go Below $200."

53. H. McCracken, "E-Reader Price Wars: You Out There, Sony?" PCWorld.com, June 23, 2010, accessed July 2, 2010, http://www.pcworld.com/article/199628/ereader_price_wars_you_out_there_sony.html?tk=hp_new.

54. B. Stone, "In Price War, E-Readers Go Below $200."; H. McCracken, "E-Reader Price Wars: You Out There, Sony?"; S. Canaves and C. Kok, "Acer, Sony Rev E-Reader Race," *Wall Street Journal*, May 27, 2010, accessed July 2, 2010, http://online.wsj.com/article/SB10001424052748704269204575270251614597606.html?KEYWORDS=e-reader+price+war.

55. D. Wakabayashi, "Hope Fades for PS3 as a Comeback Player—In Battle of the Game Consoles, Nintendo Wii and Microsoft Xbox Widen Leads over Sony's PlayStation," *Wall Street Journal*, December 29, 2008, B1; N. Wingfield, "Microsoft Cuts Xbox to $199," *Wall Street Journal*, September 4, 2008, B9; N. Wingfield, "Microsoft to Cut Xbox 360 Pro Price," *Wall Street Journal*, July 11, 2008, B6.

56. D. Wakabayashi, "Hope Fades for PS3 as a Comeback Player—In Battle of the Game Consoles, Nintendo Wii and Microsoft Xbox Widen Leads over Sony's PlayStation."

Chapter 7

1. "Swedes to Use Body Heat to Warm Offices," ABC News, accessed September 17, 2008, http://abcnews.go.com/International/wireStory?id=410819; E. Yerger, "Company in Sweden Uses Body Heat to Warm Office Building," *Unusual Things*, accessed September 17, 2008, http://www.popfi.com/2008/01/14/company-to-use-body-heat-to-warm-office-building-2; D. Chazan, "Office Block Warmed by Body Heat," BBC News, accessed September 17, 2008, http://news.bbc.co.uk/2/hi/science/nature/7233123.stm.

2. T. M. Amabile, R. Conti, H. Coon, J. Lazenby, and M. Herron, "Assessing the Work Environment for Creativity," *Academy of Management Journal* 39 (1996): 1154–1184.

3. Ibid.

4. A. H. Van de Ven and M. S. Poole, "Explaining Development and Change in Organizations," *Academy of Management Review* 20 (1995): 510–540.

5. T. M. Amabile, R. Conti, H. Coon, J. Lazenby, and M. Herron, "Assessing the Work Environment for Creativity."

6. S. McBride, "Thinking About Tomorrow: How We Watch Movies and TV," *Wall Street Journal*, January 28, 2008, R1.

7. P. Anderson and M. L. Tushman, "Managing through Cycles of Technological Change," *Research/Technology Management*, May–June 1991, 26–31.

8. R. N. Foster, *Innovation: The Attacker's Advantage* (New York: Summitt, 1986).

9. J. Burke, *The Day the Universe Changed* (Boston: Little, Brown, 1985).

10. "Industry Snapshot," *Time*, December 5, 2005, 110; W. Symonds, "Kodak: Is This the Darkest Hour?" *BusinessWeek Online*, August 8, 2006, 3.

11. M. L. Tushman, P. C. Anderson, and C. O'Reilly, "Technology Cycles, Innovation Streams, and Ambidextrous Organizations: Organization Renewal through Innovation Streams and Strategic Change," in *Managing Strategic Innovation and Change*, ed. M. L. Tushman and P. Anderson (New York: Oxford Press, 1997), 3–23.

12. C. Tribbey, "Blu Capabilities Still Up in the Air," *Home Media Magazine*, April 13–19, 2008, accessed November 17, 2009, http://www.nxtbook.com/nxtbooks/questex/hom041308/#/2.

13. W. Abernathy and J. Utterback, "Patterns of Industrial Innovation," *Technology Review* 2 (1978): 40–47.

14. C. Tribbey, "Blu Capabilities Still Up in the Air."

15. "Universal Phone Charger Approved," BBC News, October 23, 2009, accessed November 8, 2009, http://news.bbc.co.uk.

16. M. Schilling, "Technological Lockout: An Integrative Model of the Economic and Strategic Factors Driving Technology Success and Failure," *Academy of Management Review* 23 (1998): 267–284; M. Schilling, "Technology Success and

Failure in Winner-Take-All Markets: The Impact of Learning Orientation, Timing, and Network Externalities," *Academy of Management Journal* 45 (2002): 387–398.

17. S. McBride and Y. I. Kane, "As Toshiba Surrenders: What's Next for DVDs?" *Wall Street Journal*, February 18, 2008, accessed October 2, 2008, http://online.wsj.com/article/SB120321618700574049.html?mod=MKTW; Y. I. Kane, "Toshiba Regroups After Losing DVD War," *Wall Street Journal*, February 20, 2008, accessed October 2, 2008, http://online.wsj.com/article/SB120342115442976687.html?mod=googlenews.

18. T. M. Amabile, R. Conti, H. Coon, J. Lazenby, and M. Herron, "Assessing the Work Environment for Creativity."

19. Ibid.

20. J. Scanlon, "How to Build a Culture of Innovation," *Bloomberg Businessweek*, August 19, 2009, accessed August 9, 2010, http://www.businessweek.com/innovate/content/aug2009/id20090819_070601.htm.

21. M. Csikszentmihalyi, *Flow: The Psychology of Optimal Experience* (New York: Harper & Row, 1990).

22. V. Vara, "Pleasing Google's Tech-Savvy Staff," *Wall Street Journal*, March 18, 2008, B6.

23. J. S. Lublin, "A CEO's Recipe for Fresh Ideas" *Wall Street Journal*, September 2, 2008, accessed October 15, 2009, http://online.wsj.com/article/SB122030336412088091.html.

24. B. Kowitt, "Dunkin' Brands' Kitchen Crew," *Fortune*, May 24, 2010. 72–74.

25. K. M. Eisenhardt, "Accelerating Adaptive Processes: Product Innovation in the Global Computer Industry," *Administrative Science Quarterly* 40 (1995): 84–110.

26. Ibid.

27. M. Oiaga, "10 Reasons to Try Office 2010," Softpedia.com, June 19, 2010, accessed July 23, 2010, http://news.softpedia.com/news/10-Reasons-to-Try-Office-2010-145019.shtml.

28. L. Kraar, "25 Who Help the U.S. Win: Innovators Everywhere Are Generating Ideas to Make America a Stronger Competitor. They Range from a Boss Who Demands the Impossible to a Mathematician with a Mop," *Fortune*, March 22, 1991.

29. M. W. Lawless and P. C. Anderson, "Generational Technological Change: Effects of Innovation and Local Rivalry on Performance," *Academy of Management Journal* 39 (1996): 1185–1217.

30. C. Palmeri, "Sysco's Hands-On Way of Keeping Restaurants Going," *Bloomberg Businessweek*, May 7, 2009, accessed August 6, 2009, http://www.businessweek.com/magazine/content/09_20/b4131052577089.htm?chan=magazine+channel_what's+next.

31. J. Rich, "Twilight Exclusive: Chris Weitz Will Not Direct Third Film, 'Eclipse'," *Hollywood Insider*, February 21,

2009, accessed July 23, 2010, http://hollywoodinsider.ew.com/2009/02/21/twilight-chris/; G. McIntyre, "On the Set: 'New Moon' on the Rise," *Los Angeles Times*, July 19, 2009, accessed July 23, 2010, http://www.latimes.com/entertainment/news/la-ca-newmoon19-2009jul19,0,3312678,full.story; N. Sperling, "It's Official: Bill Condon Will Direct Twilight's Final Chapter 'Breaking Dawn'," *Hollywood Insider*, April 28, 2010, accessed July 23, 2010, http://hollywoodinsider.ew.com/2010/04/28/bill-condon-will-direct-twilights-final-chapter-breaking-dawn/.

32. M. Boyle, "Hershey's Arrested Development," *BusinessWeek*, October 14, 2009, accessed November 17, 2009, http://www.businessweek.com/print/innovate/content/oct2009/id20091014_976052.htm.

33. P. Strebel, "Choosing the Right Change Path," *California Management Review* (Winter 1994): 29–51.

34. W. Weitzel and E. Jonsson, "Reversing the Downward Spiral: Lessons from W. T. Grant and Sears Roebuck," *Academy of Management Executive* 5 (1991): 7–22.

35. P. Ingrassia, "How GM Lost Its Way," *Wall Street Journal*, June 2, 2009, A21.

36. W. Weitzel and E. Jonsson, "Reversing the Downward Spiral: Lessons from W. T. Grant and Sears Roebuck."

37. S. Terlep, "GM Reports First Quarterly Profit Since 2007," *Wall Street Journal*, May 18, 2010, accessed July 22, 2010, http://online.wsj.com/article/SB10001424052748703315404575252500726874 73124.html?KEYWORDS=gm+profit; J. Muller, "GM Expects Profit in 2010," *Forbes*, January 6, 2010, accessed July 22, 2010, http://www.forbes.com/2010/01/06/general-motors-ipo-business-autos-whitacre.html; Associated Press, "GM Pays Back Government Loans Early," Fox News, April 21, 2010, accessed July 22, 2010, http://www.foxnews.com/politics/2010/04/21/gm-pays-government-loans-early/?utm_source=feedburner&utm_medium=feed&utm_campaign=Feed%3A+foxnews%2Fpolitics+(Text+-+Politics).

38. K. Lewin, *Field Theory in Social Science: Selected Theoretical Papers* (New York: Harper & Brothers, 1951).

39. A. Deutschman, "Making Change: Why Is It So Darn Hard to Change Our Ways?" *Fast Company*, May 2005, 52–62.

40. K. Lewin, *Field Theory in Social Science*.

41. D. Kravets, "AP Issues Strict Facebook, Twitter Guidelines to Staff," Wired.com, June 23, 2009, accessed August 8, 2010, http://www.wired.com/threatlevel/2009/06/facebookfollow/.

42. A. B. Fisher, "Making Change Stick," *Fortune*, April 17, 1995, 121.

43. J. P. Kotter and L. A. Schlesinger, "Choosing Strategies for Change," *Harvard Business Review* (March–April 1979): 106–114; Harvard Business School Press, *Managing Change to Reduce Resistance* (Cambridge: Harvard Business School Press, 2005).

44. K. Capell "Novartis Radically Remaking Its Drug Business," *BusinessWeek*, June 22, 2009, 30–35.

45. J. Scanlon, "San Diego Zoo's Newest Exhibit: Innovation," *BusinessWeek*, October 14, 2009, accessed November 10, 2009, www.businessweek.com.

46. B. Orwall, "Disney Decides It Must Draw Artists into Computer Age," *Wall Street Journal*, October 23, 2003, A1.

47. J. P. Kotter, "Leading Change: Why Transformation Efforts Fail," *Harvard Business Review* 73, no. 2 (March–April 1995): 59.

48. G. Pitts, "A Classic Turnaround—With Some Twists," *Globe & Mail*, July 7, 2008, B1.

49. R. H. Schaffer and H. A. Thomson, "Successful Change Programs Begin with Results," *Harvard Business Review on Change* (Boston: Harvard Business School Press, 1998), 189–213.

50. "2010 Initial Quality Study Results," J.D. Power and Associates, 2010, accessed July 23, 2010, http://www.jdpower.com/autos/articles/2010-Initial-Quality-Study-Results.

51. P. Ingrassia, "Why Hyundai Is an American Hit," *Wall Street Journal*, September 14, 2009, A13.

52. R. N. Ashkenas and T. D. Jick, "From Dialogue to Action in GE Workout: Developmental Learning in a Change Process," in *Research in Organizational Change and Development*, vol. 6, ed. W. A. Pasmore and R. W. Woodman (Greenwich, CT: JAI Press, 1992), 267–287.

53. T. Stewart, "GE Keeps Those Ideas Coming," *Fortune*, August 12, 1991, 40.

54. W. J. Rothwell, R. Sullivan, and G. M. McLean, *Practicing Organizational Development: A Guide for Consultants* (San Diego, CA: Pfeiffer & Co., 1995).

55. Ibid.

Chapter 8

1. "World Investment Report, 2006," United Nations Conference on Trade & Development, accessed January 30, 2007, http://www.unctad.org/en/docs/wir2006annexes_en.pdf.

2. T. Virki, "Nokia Siemens Buys Motorola Network Ops for $1.2 Billion," Reuters, July 19, 2010, accessed July 23, 2010, http://www.reuters.com/article/idUSTRE66I24P20100719.

3. A. Cordeiro, "Hershey to Expand in Asia," *Wall Street Journal*, March 12, 2009, B5.

4. M. Kitchen, "China to Set Anti-Dumping Measures on U.S. Chicken," *Market Watch*, February 5, 2010, accessed August 3, 2010, http://www.marketwatch.com/story/china-to-set-anti-dumping-measures-on-us-chicken-2010-02-05.

5. E. L. Andrews, "U.S. Adds Tariffs on Chinese Tires," *Wall Street Journal*, September 11, 2009, accessed June 9, 2010, http://www.nytimes.com/2009/09/12/business/global/12tires.html?_r=1&scp=1&sq=tariff&st=cse.

6. K. Bradsher, "W.T.O. Rules Against China's Limits on Imports," *New York*

Times, August 12, 2009, accessed June 9, 2010, http://www.nytimes .com/2009/08/13/business/global /13trade.html?scp=3&sq=trade %20quota&st=cse.

7. T. Wright, "Pakistan Textile Workers Rally," *Wall Street Journal,* May 11, 2010, accessed June 9, 2010, http:// online.wsj.com/article/SB10001424052 7487035658045752381032716990 66 .html?KEYWORDS=quotas.

8. "Non-tariff Barriers: Red Tape, etc." World Trade Organization, accessed August 5, 2008, http://www.wto.org/english /thewto_e/whatis_e/tif_e/agrm9_e.htm.

9. J. Adams, "Taiwan Curbs U.S. Beef Imports in Latest Asia Trade Frictions," *Christian Science Monitor,* January 5, 2010, accessed July 23, 2010, http:// www.csmonitor.com/World/Asia -Pacific/2010/0105/Taiwan-curbs-US -beef-imports-in-latest-Asia-trade -frictions.

10. C. Drew, "In Ruling, W.T.O. Faults Europe Over Aid to Airbus," *New York Times,* June 30, 2010, accessed July 23, 2010, http://www.nytimes .com/2010/07/01/business/global/01wto .html.

11. "GATT/WTO," Duke Law: Library & Technology, accessed June 12, 2009, http://www.law.duke.edu.

12. P. Sonne and M. Colchester, "France, the U.K. Take Aim at Digital Pirates," *Wall Street Journal,* April 15, 2010, accessed June 9, 2010, http:// /article/SB100014240527023046042 04575181820755061494.html.

13. "The History of the European Union," *Europa—The European Union Online,* accessed August 6, 2008, http://europa .eu/abc/history/index_en.htm.

14. Ibid.

15. P. Fessler, "Proposal for New Border Bridge Draws Critics," npr.org, accessed August 6, 2008, http://www.npr.org /templates/story/story.php?storyId =10298816.

16. "Testimony of Under Secretary of Commerce for International Trade Grant D. Aldona: The Impact of NAFTA on the United States Economy," Senate Foreign Relations Committee, Subcommittee on International Economic Policy, Export and Trade Promotion, February 7, 2007.

17. L. H. Teslik, "NAFTA's Economic Impact," Council on Foreign Relations, accessed August 6, 2008, http://www.cfr .org/publication/15790/naftas_economic _impact.html#4.

18. "CAFTA-DR (Dominican Republic-Central America FTA)," Office of the United States Trade Representative, accessed June 13, 2009, http://www .ustr.gov.

19. "US Trade with the CAFTA-DR Countries," Office of the United States Trade Representative (July 2007), accessed August 6, 2008, http://www.ustr.gov /assets/Trade_Agreements/Bilateral /CAFTA/Briefing_Book/asset_upload _file601_13191.pdf.

20. UNASUR, Union of South American Nations, accessed August 6, 2008, http:// www.comunidadandina.org/ingles /sudamerican.htm.

21. "Selected Basic ASEAN Indicators, 2005," Association of Southeast Nations, accessed March 18, 2009, http://www .aseansec.org/stat/Table1.pdf; "Top Ten ASEAN Trade Partner Countries/Regions, 2005," Association of Southeast Nations, accessed March 18, 2009, http://www .aseansec.org/Stat/Table20.pdf.

22. Ibid; "ASEAN Free Trade Area (AFTA)," Association of Southeast Nations, accessed August 6, 2008, http://www .aseansec.org/12021.htm.

23. "Member Economies," Asia-Pacific Economic Cooperation, accessed August 6, 2008, http://www.apec.org/apec /member_economies/key_websites.html; "Frequently Asked Questions (FAQs)" Asia-Pacific Economic Cooperation, accessed August 6, 2008, http://www .apec.org/apec/tools/faqs.html.

24. "The Big Mac Index," *Economist,* accessed March 18, 2009, http://www .economist.com/markets/indicators /displaystory.cfm?story_id=13055650.

25. "Freer Trade Cuts the Cost of Living," World Trade Organization, accessed June 8, 2010, http://www.wto.org/english /thewto_e/whatis_e/10ben_e/10b04_e .htm.

26. E. Holmes, "How H&M Keeps Its Cool," *Wall Street Journal,* May 10, 2010, accessed July 23, 2010, http://online .wsj.com/article/SB10001424052748 7033380045752304936979114 32 .html?mod=WSJ_business _MediaMktNewsBucket&mg=com -wsj.

27. A. Singh and S. Shankar, "Tupperware Parties Help Reshape India's Kitchens," *Bloomberg Businessweek,* July 13, 2010, accessed July 23, 2010, http://www .businessweek.com/globalbiz/content /jul2010/gb20100713_165186.htm; A. Singh and S. Shankar, "Tupperware Story Throws up Some Success Mantras for Indian Market," *Economic Times,* June 11, 2010, accessed July 23, 2010, http:// economictimes.indiatimes.com/Features /Corporate-Dossier/Tupperware-story -throws-up-some-success-mantras-for -Indian-market/articleshow/6034418 .cms?curpg=1.

28. A. Sundaram and J. S. Black, "The Environment and Internal-Organization of Multinational Enterprises," *Academy of Management Review* 17 (1992): 729–757.

29. H. S. James Jr., and M. Weidenbaum, *When Businesses Cross International Borders: Strategic Alliances and Their Alternatives* (Westport, CT: Praeger Publishers, 1993).

30. J. T. Areddy, "China's Export Machine Threatened by Rising Costs," *Wall Street Journal,* June 30, 2008, A1.

31. W. Sedgwick, "Nevada Lands First Chinese Wind Turbine Factory in U.S.," Greentechnologydaily.com, March 11, 2010, accessed August 8, 2010, http:// www.greentechnologydaily.com/solar -wind/661-nevada-lands-first-chinese -wind-turbine-factory-in-us.

32. N. Becker, "Abbott in Licensing Deal with Indian Firm," *Wall Street Journal,* May 11, 2010, accessed July 23, 2010, http:// online.wsj.com/article/SB100014240527

4870425010457523827127304746 4 .html?KEYWORDS=licensing.

33. "Company Profile," Fuji Xerox, accessed June 9, 2010, http://www.fujixerox.co.jp /eng/company/profile.html.

34. A. Ustinova and S. G. Forden, "Fiat, Sollers Form $3.3 Billion Russian Car Venture," *Bloomberg Businessweek,* February 11, 2010, accessed July 23, 2010, http://www.businessweek.com /news/2010-02-11/fiat-sollers-will-set -up-2-4-billion-euro-russian-car-venture .html.

35. "Arrow, Shell Seal a Venture," *Wall Street Journal,* September 15, 2008, accessed September 18, 2008, http://online.wsj .com/article/SB122144583046434931 .html.

36. "Joint Ventures," *Encyclopedia of Business,* 2d ed., accessed August 6, 2008, http://www.referenceforbusiness.com /encyclopedia/Int-Jun/Joint-Ventures. html#WHY_JOINT_VENTURES_FAIL.

37. S. Prasso, "American Made . . . Chinese Owned," *Fortune,* May 24, 2010, 87; "About Haier" Haier.com, accessed August 8, 2010, http://www.haieramerica .com/en/aboutus/?sessid=6bad918738374 8176bddd8a3e6cf55c9.

38. M. W. Hordes, J. A. Clancy, and J. Baddaley, "A Primer for Global Start-Ups," *Academy of Management Executive* (May 1995): 7–11.

39. D. Pavlos, J. Johnson, J. Slow, and S. Young, "Micromultinationals: New Types of Firms for the Global Competitive Landscape," *European Management Journal* 21, no. 2 (April 2003): 164; B. M. Oviatt and P. P. McDougall, "Toward a Theory of International New Ventures," *Journal of International Business Studies,* (Spring 1994): 45; S. Zahra, "A Theory of International New Ventures: A Decade of Research," *Journal of International Business Studies* (January 2005): 20–28.

40. PR Newswire, "Air Lease Corporation, the New Global Aviation Venture, Is Ready for Take-Off with Substantial Financing and a Top-Flight Senior Management Team," PR Newsire, July 15, 2010, accessed July 23, 2010, http:// www.prnewswire.com/news-releases /air-lease-corporation-the-new-global -aviation-venture-is-ready-for-take -off-with-substantial-financing-and -a-top-flight-senior-management -team-98529409.html.

41. D. Lynch, "Developing Nations Poised to Challenge USA as King of the Hill," *USA Today,* February 8, 2007, B.1; N. Srinivas, "Of Carats and Calories," *Economic Times,* December 29, 2006.

42. S. Kennedy, M. Bristow, and S. Adam, "There's a New Silk Road, and It Doesn't Lead to the U.S.," *Bloomberg Business-Week,* August 9–15, 2010, 13–14.

43. P. Dvorak, "Why Multiple Headquarters Multiply," *Wall Street Journal,* November 19, 2007, B1; J. L. Yang, "Making Mergers Work," *Fortune,* November 26, 2007, 42.

44. "Customer Care in the Netherlands," The Netherlands Foreign Investment Agency, accessed June 9, 2010, http://www.nfia .com/customer_care.html.

45. J. Oetzel, R. Bettis, and M. Zenner, "How Risky Are They?" *Journal of World Business* 36, no. 2 (Summer 2001): 128–145.

46. K. D. Miller, "A Framework for Integrated Risk Management in International Business," *Journal of International Business Studies* (2nd Quarter 1992): 311.

47. A. Osborn and D. Gauthier-Villars, "Twisty Road: Renault Deal in Russia Shows Kremlin Tactics," *Wall Street Journal*, March 21, 2008, A1.

48. "Chapter 1: Political Outlook," *UAE Business Forecast Report*, (2007 1st Quarter): 5–10.

49. I. Brat, "Going Global by Going Green," *Wall Street Journal*, February 26, 2008, B1.

50. G. Hofstede, "The Cultural Relativity of the Quality of Life Concept," *Academy of Management Review* 9 (1984): 389–398; G. Hofstede, "The Cultural Relativity of Organizational Practices and Theories," *Journal of International Business Studies* (Fall 1983): 75–89; G. Hofstede, "The Interaction between National and Organizational Value Systems," *Journal of Management Studies* (July 1985): 347–357; M. Hoppe, "An Interview with Geert Hofstede," *Academy of Management Executive* (February 2004): 75–79.

51. R. Hodgetts, "A Conversation with Geert Hofstede," *Organizational Dynamics* (Spring 1993): 53–61.

52. T. Lenartowicz and K. Roth, "Does Subculture within a Country Matter? A Cross-Cultural Study of Motivational Domains and Business Performance in Brazil," *Journal of International Business Studies* 32 (2001): 305–325.

53. Associated Press, "Cultures Clash as Japanese CEO Testifies," CBSNews.com, February 24, 2010, accessed August 11, 2010, http://www.cbsnews.com/stories /2010/02/24/business/main6239892 .shtml; K. Voigt, "Toyota in Washington: A Clash of Cultures?" CNN.com, February 24, 2010, accessed August 11, 2010, http://www.cnn.com/2010/BUSINESS /02/24/money.toyoda.culture.clash/index .html.

54. J. S. Black, M. Mendenhall, and G. Oddou, "Toward a Comprehensive Model of International Adjustment: An Integration of Multiple Theoretical Perspectives," *Academy of Management Review* 16 (1991): 291–317; R. L. Tung, "American Expatriates Abroad: From Neophytes to Cosmopolitans," *Columbia Journal of World Business*, June 22, 1998, 125; A. Harzing, "The Persistent Myth of High Expatriate Failure Rates," *International Journal of Human Resource Management* 6 (1995): 457–475; A. Harzing, "Are Our Referencing Errors Undermining Our Scholarship and Credibility? The Case of Expatriate Failure Rates," *Journal of Organizational Behavior* 23 (2002): 127–148; N. Forster, "The Persistent Myth of High Expatriate Failure Rates: A Reappraisal," *International Journal of Human Resource Management* 8 (1997): 414–433.

55. J. Black, "The Right Way to Manage Expats," *Harvard Business Review* 77 (March–April 1999): 52; C. Joinson, "No Returns," *HR Magazine*, November 1, 2002, 70.

56. C. Joinson, "No Returns."

57. J. S. Black and M. Mendenhall, "Cross-Cultural Training Effectiveness: A Review and Theoretical Framework for Future Research," *Academy of Management Review* 15 (1990): 113–136.

58. K. Essick, "Executive Education: Transferees Prep for Life, Work in Far-Flung Lands," *Wall Street Journal*, November 12, 2004, A6.

59. P. W. Tam, "Culture Course—'Awareness Training' Helps U.S. Workers Better Know Their Counterparts in India," *Wall Street Journal*, May 25, 2004, B1.

60. Ibid.

61. W. Arthur Jr., and W. Bennett Jr., "The International Assignee: The Relative Importance of Factors Perceived to Contribute to Success," *Personnel Psychology* 48 (1995): 99–114; B. Cheng, "Home Truths about Foreign Postings; To Make an Overseas Assignment Work, Employers Need More Than an Eager Exec with a Suitcase. They Must Also Motivate the Staffer's Spouse," *BusinessWeek Online*, accessed March 20, 2009, http://www.businessweek.com/careers /content/jul2002/ca20020715_9110.htm.

62. M. Netz, "It's Not Judging—It's Assessing: The Truth about Candidate Assessments," *NRRE Magazine*, March 2004, accessed August 8, 2008, http://rismedia .com/wp/2004-03-03/its-not-judging-its -assessing.

63. M. Nitz, "It's Not Judging—It's Assessing: The Truth About Candidate Assessments," *NRRE Magazine*, March 2004, accessed November 14, 2010, http:// www.rismedia.com/index.php/article /articleview/5996/1/492/.

64. D. Eschbach, G. Parker, and P. Stoeberl, "American Repatriate Employees' Retrospective Assessments of the Effects of Cross-Cultural Training on Their Adaptation to International Assignments," *International Journal of Human Resource Management* 12 (2001): 270–287; "Culture Training: How to Prepare Your Expatriate Employees for Cross-Cultural Work Environments," *Managing Training & Development*, February 1, 2005.

65. T. Mohn, "The Dislocated Americans," *New York Times*, December 1, 2008, accessed July 23, 2010, http:// www.nytimes.com/2008/12/02 /business/worldbusiness/02expat .html?ref=americans_abroad.

Chapter 9

1. "Sony Corporation of America: Overview," accessed June 10, 2010, http:// www.sony.com/SCA/index.shtml.

2. M. Hammer and J. Champy, *Reengineering the Corporation: A Manifesto for Business Revolution* (New York: Harper & Row, 1993).

3. "Sara Lee Now," *Sara Lee 2009 Annual Report*, accessed November 13, 2009, http://www.saralee.com.

4. J. G. March and H. A. Simon, *Organizations* (New York: John Wiley & Sons, 1958).

5. "Fact & Figures: Our Businesses," Fast Facts, accessed November 13, 2009, http://www.utc.com.

6. "Company Overview," *UTC 2008 Annual Report*, accessed November 13, 2009, http://www.utc.com.

7. "Company Structure," About Swisscom, accessed November 14, 2009, http:// www.swisscom.ch.

8. "Our Company: The Best Brands in the World," Coca-Cola Enterprises, http:// www.cokecce.com/srclib/1.1.1.html (content no longer online).

9. "Who We Are," Procter & Gamble, accessed November 14, 2009, http://www .pg.com.

10. "Corporate Info: Corporate Structure—Four Pillars," Procter & Gamble, accessed March 20, 2009, http://www.pg.com /jobs/corporate_structure/four_pillars .jhtml; "P&G Management," Procter & Gamble, accessed March 20, 2009, http://www.pg.com/news/management /bios_photos.jhtml.

11. L. R. Burns, "Adoption and Abandonment of Matrix Management Programs: Effects of Organizational Characteristics and Interorganizational Networks," *Academy of Management Journal* 36 (1993): 106–138.

12. H. Fayol, *General and Industrial Management*, trans. C. Storrs (London: Pitman Publishing, 1949).

13. M. Weber, *The Theory of Social and Economic Organization*, trans. and ed. A. M. Henderson and T. Parsons (New York: Free Press, 1947).

14. H. Fayol, *General and Industrial Management*.

15. T. Yamada, "Corner Office: Talk to Me. I'll Turn Off My Phone," interview by A. Bryant, *New York Times*, February 27, 2010, accessed July 20, 2010, http://www.nytimes.com/2010/02/28 /business/28corner.html.

16. R. A. Guth, "Gates-Ballmer Clash Shaped Microsoft's Coming Handover," *Wall Street Journal*, June 5, 2008, A1.

17. S. Bistayi, "Delegate—Or Not?" *Forbes*, April 21, 1997, 20–21.

18. E. E. Lawler, S. A. Mohrman, and G. E. Ledford, *Creating High Performance Organizations: Practices and Results of Employee Involvement and Quality Management in Fortune 1000 Companies* (San Francisco: Jossey-Bass, 1995).

19. R. Swanborg, "The Ideal Standardization," *CIO*, October 1, 2009, 19.

20. S. Curry, "Retention Getters," *Incentive*, April 1, 2005.

21. R. W. Griffin, *Task Design* (Glenview, IL: Scott, Foresman, 1982).

22. F. Herzberg, *Work and the Nature of Man* (Cleveland, OH: World Press, 1966).

23. J. R. Hackman and G. R. Oldham, *Work Redesign* (Reading, MA: Addison-Wesley, 1980).

24. T. Burns and G. M. Stalker, *The Management of Innovation* (London: Tavistock, 1961).

25. M. Hammer and J. Champy, *Reengineering the Corporation*.

26. C. Tuna, "Remembrances: Champion of 'Re-Engineering' Saved Companies,

Challenged Thinking," *Wall Street Journal*, September 6, 2008, A12.

27. J. D. Thompson, *Organizations in Action* (New York: McGraw-Hill, 1967).

28. J. B. White, "'Next Big Thing': Re-Engineering Gurus Take Steps to Remodel Their Stalling Vehicles," *Wall Street Journal Interactive Edition*, November 26, 1996.

29. Ibid.

30. G. M. Spreitzer, "Individual Empowerment in the Workplace: Dimensions, Measurement, and Validation," *Academy of Management Journal* 38 (1995): 1442–1465.

31. M. Pincus, "Corner Office: Every Worker Should Be the C.E.O. of Something," interview by A. Bryant, *New York Times*, January 30, 2010, accessed June 8, 2010, http://www.nytimes.com/2010/01/31/business/31corner.html?pagewanted=2&ref=business.

32. M. Schrage, "I Know What You Mean, And I Can't Do Anything about It," *Fortune*, April 2, 2001, 186.

33. K. W. Thomas and B. A. Velthouse, "Cognitive Elements of Empowerment," *Academy of Management Review* 15 (1990): 666–681.

34. G. Kahn, "Making Labels for Less—Supply-Chain City Transforms Far-Flung Apparel Industry; Help for 'The Button Guy,'" *Wall Street Journal*, August 13, 2004, B1.

35. G. G. Dess, A. M. A. Rasheed, K. J. McLaughlin, and R. L. Priem, "The New Corporate Architecture," *Academy of Management Executive* 9 (1995): 7–18.

36. G. McWilliams, "Apple Uses Software, Outsourcing to Gain Share As Sony Struggles to Grow," *Wall Street Journal*, March 10, 2005, A1.

37. C. C. Snow, R. E. Miles, and H. J. Coleman Jr., "Managing 21st Century Network Organizations," *Organizational Dynamics,* (Winter 1992): 5–20.

Chapter 10

1. B. Dumaine, "The Trouble with Teams," *Fortune,* September 5, 1994, 86–92.

2. K. C. Stag, E. Salas, and S. M. Fiore, "Best Practices in Cross Training Teams," in *Workforce Cross Training Handbook*, ed. D. A. Nembhard (Boca Raton, FL: CRC Press, 2007), 156–175.

3. M. Marks, "The Science of Team Effectiveness," *Psychological Science in the Public Interest* (December 2006): pi–i.

4. J. R. Katzenback and D. K. Smith, *The Wisdom of Teams* (Boston: Harvard Business School Press, 1993).

5. S. E. Gross, *Compensation for Teams* (New York: American Management Association, 1995); B. L. Kirkman and B. Rosen, "Beyond Self-Management: Antecedents and Consequences of Team Empowerment," *Academy of Management Journal* 42 (1999): 58–74; G. Stalk and T. M. Hout, *Competing against Time: How Time-Based Competition Is Reshaping Global Markets* (New York: Free Press, 1990); S. C. Wheelwright and K. B. Clark, *Revolutionizing New Product Development* (New York: Free Press, 1992).

6. "Hertz Creates Gulf Coast Customer Care Center," *Marketwire*, July 27, 2010, accessed August 15, 2010, http://www.marketwatch.com/story/hertz-creates-gulf-coast-customer-care-center-2010-07-27?reflink=MW_news_stmp.

7. R. D. Banker, J. M. Field, R. G. Schroeder, and K. K. Sinha, "Impact of Work Teams on Manufacturing Performance: A Longitudinal Field Study," *Academy of Management Journal* 39 (1996): 867–890.

8. C. Fishman, "The Anarchist's Cookbook: John Mackey's Approach to Management Is Equal Parts Star Trek and 1970s Flashback," *Fast Company*, July 1, 2004, 70.

9. J. L. Cordery, W. S. Mueller, and L. M. Smith, "Attitudinal and Behavioral Effects of Autonomous Group Working: A Longitudinal Field Study," *Academy of Management Journal* 34 (1991): 464–476; T. D. Wall, N. J. Kemp, P. R. Jackson, and C. W. Clegg, "Outcomes of Autonomous Workgroups: A Long-Term Field Experiment," *Academy of Management Journal* 29 (1986): 280–304.

10. "Declaration of Interdependence," Whole Foods Market, accessed June 10, 2010, http://www.wholefoodsmarket.com/company/declaration.html.

11. Ibid.

12. A. Erez, J. Lepine, and H. Elms, "Effects of Rotated Leadership and Peer Evaluation on the Functioning and Effectiveness of Self-Managed Teams: A Quasi-Experiment," *Personnel Psychology* 55, no. 4 (2002): 929.

13. R. Liden, S. Wayne, R. Jaworski, and N. Bennett, "Social Loafing: A Field Investigation," *Journal of Management* 30 (2004): 285–304.

14. J. George, "Extrinsic and Intrinsic Origins of Perceived Social Loafing in Organizations," *Academy of Management Journal* 35 (1992): 191–202.

15. T. T. Baldwin, M. D. Bedell, and J. L. Johnson, "The Social Fabric of a Team-Based M.B.A. Program: Network Effects on Student Satisfaction and Performance," *Academy of Management Journal* 40 (1997): 1369–1397.

16. K. H. Price, D. A. Harrison and J. H. Gavin, "Withholding Inputs in Team Contexts: Member Composition, Interaction Processes, Evaluation Structure and Social Loafing," *Journal of Applied Psychology* 91(6) (2006): 1375–1384.

17. D. Rosensweig, "Corner Office: Remember to Thank Your Star Players," interview by A. Bryant, *New York Times*, July 9, 2010, accessed July 30, 2010, http://www.nytimes.com/2010/07/11/business/11corner.html?_r=1.

18. C. Joinson, "Teams at Work," *HR Magazine*, May 1, 1999, 30.

19. R. Wageman, "Critical Success Factors for Creating Superb Self-Managing Teams," *Organizational Dynamics* 26, no. 1 (1997): 49–61.

20. D. A. Harrison, S. Mohammed, J. E. McGrath, A. T. Florey and S. W. Vanderstoep, "Time Matters in Team Performance: Effects of Member Familiarity, Entrainment, and Task Discontinuity on Speed and Quality," *Personnel Psychology* 56, no. 3 (August 2003): 633–669.

21. M. A. Cusumano, "How Microsoft Makes Large Teams Work Like Small Teams," *Sloan Management Review* 39, no. 1 (Fall 1997): 9–20.

22. N. Wingfield, "Tech Journal: To Rebuild Windows, Microsoft Razed Walls—Three Year Effort to Create Latest Version Meant Close Collaboration Among Workers to Avoid Vista's Woes," *Wall Street Journal*, October 20, 2009, B9.

23. B. L. Kirkman and B. Rosen, "Beyond Self-Management."

24. S. Easton and G. Porter, "Selecting the Right Team Structure to Work in Your Organization," in *Handbook of Best Practices for Teams*, vol. 1, ed. G. M. Parker (Amherst, MA: Irwin, 1996).

25. R. J. Recardo, D. Wade, C. A. Mention, and J. Jolly, *Teams* (Houston: Gulf Publishing Co., 1996).

26. D. R. Denison, S. L. Hart, and J. A. Kahn, "From Chimneys to Cross-Functional Teams: Developing and Validating a Diagnostic Model," *Academy of Management Journal* 39, no. 4 (1996): 1005–1023.

27. P. Kotler, R. Wolcott, and S. Chandrasekhar, "Product Development—Playing Well with Others: How to Improve the Relationship between the Marketing and R&D Departments—And Increase the Chance of Coming Up with Successful New Products," *Wall Street Journal*, June 22, 2009, R5.

28. A. M. Townsend, S. M. DeMarie, and A. R. Hendrickson, "Virtual Teams: Technology and the Workplace of the Future," *Academy of Management Executive* 13, no. 3 (1998): 17–29.

29. J. Hyatt, "MySQL: Workers in 25 Countries with No HQ," *Fortune*, June 1, 2006, accessed August 12, 2008, http://money.cnn.com/2006/05/31/magazines/fortune/mysql_greatteams_fortune/index.htm.

30. A. M. Townsend, S. M. DeMarie, and A. R. Hendrickson, "Are You Ready for Virtual Teams?" *HR Magazine* 41, no. 9 (1996): 122–126.

31. R. S. Wellins, W. C. Byham, and G. R. Dixon, *Inside Teams* (San Francisco: Jossey-Bass, 1994).

32. A. M. Townsend, S. M. DeMarie, and A. R. Hendrickson, "Virtual Teams."

33. W. F. Cascio, "Managing a Virtual Workplace," *Academy of Management Executive* 14 (2000): 81–90.

34. R. Katz, "The Effects of Group Longevity on Project Communication and Performance," *Administrative Science Quarterly* 27 (1982): 245–282.

35. D. Mankin, S. G. Cohen, and T. K. Bikson, *Teams and Technology: Fulfilling the Promise of the New Organization* (Boston: Harvard Business School Press, 1996).

36. P. Patton, "Envisioning a Small Electric BMW for the World's Very Big Cities," *New York Times*, July 1, 2010, accessed September 1, 2010, http://www.nytimes.com/2010/07/04/automobiles/04MEGACITY.html?_r=1&ref=automobiles.

37. A. P. Ammeter and J. M. Dukerich, "Leadership, Team Building, and Team Member Characteristics in High

Performance Project Teams," *Engineering Management* 14, no. 4 (2002): 3–11.

38. K. Lovelace, D. Shapiro, and L. Weingart, "Maximizing Cross-Functional New Product Teams' Innovativeness and Constraint Adherence: A Conflict Communications Perspective," *Academy of Management Journal* 44 (2001): 779–793.

39. L. Holpp and H. P. Phillips, "When Is a Team Its Own Worst Enemy?" *Training*, September 1, 1995, 71.

40. S. Asche, "Opinions and Social Pressure," *Scientific American* 193 (1995): 31–35.

41. J. Stephens, "Corner Office: Rah-Rah Isn't for Everyone," interview by A. Bryant, *New York Times*, April 9, 2010, accessed June 11, 2010, http://www.nytimes.com/2010/04/11/business/11corner.html?pagewanted=2.

42. S. G. Cohen, G. E. Ledford, and G. M. Spreitzer, "A Predictive Model of Self-Managing Work Team Effectiveness," *Human Relations* 49, no. 5 (1996): 643–676.

43. K. Bettenhausen and J. K. Murnighan, "The Emergence of Norms in Competitive Decision-Making Groups," *Administrative Science Quarterly* 30 (1985): 350–372.

44. M. E. Shaw, *Group Dynamics* (New York: McGraw Hill, 1981).

45. S. E. Jackson, "The Consequences of Diversity in Multidisciplinary Work Teams," in *Handbook of Work Group Psychology,* ed. M. A. West (Chichester, UK: Wiley, 1996).

46. A. M. Isen and R. A. Baron, "Positive Affect as a Factor in Organizational Behavior," in *Research in Organizational Behavior* 13, ed. L. L. Cummings and B. M. Staw (Greenwich, CT: JAI Press, 1991), 1–53.

47. C. R. Evans and K. L. Dion, "Group Cohesion and Performance: A Meta Analysis," *Small Group Research* 22, no. 2 (1991): 175–186.

48. R. Stankiewicsz, "The Effectiveness of Research Groups in Six Countries," in *Scientific Productivity*, ed. F. M. Andrews (Cambridge: Cambridge University Press, 1979), 191–221.

49. F. Rees, *Teamwork from Start to Finish* (San Francisco: Jossey-Bass, 1997).

50. S. M. Gully, D. S. Devine, and D. J. Whitney, "A Meta-Analysis of Cohesion and Performance: Effects of Level of Analysis and Task Interdependence," *Small Group Research* 26, no. 4 (1995): 497–520.

51. E. Matson, "Four Rules for Fast Teams," *Fast Company*, August 1996, 87.

52. F. Tschan and M. V. Cranach, "Group Task Structure, Processes and Outcomes," in *Handbook of Work Group Psychology,* ed. M. A. West (Chichester, UK: Wiley, 1996).

53. D. E. Yeatts and C. Hyten, *High Performance Self Managed Teams* (Thousand Oaks, CA: Sage Publications, 1998); H. M. Guttman and R. S. Hawkes, "New Rules for Strategic Development," *Journal of Business Strategy* 25, no. 1 (2004): 34–39.

54. D. E. Yeatts and C. Hyten, *High Performance Self Managed Teams*; M. Guttman and R. S. Hawkes, "New Rules for Strategic Development"; J. Colquitt, R. Noe, and C. Jackson, "Justice in Teams: Antecedents and Consequences of Procedural Justice Climate," *Personnel Psychology,* April 1, 2002, 83.

55. D. S. Kezsbom, "Re-Opening Pandora's Box: Sources of Project Team Conflict in the '90s," *Industrial Engineering* 24, no. 5 (1992): 54–59.

56. A. C. Amason, W. A. Hochwarter, and K. R. Thompson, "Conflict: An Important Dimension in Successful Management Teams," *Organizational Dynamics* 24 (1995): 20.

57. A. C. Amason, "Distinguishing the Effects of Functional and Dysfunctional Conflict on Strategic Decision Making: Resolving a Paradox for Top Management Teams," *Academy of Management Journal* 39, no. 1 (1996): 123–148.

58. K. M. Eisenhardt, J. L. Kahwajy, and L. J. Bourgeois III, "How Management Teams Can Have a Good Fight," *Harvard Business Review* 75, no. 4 (July–August 1997): 77–85.

59. Ibid.

60. C. Nemeth and P. Owens, "Making Work Groups More Effective: The Value of Minority Dissent," in *Handbook of Work Group Psychology,* ed. M. A. West (Chichester, UK: Wiley, 1996).

61. J. M. Levin and R. L. Moreland, "Progress in Small Group Research," *Annual Review of Psychology* 9 (1990): 72–78; S. E. Jackson, "Team Composition in Organizational Settings: Issues in Managing a Diverse Work Force," in *Group Processes and Productivity*, ed. S. Worchel, W. Wood, and J. Simpson (Beverly Hills, CA: Sage, 1992).

62. K. M. Eisenhardt, J. L. Kahwajy, and L. J. Bourgeois III, "How Management Teams Can Have a Good Fight."

63. B. W. Tuckman, "Development Sequence in Small Groups," *Psychological Bulletin* 63, no. 6 (1965): 384–399.

64. S. E. Gross, *Compensation for Teams.*

65. J. F. McGrew, J. G. Bilotta, and J. M. Deeney, "Software Team Formation and Decay: Extending the Standard Model for Small Groups," *Small Group Research* 30, no. 2 (1999): 209–234.

66. Ibid.

67. J. R. Hackman, "The Psychology of Self-Management in Organizations," in *Psychology and Work: Productivity, Change, and Employment*, ed. M. S. Pallak and R. Perloff (Washington, DC: American Psychological Association, 1986), 85–136.

68. A. O'Leary-Kelly, J. J. Martocchio, and D. D. Frink, "A Review of the Influence of Group Goals on Group Performance," *Academy of Management Journal* 37, no. 5 (1994): 1285–1301.

69. G. Smith, "How Nucor Steel Rewards Performance and Productivity," *Business Know How*, accessed June 10, 2010, http://www.businessknowhow.com/manage/nucor.htm.

70. A. Zander, "The Origins and Consequences of Group Goals," in *Retrospections on Social Psychology*, ed. L. Festinger (New York: Oxford University Press, 1980), 205–235.

71. M. Erez and A. Somech, "Is Group Productivity Loss the Rule or the Exception? Effects of Culture and Group-Based Motivation," *Academy of Management Journal* 39, no. 6 (1996): 1513–1537.

72. S. Sherman, "Stretch Goals: The Dark Side of Asking for Miracles," *Fortune*, November 13, 1995, 231.

73. N. Bunkley, "Hyundai Says Its Cars Will Average 50 M.P.G. by 2025," *New York Times* Wheels Blog, August 4, 2010, accessed August 20, 2010, http://wheels.blogs.nytimes.com/2010/08/04/hyundai-says-its-cars-will-average-50-m-p-g-by-2025/.

74. S. Kerr and S. Landauer, "Using Stretch Goals to Promote Organizational Effectiveness and Personal Growth: General Electric and Goldman Sachs," *Academy of Management Executive* (November 2004): 134–138.

75. K. R. Thompson, W. A. Hochwarter, and N. J. Mathys, "Stretch Targets: What Makes Them Effective?" *Academy of Management Executive* 11, no. 3 (1997): 48–60.

76. B. Dumaine, "The Trouble with Teams."

77. G. A. Neuman, S. H. Wagner, and N. D. Christiansen, "The Relationship between Work-Team Personality Composition and the Job Performance of Teams," *Group & Organization Management* 24, no. 1 (1999): 28–45.

78. M. A. Campion, G. J. Medsker, and A. C. Higgs, "Relations between Work Group Characteristics and Effectiveness: Implications for Designing Effective Work Groups," *Personnel Psychology* 46, no. 4 (1993): 823–850.

79. B. L. Kirkman and D. L. Shapiro, "The Impact of Cultural Values on Employee Resistance to Teams: Toward a Model of Globalized Self-Managing Work Team Effectiveness," *Academy of Management Review* 22, no. 3 (1997): 730–757.

80. C. Fishman, "Engines of Democracy:" *Fast Company*, October 1, 1999, 174.

81. J. Bunderson and K. Sutcliffe, "Comparing Alternative Conceptualizations of Functional Diversity in Management Teams: Process and Performance Effects," *Academy of Management Journal* 45 (2002): 875–893.

82. J. Barbian, "Getting to Know You," *Training*, June 2001: 60–63.

83. G. Anders, "Companies Try to Extend Researchers' Productivity; Teams of Various Ages, Newer Hires Combat Short Spans of Inventing," *Wall Street Journal*, August 18, 2008, B5.

84. P. Sanders, "Boeing Brings in Old Hands, Gets an Earful," *Wall Street Journal*, July 19, 2010, B1.

85. J. Hackman, "New Rules for Team Building—The Times Are Changing—And So Are the Guidelines for Maximizing Team Performance," *Optimize*, July 1, 2002, 50.

86. C. Joinson, "Teams at Work."

87. K. Mollica, "Stay Above the Fray: Protect Your Time—And Your Sanity—By Coaching Employees to Deal with Interpersonal Conflicts on Their Own," *HR Magazine*, April 2005, 111.

88. E. Salas, D. DiazGranados, C. Klein, C. Burke, K. Stagl, G. Goodwin, and

S. Halpin, "Does Team Training Improve Team Performance? A Meta-Analysis," *Human Factors* 50, no. 6 (2008): 903–933.

89. S. Caudron, "Tie Individual Pay to Team Success," *Personnel Journal* 73, no. 10 (October 1994): 40.

90. Ibid.

91. S. E. Gross, *Compensation for Teams*, 85.

92. G. Ledford, "Three Case Studies on Skill-Based Pay: An Overview," *Compensation & Benefits Review* 23, no. 2 (1991): 11–24.

93. J. R. Schuster and P. K. Zingheim, *The New Pay: Linking Employee and Organizational Performance* (New York: Lexington Books, 1992).

94. S. G. Cohen and D. E. Bailey, "What Makes Teams Work: Group Effectiveness Research from the Shop Floor to the Executive Suite," *Journal of Management* 23, no. 3 (1997): 239–290.

95. R. Allen and R. Kilmann, "Aligning Reward Practices in Support of Total Quality Management," *Business Horizons* 44 (May 2001): 77–85.

Chapter 11

1. S. Bing, "The Feds Make a Pass at Hooters," *Fortune*, January 15, 1996, 82.

2. J. Helyar, "Hooters: A Case Study," *Fortune*, September 1, 2003, 140.

3. A. Samuels, "Pushing Hot Buttons and Wings," *St. Petersburg Times*, March 10, 2003, 1A.

4. J. Casale, R. Ceniceros, and M. Hofmann, "Hooters Wannabe Resists Girls-Only Policy," *Business Insurance* 43, no. 4 (2009), 23.

5. P. S. Greenlaw and J. P. Kohl, "Employer 'Business' and 'Job' Defenses in Civil Rights Actions," *Public Personnel Management* 23, no. 4 (1994): 573.

6. "Massey Settles Age Discrimination Suit for $8.75 Million," Cleveland.com, October 30, 2009, accessed September 5, 2010, http://www.cleveland.com/business/index.ssf/2009/10/massey_settles_age_discriminat.html.

7. J. L. Ledvinka, *Federal Regulation of Personnel and Human Resource Management* (Boston: Kent Publishing Co., 1982), 137–198.

8. P. S. Greenlaw and J. P. Kohl, "Employer 'Business' and 'Job' Defenses in Civil Rights Actions."

9. W. Peirce, C. A. Smolinski, and B. Rosen, "Why Sexual Harassment Complaints Fall on Deaf Ears," *Academy of Management Executive* 12, no. 3 (1998): 41–54.

10. N. Olivares-Giles, "ABM Settles Sexual Harassment Suit for $5.8 Million," *Los Angeles Times*, September 2, 2010, accessed September 6, 2010, http://articles.latimes.com/2010/sep/02/business/la-fi-0903-harass-suit-20100902.

11. W. Peirce, C. A. Smolinski, and B. Rosen, "Why Sexual Harassment Complaints Fall on Deaf Ears."

12. E. Larson, "The Economic Costs of Sexual Harassment," *Freeman* 46, August 1996, accessed June 14, 2010, http://www.fee.org/publications/the-freeman/article.asp?aid=4114.

13. G. Hyland-Savage, "General Management Perspective on Staffing: The Staffing Commandments," *On Staffing: Advice and Perspectives from HR Leaders*, ed. N. C. Buckholder, P. J. Edwards Jr., and L. Sartain (Hoboken, NJ: Wiley, 2003), 280.

14. R. D. Gatewood and H. S. Field, *Human Resource Selection* (Fort Worth, TX: Dryden Press, 1998).

15. Ibid.

16. G. Marks, "How to Surf the Resume Tsunami," *Forbes*, July 16, 2010, accessed August 23, 2010, http://www.forbes.com/2010/07/16/hiring-jobs-small-business-entrepreneurs-human-resources-gene-marks.html.

17. Griggs v. Duke Power Co., 401 U.S. 424, 436 (1971); Albemarle Paper Co. v. Moody, 422 U.S. 405 (1975).

18. "Executive Team: Bob McDonald, Biography," Procter & Gamble, January 2010, accessed July 27, 2010, http://www.pg.com/en_US/downloads/company/executive_team/bios/pg_executive_bio_bob_mcdonald.pdf.

19. B. O'Keefe, "Battle-Tested: How a Decade of War Has Created . . . A New Generation of Elite Business Leaders," *Fortune*, March 22, 2010, 108–111.

20. J. Breaugh and M. Starke, "Research on Employee Recruitment: So Many Studies, So Many Remaining Questions," *Journal of Management* 26 (2000): 405–434.

21. "Internet Recruitment Report," *NAS Insights*, accessed August 14, 2008, http://www.nasrecruitment.com/talenttips/NASinsights/InternetRecruitingReport06.pdf.

22. K. Maher, "Corporations Cut Middlemen and Do Their Own Recruiting," *Wall Street Journal*, January 14, 2003, B10.

23. S. Needleman, "Theory and Practice: Recruiters Use Search Engines to Lure Job Hunters—Cash-Strapped Companies Save with Search Ads, Scale Back on Rival Media Like Job Boards and Newspapers," *Wall Street Journal*, March 9, 2009, B4.

24. C. Camden and B. Wallace, "Job Application Forms: A Hazardous Employment Practice," *Personnel Administrator* 28 (1983): 31–32.

25. T. Minton-Eversole, "Background Screens Even More Crucial during Economic Slump," *Society for Human Resource Management*, July 30, 2008, accessed August 12, 2008, http://www.shrm.org/hrdisciplines/staffingmanagement/Pages/background.aspx.

26. S. Adler, "Verifying a Job Candidate's Background: The State of Practice in a Vital Human Resources Activity," *Review of Business* 15, no. 2 (1993/1994): 3–8.

27. "More Than 70 Percent of HR Professionals Say Reference Checking Is Effective in Identifying Poor Performers," *Society for Human Resource Management*, accessed February 3, 2005, http://www.shrm.org/press_published/CMS_011240.asp.

28. P. Babcock, "Spotting Lies: The High Cost of Careless Hiring," *HR Magazine* 48, no. 10 (October 2003).

29. M. Le, T. Nguyen, and B. Kleiner, "Legal Counsel: Don't Be Sued for Negligent Hiring," *Nonprofit World*, May 1, 2003, 14–15.

30. "Why It's Critical to Set a Policy on Background Checks for New Hires," *Managing Accounts Payable*, September 2004, 6; J. Schramm, "Future Focus: Background Checking," *HR Magazine*, January 2005.

31. K. Eaton, "If You're Applying for a Job, Censor Your Facebook Page," *Fast Company*, August 19, 2009, accessed August 10, 2010, http://www.fastcompany.com/blog/kit-eaton/technomix/if-youre-applying-job-censor-your-facebook-page.

32. C. Cohen, "Reference Checks," *CA Magazine*, November 2004, 41.

33. S. Marshall, "Spot Inflated Resumes with Simple Sleuthing," *Asian Wall Street Journal*, April 7, 2000, P3.

34. J. Hunter, "Cognitive Ability, Cognitive Aptitudes, Job Knowledge, and Job Performance," *Journal of Vocational Behavior* 29 (1986): 340–362.

35. F. L. Schmidt, "The Role of General Cognitive Ability and Job Performance: Why There Cannot Be a Debate," *Human Performance* 15 (2002): 187–210.

36. K. Murphy, "Can Conflicting Perspectives on the Role of g in Personnel Selection Be Resolved?" *Human Performance* 15 (2002): 173–186.

37. J. R. Glennon, L. E. Albright, and W. A. Owens, *A Catalog of Life History Items* (Greensboro, NC: The Richardson Foundation, 1966).

38. R. D. Gatewood and H. S. Field, *Human Resource Selection*.

39. I. Kotlyar and K. Ades, "HR Technology: Assessment Technology Can Help Match the Best Applicant to the Right Job," *HR Magazine*, May 1, 2002, 97.

40. M. S. Taylor and J. A. Sniezek, "The College Recruitment Interview: Topical Content and Applicant Reactions," *Journal of Occupational Psychology* 57 (1984): 157–168.

41. M. Harris, "Reconsidering the Employment Interview: A Review of Recent Literature and Suggestions for Future Research," *Personnel Psychology* (Winter 1989): 691–726.

42. R. Burnett, C. Fan, S. J. Motowidlo, and T. DeGroot, "Interview Notes and Validity," *Personnel Psychology* 51, no. X (1998): 375–396; M. A. Campion, D. K. Palmer, and J. E. Campion, "A Review of Structure in the Selection Interview," *Personnel Psychology* 50, no. 3 (1997): 655–702.

43. M. A. Campion, D. K. Palmer, and J. E. Campion, "A Review of Structure in the Selection Interview."

44. T. Judge, "The Employment Interview: A Review of Recent Research and Recommendations for Future Research," *Human Resource Management Review* 10, no. 4 (2000): 383–406.

45. J. Cortina, N. Goldstein, S. Payne, K. Davison, and S. Gilliland, "The Incremental Validity of Interview Scores Over and Above Cognitive Ability and Conscientiousness Scores," *Personnel Psychology* 53, no. 2 (2000): 325–351.

46. S. Livingston, T. W. Gerdel, M. Hill, B. Yerak, C. Melvin, and B. Lubinger, "Ohio's Strongest Companies All Agree

That Training Is Vital to Their Success," *Cleveland Plain Dealer*, May 21, 1997, 30S.

47. The Oil Spill Training Company, accessed August 14, 2008, http://oilspilltraining.com/home/index.asp.

48. R. Flandez, "Firms Go Online to Train Employees; Virtual Classes, Videos Give Workers Flexibility and Save Owners Money," *Wall Street Journal*, August 14, 2007, B4.

49. R. Flandez, "Chip Maker Trains in the Virtual World," *Wall Street Journal*, April 3, 2008, B6.

50. D. L. Kirkpatrick, "Four Steps to Measuring Training Effectiveness," *Personnel Administrator* 28 (1983): 19–25.

51. L. Bassi, J. Ludwig, D. McMurrer, and M. Van Buren, "Profiting from Learning: Do Firms' Investments in Education and Training Pay Off?" *American Society for Training and Development*, accessed August 14, 2008, http://www.astd.org/NR/rdonlyres/91956A5E-6E57-44-DD-AE5D-FCFFCDC11C3F/0/ASTD_Profiting_From_Learning.pdf.

52. C. Bartz, "Corner Office: Imagining a World of No Annual Reviews," interview by A. Bryant, *New York Times*, October 17, 2009, accessed July 30, 2010, http://www.nytimes.com/2009/10/18/business/18corner.html?_r=1.

53. D. Murphy, "Are Performance Appraisals Worse Than a Waste of Time? Book Derides Unintended Consequences," *San Francisco Chronicle*, September 9, 2001, W1.

54. U. J. Wiersma and G. P. Latham, "The Practicality of Behavioral Observation Scales, Behavioral Expectation Scales, and Trait Scales," *Personnel Psychology* 39 (1986): 619–628; U. J. Wiersma, P. T. Van Den Berg, and G. P. Latham, "Dutch Reactions to Behavioral Observation, Behavioral Expectation, and Trait Scales," *Group & Organization Management* 20 (1995): 297–309.

55. D. J. Schleicher, D. V. Day, B. T. Mayes, and R. E. Riggio, "A New Frame for Frame-of-Reference Training: Enhancing the Construct Validity of Assessment Centers," *Journal of Applied Psychology* (August 2002): 735–746.

56. H. H. Meyer, "A Solution to the Performance Appraisal Feedback Enigma," *Academy of Management Executive* 5, no. 1 (1991): 68–76; G. C. Thornton, "Psychometric Properties of Self-Appraisals of Job Performance," *Personnel Psychology* 33 (1980): 263–271.

57. D. A. Waldman, L. E. Atwater, and D. Antonioni, "Has 360 Feedback Gone Amok?" *Academy of Management Executive* 12, no. 2 (1998): 86–94.

58. J. Smither, M. London, R. Flautt, Y. Vargas, and I. Kucine, "Can Working with an Executive Coach Improve Multisource Feedback Ratings over Time? A Quasi-Experimental Field Study," *Personnel Psychology* (Spring 2003): 21–43.

59. A. Walker and J. Smither, "A Five-Year Study of Upward Feedback: What Managers Do with Their Results Matters," *Personnel Psychology* (Summer 1999): 393–422.

60. C. Tuna, "In Some Offices, Keeping Workers Earns a Bonus; More Firms Like Penske Tie Top Managers' Pay To Employee Retention," *Wall Street Journal*, June 30, 2008, B6.

61. Ibid.

62. G. T. Milkovich and J. M. Newman, *Compensation*, 4th ed. (Homewood, IL: Irwin, 1993).

63. J. A. Livingston, "Child Care Wages and Benefits Study," *Child Care Resource*, August 2, 2006, accessed August 14, 2008, http://www.childcareresource.org/home_announce/cc%20wages%20and%20benefits%20report.final.augst.2006.pdf.

64. "A Worthy Wage?" *American Federation of Teachers*, May 1, 2008, accessed August 14, 2008, http://www.aft.org/news/download/AFT-WorthyWage-Day2008-Ad.pdf.

65. M. L. Williams and G. F. Dreher, "Compensation System Attributes and Applicant Pool Characteristics," *Academy of Management Journal* 35, no. 3 (1992): 571–595.

66. S. Cooper and C. Debaise, "Best Ways to Pay Your Sales Staff," *Bloomberg Businessweek*, June 5, 2009, accessed September 6, 2010, http://www.businessweek.com/magazine/content/09_66/s0906028668952.htm.

67. N. Bunkley, "Ford Profit Comes as Toyota Hits a Bump," *Wall Street Journal*, January 28, 2010, accessed June 15, 2010, http://www.nytimes.com/2010/01/29/business/29ford.html?scp=3&sq=profit-sharing&st=cse.

68. L. S. Covel, "How to Get Workers to Think and Act Like Owners," *Wall Street Journal*, February 7, 2008, B6.

69. Ibid.

70. M. Bloom, "The Performance Effects of Pay Dispersion on Individuals and Organizations," *Academy of Management Journal* 42, no. 1 (1999): 25–40.

71. "Trends in CEO Pay," AFL-CIO, accessed August 11, 2010, http://www.aflcio.org/corporatewatch/paywatch/pay/index.cfm; "Employer Costs for Employee Compensation," *Economic News Release*, Bureau of Labor Statistics, June 9, 2010, accessed July 1, 2010, http://www.bls.gov/news.release/ecec.nr0.htm.

72. W. Grossman and R. E. Hoskisson, "CEO Pay at the Crossroads of Wall Street and Main: Toward the Strategic Design of Executive Compensation," *Academy of Management Executive* 12, no. 1 (1998): 43–57.

73. M. Bloom, "The Performance Effects of Pay Dispersion on Individuals and Organizations."

74. M. Bloom and J. Michel, "The Relationships among Organizational Context, Pay Dispersion, and Managerial Turnover," *Academy of Management Journal* 45 (2002): 33–42.

75. S. E. Needleman, "'The Cat Hid My Car Keys'—Excuses Workers Make," *Wall Street Journal*, May 14, 2010, accessed September 5, 2010, http://online.wsj.com/article/NA_WSJ_PUB:SB10001424052748703339304575240770333031744.html.

76. P. Michal-Johnson, *Saying Good-Bye: A Manager's Guide to Employee Dismissal* (Glenview, IL: Scott, Foresman & Co., 1985).

77. "Mass Layoffs in December 2007 and Annual Totals for 2007," *Bureau of Labor Statistics News*, January 24, 2008, accessed June 14, 2010, http://www.bls.gov/news.release/archives/mmls_01242008.pdf.

78. S. Shankland, "Yahoo Plans Layoff after Profit Plunges," cnet, April 21, 2009, accessed October 10, 2009, http://www.cnet.com.

79. S. Terlep and J. Stoll, "GM to Eliminate More Jobs as It Accelerates Downsizing," *Wall Street Journal*, June 24, 2009, B2.

80. J. R. Morris, W. F. Cascio, and C. E. Young, "Downsizing after All These Years: Questions and Answers about Who Did It, How Many Did It, and Who Benefited from It," *Organizational Dynamics* 27, no. 3 (1999): 78–87.

81. K. Maher, "Hiring Freezes Cushion New Layoffs," *Wall Street Journal*, January 24, 2008, A13.

82. E. White, "Job Ads Loosen Up, Get Real," *Wall Street Journal*, March 12, 2007, B3.

83. K. E. Mishra, G. M. Spreitzer, and A. K. Mishra, "Preserving Employee Morale during Downsizing," *Sloan Management Review* 39, no. 2 (1998): 83–95.

84. J. Hilsenrath, "Adventures in Cost Cutting," *Wall Street Journal*, May 10, 2004, R1.

85. J. Lublin and S. Thurm, "How Companies Calculate Odds in Buyout Offers," *Wall Street Journal*, March 27, 2009, B1.

86. M. Willett, "Early Retirement and Phased Retirement Programs for the Public Sector," *Benefits & Compensation Digest*, April 2005, 31.

87. J. Spiro, "How to Improve Employee Retention," *Inc.*, April 7, 2010, accessed August 5, 2010, http://www.inc.com/guides/2010/04/employee-retention.html.

88. D. R. Dalton, W. D. Todor, and D. M. Krackhardt, "Turnover Overstated: The Functional Taxonomy," *Academy of Management Review* 7 (1982): 117–123.

89. J. R. Hollenbeck and C. R. Williams, "Turnover Functionality versus Turnover Frequency: A Note on Work Attitudes and Organizational Effectiveness," *Journal of Applied Psychology* 71 (1986): 606–611.

90. C. R. Williams, "Reward Contingency, Unemployment, and Functional Turnover," *Human Resource Management Review* 9 (1999): 549–576.

Chapter 12

1. Population Division, U.S. Census Bureau, "Percent of the Projected Population by Race and Hispanic Origin for the United States: 2008 to 2050," U.S. Census Bureau, August 14, 2008, accessed November 4, 2009, http://www.census.gov/population/www/projections/tablesandcharts/table_4.xls.

2. "Quick Stats on Women Workers, 2008," United States Department of Labor,

accessed November 4, 2009, http://www
.dol.gov/wb/stats/main.htm.

3. M. Toossi, "Labor Force Projections
to 2014: Retiring Boomers," *Monthly
Labor Review* (November 2005): 25–44.

4. P. English, "The Way I Work: Paul English
of Kayak," interview by L. Welch, *Inc.*,
February 1, 2010, accessed July 27, 2010,
http://www.inc.com/magazine/20100201
/the-way-i-work-paul-english-of-kayak
.html.

5. Equal Employment Opportunity Commission, "Affirmative Action Appropriate
under Title VII of the Civil Rights Act of
1964, As Amended. Chapter XIV—Equal
Employment Opportunity Commission,
Part 1608," accessed November 5, 2009,
http://www.access.gpo.gov/nara/cfr
/waisidx_04/29cfr1608_04.html.

6. Equal Employment Opportunity Commission, "Federal Laws Prohibiting Job
Discrimination: Questions and Answers,"
accessed August 21, 2008, http://www
.eeoc.gov/facts/qanda.html.

7. A. P. Carnevale and S. C. Stone, *The
American Mosaic: An In-Depth Report
on the Future of Diversity at Work*
(New York: McGraw-Hill, 1995).

8. T. Roosevelt, "From Affirmative Action to
Affirming Diversity," *Harvard Business
Review* 68, no. 2 (1990): 107–117.

9. A. M. Konrad and F. Linnehan, "Formalized HRM Structures: Coordinating
Equal Employment Opportunity or
Concealing Organizational Practices?"
Academy of Management Journal 38,
no. 3 (1995): 787–820; for relevant
court decisions, see, e.g., *Hopwood v.
State of Texas*, 78 F.3d 932, 64 USLW
2591, 107 Ed. Law Rep. 552 (5th Cir.
(Tex.), 18 March 1996) (No. 94-50569,
94-50664). The U.S. Supreme Court has
upheld the principle of affirmative action but has struck down some specific
programs.

10. P. Schmidt, "5 More States May Curtail
Affirmative Action," *Chronicle of Higher
Education*, October 19, 2007, A1.

11. M. E. Heilman, C. J. Block, and P.
Stathatos, "The Affirmative Action
Stigma of Incompetence: Effects of
Performance Information Ambiguity,"
Academy of Management Journal 40,
no. 3 (1997): 603–625.

12. E. Orenstein, "The Business Case for Diversity," *Financial Executive*, May 2005,
22–25; G. Robinson and K. Dechant,
"Building a Business Case for Diversity,"
Academy of Management Executive 11,
no. 3 (1997): 21–31.

13. E. Esen, "2005 Workplace Diversity Practices: Survey Report," Survey conducted
by the Society for Human Resource Management, SHRM Research Department,
Alexandria, VA, October 2005, accessed
March 24, 2009, http://www.shrm.org
/research.

14. E. Orenstein, "The Business Case for
Diversity."

15. E. Esen, "2005 Workplace Diversity
Practices."

16. Ibid.

17. E. Orenstein, "The Business Case for
Diversity."

18. M. Selmi, "The Price of Discrimination:
The Nature of Class Action Employment

Discrimination Litigation and Its Effects,"
Texas Law Review, April 1, 2003, 1249.

19. P. Wright and S. P. Ferris, "Competitiveness through Management of Diversity:
Effects on Stock Price Valuation," *Academy of Management Journal* 38 (1995):
272–285.

20. Ibid.

21. E. Esen, "2005 Workplace Diversity Prac-
tices"; L. E. Wynter, "Business and Race:
Advocates Try to Tie Diversity to Profit,"
Wall Street Journal, February 7, 1996,
B1.

22. M. Angelo, "At TBS, Diversity Pays Its
Own Way," *New York Times*, May 28,
2010, accessed September 2, 2010, http://
www.nytimes.com/2010/05/30/arts
/television/30tbs.html; A. Love, "Diversity
as a Strategic Advantage," *Bloomberg
Businessweek*, May 14, 2010, accessed
August 23, 2010, http://www
.businessweek.com/managing/content
/may2010/ca20100513_748402.htm.

23. W. W. Watson, K. Kumar, and L. K.
Michaelsen, "Cultural Diversity's
Impact on Interaction Process and Performance: Comparing Homogeneous
and Diverse Task Groups," *Academy
of Management Journal* 36 (1993):
590–602; K. A. Jehn, G. B. Northcraft,
and M. A. Neale, "Why Differences
Make a Difference: A Field Study of
Diversity, Conflict, and Performance in
Workgroups," *Administrative Science
Quarterly* 44 (1999): 741–763; E.
Kearney, D. Gebert, S. Voelpel, "When
and How Diversity Benefits Teams: The
Importance of Team Members' Need
for Cognition," *Academy of Management Journal* 52 (2009): 581–598.

24. M. R. Carrell and E. E. Mann, "Defin-
ing Workplace Diversity Programs and
Practices in Organizations," *Labor Law
Journal* 44 (1993): 743–764.

25. D. A. Harrison, K. H. Price, and M. P.
Bell, "Beyond Relational Demography:
Time and the Effects of Surface- and
Deep-Level Diversity on Work Group
Cohesion," *Academy of Management
Journal* 41 (1998): 96–107.

26. D. Harrison, K. Price, J. Gavin, and A.
Florey, "Time, Teams, and Task Performance: Changing Effects of Surface- and
Deep-Level Diversity on Group Functioning," *Academy of Management Journal*
45 (2002): 1029–1045.

27. D. A. Harrison, K. H. Price, and M. P.
Bell, "Beyond Relational Demography."

28. Ibid.

29. J. Helyar and B. Cherry, "50 and Fired,"
Fortune, May 16, 2005, 78.

30. E. White, "The New Recruits: Older
Workers," *Wall Street Journal*, January
14, 2008, B3.

31. S. R. Rhodes, "Age-Related Differences in
Work Attitudes and Behavior," *Psychological Bulletin* 92 (1983): 328–367.

32. A. Fisher, "Wanted: Aging Baby-Boom-
ers," *Fortune*, September 30, 1996, 204.

33. G. M. McEvoy and W. F. Cascio, "Cumulative Evidence of the Relationship
between Employee Age and Job Performance," *Journal of Applied Psychology*
74 (1989): 11–17.

34. S. E. Sullivan and E. A. Duplaga, "Recruiting and Retaining Older Workers for

the Millennium," *Business Horizons* 40
(November 12, 1997): 65.

35. T. Maurer and N. Rafuse, "Learning, Not
Litigating: Managing Employee Development and Avoiding Claims of Age Discrimination," *Academy of Management
Executive* 15, no. 4 (2001): 110–121.

36. B. L. Hassell and P. L. Perrewe, "An Examination of Beliefs about Older Workers: Do Stereotypes Still Exist?" *Journal
of Organizational Behavior* 16 (1995):
457–468.

37. "Women's Earnings as a Percentage of
Men's, 2008," U.S. Department of Labor,
Bureau of Labor Statistics, October
14, 2009, accessed November 7, 2009,
http://www.bls.gov/opub/ted/2009
/ted_20091014_data.htm; "National
Numbers: Women-Owned Businesses
in the United States 2006," Center for
Women's Business Research, accessed
November 7, 2009, http://www.cfwbr
.org/national/index.php.

38. "Fortune 500 Women CEOs," *Fortune*,
accessed July 28, 2010, http://money.cnn
.com/galleries/2010/fortune/1004/gallery
.fortune500_women_ceos.fortune/index
.html; "2009 Catalyst Census: Fortune
500 Women Executive Officers and Top
Earners," *Catalyst*, December 2009, accessed July 27, 2010, http://www.catalyst
.org/publication/358/2009-catalyst
-census-fortune-500-women-executive
-officers-and-top-earners.

39. "Fortune 500 Women CEOs."

40. "2009 Catalyst Census: Fortune 500
Women Board Directors," *Catalyst*,
December 2009, accessed July
27, 2010, http://www.catalyst.org
/publication/357/2009-catalyst-census
-fortune-500-women-board-directors.

41. M. Bertrand and K. Hallock, "The
Gender Gap in Top Corporate Jobs,"
Industrial & Labor Relations Review
55 (2001): 3–21.

42. J. R. Hollenbeck, D. R. Ilgen, C. Ostroff,
and J. B. Vancouver, "Sex Differences in
Occupational Choice, Pay, and Worth: A
Supply-Side Approach to Understanding
the Male-Female Wage Gap," *Personnel
Psychology* 40 (1987): 715–744.

43. A. Chaker and H. Stout, "Second
Chances: After Years Off, Women
Struggle to Revive Careers," *Wall Street
Journal*, May 6, 2004, A1.

44. Korn-Ferry International, 1993.

45. Department of Industry, Labor and Human Relations, *Report of the Gover-
nor's Task Force on the Glass Ceiling
Commission* (Madison, WI: State of
Wisconsin, 1993).

46. M. Fix, G. C. Galster, and R. J. Struyk,
"An Overview of Auditing for Discrimination," in *Clear and Convincing Evidence: Measurement of Discrimination
in America*, ed. M. Fix and R. Struyk
(Washington, DC: Urban Institute Press,
1993), 1–68.

47. E. O. Wright and J. Baxter, "The Glass
Ceiling Hypothesis: A Reply to Critics,"
Gender & Society, vol. 14 (2000):
814–821.

48. B. R. Ragins, B. Townsend, and M. Mat-
tis, "Gender Gap in the Executive Suite:
CEOs and Female Executives Report on
Breaking the Glass Ceiling," *Academy*

of *Management Executive* 12 (1998): 28–42.

49. N. Lockwood, "The Glass Ceiling: Domestic and International Perspectives," *HR Magazine*, 2004 Research Quarterly, 2–10.

50. T. B. Foley, "Discrimination Lawsuits Are a Small-Business Nightmare: A Guide to Minimizing the Potential Damage," *Wall Street Journal*, September 28, 1998, 15.

51. "Charge Statistics FY 1997 through FY 2008," U.S. Equal Employment Opportunity Commission, accessed November 7, 2008, http://www.eeoc.gov.

52. "With O'Neal Out, Black Fortune 500 CEO Count Drops to Five," Diversity-Inc.com, October 29, 2007, accessed August 21, 2008, http://www.diversityinc.com/public/2651.cfm.

53. "Household Data: Annual Averages, Table 11. Employed Persons by Detailed Occupation, Sex, Race, and Hispanic or Latino Ethnicity," Bureau of Labor Statistics, accessed August 21, 2008, http://www.bls.gov/cps/cpsaat11.pdf.

54. D. A. Neal and W. R. Johnson, "The Role of Premarket Factors in Black-White Wage Differences," *Journal of Political Economy* 104, no. 5 (1996): 869–895.

55. M. Fix, G. C. Galster, and R. J. Struyk, "An Overview of Auditing for Discrimination."

56. M. Bendick Jr., C. W. Jackson, and V. A. Reinoso, "Measuring Employment Discrimination through Controlled Experiments," in *African-Americans and Post-Industrial Labor Markets*, ed. J. B. Stewart (New Brunswick, NJ: Transaction Publishers, 1997), 77–100.

57. P. B. Riach and J. Rich, "Measuring Discrimination by Direct Experimental Methods: Seeking Gunsmoke," *Journal of PostKeynesian Economics* 14, no. 2 (Winter 1991–1992): 143–150.

58. A. P. Brief, R. T. Buttram, R. M. Reizenstein, and S. D. Pugh, "Beyond Good Intentions: The Next Steps toward Racial Equality in the American Workplace," *Academy of Management Executive* 11 (1997): 59–72.

59. L. E. Wynter, "Business and Race: Federal Agencies, Spurred on by Nonprofit Groups, Are Increasingly Embracing the Use of Undercover Investigators to Identify Discrimination in the Marketplace," *Wall Street Journal*, July 1, 1998, B1.

60. "ADA Questions and Answers," U.S. Department of Justice, May 2002, accessed March 24, 2009, http://www.ada.gov.

61. "Frequently Asked Questions," *Disability Statistics: Online Resource for U.S. Disability Statistics*, accessed August 21, 2008, http://www.ilr.cornell.edu/edi/disabilitystatistics.

62. "2007 Disability Status Report: United States," Rehabilitation Research and Training Center on Disability Demographics and Statistics, accessed November 7, 2009, http://www.ilr.cornell.edu/edi/disabilitystatistics/statusreports.

63. F. Bowe, "Adults with Disabilities: A Portrait," *President's Committee on Employment of People with Disabilities* (Washington, DC: GPO, 1992); D. Braddock and L. Bachelder, *The Glass Ceiling and Persons with Disabilities*, Glass Ceiling Commission, U.S. Department of Labor (Washington, DC: GPO, 1994).

64. Louis Harris & Associates, Inc., *Public Attitudes toward People with Disabilities* (Washington DC: National Organization on Disability, 1991); Louis Harris & Associates, Inc., *The ICD Survey II: Employing Disabled Americans* (New York: 1987).

65. R. Greenwood and V. A. Johnson, "Employer Perspectives on Workers with Disabilities," *Journal of Rehabilitation* 53 (1987): 37–45.

66. "Accessibility at IBM: An Integrated Approach" IBM.com, accessed August 10, 2010, http://www-03.ibm.com/able/access_ibm/execbrief.html#recruiting; "The DiversityInc Top 10 Companies for People with Disabilities," *DiversityInc.*, May 6, 2010, accessed August 15, 2010, http://diversityinc.com/content/1757/article/7554/.

67. "Work Accommodations: Low Cost, High Impact" U.S. Department of Labor's Office of Disability Employment Policy, accessed November 7, 2009, http://www.jan.wvu.edu/media/LowCostHighImpact.doc.

68. "Study on the Financing of Assistive Technology Devices and Services for Individuals with Disabilities: A Report to the President and the Congress of the United States," National Council on Disability, accessed August 21, 2008, http://www.ncd.gov/newsroom/publications/assistive.html.

69. R. B. Cattell, "Personality Pinned Down," *Psychology Today* 7 (1973): 40–46; C. S. Carver and M. F. Scheier, *Perspectives on Personality* (Boston: Allyn & Bacon, 1992).

70. J. M. Digman, "Personality Structure: Emergence of the Five-Factor Model," *Annual Review of Psychology* 41 (1990): 417–440; M. R. Barrick and M. K. Mount, "The Big Five Personality Dimensions and Job Performance: A Meta-Analysis," *Personnel Psychology* 44 (1991): 1–26.

71. O. Behling, "Employee Selection: Will Intelligence and Conscientiousness Do the Job?," *Academy of Management Executive* 12 (1998): 77–86.

72. R. S. Dalal, "A Meta-Analysis of the Relationship between Organizational Citizenship Behavior and Counterproductive Work Behavior," *Journal of Applied Psychology*, 90 (2005): 1241–1255.

73. M. R. Barrick and M. K. Mount, "The Big Five Personality Dimensions and Job Performance."

74. Ibid.

75. Ibid.

76. D. A. Thomas and R. J. Ely, "Making Differences Matter: A New Paradigm for Managing Diversity," *Harvard Business Review* 74 (September–October 1996): 79–90.

77. E. Esen, "2005 Workplace Diversity Practices."

78. D. A. Thomas and S. Wetlaufer, "A Question of Color: A Debate on Race in the U.S. Workplace," *Harvard Business Review* 75 (September–October 1997), 118–132.

79. E. Esen, "2007 State of Workplace Diversity Management: A Survey Report by the Society for Human Resource Management," 2008, accessed November 15, 2010, http://www.shrm.org/Research/SurveyFindings/Articles/Pages/The2007StateofWorkplaceDiversityManagementSurveyReport.aspx.

80. A. Fisher, "How You Can Do Better on Diversity," *Fortune*, November 15, 2004, 60.

81. Aetna, 2005 Diversity Annual Report, http://www.aetna.com, obtained from SHRM Research Department.

82. J. R. Norton and R. E. Fox, *The Change Equation: Capitalizing on Diversity for Effective Organizational Change* (Washington, DC: American Psychological Association, 1997).

83. Ibid.

84. D. A. Thomas and R. J. Ely, "Making Differences Matter."

85. R. R. Thomas Jr., *Beyond Race and Gender: Unleashing the Power of Your Total Workforce by Managing Diversity* (New York: AMACOM, 1991).

86. Ibid.

87. S. Lubove, "Damned If You Do, Damned If You Don't: Preference Programs Are on the Defensive in the Public Sector, but Plaintiffs' Attorneys and Bureaucrats Keep Diversity Inc. Thriving in Corporate America," *Forbes*, December 15, 1997, 122.

88. W. Wright, "Corner Office: On His Team, Would You Be a Solvent, or the Glue?," interview by A. Bryant, *New York Times*, June 12, 2009, accessed November 11, 2009, http://www.nytimes.com/2009/06/14/business/14corner.html?pagewanted=1&_r=1&adxnnl=1&adxnnlx=1257959098-su4NLK/i2ml%20mP%20tPhBmXg.

89. L. S. Gottfredson, "Dilemmas in Developing Diversity Programs," in *Diversity in the Workplace*, ed. S. E. Jackson & Associates (New York: Guildford Press, 1992).

90. A. Greenwald, B. Nosek, and M. Banaji, "Understanding and Using the Implicit Association Test: I. An Improved Scoring Algorithm," *Journal of Personality & Social Psychology* (August 2003): 197–206; S. Vedantam, "See No Bias; Many Americans Believe They Are Not Prejudiced," *Washington Post*, January 23, 2005, W12.

91. A. P. Carnevale and S. C. Stone, *The American Mosaic.*

92. D. Fenn, "Diversity: More Than Just Affirmative Action," *Inc.*, July 1995, 93.

93. J. R. Joplin and C. S. Daus, "Challenges of Leading a Diverse Workforce," *Academy of Management Executive* 11 (1997): 32–47.

94. N. Byrnes and R. O. Crocket, "An Historic Succession at Xerox," *BusinessWeek*, June 8, 2009, 18–22.

95. F. Rice, "How to Make Diversity Pay, " *Fortune*, August 8, 2004, 78.

Chapter 13

1. "Motivation Matters: Encouraging Staff, Recruiting Qualified Candidates Top List

of Management Challenges," The Creative Group, September 26, 2006, www.creativegroup.com (content no longer available online).

2. J. P. Campbell and R. D. Pritchard, "Motivation Theory in Industrial and Organizational Psychology," in *Handbook of Industrial and Organizational Psychology*, ed. M. D. Dunnette (Chicago: Rand McNally, 1976).

3. C. Tuna, "Pay, Your Own Way: Firm Lets Workers Pick Salary; Big Bonus? None at All? In Throwback to '80s, Employees Make Call," *Wall Street Journal*, July 7, 2008, B6.

4. E. A. Locke, "The Nature and Causes of Job Satisfaction," in *Handbook of Industrial and Organizational Psychology*, ed. M. D. Dunnette (Chicago: Rand McNally, 1976).

5. A. H. Maslow, "A Theory of Human Motivation," *Psychological Review* 50 (1943): 370–396.

6. C. P. Alderfer, *Existence, Relatedness, and Growth: Human Needs in Organizational Settings* (New York: Free Press, 1972).

7. D. C. McClelland, "Toward a Theory of Motive Acquisition," *American Psychologist* 20 (1965): 321–333; D. C. McClelland and D. H. Burnham, "Power Is the Great Motivator," *Harvard Business Review* 54, no. 2 (1976): 100–110.

8. J. H. Turner, "Entrepreneurial Environments and the Emergence of Achievement Motivation in Adolescent Males," *Sociometry* 33 (1970): 147–165.

9. L. W. Porter, E. E. Lawler III, and J. R. Hackman, *Behavior in Organizations* (New York: McGraw-Hill, 1975).

10. C. Ajila, "Maslow's Hierarchy of Needs Theory: Applicability to the Nigerian Industrial Setting," *IFE Psychology* (1997): 162–174.

11. M. A. Wahba and L. B. Birdwell, "Maslow Reconsidered: A Review of Research on the Need Hierarchy Theory," *Organizational Behavior & Human Performance* 15 (1976): 212–240; J. Rauschenberger, N. Schmitt, and J. E. Hunter, "A Test of the Need Hierarchy Concept by a Markov Model of Change in Need Strength," *Administrative Science Quarterly* 25 (1980): 654–670.

12. E. E. Lawler III and L. W. Porter, "The Effect of Performance on Job Satisfaction," *Industrial Relations* 7 (1967): 20–28.

13. L. W. Porter, E. E. Lawler III, and J. R. Hackman, *Behavior in Organizations*.

14. M. Rogoway, "Intel's Fourth-Quarter Sales Top Forecasts—Outlook Brighter Still," OregonLive.com, January 14, 2010, accessed August 29, 2010, http://www.oregonlive.com/business/index.ssf/2010/01/intel_q4_numbers.html; M. Rogoway, "A Little More on Intel's New Bonuses," OregonLive.com, January 18, 2010, accessed August 29, 2010, http://blog.oregonlive.com/siliconforest/2010/01/a_little_more_on_intels_new_bo.html.

15. L. W. Porter, E. E. Lawler III, and J. R. Hackman, *Behavior in Organizations*.

16. D. A. Kaplan, "The Best Company to Work For," *Fortune*, February 8, 2010, 56–64.

17. RSA Vision, *Dan Pink - Drive*, video of a lecture by Daniel Pink at the Royal Society for the encouragement of Arts, Manufacture, & Commerce, London, England, January 27, 2010, accessed July 29, 2010, http://www.thersa.org/events/vision/vision-videos/dan-pink-drive.

18. C. Caggiano, "What Do Workers Want?" *Inc.*, November 1992, 101–104; "National Study of the Changing Workforce," Families and Work Institute, accessed May 31, 2005, http://www.familiesandwork.org/summary/nscw.pdf.

19. H. Dolezalek, "Good Job!: Recognition Training," *Training* (July 28, 2008).

20. R. Kanfer and P. Ackerman, "Aging, Adult Development, and Work Motivation," *Academy of Management Review* (2004): 440–458.

21. E. White, "The New Recruits: Older Workers," *Wall Street Journal*, January 14, 2008, B3.

22. J. S. Lublin, "CEO Pay Sinks Along with Profits," *Wall Street Journal*, April 3, 2009, A1.

23. J. S. Lublin, "Say on the Boss's Pay," *Wall Street Journal*, March 7, 2008, B1.

24. C. T. Kulik and M. L. Ambrose, "Personal and Situational Determinants of Referent Choice," *Academy of Management Review* 17 (1992): 212–237.

25. J. S. Adams, "Toward an Understanding of Inequity," *Journal of Abnormal Social Psychology* 67 (1963): 422–436.

26. R. A. Cosier and D. R. Dalton, "Equity Theory and Time: A Reformulation," *Academy of Management Review* 8 (1983): 311–319; M. R. Carrell and J. E. Dittrich, "Equity Theory: The Recent Literature, Methodological Considerations, and New Directions," *Academy of Management Review* 3 (1978): 202–209.

27. "Anger at 30,000 Feet," *Fortune*, December 10, 2007, 32.

28. N. Maestri, "Supreme Court Lets Stand $36 Million Family Dollar Ruling," Reuters.com, October 5, 2009, accessed January 10, 2010, http://www.reuters.com/article/domesticNews/idUSTRE59447W20091005; R. Montaigne, "Court Rejects Family Dollar Case; Store to Pay Up," *Morning Edition*, National Public Radio, October 6, 2009.

29. C. Chen, J. Choi, and S. Chi, "Making Justice Sense of Local-Expatriate Compensation Disparity: Mitigation by Local Referents, Ideological Explanations, and Interpersonal Sensitivity in China-Foreign Joint Ventures," *Academy of Management Journal* (2002): 807–817.

30. K. Aquino, R. W. Griffeth, D. G. Allen, and P. W. Hom, "Integrating Justice Constructs into the Turnover Process: A Test of a Referent Cognitions Model," *Academy of Management Journal* 40, no. 5 (1997): 1208–1227.

31. S. Needleman, "Burger Chain's Health-Care Recipe—Paying More for Insurance Cuts Turnover, Boosts Sales and Productivity," *Wall Street Journal*, August 31, 2009, B4.

32. R. Folger and M. A. Konovsky, "Effects of Procedural and Distributive Justice on Reactions to Pay Raise Decisions," *Academy of Management Journal* 32 (1989): 115–130; M. A. Konovsky, "Understanding Procedural Justice and Its Impact on Business Organizations," *Journal of Management* 26 (2000): 489–512.

33. E. Barret-Howard and T. R. Tyler, "Procedural Justice as a Criterion in Allocation Decisions," *Journal of Personality & Social Psychology* 50 (1986): 296–305; R. Folger and M. A. Konovsky, "Effects of Procedural and Distributive Justice on Reactions to Pay Raise Decisions."

34. R. Folger and J. Greenberg, "Procedural Justice: An Interpretive Analysis of Personnel Systems," in *Research in Personnel and Human Resources Management*, Vol. 3, ed. K. Rowland and G. Ferris (Greenwich, CT: JAI Press, 1985); R. Folger, D. Rosenfield, J. Grove, and L. Corkran, "Effects of 'Voice' and Peer Opinions on Responses to Inequity," *Journal of Personality & Social Psychology* 37 (1979): 2253–2261; E. A. Lind and T. R. Tyler, *The Social Psychology of Procedural Justice* (New York: Plenum Press, 1988); M. A. Konovsky, "Understanding Procedural Justice and Its Impact on Business Organizations."

35. V. H. Vroom, *Work and Motivation* (New York: John Wiley & Sons, 1964); L. W. Porter and E. E. Lawler III, *Managerial Attitudes and Performance* (Homewood, IL: Dorsey Press & Richard D. Irwin, 1968).

36. J. Galante, "Another Day, Another Virtual Dollar," *Bloomberg Businessweek*, June 21–27, 2010, 43–44.

37. P. V. LeBlanc and P. W. Mulvey, "How American Workers See the Rewards of Work," *Compensation & Benefits Review* 30 (February 1998): 24–28.

38. A. Fox, "Companies Can Benefit When They Disclose Pay Processes to Employees," *HR Magazine* 47 (July 2002): 25.

39. K. W. Thomas and B. A. Velthouse, "Cognitive Elements of Empowerment," *Academy of Management Review* 15 (1990): 666–681.

40. E. L. Thorndike, *Animal Intelligence* (New York: Macmillan, 1911).

41. S. Nassauer, "Now at Hotels: The $250 Cigarette; Major Chains Get Tough with Fines for Smoking; Busted for Butts in the Trash," *Wall Street Journal*, February 21, 2008, D1.

42. B. F. Skinner, *Science and Human Behavior* (New York: Macmillan, 1954); B. F. Skinner, *Beyond Freedom and Dignity* (New York: Bantam Books, 1971); B. F. Skinner, *A Matter of Consequences* (New York: New York University Press, 1984).

43. A. M. Dickinson and A. D. Poling, "Schedules of Monetary Reinforcement in Organizational Behavior Management: Latham and Huber Revisited," *Journal of Organizational Behavior Management* 16, no. 1 (1992): 71–91.

44. V. Bauerlein, "PepsiCo Plans Recycling Initiative," *Wall Street Journal*, April 22, 2010, accessed August 23, 2010, http://online.wsj.com/article/NA_WSJ_PUB:SB10001424052748703404004575198390481890492.html.

45. R. Ho, "Attending to Attendance," *Wall Street Journal Interactive*, December 7, 1998.

46. D. Grote, "Manager's Journal: Discipline without Punishment," *Wall Street Journal*, May 23, 1994, A14.

47. J. B. Miner, *Theories of Organizational Behavior* (Hinsdale, IL: Dryden, 1980).

48. A. M. Dickinson and A. D. Poling, "Schedules of Monetary Reinforcement in Organizational Behavior Management."

49. F. Luthans and A. D. Stajkovic, "Reinforce for Performance: The Need to Go beyond Pay and Even Rewards," *Academy of Management Executive* 13, no. 2 (1999): 49–57.

50. K. D. Butterfield, L. K. Trevino, and G. A. Ball, "Punishment from the Manager's Perspective: A Grounded Investigation and Inductive Model," *Academy of Management Journal* 39 (1996): 1479–1512.

51. R. D. Arvey and J. M. Ivancevich, "Punishment in Organizations: A Review, Propositions, and Research Suggestions," *Academy of Management Review* 5 (1980): 123–132.

52. R. D. Arvey, G. A. Davis, and S. M. Nelson, "Use of Discipline in an Organization: A Field Study," *Journal of Applied Psychology* 69 (1984): 448–460; M. E. Schnake, "Vicarious Punishment in a Work Setting," *Journal of Applied Psychology* 71 (1986): 343–345.

53. E. A. Locke and G. P. Latham, *Goal Setting: A Motivational Technique That Works* (Englewood Cliffs, NJ: Prentice-Hall, 1984); E. A. Locke and G. P. Latham, *A Theory of Goal Setting and Task Performance* (Englewood Cliffs, NJ: Prentice-Hall, 1990).

54. "Franchising—In with the New: As More Boomers Retire, Franchisers Set Their Sights on a Much Younger Crowd," *Wall Street Journal*, September 28, 2009, R9.

55. G. P. Latham and E. A. Locke, "Goal Setting—A Motivational Technique That Works," *Organizational Dynamics* 8, no. 2 (1979): 68.

56. Ibid.

Chapter 14

1. W. Bennis, "Why Leaders Can't Lead," *Training & Development Journal* 43, no. 4 (1989).

2. L. Buchanan, "How the Creative Stay Creative," *Inc.*, June 2008, 102–103.

3. A. Zaleznik, "Managers and Leaders: Are They Different?" *Harvard Business Review* 55 (1977): 76–78; A. Zaleznik, "The Leadership Gap," *The Washington Quarterly* 6 (1983): 32–39.

4. D. Welch, "Ed Whitacre's Battle to Save GM from Itself," *Bloomberg Businessweek*, April 29, 2010, accessed August 27, 2010, http://www .businessweek.com/magazine /content/10_19/b4177048204431.htm.

5. W. Bennis, "Why Leaders Can't Lead."

6. S. Berfield, "The Best of 2006: Leaders," *BusinessWeek*, December 18, 2006, 58.

7. D. Jones, "Not All Successful CEOs are Extroverts," *USA Today*, June 7, 2006, B.1.

8. Ibid.

9. M. Gladwell, "Why Do We Love Tall Men?" Gladwell.com, accessed August 27, 2008, http://www.gladwell.com/blink /blink_excerpt2.html.

10. R. J. House and R. M Aditya, "The Social Scientific Study of Leadership: Quo Vadis?" *Journal of Management* 23 (1997): 409–473; T. Judge, R. Illies, J. Bono, and M. Gerhardt, "Personality and Leadership: A Qualitative and Quantitative Review," *Journal of Applied Psychology* (August 2002): 765–782; S. A. Kirkpatrick and E. A. Locke, "Leadership: Do Traits Matter?" *Academy of Management Executive* 5, no. 2 (1991): 48–60.

11. R. J. House and R. M Aditya, "The Social Scientific Study of Leadership"; S. A. Kirkpatrick and E. A. Locke, "Leadership: Do Traits Matter?"

12. "The Best CEOs," *Barron's*, March 29, 2010, accessed August 30, 2010, http://online.barrons.com/article /SB126964409156568321.html; "Cummins Inc," *Bloomberg Businessweek*, accessed August 30, 2010, http://investing .businessweek.com/research/stocks/people /person.asp?personId=265255&ticker =CMI:US.

13. S. A. Kirkpatrick and E. A. Locke, "Leadership: Do Traits Matter?"

14. E. A. Fleishman, "The Description of Supervisory Behavior," *Journal of Applied Psychology* 37 (1953): 1–6; L. R. Katz, *New Patterns of Management* (New York: McGraw-Hill, 1961).

15. B. Einhorn, "Innovator: Jimmy Lai," *Bloomberg Businessweek*, August 26, 2010, accessed September 9, 2010, http:// www.businessweek.com/magazine /content/10_36/b4193038847783.htm.

16. N. Byrnes, "The Issue: Maintaining Employee Engagement," *Bloomberg Businessweek*, January 16, 2009, accessed August 20, 2010, http://www .businessweek.com/managing/content /jan2009/ca20090116_444132.htm.

17. P. Weissenberg and M. H. Kavanagh, "The Independence of Initiating Structure and Consideration: A Review of the Evidence," *Personnel Psychology* 25 (1972): 119–130.

18. R. J. House and T. R. Mitchell, "Path-Goal Theory of Leadership," *Journal of Contemporary Business* 3 (1974): 81–97; F. E. Fiedler, "A Contingency Model of Leadership Effectiveness," in *Advances in Experimental Social Psychology*, ed. L. Berkowitz (New York: Academic Press, 1964); V. H. Vroom and P. W. Yetton, *Leadership and Decision Making* (Pittsburgh: University of Pittsburgh Press, 1973); P. Hersey and K. H. Blanchard, *The Management of Organizational Behavior*, 4th ed. (Englewood Cliffs, NJ: Prentice Hall, 1984); S. Kerr and J. M. Jermier, "Substitutes for Leadership: Their Meaning and Measurement," *Organizational Behavior & Human Performance* 22 (1978): 375–403.

19. F. E. Fiedler and M. M. Chemers, *Leadership and Effective Management* (Glenview, IL: Scott, Foresman, 1974); F. E. Fiedler and M. M. Chemers, *Improving Leadership Effectiveness: The Leader Match Concept*, 2d ed. (New York: John Wiley & Sons, 1984).

20. F. E. Fiedler and M. M. Chemers, *Improving Leadership Effectiveness*.

21. F. E. Fiedler, "The Effects of Leadership Training and Experience: A Contingency Model Interpretation," *Administrative Science Quarterly* 17, no. 4 (1972): 455; F. E. Fiedler, *A Theory of Leadership Effectiveness* (New York: McGraw-Hill, 1967).

22. L. S. Csoka and F. E. Fiedler, "The Effect of Military Leadership Training: A Test of the Contingency Model," *Organizational Behavior & Human Performance* 8 (1972): 395–407.

23. R. J. House and T. R. Mitchell, "Path-Goal Theory of Leadership."

24. M. Conlin, "Making Pay Cuts Less Painful," *Bloomberg Businessweek*, April 23, 2009, accessed August 10, 2010, http:// www.businessweek.com/magazine /content/09_18/b4129067650111.htm.

25. R. J. House and T. R. Mitchell, "Path-Goal Theory of Leadership."

26. B. M. Fisher and J. E. Edwards, "Consideration and Initiating Structure and Their Relationships with Leader Effectiveness: A Meta-Analysis," *Proceedings of the Academy of Management*, August 1988, 201–205.

27. A. Todorova, "Company Programs Help Workers Save on Gas," *Wall Street Journal*, May 30, 2008, accessed June 18, 2009, http://www.wsj.com.

28. L. Buchanan, "Letting Employees Run the Company," *Inc.*, June 8, 2010, accessed August 30, 2010, http://www.inc.com /top-workplaces/2010/letting-employees -run-the-company.html.

29. M. Copeland, K. Crawford, J. Davis, S. Hamner, C. Hawn, R. Howe, P. Kaihla, M. Maier, O. Malik, D. McDonald, C. Null, E. Schonfeld, O. Thomas, and G. Zachary, "My Golden Rule," *Business 2.0*, December 1, 2005, 108.

30. E. White, "Art of Persuasion Becomes Key," *Wall Street Journal*, May 19, 2008, B5.

31. J. C. Wofford and L. Z. Liska, "Path-Goal Theories of Leadership: A Meta-Analysis," *Journal of Management* 19 (1993): 857–876.

32. R. J. House and R. M Aditya, "The Social Scientific Study of Leadership."

33. V. H. Vroom and A. G. Jago, *The New Leadership: Managing Participation in Organizations* (Englewood Cliffs, NJ: Prentice Hall, 1988).

34. C. Fishman, "How Teamwork Took Flight: This Team Built a Commercial Engine—and Self-Managing GE Plant—from Scratch," *Fast Company*, October 1, 1999, 188.

35. Ibid.

36. Ibid.

37. G. A. Yukl, *Leadership in Organizations*, 3rd ed. (Englewood Cliffs, NJ: Prentice Hall, 1995).

38. B. M. Bass, *Bass & Stogdill's Handbook of Leadership: Theory, Research, and Managerial Applications* (New York: Free Press, 1990).

39. R. D. Ireland and M. A. Hitt, "Achieving and Maintaining Strategic Competitiveness in the 21st Century: The Role of

Strategic Leadership," *Academy of Management Executive* 13, no. 1 (1999): 43–57.

40. P. Thoms and D. B. Greenberger, "Training Business Leaders to Create Positive Organizational Visions of the Future: Is It Successful?" *Academy of Management Journal* (Best Papers & Proceedings 1995): 212–216.

41. M. Weber, *The Theory of Social and Economic Organizations*, trans. R. A. Henderson and T. Parsons (New York: Free Press, 1947).

42. J. Clegg, "The Way Mourinho Manages," *Wall Street Journal*, June 2, 2010, accessed August 10, 2010, http://online.wsj.com/article/NA_WSJ_PUB:SB10001424052748703961204575280851972332526.html.

43. D. A. Waldman and F. J. Yammarino, "CEO Charismatic Leadership: Levels-of-Management and Levels-of-Analysis Effects," *Academy of Management Review* 24, no. 2 (1999): 266–285.

44. K. B. Lowe, K. G. Kroeck, and N. Sivasubramaniam, "Effectiveness Correlates of Transformational and Transactional Leadership: A Meta-Analytic Review of the MLQ Literature," *Leadership Quarterly* 7 (1996): 385–425.

45. J. M. Howell and B. J. Avolio, "The Ethics of Charismatic Leadership: Submission or Liberation?" *Academy of Management Executive* 6, no. 2 (1992): 43–54.

46. Ibid.

47. B. M. Bass, "From Transactional to Transformational Leadership" *Organizational Dynamics* 18, no. 3 (1990): 19–31.

48. B. M. Bass, *A New Paradigm of Leadership: An Inquiry into Transformational Leadership* (Alexandria, VA: U.S. Army Research Institute for the Behavioral and Social Sciences, 1996).

49. K. Swisher, "A Question of Management: Carol Bartz on How Yahoo's Organizational Structure Got in the Way of Innovation," *Wall Street Journal*, June 2, 2009, R4.

50. L. Buchanan, "How to Build a Beautiful Company," Inc.com, June 8, 2010, accessed July 30, 2010, http://www.inc.com/top-workplaces/2010/how-to-build-a-beautiful-company.html.

51. B. M. Bass, "From Transactional to Transformational Leadership."

Chapter 15

1. E. E. Lawler III, L. W. Porter, and A. Tannenbaum, "Manager's Attitudes toward Interaction Episodes," *Journal of Applied Psychology* 52 (1968): 423–439; H. Mintzberg, *The Nature of Managerial Work* (New York: Harper & Row, 1973).

2. J. D. Maes, T. G. Weldy, and M. L. Icenogle, "A Managerial Perspective: Oral Communication Competency Is Most Important for Business Students in the Workplace," *Journal of Business Communication* 34 (1997): 67–80.

3. R. Lepsinger and A. D. Lucia, *The Art and Science of 360 Degree Feedback* (San Francisco: Pfeiffer, 1997).

4. E. E. Jones and K. E. Davis, "From Acts to Dispositions: The Attribution Process in Person Perception," in *Advances in Experimental and Social Psychology*, vol. 2, ed. L. Berkowitz (New York: Academic Press, 1965), 219–266; R. G. Lord and J. E. Smith, "Theoretical, Information-Processing, and Situational Factors Affecting Attribution Theory Models of Organizational Behavior," *Academy of Management Review* 8 (1983): 50–60.

5. J. Zadney and H. B. Gerard, "Attributed Intentions and Informational Selectivity," *Journal of Experimental Social Psychology* 10 (1974): 34–52.

6. B. Dumaine, "Buffett's Mr. Fix-It," *Fortune*, August 16, 2010, 78–86; M.M. Rose, "NetJets Returns to Profit in First Quarter," *Columbus Dispatch*, April 22, 2010, accessed August 22, 2010, http://www.dispatch.com/live/content/business/stories/2010/04/22/netjets-returns-to-profit-in-first-quarter.html.

7. H. H. Kelly, *Attribution in Social Interaction* (Morristown, NJ: General Learning Press, 1971).

8. J. M. Burger, "Motivational Biases in the Attribution of Responsibility for an Accident: A Meta-Analysis of the Defensive-Attribution Hypothesis," *Psychological Bulletin* 90 (1981): 496–512.

9. D. A. Hofmann and A. Stetzer, "The Role of Safety Climate and Communication in Accident Interpretation: Implications for Learning from Negative Events," *Academy of Management Journal* 41, no. 6 (1998): 644–657.

10. C. Perrow, *Normal Accidents: Living with High-Risk Technologies* (New York: Basic Books, 1984).

11. A. G. Miller and T. Lawson, "The Effect of an Informational Opinion on the Fundamental Attribution Error," *Journal of Personality & Social Psychology* 47 (1989): 873–896; J. M. Burger, "Changes in Attribution Errors over Time: The Ephemeral Fundamental Attribution Error," *Social Cognition* 9 (1991): 182–193.

12. F. Heider, *The Psychology of Interpersonal Relations* (New York: Wiley, 1958); D. T. Miller and M. Ross, "Self-Serving Biases in Attribution of Causality: Fact or Fiction?" *Psychological Bulletin* 82 (1975): 213–225.

13. J. R. Larson Jr., "The Dynamic Interplay between Employees' Feedback-Seeking Strategies and Supervisors' Delivery of Performance Feedback," *Academy of Management Review* 14, no. 3 (1989): 408–422.

14. C. Hymowitz, "Mind Your Language: To Do Business Today, Consider Delayering," *Wall Street Journal*, March 27, 2006, B1.

15. G. L. Kreps, *Organizational Communication: Theory and Practice* (New York: Longman, 1990).

16. Ibid.

17. B. Salzberg, "Trusting a CEO in the Twitter Age," *Bloomberg Businessweek*, August 7, 2009, accessed August 10, 2010, http://www.businessweek.com/managing/content/aug2009/ca2009087_680028.htm?chan=careers_managing+your+company+page_top+stories.

18. L. Landro, "The Informed Patient: Hospitals Combat Errors at the 'Hand-Off,'" *Wall Street Journal*, June 28, 2006, D1.

19. G. L. Kreps, *Organizational Communication: Theory and Practice.*

20. J. Sandberg, "Ruthless Rumors and the Managers Who Enable Them," *Wall Street Journal*, October 29, 2003, B1.

21. Ibid.

22. W. Davis and J. R. O'Connor, "Serial Transmission of Information: A Study of the Grapevine," *Journal of Applied Communication Research* 5 (1977): 61–72.

23. J. Sandberg, "Ruthless Rumors and the Managers Who Enable Them."

24. K. Voight, "Office Intelligence," *Asian Wall Street Journal*, January 21, 2005, P1.

25. W. Davis and J. R. O'Connor, "Serial Transmission of Information: A Study of the Grapevine"; C. Hymowitz, "Managing: Spread the Word, Gossip Is Good," *Wall Street Journal*, October 4, 1988.

26. W. C. Redding, *Communication within the Organization: An Interpretive View of Theory and Research* (New York: Industrial Communication Council, 1972).

27. D. T. Hall, K. L. Otazo, and G. P. Hollenbeck, "Behind Closed Doors: What Really Happens in Executive Coaching," *Organizational Dynamics* 27, no. 3 (1999): 39–53.

28. J. Kelly, "Blowing the Whistle on the Boss," *PR Newswire*, November 15, 2004.

29. R. McGarvey, "Lords of Discipline," *Entrepreneur Magazine*, January 1, 2000.

30. A. Mehrabian, "Communication without Words," *Psychology Today* 3 (1968): 53; A. Mehrabian, *Silent Messages* (Belmont, CA: Wadsworth, 1971); R. Harrison, *Beyond Words: An Introduction to Nonverbal Communication* (Upper Saddle River, NJ: Prentice Hall, 1974); A. Mehrabian, *Non-Verbal Communication* (Chicago: Aldine, 1972).

31. M. L. Knapp, *Nonverbal Communication in Human Interaction*, 2nd ed. (New York: Holt, Rinehart & Winston, 1978).

32. H. M. Rosenfeld, "Instrumental Affiliative Functions of Facial and Gestural Expressions," *Journal of Personality & Social Psychology* 24 (1966): 65–72; P. Ekman, "Differential Communication of Affect by Head and Body Cues," *Journal of Personality & Social Psychology* 23 (1965): 726–735; A. Mehrabian, "Significance of Posture and Position in the Communication of Attitude and Status Relationships," *Psychological Bulletin* 71 (1969): 359–372.

33. J. Gottman and R. Levenson, "The Timing of Divorce: Predicting When a Couple Will Divorce over a 14-Year Period," *Journal of Marriage & the Family* 62 (August 2000): 737–745; J. Gottman, R. Levenson, and E. Woodin, "Facial Expressions during Marital Conflict," *Journal of Family Communication* 1, issue 1 (2001): 37–57.

34. T. Aeppel, "Career Journal: Nicknamed 'Nag,' She's Just Doing Her Job," *Wall Street Journal*, May 14, 2002, B1.

35. C. A. Bartlett and S. Ghoshal, "Changing the Role of Top Management: Beyond Systems to People," *Harvard Business Review* (May–June 1995): 132–142.

36. T. Andrews, "E-Mail Empowers, Voice-Mail Enslaves," *PC Week*, April 10, 1995, E11.
37. A. Rawlins, "There's a Message in Every Email," *Fast Company* September 2007, accessed September 3, 2008, http://www.fastcompany.com/magazine/118/theres-a-message-in-every-email.html?partner=rss-alert.
38. R. G. Nichols, "Do We Know How to Listen? Practical Helps in a Modern Age," in *Communication Concepts and Processes*, ed. J. DeVitor (Englewood Cliffs, NJ: Prentice Hall, 1971); P. V. Lewis, *Organizational Communication: The Essence of Effective Management* (Columbus, OH: Grid Publishing Company, 1975).
39. E. Atwater, *I Hear You*, revised ed. (New York: Walker, 1992).
40. R. Adler and N. Towne, *Looking Out/Looking In* (San Francisco: Rinehart Press, 1975).
41. K. Pattison, "Yahoo CEO Carol Bartz: 'I'm Just a Manager'," *Fast Company*, August 11, 2010, accessed August 20, 2010, http://www.fastcompany.com/1680546/yahoo-ceo-carol-bartz-im-just-a-manager; "Yahoo! Reports Second Quarter 2010 Results," *MarketWatch*, July 20, 2010, accessed August 20, 2010 http://www.marketwatch.com/story/yahoo-reports-third-quarter-2010-results-2010-10-19.
42. C. Gallo, "Why Leadership Means Listening," *Bloomberg Businessweek* January 31, 2007, accessed September 3, 2008, http://www.businessweek.com/smallbiz/content/jan2007/sb20070131_192848.htm.
43. B. D. Seyber, R. N. Bostrom, and J. H. Seibert, "Listening, Communication Abilities, and Success at Work," *Journal of Business Communication* 26 (1989): 293–303.
44. E. Atwater, *I Hear You*.
45. P. Sellers, A. Diba, and E. Florian, "Get Over Yourself—Your Ego Is Out Of Control. You're Screwing Up Your Career," *Fortune*, April 30, 2001, 76.
46. J. Sandberg, "Not Communicating with Your Boss? Count Your Blessings," *Wall Street Journal*, May 22, 2007, B1.
47. H. H. Meyer, "A Solution to the Performance Appraisal Feedback Enigma," *Academy of Management Executive 5*, no. 1 (1991): 68–76.
48. C. Hymowitz, "Executives Who Build Truth-Telling Cultures Learn Fast What Works," *Wall Street Journal*, June 12, 2006, B1.
49. A. Levy, "Polycom CEO Sends Companywide E-Mail after Insider Trading Case," Bloomberg.com, October 19, 2009, accessed July 30, 2010, http://www.bloomberg.com/apps/news?pid=newsarchive&sid=aZqJn4tejCDw.
50. G. Hamel, "HCL: Extreme Management Makeover," *Wall Street Journal*, July 6, 2010, accessed August 20, 2010, http://blogs.wsj.com/management/2010/07/06/hcl-extreme-management-makeover/.
51. A. Lashinsky, "Lights! Camera! Cue the CEO!" *Fortune*, August 21, 2006, 27.
52. M. Campanelli and N. Friedman, "Welcome to Voice Mail Hell: The New Technology Has Become a Barrier between Salespeople and Customers," *Sales & Marketing Management* 147 (May 1995): 98–101.
53. E. W. Morrison, "Organizational Silence: A Barrier to Change and Development in a Pluralistic World," *Academy of Management Review* 25 (2000): 706–725.
54. "Force Protection: Code of Conduct and Ethics," Force Protection, accessed June 26, 2009, http://www.forceprotectioninc.com.
55. K. Maher, "Global Companies Face Reality of Instituting Ethics Programs," *Wall Street Journal*, November 9, 2004, B8.
56. "An Inside Look at Corporate Hotlines," *Security Director's Report*, February 2007, 8.
57. J. Confino, "Guardian Employee Survey Maintains High Scores Despite Radical Restructuring," Guardian.co.uk, January 11, 2010, accessed July 15, 2010, http://www.guardian.co.uk/sustainability/corporate-social-responsibility-employee-survey-employee-engagement-sustainability.
58. C. Hymowitz, "Sometimes, Moving Up Makes It Harder to See What Goes on Below," *Wall Street Journal*, October 15, 2007, B1.
59. Ibid.
60. D. Kirkpatrick and D. Roth, "Why There's No Escaping the Blog," *Fortune (Europe)*, January 24, 2005, 64.
61. M. Bush, "How Twitter Can Help or Hurt an Airline," *Advertising Age*, July 16, 2009, Accessed August 1, 2010, http://adage.com/digital/article?article_id=137977.

Chapter 16

1. R. Leifer and P. K. Mills, "An Information Processing Approach for Deciding upon Control Strategies and Reducing Control Loss in Emerging Organizations," *Journal of Management* 22 (1996): 113–137.
2. M. Mecham and G. Norris, "Boeing Plans 8.5 Months of 787 Testing," *Aviation Week*, December 18, 2009, accessed August 1, 2010, http://www.aviationweek.com/aw/generic/story_channel.jsp?channel=comm&id=news/W787PLAN121809.xml.
3. R. Grais-Targow, "Big Salmon Exporter Fights Virus—Chile's Share of Global Output Expected to Fall; Pickup Unlikely Until 2011," *Wall Street Journal*, July 7, 2009, B6.
4. S. Michel, D. Bowen, and R. Johnston, "Business Insight (A Special Report); Customer Service: Making the Most Of Customer Complaints," *Wall Street Journal*, September 22, 2008, R4.
5. "Mobile Firms Failing on Coverage," BBC, July 14, 2010, accessed July 20, 2010, http://www.bbc.co.uk/news/10618236.
6. J. Mann, "StarCraft 2 Beta Signup Opens Today," Techspot.com, May 6, 2009, accessed July 30, 2010, http://www.techspot.com/news/34601-starcraft-2-beta-signup-opens-today.html.
7. N. Wiener, *Cybernetics; Or Control and Communication in the Animal and the Machine* (New York: Wiley, 1948).
8. P. Lyon, "First Drive: 2011 Nissan Leaf Japanese Spec," *MotorTrend*, June 28, 2010, accessed July 16, 2010, http://www.motortrend.com/roadtests/alternative/1006_2011_nissan_leaf_japanese_spec_drive/index.html.
9. P. Thurrott, "What You Need to Know about Windows 7 Beta 1," *Windows IT Pro Magazine*, February 1, 2009, 7.
10. R. Leifer and P. K. Mills, "An Information Processing Approach for Deciding upon Control Strategies and Reducing Control Loss in Emerging Organizations."
11. C. Conkey and M. Trottman, "Big Changes Called for at FAA; Top Inspector Sees Too Much Reliance on Airline Reports," *Wall Street Journal*, April 11, 2008, A4.
12. C. Bryan-Low, "Pound for Pound, a Veggie Peddler Takes on the EU—East London's Ms. Devers Snubs the Metric System; Selling by the Bowl is Alleged," *Wall Street Journal*, January 22, 2008, A1
13. Daily Mail Reporter, "'Metric Martyr' Case Dropped against 64-year-old Fruit and Veg Seller," *Mail Online*, January 13, 2009, accessed August 22, 2009, http://www.dailymail.co.uk.
14. "Speed Demons Will Meet Their Match on the Piste," *Times Online*, January 5, 2008, accessed August 11, 2009, http://travel.timesonline.co.uk.
15. A. Coombes, "Bully for You: Hair-Raising Bad-Boss Stories, and Tips on How to Cope," *MarketWatch*, July 17, 2006, accessed July 30, 2009, http://www.workplacebullying.org.
16. M. Weber, *The Protestant Ethic and the Spirit of Capitalism* (New York: Scribner's, 1958).
17. D. Hunt, "JEA Keeping a Closer Watch on Employees," Jacksonville.com/*Florida Times-Union*, March 4, 2010, accessed July 12, 2010, http://jacksonville.com/news/metro/2010-03-04/story/jea_keeping_a_closer_watch_on_employees.html.
18. "Some Details on Bedard's Contract Incentives," *Seattle Post Intelligencier*, February 9, 2010, accessed July 1, 2010, http://blog.seattlepi.com/baseball/archives/193984.asp.
19. A. DeFelice, "A Century of Customer Love: Nordstrom Is the Gold Standard for Customer Service Excellence," *CRM Magazine*, June 1, 2005, 42.
20. R. T. Pascale, "Nordstrom: Respond to Unreasonable Customer Requests!," *Planning Review* 2 (May–June 1994): 17.
21. Ibid.
22. Ibid.
23. J. R. Barker, "Tightening the Iron Cage: Concertive Control in Self-Managing Teams," *Administrative Science Quarterly* 38 (1993): 408–437.
24. N. Byrnes, "The Art of Motivation," *BusinessWeek*, May 1, 2006, 56–62.
25. J. R. Barker, "Tightening the Iron Cage."
26. C. Manz and H. Sims, "Leading Workers to Lead Themselves: The External Leadership of Self-Managed Work Teams," *Administrative Science Quarterly* 32 (1987): 106–128.
27. J. Slocum and H. A. Sims, "Typology for Integrating Technology, Organization

and Job Design," *Human Relations* 33 (1980): 193–212.

28. C. C. Manz and H. P. Sims Jr., "Self-Management as a Substitute for Leadership: A Social Learning Perspective," *Academy of Management Review* 5 (1980): 361–367.

29. C. Manz and C. Neck, *Mastering Self-Leadership*, 3rd ed. (Upper Saddle River, NJ: Pearson, Prentice Hall, 2004).

30. R. S. Kaplan and D. P. Norton, "Using the Balanced Scorecard as a Strategic Management System," *Harvard Business Review* (January–February 1996): 75–85; R. S. Kaplan and D. P. Norton, "The Balanced Scorecard: Measures That Drive Performance," *Harvard Business Review* (January–February 1992): 71–79.

31. J. R. Davis and T. Atkinson, "Need Speed? Slow Down," *Harvard Business Review*, May 2010, accessed August 1, 2010, http://hbr.org/2010/05/need-speed-slow-down/ar/1.

32. M. H. Stocks and A. Harrell, "The Impact of an Increase in Accounting Information Level on the Judgment Quality of Individuals and Groups," *Accounting, Organizations & Society*, October–November 1995, 685–700.

33. B. Morris, "Roberto Goizueta and Jack Welch: The Wealth Builders," *Fortune*, December 11, 1995, 80–94.

34. G. Colvin, "America's Best and Worst Wealth Creators: The Real Champions Aren't Always Who You Think. Here's an Eye-Opening Look at Which Companies Produce and Destroy the Most Money for Investors—Plus a New Tool for Spotting Future Winners," *Fortune*, December 18, 2000, 207.

35. E. Varon, "Strategic Planning: Implementation Is Not for the Meek," *CIO*, November 15, 2002, accessed September 5, 2008, http://www.cio.com/article/31510/Strategic_Planning_Implementation_Is_Not_for_the_Meek.

36. "Welcome Complaints," Office of Consumer and Business Affairs, accessed June 20, 2005, http://www.ocba.sa.gov.au/businessadvice/complaints/03_welcome.html.

37. C. B. Furlong, "12 Rules for Customer Retention," *Bank Marketing* 5 (January 1993): 14.

38. Customer retention graphs, accessed August 1, 2009, http://www.voxinc.com/customer-experience-graphs/impact-customer-retention.htm.

39. M. Raphel, "Vanished Customers Are Valuable Customers," *Art Business News*, June 2002, 46.

40. C. A. Reeves and D. A. Bednar, "Defining Quality: Alternatives and Implications," *Academy of Management Review* 19 (1994): 419–445.

41. "Our Achievements," Singapore Airlines, accessed September 5, 2008, http://www.singaporeair.com/saa/en_UK/content/company_info/news/achievements.jsp.

42. S. Holmes, "Creature Comforts at 30,000 feet," *BusinessWeek*, December 18, 2006, 138.

43. M. Harley, "Review: 2011 Hyundai Sonata a Sweet Addition to Mid-size Sedan Segment," Autoblog.com, February 22, 2010, accessed July 10, 2010, http://www.autoblog.com/2010/02/22/2011-hyundai-sonata-review/.

44. D. R. May and B. L. Flannery, "Cutting Waste with Employee Involvement Teams," *Business Horizons*, September–October 1995, 28–38.

45. J. Carlton, "To Cut Fuel Bills, Try High-Tech Help," *Wall Street Journal*, March 11, 2008, B3.

46. M. Warner, "Plastic Potion No. 9," *Fast Company*, September 2008, 88.

47. J. Motavalli, "See How Printer Cartridges Are Recycled," The Daily Green, April 17, 2010, accessed June 29, 2010, http://www.thedailygreen.com/living-green/blogs/cars-transportation/recycle-printer-cartridges-460410.

48. "Herman Miller Earns Design for Recycling Award," GreenerDesign, May 12, 2009, accessed July 23, 2010, http://www.greenbiz.com/news/2009/05/12/herman-miller-earns-design-recycling-award.

49. M. Conlin and P. Raeburn, "Industrial Evolution: Bill McDonough Has the Wild Idea He Can Eliminate Waste. Surprise! Business Is Listening," *BusinessWeek*, April 8, 2002, 70.

50. B. Byrne, "EU Says Makers Must Destroy Their Own Brand End-of-Life Cars," *Irish Times*, April 23, 2003, 52.

51. J. L. Schenker, "Cows to Kilowatts: A Bounty from Waste," *BusinessWeek*, December 3, 2008, accessed August 1, 2009, http://www.businessweek.com.

52. "The End of the Road: Schools and Computer Recycling," Intel, accessed September 5, 2008, http://www.intel.com/education/recycling_computers/recycling.htm.

53. P. Lima, "How to Navigate the Recycling Maze; There Are Programs Out There to Help Businesses and Consumers Get Rid of Old Equipment Responsibly," *Globe and Mail (Canada)*, March 10, 2008, B9.

Chapter 17

1. R. Lenzner, "The Reluctant Entrepreneur," *Forbes*, September 11, 1995, 162–166.

2. R. McGill Murphy, "Rising Stars," *Fortune*, September 6, 2010, 110–116.

3. R. D. Buzzell and B. T. Gale, *The PIMS Principles: Linking Strategy to Performance* (New York: Free Press, 1987); M. Lambkin, "Order of Entry and Performance in New Markets," *Strategic Management Journal* 9 (1988): 127–140.

4. G. L. Urban, T. Carter, S. Gaskin, and Z. Mucha, "Market Share Rewards to Pioneering Brands: An Empirical Analysis and Strategic Implications," *Management Science* 32 (1986): 645–659.

5. S. Nassauer, "'I Hate My Room' The Traveler Tweeted. Ka-Boom! An Upgrade!" *Wall Street Journal*, June 24, 2010, accessed August 14, 2010, http://online.wsj.com/article/NA_WSJ_PUB:SB10001424052748704256304575320730977161348.html.

6. K. Hall, "How Komatsu Innovations Keep Its Machinery Selling," *Bloomberg Businessweek*, October 1, 2009, accessed July 10, 2010, http://www.businessweek.com/globalbiz/content/sep2009/gb20090930_232338.htm?campaign_id=alerts.

7. L. Tischler, "Tech for Toques," *Fast Company*, May 1, 2006, 68.

8. "UPMC Creates Electronic Health Record," UPMC, accessed June 28, 2009, http://www.UPMC.com.

9. A. Palanjian, "Career Journal: Disasters Are Her Specialty," *Wall Street Journal*, April 7, 2009, B12.

10. S. McCartney, "The Middle Seat: Why Your Bags Aren't Better Off on Big Airline," *Wall Street Journal*, September 2, 2008, D1.

11. "2010 Census by the Numbers," U.S. Census Bureau News, March 8, 2010, accessed June 1, 2010, http://www.census.gov/newsroom/releases/pdf/cb10-ffse01.pdf.

12. "What is the WLCG?" CERN - the European Organization for Nuclear Research, accessed July 22, 2010, http://lcg.web.cern.ch/LCG/public/overview.htm.

13. "Carbonite Expands Boston Data Center," PressReleasePoint, November 2, 2009, accessed September 16, 2010, http://www.pressreleasepoint.com/carbonite-expands-boston-data-center-0.

14. M. Santosus, "Procter & Gamble's Enterprise Content Management (ECM) System," *CIO*, May 15, 2003, accessed September 12, 2008, http://www.cio.com/article/31920/Procter_Gamble_s_Enterprise_Content_Management_ECM_System; U. Kampffmeyer, "Trends in Records, Document and Enterprise Content Management," Whitepaper, S.E.R. conference, Vise-grad, September 28, 2004.

15. N. Clark, "Crash Spurs Interest in Real-Time Flight Data," *New York Times*, July 21, 2010, accessed July 29, 2010, http://www.nytimes.com/2010/07/22/business/global/22blackbox.html?_r=1&hp.

16. R. Smith, "Wireless Firms Eye 'Smart Grids'—Cellphone Carriers Cut Prices in Aggressive Push for Deals with Utilities," *Wall Street Journal*, April 16, 2009, B5.

17. S. Lubar, *Infoculture: The Smithsonian Book of Information Age Inventions* (Boston: Houghton, Mifflin, 1993).

18. Ibid.

19. A. Lavallee, "Unilever to Test Mobile Coupons—In Trial at Supermarket, Cellphones Will Be the Medium for Discount Offers," *Wall Street Journal*, May 29, 2009, B8.

20. B. Worthen, "Bar Codes on Steroids," *CIO*, December 15, 2002, 53.

21. M. Totty, "Technology (A Special Report)—Business Solutions," *Wall Street Journal*, June 2, 2009, R13.

22. M. Stone, "Scanning for Business," *PC Magazine*, May 10, 2005, 117.

23. N. Rubenking, "Hidden Messages," *PC Magazine*, May 22, 2001, 86.

24. A. Carter and D. Beucke, "A Good Neighbor Gets Better," *BusinessWeek*, June 20, 2005, 16.

25. N. Rubenking, "Hidden Messages."

26. G. Saitz, "Naked Truth—Data Miners, Who Taught Retailers to Stock Beer Near Diapers, Find Hidden Sales Trends, a Science That's Becoming Big

Business," *Star-Ledger*, August 1, 2002, 041.

27. J. Brustein, "Star Pitchers in a Duel? Tickets Will Cost More," *New York Times*, June 27, 2010, accessed August 20, 2010, http://www.nytimes.com/2010/06/28/technology/28tickets.html.

28. C. Duhigg, "What Does Your Credit-Card Company Know About You?" *New York Times Magazine*, May 12, 2009, accessed June 16, 2010, http://www.nytimes.com/2009/05/17/magazine/17credit-t.html?pagewanted=1.

29. B. Gottesman and K. Karagiannis, "A False Sense of Security," *PC Magazine*, February 22, 2005, 72.

30. F. J. Derfler Jr., "Secure Your Network," *PC Magazine*, June 27, 2000, 183–200.

31. "Authentication," Webopedia.com, accessed September 12, 2008, http://www.webopedia.com/TERM/a/authentication.html.

32. "Authorization," Webopedia.com, accessed September 12, 2008, http://www.webopedia.com/TERM/a/authorization.html.

33. L. Seltzer, "Password Crackers," *PC Magazine*, February 12, 2002, 68.

34. "Gemalto Release OTP Device for Acccess to Amazon's Web Services," DigalIDNews, September 10, 2010, accessed May 29, 2010, http://www.digitalidnews.com/2009/09/10/gemalto-releases-otp-device-for-access-to-amazons-web-services.

35. J. N. Hoover, "Stolen VA Laptop Contains Personal Data," *InformationWeek*, May 14, 2010, accessed May 28, 2010, http://www.informationweek.com/news/government/security/showArticle.jhtml?articleID=224800060.

36. C. Metz, "Total Security," *PC Magazine*, October 1, 2003, 83.

37. J. DeAvila, "Wi-Fi Users, Beware: Hot Spots are Weak Spots," *Wall Street Journal*, January 16, 2008, D1.

38. J. van den Hoven, "Executive Support Systems and Decision Making," *Journal of Systems Management* 47, no. 8 (March–April 1996): 48.

39. "Business Objects Customers Take Off with Performance Management; Management Dashboards Help Organizations Gain Insight and Optimize Performance," *Business Wire*, April 4, 2005.

40. "Intranet," Webopedia.com, accessed August 26, 2010, http://www.webopedia.com/TERM/i/intranet.html.

41. J. Ericson, "The Hillman Group Leverages Consolidated Reporting, Geographic Analysis to Support Its Hardware Manufacturing/Distribution Leadership," *Business Intelligence Review*, March 1, 2007, 12.

42. "Web Services," Webopedia, accessed April 16, 2009, http://www.webopedia.com/TERM/W/Web_Services.html.

43. M. Garry and J. Gallagher, "Food Lion Expands Data-Sharing Program," *Supermarket News*, November 10, 2008, 28.

44. Ibid.

45. "Extranet," Webopedia.com, accessed September 12, 2008, http://www.webopedia.com/TERM/E/extranet.html.

46. S. Hamm, D. Welch, W. Zellner, F. Keenan, and F. Engardio, "Down but Hardly Out: Downturn Be Damned, Companies Are Still Anxious to Expand Online," *BusinessWeek*, March 26, 2001, 126.

47. J. C. Radley, "Blockbuster Closes Stores and Adds Blockbuster Express Kiosks," Examiner.com, September 16, 2009, accessed July 5, 2010, http://www.examiner.com/x-22738-New-Haven-Movie-Examiner~y2009m9d16-Blockbuster-to-close-over-900-stores-and-add-Blockbuster-Express-kiosks.

48. S. Hamm, D. Welch, W. Zellner, F. Keenan, and F. Engardio, "Down but Hardly Out."

49. K. C. Laudon and J. P. Laudon, *Management Information Systems: Organization and Technology* (Upper Saddle River, NJ: Prentice Hall, 1996).

50. J. Borzo, "Software for Symptoms," *Wall Street Journal*, May 23, 2005, R10.

51. Ibid.

52. R. Hernandez, "American Express Authorizer's Assistant," *Business Rules Journal*, accessed September 12, 2008, http://www.bizrules.com/page/art_amexaa.htm.

Chapter 18

1. "Ryanair Celebrates 20 Years of Operations," Ryanair.com, May 31, 2005, accessed September 12, 2008, http://www.ryanair.com/site/EN/news.php?yr=05&month=may&story=reg-en-310505; "Ryanair Back in Black with €319m Profit," InsideIreland.ie, June 1, 2010, accessed July 29, 2010, http://www.insideireland.ie/index.cfm/section/news/ext/ryanair016/category/1062.

2. B. Baker, "America's Best Drive-Thru 2008 Is . . . Chick-fil-A! (Again)," *QSR Magazine*, accessed August 2, 2009, http://www.qsrmagazine.com/reports.

3. M. Richtel, "The Long-Distance Journey of a Fast-Food Order," *New York Times,* April 11, 2006, accessed September 12, 2008, http://www.nytimes.com/2006/04/11/technology/11fast.html?ei=5090&en=fba08e17788e24c9&ex=1302408000&pagewanted=all.

4. "Employment Cost Index News Release Text," Bureau of Labor Statistics, July 31, 2008, accessed September 12, 2008, http://www.bls.gov/news.release/eci.nr0.htm; "Productivity and Costs, Second Quarter 2008 Revised," Bureau of Labor Statistics, September 4, 2008, accessed September 12, 2008, http://www.bls.gov/news.release/prod2.nr0.htm.

5. "HINC-03. People in Households—Households, by Total Money Income in 2003, Age, Race, and Hispanic Origin of Householder," U.S. Census Bureau, accessed September 12, 2008, http://pubdb3.census.gov/macro/032004/hhinc/new03_001.htm.

6. "Historical Income Tables—Families: Table F-23—Families by Total Money Income, Race, and Hispanic Origin of Householder: 1967 to 2007," U.S. Census Bureau, accessed September 1, 2009, http://www.census.gov/hhes/www/income/data/historical/families/f23.xls.

7. M. Baily and M. Slaughter, "What's Behind the Recent Productivity Slowdown," *Wall Street Journal*, December 13, 2008, A15.

8. "Employment Projections, Table 1: Civilian Labor Force by Sex, Age, Race, and Hispanic Origin, 1986, 1996, 2006, and Projected 2016," *U.S. Bureau of Labor Statistics*, December 4 , 2007, accessed September 9, 2009, http://www.bls.gov.

9. "Key Development Data and Statistics: United States Data Profile," WorldBank, accessed September 9, 2009, http://web.worldbank.org.

10. "Lenovo IdeaPad S Series Netbook," accessed August 1, 2010, http://shop.lenovo.com/us/notebooks/ideapad/s-series; "Product Fact Sheet," accessed August 1, 2010, http://www-03.ibm.com/ibm/history/exhibits/pc25/pc25_fact.html.

11. R. Harbour and M. Hill, "Productivity Gap Narrows across North America and Europe," *Harbour Report*, accessed August 2, 2009, http://www.theharbourreport.com/index2.jsp (also see http://www.oliverwyman.com/ow/pdf_files/2_Productivity_Gap_Narrows_Across_North_America_and_Europe.pdf).

12. "Profiled International—America's Most Productive Companies," *Drug Week*, May 15, 2009, 265; "America's Most Productive Companies," accessed August 2, 2009, http://www.americasmostproductive.com.

13. "Study: Automakers Initial Quality Improves Considerably," *Quality Digest*, accessed August 2, 2009, http://www.qualitydigest.com; "2008 Initial Quality Study Results," accessed August 2, 2009, http://www.jdpower.com/autos/articles/2008-Initial-Quality-Study-Results.

14. "Embattled U.S. Automakers Make Substantial Gains in Initial Quality, Outpacing Industry-Wide Improvement," J.D. Power and Associates, June 22, 2009, accessed September 10, 2009, http://www.jdpower.com.

15. "Basic Concepts," American Society for Quality, accessed September 15, 2008, http://www.asq.org/glossary/q.html.

16. R. E. Markland, S. K. Vickery, and R. A. Davis, "Managing Quality," in *Operations Management: Concepts in Manufacturing and Services* (Cincinnati, OH: South-Western College Publishing, 1998).

17. REVA Electric Car Company, accessed August 2, 2009, http://www.revaindia.com.

18. "New Industrial LCD Panels with 100,000 Hour MTBF LED Backlight Systems from Toshiba America Electronic Components," *Your Industry News*, August 26, 2009, accessed September 12, 2009, http://www.yourindustrynews.com.

19. L. L. Berry and A. Parasuraman, *Marketing Services* (New York: Free Press, 1991).

20. "FAQs—General," International Organization for Standardization, accessed July 2, 2005, http://www.iso.org/iso/en/faqs/faq-general.html.

21. "ISO 9000 and ISO 14000," International Organization for Standardization,

accessed September 15, 2008, http://
www.iso.org/iso/iso_catalogue
/management_standards/iso_9000
_iso_14000.htm.

22. J. Briscoe, S. Fawcett, and R. Todd, "The Implementation and Impact of ISO 9000 among Small Manufacturing Enterprises," *Journal of Small Business Management* 43 (July 1, 2005): 309.

23. R. Henkoff, "The Not New Seal of Quality (ISO 9000 Standard of Quality Management)," *Fortune*, June 28, 1993, 116.

24. "Frequently Asked Questions about the Malcolm Baldrige National Quality Award," National Institute of Standards & Technology, accessed September 15, 2008, http://www.nist.gov/baldrige /publications/criteria.cfm.

25. Ibid.

26. Ibid.

27. "Criteria for Performance Excellence," Baldrige National Quality Program 2008, accessed September 15, 2008, http:// www.nist.gov/baldrige/publications /criteria.cfm.

28. Ibid.

29. Ibid.

30. "NIST Stock Studies Show Quality Pays (Baldrige National Quality Award)," National Institute of Standards & Technology, accessed July 2, 2005, http://www .quality.nist.gov/Stock_Studies.htm.

31. J. W. Dean Jr., and J. Evans, *Total Quality: Management, Organization, and Strategy* (St. Paul, MN: West Publishing Co., 1994).

32. J. W. Dean Jr., and D. E. Bowen, "Management Theory and Total Quality: Improving Research and Practice through Theory Development," *Academy of Management Review* 19 (1994): 392–418.

33. R. Allen and R. Kilmann, "Aligning Reward Practices in Support of Total Quality Management," *Business Horizons*, May 1, 2001, 77.

34. D. J. DeNoon, "Tylenol Recall Expands," WebMD, December 29, 2009, accessed July 10, 2010, http://arthritis.webmd .com/news/20091229/tylenol-recall -expands.

35. L. Layton, "Johnson & Johnson Division Recalls 43 OTC Medicines for Infants and Children," *Washington Post*, May 2, 2010, accessed July 11, 2010, http://www.washingtonpost.com

/wp-dyn/content/article/2010/05/01 /AR2010050103051.html.

36. "Better Teamwork When Doctors Discuss Cases," UPI.com, July 12, 2010, accessed July 15, 2010, http://www.upi .com/Health_News/2010/07/12/Better -teamwork-when-doctors-discuss-cases /UPI-81301278992189/.

37. "Table 647. Gross Domestic Product in Current and Real (2000) Dollars by Type of Product and Sector; 1990 to 2007," *The 2009 Statistical Abstract*, U.S. Census Bureau, accessed September 12, 2009, http://www.census.gov.

38. R. Hallowell, L. A. Schlesinger, and J. Zornitsky, "Internal Service Quality, Customer and Job Satisfaction: Link-ages and Implications for Management," *Human Resource Planning* 19 (1996): 20–31; J. L. Heskett, T. O. Jones, G. W. Loveman, W. E. Sasser Jr., and L. A. Schlesinger, "Putting the Service-Profit Chain to Work," *Harvard Business Review* (March–April 1994): 164–174.

39. "Unusual Perks," *Fortune*, January 29, 2009, accessed September 13, 2010, http://money.cnn.com/galleries/2009 /fortune/0901/gallery.unusual_perks .fortune/index.html.

40. R. Eder, "Customer-Easy Doesn't Come Easy," *Drug Store News*, October 21, 2002, 52.

41. G. Brewer, "The Ultimate Guide to Winning Customers: The Customer Stops Here," *Sales & Marketing Management* 150 (March 1998): 30; F. F. Reichheld, *The Loyalty Effect: The Hidden Force behind Growth, Profits, and Lasting Value*, (Cambridge, MA: Harvard Business School Press, 2001).

42. L. L. Berry and A. Parasuraman, "Listening to the Customer—The Concept of a Service-Quality Information System," *Sloan Management Review* 38, no. 3 (Spring 1997): 65; C. W. L. Hart, J. L. Heskett, and W. E. Sasser Jr., "The Profitable Art of Service Recovery," *Harvard Business Review* (July–August 1990): 148–156.

43. D. Stanley, "When Flight Diverted, Crew Ordered Pizza for Passengers," *Denver News*, May 21, 2010, accessed July 7, 2010, http://www.thedenverchannel.com /news/23620842/detail.html.

44. D. E. Bowen and E. E. Lawler III, "The Empowerment of Service Workers: What, Why, How, and When," *Sloan Management Review* 33 (Spring 1992):

31–39; D. E. Bowen and E. E. Lawler III, "Empowering Service Employees," *Sloan Management Review* 36 (Summer 1995): 73–84.

45. D. E. Bowen and E. E. Lawler III, "The Empowerment of Service Workers: What, Why, How, and When."

46. "The Way I Work: Marc Lore of Diapers. com," Inc.com, September 1, 2009, accessed September 2, 2010, http://www .inc.com/magazine/20090901/the-way -i-work-marc-lore-of-diaperscom.html.

47. G. V. Frazier and M. T. Spiggs, "Achieving Competitive Advantage through Group Technology," *Business Horizons* 39 (1996): 83–88.

48. "The Top 100 Beverage Companies: The List," *Beverage Industry*, July 2001, 30.

49. "Job Shop Hits Bull's Eye with Multitasking," *Manufacturing Engineering* (November 2008): 43–105.

50. D. Wakabayashi, "Gadget Appetite Strains Suppliers," *Wall Street Journal*, July 15, 2010, B1–2.

51. P. Ziobro, "After 10 Million Ribs, Burger King Begins to Run Out," *Wall Street Journal*, June 11, 2010, http://online .wsj.com/article/SB1000142405274 87036277045752987003298255 56 .html?KEYWORDS=burger+king.

52. D. Drickhamer, "Reality Check," *Industry Week*, November 2001, 29.

53. D. Drickhamer, "Zeroing In on World-Class," *Industry Week*, November 2001, 36.

54. J. Zeiler, "The Need for Speed," *Operations & Fulfillment*, April 1, 2004, 38.

55. "Efficient Foodservice Response (EFR)," accessed August 3, 2009, http://www .ifdaonline.org/webarticles.

56. J. R. Henry, "Minimized Setup Will Make Your Packaging Line S.M.I.L.E.," *Packaging Technology & Engineering*, February 1, 1998, 24.

57. J. Donoghue, "The Future Is Now," *Air Transport World*, April 1, 2001, 78.

58. N. Shirouzu, "Why Toyota Wins Such High Marks on Quality Surveys," *Wall Street Journal*, March 15, 2001, A1.

59. Ibid.

60. G. Gruman, "Supply on Demand; Manufacturers Need to Know What's Selling before They Can Produce and Deliver Their Wares in the Right Quantities," *Info World*, April 18, 2005.

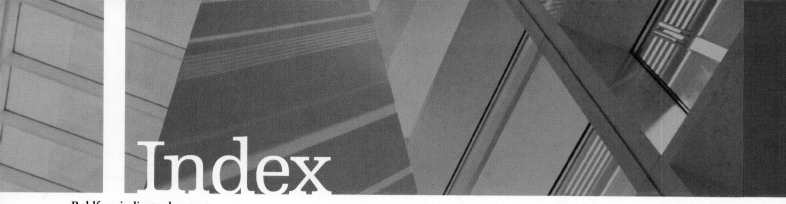

Index

Boldface indicates key term.

A

"A" decisions, 273
AB InBev, 49
Abbott Laboratories, 146
ABC, 49
Ability, 242
ABM Industries, 200, 201
Absenteeism, 225
Absolute comparison, 91
Abstract decision rules, 274
Academy of Management Executive, 23
Access and legitimacy paradigm of diversity, 235
Accommodation Assessment Teams, 232
Accommodation, structural, 191
Accommodative strategy, 77, 78
Accountability, 167, 168
Accounting and writing, invention of, 23
Accounting for Dummies, 314
Accounting the Easy Way, 314
Accurate information, 324
Accu-Screen, Inc., 206
Ace, 336
Acer, 104, 105, 116
Achievement needs, 242
Achievement-oriented leadership, 270, 271, 272
Acquisition, 108
Acquisition costs, 325
Action plan, 84
Active listening, 295
Activision Blizzard, 48
Adams, Ed, 235
Adaptability, 55
Adaptability screening, 155
Adaptation, 144
Adaptive organizations, 158–177
Addessi, Richard and Joan, 65, 66, 68, 69
Adidas, 53
Adobe PDF documents, 328
Advantage, competitive, 121
Advantage, discompetitive, 121
Adverse impact, 200
Advertisement, 204
Advertising, 51
Advise, 166
Advocacy groups, 50, 51
Adware, 331
AeroMechanical Services, 326
Aetna, 235
Affective conflict (a-type conflict), 95, 188, 189
Affiliation needs, 242
Affirmative action, 223, 224, 225
Aflac, 247
Africa, 146

Age discrimination, 198, 205, 223, 226, 227, 232, 235
discrimination, 199, 200
discrimination in training, 211
Age Discrimination in Employment Act of 1967, 199, 205
Aggression, 62
Agreeableness, 233
Agreements, trade, 143–144
AI decision style, 274
AIDS/HIV, 205
AII decision style, 274
Air France Flight 447, 326
Air Lease Corporation, 148
Air Products & Chemicals, 168, 169
Air Transport Association, 325
Airbus, 139
Airline industry, 42
Akraya, 47
Albaugh, Jim, 193
Albemarle Paper Co. v. Moody, 203
Albrecht, Chris, 73
Alderfer's ERG Theory, 242, 243
al-Farabi, 22
All (laundry detergent), 78
Allaire, Paul A., 239
Alliances, strategic, 146–147
Alteon WebSystems, 94
Amazon, 86, 102, 115, 116
Ambassador Bridge, 142
Amelio, Bill, 149
American Airlines, 248, 306, 325
American Beverage Association (ABA), 50
American Civil Rights Institute, 225
American Council of the Blind, 232
American Express card, 339
transaction processing system, 339
American Federation of Teachers, 216
American Honda, *see* Honda
American Hospital Association, 52
American Humane Association, 51
American National Standards Institute, 345
American Society for Quality, 345
American Society for Training and Development, 210, 213
American Society of Mechanical Engineers, 27
Americans with Disabilities Act of 1990, 199, 205, 231
Americans, Asian, black, Hispanic, Native, white, 223, 225
Amie Street, 101
Amount of processing in manufacturing operations, 350
AMP, 155
Analysis, situational, 102
Analyzers, 114
Andean Community, 143
Andrew, Jim, 12
Anheuser-Busch, 49

Antivirus software
corporate, 333
for PCs and email servers, 332, 333
Antonio's in Las Vegas, 324
A-Power Energy Generation Systems, 145
Apple, Inc., 11, 42, 53, 99–101, 113, 175, 315, 352
Applebee's, 115
Appleton Papers, Inc., 290
Applets, 331
Applicant selection, 204
Application forms, 204–206
Aptitude tests (specific ability tests), 207
Archer Daniels Midland, 229
ARCOS, Inc., 218
Ardila, Jaime, 164
Are We There Yet?, 226
Argentina, 143
Armed Forces Reserve, discrimination, 199
Arpey, Gerard, 306
Arrest records, 205
Arrivers, 14
Arrow Energy Ltd., 147
Arroyo, Raymond, 235
Artifacts
symbolic, 56, 57
visible, 57
Artisans, 22
ASCII (American Standard Code for Information Interchange), 328
Asda, 110
Asia, 141, 143, 146, 151
Asia-Pacific Economic Cooperation (APEC), 141, 143
Asian Americans, 223, 230
Assemble-to-order operation, 350
Assessment center, 208
Associated Press (AP), 11, 130
Association for Information and Image Management, 326
Association of Southeast Asian Nations (ASEAN), 141, 143
Association or affinity patterns, 329, 330
Assurance, 345
AT&T, 4, 14, 35, 47, 53, 106
Atlassian, 245
Attack, 115
Attensity Corporation, 48
Attention, 284
Attitudes, 227, 232
Attribution, 286
Attribution theory, 285
A-type conflict (affective conflict), 95
Australia, 143, 231
Austria, 141
Authentication, 332
Authority, 33, 166, 168, 174, 183, 184

centralized, 168, 72
Chester Barnard, 34
decentralized, 172
delegation of, 167–168
line, 166–167
organizational, 166–169
and responsibility, 31
staff, 166–167
Authority-compliance management style, 266
Authorization, 332
Authorizer's Assistant, 339
Autocratic decision rules, 273
Autocratic decisions (AI or AII), 273
AutoDesk, 280
AutoLinQ, 114
Autonomy, 171, 182, 183, 189
Average aggregate inventory, 353
Avero's Slingshot software, 324
Avoidance learning, 254
Avoidance strategy of political risk, 151
Avon, 86, 87, 201, 228
Awareness training, 238
Axcelis Technologies, 154, 155
Aziz, Gamal, 265

B

"B" decisions, 273
BA, 72
Baby boomers, 223, 227, 288
Background checks, 206–207
Background questions, interviews, 209
Bahrain, 152
Balance sheets, 313
Balanced scorecard, 311
Southwest Airlines', 312
Baldrige National Quality Award, 346
criteria for, 347
Ball Park, 160
Ballmer, Steve, 167
Bambi, 131
Banana Republic, 90
Banking system, 51
Bankruptcy, 129
Banner, David, 52
Baptist Health South Florida, 349
Bar code, 327
Barbarigo, 22
Bargaining power of buyers, 112
Bargaining power of suppliers, 112
Barnard, Chester, 34, 35
Barnes & Noble, 53, 115, 116
Barnes, Brenda, 263
Barriers
to change, 132
nontariff, 139
tariff and nontariff, 145
trade, 138–140, 143–144, 152

Review 1

Learning Outcomes

Each Review Card contains summaries for the Learning Outcomes in order by chapter section.

REVIEW 1 Management Is . . .

Good management is working through others to accomplish tasks that help fulfill organizational objectives as efficiently as possible.

REVIEW 2 Management Functions

Henri Fayol's classic management functions are known today as planning, organizing, leading, and controlling. Planning is determining organizational goals and a means for achieving them. Organizing is deciding where decisions will be made, who will do what jobs and tasks, and who will work for whom. Leading is inspiring and motivating workers to work hard to achieve organizational goals. Controlling is monitoring progress toward goal achievement and taking corrective action when needed. Studies show that performing the management functions well leads to better managerial performance.

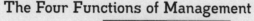

The Four Functions of Management

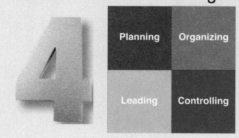

Planning Organizing

Leading Controlling

© iStockphoto.com/blackred

REVIEW 3 Kinds of Managers

There are four different kinds of managers. Top [managers are responsible for creating] a context for change, developing attitudes of co[mmitment and ownership, creating] a positive organizational culture through words a[nd actions, and monitoring their] companies' business environments. Middle managers are responsible for planning and allocating resources, coordinating and linking groups and departments, monitoring and managing the performance of subunits and managers, and implementing the changes or strategies generated by top managers. First-line managers are responsible for managing the performance of nonmanagerial employees, teaching entry-level employees how to do their jobs, and making detailed schedules and operating plans based on middle management's intermediate-range plans. Team leaders are responsible for facilitating team performance, fostering good relationships among team members, and managing external relationships.

Graphics from the chapter are often used as memory prompts to help you recall the information in the written summary.

REVIEW 4 Managerial Roles

Managers perform interpersonal, informational, and decisional roles in their jobs. In fulfilling interpersonal roles, managers act as figureheads by performing ceremonial duties, as leaders by motivating and encouraging workers, and as liaisons by dealing with people outside their units. In performing informational roles, managers act as monitors by scanning their environment for information, as disseminators by sharing information with others in their companies, and as spokespeople by sharing information with people outside their departments or companies. In fulfilling decisional roles, managers act as entrepreneurs by adapting their units to change, as disturbance handlers by responding to larger problems that demand immediate action, as resource allocators by deciding resource recipients and amounts, and as negotiators by bargaining with others about schedules, projects, goals, outcomes, and resources.

Key Terms

Management getting work done through others

Efficiency getting work done with a minimum of effort, expense, or waste

Effectiveness accomplishing tasks that help fulfill organizational objectives

Planning (management function) determining organizational goals and a means for achieving them

Organizing deciding where decisions will be made, who will do what jobs and tasks, and who will work for whom

Leading inspiring and motivating workers to work hard to achieve organizational goals

Controlling monitoring progress toward goal achie[vement and taking] correc[tive] action w[hen needed]

Key Terms from the chapter's margins appear in this column (and continue on the back of the card) in the same order in which they appear in the chapter.

Top ma[nagers] [responsib]le for the over[all...]

Middle [managers respon]sible for [...] [w]ith top man[agers ...] and impl[ement...] [for] achievin[g...]

First-li[ne managers ...] [w]ho train and s[upervise ...] of nonmanagerial employees who are directly responsible for producing the company's products or services

Team leaders managers responsible for facilitating team activities toward accomplishing a goal

Figurehead role the interpersonal role managers play when they perform ceremonial duties

Leader role the interpersonal role managers play when they motivate and encourage workers to accomplish organizational objectives

Liaison role the interpersonal role managers play when they deal with people outside their units

Monitor role the informational role managers play when they scan their environment for information

Disseminator role the informational role managers play when they share information with others in their departments or companies

Spokesperson role the informational role managers play when they share information with people outside their departments or companies

Entrepreneur role the decisional role managers play when they adapt themselves, their subordinates, and their units to change

Disturbance handler role the decisional role managers play when they respond to severe problems that demand immediate action

Resource allocator role the decisional role managers play when they decide who gets what resources and in what amounts

Negotiator role the decisional role managers play when they negotiate schedules, projects, goals, outcomes, resources, and employee raises

Technical skills the specialized procedures, techniques, and knowledge required to get the job done

Human skills the ability to work well with others

Conceptual skills the ability to see the organization as a whole, understand how the different parts affect each other, and recognize how the company fits into or is affected by its environment

Motivation to manage an assessment of how enthusiastic employees are about managing the work of others

---

How to Use this Card:

1. Look over the card to preview the new concepts you'll be introduced to in the chapter.

2. Read the chapter to fully understand the material.

3. Go to class (and pay attention).

4. Review the card one more time to make sure you've registered the key concepts.

5. Don't forget, this card is only one of many MGMT learning tools available to help you succeed in your management course.

REVIEW 5 · What Companies Look for in Managers

Companies do not want one-dimensional managers. They want managers with a balance of skills. Managers need the knowledge and abilities to get the job done (technical skills), must be able to work effectively in groups and be good listeners and communicators (human skills), must be able to assess the relationships between the different parts of their companies and the external environment and position their companies for success (conceptual skills), and should want to assume positions of leadership and power (motivation to manage). Technical skills are most important for lower-level managers, human skills are equally important at all levels of management, and conceptual skills and motivation to manage increase in importance as managers rise through the managerial ranks.

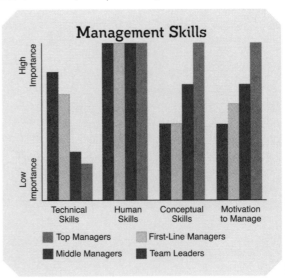

© Cengage Learning 2011

REVIEW 6 · Mistakes Managers Make

Another way to understand what it takes to be a manager is to look at the top mistakes managers make. Five of the most important mistakes made by managers are being abrasive and intimidating; being cold, aloof, or arrogant; betraying trust; being overly ambitious; and failing to deal with specific performance problems of the business.

REVIEW 7 · The Transition to Management: The First Year

Managers often begin their jobs by using more formal authority and less people management skill. However, most managers find that being a manager has little to do with "bossing" their subordinates. According to a study of managers in their first year, after six months on the job, the managers were surprised by the fast pace and heavy workload and by the fact that "helping" their subordinates was viewed as interference. After a year on the job, most of the managers had come to think of themselves not as doers but as managers who get things done through others. And, because they finally realized that people management was the most important part of their job, most of them had abandoned their authoritarian approach for one based on communication, listening, and positive reinforcement.

REVIEW 8 · Competitive Advantage through People

Why does management matter? Well-managed companies are competitive because their workforces are smarter, better trained, more motivated, and more committed. Furthermore, companies that practice good management consistently have greater sales revenues, profits, and stock market performance than companies that don't. Finally, good management matters because good management leads to satisfied employees who, in turn, provide better service to customers. Because employees tend to treat customers the same way that their managers treat them, good management can improve customer satisfaction.

Review 1

Learning Outcomes

REVIEW 1 Management Is . . .

Good management is working through others to accomplish tasks that help fulfill organizational objectives as efficiently as possible.

REVIEW 2 Management Functions

Henri Fayol's classic management functions are known today as planning, organizing, leading, and controlling. Planning is determining organizational goals and a means for achieving them. Organizing is deciding where decisions will be made, who will do what jobs and tasks, and who will work for whom. Leading is inspiring and motivating workers to work hard to achieve organizational goals. Controlling is monitoring progress toward goal achievement and taking corrective action when needed. Studies show that performing the management functions well leads to better managerial performance.

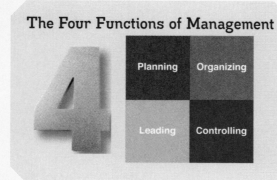

The Four Functions of Management

Planning · Organizing · Leading · Controlling

© iStockphoto.com/blackred

REVIEW 3 Kinds of Managers

There are four different kinds of managers. Top managers are responsible for creating a context for change, developing attitudes of commitment and ownership, creating a positive organizational culture through words and actions, and monitoring their companies' business environments. Middle managers are responsible for planning and allocating resources, coordinating and linking groups and departments, monitoring and managing the performance of subunits and managers, and implementing the changes or strategies generated by top managers. First-line managers are responsible for managing the performance of nonmanagerial employees, teaching entry-level employees how to do their jobs, and making detailed schedules and operating plans based on middle management's intermediate-range plans. Team leaders are responsible for facilitating team performance, fostering good relationships among team members, and managing external relationships.

REVIEW 4 Managerial Roles

Managers perform interpersonal, informational, and decisional roles in their jobs. In fulfilling interpersonal roles, managers act as figureheads by performing ceremonial duties, as leaders by motivating and encouraging workers, and as liaisons by dealing with people outside their units. In performing informational roles, managers act as monitors by scanning their environment for information, as disseminators by sharing information with others in their companies, and as spokespeople by sharing information with people outside their departments or companies. In fulfilling decisional roles, managers act as entrepreneurs by adapting their units to change, as disturbance handlers by responding to larger problems that demand immediate action, as resource allocators by deciding resource recipients and amounts, and as negotiators by bargaining with others about schedules, projects, goals, outcomes, and resources.

Key Terms

Management getting work done through others

Efficiency getting work done with a minimum of effort, expense, or waste

Effectiveness accomplishing tasks that help fulfill organizational objectives

Planning (management function) determining organizational goals and a means for achieving them

Organizing deciding where decisions will be made, who will do what jobs and tasks, and who will work for whom

Leading inspiring and motivating workers to work hard to achieve organizational goals

Controlling monitoring progress toward goal achievement and taking corrective action when needed

Top managers executives responsible for the overall direction of the organization

Middle managers managers responsible for setting objectives consistent with top management's goals and for planning and implementing subunit strategies for achieving those objectives

First-line managers managers who train and supervise the performance of nonmanagerial employees who are directly responsible for producing the company's products or services

Team leaders managers responsible for facilitating team activities toward accomplishing a goal

Figurehead role the interpersonal role managers play when they perform ceremonial duties

Leader role the interpersonal role managers play when they motivate and encourage workers to accomplish organizational objectives

Liaison role the interpersonal role managers play when they deal with people outside their units

Monitor role the informational role managers play when they scan their environment for information

Disseminator role the informational role managers play when they share information with others in their departments or companies

Spokesperson role the informational role managers play when they share information with people outside their departments or companies

Entrepreneur role the decisional role managers play when they adapt themselves, their subordinates, and their units to change

Disturbance handler role the decisional role managers play when they respond to severe problems that demand immediate action

Resource allocator role the decisional role managers play when they decide who gets what resources and in what amounts

Negotiator role the decisional role managers play when they negotiate schedules, projects, goals, outcomes, resources, and employee raises

Technical skills the specialized procedures, techniques, and knowledge required to get the job done

Human skills the ability to work well with others

Conceptual skills the ability to see the organization as a whole, understand how the different parts affect each other, and recognize how the company fits into or is affected by its environment

Motivation to manage an assessment of how enthusiastic employees are about managing the work of others

REVIEW 5 What Companies Look for in Managers

Companies do not want one-dimensional managers. They want managers with a balance of skills. Managers need the knowledge and abilities to get the job done (technical skills), must be able to work effectively in groups and be good listeners and communicators (human skills), must be able to assess the relationships between the different parts of their companies and the external environment and position their companies for success (conceptual skills), and should want to assume positions of leadership and power (motivation to manage). Technical skills are most important for lower-level managers, human skills are equally important at all levels of management, and conceptual skills and motivation to manage increase in importance as managers rise through the managerial ranks.

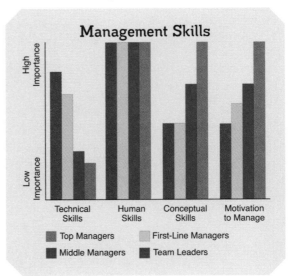

© Cengage Learning 2011

REVIEW 6 Mistakes Managers Make

Another way to understand what it takes to be a manager is to look at the top mistakes managers make. Five of the most important mistakes made by managers are being abrasive and intimidating; being cold, aloof, or arrogant; betraying trust; being overly ambitious; and failing to deal with specific performance problems of the business.

REVIEW 7 The Transition to Management: The First Year

Managers often begin their jobs by using more formal authority and less people management skill. However, most managers find that being a manager has little to do with "bossing" their subordinates. According to a study of managers in their first year, after six months on the job, the managers were surprised by the fast pace and heavy workload and by the fact that "helping" their subordinates was viewed as interference. After a year on the job, most of the managers had come to think of themselves not as doers but as managers who get things done through others. And, because they finally realized that people management was the most important part of their job, most of them had abandoned their authoritarian approach for one based on communication, listening, and positive reinforcement.

REVIEW 8 Competitive Advantage through People

Why does management matter? Well-managed companies are competitive because their workforces are smarter, better trained, more motivated, and more committed. Furthermore, companies that practice good management consistently have greater sales revenues, profits, and stock market performance than companies that don't. Finally, good management matters because good management leads to satisfied employees who, in turn, provide better service to customers. Because employees tend to treat customers the same way that their managers treat them, good management can improve customer satisfaction.

Chapter 2

Review 2

Learning Outcomes

REVIEW 1 The Origins of Management

Management as a field of study is just 125 years old, but management ideas and practices have actually been used since 5000 BCE. From ancient Sumeria to 16th-century Europe, there are historical antecedents for each of the functions of management discussed in this textbook: planning, organizing, leading, and controlling. However, there was no compelling need for managers until systematic changes in the nature of work and organizations occurred during the last two centuries. As work shifted from families to factories; from skilled laborers to specialized, unskilled laborers; from small, self-organized groups to large factories employing thousands under one roof; and from unique, small batches of production to standardized mass production; managers were needed to impose order and structure, to motivate and direct large groups of workers, and to plan and make decisions that optimized overall performance by effectively coordinating the different parts of an organizational system.

REVIEW 2 Scientific Management

Scientific management involves studying and testing different work methods to identify the best, most efficient way to complete a job. According to Frederick W. Taylor, the father of scientific management, managers should follow four scientific management principles. First, study each element of work to determine the one best way to do it. Second, scientifically select, train, teach, and develop workers to reach their full potential. Third, cooperate with employees to ensure that the scientific principles are implemented. Fourth, divide the work and the responsibility equally between management and workers. Above all, Taylor felt these principles could be used to align managers and employees by determining a fair day's work, what an average worker could produce at a reasonable pace, and a fair day's pay (what management should pay workers for that effort). Taylor felt that incentives were one of the best ways to align management and employees.

Frank and Lillian Gilbreth are best known for their use of motion studies to simplify work. Whereas Taylor used time study to determine a fair day's work based on how long it took a "first-class man" to complete each part of his job, Frank Gilbreth used film cameras and microchronometers to conduct motion studies to improve efficiency by eliminating unnecessary or repetitive motions. Henry Gantt is best known for the Gantt chart, which graphically indicates when a series of tasks must be completed to perform a job or project, but he also developed ideas regarding worker training (all workers should be trained and their managers should be rewarded for training them).

REVIEW 3 Bureaucratic and Administrative Management

Today, we associate bureaucracy with inefficiency and red tape. Yet, German sociologist Max Weber thought that bureaucracy—that is, running organizations on the basis of knowledge, fairness, and logical rules and procedures—would accomplish organizational goals much more efficiently than monarchies and patriarchies, where decisions were based on personal or family connections, personal gain, and arbitrary decision making. Bureaucracies are characterized by seven elements: qualification-based hiring; merit-based promotion; chain of command; division of labor; impartial application of rules and procedures; recording rules, procedures, and decisions in writing; and separating managers from owners. Nonetheless, bureaucracies are often inefficient and can be highly resistant to change.

The Frenchman Henri Fayol, whose ideas were shaped by his more than 20 years of experience as a CEO, is best known for developing five management functions (planning,

Key Terms

Scientific management thoroughly studying and testing different work methods to identify the best, most efficient way to complete a job

Soldiering when workers deliberately slow their pace or restrict their work outputs

Rate buster a group member whose work pace is significantly faster than the normal pace in his or her group

Motion study breaking each task or job into its separate motions and then eliminating those that are unnecessary or repetitive

Time study timing how long it takes good workers to complete each part of their jobs

Gantt chart a graphic chart that shows which tasks must be completed at which times in order to complete a project or task

Bureaucracy the exercise of control on the basis of knowledge, expertise, or experience

Integrative conflict resolution an approach to dealing with conflict in which both parties deal with the conflict by indicating their preferences and then working together to find an alternative that meets the needs of both

Organization a system of consciously coordinated activities or forces created by two or more people

System a set of interrelated elements or parts that function as a whole

Subsystems smaller systems that operate within the context of a larger system

Synergy when two or more subsystems working together can produce more than they can working apart

Closed systems systems that can sustain themselves without interacting with their environments

Open systems systems that can sustain themselves only by interacting with their environments, on which they depend for their survival

Contingency approach holds that there are no universal management theories and that the most effective management theory or idea depends on the kinds of problems or situations that managers are facing at a particular time and place

organizing, coordinating, commanding, and controlling) and fourteen principles of management (division of work, authority and responsibility, discipline, unity of command, unity of direction, subordination of individual interests to the general interest, remuneration, centralization, scalar chain, order, equity, stability of tenure of personnel, initiative, and *esprit de corps*).

REVIEW 4 Human Relations Management

Unlike most people who view conflict as bad, Mary Parker Follett believed that it should be embraced rather than avoided. Of the three ways of dealing with conflict—domination, compromise, and integration—she argued that the latter was the best because it focuses on developing creative methods for meeting conflicting parties' needs.

Elton Mayo is best known for his role in the Hawthorne Studies at the Western Electric Company. In the first stage of the Hawthorne Studies, production went up because the increased attention paid to the workers in the study and their development into a cohesive work group led to significantly higher levels of job satisfaction and productivity. In the second stage, productivity dropped because the workers had already developed strong negative norms. The Hawthorne Studies demonstrated that workers' feelings and attitudes affected their work, that financial incentives weren't necessarily the most important motivator for workers, and that group norms and behavior played a critical role in behavior at work.

Chester Barnard, president of New Jersey Bell Telephone, emphasized the critical importance of willing cooperation in organizations. In general, Barnard argued that people will be indifferent to managerial directives or orders if they (1) are understood, (2) are consistent with the purpose of the organization, (3) are compatible with the people's personal interests, and (4) can actually be carried out by those people. Acceptance of managerial authority (i.e., cooperation) is not automatic, however.

REVIEW 5 Operations, Information, Systems, and Contingency Management

Operations management uses a quantitative or mathematical approach to find ways to increase productivity, improve quality, and manage or reduce costly inventories. The manufacture of standardized, interchangeable parts, the graphical and computerized design of parts, and the accidental discovery of just-in-time inventory systems were some of the most important historical events in operations management.

Throughout history, organizations have pushed for and quickly adopted new information technologies that reduce the cost or increase the speed with which they can acquire, store, retrieve, or communicate information. Historically, some of the most important technologies that have revolutionized information management were the creation of paper and the printing press in the 14th and 15th centuries, the manual typewriter in 1850, the cash register in 1879, the telephone in the 1880s, the personal computer in the 1980s, and the Internet in the 1990s.

A system is a set of interrelated elements or parts (subsystems) that function as a whole. Organizational systems obtain inputs from both general and specific environments. Managers and workers then use their management knowledge and manufacturing techniques to transform those inputs into outputs which, in turn, provide feedback to the organization. Organizational systems must also address the issues of synergy and open *versus* closed systems.

Finally, the contingency approach to management clearly states that there are no universal management theories. The most effective management theory or idea depends on the kinds of problems or situations that managers or organizations are facing at a particular time. This means that management is much harder than it looks.

Review | 3

Chapter 3
Organizational
Environments and
Cultures

Chapter 3

Learning Outcomes

REVIEW 1 Changing Environments

Environmental change, environmental complexity, and resource scarcity are the basic components of external environments. Environmental change is the variation in a company's general and specific environments. Environmental complexity is the number and intensity of factors in the external environment. Resource scarcity is the abundance or shortage of critical resources in the external environment. As the rate of environmental change increases, as the environment becomes more complex, and as resources become more scarce, managers become less confident that they can understand, predict, and effectively react to the trends affecting their businesses. According to punctuated equilibrium theory, companies experience long periods of stability followed by short periods of dynamic, fundamental change, followed by a return to stability.

REVIEW 2 General Environment

The general environment consists of trends that affect all organizations. Because the economy influences basic business decisions, managers often use economic statistics and business confidence indices to predict future economic activity. Changes in technology, which transforms inputs into outputs, can be a benefit or a threat to a business. Sociocultural trends, such as changing demographic characteristics, affect how companies run their businesses. Similarly, sociocultural changes in behavior, attitudes, and beliefs affect the demand for businesses' products and services. Court decisions and new federal and state laws have imposed much greater political/legal responsibility on companies. The best way to manage legal responsibilities is to educate managers and employees about laws and regulations as well as potential lawsuits that could affect a business.

General and Specific Environments

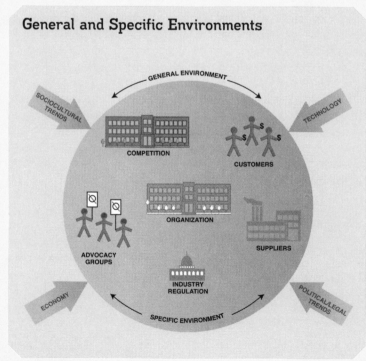

© Cengage Learning 2011

Key Terms

External environments all events outside a company that have the potential to influence or affect it

Environmental change the rate at which a company's general and specific environments change

Stable environment an environment in which the rate of change is slow

Dynamic environment an environment in which the rate of change is fast

Punctuated equilibrium theory a theory according to which companies go through long, simple periods of stability (equilibrium), followed by short periods of dynamic, fundamental change (revolution), and ending with a return to stability (new equilibrium)

Environmental complexity the number of external factors in the environment that affect organizations

Simple environment an environment with few environmental factors

Complex environment an environment with many environmental factors

Resource scarcity the abundance or shortage of critical organizational resources in an organization's external environment

Uncertainty the extent to which managers can understand or predict which environmental changes and trends will affect their businesses

General environment the economic, technological, sociocultural, and political trends that indirectly affect all organizations

Specific environment the customers, competitors, suppliers, industry regulations, and advocacy groups that are unique to an industry and directly affect how a company does business

Business confidence indices indices that show managers' level of confidence about future business growth

Technology the knowledge, tools, and techniques used to transform input into output

Competitors companies in the same industry that sell similar products or services to customers

Competitive analysis a process for monitoring the competition that involves identifying competition, anticipating their moves, and determining their strengths and weaknesses

Suppliers companies that provide material, human, financial, and informational resources to other companies

Supplier dependence the degree to which a company relies on a supplier because of the importance of the supplier's product to the company and the difficulty of finding other sources for that product

Buyer dependence the degree to which a supplier relies on a buyer because of the importance of that buyer to the supplier and the difficulty of finding other buyers for its products

Opportunistic behavior a transaction in which one party in the relationship benefits at the expense of the other

Relationship behavior mutually beneficial, long-term exchanges between buyers and suppliers

Industry regulation regulations and rules that govern the business practices and procedures of specific industries, businesses, and professions

Advocacy groups groups of concerned citizens who band together to try to influence the business practices of specific industries, businesses, and professions

Public communications an advocacy group tactic that relies on voluntary participation by the news media and the advertising industry to get the advocacy group's message out

Media advocacy an advocacy group tactic that involves framing issues as public issues; exposing questionable, exploitative, or unethical practices; and forcing media coverage by buying media time or creating controversy that is likely to receive extensive news coverage

Product boycott an advocacy group tactic that involves protesting a company's actions by convincing consumers not to purchase its product or service

Environmental scanning searching the environment for important events or issues that might affect an organization

Cognitive maps graphic depictions of how managers believe environmental factors relate to possible organizational actions

Internal environment the events and trends inside an organization that affect management, employees, and organizational culture

Organizational culture the values, beliefs, and attitudes shared by members of the organization

Organizational stories stories told by members to make sense of events and changes in an organization and to emphasize culturally consistent assumptions, decisions, and actions

Organizational heroes people celebrated for their qualities and achievements within an organization

Company mission a business's purpose or reason for existing

Consistent organizational culture when a company actively defines and teaches organizational values, beliefs, and attitudes

Behavioral addition the process of having managers and employees perform new behaviors that are central to and symbolic of the new organizational culture a company wants to create

The specific environment is made up of five components: customers, competitors, suppliers, industry regulations, and advocacy groups. Companies can monitor customers' needs by identifying customer problems after they occur or by anticipating problems before they occur. Because they tend to focus on well-known competitors, managers often underestimate their competition or do a poor job of identifying future competitors. Suppliers and buyers are very dependent on each other, and that dependence sometimes leads to opportunistic behavior, in which one party benefits at the expense of the other. Regulatory agencies affect businesses by creating rules and then enforcing them. Advocacy groups cannot regulate organizations' practices. Nevertheless, through public communications, media advocacy, and product boycotts, they try to convince companies to change their practices.

REVIEW 4 Making Sense of Changing Environments

Managers use a three-step process to make sense of external environments: environmental scanning, interpreting information, and acting on threats and opportunities. Managers scan their environments in order to keep up to date on factors influencing their industries, to reduce uncertainty, and to detect potential problems. When managers identify environmental events as threats, they take steps to protect their companies from harm. When managers identify environmental events as opportunities, they formulate alternatives for taking advantage of them to improve company performance. Using cognitive maps can help managers visually summarize the relationships between environmental factors and the actions they might take to deal with them.

REVIEW 5 Organizational Cultures: Creation, Success, and Change

Organizational culture is the set of key values, beliefs, and attitudes shared by members of an organization. Organizational cultures are often created by company founders and then sustained through repetition of organizational stories and recognition of organizational heroes. Adaptable cultures that promote employee involvement, make clear the organization's strategic purpose and direction, and actively define and teach organizational values and beliefs that can help companies achieve higher sales growth, return on assets, profits, quality, and employee satisfaction. Organizational cultures exist on three levels: the surface level, where visible artifacts and behaviors can be observed; just below the surface, where values and beliefs are expressed; and deep below the surface, where unconsciously held assumptions and beliefs exist. Managers can begin to change company cultures by focusing on the top two levels. Techniques for changing organizational cultures include using behavioral substitution and behavioral addition, changing visible artifacts, and selecting job applicants who have values and beliefs consistent with the desired company culture.

Behavioral substitution the process of having managers and employees perform new behavior central to the new organizational culture in place of behaviors that were central to the old organizational culture

Visible artifacts visible signs of an organization's culture, such as the office design and layout, company dress code, and company benefits and perks

Three Levels of Organizational Culture

SEEN (Surface level)	• Symbolic artifacts such as dress codes • Workers' and managers' behaviors
HEARD (Expressed values & beliefs)	• What people say • How decisions are made and explained
BELIEVED (Unconscious assumptions & beliefs)	• Widely shared assumptions and beliefs • Buried deep below surface • Rarely discussed or thought about

Learning Outcomes

REVIEW 1 Workplace Deviance

Ethics is the set of moral principles or values that define right and wrong. Workplace deviance is behavior that violates organizational norms about right and wrong and harms the organization or its workers. There are four different types of workplace deviance. Production deviance and property deviance harm the company, whereas political deviance and personal aggression harm individuals within the company.

REVIEW 2 U.S. Sentencing Commission Guidelines for Organizations

Under the U.S. Sentencing Commission Guidelines, companies can be prosecuted and fined up to $300 million for employees' illegal actions. Fines are computed by multiplying the base fine by a culpability score. Companies that establish compliance programs to encourage ethical behavior can reduce their culpability scores and their fines.

REVIEW 3 Influences on Ethical Decision Making

Three factors influence ethical decisions: the ethical intensity of the decision, the moral development of the manager, and the ethical principles used to solve the problem. Ethical intensity is high when decisions have large, certain, immediate consequences and when the decision maker is physically or psychologically close to those affected by the decision. There are three levels of moral development. At the preconventional level, decisions are made for selfish reasons. At the conventional level, decisions conform to societal expectations. At the postconventional level, internalized principles are used to make ethical decisions. Each of these levels has two stages within it. Managers can use a number of different principles when making ethical decisions: long-term self-interest, personal virtue, religious injunctions, government requirements, utilitarian benefits, individual rights, and distributive justice.

REVIEW 4 Practical Steps to Ethical Decision Making

Employers can increase their chances of hiring ethical employees by testing all job applicants. Most large companies now have corporate codes of ethics. In addition to offering general rules, ethics codes must also provide specific, practical advice. Ethics training seeks to increase employees' awareness of ethical issues; make ethics a serious, credible factor in organizational decisions; and teach employees a practical model of ethical decision making. The most important factors in creating an ethical business climate are the personal examples set by company managers, the involvement of management in the company ethics program, a reporting system that encourages whistleblowers to report potential ethics violations, and fair but consistent punishment of violators.

REVIEW 5 To Whom Are Organizations Socially Responsible?

Social responsibility is a business's obligation to benefit society. According to the shareholder model, a company's only social responsibility is to maximize shareholder wealth by maximizing company profits. According to the stakeholder model, companies must satisfy the needs and interests of multiple corporate stakeholders, not just shareholders. The needs of primary stakeholders, on which the organization relies for its existence, take precedence over those of secondary stakeholders.

REVIEW 6 For What Are Organizations Socially Responsible?

Companies can best benefit their stakeholders by fulfilling their economic, legal, ethical, and discretionary responsibilities. Being profitable, or meeting its economic responsibility,

Key Terms

Ethics the set of moral principles or values that defines right and wrong for a person or group

Ethical behavior behavior that conforms to a society's accepted principles of right and wrong

Workplace deviance unethical behavior that violates organizational norms about right and wrong

Production deviance unethical behavior that hurts the quality and quantity of work produced

Property deviance unethical behavior aimed at the organization's property or products

Employee shrinkage employee theft of company merchandise

Political deviance using one's influence to harm others in the company

Personal aggression hostile or aggressive behavior toward others

Ethical intensity the degree of concern people have about an ethical issue

Magnitude of consequences the total harm or benefit derived from an ethical decision

Social consensus agreement on whether behavior is bad or good

Probability of effect the chance that something will happen and then harm others

Temporal immediacy the time between an act and the consequences the act produces

Proximity of effect the social, psychological, cultural, or physical distance between a decision maker and those affected by his or her decisions

Concentration of effect the total harm or benefit that an act produces on the average person

Preconventional level of moral development the first level of moral development in which people make decisions based on selfish reasons

Conventional level of moral development the second level of moral development in which people make decisions that conform to societal expectations

Postconventional level of moral development the third level of moral development in which people make decisions based on internalized principles

Principle of long-term self-interest an ethical principle that holds that you should never take any action that is not in your or your organization's long-term self-interest

Principle of personal virtue an ethical principle that holds that you should never do anything that is not honest, open, and truthful and that you would not be glad to see reported in the newspapers or on TV

Principle of religious injunctions an ethical principle that holds that you should never take any action that is not kind and that does not build a sense of community

Principle of government requirements an ethical principle that holds that you should never take any action that violates the law, for the law represents the minimal moral standard

Principle of utilitarian benefits an ethical principle that holds that you should never take any action that does not result in greater good for society

Principle of individual rights an ethical principle that holds that you should never take any action that infringes on others' agreed-upon rights

Principle of distributive justice an ethical principle that holds that you should never take any action that harms the least fortunate among us: the poor, the uneducated, the unemployed

Overt integrity test a written test that estimates job applicants' honesty by directly asking them what they think or feel about theft or about punishment of unethical behaviors

Personality-based integrity test a written test that indirectly estimates job applicants' honesty by measuring psychological traits such as dependability and conscientiousness

Whistleblowing reporting others' ethics violations to management or legal authorities

Social responsibility a business's obligation to pursue policies, make decisions, and take actions that benefit society

Shareholder model a view of social responsibility that holds that an organization's overriding goal should be to maximize profit for the benefit of shareholders

Stakeholder model a theory of corporate responsibility that holds that management's most important responsibility, long-term survival, is achieved by satisfying the interests of multiple corporate stakeholders

Stakeholders persons or groups with a "stake" or legitimate interest in a company's actions

Primary stakeholder any group on which an organization relies for its long-term survival

Secondary stakeholder any group that can influence or be influenced by a company and can affect public perceptions about its socially responsible behavior

is a business's most basic social responsibility. Legal responsibility consists of following a society's laws and regulations. Ethical responsibility means not violating accepted principles of right and wrong when doing business. Discretionary responsibilities are social responsibilities beyond basic economic, legal, and ethical responsibilities.

REVIEW 7 Responses to Demands for Social Responsibility

Social responsiveness is a company's response to stakeholders' expectations concerning socially responsible behavior. There are four social responsiveness strategies. When a company uses a reactive strategy, it denies responsibility for a problem. When it uses a defensive strategy, it takes responsibility for a problem but does the minimum required to solve it. When a company uses an accommodative strategy, it accepts responsibility for problems and does all that society expects to solve them. Finally, when a company uses a proactive strategy, it does much more than expected to solve social responsibility problems.

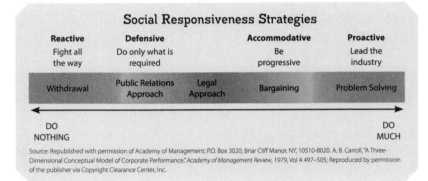

Social Responsiveness Strategies

Reactive	Defensive		Accommodative	Proactive
Fight all the way	Do only what is required		Be progressive	Lead the industry
Withdrawal	Public Relations Approach	Legal Approach	Bargaining	Problem Solving

DO NOTHING ————————————————→ DO MUCH

Source: Republished with permission of Academy of Management; P.O. Box 3020, Briar Cliff Manor, NY, 10510-8020. A. B. Carroll, "A Three-Dimensional Conceptual Model of Corporate Performance," *Academy of Management Review*, 1979, Vol 4 497–505; Reproduced by permission of the publisher via Copyright Clearance Center, Inc.

REVIEW 8 Social Responsibility and Economic Performance

Does it pay to be socially responsible? Studies show that there is generally no tradeoff between social responsibility and economic performance. In most circumstances, there is generally a small positive relationship between social responsibility and economic performance that becomes stronger when a company or its products have a positive reputation. Social responsibility, however, does not guarantee profitability as socially responsible companies experience the same ups and downs as other companies.

Economic responsibility the expectation that a company will make a profit by producing a valued product or service

Legal responsibility a company's social responsibility to obey society's laws and regulations

Ethical responsibility a company's social responsibility not to violate accepted principles of right and wrong when conducting business

Discretionary responsibility the expectation that a company will voluntarily serve a social role beyond its economic, legal, and ethical responsibilities

Social responsiveness refers to a company's strategy for responding to stakeholders' expectations concerning economic, legal, ethical, or discretionary responsibility

Reactive strategy a social responsiveness strategy in which a company does less than society expects

Defensive strategy a social responsiveness strategy in which a company admits responsibility for a problem but does the least required to meet societal expectations

Accommodative strategy a social responsiveness strategy in which a company accepts responsibility for a problem and does all that society expects to solve that problem

Proactive strategy a social responsiveness strategy in which a company anticipates responsibility for a problem before it occurs and does more than society expects to address the problem

Learning Outcomes

REVIEW 1 Benefits and Pitfalls of Planning

Planning is choosing a goal and developing a method or strategy for achieving it. Planning is one of the best ways to improve organizational and individual performance. It encourages people to work harder (intensified effort), to work hard for extended periods (persistence), to engage in behaviors directly related to goal accomplishment (directed behavior), and to think of better ways to do their jobs (task strategies). However, planning also has three potential pitfalls. Companies that are overly committed to their plans may be slow to adapt to environmental changes. Planning is based on assumptions about the future, and when those assumptions are wrong, plans can fail. Finally, planning can fail when planners are detached from the implementation of their plans.

REVIEW 2 How to Make a Plan That Works

There are five steps to making a plan that works: (1) Set S.M.A.R.T. goals—goals that are **S**pecific, **M**easurable, **A**ttainable, **R**ealistic, and **T**imely. (2) Develop commitment to the goals. Managers can increase workers' goal commitment by encouraging their participation in goal setting, making goals public, and getting top management to show support for goals. (3) Develop action plans for goal accomplishment. (4) Track progress toward goal achievement by setting both proximal and distal goals and by providing workers with regular performance feedback. (5) Maintain flexibility by keeping options open.

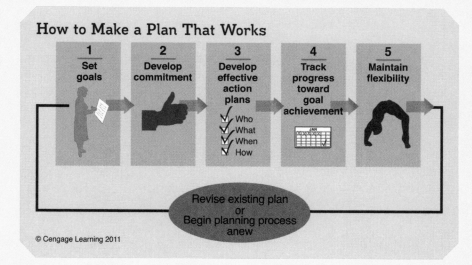

How to Make a Plan That Works

1 Set goals

2 Develop commitment

3 Develop effective action plans — Who / What / When / How

4 Track progress toward goal achievement

5 Maintain flexibility

Revise existing plan or Begin planning process anew

© Cengage Learning 2011

REVIEW 3 Planning from Top to Bottom

Proper planning requires that the goals at the bottom and middle of the organization support the objectives at the top of the organization. The goals at the top will be longer range than those at the bottom, as shown in the exhibit on the reverse. Top management develops strategic plans, which start with the creation of an organizational purpose and strategic objectives. Middle managers use techniques such as management by objectives (MBO) to develop tactical plans that direct behavior, efforts, and priorities. Finally, lower-level managers develop operational plans that guide daily activities in producing or delivering an organization's products and services. There are three kinds of operational plans: single-use plans, standing plans (policies, procedures, and rules and regulations), and budgets.

Planning choosing a goal and developing a method or strategy to achieve that goal

S.M.A.R.T. goals goals that are specific, measurable, attainable, realistic, and timely

Goal commitment the determination to achieve a goal

Action plan the specific steps, people, resources, and time period needed to accomplish a goal

Proximal goals short-term goals or subgoals

Distal goals long-term or primary goals

Options-based planning maintaining flexibility by making small, simultaneous investments in many alternative plans

Slack resources a cushion of extra resources that can be used with options-based planning to adapt to unanticipated change, problems, or opportunities

Strategic plans overall company plans that clarify how the company will serve customers and position itself against competitors over the next two to five years

Purpose statement a statement of a company's purpose or reason for existing; often referred to as an *organizational mission* or *vision*

Strategic objective a statement of a company's overall goal that unifies company-wide effort toward its vision, stretches and challenges the organization, and possesses a finish line and a time frame

Tactical plans plans created and implemented by middle managers that specify how the company will use resources, budgets, and people over the next six months to two years to accomplish specific goals within its strategic objective

Management by objectives (MBO) a four-step process in which managers and employees discuss and select goals, develop tactical plans, and meet regularly to review progress toward goal accomplishment

Operational plans day-to-day plans, developed and implemented by lower-level managers, for producing or delivering the organization's products and services over a 30-day to six-month period

Single-use plans plans that cover unique, one-time-only events

Standing plans plans used repeatedly to handle frequently recurring events

Policy a standing plan that indicates the general course of action that should be taken in response to a particular event or situation

Procedure a standing plan that indicates the specific steps that should be taken in response to a particular event

Rules and regulations standing plans that describe how a particular action should be performed or what must happen or not happen in response to a particular event

Budgeting quantitative planning through which managers decide how to allocate available money to best accomplish company goals

Decision making the process of choosing a solution from available alternatives

Rational decision making a systematic process of defining problems, evaluating alternatives, and choosing optimal solutions

Problem a gap between a desired state and an existing state

Decision criteria the standards used to guide judgments and decisions

Absolute comparison a process in which each criterion is compared to a standard or ranked on its own merits

Relative comparison a process in which each criterion is compared directly to every other

Maximizing choosing the best alternative

Satisficing choosing a "good enough" alternative

Groupthink a barrier to good decision making caused by pressure within a group for members to agree with each other

C-type conflict (cognitive conflict) disagreement that focuses on problem- and issue-related differences of opinion

A-type conflict (affective conflict) disagreement that focuses on individual or personal issues

Devil's advocacy a decision-making method in which an individual or a subgroup is assigned the role of critic

Nominal group technique a decision-making method that begins and ends by having group members quietly write down and evaluate ideas to be shared with the group

Delphi technique a decision-making method in which members of a panel of experts respond to questions and to each other until reaching agreement on an issue

Brainstorming a decision-making method in which group members build on each others' ideas to generate as many alternative solutions as possible

Electronic brainstorming a decision-making method in which group members use computers to build on each others' ideas and generate many alternative solutions

Production blocking a disadvantage of face-to-face brainstorming in which a group member must wait to share an idea because another member is presenting an idea

Evaluation apprehension fear of what others will think of your ideas

Planning from Top to Bottom

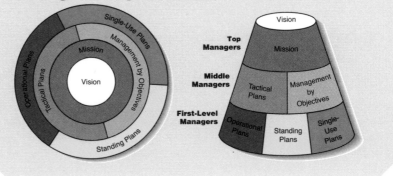

REVIEW 4 Steps and Limits to Rational Decision Making

Rational decision making is a six-step process in which managers define problems, evaluate alternatives, and compute optimal solutions. Step 1 is identifying and defining the problem. Problems are gaps between desired and existing states. Managers won't begin the decision-making process unless they are aware of the gap, motivated to reduce it, and possess the necessary resources to fix it. Step 2 is defining the decision criteria used to judge alternatives. In Step 3, an absolute or relative comparison process is used to rate the importance of the decision criteria. Step 4 involves generating many alternative courses of action (i.e., solutions). Potential solutions are assessed in Step 5 by systematically gathering information and evaluating each alternative against each criterion. In Step 6, criterion ratings and weights are used to compute the weighted average for each alternative course of action. Rational managers then choose the alternative with the highest value.

The rational decision-making model describes how decisions should be made in an ideal world without constraints. However, managers' limited resources, incomplete and imperfect information, and limited decision-making capabilities restrict their decision-making processes in the real world.

6 Steps of the Rational Decision-Making Process

1. Define the Problem
2. Identify Decision Criteria
3. Weight the Criteria
4. Generate Alternative Courses of Action
5. Evaluate Each Alternative
6. Compute the Optimal Decision

REVIEW 5 Using Groups to Improve Decision Making

When groups view problems from multiple perspectives, use more information, have a diversity of knowledge and experience, and become committed to solutions they help choose, they can produce better solutions than do individual decision makers. However, group decisions can suffer from these disadvantages: groupthink, slowness, discussions dominated by just a few individuals, and unfelt responsibility for decisions. Group decisions work best when group members encourage c-type (cognitive) conflict. Group decisions don't work as well when groups become mired in a-type (affective) conflict. The devil's advocacy approach improves group decisions because it brings structured c-type conflict into the decision-making process. By contrast, the nominal group technique improves decision making by reducing a-type conflict. Because it overcomes the problems of production blocking and evaluation apprehension, electronic brainstorming is more effective than face-to-face brainstorming.

Learning Outcomes

Sustainable Competitive Advantage

Firms can use their resources to create and sustain a competitive advantage, that is, to provide greater value for customers than competitors can. A competitive advantage becomes sustainable when other companies cannot duplicate the benefits it provides and have, for now, stopped trying. Four conditions must be met if a firm's resources are to be used to achieve a sustainable competitive advantage. The resources must be valuable, rare, imperfectly imitable, and nonsubstitutable.

REVIEW 2 Strategy-Making Process

The first step in strategy making is determining whether a strategy needs to be changed to sustain a competitive advantage. The second step is to conduct a situational (SWOT) analysis that examines internal strengths and weaknesses as well as external threats and opportunities. The third step involves choosing a strategy. Strategic reference point theory suggests that when companies are performing better than their strategic reference points, top management will typically choose a risk-averse strategy. When performance is below strategic reference points, risk-seeking strategies are more likely to be chosen.

REVIEW 3 Corporate-Level Strategies

Corporate-level strategies, consisting of portfolio strategies and grand strategies, help managers determine what businesses they should be in. Portfolio strategy focuses on lowering business risk by being in multiple, unrelated businesses and by investing the cash flows from slow-growth businesses into faster-growing businesses. One portfolio strategy is based on the BCG matrix. The most successful way to use the portfolio approach to corporate strategy is to reduce risk through related diversification.

The three kinds of grand strategies are growth, stability, and retrenchment/recovery. Companies can grow externally by merging with or acquiring other companies, or they can grow internally through direct expansion or creating new businesses. Companies choose a stability strategy when their external environment changes very little or after they have dealt with periods of explosive growth. Retrenchment strategy, shrinking the size or scope of a business, is used to turn around poor performance. If retrenchment works, it is often followed by a recovery strategy that focuses on growing the business again.

Corporate-Level Strategies

Portfolio Strategies	Grand Strategies
Acquisitions, unrelated diversification, related diversification, single businesses	Growth
	Stability
	Retrenchment/recovery
Boston Consulting Group matrix • Stars • Question marks • Cash cows • Dogs	

© Cengage Learning 2011

REVIEW 4 Industry-Level Strategies

The five industry forces determine an industry's overall attractiveness to corporate investors and its potential for long-term profitability. Together, a high level of these elements combine to increase competition and decrease profits. Industry-level strategies focus on how companies choose to compete in their industries. The three positioning strategies can help companies protect themselves from the negative effects of industry-wide competition. The four adaptive strategies help companies adapt to changes in the external environment. Defenders want to defend their current strategic positions. Prospectors look

Key Terms

Resources the assets, capabilities, processes, information, and knowledge that an organization uses to improve its effectiveness and efficiency, create and sustain competitive advantage, and fulfill a need or solve a problem

Competitive advantage providing greater value for customers than competitors can

Sustainable competitive advantage a competitive advantage that other companies have tried unsuccessfully to duplicate and have, for the moment, stopped trying to duplicate

Valuable resources resources that allow companies to improve efficiency and effectiveness

Rare resources resources that are not controlled or possessed by many competing firms

Imperfectly imitable resources resources that are impossible or extremely costly or difficult for other firms to duplicate

Nonsubstitutable resources resources that produce value or competitive advantage and have no equivalent substitutes or replacements

Competitive inertia a reluctance to change strategies or competitive practices that have been successful in the past

Strategic dissonance a discrepancy between a company's intended strategy and the strategic actions managers take when implementing that strategy

Situational (SWOT) analysis an assessment of the strengths and weaknesses in an organization's internal environment and the opportunities and threats in its external environment

Distinctive competence what a company can make, do, or perform better than its competitors

Core capabilities the internal decision-making routines, problem-solving processes, and organizational cultures that determine how efficiently inputs can be turned into outputs

Strategic group a group of companies within an industry that top managers choose to compare, evaluate, and benchmark strategic threats and opportunities

Core firms the central companies in a strategic group

Secondary firms the firms in a strategic group that follow strategies related to but somewhat different from those of the core firms

Strategic reference points the strategic targets managers use to measure whether a firm has developed the core competencies it needs to achieve a sustainable competitive advantage

Corporate-level strategy the overall organizational strategy that addresses the question "What business or businesses are we in or should we be in?"

Diversification a strategy for reducing risk by owning a variety of items (stocks or, in the case of a corporation, types of businesses) so that the failure of one stock or one business does not doom the entire portfolio

Portfolio strategy a corporate-level strategy that minimizes risk by diversifying investment among various businesses or product lines

Acquisition the purchase of a company by another company

Unrelated diversification creating or acquiring companies in completely unrelated businesses

BCG matrix a portfolio strategy, developed by the Boston Consulting Group, that categorizes a corporation's businesses by growth rate and relative market share and helps managers decide how to invest corporate funds

Star a company with a large share of a fast-growing market

Question mark a company with a small share of a fast-growing market

Cash cow a company with a large share of a slow-growing market

Dog a company with a small share of a slow-growing market

Related diversification creating or acquiring companies that share similar products, manufacturing, marketing, technology, or cultures

Grand strategy a broad corporate-level strategic plan used to achieve strategic goals and guide the strategic alternatives that managers of individual businesses or subunits may use

Growth strategy a strategy that focuses on increasing profits, revenues, market share, or the number of places in which the company does business

Stability strategy a strategy that focuses on improving the way in which the company sells the same products or services to the same customers

Retrenchment strategy a strategy that focuses on turning around very poor company performance by shrinking the size or scope of the business

Recovery the strategic actions taken after retrenchment to return to a growth strategy

Industry-level strategy a corporate strategy that addresses the question "How should we compete in this industry?"

Character of the rivalry a measure of the intensity of competitive behavior between companies in an industry

Threat of new entrants a measure of the degree to which barriers to entry make it easy or difficult for new companies to get started in an industry

for new market opportunities by bringing innovative new products to market. Analyzers minimize risk by following the proven successes of prospectors. Reactors do not follow a consistent strategy but instead react to changes in the external environment after they occur.

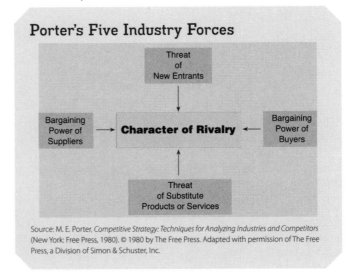

Porter's Five Industry Forces

Source: M. E. Porter, *Competitive Strategy: Techniques for Analyzing Industries and Competitors* (New York: Free Press, 1980). © 1980 by The Free Press. Adapted with permission of The Free Press, a Division of Simon & Schuster, Inc.

REVIEW 5 Firm-Level Strategies

Firm-level strategies are concerned with direct competition between firms. Market commonality and resource similarity determine whether firms are in direct competition and thus likely to attack each other and respond to each other's attacks. In general, the more markets in which there is product, service, or customer overlap and the greater the resource similarity between two firms, the more intense the direct competition between them.

Threat of substitute products or services a measure of the ease with which customers can find substitutes for an industry's products or services

Bargaining power of suppliers a measure of the influence that suppliers of parts, materials, and services to firms in an industry have on the prices of these inputs

Bargaining power of buyers a measure of the influence that customers have on a firm's prices

Cost leadership the positioning strategy of producing a product or service of acceptable quality at consistently lower production costs than competitors can, so that the firm can offer the product or service at the lowest price in the industry

Differentiation the positioning strategy of providing a product or service that is sufficiently different from competitors' offerings so that customers are willing to pay a premium price for it

Focus strategy the positioning strategy of using cost leadership or differentiation to produce a specialized product or service for a limited, specially targeted group of customers in a particular geographic region or market segment

Defenders firms that adopt an adaptive strategy aimed at defending strategic positions by seeking moderate, steady growth and by offering a limited range of high-quality products and services to a well-defined set of customers

Prospectors firms that adopt an adaptive strategy that seeks fast growth by searching for new market opportunities, encouraging risk taking, and being the first to bring innovative new products to market

Analyzers firms that adopt an adaptive strategy that seeks to minimize risk and maximize profits by following or imitating the proven successes of prospectors

Reactors firms that take an adaptive strategy of not following a consistent strategy, but instead reacting to changes in the external environment after they occur

Firm-level strategy a corporate strategy that addresses the question "How should we compete against a particular firm?"

Direct competition the rivalry between two companies that offer similar products and services, acknowledge each other as rivals, and react to each other's strategic actions

Market commonality the degree to which two companies have overlapping products, services, or customers in multiple markets

Resource similarity the extent to which a competitor has similar amounts and kinds of resources

Attack a competitive move designed to reduce a rival's market share or profits

Response a competitive countermove, prompted by a rival's attack, to defend or improve a company's market share or profit

Learning Outcomes

REVIEW 1 Why Innovation Matters

Technology cycles typically follow an S-curve pattern of innovation. Early in the cycle, technological progress is slow, and improvements in technological performance are small. As a technology matures, however, performance improves quickly. Finally, as the limits of a technology are reached, only small improvements occur. At this point, significant improvements in performance must come from new technologies. The best way to protect a competitive advantage is to create a stream of innovative ideas and products. Innovation streams begin with technological discontinuities that create significant breakthroughs in performance or function. Technological discontinuities are followed by discontinuous change, in which customers purchase new technologies and companies compete to establish the new dominant design. Dominant designs emerge because of critical mass, because they solve a practical problem, or because of the negotiations of independent standards bodies. Because technological innovation both enhances and destroys competence, companies that bet on the wrong design often struggle, while companies that bet on the eventual dominant design usually prosper. When a dominant design emerges, companies focus on incremental change, lowering costs, and making small but steady improvements in the dominant design. This focus continues until the next technological discontinuity occurs.

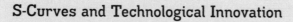

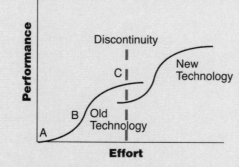

S-Curves and Technological Innovation

Source: R. N. Foster, *Innovation: The Attacker's Advantage* (New York: Summitt, 1986).

REVIEW 2 Managing Innovation

To successfully manage innovation streams, companies must manage the sources of innovation and learn to manage innovation during both discontinuous and incremental change. Since innovation begins with creativity, companies can manage the sources of innovation by supporting a work environment in which creative thoughts and ideas are welcomed, valued, and encouraged. Creative work environments provide challenging work; offer organizational, supervisory, and work group encouragement; allow significant freedom; and remove organizational impediments to creativity.

Discontinuous and incremental change require different strategies. Companies that succeed in periods of discontinuous change typically follow an experiential approach to innovation. The experiential approach assumes that intuition, flexible options, and hands-on experience can reduce uncertainty and accelerate learning and understanding. A compression approach to innovation works best during periods of incremental change.

Organizational innovation the successful implementation of creative ideas in organizations

Creativity the production of novel and useful ideas

Organizational change a difference in the form, quality, or condition of an organization over time

Technology cycle a cycle that begins with the birth of a new technology and ends when that technology reaches its limits and is replaced by a newer, substantially better technology

S-curve pattern of innovation a pattern of technological innovation characterized by slow initial progress, then rapid progress, and then slow progress again as a technology matures and reaches its limits

Innovation streams patterns of innovation over time that can create sustainable competitive advantage

Technological discontinuity when a scientific advance or a unique combination of existing technologies creates a significant breakthrough in performance or function

Discontinuous change the phase of a technology cycle characterized by technological substitution and design competition

Technological substitution the purchase of new technologies to replace older ones

Design competition competition between old and new technologies to establish a new technological standard or dominant design

Dominant design a new technological design or process that becomes the accepted market standard

Technological lockout when a new dominant design (i.e., a significantly better technology) prevents a company from competitively selling its products or makes it difficult to do so

Incremental change the phase of a technology cycle in which companies innovate by lowering costs and improving the functioning and performance of the dominant technological design

Creative work environments workplace cultures in which workers perceive that new ideas are welcomed, valued, and encouraged

Flow a psychological state of effortlessness, in which you become completely absorbed in what you're doing and time seems to pass quickly

Experiential approach to innovation an approach to innovation that assumes a highly uncertain environment and uses intuition, flexible options, and hands-on experience to reduce uncertainty and accelerate learning and understanding

Design iteration a cycle of repetition in which a company tests a prototype of a new product or service, improves on that design, and then builds and tests the improved prototype

Product prototype a full-scale, working model that is being tested for design, function, and reliability

Testing the systematic comparison of different product designs or design iterations

Milestones formal project review points used to assess progress and performance

Multifunctional teams work teams composed of people from different departments

Compression approach to innovation an approach to innovation that assumes that incremental innovation can be planned using a series of steps and that compressing those steps can speed innovation

Generational change change based on incremental improvements to a dominant technological design such that the improved technology is fully backward compatible with the older technology

Organizational decline a large decrease in organizational performance that occurs when companies don't anticipate, recognize, neutralize, or adapt to the internal or external pressures that threaten their survival

Change forces forces that produce differences in the form, quality, or condition of an organization over time

Resistance forces forces that support the existing state of conditions in organizations

Resistance to change opposition to change resulting from self-interest, misunderstanding and distrust, and a general intolerance for change

Unfreezing getting the people affected by change to believe that change is needed

Change intervention the process used to get workers and managers to change their behavior and work practices

Refreezing supporting and reinforcing new changes so that they stick

Coercion using formal power and authority to force others to change

Results-driven change change created quickly by focusing on the measurement and improvement of results

General Electric workout a three-day meeting in which managers and employees from different levels and parts of an organization quickly generate and act on solutions to specific business problems

Organizational development a philosophy and collection of planned change interventions designed to improve an organization's long-term health and performance

Change agent the person formally in charge of guiding a change effort

This approach assumes that innovation can be planned using a series of steps and that compressing the time it takes to complete those steps can speed up innovation.

REVIEW 3 Organizational Decline: The Risk of Not Changing

The five-stage process of organizational decline begins when organizations don't recognize the need for change. In the blinded stage, managers fail to recognize the changes that threaten their organization's survival. In the inaction stage, management recognizes the need to change but doesn't act, hoping that the problems will correct themselves. In the faulty action stage, management focuses on cost cutting and efficiency rather than facing up to the fundamental changes needed to ensure survival. In the crisis stage, failure is likely unless fundamental reorganization occurs. Finally, in the dissolution stage, the company is dissolved through bankruptcy proceedings; by selling assets to pay creditors; or through the closing of stores, offices, and facilities. If companies recognize the need to change early enough, however, dissolution may be avoided.

REVIEW 4 Managing Change

The basic change process involves unfreezing, change, and refreezing. Resistance to change stems from self-interest, misunderstanding, and distrust as well as a general intolerance for change. It can be managed through education and communication, participation, negotiation, top management support, and coercion. Knowing what *not* to do is as important as knowing what to do to achieve successful change. Managers should avoid these errors when leading change: not establishing urgency, not creating a guiding coalition, lacking a vision, undercommunicating the vision, not removing obstacles to the vision, not creating short-term wins, declaring victory too soon, and not anchoring changes in the corporation's culture. Finally, managers can use a number of change techniques. Results-driven change and the GE workout reduce resistance to change by getting change efforts off to a fast start. Organizational development is a collection of planned change interventions (large system, small group, person-focused), guided by a change agent, that are designed to improve an organization's long-term health and performance.

General Steps for Organizational Development Interventions

1. Entry	A problem is discovered and the need for change becomes apparent. A search begins for someone to deal with the problem and facilitate change.
2. Startup	A change agent enters the picture and works to clarify the problem and gain commitment to a change effort.
3. Assessment & feedback	The change agent gathers information about the problem and provides feedback about it to decision makers and those affected by it.
4. Action planning	The change agent works with decision makers to develop an action plan.
5. Intervention	The action plan, or organizational development intervention, is carried out.
6. Evaluation	The change agent helps decision makers assess the effectiveness of the intervention.
7. Adoption	Organizational members accept ownership and responsibility for the change, which is then carried out through the entire organization.
8. Separation	The change agent leaves the organization after first ensuring that the change intervention will continue to work.

Source: W. J. Rothwell, R. Sullivan, and G. M. McLean, *Practicing Organizational Development: A Guide for Consultants* (San Diego: Pfeiffer & Co., 1995).

Review | 8

Learning Outcomes

REVIEW 1   Global Business, Trade Rules, and Trade Agreements

Today, there are 79,000 multinational corporations worldwide; just 3.1 percent are based in the United States. Global business affects the United States in two ways: through direct foreign investment in the United States by foreign companies, and through U.S. companies' investment in businesses in other countries. U.S. direct foreign investment throughout the world amounts to more than $2.8 trillion per year, whereas direct foreign investment by foreign companies in the United States amounts to more than $2.1 trillion per year. Historically, tariffs and nontariff trade barriers such as quotas, voluntary export restraints, government import standards, government subsidies, and customs classifications have made buying foreign goods much harder or more expensive than buying domestically produced products. In recent years, however, worldwide trade agreements such as GATT and the WTO, along with regional trading agreements like the Maastricht Treaty of Europe, NAFTA, CAFTA-DR, UNASUR, ASEAN, and APEC have substantially reduced tariffs and nontariff barriers to international trade. Companies have responded by investing in growing markets in Asia, Eastern Europe, and Latin America. Consumers have responded by purchasing products based on value rather than geography.

REVIEW 2   Consistency or Adaptation?

Global business requires a balance between global consistency and local adaptation. Global consistency means using the same rules, guidelines, policies, and procedures in each location. Managers at company headquarters like global consistency because it simplifies decisions. Local adaptation means adapting standard procedures to differences in markets. Local managers prefer a policy of local adaptation because it gives them more control. Not all businesses need the same combination of global consistency and local adaptation. Some thrive by emphasizing global consistency and ignoring local adaptation. Others succeed by ignoring global consistency and emphasizing local adaptation.

REVIEW 3   Forms for Global Business

The phase model of globalization says that, as companies move from a domestic to a global orientation, they use these organizational forms in sequence: exporting, cooperative contracts (licensing and franchising), strategic alliances, and wholly owned affiliates. Yet not all companies follow the phase model. For example, global new ventures are global from their inception.

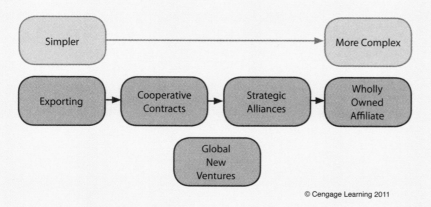

© Cengage Learning 2011

Key Terms

Global business the buying and selling of goods and services by people from different countries

Multinational corporation a corporation that owns businesses in two or more countries

Direct foreign investment a method of investment in which a company builds a new business or buys an existing business in a foreign country

Trade barriers government-imposed regulations that increase the cost and restrict the number of imported goods

Protectionism a government's use of trade barriers to shield domestic companies and their workers from foreign competition

Tariff a direct tax on imported goods

Nontariff barriers nontax methods of increasing the cost or reducing the volume of imported goods

Quota a limit on the number or volume of imported products

Voluntary export restraints voluntarily imposed limits on the number or volume of products exported to a particular country

Government import standard a standard ostensibly established to protect the health and safety of citizens but, in reality, often used to restrict or ban imports

Subsidies government loans, grants, and tax deferments given to domestic companies to protect them from foreign competition

Customs classification a classification assigned to imported products by government officials that affects the size of the tariff and imposition of import quotas

General Agreement on Tariffs and Trade (GATT) a worldwide trade agreement that reduced and eliminated tariffs, limited government subsidies, and established protections for intellectual property

World Trade Organization (WTO) as the successor to GATT, the only international organization dealing with the global rules of trade between nations

Regional trading zones areas in which tariff and nontariff barriers on trade between countries are reduced or eliminated

Maastricht Treaty of Europe a regional trade agreement between most European countries

North American Free Trade Agreement (NAFTA) a regional trade agreement between the United States, Canada, and Mexico

Central America Free Trade Agreement (CAFTA-DR) a regional trade agreement between Costa Rica, the Dominican Republic, El Salvador, Guatemala, Honduras, Nicaragua, and the United States

Union of South American Nations (UNASUR) a regional trade agreement between Argentina, Brazil, Paraguay, Uruguay, Venezuela, Bolivia, Colombia, Ecuador, Peru, Guyana, Suriname, and Chile

Association of Southeast Asian Nations (ASEAN) a regional trade agreement between Brunei Darussalam, Cambodia, Indonesia, Lao PDR, Malaysia, Myanmar, the Philippines, Singapore, Thailand, and Vietnam

Asia-Pacific Economic Cooperation (APEC) a regional trade agreement between Australia, Canada, Chile, the People's Republic of China, Hong Kong, Japan, Mexico, New Zealand, Papua New Guinea, Peru, Russia, South Korea, Taiwan, the United States, and all members of ASEAN, except Cambodia, Lao PDR, and Myanmar

Global consistency when a multinational company has offices, manufacturing plants, and distribution facilities in different countries and runs them all using the same rules, guidelines, policies, and procedures

Local adaptation when a multinational company modifies its rules, guidelines, policies, and procedures to adapt to differences in foreign customers, governments, and regulatory agencies

Exporting selling domestically produced products to customers in foreign countries

Cooperative contract an agreement in which a foreign business owner pays a company a fee for the right to conduct that business in his or her country

Licensing an agreement in which a domestic company, the licensor, receives royalty payments for allowing another company, the licensee, to produce the licensor's product, sell its service, or use its brand name in a specified foreign market

Franchise a collection of networked firms in which the manufacturer or marketer of a product or service, the franchisor, licenses the entire business to another person or organization, the franchisee

Strategic alliance an agreement in which companies combine key resources, costs, risk, technology, and people

Joint venture a strategic alliance in which two existing companies collaborate to form a third, independent company

Wholly owned affiliates foreign offices, facilities, and manufacturing plants that are 100 percent owned by the parent company

---

REVIEW 4 Finding the Best Business Climate

The first step in deciding where to take your company global is finding an attractive business climate. Be sure to look for a growing market where consumers have strong purchasing power and foreign competitors are weak. When locating an office or manufacturing facility, consider both qualitative and quantitative factors. In assessing political risk, be sure to examine both political uncertainty and policy uncertainty. If the location you choose has considerable political risk, you can avoid it, try to control the risk, or use a cooperation strategy.

REVIEW 5 Becoming Aware of Cultural Differences

National culture is the set of shared values and beliefs that affects the perceptions, decisions, and behavior of the people from a particular country. The first step in dealing with culture is to recognize meaningful differences such as power distance, individualism, masculinity, uncertainty avoidance, and short-term/long-term orientation. Cultural differences should be carefully interpreted because they are based on generalizations rather than specific individuals. Adapting managerial practices to cultural differences is difficult because policies and practices can be perceived differently in different cultures.

REVIEW 6 Preparing for an International Assignment

Many expatriates return prematurely from international assignments because of poor performance. This is much less likely to happen if employees receive linguistic and cross-cultural training, such as documentary training, cultural simulations, or field experiences, before going on assignment. Adjustment of expatriates' spouses and families, which is the most important determinant of success in international assignments, can be improved through adaptability screening and language and cross-cultural training.

Global new ventures new companies that are founded with an active global strategy and have sales, employees, and financing in different countries

Purchasing power a comparison of the relative cost of a standard set of goods and services in different countries

Political uncertainty the risk of major changes in political regimes that can result from war, revolution, death of political leaders, social unrest, or other influential events

Policy uncertainty the risk associated with changes in laws and government policies that directly affect the way foreign companies conduct business

National culture the set of shared values and beliefs that affects the perceptions, decisions, and behavior of the people from a particular country

Expatriate someone who lives and works outside his or her native country

Learning Outcomes

REVIEW 1 Departmentalization

There are five traditional departmental structures: functional, product, customer, geographic, and matrix. Functional departmentalization is based on the different business functions or types of expertise used to run a business. Product departmentalization is organized according to the different products or services a company sells. Customer departmentalization focuses its divisions on the different kinds of customers a company has. Geographic departmentalization is based on the different geographic areas or markets in which the company does business. Matrix departmentalization is a hybrid form that combines two or more forms of departmentalization, the most common being the product and functional forms. There is no single best departmental structure. Each structure has advantages and disadvantages.

REVIEW 2 Organizational Authority

Organizational authority is determined by the chain of command, line versus staff authority, delegation, and the degree of centralization in a company. The chain of command vertically connects every job in the company to higher levels of management and makes clear who reports to whom. Managers have line authority to command employees below them in the chain of command but have only staff, or advisory, authority over employees not below them in the chain of command. Managers delegate authority by transferring to subordinates the authority and responsibility needed to do a task; in exchange, subordinates become accountable for task completion. In centralized companies, most authority to make decisions lies with managers in the upper levels of the company. In decentralized companies, much of the authority is delegated to the workers closest to the problems, who can then make the decisions necessary for solving the problems themselves.

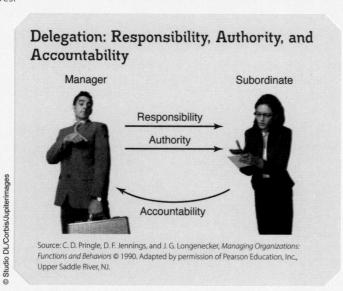

Delegation: Responsibility, Authority, and Accountability

Manager   Subordinate

Responsibility →
Authority →
← Accountability

Source: C. D. Pringle, D. F. Jennings, and J. G. Longenecker, *Managing Organizations: Functions and Behaviors* © 1990. Adapted by permission of Pearson Education, Inc., Upper Saddle River, NJ.

© Studio DL/Corbis/Jupiterimages

REVIEW 3 Job Design

Companies use specialized jobs because they are economical and easy to learn and don't require highly paid workers. However, specialized jobs aren't motivating or particularly satisfying for employees. Companies have used job rotation, job enlargement, job

Key Terms

Organizational structure the vertical and horizontal configuration of departments, authority, and jobs within a company

Organizational process the collection of activities that transform inputs into outputs that customers value

Departmentalization subdividing work and workers into separate organizational units responsible for completing particular tasks

Functional departmentalization organizing work and workers into separate units responsible for particular business functions or areas of expertise

Product departmentalization organizing work and workers into separate units responsible for producing particular products or services

Customer departmentalization organizing work and workers into separate units responsible for particular kinds of customers

Geographic departmentalization organizing work and workers into separate units responsible for doing business in particular geographic areas

Matrix departmentalization a hybrid organizational structure in which two or more forms of departmentalization, most often product and functional, are used together

Simple matrix a form of matrix departmentalization in which managers in different parts of the matrix negotiate conflicts and resources

Complex matrix a form of matrix departmentalization in which managers in different parts of the matrix report to matrix managers, who help them sort out conflicts and problems

Authority the right to give commands, take action, and make decisions to achieve organizational objectives

Chain of command the vertical line of authority that clarifies who reports to whom throughout the organization

Unity of command a management principle that workers should report to just one boss

Line authority the right to command immediate subordinates in the chain of command

Staff authority the right to advise, but not command, others who are not subordinates in the chain of command

Line function an activity that contributes directly to creating or selling the company's products

Staff function an activity that does not contribute directly to creating or selling the company's products, but instead supports line activities

Delegation of authority the assignment of direct authority and responsibility to a subordinate to complete tasks for which the manager is normally responsible

Centralization of authority the location of most authority at the upper levels of the organization

Decentralization the location of a significant amount of authority in the lower levels of the organization

Standardization solving problems by consistently applying the same rules, procedures, and processes

Job design the number, kind, and variety of tasks that individual workers perform in doing their jobs

Job specialization a job composed of a small part of a larger task or process

Job rotation periodically moving workers from one specialized job to another to give them more variety and the opportunity to use different skills

Job enlargement increasing the number of different tasks that a worker performs within one particular job

Job enrichment increasing the number of tasks in a particular job and giving workers the authority and control to make meaningful decisions about their work

Job characteristics model (JCM) an approach to job redesign that seeks to formulate jobs in ways that motivate workers and lead to positive work outcomes

Internal motivation motivation that comes from the job itself rather than from outside rewards

Skill variety the number of different activities performed in a job

Task identity the degree to which a job, from beginning to end, requires the completion of a whole and identifiable piece of work

Task significance the degree to which a job is perceived to have a substantial impact on others inside or outside the organization

Autonomy the degree to which a job gives workers the discretion, freedom, and independence to decide how and when to accomplish the job

Feedback the amount of information the job provides to workers about their work performance

Mechanistic organization an organization characterized by specialized jobs and responsibilities; precisely defined, unchanging roles; and a rigid chain of command based on centralized authority and vertical communication

Organic organization an organization characterized by broadly defined jobs and responsibility; loosely defined, frequently changing roles; and decentralized authority and horizontal communication based on task knowledge

Intraorganizational process the collection of activities that take place within an organization to transform inputs into outputs that customers value

Reengineering fundamental rethinking and radical redesign of business processes to achieve dramatic improvements in critical measures of performance, such as cost, quality, service, and speed

enrichment, and the job characteristics model to make specialized jobs more interesting and motivating. The goal of the job characteristics model is to make jobs intrinsically motivating. For this to happen, jobs must be strong on five core job characteristics (skill variety, task identity, task significance, autonomy, and feedback), and workers must experience three critical psychological states (knowledge of results, responsibility for work outcomes, and meaningful work). If jobs aren't internally motivating, they can be redesigned by combining tasks, forming natural work units, establishing client relationships, vertical loading, and opening feedback channels.

REVIEW 4 — Intraorganizational Processes

Today, companies are using reengineering and empowerment to change their intraorganizational processes. Reengineering changes an organization's orientation from vertical to horizontal and its work processes by decreasing sequential and pooled interdependence and by increasing reciprocal interdependence. Reengineering promises dramatic increases in productivity and customer satisfaction, but it has been criticized as simply an excuse to cut costs and lay off workers. Empowering workers means taking decision-making authority and responsibility from managers and giving it to workers. Empowered workers develop feelings of competence and self-determination and believe that their work has meaning and impact.

REVIEW 5 — Interorganizational Processes

Organizations are using modular and virtual organizations to change interorganizational processes. Because modular organizations outsource all noncore activities to other businesses, they are less expensive to run than traditional companies. However, modular organizations require extremely close relationships with suppliers, may result in a loss of control, and could create new competitors if the wrong business activities are outsourced. Virtual organizations participate in a network in which they share skills, costs, capabilities, markets, and customers. Virtual organizations can reduce costs, respond quickly, and, if they can successfully coordinate their efforts, produce outstanding products and service.

Reengineering and Task Interdependence

Pooled Interdependence

Finished Product

Sequential Interdependence

Finished Product

Reciprocal Interdependence

Finished Product

© Cengage Learning 2011

Task interdependence the extent to which collective action is required to complete an entire piece of work

Pooled interdependence work completed by having each job or department independently contribute to the whole

Sequential interdependence work completed in succession, with one group's or job's outputs becoming the inputs for the next group or job

Reciprocal interdependence work completed by different jobs or groups working together in a back-and-forth manner

Empowering workers permanently passing decision-making authority and responsibility from managers to workers by giving them the information and resources they need to make and carry out good decisions

Empowerment feelings of intrinsic motivation, in which workers perceive their work to have impact and meaning and perceive themselves to be competent and capable of self-determination

Interorganizational process a collection of activities that take place among companies to transform inputs into outputs that customers value

Modular organization an organization that outsources noncore business activities to outside companies, suppliers, specialists, or consultants

Virtual organization an organization that is part of a network in which many companies share skills, costs, capabilities, markets, and customers to collectively solve customer problems or provide specific products or services

Learning Outcomes

REVIEW 1 The Good and Bad of Using Teams

In many industries, teams are growing in importance because they help organizations respond to specific problems and challenges. Teams have been shown to increase customer satisfaction (specific customer teams), product and service quality (direct responsibility), and employee job satisfaction (cross-training, unique opportunities, and leadership responsibilities). Although teams can produce significant improvements in these areas, using teams does not guarantee these positive outcomes. Teams and teamwork have the disadvantages of initially high turnover and social loafing (especially in large groups). Teams also share many of the advantages (multiple perspectives, generation of more alternatives, and more commitment) and disadvantages (groupthink, time, poorly run meetings, domination by a few team members, and weak accountability) of group decision making. Teams should be used for a clear purpose, when the work requires that people work together, when rewards can be provided for both teamwork and team performance, when ample resources can be provided, and when teams can be given clear authority over their work.

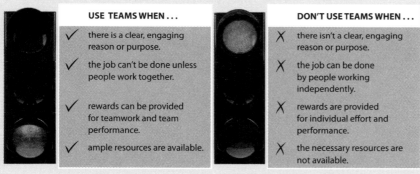

When to Use and When Not to Use Teams

USE TEAMS WHEN . . .	DON'T USE TEAMS WHEN . . .
✓ there is a clear, engaging reason or purpose.	✗ there isn't a clear, engaging reason or purpose.
✓ the job can't be done unless people work together.	✗ the job can be done by people working independently.
✓ rewards can be provided for teamwork and team performance.	✗ rewards are provided for individual effort and performance.
✓ ample resources are available.	✗ the necessary resources are not available.

Source: R. Wageman, "Critical Success Factors for Creating Superb Self-Managing Teams," *Organizational Dynamics* 26, no. 1 (1997): 49–61.

© iStockphoto.com/Serdar Yagci

REVIEW 2 Kinds of Teams

Companies use different kinds of teams to make themselves more competitive. Autonomy is the key dimension that makes teams different. Traditional work groups (which execute tasks) and employee involvement groups (which make suggestions) have the lowest levels of autonomy. Semi-autonomous work groups (which control major direct tasks) have more autonomy, while self-managing teams (which control all direct tasks) and self-designing teams (which control membership and how tasks are done) have the highest levels of autonomy. Cross-functional, virtual, and project teams are common but are not easily categorized in terms of autonomy. Cross-functional teams combine employees from different functional areas to help teams attack problems from multiple perspectives and generate more ideas and solutions. Virtual teams use telecommunications and information technologies to bring coworkers together, regardless of physical location or time zone. Virtual teams reduce travel and work time, but communication may suffer since team members don't work face-to-face. Finally, project teams are used for specific, one-time projects or tasks that must be completed within a limited time. Project teams reduce communication barriers and promote flexibility; teams and team members are reassigned to their departments or new projects as old projects are completed.

Key Terms

Work team a small number of people with complementary skills who hold themselves mutually accountable for pursuing a common purpose, achieving performance goals, and improving interdependent work processes

Cross-training training team members to do all or most of the jobs performed by the other team members

Social loafing behavior in which team members withhold their efforts and fail to perform their share of the work

Traditional work group a group composed of two or more people who work together to achieve a shared goal

Employee involvement team a team that provides advice or makes suggestions to management concerning specific issues

Semi-autonomous work group a group that has the authority to make decisions and solve problems related to the major tasks of producing a product or service

Self-managing team a team that manages and controls all of the major tasks of producing a product or service

Self-designing team a team that has the characteristics of self-managing teams but also controls team design, work tasks, and team membership

Cross-functional team a team composed of employees from different functional areas of the organization

Virtual team a team composed of geographically and/or organizationally dispersed coworkers who use telecommunication and information technologies to accomplish an organizational task

Project team a team created to complete specific, one-time projects or tasks within a limited time

Norms informally agreed-on standards that regulate team behavior

Cohesiveness the extent to which team members are attracted to a team and motivated to remain in it

Forming the first stage of team development, in which team members meet each other, form initial impressions, and begin to establish team norms

Storming the second stage of team development, characterized by conflict and disagreement, in which team members disagree over what the team should do and how it should do it

Norming the third stage of team development, in which team members begin to settle into their roles, group cohesion grows, and positive team norms develop

Performing the fourth and final stage of team development, in which performance improves because the team has matured into an effective, fully functioning team

Structural accommodation the ability to change organizational structures, policies, and practices in order to meet stretch goals

Bureaucratic immunity the ability to make changes without first getting approval from managers or other parts of an organization

Individualism-collectivism the degree to which a person believes that people should be self-sufficient and that loyalty to oneself is more important than loyalty to team or company

Team level the average level of ability, experience, personality, or any other factor of a team

Team diversity the variances or differences in ability, experience, personality, or any other factor of a team

Interpersonal skills skills, such as listening, communicating, questioning, and providing feedback, that enable people to have effective working relationships with others

Skill-based pay compensation system that pays employees for acquiring additional skills or knowledge

Gainsharing a compensation system in which companies share the financial value of performance gains, such as productivity, cost savings, or quality, with their workers

Work-Team Characteristics

The most important characteristics of work teams are team norms, cohesiveness, size, conflict, and development. Norms let team members know what is expected of them and can influence team behavior in positive and negative ways. Positive team norms are associated with organizational commitment, trust, and job satisfaction. Team cohesiveness helps teams retain members, promotes cooperative behavior, increases motivation, and facilitates team performance. Attending team meetings and activities, creating opportunities to work together, and engaging in non-work activities can increase cohesiveness. Team size has a curvilinear relationship with team performance: teams that are very small or very large do not perform as well as moderate-sized teams of six to nine members. Teams of this size are cohesive and small enough for team members to get to know each other and contribute in a meaningful way but are large enough to take advantage of team members' diverse skills, knowledge, and perspectives. Conflict and disagreement are inevitable in most teams. The key to dealing with team conflict is to maximize cognitive conflict, which focuses on issue-related differences, and minimize affective conflict, the emotional reactions that occur when disagreements become personal rather than professional. As teams develop and grow, they pass through four stages of development: forming, storming, norming, and performing. If a team is not managed well, its performance may decline after a period of time as the team regresses through the stages of de-norming, de-storming, and de-forming.

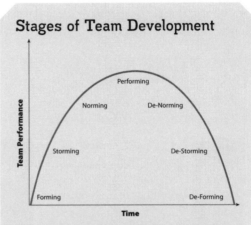

Stages of Team Development

Sources: J. F. McGrew, J. G. Bilotta, and J. M. Deeney, "Software Team Formation and Decay: Extending the Standard Model for Small Groups," *Small Group Research* 30, no. 2 (1999): 209–234; B. W. Tuckman, "Development Sequence in Small Groups," *Psychological Bulletin* 63, no. 6 (1965): 384–399.

Enhancing Work-Team Effectiveness

Companies can make teams more effective by setting team goals and managing how team members are selected, trained, and compensated. Team goals provide a clear focus and purpose, reduce the incidence of social loafing, and lead to higher team performance 93 percent of the time. Extremely difficult stretch goals can be used to motivate teams as long as teams have autonomy, control over resources, structural accommodation, and bureaucratic immunity. Not everyone is suited for teamwork. When selecting team members, companies should select people who have a preference for teamwork (individualism-collectivism) and should consider team level (average ability of a team) and team diversity (different abilities of a team). Organizations that successfully use teams provide thousands of hours of training to make sure that teams work. The most common types of team training are for interpersonal skills, decision-making and problem-solving skills, conflict resolution, technical training to help team members learn multiple jobs (i.e., cross-training), and training for team leaders. Employees can be compensated for team participation and accomplishments in three ways: skill-based pay, gainsharing, and nonfinancial rewards.

Learning Outcomes

REVIEW 1 Employment Legislation

Human resource management is subject to numerous major federal employment laws and subject to review by several federal agencies. In general, these laws indicate that sex, age, religion, color, national origin, race, disability, and pregnancy may not be considered in employment decisions unless these factors reasonably qualify as BFOQs. Two important criteria, disparate treatment (intentional discrimination) and adverse impact (unintentional discrimination), are used to decide whether companies have wrongly discriminated against someone. The two kinds of sexual harassment are quid pro quo sexual harassment and hostile work environment.

REVIEW 2 Recruiting

Recruiting is the process of finding qualified job applicants. The first step in recruiting is to conduct a job analysis, which is used to write a job description of basic tasks, duties, and responsibilities and to write job specifications indicating the knowledge, skills, and abilities needed to perform the job. Whereas internal recruiting involves finding qualified job applicants from inside the company, external recruiting involves finding qualified job applicants from outside the company.

REVIEW 3 Selection

Selection is the process of gathering information about job applicants to decide who should be offered a job. Accurate selection procedures are valid, are legally defendable, and improve organizational performance. Application forms and résumés are the most common selection devices. Managers should check references and conduct background checks even though previous employers are often reluctant to provide such information for fear of being sued for defamation. Unfortunately, without this information, other employers are at risk of negligent hiring lawsuits. Selection tests generally do the best job of predicting applicants' future job performance. The three kinds of job interviews are unstructured, structured, and semistructured interviews.

REVIEW 4 Training

Training is used to give employees the job-specific skills, experience, and knowledge they need to do their jobs or improve their job performance. To make sure training dollars are well spent, companies need to determine specific training needs, select appropriate training methods, and then evaluate the training.

The Human Resource Management Process

© Cengage Learning 2011

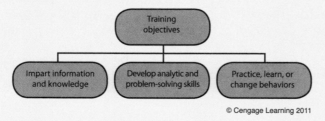

© Cengage Learning 2011

Key Terms

Human resource management (HRM) the process of finding, developing, and keeping the right people to form a qualified work force

Bona fide occupational qualification (BFOQ) an exception in employment law that permits sex, age, religion, and the like to be used when making employment decisions, but only if they are "reasonably necessary to the normal operation of that particular business"; strictly monitored by the Equal Employment Opportunity Commission

Disparate treatment intentional discrimination that occurs when people are purposely not given the same hiring, promotion, or membership opportunities because of their race, color, sex, age, ethnic group, national origin, or religious beliefs

Adverse impact unintentional discrimination that occurs when members of a particular race, sex, or ethnic group are unintentionally harmed or disadvantaged because they are hired, promoted, or trained (or any other employment decision) at substantially lower rates than others

Four-fifths (or 80 percent) rule a rule of thumb used by the courts and the EEOC to determine whether there is evidence of adverse impact; a violation of this rule occurs when the selection rate for a protected group is less than 80 percent or four-fifths of the selection rate for a nonprotected group

Sexual harassment a form of discrimination in which unwelcome sexual advances, requests for sexual favors, or other verbal or physical conduct of a sexual nature occurs while performing one's job

Quid pro quo sexual harassment a form of sexual harassment in which employment outcomes, such as hiring, promotion, or simply keeping one's job, depend on whether an individual submits to sexual harassment

Hostile work environment a form of sexual harassment in which unwelcome and demeaning sexually related behavior creates an intimidating and offensive work environment

Recruiting the process of developing a pool of qualified job applicants

Job analysis a purposeful, systematic process for collecting information on the important work-related aspects of a job

Job description a written description of the basic tasks, duties, and responsibilities required of an employee holding a particular job

Job specifications a written summary of the qualifications needed to successfully perform a particular job

Internal recruiting the process of developing a pool of qualified job applicants from people who already work in the company

External recruiting the process of developing a pool of qualified job applicants from outside the company

Selection the process of gathering information about job applicants to decide who should be offered a job

Validation the process of determining how well a selection test or procedure predicts future job performance; the better or more accurate the prediction of future job performance, the more valid a test is said to be

Employment references sources such as previous employers or coworkers who can provide job-related information about job candidates

Background checks procedures used to verify the truthfulness and accuracy of information that applicants provide about themselves and to uncover negative, job-related background information not provided by applicants

Specific ability tests (aptitude tests) tests that measure the extent to which an applicant possesses the particular kind of ability needed to do a job well

Cognitive ability tests tests that measure the extent to which applicants have abilities in perceptual speed, verbal comprehension, numerical aptitude, general reasoning, and spatial aptitude

Biographical data (biodata) extensive surveys that ask applicants questions about their personal backgrounds and life experiences

Work sample tests tests that require applicants to perform tasks that are actually done on the job

Assessment center a series of managerial simulations, graded by trained observers, that is used to determine applicants' capability for managerial work

Interview a selection tool in which company representatives ask job applicants job-related questions to determine whether they are qualified for the job

Unstructured interviews interviews in which interviewers are free to ask the applicants anything they want

Structured interviews interviews in which all applicants are asked the same set of standardized questions, usually including situational, behavioral, background, and job-knowledge questions

Training developing the skills, experience, and knowledge employees need to perform their jobs or improve their performance

---

REVIEW 5 Performance Appraisal

The keys to successful performance appraisal are accurately measuring job performance and effectively sharing performance feedback with employees. Organizations should develop good performance appraisal scales; train raters how to accurately evaluate performance; and impress upon managers the value of providing feedback in a clear, consistent, and fair manner, as well as setting goals and monitoring progress toward those goals.

REVIEW 6 Compensation and Employee Separation

Compensation includes both the financial and the nonfinancial rewards that organizations give employees in exchange for their work. There are three basic kinds of compensation decisions: pay level, pay variability, and pay structure. Employee separation is the loss of an employee, which can occur voluntarily or involuntarily. Companies use downsizing and early retirement incentive programs (ERIPs) to reduce the number of employees in the organization and lower costs. However, companies generally try to keep the rate of employee turnover low to reduce costs associated with finding and developing new employees. Functional turnover, on the other hand, can be good for organizations.

Needs assessment the process of identifying and prioritizing the learning needs of employees

Performance appraisal the process of assessing how well employees are doing their jobs

Objective performance measures measures of job performance that are easily and directly counted or quantified

Behavioral Observation Scale (BOS) a rating scale that indicates the frequency with which workers perform specific behaviors that are representative of the job dimensions critical to successful job performance

Rater training training performance appraisal raters in how to avoid rating errors and increase rating accuracy

360-degree feedback a performance appraisal process in which feedback is obtained from the boss, subordinates, peers and coworkers, and the employees themselves

Compensation the financial and nonfinancial rewards that organizations give employees in exchange for their work

Employee separation the voluntary or involuntary loss of an employee

Job evaluation a process that determines the worth of each job in a company by evaluating the market value of the knowledge, skills, and requirements needed to perform it

Piecework a compensation system in which employees are paid a set rate for each item they produce

Commission a compensation system in which employees earn a percentage of each sale they make

Profit sharing a compensation system in which a company pays a percentage of its profits to employees in addition to their regular compensation

Employee stock ownership plan (ESOP) a compensation system that awards employees shares of company stock in addition to their regular compensation

Stock options a compensation system that gives employees the right to purchase shares of stock at a set price, even if the value of the stock increases above that price

Wrongful discharge a legal doctrine that requires employers to have job-related reasons to terminate employees

Downsizing the planned elimination of jobs in a company

Outplacement services employment-counseling services offered to employees who are losing their jobs because of downsizing

Early retirement incentive programs (ERIPs) programs that offer financial benefits to employees to encourage them to retire early

Phased retirement employees transition to retirement by working reduced hours over a period of time before completely retiring

Employee turnover loss of employees who voluntarily choose to leave the company

Functional turnover loss of poor-performing employees who voluntarily choose to leave a company

Dysfunctional turnover loss of high-performing employees who voluntarily choose to leave a company

Review | 12

Chapter 12
Managing
Individuals and a
Diverse Work Force

Chapter 12

Learning Outcomes

REVIEW 1 | Diversity: Differences That Matter

Diversity exists in organizations when there are demographic, cultural, and personal differences among the employees and the customers. A common misconception is that workplace diversity and affirmative action are the same. However, affirmative action is more narrowly focused on demographics; is required by law; and is used to punish companies that discriminate on the basis of race/ethnicity, religion, sex, or national origin. By contrast, diversity is broader in focus (going beyond demographics); voluntary; more positive in that it encourages companies to value all kinds of differences; and, at this time, substantially less controversial than affirmative action. Affirmative action and diversity thus differ in purpose, practice, and the reactions they produce. Diversity also makes good business sense in terms of reducing costs (decreasing turnover and absenteeism and avoiding lawsuits), attracting and retaining talent, and driving business growth (improving marketplace understanding and promoting higher-quality problem solving).

REVIEW 2 | Surface-Level Diversity

Age, sex, race/ethnicity, and physical and mental disabilities are dimensions of surface-level diversity. Because those dimensions are (usually) easily observed, managers and workers tend to rely on them to form initial impressions and stereotypes. Sometimes this can lead to age, sex, racial/ethnic, or disability discrimination (i.e., treating people differently) in the workplace. In general, older workers, women, people of color or different national origins, and people with disabilities are much less likely to be hired or promoted than are white males. This disparity is often due to incorrect beliefs or stereotypes such as "job performance declines with age," or "women aren't willing to travel on business," or "workers with disabilities aren't as competent as able workers." To reduce discrimination, companies can determine the hiring and promotion rates for different groups, train managers to make hiring and promotion decisions on the basis of specific criteria, and make sure that everyone has equal access to training, mentors, reasonable work accommodations, and assistive technology. Finally, companies need to designate a go-to person to whom employees can talk if they believe they have suffered discrimination.

REVIEW 3 | Deep-Level Diversity

Deep-level diversity matters because it can reduce prejudice, discrimination, and conflict while increasing social integration. It consists of dispositional and personality differences that can be recognized only through extended interaction with others. Research conducted in different cultures, settings, and languages indicates that there are five basic dimensions of personality: extraversion, emotional stability, agreeableness, conscientiousness, and openness to experience. Of these, conscientiousness is perhaps the most important because conscientious workers tend to be better performers on virtually any job. Extraversion is also related to performance in jobs that require significant interaction with others.

REVIEW 4 | Managing Diversity

The three paradigms for managing diversity are the discrimination and fairness paradigm (equal opportunity, fair treatment, strict compliance with the law), the access and legitimacy paradigm (matching internal diversity to external diversity), and the learning and effectiveness paradigm (achieving organizational plurality by integrating deep-level diversity into the work of the organization). Unlike the other paradigms that focus on

Key Terms

Diversity a variety of demographic, cultural, and personal differences among an organization's employees and customers

Affirmative action purposeful steps taken by an organization to create employment opportunities for minorities and women

Surface-level diversity differences such as age, sex, race/ethnicity, and physical disabilities that are observable, typically unchangeable, and easy to measure

Deep-level diversity differences such as personality and attitudes that are communicated through verbal and nonverbal behaviors and are recognized only through extended interaction with others

Social integration the degree to which group members are psychologically attracted to working with each other to accomplish a common objective

Age discrimination treating people differently (e.g., in hiring and firing, promotion, and compensation decisions) because of their age

Sex discrimination treating people differently because of their sex

Glass ceiling the invisible barrier that prevents women and minorities from advancing to the top jobs in organizations

Racial or ethnic discrimination treating people differently because of their race or ethnicity

Disability a mental or physical impairment that substantially limits one or more major life activities

Disability discrimination treating people differently because of their disabilities

Disposition the tendency to respond to situations and events in a predetermined manner

Personality the relatively stable set of behaviors, attitudes, and emotions displayed over time that makes people different from each other

Extraversion the degree to which someone is active, assertive, gregarious, sociable, talkative, and energized by others

Emotional stability the degree to which someone is not angry, depressed, anxious, emotional, insecure, or excitable

Agreeableness the degree to which someone is cooperative, polite, flexible, forgiving, good-natured, tolerant, and trusting

Conscientiousness the degree to which someone is organized, hardworking, responsible, persevering, thorough, and achievement oriented

Openness to experience the degree to which someone is curious, broadminded, and open to new ideas, things, and experiences; is spontaneous; and has a high tolerance for ambiguity

Organizational plurality a work environment in which (1) all members are empowered to contribute in a way that maximizes the benefits to the organization, customers, and themselves, and (2) the individuality of each member is respected by not segmenting or polarizing people on the basis of their membership in a particular group

Awareness training training that is designed to raise employees' awareness of diversity issues and to challenge the underlying assumptions or stereotypes they may have about others

Skills-based diversity training training that teaches employees the practical skills they need for managing a diverse work force, such as flexibility and adaptability, negotiation, problem solving, and conflict resolution

surface-level differences, the learning and effectiveness program values common ground, distinguishes between individual and group differences, minimizes conflict and divisiveness, and focuses on bringing different talents and perspectives together. What principles can companies use when managing diversity? Follow and enforce federal and state laws regarding equal employment opportunity. Treat group differences as important but not special. Find the common ground. Tailor opportunities to individuals, not groups. Reexamine, but maintain, high standards. Solicit negative as well as positive feedback. Set high but realistic goals. The two types of diversity training are awareness training and skills-based diversity training. Companies also manage diversity through diversity audits and diversity pairing and by having top executives experience what it is like to be in the minority.

Diversity audits formal assessments that measure employee and management attitudes, investigate the extent to which people are advantaged or disadvantaged with respect to hiring and promotions, and review companies' diversity-related policies and procedures

Diversity pairing a mentoring program in which people of different cultural backgrounds, sexes, or races/ethnicities are paired so that they can get to know each other and change any stereotypical beliefs and attitudes

Paradigms for Managing Diversity

DIVERSITY PARADIGM	FOCUS	SUCCESS MEASURED BY	BENEFITS	LIMITATIONS
Discrimination & Fairness	Equal opportunity, Fair treatment, Recruitment of minorities, Strict compliance with laws	Recruitment, promotion, and retention goals for underrepresented group	Fairer treatment, Increased demographic diversity	Focus on surface-level diversity
Access & Legitimacy	Acceptance and celebration of differences	Diversity in company matches diversity of primary stakeholders	Establishes a clear business reason for diversity	Focus on surface-level diversity
Learning & Effectiveness	Integrating deep-level differences into organization	Valuing people on the basis of individual knowledge, skills, and abilities	Values common ground, Distinction between individual and group differences, Less conflict, backlash, and divisiveness, Bringing different talents and perspectives together	Focus on deep-level diversity, which is more difficult to measure and quantify

© Cengage Learning 2011

Learning Outcomes

REVIEW 1 Basics of Motivation

Motivation is the set of forces that initiates, directs, and makes people persist in their efforts over time to accomplish a goal. Managers often confuse motivation and performance, but job performance is a multiplicative function of motivation times ability times situational constraints. Needs are the physical or psychological requirements that must be met to ensure survival and well-being. Different motivational theories (Maslow's Hierarchy of Needs, Alderfer's ERG Theory, and McClelland's Learned Needs Theory) specify a number of different needs. However, studies show that there are only two general kinds of needs, lower-order needs and higher-order needs. Both extrinsic and intrinsic rewards motivate people.

MOTIVATING TO INCREASE EFFORT

- **Start by asking people what their needs are.**
- **Satisfy lower-order needs first.**
- **Expect people's needs to change.**
- **As needs change and lower-order needs are satisfied, satisfy higher-order needs by looking for ways to allow employees to experience intrinsic rewards.**

REVIEW 2 Equity Theory

The basic components of equity theory are inputs, outcomes, and referents. After an internal comparison in which employees compare their outcomes to their inputs, they then make an external comparison in which they compare their O/I ratio with the O/I ratio of a referent, a person who works in a similar job or is otherwise similar. When their O/I ratio is equal to the referent's O/I ratio, employees perceive that they are being treated fairly. But, when their O/I ratio is lower than or higher than their referent's O/I ratio, they perceive that they have been treated inequitably or unfairly. There are two kinds of inequity: underreward and overreward. Underreward, which occurs when a referent's O/I ratio is higher than the employee's O/I ratio, leads to anger or frustration. Overreward, which occurs when a referent's O/I ratio is lower than the employee's O/I ratio, can lead to guilt but only when the level of overreward is extreme.

MOTIVATING WITH EQUITY THEORY

- **Look for and correct major inequities.**
- **Reduce employees' inputs.**
- **Make sure decision-making processes are fair.**

REVIEW 3 Expectancy Theory

Expectancy theory holds that three factors affect the conscious choices people make about their motivation: valence, expectancy, and instrumentality. Expectancy theory holds that all three factors must be high for people to be highly motivated. If any one of these factors declines, overall motivation will decline, too.

MOTIVATING WITH EXPECTANCY THEORY

- **Systematically gather information to find out what employees want from their jobs.**
- **Take specific steps to link rewards to individual performance in a way that is clear and understandable to employees.**
- **Empower employees to make decisions if management really wants them to believe that their hard work and effort will lead to good performance.**

Key Terms

Motivation the set of forces that initiates, directs, and makes people persist in their efforts to accomplish a goal

Needs the physical or psychological requirements that must be met to ensure survival and well-being

Extrinsic reward a reward that is tangible, visible to others, and given to employees contingent on the performance of specific tasks or behaviors

Intrinsic reward a natural reward associated with performing a task or activity for its own sake

Equity theory a theory that states that people will be motivated when they perceive that they are being treated fairly

Inputs in equity theory, the contributions employees make to the organization

Outcomes in equity theory, the rewards employees receive for their contributions to the organization

Referents in equity theory, others with whom people compare themselves to determine if they have been treated fairly

Outcome/input (O/I) ratio in equity theory, an employee's perception of how the rewards received from an organization compare with the employee's contributions to that organization

Underreward a form of inequity in which you are getting fewer outcomes relative to inputs than your referent is getting

Overreward a form of inequity in which you are getting more outcomes relative to inputs than your referent

Distributive justice the perceived degree to which outcomes and rewards are fairly distributed or allocated

Procedural justice the perceived fairness of the process used to make reward allocation decisions

Expectancy theory a theory that states that people will be motivated to the extent to which they believe that their efforts will lead to good performance, that good performance will be rewarded, and that they will be offered attractive rewards

Valence the attractiveness or desirability of a reward or outcome

Expectancy the perceived relationship between effort and performance

Instrumentality the perceived relationship between performance and rewards

Reinforcement theory a theory that states that behavior is a function of its consequences, that behaviors followed by positive consequences will occur more frequently, and that behaviors followed by negative consequences, or not followed by positive consequences, will occur less frequently

Reinforcement the process of changing behavior by changing the consequences that follow behavior

Reinforcement contingencies cause-and-effect relationships between the performance of specific behaviors and specific consequences

Schedule of reinforcement rules that specify which behaviors will be reinforced, which consequences will follow those behaviors, and the schedule by which those consequences will be delivered

Positive reinforcement reinforcement that strengthens behavior by following behaviors with desirable consequences

Negative reinforcement reinforcement that strengthens behavior by withholding an unpleasant consequence when employees perform a specific behavior

Punishment reinforcement that weakens behavior by following behaviors with undesirable consequences

Extinction reinforcement in which a positive consequence is no longer allowed to follow a previously reinforced behavior, thus weakening the behavior

Continuous reinforcement schedule a schedule that requires a consequence to be administered following every instance of a behavior

Intermittent reinforcement schedule a schedule in which consequences are delivered after a specified or average time has elapsed or after a specified or average number of behaviors has occurred

Fixed interval reinforcement schedule an intermittent schedule in which consequences follow a behavior only after a fixed time has elapsed

Variable interval reinforcement schedule an intermittent schedule in which the time between a behavior and the following consequences varies around a specified average

Fixed ratio reinforcement schedule an intermittent schedule in which consequences are delivered following a specific number of behaviors

Variable ratio reinforcement schedule an intermittent schedule in which consequences are delivered following a different number of behaviors, sometimes more and sometimes less, that vary around a specified average number of behaviors

Goal a target, objective, or result that someone tries to accomplish

Goal-setting theory a theory that states that people will be motivated to the extent to which they accept specific, challenging goals and receive feedback that indicates their progress toward goal achievement

REVIEW 4 Reinforcement Theory

Reinforcement theory says that behavior is a function of its consequences. Reinforcement has two parts: reinforcement contingencies and schedules of reinforcement. The four kinds of reinforcement contingencies are positive reinforcement and negative reinforcement, which strengthen behavior, and punishment and extinction, which weaken behavior. There are two kinds of reinforcement schedules, continuous and intermittent; intermittent schedules, in turn, can be divided into fixed and variable interval schedules and fixed and variable ratio schedules.

REVIEW 5 Goal-Setting Theory

A goal is a target, objective, or result that someone tries to accomplish. Goal-setting theory says that people will be motivated to the extent to which they accept specific, challenging goals and receive feedback that indicates their progress toward goal achievement. The basic components of goal-setting theory are goal specificity, goal difficulty, goal acceptance, and performance feedback. Goal specificity is the extent to which goals are detailed, exact, and unambiguous. Goal difficulty is the extent to which a goal is hard or challenging to accomplish. Goal acceptance is the extent to which people consciously understand and agree to goals. Performance feedback is information about the quality or quantity of past performance and indicates whether progress is being made toward the accomplishment of a goal.

Motivating with the Integrated Model

MOTIVATING WITH	MANAGERS SHOULD . . .
THE BASICS	• Ask people what their needs are. • Satisfy lower-order needs first. • Expect people's needs to change. • As needs change and lower-order needs are satisfied, satisfy higher-order needs by looking for ways to allow employees to experience intrinsic rewards.
EQUITY THEORY	• Look for and correct major inequities. • Reduce employees' inputs. • Make sure decision-making processes are fair.
EXPECTANCY THEORY	• Systematically gather information to find out what employees want from their jobs. • Take specific steps to link rewards to individual performance in a way that is clear and understandable to employees. • Empower employees to make decisions if management really wants them to believe that their hard work and efforts will lead to good performance.
REINFORCEMENT THEORY	• Identify, measure, analyze, intervene, and evaluate critical performance-related behaviors. • Don't reinforce the wrong behaviors. • Correctly administer punishment at the appropriate time. • Choose the simplest and most effective schedules of reinforcement.
GOAL-SETTING THEORY	• Assign specific, challenging goals. • Make sure workers truly accept organizational goals. • Provide frequent, specific, performance-related feedback.

© Cengage Learning 2011

Goal specificity the extent to which goals are detailed, exact, and unambiguous

Goal difficulty the extent to which a goal is hard or challenging to accomplish

Goal acceptance the extent to which people consciously understand and agree to goals

Performance feedback information about the quality or quantity of past performance that indicates whether progress is being made toward the accomplishment of a goal

Learning Outcomes

REVIEW 1 Leaders versus Managers

Management is getting work done through others; leadership is the process of influencing others to achieve group or organizational goals. Leaders are different from managers. The primary difference is that leaders are concerned with doing the right thing, while managers are concerned with doing things right. Organizations need both managers and leaders. But, in general, companies are overmanaged and underled.

REVIEW 2 Who Leaders Are and What Leaders Do

Trait theory says that effective leaders possess traits or characteristics that differentiate them from nonleaders. Those traits are drive, the desire to lead, honesty/integrity, self-confidence, emotional stability, cognitive ability, and knowledge of the business. These traits alone aren't enough for successful leadership; leaders who have many or all of them must also behave in ways that encourage people to achieve group or organizational goals. Two key leader behaviors are initiating structure, which improves subordinate performance, and consideration, which improves subordinate satisfaction. There is no ideal combination of these behaviors. The best leadership style depends on the situation.

REVIEW 3 Putting Leaders in the Right Situations: Fiedler's Contingency Theory

Fiedler's contingency theory assumes that leaders are effective when their work groups perform well, that leaders are unable to change their leadership styles, that leadership styles must be matched to the proper situations, and that favorable situations permit leaders to influence group members. According to the Least Preferred Coworker (LPC) scale, there are two basic leadership styles. People who describe their LPC in a positive way have a relationship-oriented leadership style. By contrast, people who describe their LPC in a negative way have a task-oriented leadership style. Situational favorableness, which occurs when leaders can influence followers, is determined by leader-member relations, task structure, and position power. In general, relationship-oriented leaders with high LPC scores are better leaders under moderately favorable situations, whereas task-oriented leaders with low LPC scores are better leaders in highly favorable and unfavorable situations. Since Fiedler assumes that leaders are incapable of changing their leadership styles, the key is to accurately measure and match leaders to situations or to teach leaders how to change situational factors. Though matching or placing leaders in appropriate situations works well, reengineering situations to fit leadership styles doesn't because the complexity of the model makes it difficult for people to understand.

Matching Leadership Styles to Situations

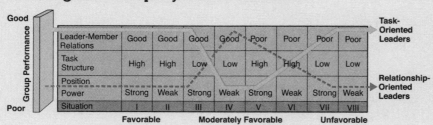

Leader-Member Relations	Good	Good	Good	Good	Poor	Poor	Poor	Poor
Task Structure	High	High	Low	Low	High	High	Low	Low
Position Power	Strong	Weak	Strong	Weak	Strong	Weak	Strong	Weak
Situation	I	II	III	IV	V	VI	VII	VIII

Favorable — Moderately Favorable — Unfavorable

Good ↔ Poor Group Performance

Task-Oriented Leaders

Relationship-Oriented Leaders

© Cengage Learning 2011

Key Terms

Leadership the process of influencing others to achieve group or organizational goals

Trait theory a leadership theory that holds that effective leaders possess a similar set of traits or characteristics

Traits relatively stable characteristics, such as abilities, psychological motives, and consistent patterns of behavior

Initiating structure the degree to which a leader structures the roles of followers by setting goals, giving directions, setting deadlines, and assigning tasks

Consideration the extent to which a leader is friendly, approachable, and supportive and shows concern for employees

Leadership style the way a leader generally behaves toward followers

Contingency theory a leadership theory that states that in order to maximize work group performance, leaders must be matched to the situations that best fit their leadership styles

Situational favorableness the degree to which a particular situation either permits or denies a leader the chance to influence the behavior of group members

Leader-member relations the degree to which followers respect, trust, and like their leaders

Task structure the degree to which the requirements of a subordinate's tasks are clearly specified

Position power the degree to which leaders are able to hire, fire, reward, and punish workers

Path-goal theory a leadership theory that states that leaders can increase subordinate satisfaction and performance by clarifying and clearing the paths to goals and by increasing the number and kinds of rewards available for goal attainment

Directive leadership a leadership style in which the leader lets employees know precisely what is expected of them, gives them specific guidelines for performing tasks, schedules work, sets standards of performance, and makes sure that people follow standard rules and regulations

Supportive leadership a leadership style in which the leader is friendly and approachable, shows concern for employees and their welfare, treats them as equals, and creates a friendly climate

Participative leadership a leadership style in which the leader consults employees for their suggestions and input before making decisions

Achievement-oriented leadership a leadership style in which the leader sets challenging goals, has high expectations of employees, and displays confidence that employees will assume responsibility and put forth extraordinary effort

Normative decision theory a theory that suggests how a leader can determine an appropriate amount of employee participation when making decisions

Strategic leadership the ability to anticipate, envision, maintain flexibility, think strategically, and work with others to initiate changes that will create a positive future for an organization

Visionary leadership leadership that creates a positive image of the future that motivates organizational members and provides direction for future planning and goal setting

Charismatic leadership the behavioral tendencies and personal characteristics of leaders that create exceptionally strong relationships between them and their followers

Ethical charismatics charismatic leaders who provide developmental opportunities for followers, are open to positive and negative feedback, recognize others' contributions, share information, and have moral standards that emphasize the larger interests of the group, organization, or society

Unethical charismatics charismatic leaders who control and manipulate followers, do what is best for themselves instead of their organizations, want to hear only positive feedback, share only information that is beneficial to themselves, and have moral standards that put their interests before everyone else's

Transformational leadership leadership that generates awareness and acceptance of a group's purpose and mission and gets employees to see beyond their own needs and self-interests for the good of the group

Transactional leadership leadership based on an exchange process, in which followers are rewarded for good performance and punished for poor performance

REVIEW 4 Adapting Leader Behavior: Path-Goal Theory

Path-goal theory states that leaders can increase subordinate satisfaction and performance by clarifying and clearing the paths to goals and by increasing the number and kinds of rewards available for goal attainment. For this to work, however, leader behavior must be a source of immediate or future satisfaction for followers and must complement and not duplicate the characteristics of followers' work environments. In contrast to Fiedler's contingency theory, path-goal theory assumes that leaders can and do change their leadership styles (directive, supportive, participative, and achievement-oriented), depending on their subordinates (experience, perceived ability, and internal or external locus of control) and the environment in which those subordinates work (task structure, formal authority system, and primary work group).

REVIEW 5 Adapting Leader Behavior: Normative Decision Theory

The normative decision theory helps leaders decide how much employee participation should be used when making decisions. Using the right degree of employee participation improves the quality of decisions and the extent to which employees accept and are committed to decisions. The theory specifies five different decision styles or ways of making decisions: autocratic decisions (AI or AII), consultative decisions (CI or CII), and group decisions (GII). The theory improves decision quality via decision rules concerning quality, leader information, subordinate information, goal congruence, and problem structure. The theory improves employee commitment and acceptance via decision rules related to commitment probability, subordinate conflict, and commitment requirement. These decision rules help leaders improve decision quality and follower acceptance and commitment by eliminating decision styles that don't fit the decision or situation the group or organization is facing. Normative decision theory operationalizes these decision rules in the form of yes/no questions, as shown in the decision tree displayed in Exhibit 14.8.

REVIEW 6 Visionary Leadership

Strategic leadership requires visionary leadership, which can be charismatic or transformational. Visionary leadership creates a positive image of the future that motivates organizational members and provides direction for future planning and goal setting. Charismatic leaders have strong, confident, dynamic personalities that attract followers, enable the leader to create strong bonds, and inspire followers to accomplish the leader's vision. Followers of ethical charismatic leaders work harder, are more committed and satisfied, are better performers, and are more likely to trust their leaders. Followers can be just as supportive and committed to unethical charismatics, but these leaders can pose a tremendous risk for companies. Unethical charismatics control and manipulate followers and do what is best for themselves instead of their organizations. Transformational leadership goes beyond charismatic leadership by generating awareness and acceptance of a group's purpose and mission and by getting employees to see beyond their own needs and self-interests for the good of the group. The four components of transformational leadership are charismatic leadership or idealized influence, inspirational motivation, intellectual stimulation, and individualized consideration.

Learning Outcomes

REVIEW 1 Perception and Communication Problems

Perception is the process by which people attend to, organize, interpret, and retain information from their environments. Perception is not a straightforward process. Because of perceptual filters such as selective perception and closure, people exposed to the same information or stimuli often end up with very different perceptions and understandings. Perception-based differences can also lead to differences in the attributions (internal or external) that managers and workers make when explaining workplace behavior. In general, workers are more likely to explain behavior from a defensive bias, in which they attribute problems to external causes (i.e., the situation). Managers, on the other hand, tend to commit the fundamental attribution error, attributing problems to internal causes (i.e., the worker made a mistake or error). Consequently, when things go wrong, it's common for managers to blame workers and for workers to blame the situation or context in which they do their jobs. Finally, this problem is compounded by a self-serving bias that leads people to attribute successes to internal causes and failures to external causes. So, when workers receive negative feedback from managers, they may become defensive and emotional and not hear what their managers have to say. In short, perceptions and attributions represent a significant challenge to effective communication and understanding in organizations.

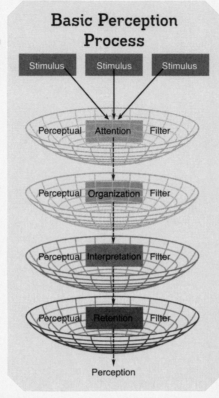

Basic Perception Process

Stimulus   Stimulus   Stimulus

Perceptual   Attention   Filter

Perceptual   Organization   Filter

Perceptual   Interpretation   Filter

Perceptual   Retention   Filter

Perception

© Cengage Learning 2011

REVIEW 2 Kinds of Communication

Organizational communication depends on the communication process, formal and informal communication channels, one-on-one communication, and nonverbal communication. The major components of the communication process are the sender, the receiver, noise, and feedback. Senders often mistakenly assume that they can pipe their intended messages directly into receivers' heads with perfect clarity. Formal communication channels such as downward,

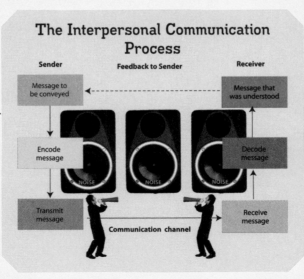

The Interpersonal Communication Process

Sender   Feedback to Sender   Receiver

Message to be conveyed   Message that was understood

Encode message   Decode message

NOISE   NOISE   NOISE

Transmit message   Receive message

Communication channel

© Burke/Triolo Productions/Brand X Pictures/Jupiterimages / © TongRo Image Stock/Jupiterimages

Key Terms

Communication the process of transmitting information from one person or place to another

Perception the process by which individuals attend to, organize, interpret, and retain information from their environments

Perceptual filters the personality-, psychology-, or experience-based differences that influence people to ignore or pay attention to particular stimuli

Selective perception the tendency to notice and accept objects and information consistent with our values, beliefs, and expectations while ignoring, screening out, or not accepting inconsistent stimuli or information

Closure the tendency to fill in gaps of missing information by assuming that what we don't know is consistent with what we already know

Attribution theory a theory that states that we all have a basic need to understand and explain the causes of other people's behavior

Defensive bias the tendency for people to perceive themselves as personally and situationally similar to someone who is having difficulty or trouble

Fundamental attribution error the tendency to ignore external causes of behavior and to attribute other people's actions to internal causes

Self-serving bias the tendency to overestimate our value by attributing successes to ourselves (internal causes) and attributing failures to others or the environment (external causes)

Encoding putting a message into a written, verbal, or symbolic form that can be recognized and understood by the receiver

Decoding the process by which the receiver translates the written, verbal, or symbolic form of a message into an understood message

Feedback to sender in the communication process, a return message to the sender that indicates the receiver's understanding of the message

Noise anything that interferes with the transmission of the intended message

Jargon vocabulary particular to a profession or group

Formal communication channels the system of official channels that carry organizationally approved messages and information

Downward communication communication that flows from higher to lower levels in an organization

Upward communication communication that flows from lower to higher levels in an organization

Horizontal communication communication that flows among managers and workers who are at the same organizational level

Informal communication channel (grapevine) the transmission of messages from employee to employee outside of formal communication channels

Coaching communicating with someone for the direct purpose of improving the person's on-the-job performance or behavior

Counseling communicating with someone about non–job-related issues that may be affecting or interfering with the person's performance

Nonverbal communication any communication that doesn't involve words

Kinesics movements of the body and face

Paralanguage the pitch, rate, tone, volume, and speaking pattern (i.e., use of silences, pauses, or hesitations) of one's voice

Communication medium the method used to deliver an oral or written message

Hearing the act or process of perceiving sounds

Listening making a conscious effort to hear

Active listening assuming half the responsibility for successful communication by actively giving the speaker nonjudgmental feedback that shows you've accurately heard what he or she said

Empathetic listening understanding the speaker's perspective and personal frame of reference and giving feedback that conveys that understanding to the speaker

Destructive feedback feedback that disapproves without any intention of being helpful and almost always causes a negative or defensive reaction in the recipient

Constructive feedback feedback intended to be helpful, corrective, and/or encouraging

Collaborative discussion sites Web- or software-based discussion tools that allow employees to ask questions and share knowledge

upward, and horizontal communication carry organizationally approved messages and information. By contrast, the informal communication channel, called the "grapevine," arises out of curiosity and is carried out through gossip or cluster chains. There are two kinds of one-on-one communication. Coaching is used to improve on-the-job performance, while counseling is used to communicate about non–job-related issues affecting job performance. Nonverbal communication, such as kinesics and paralanguage, accounts for as much as 93 percent of the transmission of a message's content.

REVIEW 3 Managing One-on-One Communication

One-on-one communication can be managed by choosing the right communication medium, being a good listener, and giving effective feedback. Managers generally prefer oral communication because it provides the opportunity to ask questions and assess nonverbal communication. Oral communication is best suited to complex, ambiguous, or emotionally laden topics. Written communication is best suited for delivering straightforward messages and information. Listening is important for managerial success, but most people are terrible listeners. To improve your listening skills, choose to be an active listener (clarify responses, paraphrase, and summarize) and an empathetic listener (show your desire to understand, reflect feelings). Feedback can be constructive or destructive. To be constructive, feedback must be immediate, focused on specific behaviors, and problem-oriented.

REVIEW 4 Managing Organization-Wide Communication

Managers need methods for managing organization-wide communication and for making themselves accessible so that they can hear what employees throughout their organizations are feeling and thinking. Email, collaborative discussion sites, televised/videotaped speeches and conferences, and broadcast voice mail make it much easier for managers to improve message transmission and get the message out. By contrast, anonymous company hotlines, survey feedback, frequent informal meetings, and surprise visits help managers avoid organizational silence and improve reception by giving them the opportunity to hear what others in the organization think and feel. Monitoring internal and external blogs is another way to find out what people are saying and thinking about your organization.

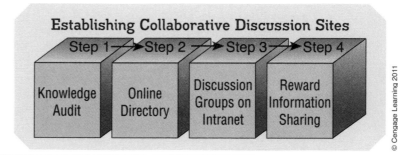

Establishing Collaborative Discussion Sites

Step 1 → Step 2 → Step 3 → Step 4

Knowledge Audit | Online Directory | Discussion Groups on Intranet | Reward Information Sharing

© Cengage Learning 2011

Televised/videotaped speeches and meetings speeches and meetings originally made to a smaller audience that are either simultaneously broadcast to other locations in the company or videotaped for subsequent distribution and viewing

Organizational silence when employees withhold information about organizational problems or issues

Company hotlines phone numbers that anyone in the company can call anonymously to leave information for upper management

Survey feedback information that is collected from surveys given to organizational members and then compiled, disseminated, and used to develop action plans for improvement

Blog a personal website that provides personal opinions or recommendations, news summaries, and reader comments

Chapter 16

Review | 16

Learning Outcomes

REVIEW 1 The Control Process

The control process begins by setting standards and then measuring performance and comparing performance to the standards. The better a company's information and measurement systems, the easier it is to make these comparisons. The control process continues by identifying and analyzing performance deviations and then developing and implementing programs for corrective action. Control is a continuous, dynamic, cybernetic process, not a one-time achievement or result. Control requires frequent managerial attention. The three basic control methods are feedback control (after-the-fact performance information), concurrent control (simultaneous performance information), and feedforward control (preventive performance information). Control has regulation costs and unanticipated consequences and therefore isn't always worthwhile or possible.

REVIEW 2 Control Methods

There are five methods of control: bureaucratic, objective, normative, concertive, and self-control (self-management). Bureaucratic and objective controls are top-down, management-based, and measurement-based. Normative and concertive controls represent shared forms of control because they evolve from company-wide or team-based beliefs and values. Self-control, or self-management, is a control system in which managers and workers control their own behavior.

Bureaucratic control is based on organizational policies, rules, and procedures. Objective control is based on reliable measures of behavior or outputs. Normative control is based on strong corporate beliefs and careful hiring practices. Concertive control is based on the development of values, beliefs, and rules in autonomous work groups. Self-control is based on individuals setting their own goals, monitoring themselves, and rewarding or punishing themselves with respect to goal achievement.

Nordstrom's Employee Handbook

Welcome to Nordstrom. We're glad to have you with our company. Our Number One goal is to provide outstanding customer service. Set both your personal and professional goals high. We have great confidence in your ability to achieve them.

Nordstrom Rules:

Rule #1: Use your good judgment in all situations.

There will be no additional rules. Please feel free to ask your department manager, store manager, or division general manager any question at any time.

Source: S. Williford, "Nordstrom Sets the Standard for Customer Service," *Memphis Business Journal*, July 1, 1996, 21.

Key Terms

Control a regulatory process of establishing standards to achieve organizational goals, comparing actual performance to the standards, and taking corrective action when necessary

Standards a basis of comparison for measuring the extent to which various kinds of organizational performance are satisfactory or unsatisfactory

Benchmarking the process of identifying outstanding practices, processes, and standards in other companies and adapting them to your company

Cybernetic the process of steering or keeping on course

Feedback control a mechanism for gathering information about performance deficiencies after they occur

Concurrent control a mechanism for gathering information about performance deficiencies as they occur, thereby eliminating or shortening the delay between performance and feedback

Feedforward control a mechanism for monitoring performance inputs rather than outputs to prevent or minimize performance deficiencies before they occur

Control loss the situation in which behavior and work procedures do not conform to standards

Regulation costs the costs associated with implementing or maintaining control

Cybernetic feasibility the extent to which it is possible to implement each step in the control process

Bureaucratic control the use of hierarchical authority to influence employee behavior by rewarding or punishing employees for compliance or noncompliance with organizational policies, rules, and procedures

Objective control the use of observable measures of worker behavior or outputs to assess performance and influence behavior

Behavior control the regulation of the behaviors and actions that workers perform on the job

Output control the regulation of workers' results or outputs through rewards and incentives

Normative control the regulation of workers' behavior and decisions through widely shared organizational values and beliefs

Concertive control the regulation of workers' behavior and decisions through work group values and beliefs

Self-control (self-management) a control system in which managers and workers control their own behavior by setting their own goals, monitoring their own progress, and rewarding themselves for goal achievement

Balanced scorecard measurement of organizational performance in four equally important areas: finances, customers, internal operations, and innovation and learning

Suboptimization performance improvement in one part of an organization at the expense of decreased performance in another part

Cash flow analysis a type of analysis that predicts how changes in a business will affect its ability to take in more cash than it pays out

Balance sheets accounting statements that provide a snapshot of a company's financial position at a particular time

Income statements accounting statements, also called *profit-and-loss statements*, that show what has happened to an organization's income, expenses, and net profit over a period of time

Financial ratios calculations typically used to track a business's liquidity (cash), efficiency, and profitability over time compared to other businesses in its industry

Budgets quantitative plans through which managers decide how to allocate available money to best accomplish company goals

Economic value added (EVA) the amount by which company profits (revenues, minus expenses, minus taxes) exceed the cost of capital in a given year

Customer defections a performance assessment in which companies identify which customers are leaving and measure the rate at which they are leaving

Value customer perception that the product quality is excellent for the price offered

When to Use Different Methods of Control

BUREAUCRATIC CONTROL	• When it is necessary to standardize operating procedures • When it is necessary to establish limits
BEHAVIOR CONTROL	• When it is easier to measure what workers do on the job than what they accomplish on the job • When cause–effect relationships are clear; that is, when companies know which behaviors will lead to success and which won't • When good measures of worker behavior can be created
OUTPUT CONTROL	• When it is easier to measure what workers accomplish on the job than what they do on the job • When good measures of worker output can be created • When it is possible to set clear goals and standards for worker output • When cause–effect relationships are unclear
NORMATIVE CONTROL	• When organizational culture, values, and beliefs are strong • When it is difficult to create good measures of worker behavior • When it is difficult to create good measures of worker output
CONCERTIVE CONTROL	• When responsibility for task accomplishment is given to autonomous work groups • When management wants workers to take ownership of their behavior and outputs • When management desires a strong form of worker-based control
SELF-CONTROL	• When workers are intrinsically motivated to do their jobs well • When it is difficult to create good measures of worker behavior • When it is difficult to create good measures of worker output • When workers have or are taught self-control and self-leadership skills

Sources: L. J. Kirsch, "The Management of Complex Tasks in Organizations: Controlling the Systems Development Process," *Organization Science* 7 (1996): 1–21; S. A. Snell, "Control Theory in Strategic Human Resource Management: The Mediating Effect of Administrative Information," *Academy of Management Journal* 35 (1992): 292–327.

Each of these control methods may be more or less appropriate depending on the circumstances.

REVIEW 3 What to Control?

Deciding what to control is just as important as deciding whether to control or how to control. In most companies, performance is measured using financial measures alone. However, the balanced scorecard encourages managers to measure and control company performance from four perspectives: financial, customer, internal, and innovation and learning. Traditionally, financial control has been achieved through cash flow analysis, balance sheets, income statements, financial ratios, and budgets. (For a refresher on these traditional financial control tools, see the Financial Review Card.) Another way to measure and control financial performance is to evaluate economic value added (EVA). Unlike traditional financial measures, EVA helps managers assess whether they are performing well enough to pay the cost of the capital needed to run the business. Instead of using customer satisfaction surveys to measure performance, companies should pay attention to customer defections, as customers who leave are more likely to speak up about what the company is doing wrong. From the internal perspective, performance is often measured in terms of quality, which is defined in three ways: excellence, value, and conformance to specifications. Minimizing waste has become an important part of innovation and learning in companies. The four levels of waste minimization are waste prevention and reduction, recycling and reuse, waste treatment, and waste disposal.

Conformance to Specifications Checklist for Buying Fresh Fish

FRESH WHOLE FISH	ACCEPTABLE	NOT ACCEPTABLE
Gills	✓ bright red, free of slime, clear mucus	✗ brown to grayish, thick, yellow mucus
Eyes	✓ clear, bright, bulging, black pupils	✗ dull, sunken, cloudy, gray pupils
Smell	✓ inoffensive, slight ocean smell	✗ ammonia, putrid smell
Skin	✓ opalescent sheen, scales adhere tightly to skin	✗ dull or faded color, scales missing or easily removed
Flesh	✓ firm and elastic to touch, tight to the bone	✗ soft and flabby, separating from the bone
Belly cavity	✓ no viscera or blood visible, lining intact, no bone protruding	✗ incomplete evisceration, cuts or protruding bones, off-odor

Sources: "A Closer Look: Buy It Fresh, Keep It Fresh," *Consumer Reports Online*, accessed June 20, 2005, http://www.seagrant.sunysb.edu/SeafoodTechnology /SeafoodMedia/CR02-2001/CR-SeafoodII020101.htm; "How to Purchase: Buying Fish," AboutSeaFood, accessed June 20, 2005, http://www.aboutseafood.com /faqs/purchase1.html.

© iStockphoto.com/Valeriy Evlakhov

Basic Accounting Tools for Controlling Financial Performance

STEPS FOR A BASIC CASH FLOW ANALYSIS

1. Forecast sales (steady, up, or down).

2. Project changes in anticipated cash inflows (as a result of changes).

3. Project anticipated cash outflows (as a result of changes).

4. Project net cash flows by combining anticipated cash inflows and outflows.

PARTS OF A BASIC BALANCE SHEET (ASSETS = LIABILITIES + OWNER'S EQUITY)

1. Assets
   a. Current assets (cash, short-term investment, marketable securities, accounts receivable, etc.)
   b. Fixed assets (land, buildings, machinery, equipment, etc.)

2. Liabilities
   a. Current liabilities (accounts payable, notes payable, taxes payable, etc.)
   b. Long-term liabilities (long-term debt, deferred income taxes, etc.)

3. Owner's Equity
   a. Preferred stock and common stock
   b. Additional paid-in capital
   c. Retained earnings

BASIC INCOME STATEMENT

```
  SALES REVENUE
− sales returns and allowances
+ other income
= NET REVENUE
− cost of goods sold (beginning inventory, costs of goods purchased, ending inventory)
= GROSS PROFIT
− total operating expenses (selling, general, and administrative expenses)
= INCOME FROM OPERATIONS
− interest expense
= PRETAX INCOME
− income taxes
= NET INCOME
```

Common Kinds of Budgets

Revenue Budgets—used to project or forecast future sales.	• Accuracy of projection depends on economy, competitors, sales force estimates, etc. • Determined by estimating future sales volume and sales prices for all products and services.
Expense Budgets—used within departments and divisions to determine how much will be spent on various supplies, projects, or activities.	• One of the first places that companies look for cuts when trying to lower expenses.
Profit Budgets—used by profit centers, which have "profit and loss" responsibility.	• Profit budgets combine revenue and expense budgets into one budget. • Typically used in large businesses with multiple plants and divisions.
Cash Budgets—used to forecast how much cash a company will have on hand to meet expenses.	• Similar to cash-flow analyses. • Used to identify cash shortfalls, which must be covered to pay bills, or cash excesses, which should be invested for a higher return.
Capital Expenditure Budgets—used to forecast large, long-lasting investments in equipment, buildings, and property.	• Help managers identify funding that will be needed to pay for future expansion or strategic moves designed to increase competitive advantage.
Variable Budgets—used to project costs across varying levels of sales and revenues.	• Important because it is difficult to accurately predict sales revenue and volume. • Lead to more accurate budgeting with respect to labor, materials, and administrative expenses, which vary with sales volume and revenues. • Build flexibility into the budgeting process.

Common Financial Ratios

RATIOS	FORMULA	WHAT IT MEANS	WHEN TO USE
LIQUIDITY RATIOS			
Current Ratio	$\dfrac{\text{Current Assets}}{\text{Current Liabilities}}$	• Whether you have enough assets on hand to pay for short-term bills and obligations. • Higher is better. • Recommended level is two times as many current assets as current liabilities.	• Track monthly and quarterly. • Basic measure of your company's health.
Quick (Acid Test) Ratio	$\dfrac{\text{(Current Assets} - \text{Inventories)}}{\text{Current Liabilities}}$	• Stricter than current ratio. • Whether you have enough (i.e., cash) to pay short-term bills and obligations. • Higher is better. • Recommended level is one or higher.	• Track monthly. • Also calculate quick ratio with potential customers to evaluate whether they're likely to pay you in a timely manner.
LEVERAGE RATIOS			
Debt to Equity	$\dfrac{\text{Total Liabilities}}{\text{Total Equity}}$	• Indicates how much the company is leveraged (in debt) by comparing what is owed (liabilities) to what is owned (equity). • Lower is better. A high debt-to-equity ratio could indicate that the company has too much debt. • Recommended level depends on industry.	• Track monthly. • Lenders often use this to determine the creditworthiness of a business (i.e., whether to approve additional loans).
Debt Coverage	$\dfrac{\text{(Net Profit} + \text{Noncash Expense)}}{\text{Debt}}$	• Indicates how well cash flow covers debt payments. • Higher is better.	• Track monthly. • Lenders look at this ratio to determine if there is adequate cash to make loan payments.
EFFICIENCY RATIOS			
Inventory Turnover	$\dfrac{\text{Cost of Goods Sold}}{\text{Average Value of Inventory}}$	• Whether you're making efficient use of inventory. • Higher is better, indicating that inventory (dollars) isn't purchased (spent) until needed. • Recommended level depends on industry.	• Track monthly by using a 12-month rolling average.
Average Collections Period	$\dfrac{\text{Accounts Receivable}}{\text{(Annual Net Credit Sales Divided by 365)}}$	• Shows on average how quickly your customers are paying their bills. • Recommended level is no more than 15 days longer than credit terms. If credit is net 30 days, then average should not be longer than 45 days.	• Track monthly. • Use to determine how long company's money is being tied up in customer credit.
PROFITABILITY RATIOS			
Gross Profit Margin	$\dfrac{\text{Gross Profit}}{\text{Total Sales}}$	• Shows how efficiently a business is using its materials and labor in the production process. • Higher is better, indicating that a profit can be made if fixed costs are controlled.	• Track monthly. • Analyze when unsure about product or service pricing. • Low margin compared to competitors means you're underpricing.
Return on Equity	$\dfrac{\text{Net Income}}{\text{Owner's Equity}}$	• Shows what was earned on your investment in the business during a particular period. Often called "return on investment." • Higher is better.	• Track quarterly and annually. • Use to compare to what you might have earned on the stock market, bonds, or government Treasury bills during the same period.

Learning Outcomes

REVIEW 1 Strategic Importance of Information

The first company to use new information technology to substantially lower costs or differentiate products or services often gains a first-mover advantage, higher profits, and a larger market share. Creating a first-mover advantage can be difficult, expensive, and risky, however. According to the resource-based view of information technology, sustainable competitive advantage occurs when information technology adds value, is different across firms, and is difficult to create or acquire.

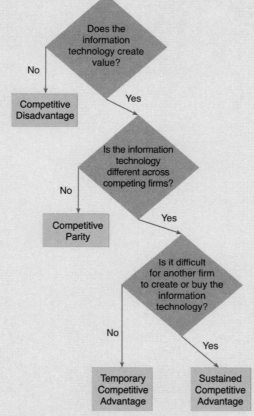

Using Information Technology to Sustain a Competitive Advantage

Source: Adapted from F. J. Mata, W. L. Fuerst, and J. B. Barney, "Information Technology and Sustained Competitive Advantage: A Resource-Based Analysis," *MIS Quarterly* 19, no. 4 (December 1995): 487–505. Reprinted by special permission by the Society for Information Management and the Management Information Systems Research Center at the University of Minnesota.

REVIEW 2 Characteristics and Costs of Useful Information

Raw data are facts and figures. Raw data do not become information until they are in a form that can affect decisions and behavior. For information to be useful, it has to be reliable and valid (accurate), of sufficient quantity (complete), pertinent to the problems you're facing (relevant), and available when you need it (timely). Useful information is not cheap. The five costs of obtaining good information are the costs of acquiring, processing, storing, retrieving, and communicating information.

REVIEW 3 Capturing, Processing, and Protecting Information

Electronic data capture (using bar codes, radio frequency identification [RFID] tags, scanners, or optical character recognition), is much faster, easier, and cheaper than manual data capture. Processing information means transforming raw data into meaningful information that can be applied to business decision making. Data mining helps managers with this transformation by discovering unknown patterns and relationships in data. Supervised data mining looks for patterns specified by managers, while unsupervised

Key Terms

Moore's law the prediction that the cost of computing will drop by 50 percent about every 2 years as computer-processing power doubles

Raw data facts and figures

Information useful data that can influence people's choices and behavior

First-mover advantage the strategic advantage that companies earn by being the first to use new information technology to substantially lower costs or to make a product or service different from that of competitors

Acquisition cost the cost of obtaining data that you don't have

Processing cost the cost of turning raw data into usable information

Storage cost the cost of physically or electronically archiving information for later use and retrieval

Retrieval cost the cost of accessing already-stored and processed information

Communication cost the cost of transmitting information from one place to another

Bar code a visual pattern that represents numerical data by varying the thickness and pattern of vertical bars

Radio frequency identification (RFID) tags tags containing minuscule microchips that transmit information via radio waves and can be used to track the number and location of the objects into which the tags have been inserted

Electronic scanner an electronic device that converts printed text and pictures into digital images

Optical character recognition the ability of software to convert digitized documents into ASCII (American Standard Code for Information Interchange) text or PDF documents that can be searched, read, and edited by word processing and other kinds of software

Processing information transforming raw data into meaningful information

Data mining the process of discovering patterns and relationships in large amounts of data

Data warehouse stores huge amounts of data that have been prepared for data mining analysis by being cleaned of errors and redundancy

Supervised data mining the process when the user tells the data mining software to look and test for specific patterns and relationships in a data set

Unsupervised data mining the process when the user simply tells the data mining software to uncover whatever patterns and relationships it can find in a data set

Association or affinity patterns when two or more database elements tend to occur together in a significant way

Sequence patterns when two or more database elements occur together in a significant pattern, but one of the elements precedes the other

Predictive patterns patterns that help identify database elements that are different

Data clusters when three or more database elements occur together (i.e., cluster) in a significant way

Protecting information the process of ensuring that data are reliably and consistently retrievable in a usable format for authorized users but no one else

Authentication making sure potential users are who they claim to be

Authorization granting authenticated users approved access to data, software, and systems

Two-factor authentication authentication based on what users know, such as a password, and what they have in their possession, such as a secure ID card or key

Biometrics identifying users by unique, measurable body features, such as fingerprint recognition or iris scanning

Firewall a protective hardware or software device that sits between the computers in an internal organizational network and outside networks, such as the Internet

Virus a program or piece of code that, against your wishes, attaches itself to other programs on your computer and can trigger anything from a harmless flashing message to the reformatting of your hard drive to a systemwide network shutdown

Data encryption the transformation of data into complex, scrambled digital codes that can be unencrypted only by authorized users who possess unique decryption keys

Virtual private network (VPN) software that securely encrypts data sent by employees outside the company network, decrypts the data when they arrive within the company computer network, and does the same when data are sent back to employees outside the network

Secure sockets layer (SSL) encryption Internet browser–based encryption that provides secure off-site Web access to some data and programs

data mining looks for four general kinds of data patterns: association or affinity patterns, sequence patterns, predictive patterns, and data clusters. Protecting information ensures that data are reliably and consistently retrievable in a usable format by authorized users but no one else. Authentication and authorization, firewalls, antivirus software for PCs and corporate email and network servers, data encryption, virtual private networks (VPNs), and Web-based secure sockets layer (SSL) encryption are some of the best ways to protect information. Be careful when using wireless networks, which are easily compromised even when security and encryption protocols are in place.

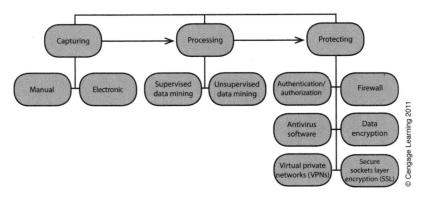

© Cengage Learning 2011

REVIEW 4 Accessing and Sharing Information and Knowledge

Executive information systems, intranets, and corporate portals facilitate internal sharing and access to company information and transactions. Electronic data interchange and the Internet allow external groups like suppliers and customers to easily access company information. Both decrease costs by reducing or eliminating data entry, data errors, and paperwork and by speeding up communication. Organizations use decision support systems and expert systems to capture and share specialized knowledge with nonexpert employees.

Executive information system (EIS) a data processing system that uses internal and external data sources to provide the information needed to monitor and analyze organizational performance

Intranets private company networks that allow employees to easily access, share, and publish information using Internet software

Corporate portal a hybrid of executive information systems and intranets that allows managers and employees to use a Web browser to gain access to customized company information and to complete specialized transactions

Electronic data interchange (EDI) when two companies convert their purchase and ordering information to a standardized format to enable the direct electronic transmission of that information from one company's computer system to the other company's computer system

Web services using standardized protocols to describe and transfer data from one company in such a way that those data can automatically be read, understood, transcribed, and processed by different computer systems in another company

Extranets networks that allow companies to exchange information and conduct transactions with outsiders by providing them direct, Web-based access to authorized parts of a company's intranet or information system

Knowledge the understanding that one gains from information

Decision support system (DSS) an information system that helps managers understand specific kinds of problems and potential solutions and analyze the impact of different decision options using "what if" scenarios

Expert system an information system that contains the specialized knowledge and decision rules used by experts and experienced decision makers so that nonexperts can draw on this knowledge base to make decisions

Learning Outcomes

REVIEW 1 Productivity

Productivity is a measure of how many inputs it takes to produce or create an output. The greater the output from one input, or the fewer inputs it takes to create an output, the higher the productivity. Partial productivity measures how much of a single kind of input, such as labor, is needed to produce an output. Multifactor productivity is an overall measure of productivity that indicates how much labor, capital, materials, and energy are needed to produce an output.

$$\text{Partial Productivity} = \frac{\text{Outputs}}{\text{Single Kind of Input}}$$

$$\frac{\text{Multifactor}}{\text{Productivity}} = \frac{\text{Outputs}}{(\text{Labor} + \text{Capital} + \text{Materials} + \text{Energy})}$$

REVIEW 2 Quality

Quality can mean that a product or service is practically free of deficiencies or has characteristics that satisfy customer needs. Quality products usually possess three characteristics: reliability, serviceability, and durability. Quality service includes reliability, tangibles, responsiveness, assurance, and empathy. ISO 9000 is a series of five international standards for achieving consistency in quality management and quality assurance, while ISO 14000 is a set of standards for minimizing an organization's harmful effects on the environment. The Baldrige National Quality Award recognizes U.S. companies for their achievements in quality and business performance. Each year, up to three Baldrige Awards may be given in the categories of manufacturing, service, small business, education, and health care. Total quality management (TQM) is an integrated organization-wide strategy for improving product and service quality. TQM is based on three mutually reinforcing principles: customer focus and satisfaction, continuous improvement, and teamwork.

REVIEW 3 Service Operations

Services are different from goods. Goods are produced, tangible, and storable. Services are performed, intangible, and perishable. Likewise, managing service operations is different from managing production operations. The service-profit chain indicates that success begins with internal service quality, meaning how well management treats employees. Internal service quality leads to employee satisfaction and service capability, which, in turn, lead to high-value service to customers, customer satisfaction, customer loyalty, and long-term profits and growth. Keeping existing customers is far more cost-effective than finding new ones. Consequently, to prevent disgruntled customers from

Service-Profit Chain

Internal Service Quality

Employee Satisfaction

Service Capability

High Value Service

= ✔ Customer Satisfaction ✔ Customer Loyalty lead to

Upper Management   Employees   Customers

Profit and Growth

Sources: R. Hallowell, L. A. Schlesinger, and J. Zornitsky, "Internal Service Quality, Customer and Job Satisfaction: Linkages and Implications for Management," *Human Resource Planning* 19 (1996): 20–31; J. L. Heskett, T. O. Jones, G. W. Loveman, W. E. Sasser Jr., and L. A. Schlesinger, "Putting the Service-Profit Chain to Work," *Harvard Business Review* (March–April 1994): 164–174.

Key Terms

Productivity a measure of performance that indicates how many inputs it takes to produce or create an output

Partial productivity a measure of performance that indicates how much of a particular kind of input it takes to produce an output

Multifactor productivity an overall measure of productivity that indicates how much labor, capital, materials, and energy it takes to produce an output

Quality a product or service free of deficiencies, or the characteristics of a product or service that satisfy customer needs

ISO 9000 a series of five international standards, from ISO 9000 to ISO 9004, for achieving consistency in quality management and quality assurance in companies throughout the world

ISO 14000 a series of international standards for managing, monitoring, and minimizing an organization's harmful effects on the environment

Total quality management (TQM) an integrated, principle-based, organization-wide strategy for improving product and service quality

Customer focus an organizational goal to concentrate on meeting customers' needs at all levels of the organization

Customer satisfaction an organizational goal to provide products or services that meet or exceed customers' expectations

Continuous improvement an organization's ongoing commitment to constantly assess and improve the processes and procedures used to create products and services

Variation a deviation in the form, condition, or appearance of a product from the quality standard for that product

Teamwork collaboration between managers and nonmanagers, across business functions, and between companies, customers, and suppliers

Service recovery restoring customer satisfaction to strongly dissatisfied customers

Make-to-order operation a manufacturing operation that does not start processing or assembling products until a customer order is received

Assemble-to-order operation a manufacturing operation that divides manufacturing processes into separate parts or modules that are combined to create semicustomized products

Make-to-stock operation a manufacturing operation that orders parts and assembles standardized products before receiving customer orders

Manufacturing flexibility the degree to which manufacturing operations can easily and quickly change the number, kind, and characteristics of products they produce

Continuous-flow production a manufacturing operation that produces goods at a continuous, rather than a discrete, rate

Line-flow production manufacturing processes that are preestablished, occur in a serial or linear manner, and are dedicated to making one type of product

Batch production a manufacturing operation that produces goods in large batches in standard lot sizes

Job shops manufacturing operations that handle custom orders or small batch jobs

Inventory the amount and number of raw materials, parts, and finished products that a company has in its possession

Raw material inventories the basic inputs in a manufacturing process

Component parts inventories the basic parts used in manufacturing that are fabricated from raw materials

Work-in-process inventories partially finished goods consisting of assembled component parts

Finished goods inventories the final outputs of manufacturing operations

Average aggregate inventory average overall inventory during a particular time period

Stockout the situation in which a company runs out of finished product

Inventory turnover the number of times per year that a company sells or "turns over" its average inventory

Ordering cost the costs associated with ordering inventory, including the cost of data entry, phone calls, obtaining bids, correcting mistakes, and determining when and how much inventory to order

Setup cost the costs of downtime and lost efficiency that occur when a machine is changed or adjusted to produce a different kind of inventory

Holding cost the cost of keeping inventory until it is used or sold, including storage, insurance, taxes, obsolescence, and opportunity costs

Stockout costs the costs incurred when a company runs out of a product, including transaction costs to replace inventory and the loss of customers' goodwill

Economic order quantity (EOQ) a system of formulas that minimizes ordering and holding costs and helps determine how much and how often inventory should be ordered

leaving, some companies are empowering service employees to perform service recovery—restoring customer satisfaction to strongly dissatisfied customers—by giving employees the authority and responsibility to immediately solve customer problems. The hope is that empowered service recovery will prevent customer defections.

REVIEW 4 Manufacturing Operations

Manufacturing operations produce physical goods. Manufacturing operations can be classified according to the amount of processing or assembly that occurs after receiving an order from a customer.

Manufacturing operations can also be classified in terms of flexibility, the degree to which the number, kind, and characteristics of products can easily and quickly be changed. Flexibility allows companies to respond quickly to competitors and customers and to reduce order lead times, but it can also lead to higher unit costs.

REVIEW 5 Inventory

There are four kinds of inventory: raw materials, component parts, work-in-process, and finished goods. Because companies incur ordering, setup, holding, and stockout costs when handling inventory, inventory costs can be enormous. To control those costs, companies measure and track inventory in three ways: average aggregate inventory, weeks of supply, and turnover. Companies meet the basic goals of inventory management (avoiding stockouts and reducing inventory without hurting daily operations) through economic order quantity (EOQ) formulas, just-in-time (JIT) inventory systems, and materials requirement planning (MRP).

$$EOQ = \sqrt{\frac{2DO}{H}}$$

Use EOQ formulas when inventory levels are independent, and use JIT and MRP when inventory levels are dependent on the number of products to be produced.

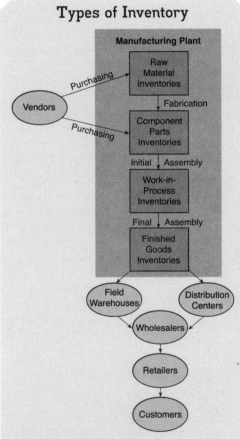

Types of Inventory

Source: R. E. Markland, S. K. Vickery, and R. A. Davis, *Operations Management*, 2nd ed. (Mason, OH: South-Western, 1998). Reprinted with permission.

Just-in-time (JIT) inventory system an inventory system in which component parts arrive from suppliers just as they are needed at each stage of production

Kanban a ticket-based system that indicates when to reorder inventory

Materials requirement planning (MRP) a production and inventory system that determines the production schedule, production batch sizes, and inventory needed to complete final products

Independent demand system an inventory system in which the level of one kind of inventory does not depend on another

Dependent demand system an inventory system in which the level of inventory depends on the number of finished units to be produced